WÖRTERBUCH
FÜR DAS BANK- UND BÖRSENWESEN

DICTIONARY
OF BANKING AND STOCK TRADING

HANS E. ZAHN

WÖRTERBUCH
FÜR DAS BANK- UND BÖRSENWESEN

DEUTSCH – ENGLISCH
ENGLISCH – DEUTSCH

3., aktualisierte und erweiterte Auflage

FRITZ KNAPP VERLAG  FRANKFURT AM MAIN

HANS E. ZAHN

DICTIONARY
OF BANKING AND STOCK TRADING

GERMAN – ENGLISH
ENGLISH – GERMAN

Third Edition

FRITZ KNAPP VERLAG  FRANKFURT AM MAIN

ISBN 3-7819-2022-4

1. Auflage 1982
2. Auflage 1983
3. Auflage 1984

Copyright 1984 by Fritz Knapp Verlag, Frankfurt am Main
Gesamtherstellung: Beltz Offsetdruck, Hemsbach
Umschlagentwurf: Manfred Jung, Frankfurt am Main

Printed in Germany

VORWORT
ZUR DRITTEN AUFLAGE

Der Erfolg der beiden vorangegangenen Auflagen ermutigte Autor und Verlag, das Wörterbuch für das Bank- und Börsenwesen in seiner dritten Auflage wesentlich zu erweitern.

Die praxisbezogene Konzeption wurde beibehalten, d. h. Texte und Verträge aus der täglichen Bankpraxis sowie die Berichte einschlägiger Fachzeitschriften über das internationale Kredit- und Börsengeschäft bildeten die Arbeitsunterlagen. Es sei an dieser Stelle darauf hingewiesen, daß sich das vorliegende Wörterbuch als ein Spezialwörterbuch versteht, bei dem auf die Aufnahme von Begriffen aus anderen Wirtschaftsbereichen bewußt verzichtet wurde. Um es durch einen niedrigen Preis einem möglichst breiten Benutzerkreis zugänglich zu machen, war eine Begrenzung der Seitenzahl unumgänglich. Diese Notwendigkeit einerseits sowie der hohe Anfall von Übersetzungen in die englische Sprache andererseits, zwangen den Verfasser, das Wörterbuch mit einem wesentlich umfangreicheren deutsch-englischen Teil zu konzipieren.

Zielgruppe des vorliegenden Wörterbuches sind in erster Linie die Mitarbeiter der Kreditinstitute und Übersetzer, die täglich oder gelegentlich mit den beiden Sprachen arbeiten. Der Verfasser hofft, daß ihnen das Wörterbuch für das Bank- und Börsenwesen gute Dienste leisten wird, bittet jedoch zu bedenken, daß ein Spezial-Wörterbuch naturgemäß nicht alle Übersetzungswünsche befriedigen kann.

Bad Nauheim, September 1984　　　　　　　　　Hans E. Zahn

PREFACE TO THE THIRD EDITION

The success of the two previous editions encouraged both the author and the publisher to present this substantially enlarged third edition.

The focus of earlier editions on current usage and practice has been maintained. The author's primary sources were therefore documentation used by the banks themselves, financial dailies and reports of international lending activities and stock market operations.

This is a specialist dictionary and economic terms from outside banking and stock trading have been omitted deliberately. The higher demand for translations into English from German has been met by devoting a greater amount of the limited space available to the German-English section.

The dictionary has been designed to meet the needs of bankers and translators who deal daily or occasionally with the two languages and the author hopes that the dictionary will prove useful to all professions dealing with banking and stock trading. It should be remembered, however, that a specialist dictionary such as this is not able to cover more general vocabulary.

Bad Nauheim, September 1984   H. E. Zahn

HINWEISE ZUR BENUTZUNG

Der Gedankenstrich steht für das vorangegangene Stichwort. Alle Eintragungen sind alphabetisch geordnet, d. h. Adjektive und Verben werden unter ihrem jeweiligen Anfangsbuchstaben und nicht als substantivische Erweiterungen eingeordnet.

Ergeben die Pluralformen von Substantiven ergänzende oder weitere Übersetzungsmöglichkeiten, so werden diese unmittelbar unter dem Singular angeführt. Als Übersetzungshilfen werden bei einer Reihe von Substantiven und Verben Satzbeispiele angegeben. Abkürzungen von Institutionen und Organisationen werden im Hauptteil zusammen mit Querverweisen angeführt, die auf die vollständigen Eigennamen hinweisen. Querverweise zeigen aber auch Synonyma oder inhaltliche Zusammenhänge auf.

Bei den in Klammern stehenden Begriffen handelt es sich entweder um Synonyma von unmittelbar vorangehenden Wörtern oder um Erläuterungen zu den in die jeweils andere Sprache übertragenen Begriffen. Hat ein Stichwort mehrere Bedeutungen im Bank- und Börsenwesen, so werden diese durch die Buchstaben a, b, c verdeutlicht. Das auf ein deutsches Stichwort gelegentlich folgende zusätzliche Substantiv verweist auf den bank- oder börsenspezifischen Kontext des Begriffes.

NOTES TO THE USER OF THE DICTIONARY

The dash always stands for the preceding headword. All entries follow one another in alphabetical order, i. e. adjectives and verbs are entered at their proper alphabetical place and not as subdivisions of nouns.

Plural forms of nouns, implying a meaning additional or complementary to the singular, are listed immediately below the singular. A number of nouns and verbs have been complemented by phrases to illustrate their use. Abbreviations of institutions and organisations are given in their proper alphabetical position together with a cross reference indicating where the full name of the institution or organisation in question is listed.

Words bracketed represent either synonyms of translations immediately preceding or explanations on the terms translated.

Where an entry has several possible interpretations, the different meanings are preceded by the letters a, b, c. In the German-English section of the dictionary, the German entry is often followed by another noun in order to clarify the precise banking or stock exchange meaning of the translated term.

WÖRTERBUCH
FÜR DAS BANK- UND BÖRSENWESEN

DEUTSCH – ENGLISCH

A

abbröckeln to crumble, to ease, to slip, to drift easier

abbuchen to debit; im Lastschriftverfahren: to debit directly, to debit under a preauthorized payment mandate; Verlust: to write (to charge) off

Abbuchung debit; im Lastschriftverfahren: direct debit, direct debiting (Br), preauthorized payment (US); Verlust: writing off, charge-off

Abbuchungsermächtigung direct debit authorisation (Br), preauthorized payment mandate (US)

abdecken Risiko: to hedge, to cover, to provide cover for; Kredit: to repay, to clean up

Abdeckung hedging, covering, providing cover for; repayment

Rückstellungen zur - in- und ausländischer Kreditrisiken provisions to cover domestic and foreign loan risks

- eines Kredites repayment (cleanup) of a loan
- des Währungsrisikos hedging the exchange (currency) risk
- des Verlustrisikos hedging (covering) the exposure to loss

abdisponieren to withdraw, to transfer (to branch off) to another account

Abend-Kassenbestände overnight cash holdings

Abfinanzierung repayment of equity

abfinden Aktionäre, Gesellschafter: to buy out; Gläubiger: to pay off; entschädigen: to indemnify

Abfindung (a) buying out, buyout; (b) paying off; (c) indemnification

Abfindungs
- angebot offer to shareholders, take-over bid
- anspruch claim to compensation (indemnification)
- werte Wertpapiere: take-over (bid) candidates

Abfluß outflow, efflux
- von Spareinlagen savings outflow, drain on savings deposits

abführen to transfer, to pay over

an die Muttergesellschaft - to upstream, to transfer to the parent

Abgabedruck unter starken - geraten to come under heavy selling pressure

Abgaben von Wertpapieren: sales, selling
- bei geringen Umsätzen selling in light (quiet) trading

Abgabensaldo net selling

Abgabensätze selling rates (i.e. interest rates charged by Bundesbank for money market instruments)

Abgang deduction; disposal
- der Bezugsrechte (Dividende) deduction of rights (dividend), markdown ex rights (ex dividend)
- von Gegenständen des Anlagevermögens disposal of fixed assets

abgeben an den Markt: to sell in the market

abgrenzen to defer

abgegrenzte Erträge (Kosten) deferred income (charges)

Abgrenzung deferment

Abgrenzungsposten deferred item

Abgrenzungszinsen deferred interest

abhängiges Unternehmen controlled company

abheben to withdraw; to draw money at the bank

Abhebung withdrawal; drawing money at the bank
- en gegen Vorlage des Sparbuches withdrawals against presentation (on production) of the passbook

Ablauf expiration, lapse
- der Festlegungsfrist expiration of the blocking period (of the fixed-rate period)

ablaufen to expire, to fall due, to mature

ablösen Anleihe: to redeem, to retire; Kredit, Hypothek: to repay, to pay off; durch Umschuldung: to refund, to reschedule

Ablösung redemption, retirement; repayment; rescheduling

vorzeitige - early retirement, premature redemption
- aus einbehaltenen Gewinnen retirement out of retained earnings

Ablösungs
- finanzierung take-out (consolidation) financing
- fonds redemption (sinking)fund
- recht Anleihe: call privilege, right to call in a bond; Schuld: right to repay a debt

abrechnen to settle; Schecks: to clear; Wechsel: to discount; Wertpapiergeschäft: to settle; berechnen: to invoice

Abrechnung settlement; clearing; discounting; invoicing; Aufstellung: statement; Wertpapierabrechnung:contract note

- der zum Diskont eingereichten Wechsel settlement of bills presented for discount
- der Kauf- und Verkaufsaufträge am gleichen Tag same-day settlement of buying and selling orders
- en im Bereich Anlagenbau sales in the plant engineering sector
- von Schecks und Überweisungen clearing of cheques and bank giro credits

Abrechnungs
- kurs settlement price (rate)
- mitglieder clearing house members
- papiere clearing instruments
- salden clearing balances
- spitzen settlement fractions
- stelle clearing house (office); für Wertpapiere: stock clearing agency
- valuta (a) settlement currency; (b) settlement date
- verkehr clearing transactions
- zeitraum settlement (accounting) period

Abruf call, calling for; drawing
- der zweiten Kredittranche drawing on the second loan tranche
- von Tagesgeldern calling for overnight funds

abrufen to call, to call for; to draw on

die Lieferung der Stücke - to call for delivery of the securities

den nicht in Anspruch genommenen Teil des Krediges - to draw on the uncalled portion of the loan

abrunden eine Summe: to round down

seine Beteiligungen in der Kreditwirtschaft - to round out its finance interests

abrutschen in die roten Zahlen: to slide into the red

Absatz der Neuemissionen new issue sales (selling)

2

Absatz
- finanzierung   sales financing
- kredit   sales credit
- von Sparbriefen   sale of savings bonds

Abschlag   discount; Dividendenabschlag: deduction of dividend, quotation ex dividend; Kursabschlag: price markdown

- auf den Emissionskurs   discount from the offering price
- von -1 im Interbanken-Handel   discount of 1 in interbank trading

mit einem - von 0,5 % handeln   to trade at a discount of -.5%

Abschlags
- dividende   interim dividend, dividend on account
- zahlung   payment on account, instalment, progress payment

abschließen   Effektengeschäft: to conclude, to strike a bargain, to settle; Konto zum Quartalsende: to balance an account; Konto löschen: to close (to close out) an account

Abschluß   transaction, bargain, deal; conclusion, settlement; eines Unternehmens: annual financial statements

die Einzelheiten des -es festhalten   to set out the details of the transaction

nach - des Geschäftes zwischen A und B   once A and B have struck the bargain

- eines Kontos jeweils zum Quartalsende   balancing the account at the end of each quarter
- des Vertrages   conclusion of contract
- über mehrere Millionen   multi-million deal

Abschlüsse
- bei Kurzläufern (Langläufern)   dealings in shorts (longs)
- auf neue Rechnung   dealings (transactions) for new account
- erfolgen zum Basispreis   bargains are done at the striking price

die erzielten -   business done, bargains struck, sales

Abschluß
- bereitschaft von Darlehensinteressenten: propensity to take out a loan
- buchung   (a) closing entry; (b) entry covering interest and charges; balancing entry
- erläuterungen   notes to the financial statements
- kurs   contract (settlement) price
- posten   bei einem Bankkonto: interest and charges
- prüfer   auditor
- prüfung   audit of the annual accounts
- rechnung   closing statement; Bankkonto: statement of interest and charges; Effektengeschäft: contract (settlement) note
- saldo   closing balance
- tag   settlement day; Bilanz: balance sheet day
- vollmacht   authority to contract, contractual power
- zahlen   balance sheet figures
- zeitpunkt   date of accounts

Abschnitt   Wechsel: bill; Stückelung: denomination

abschöpfen   to skim off, to siphon off, to absorb

Abschöpfung   skimming off, siphoning off (e.g. surplus liquidity)

3

Abschöpfungsdauerauftrag   standing order for regular savings

abschreiben   to depreciate, to write down, to write off

degressiv -   to depreciate on diminishing values

linear -   to depreciate on a straight line basis

progressiv -   to depreciate on a rising scale

in gleichen Raten während der geschätzten Nutzungsdauer -   to write down in equal instalments over the estimated working life

ein Kreditengagement -   to write off a loan

Abschreibung (en) depreciation(s), write-down(s), write-off(s)

- auf Beteiligungen   write-offs on trade investments
- auf Finanzanlagen   depreciation on (of) financial assets
- auf den Rentenbestand   bond write-offs, write-offs on fixed-income securities
- auf Sachanlagen   depreciation on (of) fixed assets
- und Wertberichtigungen auf Forderungen   einer Bank: write-offs and provisions for possible loan losses

Abschreibungs
- bedarf   write-off requirements
- betrag   depreciation allowance
- gesellschaft   tax loss company
- satz   depreciation rate
- vergünstigungen   special depreciation allowances
- zeitraum   depreciation age

abschwächen, sich   to turn lower, to ease, to slither

sich gegen Ende der Börsensitzung -   to skid late in the session

Abschwächung   Konjunktur: slowdown; Kurse: easing, drifting lower, sagging

Abschwung   downturn, slump, downswing

absichern   (a) to hedge, to safeguard, to cover; (b) to provide security for, to guarantee

Absicherung   (a) hedging, safeguarding, hedge; (b) providing security for

grundbuchliche -   security by way of a land charge

- eines Kreditengagements   providing security for a loan
- in- und ausländischer Kreditrisiken   hedging domestic and foreign loan risks
- von Wechselkursschwankungen   hedge (safeguard) against exchange rate fluctuations

Absicherungsmöglichkeiten
(a) hedging opportunities (facilities); (b) security arrangements

absoluter Tiefstand   all-time low, lowest-ever level, rock-bottom

abstellen auf   to gear, to tailor to

die Zinssätze auf die gegenwärtige Marktsituation -   to gear interest rates to the present state of the market

abstimmen   to vote; Konten: to reconcile, to agree, to collate

abstoßen   Wertpapiere: to unload holdings, to sell off (out)

abtreten   to assign

Abtretung   assignment

Abtretungs
- anzeige   notice (notification) of assignment
- ausschluß   precluding the right to assign, non-assignability

- erklärung   declaration of assignment
- urkunde   deed of assignment
- verbotsklausel   non-assignment clause

abwälzen   to pass on
höhere Refinanzierungskosten auf die Kunden -   to pass on higher funding costs to customers

abwartend   die Anleger verhielten sich abwartend: investors remained on the sidelines

Abwärtsfloaten   downward float

Abwärtstrend   downward trend

Abweichungs
- indikator   EWS: divergence indicator
- schwelle   EWS: divergence threshold
- spanne   EWS: divergence margin

abwenden   die Zahlungsunfähigkeit des Kreditnehmers: to avert default on a loan

abwerfen   to yield, to provide
eine geringe Rendite -   to provide a bad return

abwerten   to devalue

Abwertung   devaluation

abwertungsverdächtig   devaluation-prone

Abwesenheitsprotest   noting a bill in absence of the drawee

abwickeln   begleichen:to settle; Inkasso, Kredit: to process, to handle; Unternehmen: to wind up, to dissolve, to liquidate

Abwicklung   settlement; processing, handling; winding-up, liquidation

- eines Kreditengagements   loan processing, processing of a loan commitment
- von Termingeschäften   handling of forward transactions, settlement of futures contracts

Abwicklungs
- bank   im Dokumentengeschäft: settling (settlement) bank
- stelle   settling(processing)agent
- termin   settlement date

abwürgen
die Nachfrage nach Konsumentenkrediten -   to choke off the consumer loan demand

abzahlen   to pay off, to repay, to settle; in Raten: to pay by instalments

Abzahlung   paying off, repayment; payment by instalments

Abzahlungshypothek   instalment mortgage

abzinsen   to discount

Abzinsung   discounting

Abzinsungs
- betrag   discount
- papiere   securities sold at a discount (e.g. zero bonds)
- satz   discounting rate
- typ   type of discounted savings bond

Abzweiglimit   sub-limit

addiertes Geschäftsvolumen   overall business volume

Adresse, erste   in der Regel: prime (first-rate) borrower; allgemein auch: blue-chip (highly valued) customer

Adressenliste   schedule of borrowers

Agio   premium
- erträge /-gewinne   premiums received

akkreditieren to open a documentary credit

Akkreditierter beneficiary under a documentary credit, accreditee

Akkreditiv documentary credit, credit, letter of credit
- ablauf expiry of a documentary credit
- abteilung documentary credits department
- abwicklung handling (processing) of a credit
- änderung amendment to a documentary credit
- ansprüche rights (claims) under a documentary credit
- anzeige notification of credit
- auftrag credit application, instructions to open a documentary credit
- auftraggeber applicant for the credit
- ausnutzung drawing on a documentary credit
- auszahlungsanspruch right to payment under a credit
- avisierung advising a documentary credit
- bank issuing (opening) bank
- bedienung payment under a documentary credit
- bedingungen terms and conditions of a documentary credit; credit terms
- begünstigter beneficiary under a documentary credit, accreditee
- bestätigung credit confirmation
- betrag amount of a credit
- bevorschussung advance against a documentary credit; packing (anticipatory) credit
- brief letter of credit
- deckung credit cover; cover for a documentary credit
- deckungskonto credit cover account
- dokumente credit documents; documents called for in a credit
- erlös credit proceeds
- ermächtigung letter of authority
- eröffnende Bank issuing (opening) bank
- eröffnung credit opening; opening of a documentary credit
- eröffnungsauftrag credit application
- gemäße /-gerechte Dokumente documents in accordance with the terms and conditions of the documentary credit
- geschäft documentary credit transaction/s
- gültigkeit validity of a credit
- hinauslegung credit accommodation (opening)
- inanspruchnahme drawing on a credit
- klausel documentary credit clause; clause stipulating payment by documentary credit
- leistung payment under a credit; effecting (making) payment under a credit
- mäßigkeit der Dokumente prüfen to check whether the documents are in accordance with the terms and conditions of the documentary credit
- mit aufgeschobener Zahlung deferred payment credit
- partei party to a documentary credit
- steller applicant for the credit
- stellung issuance (opening) of a documentary credit
- übertragung transferring a documentary credit, transfer of a credit

- verfalldatum   expiry date of a credit
- verkehr   documentary credit operations
- verlängerung   extending the term (life) of a credit
- versprechen   credit undertaking
- währung   credit currency
- zahlstelle   paying bank
- ziehung   drawing under a documentary credit

akquirieren   to solicit (to source) new business

Akquisition   soliciting (sourcing) new business

Akquisitions
- bemühungen   efforts to win new customers, efforts to solicit business
- strategie   soliciting (sourcing) strategy

Aktie   share (Br), stock (US)

Aktien
- abschlag   share discount, discount on shares (stock)
- analyse   stock analysis
- anlage   investment in equities (shares, stocks)
- aufschlag   share (stock) premium
- ausgabe   share issue, equity offering
- austausch   exchange of shares, stock swap
- baisse   slump in the stock market, sharp drop in equity prices
- bestand   holding of shares, shareholding, stockholding, stock portfolio
- beteiligung   equity holding (interest), shareholding, share stake
- bewertung   share (stock) rating
- bezugsrecht   stock right
- börse   stock exchange
- buch   share (stock) ledger, stockholders' ledger
- einziehung   calling in shares, stock retirement
- emission   share (stock) issue, equity offering
- einziehung   calling in shares, stock retirement
- emission   share (stock) issue, equity offering
- emissionsagio   share (stock) premium, premium on an equity offering
- finanzierung   equity financing
- flaute   stalemate in the equity (stock) market
- fonds   equity (stock) fund
- gattung   class of shares, stock category
- gesellschaft   public limited company (Br); stock corporation (US)
- gesetz   German Stock Corporation Law; Companies Act (Br); Corporation Law (US)
- handel   share (equity) trading, stock trading (dealings)
- hausse   upsurge in share prices, bull market in equities, rocketing (soaring) equity prices, bull run in the stock market
- index   share price index, stock index
- kapital   share (stock) capital, equity
- kapitalverzinsung   return on stockholders' equity
- kategorie   class of shares, stock category
- kurs   share (stock) certificate

7

- mantel share (stock) certificate
- mehrheit majority shareholding, majority of shares
- mit Konsortialbindung shares tied to syndicate transactions
- notierung share price quotation
- optionshandel stock option trade
- order instructions to buy or sell shares, buy or sell order
- paket share block, block of shares
- plazierung share (stock) placing, stock floatation
- portefeuille stock (equity) portfolio, portfolio of shares
- promesse scrip certificate
- recht stock corporation law
- register shareholders' ledger
- rendite stock yield
- sparen equity saving
- spitze fraction
- split share (stock) split
- streubesitz widely spread shareholdings
- übernahme stock take-over
- tausch stock swap, equity switching, exchange of shares
- tauschangebot share (stock) exchange offering
- umlauf total shares outstanding
- umtausch exchange of shares, stock swap
- urkunde share certificate
- zusammenlegung stock consolidation; consolidation of shares

Aktionär shareholder, stockholder

Aktionärs
- banken shareholding banks
- brief newsletter to shareholders
- gruppe class of shareholders, stockholder group
- rechte shareholders' rights
- versammlung shareholders' (stockholders') meeting

Aktiva assets

aktiv
-e Handelsbilanz trade balance surplus
-e Leistungsbilanz current account surplus

Aktiv
- geschäft lending business (operations)
- grenze upper lending limit
- hypotheken mortgage lendings

aktivieren to capitalise, to carry (to report) as assets

aktivierte Eigenleistungen company-produced additions to assets

Aktivierung capitalisation, carrying as assets

Aktivierung von Fremdkapitalzinsen capitalising interest on outside capital

Aktiv
- konditionen lending terms (rates)
- kundschaft borrowing customers, borrowers
- saldo credit (favourable) balance, surplus
- steuerung asset management
- tilgungen loan repayments
- überhang surplus of lendings, im Geldhandel: net selling (lending) position

- wechsel   bills receivable
- zins   (a) loan interest rate;
  (b) interest receivable
- zinsmarge   lending interest margin
- zinsüberschuß   net interest income from lendings

Akzept   acceptance
- akkreditiv   documentary acceptance credit
- austausch   interbank exchange of own acceptances
- einholung   presentation for acceptance, obtaining acceptance
- gebende Bank   accepting bank
- kredit   acceptance credit
- leistung   acceptance, effecting acceptance
- linie   acceptance line
- meldung   notification of acceptance
- provision   acceptance commission
- verbindlichkeiten   acceptance liabilities
- verweigerung   non-acceptance
- vorlage   presentation for acceptance
- zusage   undertaking (commitment) to accept

alleinvertretungsberechtigt
holding sole power of representation

Allgemeine Kreditvereinbarungen
(IWF)   General Arrangement to Borrow

Alt-Bestand   loans extended in previous years

Alt-Emission   secondary market issue

alte Rechnung   previous account

Alt-Schulden   debts contracted prior to ...

Amortisations
- anleihe   redemption loan
- fonds   sinking fund
- hypothek   amortising (instalment) mortgage

AMR → Anweisung der Deutschen Bundesbank über Mindestreserven

amtlich
- er Kurs   official price (rate)
- es Kursblatt   Official List
- er Markt   official market
- e Notierung   official quotation
- er Wechselkurs   official exchange rate
- nicht notierte Wertpapiere   unlisted securities

anbieten   im Weg der Daueremission: to offer by way of tap issues; im Tenderverfahren: to offer for sale by tender

Anderdepot   securities escrow account

Anderkonto   escrow account

andienen   Dokumente: to tender documents; zum Verkauf: to offer for sale

Andienung zur Einsichtnahme
tendering (submittal) for inspection

Aneignungsermächtigung   im Effektengeschäft: authorisation for the safekeeping of securities by foreign correspondents

Anerkenntnis   acknowledgement; Auszug, Saldo: confirmation of balance

anfallen   Zinsen: to accrue, to accumulate

Anfangs
- belastung   initial debt service, initial interest and redemption payments

9

- gewinne   Börse: early gains, gains on early trading
- kapital   initial capital
- kurs   opening price
- tilgungssatz   initial redemption rate
- verzinsung   initial interest return; Anleihe: initial coupon

Anfordern, auf erstes - zahlen   to pay upon the first call (request)

angebotene Gelder   money (funds) on offer

Angebots
- druck   Börse: selling pressure
- palette einer Bank   range of services offered by a bank
- überhang   Börse: surplus of offerings (of sell orders)

angefallene Stückzinsen   interest accrued

Angeld   earnest money

angemessene Risikovorsorge treffen   to provide adequately against lending risks

Angemessenheit des Eigenkapitals   capital adequacy; adequacy of capital and reserves

angespannt
- er Geldmarkt   tight money market
- e Liquiditätslage   stringent (tight) liquidity position

Angliederungsfinanzierung   take-over financing

angreifen   Rücklagen: to tap the reserves, to dip into the surplus

Angstklausel   non-liability clause

Angstverkäufe   panic selling

anhaltende Kurserholung   sustained rally

anheben   Kurs: to mark up; Dividende, Diskontsatz: to increase, to lift

Anhebung   marking up; lifting, increase

Ankaufs
- garantie   undertaking to buy, purchase guarantee
- kurs / - satz   buying rate
- zusage   (a) undertaking to buy; (b) assurance of rediscount

ankündigen   eine Dividende: to declare a dividend; mit Plus (Minus): to mark up (down)

ankurbeln   Konjunktur: to stimulate economic activity, to prime the pump

Anlage   investment; im Geldhandel: placing funds (money), depositing funds
- bedarf   (a) investment requirements; (b) funds available for investment
- berater   investment advisor
- beratung   investment counselling
- bereitschaft   propensity (willingness) to invest
- betrag   amount invested
- bewertung   des Anlagevermögens: asset valuation; von Wertpapieren: investment rating (appraisal), evaluation of securities
- empfehlungen   securities recommended for investment
- erfolg   investment performance, capital payout and capital appreciation
- ergebnis   investment performance
- erträge   investment income
- form   type of investment, investment vehicle

- in Aktien   equity investment, investment in shares (stocks)
- investitionen   fixed asset investments, capital equipment spending
- kapital   (a) fixed assets; (b) funds (capital) available for investment
- käufe   portfolio buying
- möglichkeiten   investment opportunities, outlet for funds
- nehmer   im Geldhandel: buyer, borrower

Anlagen
- erneuerung   asset replacement
- finanzierung   asset financing
- intensität   ratio of fixed assets to total assets
- rechnung   asset accounting
- wirtschaft   asset management
- zugänge   asset additions

Anlage
- palette   range (spectrum) of investment vehicles
- papiere   investment (portfolio) securities
- plan   formula plan
- politik   investment policy
- publikum   investing public
- risiko   investment risk
- schwerpunkt   principal investment objective, main area of investments
- spielraum   investment leeway
- streuung   spreading of investments, investment spread (diversification)
- studie   investment analysis
- suchendes Kapital   money seeking investment
- transparenz   investment transparency
- vermögen   fixed assets; eines Investmentfonds: fund's assets
- vorschriften für Kreditinstitute: provisions designed to safeguard the liquidity of banks
- werte   top quality stocks, blue chips
- wertminderung   capital depreciation
- wertpapiere zum Einstandspreis oder darunter (zum Marktwert) investment securities, at cost or less (at market price)
- wertsteigerung   capital appreciation
- ziel   investment objective

Anlaufdividende   start-up dividend

anlegen   to invest, to commit funds to

Anleger   (a) investor; (b) investing public
- gruppe   group (class) of investors
- interesse   buying (investment) interest
- interesse konzentrierte sich auf Chemiewerte   investment interest centered on chemicals
- publikum   investing public, investors

Anleihe   loan, bond
- ablösung   bond redemption, redemption of a loan
- agio   loan (bond) premium
- ausstattung   bond (loan) terms, bond features
- bedarf   bond borrowing requirements
- bedingungen   loan (bond) terms
- begebung   floating of a loan, bond floatation
- bewertung   bond rating; rating a bond issue
- der öffentlichen Hand   public bond

- dienst   debt service, loan service, redemption and coupon service; servicing a bond
- emission   bond (loan) issue
- erlös   bond (loan) proceeds
- finanzierung   bond financing, financing through bond issues
- geschäft   bond issuing operations
- inhaber   bondholder
- kapital   loan capital
- konsortium   loan syndicate
- konversion   bond conversion
- kosten   bond issuing costs, floatation costs
- kündigung   calling in a bond; bond redemption notice, call for redemption
- kurs   bond price (quotation); price quoted for a bond
- laufzeit   life (term) of a bond
- mantel   bond certificate
- mit Umtauschrecht   bond with conversion privilege
- mit variabler Verzinsung   floating rate bond
- modalitäten   bond terms, loan (bond) features
- politik   bond issuing policy
- portefeuille   bond portfolio
- rendite   bond yield
- schein   loan (bond)certificate
- schuld   loan debt
- schuldner   loan debtor, borrower
- stopp   issuing ban (freeze)
- stückelung   bond denomination
- tilgung   loan (bond) redemption; redeeming a bond
- tilgungsfonds   sinking fund
- treuhänderschaft   loan trusteeship
- umlauf   bonds outstanding
- umschuldung   refunding a bond issue
- unterbringung   placing a bond issue
- verbindlichkeiten   bonds payable
- verschuldung   bond indebtedness
- vertrag   loan agreement, bond indenture
- verzinsung   bond coupon
- zeichnungskurs   bond subscription price
- zins / -zinssatz   coupon, bond (loan) interest rate
- zinsen   loan (bond) interest
- zuteilung   loan allotment

<u>anmelden</u>   Konkursforderung: to lodge a proof, to prove

<u>Annäherungskurs</u>   approximate price

<u>Annahme</u>   acceptance; accepting
- erklärung   acceptance, undertaking to accept
- gebot   duty to accept
- stelle   Emission, Umtausch von Optionsscheinen: receiving agent

<u>annehmen</u>   to accept; to honour

<u>Annuität</u>   (a) annual interest and redemption payments, annual debt service; (b) annuity

<u>Annuitäten</u>
- anleihe   annuity loan, perpetual bond
- darlehen   annuity loan
- hypothek   redemption mortgage

<u>anpassen</u>   to adapt, to adjust; to renegotiate; to realign

<u>Anpassung</u>   adaptation, adjustment; realignment, renegotiation
- der Leitkurse (EWS)   realignment of central rates
- des Zinssatzes an veränderte Geldmarktbedingungen   adjusting the interest rate to changed conditions in the money market

<u>Anpassungsdarlehen</u> /<u>Anpassungsgeschäft</u>   renegotiated loan/lendings

<u>anrechenbar</u> (a) counting towards; (b) allowable as a deduction, deductible from the taxable income; (c) chargeable

- e Körperschaftssteuer income tax credit (i.e. corporation tax paid by the distributing company is deductible from the shareholder's income tax load)

<u>anrechnen</u> (a) to count towards, to credit; (b) to deduct; (c) to charge; (d) to set off, to net against

auf die Kapitalbasis - to count towards the capital resources

auf die Einkommensteuerschuld - to deduct from the income tax load

Zinsen und Provisionen - to charge interest and commission

auf den ausstehenden Betrag - to set off against the amount outstanding

auf das Rediskontkontingent - to net against the rediscount quota

<u>Anrechnung</u> counting towards; deducting, deduction; charging; setting off against

Satzbeispiele siehe anrechnen

<u>anrechnungsberechtigter Aktionär</u> shareholder entitled to an income tax credit (⟶ anrechenbare Körperschaftssteuer)

<u>Anrechnungsverfahren</u> tax credit system

<u>Anrechnungswert</u> amount counting towards; attributable value; amount allowable as a deduction, deduction; amount (value) to be set off

<u>Anrechtsschein</u> warrant, scrip certificate

<u>Anreicherungsfonds</u> growth fund

<u>Ansatz</u> in der Bilanz: amount stated (reported), carrying value

<u>anschaffen</u> to deliver; to remit; to provide cover

<u>Anschaffung</u> delivery, provision of cover, remittance

- der Deckung provision of cover, remitting cover funds

- der effektiven Stücke physical delivery of the securities

- des fehlenden Betrages remittance of the amount not yet transferred

<u>Anschaffungs</u>
- darlehen personal loan; personal instalment credit

- geschäfte bei Wertpapieren: securities transactions for third-party account

- kosten Wertpapiere: cost price Anlagen: cost of acquisition

- kostenprinzip historical cost principle

- wert, zum - at cost

<u>Anschluß</u>
- aufträge Börse: follow-through support, follow-up orders

- finanzierung follow-up (follow-on) financing

- kredit follow-up loan

<u>ansetzen</u> in der Bilanz: to state, to report; im Budget: to appropriate

nach dem Niederstwertprinzip - to state (to value) at the lower of cost or market

<u>Anspannung</u> Geldmarkt: tightness (constraint) in the money market; Konjunktur: economic strains; Liquidität: liquidity squeeze

<u>Anspannungskoeffizient</u> debt/equity ratio

<u>ansparen</u> to save up

<u>Ansparleistung</u> (a) savings avail-

Anspruch claim, right; title; entitlement

Anspruch, in - nehmen
den Kapitalmarkt: to tap the capital market, to call on the capital market
eine Kreditlinie: to draw on a credit line
aus einer Garantie: to call on a guarantee, to call upon the guarantor

Anspruchsberechtigter rightful claimant, beneficiary

Ansprüche an den Kapitalmarkt callings on the capital market

Ansprüche aus laufender Rechnung claims arising from current accounts

Anteil share; Beteiligung: interest, stake, share, holding; Fondsanteil:unit (Br),share(US)

Anteile im Fremdbesitz minority interests

Anteil
- inhaber von Fondsanteilen: unitholder, shareholder
- papiere shares, equities
- schein Fondsanteil: unit, share certificate

Anteils
- bestand unitholding, shareholding
- bruchteile fractional units (shares)
- eigner eines Unternehmens: shareholder, partner
- mäßige Erhöhung der Kreditlinien increase in (stepping up) credit lines on a pro rata basis
- mehrheit majority of shares
- register unit (share)register

- rückgaben unit (share) redemptions, units redeemed
- umlauf units (shares) outstanding
- zeichner subscriber to units, share applicant
- zeichnung subscription of (application for) units
- zertifikat share (unit) certificate

Antrag application, request
- auf Börseneinführung application for listing
- auf Konkurseröffnung petition in bankruptcy

Antriebskräfte impellent (stimulating) forces

Anweisung der Deutschen Bundesbank über Mindestreserven minimum reserve directives of the German Central Bank

Anzahlung downpayment, payment on account

Anzahlungsaval /-bürgschaft/-garantie downpayment guarantee, advance payment guarantee

Anzeigepflicht duty to report (to notify)
- für Großkredite duty to report loans for DM 1 million or more to the Bundesbank and the Banking Supervisory Authority

Anzeigetafel Börse: quotations board

Anzeigevorschriften notification provisions

anziehen Kurse: to firm, to move up (ahead), to harden, to advance
- auf breiter Front to harden across the board
- gegen Schluß der Börsensitzung to pick up at the close of trading

Anziehen
- der Kurse hardening of (advance in) prices
- der Zinsschraube tightening of the interest screw

Arbitragewerte arbitrage stocks

arrangieren einen Kredit: to arrange a loan

Arrondierungskäufe rounding off buying

aufbringen Gelder: to raise (to obtain, to generate) funds

auffächern to spread, to diversify

auffangen Kursverluste: to cushion (to absorb) price losses

auffordern zur Einzahlung auf Aktien: to call on shares

Aufforderung request, call

Aufgabe (a) accounting advice, voucher; (b) name of contracting party

Aufgabemakler unofficial broker dealing for own account (name and address of his contracting party must be released within the following 24 hours)

Aufgeld für vorzeitige Tilgung premium on early redemption

aufgenommene Gelder funds borrowed, borrowings

aufgenommene Tagesgelder overnight money borrowed (bought)

aufgerufene Wertpapiere (a) securities called for redemption; (b) securities advertised as lost

Aufkauf acquisition, take-over, buying up

Aufkäufe am Markt buying in the market

aufkaufen to take over, to buy up
Aktien an der Börse - to buy up shares on the stock exchange
ein Unternehmen - to acquire (to take over) a company

Aufkäufer an der Börse: buyer, speculative buyer (operator)

aufkündigen to terminate, to cancel; Kredit, Anleihe: to call in a loan

Aufkündigung termination, cancellation; calling in

Auflagen für den Kreditnehmer constraints on the borrower, restrictive loan provisions

auflassen to convey, to transfer

Auflassung von Grundbesitz: conveyance, transfer
- über $3Mrd. für den Internationalen Währungsfonds central bank governors' agreement to a $3bn loan for the International Monetary Fund

auflaufen to accrue, to accumulate
Dividenden - lassen to allow dividends to accumulate

Auflaufen von Zinsen: accrual (accumulation) of interest

auflegen to launch, to float
eine Anleihe - to float a loan, to launch a bond issue
einen Investmentfonds - to launch a unit trust
im Wege der Privatplazierung - to float as private placement
zur Zeichnung - to offer for subscription, to invite subscriptions

aufliegen zur Einsichtnahme: to be available (open) for inspection
zur Zeichnung: to be offered for subscription

auflösen Wertpapierbestände: to liquidate, to square; Unternehmen: to dissolve, to wind up; Rückstellungen: to write back auflösende Bestimmung resolutive condition

Auflösung liquidation; dissolution; writing back
- eines Unternehmens winding up (dissolution of) a company
- von Rückstellungen / Sammelwertberichtigungen writing back provisions / general loan loss provisions

Aufnahme
- eines Darlehens/Kredites raising a loan, taking out a loan, borrowing
- kreditkonformer Dokumente taking up documents which are in accordance with the terms and conditions of the credit
- von Tagesgeld overnight borrowing, buying (borrowing) overnight money
- von Termingeld buying (borrowing) term money

Aufnahmebedingungen terms of subscription, underwriting terms

aufnahmebereite Anleger investors willing to take stocks

aufnahmefähiger Markt ready market, receptive market

Aufnahme
- fähigkeit absorbing capacity, market receptivity
- saldo bei Wertpapieren: net buying
- zusage im Dokumentengeschäft: undertaking to take up documents

aufnehmen to raise; to take up
  am Kapitalmarkt - to raise (to borrow) in the capital market, to tap the capital market, to call on the capital market
  die Dokumente - to take up (to accept) the documents

einen Kredit - to raise (to contract) a loan, to borrow, to take out a loan
einen Wechsel bei Fälligkeit - to honour (to meet) a bill upon maturity

aufrechnen to set off (to net) against, to balance
  Guthaben- und Schuldzinsen - to net interest income against interest payable

aufrufen to call
  zur Tilgung - to call in (up) for redemption, to give notice of redemption

aufrunden to round up, to revise upwards

Aufschlag premium, markup; spread
- auf die Prime Rate premium above the prime rate, increment above prime
- von 1% auf Sechsmonats-Libor spread (margin) of 1% over six-month Libor

aufschwänzen to corner

Aufschwung upturn, upswing

Aufsichtsrat Supervisory Board

Aufstockung increase, rise
- des Kapitals capital increase
- der Mitgliedsquoten (IWF) increase in members' quotas (subscriptions)

Auftraggeber principal, party ordering, remitter; Akkreditiv: applicant for the credit

Auftrags
- bestand orders in (on) hand
- geschäft commission business
- papiere documents accepted for collection
- polster backlog of orders in hand
- wert Börse: transaction value

<u>auftreten</u> am Geldmarkt: to operate in the money market

<u>Aufwand</u> expenditure

- für die Risikovorsorge im Kreditgeschäft loan loss provisions

<u>Aufwands</u>
- konten expense accounts

- rückstellungen provisions for operating expenses

- zinsen interest paid

<u>Aufwärtsbewegung /-trend</u> upward trend

- am Aktienmarkt uptrend (surge) in the equity market

<u>Aufwendungen</u> expenditure, charges

- für Dienstleistungsgeschäfte service charges paid

- für Altersversorgung und Unterstützung expenditure on pension plans and employee benefits

- saldiert mit Erträgen net expenses

- aus Verlustübernahmen losses incurred under profit and loss transfer agreements

<u>aufwerten</u> to revalue

<u>Aufwertung</u> revaluation

<u>Aufwertungs</u>
- druck upward exchange rate pressure, revaluation pressure

- satz revaluation rate

- verdächtig revaluation-prone

- verlust loss on revaluation

<u>Auf-Widerruf-Auftrag</u> Börse: good till cancel order, GTC order

<u>aufzinsen</u> to add on interest, to mark up for interest accruing

<u>Aufzinsung</u> adding on interest

<u>Ausbau</u> intensification, strengthening

- des Dienstleistungsgeschäftes increase in the range of services offered

<u>ausbauen</u> to intensify, to strengthen Kundenbeziehungen - to solidify and extend customer relationships

<u>ausbuchen</u> to write off, to charge off; ein Konto: to balance (to settle) an account

<u>Ausbuchung</u> write-off, writing off, charge-off; settlement

- uneinbringlicher Forderungen writing off irrecoverable debts

<u>Ausbuchungsbedarf</u> write-off requirements

<u>Ausbuchungskompetenz</u> write-off powers

<u>Ausfall</u> (a) loss, default, non-payment, failure to pay; (b) Fehlbetrag: shortage, deficit; (c) der Dividende: passing the dividend

<u>Ausfälle im Kreditgeschäft</u> loan losses

<u>Ausfall</u>
- bürgschaft certificate (letter) of indemnity, indemnity bond

- erfahrungswerte loan loss experience

- quote im Kreditgeschäft loan loss ratio, charge-off rate, default rate, delinquency rate (US)

- risiko default risk, risk of loss (default), loan loss risk

<u>ausfertigen</u> Urkunde: to execute

<u>Ausfertigung</u> execution; Abschrift, Exemplar: copy; Wechselausfertigung: first, second or third of exchange

<u>Ausfuhr</u>
- bürgschaft export guarantee

- deckung provision of cover for exports

17

ausführen to implement; **Effektenauftrag:** to execute, to carry out

Ausfuhr
- **finanzierung** export financing
- **garantie /-gewährleistung** export guarantee
- **kreditdeckung** export loan guarantee
- **kreditversicherung** export credit insurance

Ausführung implementation; execution, carrying out

Ausführungs
- **anzeige** advice of deal, contract note, order ticket
- **börse** trading exchange

Ausgabe issue, issuing, offering
- **abschlag** offering discount
- **aufgeld** offering premium
- **aufschlag** load, loading charge, front-end load, marketing fee, selling markup
- **bedingungen** terms of issue, offering (issuing) terms
- **genehmigung** issuing approval
- **kurs** issuing (offering) price
- **preis bei Fondsanteilen:** unit offering price, selling (offer) price
- **von Gratisaktien** capitalisation issue, scrip issue
- **von jungen Aktien** issue of new shares

ausgeloste Anleihe bond drawn

ausgereichte Darlehen loans extended, lendings

ausgereizte Aktien stocks without price potential (without upside potential)

ausgewiesene eigene Mittel share capital and reserves stated in the annual accounts

Ausgleich (a) settlement, repayment balancing, squaring; (b) setting off against; (c) compensation for, covering
- **eines Kontos** (a) settling the debit balance of an account; (b) balancing (squaring) an account
- **einer Rechnung** settlement (payment) of an invoice
- **des Sollsaldos mit einem Guthaben** setting off (repaying) a debit balance against a credit
- **der Zinsverluste** covering the loss of interest

ausgleichen (a) to settle, to balance, to square; (b) to set off against; (c) to compensate for, to cover

Ausgleichs
- **buchung** balancing entry, counter-entry
- **forderungen** recovery claims
- **posten** adjustment (balancing) item
- **posten für Anteile im Fremdbesitz** minority interests
- **zahlung** compensation (compensatory) payment; payment in settlement of

ausgliedern einen Unternehmensbereich: to spin (to hive) off

Aushändigung der Dokumente: delivery of the documents

auskehren to pay, to clear (to pay) off

Auskunft information; **über einen Bankkunden:** status report (information) (Br); credit position report (US)

Auskunfts
- **einholung** making a status enquiry on a customer; obtaining information on
- **ersuchen** status enquiry; request to disclose information

- pflicht duty to furnish the information requested

Ausländer
- depot non-resident securities account
- DM-Konto non-resident DM-account
- konvertibilität non-resident convertibility

Auslands
- anleihe external DM-bond (floated by foreign issuers in Germany); external loan
- ausfälle im Kreditgeschäft: foreign loan losses
- beteiligungen foreign shareholdings (interests), trade investments abroad
- bond foreign currency bond (floated by German issuers abroad)
- einlagen non-resident deposits
- engagements im Kreditgeschäft: foreign lendings (commitments), lendings to foreign customers, international exposure
  an der Börse: foreign buying
- gelder foreign funds
- geschäft (a) international business (operations), international banking; bei Wertpapieren: (b) securities bought or sold abroad; (c) securities bought or sold for account of non-residents at home
- interesse Börse: foreign buying interest
- investitionen foreign investments, investments abroad
- investmentgesetz law governing the sale of foreign mutual fund shares
- kapital foreign capital
- käufe Börse: foreign (overseas - Br) buying
- korrespondent Bankverbindung: correspondent abroad
- kredit an das Ausland: foreign loan (lending); Kreditaufnahme im Ausland: foreign borrowing, borrowing abroad, loan raised abroad
- kreditgeschäft international lending business
- kreditportefeuille /-volumen foreign loan portfolio, international exposure
- niederlassung foreign branch
- obligo foreign commitments (lendings), international exposure
- repräsentanz representative office abroad
- saldo net external position
- scheck foreign currency cheque
- status statement of foreign borrowings and lendings
- stücke German securities held abroad
- tätigkeit einer Bank: international operations
- verkäufe Börse: foreign selling
- verschuldung external indebtedness
- verwahrung safe custody (safekeeping) abroad
- währung foreign currency
- wechsel foreign currency bill
- werte foreign stocks (securities, issues)
- zahlung (a) foreign payment (transfer); (b) payment received from abroad
- zahlungsverkehr international payments

Auslastungsgrad capacity usage ratio, capacity utilisation rate
- der Anlagen plant utilisation factor

auslaufende Pensionsgeschäfte expiring sale and repurchase agreements ausleihen to lend

Ausleihfrist lending period (term), life of a loan

Ausleihquote lending ratio; ratio of lendings to total assets plus endorsement liabilities

Ausleihungen lendings
- an Dienstleistungsunternehmen lendings to service companies
- an freie Berufe lendings to self-employed
- an Gruppengesellschaften lendings to (due from) group companies
- an die Privatkundschaft (Firmenkundschaft) lendings to private (corporate) customers

Ausleih-/Ausleihungsvolumen total lendings, lending (loan) portfolio

ausliefern to deliver

Auslieferung delivery
- effektiver Stücke physical delivery; delivery of the share certificates

auslosbar drawable; redeemable by drawings

auslosen to draw, to draw by lots

auslösen
  eine Spekulation in Bauwerten - to spark off speculative activity in buildings

  Verkaufsdruck - to trigger selling pressure

Auslosung drawing, drawing lots
  Tilgung durch - redemption by drawing lots

Auslosungs
- anleihe bond (loan) redeemable by drawings
- anzeige notice of drawing

- kurs drawing price
- liste list of drawings, list of bonds drawn
- nummern numbers drawn
- termin drawing date

ausmachen to amount to, to total

ausmachender Betrag (a) actual proceeds (cost); (b) total cost

Ausnahmekonditionen/ -sätze preferential (concessional) rates

ausnutzen to draw on, to make use of, to utilise

Ausnutzung drawing, utilisation
- einer Kreditlinie drawing(s) on a credit line

ausreichen einen Kredit: to extend a loan, to lend

Ausreichung extension, extending, lending

  die erfolgten -en lendings made, loans extended
- von Festsatzkrediten extending fixed-rate loans
- von Darlehen extension of loans, loan accommodations

ausschließlich
- Bezugsrechte ex rights
- Geber im Geldhandel: net sellers (lenders)
- Nehmer im Geldhandel: net buyers (borrowers)
- Ziehung ex drawing

Ausschließlichkeitserklärung borrower's commitment to route all banking transactions through the lending bank

ausschreiben to invite tenders for, to offer

Ausschreibung invitation for tenders, invitation to tender

- von Kassenobligationen   note tender

Ausschreibungsgarantie   tender guarantee

ausschütten   to distribute, to pay a dividend

Ausschüttung   distribution, amount distributed, dividend, payout

- en einschließlich Steuergutschrift   grossed up distributions

Ausschüttungs
- anspruch, mit - ab ...   carrying dividend rights as of ...
- bedarf   dividend requirements
- belastung   tax (charges) levied on distributions

ausschüttungsfähiger Gewinn   distributable (attributable) profit, profit for distribution, profit available to shareholders

Ausschüttungssatz   rate of distribution, dividend rate

Außen
- beitrag   current account surplus
- bezirksverkehr   money transmission orders routed through two or more Central Savings Banks (⟶ Bezirksverkehr)
- finanzierung   external financing
- handelsfinanzierung   foreign trade financing
- handelsüberschuß   foreign (external) trade surplus
- stände   receivables
- wert   einer Währung: external value of a currency
- wirtschaftsgesetz   Foreign Trade and Payments Law
- wirtschaftsposition   foreign trade position

außerbörslich
- handeln   to trade off the floor (off the board)
- er Handel   off-floor trading (dealings), off-board trading
- e Notierung   off-board price, free market quotation, street price

außergerichtlicher Vergleich   out-of-court settlement, voluntary adjustment (US)

Außerkurssetzung   invalidation of securities

außerordentlich
- e Aufwendungen   extraordinary (non-recurrent) expenses
- e Belastungen   extraordinary charges (e.g. write-offs or loan losses)
- e Rechnung   extraordinary account (statement)

außerplanmäßig
- e Abschreibungen   special write-offs
- e Ausgaben   extra-budgetary expenditure
- e Tilgung   Anleihe: unscheduled redemption; Kredit: special (unscheduled) repayment

äußerste Konditionen   most keenly priced terms

aussetzen   Kursnotierung: to suspend the quotation

aussondern   beim Konkursverfahren: to settle separately

Aussonderung   separate settlement, separation

Aussonderungsrecht   right of separation, right to separate settlement

ausstatten

die Anleihe ist mit einem hohen Zinssatz ausgestattet   the bond carries a high coupon die Bezugsrechtsscheine sind mit Stimmrechten ausgestattet the warrants carry voting rights

mit Dividendenansprüchen ausgestattet bearing dividend, carrying dividend rights

mit Kapital - to provide funds (capital)

ausgestattet mit einer Laufzeit von zehn Jahren with a life of ten years, running for ten years

ausgestattet mit einer Restlaufzeit von zwei Jahren having two years to run to maturity

finanziell gut ausgestattetes Unternehmen company operating on a sound financial basis

Ausstattung provision

- einer Anleihe bond (loan) terms, bond features

- mit Eigenmitteln availability of internally generated funds, capital resources available

ausstellen to issue; Schecks, Wechsel: to write, to draw

Aussteller issuer, drawer, writer

Ausstellerobligo drawer's liability

Ausstellung drawing, writing

austauschen Wertpapiere: to exchange (to swap) ... for ...

Austausch exchange, swap

ausüben von Bezugsrechten: to exercise (to take up) subscription rights

Ausübung exercise, taking up

auswärtige Institute out-of-town banks

Ausweichpreis fictitious price

Ausweis statement; Bankausweis: return

ausweisen in der Bilanz: to state, to carry, to show

zu den Gestehungskosten - to carry at cost

einen Gewinn - to show a profit

ausweiten to increase, to expand

Ausweitung increase, expansion

- der Barausleihungen increase in cash loans

- des Kreditvolumens expansion of the loan portfolio

- der Zinsspanne widening of the interest margin

Auswirkungen auf die Kreditnachfrage: impact (repercussions) on the demand for credit

auszahlen to pay, to pay out, to disburse; to buy out, to pay off

ein Darlehen - to disburse (to pay out) a loan

einen Gesellschafter - to buy out (to pay off) a partner

gegen Vorlage der Dokumente - to pay against presentation of the documents

Auszahlplan withdrawal plan

Auszahlung payment, disbursement; paying off

- en auf bereits zugesagte Darlehen disbursements on loans already committed

- des Darlehens an den Kreditnehmer disbursement of the loan; crediting the borrower's account with the loan proceeds

- en aus dem Kredit disbursements under the loan agreement

mit 100 % - loan proceeds being paid in full

mit 95 % - loan proceeds being paid at a 5 % discount

Auszahlungs
- anspruch right to payment (disbursement)

22

- anweisung disbursement (payment) instructions, payment order

- bedingungen für Hypothekenkredite: mortgage loan terms

- betrag amount paid out; bei einem Kredit: net loan proceeds

- bewilligung authorisation of payment (disbursement); placing the loan principal at the borrower's disposal

- disagio discount deducted from the loan principal

- ermächtigung bei einem Akkreditiv: authority to pay

- kurs disbursement rate (i.e. loan principal less discount)

- mittel loan funds; funds required for disbursements

- platz place of payment

- sperre payment stop; Scheck: countermand of payment

- überhang net lendings, lending surplus

- verlust discount deducted from the loan principal

- verpflichtungen disbursement (lending) commitments

- volumen total amount of new loans extended

- wert net loan proceeds

- zusage payment undertaking, undertaking to pay; Kredit: loan undertaking

Auszug Depotauszug: statement of securities; Kontoauszug: statement of account

Automation im Bankwesen automation in banking

automatisierte Bankkundenbedienung automated servicing of bank customers

Automobilaktien motors, automobile shares (stocks)

Aval guarantee

- akzept guarantee acceptance

- auftrag instructions to provide a guarantee

- gemeinschaftskredit syndicated guarantee credit

- hinauslegung extending a guarantee credit, guarantee accommodation

avalieren to guarantee

Aval

- inanspruchnahme calling on a guarantee

- konto guarantee account

- kredit guarantee credit; credit by way of guarantee

- kreditgebendes Institut guarantor bank

- kreditgeber guarantor

- kreditnehmer guarantee

- laufzeit life (term) of a guarantee

- linie guarantee line

- nutzen guarantee commission

- obligo guarantee commitments

- provision guarantee commission

- provisionseinnahmen guarantee commission income

- stellung /-übernahme extending a guarantee credit; furnishing a guarantee

- vermerk guarantee undertaking

- verpflichtung commitment (undertaking) to guarantee

- verpflichtungen commitments under guarantees furnished

avisierende Bank advising bank

Avisierung des Akkreditivs an den Begünstigten advising the credit to the beneficiary

B

<u>b</u> → bezahlt

<u>B</u> → Brief

<u>-B</u> → gestrichen, Brief

<u>Baisse</u> sharp drop (fall), downhill slide, nosedive of stock (and/or bond) prices
- engagement bear commitment, bear (short) position
- manöver bear raid
- markt bear (depressed) market
- position bear account (position)
- spekulant bear, short seller
- stimmung bearish mood
- verkauf bear sale
- verkäufer bear, short seller

<u>Baissier</u> bear

<u>Bandbreite</u> spread, margin, range
- n der Wechselkurse margins of fluctuation, bands of permitted fluctuation

<u>Bank</u> bank, banking organisation
- adresse bank name (e.g. in the bond market)

    erste Bankadresse prime bank
- aktien banks, bank shares (stocks)
- akzept bank (banker's) acceptance
- an-Bank-Kredit interbank lending (loan)
- angestellter bank official, bank employee
- auskunft banker's reference (opinion), status report
- ausweis bank return
- auszug bank statement, statement of account
- automation automation in banking
- aval bank guarantee
- bei-Bank-Einlagen interbank deposits
- beteiligungen banking interests, bank holdings
- betrieb banking, banking business (operations); Unternehmen: bank, banking organisation
- bilanz bank balance sheet
- bilanzierungsrichtlinien bank accounting rules
- bürgschaft bank guarantee, banker's bond
- dienstleistung banking service (facility, product)
- dienstleistungsautomat automated teller machine
- diskont (a) bank discount rate; (b) Central Bank's discount rate
- einlagen bank deposits
- einlagenschutz bank deposit protection
- einlagensicherung bank deposit insurance
- einlagensicherungsfonds bank deposit insurance fund
- einzugsverfahren direct debiting system, direct debiting to a bank account
- emblem bank logo

<u>Banken</u>
- abrechnungsstelle bankers' clearing house
- apparat banking system, banks

Banken
- aufsicht   bank supervision; supervising (monitoring) the banking industry
- aufsichtsbehörde   banking supervisory authority
- bereich   (a) banking industry (sector); (b) Börse: banks, bank shares (stocks)
- beschäftigungskartei   register of (a bank's) correspondents
- bonifikation   Emission: selling commission, allowance
- clearing   interbank clearing
- einlagen   deposits by banks
- gelder   interbank money
- gesetzgebung   bank (banking) regulation, regulation of the banking industry (US); legislation on banks
- gruppe (-konsortium)   banking syndicate, group of banks
- liquidität   bank liquidity, liquidity of the banking system
- markt   (a) interbank market; (b) Börse: bank stocks
- pfandrecht   banker's lien
- publikum   Börse: bank traders
- sektor   banking sector
- selbstbehalt   bank's franchise
- stimmrecht   authority of the bank to vote the shares of its customers held under its management
- system   banking system
- tag   bankers' congress

Bank
- feiertag   bank holiday
- finanzierung   financing through a bank
- garantie   bank guarantee, banker's bond
- gebühren   bank charges
- geheimnis   banking secrecy
- geld   bank (deposit) money
- gepflogenheiten   banking customs
- geschäft   (a) banking business (operations); (b) banking transaction
- gewerbe   banking industry, banks
- giro   bank endorsement
- gläubiger   bank creditor
- guthaben   money in the bank; Bilanzposten; cash in banks
- haus   banker, banking organisation
- kaufmann   (a) bank officer; (b) banker, fully trained bank officer
- konditionen   banking terms, bank's terms of business (business conditions)
- konto   bank account
- kredit   bank loan (credit), bank advance (accommodation)
- kredite an den privaten Sektor   bank lendings to the private sector
- kredit mit festem (variablem) Zinssatz   fixed-rate (floating--rate) bank loan
- kreise   banking community
- lehre   student apprenticeship (training period) in banking
- lehrling   student apprentice, trainee
- leistungen   bank services (products), banking facilities
- leitzahl   bank code

bankmäßige
- Kreditbesicherung   providing (putting up) bankable security for a loan
- Sicherheit   bankable security, bank collateral, banking security
- Zahlung   payment through a bank

Bank
- nebenleistungen   incidental banking services, bank-related services

Bank
- nebenplatz secondary bank place (i.e. city without Bundesbank office)
- notenprivileg note-issuing privilege
- obligation bank bond
- platz (a) banking centre; (b) city in which Bundesbank operates an office
- politik banking policy
- praxis banking practice
- produkt banking product
- prokurist assistant manager, authorised signatory
- provision banking commission
- prüfung bank audit
- publizität disclosure requirements to be observed by banks
- rate central bank's discount rate
- referenz banker's reference
- regel → goldene Bankregel
- rembours bank documentary credit
- schalter counters
- schalterhalle banking hall
- schalterstunden banking (office) hours
- scheck bank cheque, banker's draft
- schließfach safe deposit box
- schuldverschreibung bank bond
- sicherheit bank security, bank collateral
- spesen bank charges
- stellendichte banking density
- stellennetz banking network
- tag banking day
- überweisung bank transfer, payment through a bank, bank giro credit, bank credit transfer (Br)
- üblich customary in banking, in line with banking practice
- usancen banking customs
- valoren bank valuables
- verbindlichkeiten due to banks
- verbindung der Bank: correspondent bank; des Kunden: banking connection
- verkehr interbank dealings; banking operations
- verwandte Dienstleistungen near-banking services
- vollmacht power to operate a bank account; account mandate
- vorauskredit bridging loan (extended by a bank)
- wechsel bank bill (draft)
- werte banks, bank shares
- wesen banking industry, banking
- woche bank return week
- wochenstichtag weekly bank return date
- ziehung bank draft
- zinsen bank interest
- zinssatz auf Einlagen: bank deposit rate; auf Kredite: bank lending rate
- zu-Bank Einlagen interbank deposits
- zu-Bank Fazilität interbank credit line

Bar
- abhebung (a) cash drawing; (b) drawing money at a bank
- akkreditiv cash documentary credit
- ausleihungen cash lendings
- ausschüttung cash distribution (payout)
- auszahlung payment in cash, cash disbursement
- bestände cash holdings, cash in tills
- debitoren cash lendings
- dividende cash dividend
- einforderung cash call, calling in cash

- einlage   cash contribution, contribution in cash
- einschuß   putting up cash resources (cash assets); Effektenkredit: margin
- einschußsätze   margin requirements
- einzahlung   cash deposit (payment)
- entnahme   cash drawing (withdrawal)
- gebot   cash bid
- geld   cash; notes and coin

bargeldlos   cashless
-e Gehaltszahlung   cashless pay; salary payment by bank giro credit
-e Zahlung   cashless payment, bank giro credit
-er Zahlungsverkehr   cashless payments, bank giro credit system

Bar
- guthaben   cash in (on) hand, cash assets
- inanspruchnahme Kredit: cash drawdown (drawing), drawdown in cash
- kapitalerhöhung   capital increase for cash, cash capital increase
- kapitalerhöhung bei Einräumung eines Bezugsrechtes im Verhältnis 10:1   cash capital increase on the basis of a one for ten rights issue
- kredit   cash advance (loan)
- kreditinanspruchnahme   drawing on a cash loan; cash drawing
- kreditrahmen   cash credit line
- liquidität   liquid cash resources
- mittel   cash (liquid) funds, available cash

- regulierung   cash settlement

Barren   bar
- gold   gold bullion

Bar
- reserve   cash reserve assets; cash in hand plus central bank and postal cheque account balances
- scheck   cash (open) cheque
- überschuß   cash surplus
- vermögen   cash (liquid) assets
- wert   cash value, current (market) value
- zahlung gegen Dokumente   cash against documents
- zahlungsverkehr   cash transactions
- zeichner   cash subscriber

Basis
- gesellschaft   holding company operating abroad
- preis   Optionsgeschäft: striking (exercise) price
- punkt   basis point
- trend   basic trend
- währung   reference currency

Bassin
- übereignung   assignment of goods to a trustee
- vertrag   deed of multiple assignment (goods assigned under this deed to a trustee serve as collateral for several lendings)

Bau
- aktien   building shares (stocks), buildings, constructions
- darlehen   building loan
- finanzierung   construction financing
- finanzierungskredit   building (construction) loan, housing loan
- finanzierungsmittel   building (housing) finance

- gelder   building finance, building (housing) loans
- geldkredit   interim building loan
- gewerbe   building industry
- kostenindex   construction cost index
- kostenzuschüsse   building cost subsidies
- nebenwerte   building-related stocks
- sicherungshypothek   builder's lien

Bauspar
- bedingungen   building society terms, savings and loan contract terms
- darlehen   building society loan
- einlagen   building society deposits

Bausparen   saving with building societies; investment in savings and loan contracts offered by building societies

Bausparer   building society depositor

Bauspar
- finanzierung   financing with building society funds, building society finance
- gelder   building society funds (finance)
- guthaben   amount saved under a savings and loan contract
- kasse   building society (Br), building and loan association, homestead association (US)
- kassenmittel   building society funds
- prämie   bonus paid on building society deposits
- summe   principal stipulated under a savings and loan contract
- vertrag   savings and loan contract

- zinsen   building society interest (rates)

Bau
- wechsel   building bill
- werte   building shares (stocks), buildings, constructions
- zinsen   (a) interest paid to shareholders until commencement of company's operations; (b) building loan rates
- zwischenkredit   interim building loan

b.a.w.-Konditionen   terms (rates) valid until further notice

beanspruchen   (a) to claim, to require; (b) to make use of, to take recourse to

Beanspruchung   claim; making use of; recourse; pressure, strain
- der Finanzmärkte   pressure exerted on the financial markets
- der Kapitalmärkte   borrowings in the capital markets, calling on (tapping) the capital markets
- eines kurzfristigen Überziehungskredites   drawing on (recourse to) a short-term overdraft facility

bearbeiten   to handle, to process

Bearbeitung   handling, processing
 die für die - des Kredites in Rechnung gestellten Gebühren
 the fees charged for the processing of the loan

Bearbeitungs
- gebühr   processing fee, handling charge
- provision   handling commission

beauftragen   to instruct, to direct, to commission, to mandate

mit der Eröffnung des Akkreditivs - to instruct XYZ to open (to issue) the documentary credit

mit dem Inkasso -   to entrust with the collection, to instruct to collect

beauftragte Bank (a) paying bank;
(b) bank instructed to ..

Bedarf an zusätzlichen Krediten
additional borrowing requirements

Bedarfsspitzen peak borrowing
requirements

bedecken Kundeneinlagen bedecken
die Bilanzsumme mit 40 %
customer deposits account for
40 % of total assets

Bedenkfrist Wechselrecht: grace
period

bedienen to service

ein Akkreditiv - to pay under a
documentary credit

die Aktionäre - to distribute
(to pay) a dividend to shareholders

eine Anleihe - to service a bond
(a loan)

die Forderungen der Kreditgeber -
to service the claims of the
lenders

einen Hypothekenkredit - to
service a mortgage loan

das Kapital - to pay a dividend
on the capital stock

die Rücklagen - to transfer (to
allocate) to reserves

Bedienung service, servicing;
paying, payment; transfer

Bedienungsquote servicing ratio

bedingt

- e Annahme qualified acceptance

- es Indossament conditional
endorsement

- es Kapital contingent capital

- e Kapitalerhöhung contingent
capital increase (i.e.capital
increase depending on the
exercise of conversion rights)

spekulativ - of a speculative
nature, speculation-induced

Bedingung (a) condition; (b)
stipulation, provision

- en für Festsatzkredite terms
governing fixed-rate loans

- en für den Zahlungsverkehr
provisions governing payment
transactions

Bedingungsanpassung bei Krediten:
adjustment of the loan terms

befestigen, sich - Kurse: to
stiffen, to harden, to firm up, to
pick up;geringfügig: to edge higher

beflügeln den Aktienmarkt: to
propel the stock market; die
Börsenphantasie: to capture investors' imagination

befreien von der Haftung: to
discharge (to release) from
liability; von einer Steuer: to
exempt from a tax

Befreiung discharge, release;
exemption

befriedigen to satisfy, to meet

die Forderungen der Bank müssen
voll befriedigt werden the bank's
claims must be satisfied in full

die Gläubiger - to pay off the
creditors

die Käufernachfrage - to satisfy (to meet) buying demand

eine starke Kreditnachfrage - to
meet a strong loan demand

Befriedigung satisfaction

- der Ansprüche gegenüber dem Kreditnehmer satisfaction of claims
against the borrower

- aus Pfand- oder anderen Sicherungsrechten satisfaction of claims
by realising liens or other
security interests

befristen to limit, to set (to
fix)a time limit

befristet

- e Einlagen term (time) deposits

- e Forderungen an ausländische Banken   term lendings to foreign banks
- er Kredit   term (time) loan
- e Mittel   term money (funds)
- e Verbindlichkeiten   term (time) liabilities

Befristung   (a) setting a time limit; agreeing on a fixed period; (b) duration, maturity

- der Inanspruchnahmen   setting a time limit for drawings
- des Kreditangebotes   duration of the loan offer; time limit set for the acceptance of the loan offer

mit einer - von zwölf Monaten   running for twelve months

begebbar   negotiable, marketable

begeben   Dokumente: to negotiate; Emission: to float, to issue, to launch

Begebung   negotiation; floatation; launching (in the market)
Begebungs-
- fähigkeit   (a) negotiability; floatation power
- konsortium   selling group
- kosten   floatation (issuing) costs
- kurs   issuing (offering)price

begleichen   to settle, to pay

Begleichung   settlement, payment
- der fälligen Zins- und Tilgungsleistungen   settlement of interest and principal payments falling due

Begleitdokumente   supporting documents

Begrenzung der Hypothekenkreditaufnahme   mortgage lending squeeze; putting a ceiling on mortgage lending

behaupten, sich -   Kurse: to hold steady

behauptet   maintained, steady

Beherrschungsvertrag   controlling agreement

Beinahe-Geld   near-money

bei Sicht   at sight
- zahlbare Dokumente   documents payable at sight

Beistandskredit   stand-by credit

beitreibbare Forderung   recoverable debt

beitreiben   to recover, to collect
eine Darlehensforderung gerichtlich -   to recover a loan by legal process

Beitreibung   recovery, collection

Beitreibungsverfahren   recovery proceedings

belasten   (a) to debit; (b) to burden
die Börse -   to weigh down (to depress, to plague) the market

das Konto des Kreditnehmers -   to debit (to enter to the debit of) the borrower's account

eine Liegenschaft -   to encumber property

Zinsen vierteljährlich -   to debit (to charge) interest every three months

hypothekarisch -   to mortgage

den Markt zusätzlich -   to put added pressure on the market

belastender Faktor   Börse: market depressant

Belastung   (a) debit; (b) burden; (c) charge
- mit Hypotheken   mortgage charge
- des Marktes   strain (pressure) coming to bear on the market

- mit EEV-Steuern income, profit and property tax load
- mit Zins und Tilgung debt service load; interest and redemption payments
- en aus Einzelwertberichtigungen charges for specific bad and doubtful debt provisions
- en im außerordentlichen Geschäft extraordinary charges (mainly loan losses or bond write-off requirements)

Belastungs
- anzeige debit advice (note)
- faktoren Börse: depressive factors, depressants
- festschreibung establishment of fixed interest and principal payments
- grenze encumbrance limit

beleben to revive, to invigorate, to stimulate; to rise, to increase

Belebung revival, stimulation; increase, upturn
- der Konjunktur revival of economic activity, economic upswing
- der Kreditnachfrage upturn (revival) in loan demand

Beleg (supporting) voucher

belegen
langfristige Ausleihungen - 40 % des Kreditvolumens long-term lendings account for 40 % of the loan portfolio
mit einer Garantie - to provide (to furnish) a guarantee
mit Mindestreserven - to establish (to impose) reserve requirements for

beleglos paperless, voucherless
- er Datenträgeraustausch magnetic tape clearing

- er Zahlungsverkehr paperless payments

Belegschaftsaktien staff shares, employee shares (stock)
2000 - wurden ausgegeben 2,000 shares were issued under the staff share option scheme

beleihbar qualifying as security for, eligible as collateral

beleihen to lend against (on), to advance money against
Grundbesitz - to lend against real (landed) property
das Umlaufvermögen bis zur Hälfte - to lend up to half of the current assets
Wertpapiere mit 60 % - to lend up to 60 p.c. of the securities' market value

Beleihung lending on (against)
Beleihungs
- grenze lending limit
- grundsätze lending principles
- objekt property serving as security (collateral)
- quote loan-to-value ratio, percentage advance, percentage advanced against (e.g. the market value of securities)
- quote bei börsennotierten Wertpapieren loan-to-value ratio on listed securities
- raum für erststellige Belastungen margin for lendings against senior charges
- satz Beleihungsquote
- stopp lending freeze
- verzeichnis register of properties serving as security
- wert lending (collateral) value, hypothecation value

Benehmen herstellen bei einer Emission: agreement on the loan terms (on the coupon)

benutzbar

  das Akkreditiv ist durch Tratten-negoziierung - the documentary credit is available by negotiation of drafts

  gegen Vorlage der folgenden Dokumente - available against presentation of the following documents

benutzbar stellen to make available

  einen Kredit - bei to allow drawings against (on) the loan with ...

beraten to counsel, to advise

Beratung der Kunden: counselling of customers

Beratungsleistungen counselling services

berechnen in Rechnung stellen: to charge; errechnen: to calculate, to compute

Berechnung charging; calculation

  halbjährliche - von Zinsen charging interest every six months

Berechnungs

- grundlage basis of computation
- zeitraum period of computation

berechtigen zu Verfügungen über ein Konto: to authorise to draw on an account

Berechtigungsschein Börse: warrant, scrip

Bereich (a) sector, area, field; (b) industry; (c) division

  Ausleihungen im langfristigen - long-term lendings

  der Banken- tendierte nach Gewinnmitnahmen schwächer bank stocks declined on profit-taking

  Entwicklungen im Privatkunden-developments in the retail banking sector

  Neuausrichtung des -es Inlandskredite realignment of the domestic lending division

  Notierungen im kurzfristigen - quotations (prices) at the short end of the market

  in andere -e des Marktes umschichten to switch into other sectors (segments) of the market

bereinigen to settle, to clear; to adjust

bereinigt

- e Bilanzsumme total assets less intangible assets
- er Index adjusted index
- es Kapital total capital stock less intangible assets

  saison- seasonally adjusted

Bereitschaft zu zusätzlichen Krediten willingness to extend further credit

bereitstehen zur Anlage bereitstehende Mittel: funds available for investment

bereitstellen to provide, to supply; to extend, to accommodate; to make (to hold) available

  gegen die Garantie der Muttergesellschaft - to make available (to extend) against the parent's guarantee

  auf gedeckter Basis - to extend on a secured basis, to extend (to lend) against collaterals

  Haushaltsmittel - to appropriate budget funds

  Kapital - to provide capital (funds), to commit funds

  einen Kredit - to extend (to grant, to accommodate) a loan

Bereitstellung provision, supply; extension; making available

- eines Festsatzkredites extending (providing, granting) a fixed-rate loan, accommodation (extension) of a fixed-rate loan

- zusätzlicher Kredite extending further credit; providing additional finance
- des Krediets erfolgt auf einem Sonderkonto the loan proceeds will be credited to a special loan account; the loan will be made available on a special loan account
- von Mitteln / Geldern provision (commitment) of funds
- der ersten Tranche provision (payment) of the first tranche
- für einen bestimmten Zweck allocation for a particular purpose, earmarking

Bereitstellungs
- fonds appropriation fund
- provision commitment commission, availability fee
- verpflichtung commitment to extend
- zinsen commitment interest

berichtigen to correct, to adjust; stornieren (eine Buchung): to reverse

Berichtigung correction, adjustment; Stornierung: reversal

Berichtigungs
- aktien bonus shares
- aktienemission capitalisation issue, scrip issue
- bedarf im Kreditgeschäft loan loss requirements
- buchung rectifying (adjustment) entry; Storno: reversal entry

Bericht report; account

Berichts
- pflichten disclosure (reporting) requirements
- pflichtiges Wertpapiergeschäft securities transaction subject to disclosure
- termin reporting date

- zeitraum reporting period, period under review

Berufshandel professional traders (operators)

beschaffen Mittel, Kredite: to raise, to procure, to generate, to obtain

Beschaffung raising, procurement, generating
- von Geldern auf dem Kapitalmarkt raising funds in the capital market
- von Zentralbankgeld borrowing (buying) central bank funds

Beschaffungskosten der Bank cost of funds to the bank

Beschäftigungslage im verarbeitenden Gewerbe capacity utilisation in the manufacturing sector

beschleunigen to accelerate
der Abwärtstrend beschleunigte sich the downturn gathered momentum

Beschlußfassung über die Verwendung des Bilanzgewinnes resolution on the appropriation of profits

beschränkt limited, restricted
- er Handel restricted dealings
- e Konvertierbarkeit limited convertibility
- e Zuteilung scaling down, limited allotment

Beschränkung limitation, restriction, squeeze, cutting down on
- der Hypothekenkreditaufnahme mortgage credit squeeze, tightening of mortgage lending
- des Kapitalverkehrs restrictions on capital flows (movements)
- der Kreditaufnahme im Ausland restrictions on borrowings abroad

- der Kreditvergabe   lending restrictions, credit tightening
- des Notenbankkredites   restrictions on central bank borrowings
- der Rediskontkontingente   limitation of rediscount quotas

besichern   to provide (to furnish) security, to put up security, to collateralise

Besicherung   provision of security, securing, putting up security, collateralisation
- erfolgt durch eine erstrangige Hypothek   security will be provided by a senior mortgage
- von Fremdwährungskrediten   provision of security for foreign currency lendings

Besicherungs
- form   security device, type of collateral
- wert   collateral value, hypothecation value

Besitz   (a) possession; (b) ownership; (c) estate, property
- anspruch   title
- gesellschaft   holding company
- verhältnisse   ownership structure

Besserungsschein   undertaking to repay

Bestand   holdings, portfolio
- an Hypothekendarlehen   mortgage loan portfolio, total mortgage lendings
- an festverzinslichen Papieren   holdings of fixed income securities
- an Wertberichtigungen   loan loss provisions

Bestände
- im kurz- und mittelfristigen Geschäft   short and medium term lendings

Bestands
- aufstockung   increase in holdings
- ausweitung im Kreditgeschäft   increase in total lendings
- ermittlungsverfahren   valuation of holdings
- minderung   decrease in holdings
- zuwachs bei Spareinlagen   growth in savings deposits

bestätigende Bank   confirming bank

bestätigtes Akkreditiv   confirmed documentary credit

bestätigter Scheck   certified cheque

Bestätigung   confirmation, confirming
- eines Akkreditives   confirming a documentary credit
- der Ordnungsmäßigkeit der Dokumente   certificate of compliance; confirming that the documents are in accordance with the terms and conditions of the credit
- einer Unterschrift   confirming the genuineness of a signature; certifying a signature

Bestätigungs
- provision   confirming commission
- vermerk   des Buchprüfers: audit certificate; auf einem Scheck: undertaking to pay (to honour) a cheque

Bestellerkredit   buyer's credit

Bestellung   (a) appointment, nomination; (b) taking out
- eines Bevollmächtigten   appointment of a proxy
- einer Hypothek   taking out (creation) of a mortgage

bestens   at best, at the market

Bestensorder   order to buy (to sell) at best, market order

Besteuerung an der Quelle   taxation at source

bestimmen   to stipulate, to provide for; Kurs: to determine durch Angebot und Nachfrage bestimmter Kurs   price determined by supply and demand

Bestimmung   Kurs, Zinssatz: determination; Vertrag: provision, clause

beteiligen, sich - to participate, to acquire an interest in

Beteiligung   participation, interest; investment

- an einer Gesellschaft   interest (stake, share, shareholding) in a company

- am Gewinn   share in profits, profit-sharing

- an einem Konsortium   share (participation) in a syndicate

Beteiligungen   Bilanzposten: investments, trade investments

- zum Ankaufswert, abzüglich Abschreibungen und Rückstellungen investments at cost, less amounts written off and provisions

- zum Buchwert   investments at amortised cost

- zu Einstandspreisen   investments at cost

Beteiligungs

- anteil   interest held, stake, investment, shareholding

- bank   associated bank

- besitz   trade investment portfolio, shareholdings

- erträge   income from trade investments

- finanzierung   equity financing

- fonds   equity fund, venture capital fund

- garantie-Gemeinschaft   equity guaranteeing society

- geber   investor

- gesellschaft   (a) associated company; (b) holding company; (c) Kapitalbeteiligungsgesellschaft: venture capital company

- kapital   equity finance, venture capital, development capital

- käufe   acquisition of shareholdings

- papiere   investment securities

- portefeuille   trade investment portfolio; total investments

- rechte   equities; investments

- vermittlung   equity investment service; venture capital service

- vertrag   joint venture agreement

- zugänge   investment additions

betreuen   to service, to serve

Betreuung   der Privatkunden servicing private customers

Betreuungskapazität   servicing potential

Betreuungskosten   cost of servicing

Betriebs

- aufwand   operating cost (expenses)

- ergebnis   operating profit (loss), income (loss) from operations

- ergebnis vor Afa   operating profit (loss) before depreciation for wear and tear

- ergebnisquote   profit ratio (operating profit as a percentage of the average business volume)

- ergebnisrechnung   operating income statement

- fremde Aufwendungen (Erträge) non-operating expenses (earnings)

- gesellschaft   operating (managing) company

- gewinn   operating (trading) profit

- gewöhnliche Nutzungsdauer   operating life expectancy

- grundstücke   operating premises

- handelsspanne   operating margin

- internes Informationssystem in-house information system
- kapazität operating capacity
- kapital working capital
- koeffizient working (operating) ratio
- kosten operating cost, cost of operations
- kredit operating loan, short-term loan, business credit
- mittel working (operating) funds
- mittelkredit business (operating) loan, development loan
- mittelrücklage operating cash reserve
- stätte Steuergesetzgebung: permanent establishment
- überschuß trading profit; →Teilbetriebsergebnis
- und Geschäftsausstattung plant and office equipment

beurkunden to authenticate, to verify; notariell: to notarise

Beurkundung authentication, verification; notarisation

beurteilen to judge; to assess, to rate, to evaluate

Beurteilung judgement, opinion; assessment, rating, evaluation
- der Kreditwürdigkeit assessment of (assessing) the credit-worthiness, credit evaluation
- des Länderrisikos country risk assessment
- von Mitarbeitern staff appraisal (assessment), merit rating

bevollmächtigen to authorise, to empower

Bevollmächtigter attorney, authorised person (signatory), donee; bei Stimmrechten: proxy

Bevollmächtigung authorisation, power of attorney, proxy

bevorrechtigt preferential, prior, privileged, senior
- sein to rank prior to, to be senior to, to rank preferentially
- er Gläubiger preferential creditor (Br), prior (preferred) creditor, prior claimant (US)
- e Konkursforderungen preferential debts (Br), prior claims (US)

Bevorrechtigung giving preference, priority
- von Lohn- und Gehaltsforderungen in einem Konkursverfahren priority for wages and salaries
- bestimmter Gläubiger privilege of priority enjoyed by certain creditors

bevorschussen to advance, to lend against

Bevorschussung advance, lending
- von Dokumenten advance against (on) documents
- von Forderungen lending against accounts receivable
- eines Nachlasses probate advance
- von Warenbeständen inventory lending, lending against stocks

bevorzugt preferential, preferred, privileged
- e Befriedigung preferential payment
- er Kunde valued customer

Bewegungsbilanz statement of funds, statement of sources and application

bewerten to value, to evaluate; to assess, to rate
 höher (niedriger) - im Kurs: to mark up (down)
 zu den Gestehungskosten - to value at cost

unter dem Marktpreis - to value below market price

Bewertung   valuation, evaluation; assessment, rating

- von Aktien (Anleihen)   stock (bond) rating

- zu den Anschaffungskosten   valuation at cost

- von Außenständen   valuation of accounts receivable

- zum Niederstwertprinzip   valuation at the lower of cost or market

- von Wertpapieren   bilanzmäßig: valuation; im Hinblick auf die Bonität: rating

- zum Wiederbeschaffungspreis   valuation at replacement cost

Bewertungs

- abschlag   write-down

- änderung   change in valuation; valuation adjustment

- bedarf im Kreditgeschäft   charges for bad and doubtful debt provisions

- grundsätze   valuation standards, principles of valuation

- stichtag   valuation date

- vorschriften   valuation provisions (rules)

- wahlrechte   valuation options

- zahlen   im Kreditgeschäft: rating ratios

bewilligen   to approve; to appropriate

Bewilligung   appropriation; approval

- eines Kredites   loan approval; approving a loan application

Bewilligungs

- ausschuß   loans committee; appropriations committee

- befugnisse   approval powers

- volumen   loans approved (accommodated, granted)

bezahlt (b)   market cleared; all buying and selling orders were executed at the current published quotation

bezahlt, Brief (bB)   sellers over; orders at best were executed, but selling orders at limit exceeded demand at the close of the session

bezahlt, Brief repartiert (bB rep.)   substantial surplus of selling orders necessitated a scale-down

bezahlt, Geld (bG)   buyers over; orders at best were executed, but buying orders at limit exceeded selling orders at the close of the session

bezahlt, Geld repartiert (bG rep.)   substantial surplus of buying orders necessitated a scale-down

Bezahltmeldung   confirmation (advice) of payment

Bezirksverkehr   money transmission orders routed through one Central Savings Bank only (⟶ Außenbezirksverkehr)

bezogene Bank   drawee bank

Bezogenen-Obligo   drawee's liability ledger

Bezogener   drawee

Bezug   subscription

die Anleihe zum - anbieten   to offer the bond for subscription

Bezugnahmeprospekt   abridged prospectus (based upon a prospectus published only a few months ago)

Bezugs

- aktien   new shares, shares offered under subscription or conversion options

- angebot   rights offering (offer), rights issue

- aufforderung   invitation to subscribe

- bedingungen terms of subscription
- berechtigt (a) entitled to subscribe; (b) entitled to dividends
- frist subscription period
- kurs subscription price

Bezugsrechte subscription rights, rights, stock rights

mit (ohne) - cum (ex) rights

rechnerischer Wert eines -es theoretical value of a right

Bezugsrechts
- abschlag ex-rights markdown, deduction of subscription rights, ex-rights quotation
- angebot rights letter, rights offering
- ankündigung rights issue announcement
- anwärter rights candidate
- ausübung exercise of subscription rights
- ausweis subscription warrant
- emission rights issue
- handel rights trading, trading of subscription rights
- inhaber rights holder
- nachweis evidence of rights entitlement
- notierung rights quotation
- schein warrant; subscription warrant
- wert (a) rights value; (b) security (stock) carrying subscription rights

Bezugs
- stelle rights agent; subscription agent
- tag day of subscription
- verhältnis, 6:1 one for six subscription ratio

bG ⟶ bezahlt, Geld

bG rep. ⟶ bezahlt, Geld repartiert

B-Geschäft instalment credit extended through the agency of the selling company

Bietfrist bidding period

Bietungsaval /-bürgschaft/-garantie bid bond

Bietungskonsortium bidding syndicate

Bilanz balance sheet, annual financial statements (Br), statement of condition (US)
- anmerkungen notes to the financial statements
- der laufenden Posten current account, balance on current account
- gewinn net income for the year

bilanzieren (a) to draw up a balance sheet; (b) to report (to state, to show) in the balance sheet

Bilanzierungsgrundsätze principles (standards) of statement presentation, reporting (accounting) principles

Bilanz
- kennzahlen balance sheet ratios
- kontinuität consistency in statement presentation
- kosmetik window-dressing
- kurs book value
- struktur balance sheet pattern, set-up of the balance sheet
- summe total assets, balance sheet total
- summenwachstum increase in total assets
- verlust net loss for the year
- verschleierung window-dressing
- vorlage presentation of the annual accounts

- wachstum   increase in total assets
- wert   carrying value

bilden   to set up, to make

Rückstellungen -   to set up (to make) provisions

die Zinsen - sich frei nach Angebot und Nachfrage   interest rates are determined by supply and demand

Bildschirm
- gerät   visual display unit
- technologie   viewdata technology
- text   viewdata, teletext

billiges Geld   cheap (easy) money

billiger Kredit   low-interest loan

billigst   at best

binden   (a) to tie to, to link to, to peg to; (b) to lock in, to lock up, to tie up; (c) to bind

an den Diskontsatz -   to tie to the discount rate

längerfristig -   to tie up (to invest) for a longer term

den Zinssatz -   to lock in the interest rate

bindend   binding

Bindung   (a) linking to, tying to, pegging to; (b) locking in (up), tying up; (c) commitment
- an einen Index   linking to an index
- des Kontoguthabens   tying up (blocking) the account balance
- der Kreditzusage an eine erstklassige Sicherheit   pegging (subjecting) the loan undertaking to a first-rate collateral
- an den Lombardsatz   linking to the Lombard rate
- der bereitgestellten Mittel   earmarking of the funds provided; allocating (setting aside) the funds for a particular purpose
- des Zinssatzes auf fünf Jahre   locking in the interest rate for five years; arranging a fixed-rate period for five years
- der Zinssätze im Hypothekenkreditgeschäft   locking in mortgage lending rates; establishment of fixed mortgage loan rates

Bindungsfrist (Bindungsdauer)   fixed-rate period, lock-in (lock-up) period

Hypotheken mit fünfjährigen -en   mortgages with rates fixed (locked in) for five years

Neuzusagen im Baufinanzierungsbereich mit kurzen -en   new construction lendings carrying short fixed-rate periods

die -en bei Festgeldanlagen schwanken zwischen ... und ...   term money maturities range from .. to ..

die -en bei Kündigungsgeldern   the fixed-rate periods arranged for notice deposits

Binnenwert einer Währung: internal value of a currency

Bista   balance sheet statistics

Blanko
- benachrichtigungsschreiben   blank notification letter
- indossament   endorsement in blank
- kredit   unsecured credit (loan)
- scheck   blank cheque
- überziehungskredit   unsecured overdraft
- verkauf   short sale
- verkäufer   short seller
- wechsel   blank bill of exchange

Blockfloating   joint floating, common float

blockieren   Guthaben, Konto: to block, to tie up, to freeze

Boden gegenüber den Hauptwährungen an - verlieren to lose ground against the major currencies

Bodenkreditinstitut mortgage bank, land credit bank

Bodensatz core (permanent) deposits, deposit base

Bodenwert land value

Bogen coupon sheet

Bogenerneuerungsdienst coupon renewal service

Bonifikation bei einer Emission: selling commission bei Spareinlagen: interest bonus

Bonifikations

- abkommen commission agreement

- abschlag deduction of (for) selling commission

- sperre period during which the selling commission is blocked (must be repaid if securities are returned to the issuer at a price below par during this period)

bonifizieren Spareinlagen: to pay (to grant) an interest bonus, to pay a special interest rate

bonifizierte Spareinlagen bonus--carrying savings deposits

Bonität credit-worthiness, standing, rating, quality

- der abgetretenen Forderungen quality of receivables assigned

- des Kreditnehmers prüfen to check (to assess) the credit--worthiness of the borrower

- der verpfändeten Wertpapiere rating of the securities pledged

Bonitäts

- einstufung Anleihe: bond rating; eines Kreditnehmers: assessment (rating) of a borrower

- erklärung statement (letter) of solvency

- prüfung credit investigation, credit assessment, checking the borrower's credit-worthiness

- risiko credit risk

- skala rating table

Börse Warenbörse: commodity exchange; Wertpapierbörse: stock exchange, stock market

Börsen

- abschluß bargain, deal

- abschlüsse business (bargains) done, stock exchange dealings (transactions)

- anleger stock market investors

- aufsichtsbehörde Stock Exchange Supervisory Board; Securities and Exchange Commission (US)

- aufträge stock market orders; buying and selling orders

- auftragsbuch stock order book

- bedingungen stock exchange rules

- bericht stock exchange news, stock market report

- besuch, Zulassung zum Börsenbesuch mit Handelsbefugnis admission to the trading floor

- besucher mit Handelsbefugnis member of the stock exchange, person admitted to the trading floor

- bewertung stock market valuation (rating); market capitalisation

- einführung stock exchange introduction, admission to listing on the stock exchange

- einführungen von Unternehmen company launchings on the stock market

- einführungsgebühren listing charges
- einführungsprospekt listing prospectus
- einführungsprovision listing commission
- erholung rally (upturn) in the stock market, stock market recovery
- eröffnung opening of the session
- fähig (a) marketable, negotiable on the stock exchange; (b) qualifying for a stock exchange listing
- flaute stalemate in the stock market, market dullness (depression)
- gängige Papiere marketable (negotiable) securities
- gerüchte stock market rumours
- geschäft bargain, deal, business done
- geschäfte stock exchange dealings (business, operations)
- geschehen stock market activities, trading on the stock exchange
- gesetz German Stock Exchange Law
- grundstimmung underlying market sentiment, basic tone of the stock market
- handel stock exchange trading (dealings), trading on the stock exchange
- handel, Zulassung zum Börsenhandel: admission to trading on the stock exchange, admission to the trading floor
- händler stock market dealer
- hausse bull market, upsurge of prices in the stock market, soaring (rocketing) equity prices
- index stock exchange index, market average
- interesse Fahrzeugwerte standen im Mittelpunkt des Börseninteresses motors held the limelight throughout the session
  das Börseninteresse konzentrierte sich auf Spekulationswerte buying interest centered on speculative counters
- kapitalisierung (a) eines Unternehmens: market capitalisation; (b) insgesamt: total market value of listed stocks
- klima tone of the market, market sentiment (climate, mood)
- krach stock exchange crash, collapse of the stock market
- kreise stock market community
- kurs stock exchange price (quotation), market price
- kursblatt List of Quotations
- kursblatt, amtliches Stock Exchange List, Stock Exchange Daily Official List
- kurswert stock exchange value, market value
- makler stockbroker

börsenmäßig

- lieferbare Aktien good delivery stock
- e Lieferbarkeit der jungen Aktien gewährleisten to assure the delivery of marketable certificates for the new shares
- er Verkauf selling (sale) through the stock exchange

Börsen

- mitglied member of the stock exchange
- nachrichten stock exchange news (intelligence)
- notiertes Unternehmen listed corporation
- notierung (a) listing on the stock exchange; (b) stock exchange quotation, market quotation

- order stock exchange order, instructions to buy or sell securities
- ordnung stock exchange rules and regulations
- organ body of the stock exchange
- papiere exchange-traded stock, listed (quoted) securities
- pflichtblatt journal for statutory stock market advertisements
- phantasie speculative hopes, speculation
- platz der Londoner Börsenplatz the London Stock Exchange
- preis stock market price
- publikum stock market investors
- raum trading floor
- reife Erfüllung der Börsenreife meeting the requirements for going public
- saal trading floor
- schiedsgericht arbitration panel of the stock exchange
- schluß (a) trading lot (unit), contract; (b) close (closing) of the session, market close
- schlußkurs closing quotation (price), price at the close of the market
- schwäche market weakness, subdued market sentiment
- sitzung stock exchange session, market hours
- spekulant speculator, punter, market jobber
- spekulation speculation on the stock exchange, market jobbery, stockjobbing
- stand pitch, trading post
- stimmung market sentiment, market mood, tone of the market
- stunden trading hours, session

- tag trading day, market day
- tendenz stock market trend
- termingeschäft forward (time) bargain, futures contract
- terminhandel futures trading
- titel exchange-traded stock, stock exchange securities
- umsätze stock exchange turnover, activity in the stock market
- umsatzsteuer stock transfer tax
- umsatzsteuervergütung refund of stock transfer tax
- usancen customs and practices of the stock exchange
- versammlung trading session
- vertreter dealer (dealing for account of the bank he is employed with)
- vorstand stock exchange council
- wert (a) stock market value, market price; (b) transaction value; (c) market capitalisation
- werte quoted (listed) securities
- zeit trading hours, session
- zulassung (a) admission to listing on the stock exchange; (b) admission to the trading floor
- zulassungsausschuß listing committee
- zulassungsstelle listing agent
- zulassungsverfahren listing procedure
- zulassungsvorschriften listing requirements
- zwang duty to route securities transactions through the stock exchange

Börsianer stock exchange operator, market operator

Botengeschäfte dealings for account of another bank

Branchenindex   sector index, industry index

brachliegende Gelder   idle (unemployed, dormant) funds

breite Anlagenstreuung   broad portfolio diversification, wide investment spread

breitgestreut

- er Aktienbesitz   widespread shareholdings, broadly diversified (widely disseminated) stock portfolio

- es Kreditportefeuille   broadly spread loan portfolio

- e Syndizierung   broad syndication

bremsen   to curb, to check

   das Geldmengenwachstum -   to put a brake on the rising money supply

   den Zinsauftrieb -   to check the upsurge in interest rates

Brief   offered, asked; Kurszusatz bei Aktien: sellers over

- grundschuld   certified land charge

- hypothek   certified mortgage

- kurs   asked (offered) price; bei Devisen: selling rate

bringen eine Verzinsung von 6 % -   to yield a 6 p.c. return

Bruchzins   broken interest

Brutto

- abrechnung   gross settlement (i.e. market price plus commission and charges)

- absatz festverzinslicher Wertpapiere   gross sales of fixed-income securities

- anlageinvestitionen   gross investment in fixed assets

- dividende   gross dividend, pre-tax dividend

- inanspruchnahme der Kreditmärkte   gross borrowings in the financial markets
- leistung   gross performance
- rendite   gross yield (return), pre-tax yield
- verzinsung   gross interest return
- zinsspanne   gross interest margin

Btx (Bildschirmtext)   teletext, viewdata

buchen   to enter, to post

   als Aufwand -   to charge to expenditure

   als Gewinn -   to enter on the profit side

Buch

- forderungen   accounts receivable
- führungsrichtlinien   accounting standards
- geld   deposit (bank) money
- gewinn   book profit
- hypothek   registered mortgage
- kredit   book credit; current account credit
- prüfer   auditor
- saldo   ledger balance
- schulden   book debts; accounts payable

Buchung   (a) entering to an account, posting; (b) in einem Kontoauszug: entry

Buchungs

- aufgabe   accounting advice
- beleg   accounting voucher
- fehler   accounting error
- gebühr   bei Bank-Kontokorrentkonten: entry fee, transaction fee
- posten   entry, accounting entry
- schnitt   accounting close
- stand   balance in the account

Buchverlust book loss

Buchwert book value; net asset value

budgetierte Bilanz (Erfolgsrechnung) budgeted balance sheet (income statement)

Budgetierung budgeting

Bundes
- anleihe Federal bond, government bond
- anleihekonsortium Federal bond syndicate
- aufsichtsamt für das Kreditwesen Federal Banking Supervisory Authority
- bahnanleihe Federal Railway bond

Bundesbank Bundesbank, German Central Bank
  die - mußte zur Marktberuhigung DM 12 Mio aufnehmen the Bundesbank bought DM 12m worth of bonds to steady the market
  die - gab DM 10 Mio an den Markt ab the Bundesbank supplied the market with DM 10m
  die - intervenierte massiv an den Devisenmärkten the Bundesbank intervened heavily in the foreign exchange markets

Bundesbank
- ausweis Bundesbank return
- fähig rediscountable at the Bundesbank; eligible as collateral for Bundesbank borrowings
- fähiger Wechsel eligible bill, bill eligible for rediscount at (with) the Bundesbank
- gewinn Bundesbank profits
- giro Bundesbank transfer
- guthaben Bundesbank balances, balances maintained with Bundesbank

- instrumentarium Bundesbank policy instruments
- intervention Bundesbank intervention, intervention by Bundesbank
- kredit (a) Bundesbank lending, Bundesbank loan; (b) borrowing with Bundesbank
- lombardkredit Bundesbank lending against security, Bundesbank Lombard facility
- stelle Bundesbank Office
- stützungskäufe support-buying (buying-in) by Bundesbank
- unterstützung durch Wechselpensionsgeschäfte Bundesbank support by way of repurchase agreements on bills

Bundes
- bürgschaft Federal Government guarantee
- deckung Federal guarantee cover, provision of Federal insurance cover
- emittent issuer of Federal bonds
- garantie → Bundesbürgschaft
- obligation Federal treasury bond
- postanleihe Federal Post Office bond
- schätze Federal savings bonds
- schatzanweisung Federal treasury note
- schatzbrief Federal savings bond
- schatzwechsel Federal treasury bill
- schuldbrief Federal debt certificate
- schuldbuch Federal debt register
- schuldenverwaltung Federal Debt Administration
- verbürgter Exportkredit government-guaranteed export credit, export credit provided with government insurance cover
- wertpapiere Federal government securities

Bürge   guarantor

Bürgschaft   guarantee (Br), guaranty (US), surety

Bürgschafts
- akzept   guarantee acceptance
- erklärung   guarantee (surety) bond
- hinterlegung   deposit of (depositing) a guarantee
- kredit   guarantee credit
- kündigung   calling in a guarantee, notice of termination of a guarantee
- leistung   furnishing a guarantee, provision of a guarantee
- nehmer   guarantee
- plafond   guarantee limit (line)
- provision   guarantee commission
- rahmen   guarantee line
- übernahme   furnishing a guarantee, guarantee undertaking
- urkunde   guarantee (surety) bond, surety deed
- verpflichtungen   guarantee (surety) commitments
- vertrag   guarantee agreement, deed of suretyship
- volumen   total guarantees furnished
- wechsel   guarantee bill
- zusage   guarantee undertaking, undertaking to guarantee

Bürohandel   Wertpapiere: unofficial dealings

C

Chefhändler   chief dealer

Chemie-Nebenwerte   second-line chemicals

Chemiewerte   chemicals, chemical stocks

C-Geschäft   instalment credit against bills of exchange

Clearing
- forderungen   clearing receivables
- guthaben   clearing balances (assets)
- stelle   clearing house
- verkehr   clearing transactions

Courtage   brokerage, broker's fee
- rechnung   brokerage statement
- satz   brokerage rate

D

Dachfonds   fund of funds

Damnum   discount

dämpfen   to curb, to damp down, to check

   den Zinsauftrieb - to check the upsurge in interest rates

Darlehen   loan, advance

- mit kurzen Anpassungsfristen   loans renegotiable after short periods

Darlehens

- abgeld   loan discount, discount deducted from the loan principal
- abruf   drawing on a loan, calling up the loan funds
- antrag   loan application
- ausreichung   loan extension (accommodation), extending a loan
- auszahlung   loan disbursement, disbursing a loan
- auszahlung erfolgt auf Konto Nr..   the loan proceeds will be credited to account No..
- auszahlungen insgesamt: total amount of loans disbursed
- beschaffung   raising a loan
- bestand   loan portfolio, total lendings
- betrag   loan amount, loan principal
- bewilligung   (a) loan approval; (b) loan extension (accommodation)
- fälligkeit   loan maturity; loan due for repayment on
- forderung der Bank   bank's claim under a loan agreement
- forderungen abzüglich Wertberichtigungen   loans less provisions
- geber   lender
- gelder   loan funds (finance), loanable funds
- geschäft   lending business (operations, activities)
- gewährung   loan extension (accommodation), extending a loan
- hingabe   loan extension
- konditionen   loan (lending)terms
- konto   loan account
- kosten   loan charges
- kündigung   calling in a loan, terminating a loan agreement
- laufzeit   life (term) of a loan, loan maturity
- leistungen   principal and interest payments (on a loan)
- mittel   loan funds (finance), loanable funds
- nachfrage   loan demand, demand for loans
- nehmer   borrower
- nennbetrag   loan principal
- neugeschäft /-neuzusagen   new loans extended, new loan commitments
- politik   lending policy
- prolongation   loan renewal, renewing a loan
- risiko   loan risk
- sicherheit   loan collateral, security (collateral) provided for a loan
- stock   loan portfolio, total lendings
- streckung   stretching out the repayment of a loan, extending the loan maturity

47

- stundung   loan respite, debt deferral, deferring repayments due
- tätigkeit   lending activities (operations, business)
- tilgung   loan repayment, repaying a loan
- tilgungen   ingesamt: total amount of loans repaid, total repayments
- tilgungssatz   loan repayment rate, principal repayment rate
- urkunde   loan deed
- valuta   (a) loan proceeds; (b) loan currency
- valutierung   disbursement of the loan proceeds; allowing drawdowns on a loan
- vergabe   loan accommodation
- verpflichtung   der Bank: loan commitment; des Kreditnehmers: borrower's commitments under the loan, principal and interest to be paid by the borrower
- vertrag   loan agreement
- zinsen   loan interest, interest charged for a loan
- zinssatz   loan interest rate, lending rate
- zusage   loan undertaking, undertaking to extend a loan; loan commitment
- zusagen   insgesamt: total loan commitments

Datenschutz   data privacy, data protection

Datenübermittlung   data transmission

Datowechsel   after-date bill

Dauer
- auftrag   standing order
- emission   tap issue
- emittent   tap issuer
- finanzierungsmittel   long-term finance

- globalurkunde   permanent global certificate
- konsortium   standing loan syndicate
- nehmer   im Geldmarkt: permanent buyer (borrower)

Debet   debit
- saldo   debit balance
- zins   debit interest
- zinssatz   lending rate, loan interest rate

Debitoren   debtors; Bank: loans and advances, lendings
- aufstellung   (a) list of accounts receivable; (b) statement of loans extended
- ausfälle   loan charge-offs, loan losses
- finanzierung   lending against accounts receivable
- geschäft   lending business (operations)
- kontrolle   supervision of loan commitments, monitoring lendings
- kunden   borrowing customers
- länder   debtor(borrowing)countries
- risiko   risk of default
- sätze   lending rates
- verluste   loan losses (charge-offs)
- ziehung   bank bill drawn on a customer

debitorisch
- es Geschäft   lending business
- es Konto   debtor (overdraft) account; account run on a borrowing basis

decken   (a) to cover, to hedge, to provide cover; (b) to insure, to guarantee

Deckung   (a) cover, covering; hedge, hedging; providing cover; (b) insurance, insuring; guarantee

48

Deckung

- des Kreditbedarfs   covering the borrowing requirements
- der Kreditfristen auf der Aktiv- und Passivseite   matching lendings against deposits
- des Refinanzierungsbedarfs   covering funding (refinancing) requirements
- für ausgestellte Schecks   cover for cheques written
- des Währungsrisikos   hedging the currency risk
- des Zinsrisikos   hedging the interest rate risk

in - nehmen   to cover; Exportkredite: to provide cover, to provide insurance cover, to provide guarantees

zur - der in Anspruch genommenen Beträge   to cover any amounts drawn

in - genommene Geschäfte   transactions covered (hedged)

in - genommener Kredit   loan for which insurance cover (for which a guarantee) has been provided

- erfolgt auf dem Konto Nr..   cover(reimbursement) will be provided on account No..; cover funds will be remitted to account No.. with ..

die Einlösung mangels - verweigern   to refuse payment for lack of cover, to dishonour for want of cover

Deckungs

- anschaffung   (a) provision of cover, remitting cover; (b) im Sinne von Rückerstattung: reimbursement
- antrag   application for the provision of cover; guarantee application
- anweisungen   covering (reimbursement) instructions; instructions for providing cover
- art   type of cover; covering (hedging) device; method of reimbursement
- beitrag   profit contribution; variable gross margin
- beschränkungen   cover restrictions; restraints on covering transactions
- bestätigung   cover note
- darlehen   covering loan
- einkauf   covering purchase

deckungsfähig   eligible for cover, insurable

- e Risiken   insurable risks
- e Wertpapiere   fixed-income securities bought and sold by the Bundesbank in the open market (securities eligible for note coverage)

Deckungs

- fonds   cover fund
- forderungen   cover (reimbursement) claims
- garantie   undertaking to cover (to guarantee)
- gegenstand   property (interest) subject to cover
- geschäft   covering (hedging) transaction
- grad   (a) liquidity ratio; (b) cover (covering) ratio; (c) degree of cover provided
- grenze   cover (guarantee) limit
- guthaben   compensating balances
- kapital   cover (guarantee) funds
- kauf   covering purchase, covering positions
- käufe vornehmen   für Leerverkäufe: to run cover, to cover positions; in Erwartung eines Kursanstieges: to buy ahead of an upsurge in prices
- kongruenz im Hypothekengeschäft   mortgage lendings matched against mortgage bonds issued

- konto cover (reimbursement) account; guarantee account
- linie im Kreditgeschäft: support line, back-up line
- masse cover funds
- mittel (a) cover funds; (b) guarantee funds; (c) Haushalt: receipts, revenue
- papiere securities pledged as collateral
- pflichtig requiring cover
- politik guarantee policy
- prüfung checking the cover
- quote cover (covering) ratio; guarantee ratio
- register register of mortgages which serve as cover for mortgage bonds issued
- stock cover (guarantee) funds
- stockfähigkeit eligibility of securities as cover funds
- stopp cover freeze, refusal to provide further cover
- urkunde cover note, insurance certificate
- verhältnis cover (covering) ratio
  bei Kundenkrediten: ratio of customer lendings to customer deposits
  im Interbankgeschäft: ratio of interbank lendings to interbank borrowings
- verkauf covering sale
- verpflichtung undertaking to cover; undertaking to provide cover (a guarantee)
- werte covering assets
- zusage cover note

Defektivzinsen bond interest payable from deposit of the purchase price until the first coupon date

defizitäre Leistungsbilanz
current account deficit, adverse current account

degressive Abschreibung declining balance depreciation, diminishing balance depreciation

degressives Tilgungsdarlehen loan (financing) scheme geared to the requirements of the diminishing balance depreciation

Delkredere
- fall loan loss
- fonds contingencies fund
- reserve /-rückstellung loan loss reserve, provision for bad debts
- risiko credit risk
- versicherung credit insurance

Deponent depositor

Deport backwardation
- geschäft backwardation transaction (business)
- satz backwardation rate

Depositalschein deposit (custody) receipt

Depositen deposits
- banken deposit banks
- buch passbook
- geschäft deposit business (operations)
- kasse city branch
- vermerk note indicating the place of deposit

Depot securities account, custody account; securities portfolio

Depot A ⟶ Eigendepot
Depot B ⟶ Anderdepot
Depot C ⟶ Pfanddepot
Depot D ⟶ Sonderpfanddepot

Depot
- abstimmung securities (custody) account reconciliation

Depot
- abteilung   securities administration department; custodial services
- anteil   share in a securities account
- aufstellung   statement of securities; list of securities held under a securities portfolio
- ausgang   securities sold (withdrawn); outgoing securities
- ausgangskontrolle   outgoing securities control
- auszug   securities account statement, custody account statement; statement of securities
- bank   custodian bank, depositary bank, depository
- bankgarantie   custodian bank's guarantee, depositary bond
- belastung   securities account debit; debiting a securities account
- bescheinigung   deposit (custody) receipt
- bestand   securities account balance; market value of the securities held in a portfolio
- buch   custody accounts ledger
- buchführung   securities (custody) accounting
- buchhaltung   securities (custody) accounts department
- buchung   securities account entry; entering in (posting to) a securities account
- deckung   securities account cover
- deckung anschaffen   to deliver securities in cover of ...; to provide securities account cover
- dispositionen   portfolio arrangements (management); buying and/or selling of securities
- eingang   securities deposited (purchased); securities added to a portfolio; incoming securities
- eingangskontrolle   incoming securities control
- einlieferung   deposit of securities; placing securities for safekeeping
- führung   (a) administration of securities (custody) accounts; (b) conduct (maintenance) of a securities account; (c) portfolio management
- gebühren   custodian fees, custody charges
- geschäft   custody business (operations, activities), custodial services; administration of securities and safekeeping of valuables
- gesetz   Safe Custody Law
- güter   custody items; property (assets) held in safekeeping
- gutschrift   securities account credit; crediting a securities account
- handhabung   securities account administration; processing of custody accounts
- hinterlegung   deposit into a custody account; placing for safekeeping
- inhaber   securities account holder
- karte   securities account card
- konto   securities account; custody account
- kontoinhaber   securities account holder
- kunden   holder of securities accounts
- lastschrift   securities account debit
- mäßige Verbuchung   entry in a securities account; posting to a securities (custody) account
- memorial / -primanote   securities account ledger

- prüfung securities account audit; audit of custody operations
- schein deposit (custody) receipt
- sperre blocking a securities (custody) account; portfolio blocking
- stände custody account balances
- stelle (a) custodian, depository, depositary bank; (b) place of deposit (of custody)
- stimmrecht authority of the bank to vote the shares of its customers held under its management
- stücke securities held in a portfolio (in a custody account); items (property) held in safekeeping
- tagesauszug daily securities account statement
- übereignung assignment of a securities portfolio
- übertragung / - umbuchung transfer of securities; transfer of a custody account
- umschichtung portfolio (investment) shift; restructuring a portfolio; portfolio switching
- veränderungen changes in a securities portfolio; portfolio changes
- verpfändung pledging of a securities portfolio
- vertrag custody agreement
- verwahrte Stücke securities held in safekeeping (in custody)
- verwahrung holding in safekeeping (in custody); custodyship
- verwalter (a) custodian, depositary bank; (b) portfolio manager
- verwaltung (a) custodial services; administration of securities; (b) im Sinne von Vermögensverwaltung: management of a securities portfolio
- wechsel collateral bill; bill deposited as security
- wert value of a securities portfolio
- werte securities held in a portfolio; securities held in safekeeping
- wertsteigerung portfolio appreciation

Devisen foreign exchange, foreign currency
- abflüsse currency outflow
- abrechnung foreign exchange contract (settlement) note; Abteilung: foreign exchange settlements department
- angebot currency supply
- ankauf buying foreign currencies, currency buying
- ankaufskurs buying rate
- arbitrage currency arbitrage, arbitration of exchange
- aufgeld exchange premium, premium on exchange
- ausgaben foreign exchange expenditure (disbursements)
- ausgleichsabkommen exchange offset agreement
- behörden exchange control authorities; currency holdings
- bestände foreign exchange holdings, currency holdings
- bestimmungen exchange control regulations, currency regulations
- betrag foreign currency amount
- bewirtschaftung exchange control
- bilanz net foreign exchange movements
- bindung tying up foreign exchange
- börse foreign exchange market

- buchhaltung currency accounting
- defizit foreign exchange deficit (shortage)
- defizitland exchange deficit country
- dispositionen foreign exchange (currency) management, foreign exchange dealing (trading)
- dispositionsabteilung foreign exchange dealing department, currency trading desk
- eigenhandel foreign exchange dealings for own account
- eingänge currency inflow
- einnahmen foreign exchange receipts
- genehmigung exchange control permit; exchange authorisation
- gesamtposition overall exchange position
- gesetzgebung exchange control legislation
- guthaben currency (exchange) assets, foreign exchange holdings
- handel foreign exchange trading (dealings)
- handelsabteilung foreign exchange dealing department, currency trading desk
- handelserträge income from foreign exchange dealings
- händler foreign exchange dealer
- kassageschäft spot exchange deal
- kassahandel spot exchange dealings
- kassakurs spot exchange rate
- kassamarkt spot exchange market
- knappheit shortage of foreign exchange
- kontrolle exchange control
- kredit currency loan

Devisenkurs exchange rate
- bildung exchange rate determination
- feststellung fixing of the exchange rates
- notierung exchange rate quotation, currency quotation
- sicherung rate hedging; hedging the exchange rate; forward exchange covering (guarantee)
- zettel currency quotations list

Devisen
- leihe currency borrowing abroad
- makler currency broker
- markt foreign exchange market
- marktintervention intervention in the foreign exchange market; operating on the foreign exchanges
- mittelkurs mean rate of exchange
- nachfrage currency demand
- netting currency netting
- pensionsgeschäft currency repurchase agreement
- politik foreign exchange policy
- position foreign exchange position; currency position
- positionsmeldung exchange position return
- provision foreign exchange commission
- recht exchange control regulations
- rechtliche Genehmigung exchange control approval
- reserven foreign exchange reserves, currency reserves
- skontro currency ledger
- spekulation currency speculation; speculation on the foreign exchange markets
- swapgeschäft / -tauschgeschäft currency swap transaction

Devisentermin
- geschäft   forward exchange deal, exchange (currency) futures contract
- handel   forward exchange dealing, currency futures trading
- markt   forward exchange market, currency futures market

Devisen
- transaktion   foreign exchange deal, currency transaction
- überschuß   surplus of foreign exchange, currency surplus
- überschußland   exchange surplus country
- verkauf   selling foreign currencies, currency selling
- verkaufskurs   selling rate
- wechsel   currency bill
- werte   foreign currency assets
- zuflüsse   currency inflow

Dienstleistungs
- angebot   range of services offered, service offerings
- bereich   services sector
- betrieb   service undertaking
- bilanz   invisible balance
- bilanzüberschuß   surplus of invisibles
- geschäft   (a) service offering, service offered; (b) servicing (service) transactions
- palette   range of services offered, portfolio of services
- sektor   tertiary industry, services sector
- verkehr   service transactions

dinglich
- besichern   to secure by real security, to secure by mortgage (by a land charge)
- e Besicherung   provision of real security
- e Sicherheit   real security

Direkt
- andienung   direct tendering
- anschaffung beim Begünstigten   direct remittance to the beneficiary
- emission   direct offering
- kredite aufgenommene: direct borrowings; gewährte: direct lendings
- plazierung   direct placing (negotiation)

Disagio   discount

das von dem Darlehensnennbetrag in Abzug gebrachte -   the discount deducted from the loan principal

Disagio
- darlehen   loan extended at a discount
- erträge   discounts received
- gewinn   gain on redemption

Diskont
- amortisationssatz   discounted rate of return
- änderung   change in the discount rate
- aufwendungen   discounts allowed (paid)
- bank   discounting bank (banker)
- einreichung   presentation for discount
- erhöhung   increase in the discount rate
- erlös   discounting proceeds; proceeds of a bill discounted
- erträge   discounts earned (received)
- fähig   discountable, eligible for discount
- fähigkeit   discountability
- geber   discounter
- gefälle   discount rate differential (gap)
- geschäft   discounting of bills

- grenze   discount ceiling
  (limit)

diskontieren   to discount

diskontierende Bank   discounting banker

diskontierter Barwert einer Forderung   discounted cash value of a receivable

Diskontierung   discounting
- von Buchforderungen   discounting accounts receivable
- von Wechseln   discounting (of) bills

Diskontierungs
- erlös   discounting proceeds
- line   discount facility, discount credit line
- zusage   undertaking to discount

Diskontkredit   discount credit
- gewährung   extending a discount credit (facility)
- zusage   undertaking to extend a discount credit

Diskont
- linie   discount credit line
- markt   discount market
- material   bills; bills presented for discount
- nota   discount settlement note, statement of discount
- politik   discount policy
- portefeuille   portfolio of bills discounted
- provision   discount commission
- rechnung   statement of discount

Diskontsatz   discount rate
 Erhöhung des -es   increase in the discount rate, lifting the discount rate
 Senkung des -es   discount rate cut, lowering the discount rate

Diskont
- schraube   discount rate screw
- spesen   discount charges
- tage   discount days
- wechsel   discounted bill
- zusage   discount undertaking, undertaking to discount

Disponent   officer in charge; im Geld-/Devisenhandel: dealer, chief dealer

Disponenten-Kreise   dealing community

disponieren   to arrange, to make arrangements for, to provide for, to manage, to plan
 im Geldhandel: to deal, to trade, to make arrangements
 über das gekündigte Guthaben - to withdraw (to dispose of) the funds for which notice of withdrawal has been given
 über ein Konto - to draw on an account
 langfristig -   bei Wertpapieren: to invest for the long term

Dispositionen   arrangements, management, planning
 im Devisenhandel: dealings, deals, buying and/or selling, money (foreign exchange) management
 Kontoverfügungen: drawings on an account
 bei Wertpapieren: investment instructions, investment arrangements (decisions); selling and buying securities; placing orders for the purchase or sale of securities
 des Berufshandels: professional buying and selling

Dispositions
- befugnisse   approval (discretionary) powers
- berechtigung   bei einem Konto: drawing powers

- gepflogenheiten dealing (trading) practices
- kredit / Dispo-Kredit overdraft facility, personal credit line, drawing credit
- möglichkeiten leeway
- papiere documents of title
- rahmen bei einem Kredit: credit limit (line), drawing line; im Hinblick auf Befugnisse: approval powers
- vollmacht discretionary powers
- volumen funds available (e.g. for investment in securities)

Distanz

- geschäft non-local transaction
- scheck out-of-town cheque
- wechsel out-of-town bill

Dividende dividend

ex -   ex dividend

mit -   cum dividend

- einschließlich Steuergutschrift grossed up dividend

Dividenden

- abgabe dividend tax
- abschlag quotation ex dividend, ex-dividend markdown; marking ex dividend; deduction of dividend
- abschnitt dividend coupon
- angleichung dividend rate adjustment
- ankündigung dividend statement, dividend notice
- aufkommen dividends received
- auf Stammaktien ordinary dividends
- aufstockung increase in dividend, dividend rise, lifting (increasing) the dividend rate
- aufwand dividends paid (distributed)
- ausfall passing (omission) of a dividend
- ausschüttung dividend distribution (payout, disbursement)
- auszahlung dividend payment
- bekanntmachung dividend notice
- berechtigt bearing dividend, carrying dividend rights
- berechtigung, mit Dividendenberechtigung ab .. ranking for dividend as of ..
- berechtigungsschein dividend warrant
- bogen dividend coupon sheet
- deckung dividend cover; profit/dividend ratio
- erhöhung dividend increase
- erklärung dividend statement (announcement)
- erträge dividend income, dividends earned (received)
- forderungen dividends receivable
- garantie dividend guarantee
- gutschrift dividend cheque; dividend credit; crediting the dividend
- inkasso collection of a dividend
- kontinuität continuity of dividend payments; unbroken dividend record
- kürzung dividend cut; lowering the dividend rate
- papiere shares, equities
- politik dividend policy
- rechte dividend rights
- rendite dividend yield
- rückstände dividend arrears
- satz dividend rate
- schein dividend coupon
- scheinbogen coupon sheet
- scheineinreichung presentation of coupons, depositing coupons
- senkung dividend cut; lowering the dividend rate
- stopp dividend freeze

Dividenden
- summe   dividend amount; dividend total
- termin   dividend due date
- vorrecht   preferential right to a dividend
- werte   shares, equities
- zahlstelle   dividend paying agent
- zahlung   dividend payment
- zahlungen wiederaufnehmen   to return to the dividend list

dokumentär   documentary
- es Inkasso   documentary collection
- e Zahlung   documentary payment, payment against documents

Dokumente   documents
- gegen Akzept   documents against acceptance (D/A)
- gegen Zahlung (Kasse gegen Dokumente)   documents against payment (D/P)

Dokumenten
- akkreditiv   documentary credit
- andienung   tendering (submitting) of documents
- ankaufszusage   undertaking to negotiate documents
- aufnahme   taking up documents
- bearbeitung   handling of documents, processing documents
- bevorschussung   advance (lending) against documents
- einlösung   honouring documents
- einreichung   presentation of documents, presenting documents
- freigabe   release of the documents
- gegenwert   proceeds of the documents; currency equivalent of the documents
- geschäft   documentary business (transactions)
- inkasso   documentary collection; collection against documents
- negoziierung   negotiation of (negotiating) documents
- prüfung   checking the documents, examination of the documents
- tratte   documentary draft
- übergabe   surrender of the documents
- vorlage   presentation of the documents, presenting the documents
- weiterleitung   passing on the documents to

Dollar
- abfluß   dollar drain (outflow)
- angebot   dollar supply
- anleihe   dollar bond, dollar debt
- emission   dollar issue, dollar--denominated issue, dollar offering
- erlös   dollar proceeds
- hausse   sharp rise (upsurge) in the dollar
- kurs   dollar exchange rate, dollar rate
- mittelkurs   mean dollar exchange rate
- nachfrage   dollar demand
- notierung   dollar exchange rate
- rembours   dollar acceptance credit
- stärke   strength of the dollar
- titel   dollar securities
- überhang   surplus dollar holdings
- zinsen   dollar interest rates
- zufluß   influx of dollars, dollar inflow

domizilieren   to be domiciled

Domizilierung   domicilation

Domizil
- provision   domicile commission
- stelle   domicile; place for presentation
- wechsel   domiciled bill

Doppelbesteuerungsabkommen   double taxation convention (agreement)

doppelstufige Sanierung   capital write-down followed by an immediate capital increase

doppelte Minusankündigung   sharp share price markdown (as a rule by more than 10 p.c.)

doppelte Plusankündigung   sharp share price markup (as a rule by more than 10 p.c.)

doppelt gespannter Kurs   quarter spread of the fixing

Doppelwährungssystem   dual currency system

Doppelzahlung   duplicate payment

Dotationskapital   equity; capital provided (allocated)

Dotationsmittel   funds provided; für eine Anleihe: debt service funds

dotieren   to allocate, to provide funds for, to transfer

die Rücklagen -   to allocate (to transfer) to the reserves

Sparkonten -   to invest (to deposit) in savings accounts

Dotierung   allocation, provision (transfer) of funds

Draufgeld   earnest money

Dreimonatsgeld   three months' money

Dreimonatswechsel   three months' bill

Drittausfertigung   Wechsel: third of exchange

Drittschuldner   third-party debtor

Drittverwahrer   third-party custodian

drosseln   to curb, to curtail, to restrict

Druck

die DM stand unter starkem - an den internationalen Devisenmärkten   the deutschmark came under heavy pressure in the international foreign exchange markets

- auf die Zinsspannen   squeeze (pressure) on interest margins

drücken

auf die Aktienkurse -   to depress (to weigh down, to force down) equity prices

steigende Betriebskosten - auf die Gewinne   rising operating expenses are squeezing earnings

die Konditionen -   to bring down (to ratchet down) the pricing

dünne Kapitaldecke   thin capital base

Durchbruch   der erhoffte Durchbruch am Rentenmarkt   the hoped-for breakthrough in the bond market

Durchhandeln am Geldmarkt   hard arbitrage, round tripping; borrowing from a bank and re-lending the money at a profit on the interbank market

Durchkonnossement   through bill of lading

durchlaufender Kredit   transmitted loan; loan extended by a government or public body through the agency of a bank (the bank does not assume the credit risk; ⟶ Durchleitkredit)

durchlaufendes Geschäft   einer Bank: non-lending transactions

durchlaufender Posten self-
-balancing item, on-and-off
item

durchleiten to pass on, to transmit; Kredit: to extend a loan under a public lending scheme

Durchleitgelder transmitted funds

Durchleitkredit / durchgeleiteter Kredit loan extended by a bank under a public lending scheme (the lending bank assumes the credit risk; ⟶ durchlaufender Kredit)

Durchleitungs

- bank transmitting bank; bank extending a loan under a public lending scheme

- marge transmitting bank's spread (turn)

- stelle transmitting agent; ⟶ Durchleitungsbank

Durchlieferverfahren transactions in securities not eligible for collective safekeeping

Durchschnitt average

Durchschnitts

- kurs average price (rate)

- laufzeit average life (term)

- rendite average yield

- valuta (-verfallzeit) average due date

dynamische Tilgung redemption rates increasing over the life of the loan

E

echtes Factoring   old-line factoring

Eckzins   basic rate of interest

ECU-Leitkurs   ECU central rate

Edelmetall   precious metals; Gold und Silber: bullion
- handel   precious metals trade, bullion trade
- lombardierung   lending on precious metals
- markt   bullion market, market in precious metals

EEV-Steuern   income, profit, and property taxes

Effekten   securities
- abrechnung   contract note, bought or sold note
- abteilung   securities department
- anlage   investment in securities
- arbitrage   stock arbitrage
- auftrag   buying or selling order
- ausgang   securities delivered (sold); outgoing securities
- beleihung   lending on (against) securities
- beratung   investment counselling
- besitz   securities portfolio, securities holdings
- bestand   holding of securities, securities holdings
- börse   stock exchange
- depot   securities portfolio (account)
- diskont   (a) discounting of securities (i.e. repurchase of securities prior to repayment); (b) security discount rate
- eigengeschäft   own-account deal in securities
- eigenhandelsgeschäfte   own-account trading; security trading for own account
- eingang   securities received (purchased); incoming securities
- emission   securities issue (offering)
- ferngiroverkehr   out-of-town clearing transactions in securities
- geschäft   securities transaction (deal), transaction in securities
- geschäfte   dealings in securities, securities trading (transactions)
- girobank   securities depositary bank
- girodepot   securities account with a securities depositary bank
- giroverkehr   security clearing; clearing transactions in securities
- handel   securities (security) trading, dealings in securities
- handelsbestand   securities trading portfolio
- händler   securities dealer
- kaufabrechnung   bought note
- kaufauftrag   buy order
- kenn-Nummer   securities code number
- kommissionär   agent (i.e. bank buying or selling securities in its own name but for account of a customer)
- kommissionsgeschäft   buying and selling securities for account of customers, agency transactions in securities

- konto   securities account
- kredit   (a) loan on (against) securities; (b) loan to purchase stock; securities market credit
- lombard   loan on (against) securities
- lombardierung   lending against securities
- nachfrage   demand for securities
- pensionierung   pledging and/or selling of securities under repurchase agreements
- pensionsgeschäft   sale and repurchase agreement in securities; im allgemeinen nur: repurchase agreement
- platzgiroverkehr   town clearing transactions in securities
- plazierung   placing (placement) of securities
- portefeuille   securities portfolio
- provision   securities commission
- scheck   securities transfer order
- skontro   securities ledger
- substitution   security replacement
- termingeschäft   forward transaction (deal) in securities
- termingeschäfte   securities traded for future delivery; futures contracts in securities
- übertragung   transfer of securities
- verkauf   security sale; selling securities
- verkaufsabrechnung   sold note
- verkaufsauftrag   sell (selling) order
- verpfändung   pledging (of) securities
- verwahrung   safekeeping of securities, security custody

- verwaltung   securities administration

effektive Darlehenskosten   true cost of a facility

effektive Lieferung (Übergabe)   physical(constructive,actual)delivery

effektive Stücke   physical securities (certificates)

effektive Zinsbelastung   effective interest load

Effektivverzinsung   effective (real) interest return

Effektivzinssatz   effective interest rate

eigen
- e Aktien einer AG: treasury stock; stock held in treasury
- e Akzepte   own acceptances
- e Effekten   trading-account securities
- e Mittel   share capital and reserves; capital resources; internally generated funds
- e Schuldverschreibungen   own debentures
- e Ziehung   own drawing

Eigen
- besitz   own holdings
- bestände   bank-owned security holdings
- depot   trading-account securities portfolio
- emission   own issue (offering)
- finanzierung   financing from funds generated internally, self-financing
- finanzierungskraft   self-financing power
- geschäft   own-account deal, transaction for own account
- handel   trading (dealings) for own account

Eigenhandelsgewinne   income from trading for own account

Eigenhändler   trader (dealer) for own account; jobber

Eigenkapital   im bilanziellen Kontext: share capital and reserves; net worth; shareholders' equity; jedoch oft nur: capital oder equity

- anteil   equity interest (stake)
- aufbringung   putting up capital (equity)
- ausstattung   capital resources available; total amount of capital and reserves; total net worth
- basis   capital (equity) base
- berechnung   calculation of capital and reserves
- beteiligung   equity interest (stake)
- bildung   equity (net worth) formation
- deckung   capital (equity) cover
- grundsätze   capital adequacy requirements; net worth requirements
- hilfeprogramm   equity assistance scheme
- konsolidierung   equity funding
- polster   capital cushion
- quote   (a) einer Bank: equity/assets ratio; ratio of share capital and reserves to total assets; (b) bei einer Baufinanzierung: downpayment; borrower's capital contribution
- schwäche   capital inadequacy; inadequate position on share capital and reserves
- surrogate   surrogate forms of capital
- verzehr   capital depreciation (loss)

- verzinsung   return on net worth, return on shareholders' equity

Eigenleistung   bei einer Baufinanzierung: downpayment; borrower's capital contribution (resources)

eine - von 10 % des Kaufpreises erbringen   to put down 10 % of the purchase price

Eigenmittel   im bilanziellen Kontext: share capital and reserves; net worth; shareholders' equity; im allgemeinen Sprachgebrauch: capital resources; internally generated funds

Investitionen aus -n finanzieren   to finance investments from funds generated internally

Eigenmittelausstattung   capital resources available; total amount of capital and reserves

Eigenmittelquote   debt/equity ratio

Eigennutzung   owner-occupation

eigengenutztes Haus   owner-occupied home

eigenständiger Schuldner   debtor in its own right

Eigentümer   owner, proprietor

- grundschuld   land charge taken out in the proprietor's name
- risiko   owner's risk

Eigentums

- ansprüche   ownership claims, claims to ownership, title to property
- anteil   ownership interest, proprietary interest
- nachweis   evidence of title (ownership)
- recht   title, ownership, proprietary interest
- übergang   passing of ownership

- übertragung transfer of ownership, transfer of title, conveyance of property
- urkunde title deed
- vorbehalt reservation of ownership, title exception
- vorbehaltswaren goods subject to reservation of ownership

eigenverwahrte Aktien shares held in self-custody

Eigenverwahrung self-custody

Eigenwechsel promissory note

Eilüberweisungsverkehr express money transmission service; express payments

einberufen eine Hauptversammlung: to call (to convene) a general meeting

Einberufung convening, convocation

Einberufungsbekanntmachung notice of meeting, convening notice

Einbeziehungsantrag application for quotation in the over-the-counter market

einbezogene Werte securities listed in the over-the-counter market

einbrechen Kurse: to drop (to fall) sharply

einbringen Kapital: to put up, to bring into, to invest
Gewinn: to yield, to produce

1 Mio $ in die neue Gesellschaft - to put up $ 1m of capital for the new company

Einbringung putting up, contribution

- von bereits abgebuchten Kreditforderungen recoveries on loans previously charged off

einbüßen einige Punkte (im Kurs): to shed (to relinquish) some points

eindämmen to curb, to check

eindecken

ausgereichte Mittel mit kongruenter Laufzeit wieder - to fund (to cover) lendings at matching maturities

sich billig - Börse: to buy in at low prices

sich in Erwartung eines Kursanstiegs - to buy ahead of a possible upsurge in prices

Eindruck

unter dem - einer möglichen Anhebung des Lombardsatzes amid market speculation on a possible rise of the Lombard rate

unter dem - eines baldigen Nachgebens der Zinssätze anziehen to advance on hopes of an early downturn in interest rates

einfaches Inkasso clean collection

einfahren Gewinn: to turn in a profit of ..

einfordern to call in, to call up

Einforderung calling in, call on

- von noch nicht eingezahlten Zeichnungen call on unpaid subscriptions

- von Mindestreserven call on (of) minimum reserves

einführen an der Börse: to introduce on the stock exchange, to admit to the Official List, to launch

Einführung introduction (listing) on the stock exchange, launching

- in den amtlichen Handel admitting securities to official quotation

Einführungs

- bekanntmachung listing announcement

63

- konsortium listing syndicate
- kurs issuing (offering) price
- prospekt listing prospectus
- provision listing commission
- tag first day of listing

Eingang vorbehalten due payment provided

eingefrorene Guthaben blocked assets (funds)

eingeschränkt
- e Bankvollmacht restricted account mandate; account mandate (power of attorney) limited to specific transactions
- er Bestätigungsvermerk qualified audit certificate
- es Indossament qualified endorsement

eingezahlt
- es Aktienkapital paid-up share capital
- e Rücklagen capital surplus

eingliedern to integrate, to absorb

Einheitliche Richtlinien und Gebräuche für Dokumentenakkreditive Uniform customs and practice for documentary credits

Einheitliche Richtlinien für Inkassi Uniform rules for collections

einheitliche Zinssätze uniform interest rates

Einheits
- hypothek consolidated mortgage
- konditionen uniform (standard) terms and rates
- konsortium underwriting and selling group
- kurs current published quotation, daily quotation
- satz uniform rate

einholen
  das Akzept - to obtain (to ensure) the acceptance
  eine Bankauskunft über einen Kunden - to make a status enquiry on a customer

Einkaufs
- kommission agency transaction; instructions to buy on a commission basis
- kommissionär buying agent (i.e. bank buying securities in its own name but for account of a customer)
- kommittent principal; securities account holder instructing the bank to buy

Einkünfte income, receipts
- aus Kapitalvermögen investment income

Einlage (a) deposit; (b) capital contribution, capital invested

Einlagen
- abfluß deposit drain
- abgänge outflow of deposits
- beschaffung am Markt raising deposits in the market
- bestand total deposits
- bonifikation (a) interest bonus; (b) paying an interest bonus
- fristigkeit maturity pattern of deposits
- geschäft deposit banking, deposit-taking business, deposit operations
- kunde depositing customer
- mit dreimonatiger Kündigungsfrist three-month notice deposits
- mit fester Laufzeit term (time) deposits
- mix deposit mix

- schutz   deposit protection (insurance), protection of deposits
- sicherheit   safety of deposits
- sicherung   deposit insurance
- sicherungsfonds   deposit insurance fund
- struktur   pattern of deposits
- überschuß   surplus of deposits
- volumen   total deposits, deposit volume
- volumen je Kunde   deposits per customer
- von Privatkunden   retail deposits
- zins   interest on deposits
- zinssatz   deposit rate
- zugang / - zuwachs   growth in deposits, inflow of deposits; new net deposits

Einlagerungskredit   stock-piling loan

Einlagerungswechsel   storage bill

Einlegen der Stücke in das Sonderdepot   depositing the securities in the special custody account

Einleger   depositor

Einlegerstruktur   depositor pattern

einliefern   to deposit, to lodge, to hand over

Einlieferer   depositor

Einlieferung   deposit, depositing, lodgement, handing over

- in das Depot   placing in a custody account, deposit into a custody account
- in den Sammelbestand   adding to the collective holdings
- des Verwahrstückes   handing over (depositing) the property to be held in safekeeping

Einlieferungs
- bestätigung   deposit (custody) receipt
- scheck   deposit form

einlösen   Schecks,Wechsel:to honour, to pay, to meet; Kupons: to cash, to collect; Anleihen: to redeem

einlösende Bank   paying bank

Einlösung   paying, payment; cashing; redemption
- bei Fälligkeit   redemption upon maturity
- eines Schecks bei Vorlage   paying (honouring) a cheque upon presentation

Einlösungs
- bedingungen   Anleihe: terms of redemption
- ermächtigung   authority to pay
- fonds   Anleihe: sinking (redemption) fund
- gebühr   bei Schecks: cashing charge; bei Kupons: collection fee
- gewinn   gain on redemption
- kurs   redemption (repayment) price
- mittel   redemption funds
- provision   (a) payment (cashing) commission; (b) redemption commission
- stelle   paying agent, coupon paying agent
- stopp   payment stop, countermand of payment
- versprechen   undertaking to pay (to honour)
- verweigerung   non-payment, refusal to pay (to honour)
- zusage   undertaking to pay (to honour)

65

Einmalemittenten occasional issuers (floating loans only through the agency of an underwriting syndicate; issue by prospectus)

einmalige Aufwendungen non-recurrent expenditure

einmalige Zahlung non-recurrent (one-off) payment

einpendeln der Kurs pendelte sich bei 152 DM ein   the price settled down at 152 DM

einräumen einen Kredit: to extend (to grant) a loan

Einräumung extension, extending, granting, accommodation

- eines Kontokorrentkredites extending an overdraft facility

Einrede der Vorausklage bei Garantien: guarantor's right to refuse payments until the creditor has definitively failed in obtaining payment from the debtor

einreichen

einen Kreditantrag - to file (to submit) a loan application

Schecks zum Inkasso - to pay in (to deposit) cheques for collection

Wechsel zum Diskont - to present (to tender) bills for discount

Wertpapiere zur Verwahrung - to lodge (to deposit) securities for safekeeping

einreichende Bank presenting bank

Einreicher presenter, presenting party, depositor

- bank   presenting (remitting) bank
- obligo bei Wechseldiskontierungen: liability ledger on bills

Einreichungsfrist presentation period; period for presentation

einrichten to open, to establish, to set up

Einrichtung opening, establishment, setting up

- eines Akkreditivs opening (establishment) of a credit
- eines Kontos opening an account
- einer Kreditlinie setting up a credit line

einschätzen to assess, to appraise

Einschätzung des Kreditrisikos assessment (appraisal) of the lending risk

einschießen to contribute, to inject, to infuse

einschließlich

- Auslosungsbetrag cum drawing
- Bezugsrechte cum rights, rights on
- Dividende cum dividend, dividend on

einschränken to restrict, to limit; to qualify

einschränkende Bestimmung restrictive clause (covenant)

Einschränkung restriction, limitation

- der Ausleihungen lending squeeze, restrictions on lendings
- des Bestätigungsvermerks accounts qualification, adverse opinion

Einschuß bei einem Effektenkredit: margin; von Kapital: capital (equity) injection, infusion of capital

einsehen /Einsicht nehmen in das Grundbuch: to search the land register, to make a search on the land register

Einstandspflicht liability to assessments

Einstandspreis /-wert   cost price

Einstandszins   historical interest rate

einstellen

  in die Bilanz -   to state (to report) in the balance sheet

  in die Rücklagen -   to transfer (to allocate) to the reserves

  Zahlungen -   to suspend (to stop) payments

Einstellung   transfer, allocation; suspension

- in die Pauschalwertberichtigung   transfer to the general provision for bad and doubtful debts

- in freie Rücklagen aus dem Jahresüberschuß   net income transferred to retained earnings

- in offene Rücklagen   transfers to surplus

- in Sonderposten mit Rücklagenanteil   transfer to special reserves

- der Zins- und Tilgungszahlungen für die Kredite   suspending (suspension of) payments of interest and principal on the loans

einstufen   to grade, to rate, to classify

Einstufung   grading, classification, rating

- einer Anleihe   rating of a bond

- des Länderrisikos   rating (assessing) the country risk

eintauschen   to swap, to exchange

  Stammaktien gegen Festverzinsliche -   to swap common stocks for fixed-rate debt

eintragen   to register, to record, to enter

Eintragung   registration, recording, entering

- im Grundbuch   registration with the land registry, recording in the land register

- einer Grundschuld   registration (recording) of a land charge

- im Handelsregister   entry on (in)the Register of Companies

- der Löschung   registration of satisfaction; entry of satisfaction of mortgage

Eintragungs

- antrag   application for registration

- bestätigung   certificate of registration

- bewilligung   registration consent; authority to register

eintragungsfähiges Recht   registrable title

Eintragungsgebühr   registration (recording) fee

eintragungspflichtig   registrable, subject to registration

einwandfreie Kontoführung   proper conduct of an account

einzahlen   to deposit, to pay into

  auf ein Konto -   to pay into an account

Einzahlung   paying in, depositing; deposit, payment, inpayment

  regelmäßige -en auf ein Konto   regular deposits in (into) an account

- en auf Aktien abrufen   to call on shares

- en auf Bausparkassenkonten   payments into building society accounts

- en und Auszahlungen   deposits and disbursements; paying and receiving funds

Einzahlungs

- aufforderung   call to pay up; call letter

67

- automat   auto depositor
- beleg   paying-in slip, deposit (inpayment) slip
- pflicht der Aktionäre   stockholders' call liability
- quote   percentage paid up
- überschuß   net deposits; surplus of deposits
- verpflichtung   call commitment (liability)
- verpflichtungen auf nicht voll eingezahlte Aktien   commitments for uncalled payments on partly paid shares

Einzel
- abschreibung   separate (individual) write-off
- aktionär   individual (single) shareholder
- auslosungsrecht   special drawing right (i.e. number-linked drawings as opposed to series-linked drawings)
- bewertung   separate (individual) valuation
- engagement   individual loan commitment, individual (separate) exposure
- firma   sole proprietorship (tradeship)
- heiten der Zahlung (des Vorganges)   payment (transaction) details
- kaufmann   sole trader
- kreditversicherung   individual solvency insurance
- prokura   general power of attorney (to act for the company)
- prokurist   executive holding a general power of attorney (to act for the company)
- schuldbuchforderung   allocated government-inscribed debt
- stücke   odd lots (securities); securities held separately

- unternehmung   sole proprietorship
- urkunde   individual bond certificate
- verfügungsberechtigung über ein Bankkonto: authority (power) to draw singly on an account
- vertretungsberechtigung   authority to act singly (on behalf of the company)
- verwahrte Stücke   securities held separately; securities held under allocated accounts
- verwahrung   individual safekeeping; individual custody; holding separately; holding under an allocated account
- vollmacht   special power of attorney
- vorschuß   special (separate) advance
- wertberichtigte Forderungen   lendings for which specific loan loss provisions have been made
- wertberichtigung   specific provision for bad and doubtful debts; specific loan loss provision
- zeichnungsberechtigter   signatory (person) authorised to sign singly
- zeichnungsberechtigung   authority to sign singly

einziehen   to collect; to recover

Forderungen -   to collect (to recover) debts

Kupons -   to cash coupons

Schecks -   to collect (to cash) cheques

Wertpapiere -   to call in (to redeem) securities

im Wege des Lastschriftverfahrens -   to collect payments due under a direct debit mandate (Br); to collect payments due under a pre-authorized payment mandate (US)

Einziehung/Einzug   collection, collecting; recovery

Einzug
- von Forderungen   debt collection; collecting (collection of) accounts receivable
- von Forderungen mittels Lastschriften   collecting payments due under a direct debit mandate (under a preauthorized payment mandate)
- der fällig werdenden Kupons   encashment of coupons falling due for payment
- von beleglosen Lastschriften   collection of paperless direct debits; collection of paperless preauthorized payments
- von Noten   calling in bank notes; withdrawing bank notes from circulation

Einzugs
- auftrag   (a) collection order, instructions to collect; (b) direct debit mandate (Br), preauthorized payment mandate (US)
- bank   collecting bank
- ermächtigung   direct debit authorisation (mandate) (Br); preauthorized payment mandate (US)
- ermächtigungsverfahren   direct debiting system, preauthorized payments system
- gebiet   catchment area
- gebühren / - kosten   collection charges
- verfahren   direct debiting procedure (Br), preauthorized payments system (US)
- vollmacht   authority to collect
- weg   collection channels

Elan   Börse: momentum

elektronisches Geld   electronic money

elektronisches Übertragungssystem   electronic delivery system

elektronischer Zahlungsverkehr   electronic funds transfer

elektronisches Zahlungsverkehrssystem   electronic funds transfer system (EFTS)

Elektrowerte   electricals; electrical shares (stocks)

Elferausschuß   Central Capital Market Committee

Emission   issue, offering; Vorgang: issuing, floating, offering, launching an issue
- von variabel verzinslichen Anleihen   issue of floating rate bonds
- en am Euroanleihemarkt   issues in the Eurobond market
- auf dem Submissionsweg   issue by tender
- von Vorzugsaktien   preference stock issue; issuing (offering) preference shares
- von festverzinslichen Werten   issue of fixed-income securities
- en im Dollarbereich begeben   to launch (to float) dollar-denominated issues

die - hat eine Laufzeit von sieben Jahren und wird mit 9 % p.a. verzinst   the issue has a seven-year life and pays a 9 p.c. coupon (and carries a 9 p.c. coupon)

die - wurde mit einem Abschlag von 1 % gehandelt   the issue traded at a 1 p.c. discount

eine - fest übernehmen   to underwrite an issue

eine - kommissionsweise übernehmen   to take up an issue on a commission basis; wenn das Emissionskonsortium das Absatzrisiko trägt: to sponsor an issue

eine - zur Verkaufsvermittlung übernehmen   to sell an issue on a best efforts basis

Emissions
- abteilung   new issues department
- abwicklung   handling of an issue, launching of an issue
- adresse, erstklassige   first--rate name in the primary market, prime borrower, prime issuer
- agio (-aufgeld)   issuing premium
- angebot   offering; offer to launch a bond
- ankündigung   new issue announcement
- auflegung   launching (floating) of an issue
- bank   (a) investment bank, underwriting house; (b) Notenbank: bank of issue, issuing bank
- bedarf   new issue requirements
- bedingungen   terms of an issue, offering terms, bond features
- betrag   (a) amount of an issue, principal; (b) issuing total
- beträge, die nicht bei Anlegern untergebracht werden konnten   securities not taken up by investors
- dauer   issuing (offering) period
- disagio   issuing discount
- erfolg gewährleisten   to guarantee the success of an issue
- erlös   proceeds of an issue, issuing proceeds
- fähiges Unternehmen   company having access to the primary market
- fahrplan   issuing timetable (calendar), timetable of new issues
- form   type of offering
- genehmigung   issuing approval, authority to issue (to launch a bond)
- geschäft   issuing business (operations), new issue activities; investment banking
- haus   investment bank, issuing (underwriting) house
- höhe   size (magnitude) of an issue
- jahr   year of issue
- kalender   issuing timetable (calendar), calendar of new issues
- käufer   investor, buyer of an issue
- konditionen   terms of an issue, offering terms
- konsortium   issuing (underwriting) syndicate
- kontrolle   control of new issues, steering of the primary market
- kosten   issuing (floatation) cost, offering cost
- kredit   (a) standing (rating) of the issuer, rating of the borrower; (b) standing of the investment bank (of the underwriter); (c) borrowing (raising funds) through a capital issue
- kurs   issuing (issue, offering) price
- markt   primary market
- merkmale   features (characteristics) of an issue, bond features
- paket   issue (loan) package
- pause   halt in new issues, temporary issuing freeze
- plazierung   placing (of) an issue
- politik   new issue policy
- preis   issuing (offering) price
- prospekt   issuing (underwriting) prospectus, offering prospectus
- prospekt, vorläufiger   red herring

- quote   underwriting share, share in an issue
- rendite   issuing yield, yield upon issue
- risiko   issuing (underwriting) risk
- schuldner   issue (bond) debtor
- sperre   ban on new issues, issuing freeze
- standing ⟶ Emissionskredit
- summe   amount of an issue; issuing total
- tätigkeit   issuing (new issue) activities
- tätigkeit am Eurokapitalmarkt   issuing activity (underwriting operations) in the Eurobond market
- technik   issuing (investment banking) techniques
- überhang   placing backlog, oversupply of new issues
- übernahme   underwriting (of) an issue, taking up an issue
- übernahme auf Kommissionsbasis   taking up an issue on a commission basis; falls das Konsortium das Absatzrisiko trägt: sponsoring an issue
- übernahme zur Verkaufsvermittlung   taking up an issue and selling it on a best efforts basis
- umlauf   total bonds issued; bonds outstanding
- unterbringung   placing an issue
- unternehmer   underwriter, underwriting (issuing) house
- verfahren   issuing (offering) procedure
- vergütung   underwriting commission
- vertrag   underwriting agreement
- verwaltung   administration of capital issues

- volumen einer Anleihe: loan principal, total amount issued; aller begebenen Anleihen: issuing total (volume, activity)
- vorhaben   new issue project
- währung   issuing (offering) currency
- welle   spate of new issues
- zeitpunkt   launching date, date of issue; den Emissionszeitpunkt abstimmen   to agree the timing of the issue with ..

Emittent   issuer

Emittentenrisiko   issuer's risk

emittieren   to issue, to float, to offer, to launch

eine variabel verzinsliche Anleihe mit siebenjähriger Laufzeit - to launch a seven-year floater

über pari -   to issue above par, to offer at a premium

unter pari -   to issue below par, to offer at a discount

zum Nennwert -   to issue at par, to offer at par

emittierende Gesellschaft   issuing company

emporschnellen   Kurse: to soar, to rocket, to zoom

Ende   Zinsen am kurzen (langen) - short-term (long-term) interest rates

enden   der Kreditvertrag endet am ..   the loan agreement runs out (expires) on ..

endfällige Stücke   securities due for redemption

Endfälligkeit   final maturity

Endkreditnehmer   ultimate borrower

Energiewerte   resource stock

Engagement   allgemein: commitment, involvement; im Kreditgeschäft: loan commitment, exposure, lending; im Wertpapiergeschäft: investment, holdings, exposure

Engagement

- in Aktien stock exposure, investment in stocks
- in Dollartiteln investment in dollar securities; buying of dollar securities
- in Fremdwährungen foreign currency exposure, exposure in (holdings of) foreign currencies
- im Hypothekenbereich mortgage loan exposure (commitments), mortgage lendings, mortgage loan portfolio
- in langfristigen Krediten long-term loan exposure, long-term lendings
- im Privatkundenbereich involvement in retail banking
- in Rentenwerten bond exposure, investments in bonds, bond holdings

Abbau der -s in kurzfristigen Titeln reducing the holdings of short-term bonds, cutting back the exposure in short-term bonds

Aufstellung unserer Länder- s list of our exposure (lendings) to sovereign borrowers

Gesamtsumme der -s gegenüber Nichtbanken total lendings to non-bank customers

Prüfung eines -s checking the credit-worthiness of a borrower, credit investigation (assessment)

teilweise Rückführung des -s partial repayment of the loan facility, reduction of the loan exposure

Überprüfung unseres -s reviewing our loan exposure

Verringerung des -s in Aktienwerten reducing the exposure to stocks

sich mit neuen -s zurückhalten to be careful about new lendings

engagieren

wir sind mit ungefähr DM 3 Mio engagiert our exposure totals approximately DM 3m, we are committed with approximately DM 3m

sich stärker im Firmenkundengeschäft - to expand the corporate banking activities

sich mit neuen Krediten - to increase the loan exposure, to extend fresh money

enger Markt narrow (limited, tight, thin) market

entfallen

30 % der Neuausleihungen entfielen auf langfristige Kredite long-term loans accounted for 30 p.c. of new lendings; long-term loans made up 30 p.c. of new lendings

entlassen

aus einer Garantie - to release from a guarantee

aus der Haftung - to discharge from liability

Entnahme withdrawal, drawing

- aus einem Depot withdrawal from a securities account, sale against (transfer from) a securities account

- n der Gesellschafter drawings by the partners

- aus der gesetzlichen Rücklage drawing on statutory reserves

entnommener Gewinn profit (income) withdrawn, distributed profit

entnommene Stücke securities sold (withdrawn); securities transferred

entschädigen to indemnify, to compensate for

Entschädigung indemnity, indemnification, compensation

Entschädigung für die vorzeitige Rückzahlung: prepayment indemnity

entschulden to clear (to repay) the debts

Entschuldung debt clearance, repayment of debts

entsprechen

den Akkreditivbedingungen - to comply with (to observe) the terms and conditions of the documentary credit

der Marktnachfrage - to meet the market demand

entsprechend Ihren Weisungen in accordance with your instructions

die Zinssätze - den Marktgegebenheiten the interest rates are in line with market conditions (reflect the conditions in the market)

entstehen to incur, to accrue; to arise

die dem Kreditgeber entstandenen Kosten the costs incurred by the lender

für den entstandenen Schaden haften to be liable for the damage caused

Entwicklung development, trend, tendency

- en im Privatkundengeschäft developments in retail banking

Unsicherheit über die weitere - der Zinssätze uncertainty over the direction of interest rates (over the further trend in interest rates)

entziehen to drain, to skim (to siphon) off

dem Bankensystem Liquidität - to drain liquidity from the banking system

erbringen to yield, to produce

den Beweis - to furnish proof

einen angemessenen Gewinn - to yield a fair return

eine 8 %ige Rendite - to offer (to bring, to carry) a 9 p.c. yield

die gewünschte Verzinsung - to produce the desired return

erfahren einen neuen Auftrieb erfahren to experience a new upsurge

Erfahrung im Kreditgeschäft: lending experience

erfassen

alle Marktbereiche wurden von der Aufwärtsbewegung erfaßt all market sectors were caught up in the buoyancy

Erfolg (a) profit, performance; (b) success

die Neuemission verzeichnete einen großen - the new issue was extremely well received

die Bank arbeitet mit ausgezeichnetem - the bank has an excellent performance record

erfolgen

Abschlüsse - in vier Währungen contracts are traded in four currencies

die Zahlung erfolgt in US Dollar payment will be made in US dollars

Erfolgs

- analyse profit (performance) analysis

- aussichten kleinere Emissionen haben größere Erfolgsaussichten smaller issues stand a better chance of success

- beteiligung profit-sharing

- bilanz statement of income

- faktoren profit factors

- konten income accounts

73

<u>Erfolgskontrolle</u> performance control

<u>erfolgsneutral</u> neutral in its effects on profits

<u>Erfolgsrechnung</u> income statement (account), profit and loss account

<u>erforderlich</u>

die für die Fortsetzung unseres Engagements unbedingt -en Tilgungszahlungen the repayments essential to continuing our loan accommodation

die nach dem Verzug des Kreditnehmers -en Maßnahmen the measures necessary to respond to the default of the borrower

<u>erfüllen</u> Börsengeschäfte: to settle, to execute; Verpflichtungen: to meet, to fulfill, to carry out, to perform

<u>Erfüllung</u> fulfillment, meeting, performance; settlement, execution

- von Börsengeschäften durch Depotgutschrift settling transactions in securities through crediting the relevant securities accounts
- des Mindestreservesolls meeting reserve requirements
- der vertraglichen Verpflichtungen fulfillment (fulfilling) contractual obligations
- des Vertrages performance (execution) of contract

<u>Erfüllungs</u>

- garantie performance bond
- ort place of performance
- risiko settlement risk
- Statt, an Erfüllungs-Statt annehmen to accept in place of payment (in lieu of performance)
- tag date of performance; settlement day

<u>Ergebnis</u> (a) profit, income (or loss), profits performance, operating results; (b) outcome, result

- im Dienstleistungsbereich income from service transactions
- vor Ertragssteuern und Anteilen Dritter profit before income taxes and minority interests
- im zinsabhängigen Geschäft profit from interest-related transactions
- im Kreditgeschäft performance of lending operations
- im Privatkundenbereich performance in the retail banking sector, figures on the retail business
- nach Risikovorsorge profit after bad debt provisioning
- nach Steuern und Anteilen Dritter net income; income after taxes and minority interests

im - verrechnen to charge (or to credit) to operations

<u>Ergebnis</u>

- abführungsvertrag profit and loss transfer agreement
- beitrag profit contribution
- orientierte Gewinnbeteiligung profit-linked (performance--linked) profit-sharing scheme
- rechnung income statement, profit and loss account
- steuerung performance control
- übernahmevertrag profit and loss pooling agreement

<u>erhaltene Anzahlungen</u> advances received

<u>erheben</u>

Klage gegen den Kreditnehmer - to bring an action against the borrower

Kontoführungsgebühren - to charge account-maintenance fees

Protest - to lodge a protest

erhöhen

die Bilanzsumme erhöhte sich um 2,1% auf DM 80 Mio   total assets rose 2.1p.c. to DM 80m

die Bundesbank erhöhte den Diskontsatz von 6 auf 7%   the Bundesbank lifted the discount rate from 6 to 7 p.c.

der Konzernumsatz erhöhte sich um DM 8 Mio gegenüber dem Vorjahr   group sales were DM 8m ahead of the results achieved a year earlier

letztes Jahr erhöhte sich der Provisionsüberschuß um 5%   last year saw an increase in net commission income by 5 p.c.

die Umsatzerlöse erhöhten sich von DM 12 auf DM 32 Mio   sales revenue climbed (moved ahead) from DM 12 to DM 32m

Erhöhung   increase, rise, advance; increasing, lifting

es wird eine - des Lombardsatzes um 1% erwartet   the Lombard rate is expected to increase by 1p.c.

eine - von 2% gegenüber dem Vorjahr   an increase of 2 p.c. over last year's level

- des Vorsteuer-Gewinnes von .. auf ..   increase (rise) in pre-tax profits from .. to ..

erholen   (a) Kurse: to recover, to rally, to perk up; (b) sich erholen (im Dokumentengeschäft): to obtain reimbursement

.. erholten sich um 8 auf 140DM   .. recovered 8 to 140DM

sich auf die ausländische Bank -   to obtain reimbursement from the foreign bank

Fahrzeugwerte erholten sich nach Käufen des Berufshandels   motors rallied on professional buying

sich geringfügig -   to recover marginally

die Konjunktur beginnt sich zu -   economic activity begins perking up

Erholung   (a) recovery, rally; (b) obtaining reimbursement

- am Aktienmarkt   stock market rally; recovery (rally) in equity prices

Erinnerungsschreiben   chaser, reminder

Erinnerungswert   residual (notional) value

erkennen   ein Konto: to credit an account, to enter to the credit of an account

erklären   to declare, to state

die Bereitschaft zur Bürgschaftsübernahme -   to state its willingness to furnish a guarantee

unser erklärtes Ziel ist die Rückführung des Engagements   our stated goal is to reduce the exposure

Erklärung   statement, declaration

erklimmen   to soar, to climb

erlassen   Zinsen, Verbindlichkeiten: to remit, to waive

erleichtern   (a) to ease, to relax; (b) to facilitate

Erleichterung   easing, relaxation; facilitating

- der Kreditaufnahme / - der Kreditkonditionen   easing of loan terms

- des Zahlungsverkehrs unter Banken   facilitating interbank payments

Erlös   proceeds

erlöschen   to expire, to run out, to lapse

erloschene Kontovollmacht   lapsed authority (to operate the account)

ermächtigen   to authorise, to entitle, to empower

zu Verfügungen über das Konto -   to authorise to draw on the account (to operate the account)

ermäßigen to reduce, to lower
 die Bundesbank ermäßigte den Diskontsatz auf 6 % the Bundesbank lowered the discount rate to 6 %
 ... ermäßigten sich um 5 auf 90DM
 ... slipped (gave up) 5 to 90DM

Ermäßigung reduction, lowering

Ermessen judgement, discretion
 eine nach dem alleinigen - der Bank angemessene Sicherheit für die Verbindlichkeiten a security which in the sole judgement of the bank is good and adequate to secure the obligations

Ermessens
- befugnisse discretionary powers
- spielraum discretionary leeway

ermitteln to determine, to establish; to calculate

Erneuerung der Kreditzusage renewal of the loan undertaking

Erneuerungsschein renewal coupon

erneut nachgeben Kurse: to retreat afresh

eröffnen to open; to set up
 im Auftrag von .. eröffnen wir hiermit unser unwiderrufliches Akkreditiv zu Ihren Gunsten by order of .. we hereby open our irrevocable documentary credit in your favour
 die Börse eröffnete geringfügig schwächer the stock market opened a shade lower
 die Börse eröffnete bei lebhaften Umsätzen fester the stock market opened higher in brisk trading
 ein Konto bei einer Bank - to open an account with a bank
 Repräsentanzen im Ausland - to set up representative offices abroad

Eröffnung opening; setting up

Eröffnungs
- bank opening (issuing) bank
- kurs opening price
- schreiben Akkreditiv: advice of the credit

erreichen to reach, to arrive at
 die Börsenumsätze werden bald DM .. - stock market turnover will soon hit DM ..
 die Exporte erreichten nahezu DM .. exports came to nearly DM ..
 die Kreditaufnahmen am Kapitalmarkt haben einen neuen Höchststand erreicht borrowings in the capital market reached a new peak (record level)

Ersatz replacement, substitute
- investitionen expenditure on plant replacements
- scheck replacement cheque
- stücke Wertpapiere: replacement certificates

Erschließungsgarantie development guarantee

erschüttern der Zusammenbruch von XYZ erschütterte das Kreditgewerbe the collapse of XYZ rocked the banking system

Ersparnisbildung formation of savings

Erstabsatz im Wertpapiergeschäft: new issue business
- von Pfandbriefen sale of newly issued mortgage bonds

Erstausgabepreis issuing (subscription) price, initial offering price

Erstausreichung initial extension (accommodation)

Erstausstattung Wechsel: first of exchange

Erstbegünstigter first beneficiary

erste Adresse   prime name; prime borrower (issuer)

erstellen einen Depotauszug: to prepare a securities account statement

Ersterwerb im Emissionsgeschäft: purchase of newly issued securities

erstklassig first-rate, top-quality, first-class
- e Anleiheadresse first-rate name in the bond market, prime issuer
- e Bonität unquestionable financial soundness
- e Bonitätsbeurteilung (Bewertung) premium rating
- e Geldmarktpapiere top-quality commercial paper
- er Kreditnehmer prime borrower
- er staatlicher Kreditnehmer AAA sovereign borrower
- er Wechsel   prime bill
- e Wertpapiere first-class securities

erststellig
- er Beleihungsraum margin for lendings against first-rank security
- e Grundschuld first lien on land, senior land charge
- e Hypothek first (senior) mortgage
- es Hypothekendarlehen first (senior) mortgage loan

Erst(-unternehmens)konsolidierung initial consolidation (i.e. the difference between the costs of acquisition of subsidiaries and the parent company's share in its equity at the time of acquisition)

Erstverwahrer original custodian, original depository

Erstzeichner original subscriber

Ertrag income, proceeds; Rendite: yield, return

Erträge earnings, income, gains
- aus dem Abgang von Gegenständen des Anlagevermögens gains on disposal of fixed assets
- aus der Auflösung von Sonderposten mit Rücklageanteil gain from writing back special reserves
- aus Beteiligungen income from trade investments, income from subsidiaries and affiliates
- aus Dienstleistungsgeschäften income from service transactions
- aus dem Kreditgeschäft earnings from lendings
- aus frei gewordenen Wertberichtigungen gains on loan loss provisions no longer required

Erträgnis
- aufstellung list of coupon and dividend payments
- ausschüttung income (dividend) payout
- gutschrift (a) dividend; (b) coupon payment; (c) income from securities
- schein coupon

ertragsabhängige Steuern earnings-linked taxes

Ertrags
- ausfall loss (shortage) of earnings
- ausschüttung distribution of income
- besserung improvement in earnings
- delle dent in earnings
- einbruch sharp drop (setback) in earnings
- entwicklung earnings trend, development in earnings; earnings history
- kraft earnings power
- lage earnings situation (position)

- lage wurde als zufriedenstellend bezeichnet earnings were termed satisfactory

ertragsorientierte Konditionengestaltung earnings-orientated pricing

Ertrags
- quelle source of earnings
- rechnung income statement
- rückgang earnings setback, downturn (decline) in earnings
- schein coupon
- spanne earnings spread (ratio of ⟶Teilbetriebsergebnis before write-offs to the average business volume)
- steigerung increase in earnings, earnings rise (surge)
- steuerung der Filialen control of branch earnings
- wert bei Baufinanzierungen: capitalised annual income
- wiederanlage reinvestment of income distributed
- zinsen interest received
- zuwachs earnings gain

erwarten to expect, to anticipate

wir - einen Anstieg der Zinssätze we expect interest rates to climb

den erwarteten Kreditbedarf decken to meet the projected borrowing requirements

Erwartung expectation, anticipation

das Ergebnis im Privatkundengeschäft ist hinter den -en zurückgeblieben the performance of retail operations has fallen short of expectations

erweisen die Emission erwies sich als Erfolg the issue turned out to be a success

erweitern das Dienstleistungsangebot der Filialen - to extend the range of services offered by the branches

erweiterte Bandbreiten widened parity bands

erweiterter Geldhandel money market dealings between banks and non-banks

erweiterter Zugang zu den Fondsmitteln (des IWF) extended access to the Fund's (IMF) resources

Erweiterung extension
- ihrer Dienstleistungspalette extension of its range of services
- der Kapitaldecke broadening of the equity base

erwerben to acquire, to purchase

eine 30%ige Beteiligung - to take a 30 p.c. shareholding in .., to acquire a 30 p.c. stake in ..

erwirtschaftetes Eigenkapital earned surplus

erworbene Geschäftswerte acquired goodwill

erzielen

die Gesellschaft erzielte ein hervorragendes Ergebnis the company performed strongly

eine endgültige Regelung über die beabsichtigte Kreditaufnahme - to reach a final agreement on the intended borrowing

E- Scheck ⟶ Effektenscheck

Euro
- Anleihemarkt Eurobond market
- Bondmarkt, am Eurobond-Markt auflegen to float in (to launch on) the Eurobond market
- Dollareinlagen Eurodollar deposits
- Dollarkredit Eurodollar borrowing
- Dollarmarkt Eurodollar market
- Emission Euroloan, Euroissue
- Emissionswährung Euroissue currency

- Geldleihe Euroloan
- Geldmarkt Euromoney market
- Kapitalmarkt Eurocapital market
- Konsortialkredit syndicated Euroloan
- Kreditaufnahme borrowing in the Euromarket
- Kreditgeschäft Eurolending business (operations)
- Kreditsyndizierung Eurocredit syndication
- Terminzinsen Euro term money rates
- Währungskredit Eurocurrency loan
- Währungsmarkt Eurocurrency market
- Zinsen Euromarket interest rates

Europäisch
- e Rechnungseinheit European Unit of Account
- e Währungseinheit European Currency Unit
- es Währungssystem European Monetary System
- er Wechselkursverbund European Currency Snake

Eventualobligo contingent commitment

Eventualverbindlichkeiten contingent liabilities

Evidenzzentrale credit reporting agency

Existenzgründung business start-up

Existenzgründungs-Darlehen business start-up loan, development loan

exponieren mit DM 2 Mio exponiert sein to be committed with DM 2m

Exportkreditversicherung export credit insurance

Exportpauschaldeckung export blanket coverage

ex Berichtigungsaktien (exBA) ex scrip issue, ex capitalisation issue (x.cp.)

ex Bezugsrecht (exB) ex rights (x.r.)

ex Dividende (exD) ex dividend, ex coupon (x.d.)

ex Dividende notiert werden to go (to be quoted) ex dividend

ex Gratisaktien ex capitalisation issue (x.cp.)

ex Ziehung (exZ) ex drawing

F

Fahrplan im Emissionsgeschäft: issuing calendar (timetable)

Fahrzeugwerte motors

fällig payable, due
- e Stücke securities due for redemption
- bei Vorlage payable upon presentation

fällig stellen
  einen Kredit - to call in a loan
  zur sofortigen Rückzahlung - to call for immediate repayment

fällig werden to fall (to become) due, to mature

Fälligkeit maturity, due date
- eines Kupons coupon due date
- drei Monate nach Ausstellungsdatum maturity three months after date of issue

Fälligkeitenliste maturity schedule

Fälligkeits
- fächer range of maturities
- factoring maturity factoring
- gliederung maturity breakdown (spacing)
- hypothek mortgage falling due on a fixed date
- termin maturity, due date, date of maturity

falsche Wertstellung incorrect (wrong) value date

Farbennachfolger Hoechst, Bayer, BASF stocks

Farbenwerte chemicals

Farbklausel im Akkreditivgeschäft: green (red) clause

favorisiert
- e Titel market favourites
  Bankenwerte wurden - banks were in strong demand

Fazilität facility, loan (credit) facility

federführend
- e Bank lead bank, lead manager
- zeichnen to lead, to lead-manage, to manage

Federführer lead manager, lead bank, syndicate manager

Federführung lead management
  ein Konsortium unter - der ... a syndicate led by ...

Fehlbuchung wrong entry (post); amount posted to the wrong account; misposting

fehlend
- e Anschlußaufträge ließen die Kurse nachgeben prices drifted lower on lack of follow-through support
- e Deckung lack of cover, lacking cover
- es Interesse der privaten Anleger lacking retail investment interest

Fehleranzeige error notification

fehlgeleitete Überweisung misdirected money transfer

Fernscheck out-of-town cheque

Fernzahlungsverkehr   out-of-town
  payments

fest   firm, strong
- e Börse   strong (firm) market
- e Grundstimmung   firm undertone, firm underlying sentiment
- e Kurse   firm (strong) prices
- er Rentenmarkt   firm bond market
- er Schluß   firm closing
- e Übernahme   firm underwriting
- er Wechselkurs   fixed exchange rate

die Ausleihungen - refinanzieren   to fund the lendings at a fixed rate

die Aktienkurse tendierten weiterhin - equities continued (remained) firm

Bankenwerte waren gegen Schluß der Börsensitzung geringfügig - er   banks were marginally higher at the close of the session

Maschinenbauwerte tendierten bei lebhaften Umsätzen - er   engineerings turned (edged) higher in active trading

Fest
- darlehen   fixed-rate loan
- gebot   firm bid
- geld   term (time) deposits, fixed-term deposits
- geldanlage   term (time) deposit investment
- geldkonto   term (time) deposit account
- geldrendite   term money yield
- geldunterlegung   term (time) deposits serving as security for a loan
- geschäft   (a) firm bargain; (b) fixed-rate lendings

festgeschriebener Zinssatz   fixed interest rate, locked-in rate

festigen   to strengthen, to cement

seine Marktposition weiter - to further strengthen its position in the market

Fest
- jahre   call-free years
- konditionen   fixed terms, fixed rate
- kosten   fixed cost
- kostenbelastung   fixed cost charge
- kredit   fixed-rate loan
- laufzeit   fixed term (maturity)

festlegen   (a) to tie up; to invest (to deposit) for a fixed period; (b) to establish, to fix, to set out; (c) to lay down, to stipulate

die Anleger legen ihre Barmittel für längere Zeiträume fest   investors tie up their cash for longer periods

die genauen Konditionen sind im Kreditvertrag festgelegt   the full terms are set out in the loan agreement

Festlegung   (a) tying up, investing for a fixed period; (b) establishment, fixing, setting out
- der Anleihekonditionen   pricing of an issue, establishment of the bond terms, bond (loan) pricing
- der Bereitstellungsprovision   commitment fee pricing, fixing the commitment fee
- der Kreditkonditionen   establishment of the loan terms, setting out the terms of a credit facility
- der Spareinlagen auf vier Jahre   tying up the savings for a period of four years

Festlegungsdauer   (a) investment term, fixed period of investment; (b) bei Sparverträgen: blocking period

Festsatz fixed rate, locked-in (locked-up) rate

4-Jahres-Festsätze interest rates locked in for four years, fixed interest rates for four years

Festsatzbereich fixed-rate lendings, fixed-rate lending (loan) sector

die Ausleihungen im Festsatzbereich stiegen um 8 % fixed--rate lendings (business on the fixed-rate side) rose by 8 p.c.

Festsatzkredit fixed-rate loan

festschreiben

einen Zinssatz - to lock in an interest rate, to establish a fixed rate

Wertpapiere aufgrund von Prämiensparverträgen - to block securities under bonus-carrying savings schemes

Festschreibung

- der Konditionen establishing fixed loan terms, locking in (up) the loan terms

- von Wertpapieren blocking (of) securities

- des Zinssatzes auf zwei Jahre locking in (up) the interest rate for two years, establishing a fixed interest rate for two years

Festschreibungsfrist fixed-rate period, locking-in period; blocking period

festsetzen Konditionen: to fix, to establish; Kurse: to fix, to determine

Festsetzung fixing, determination, establishment

feststellen Kurs: to fix, to determine; Bilanz: to approve

Festübernahme Emission: firm underwriting

festverzinslich fixed-interest, fixed-interest-bearing, fixed--income

- e Anleihe fixed-income (fixed-coupon) bond

- e Kapitalanlagen fixed-income investments

Festverzinsliche fixed-income (fixed-interest) securities, fixed-interest-bearing bonds

Festzins

- aktiva einer Bank: fixed-rate lendings

- hypothek fixed-rate mortgage

- kredit fixed-rate loan

- satz fixed interest rate

- sparen fixed-rate saving

- vereinbarung fixed-rate agreement

Feuerwehrfonds   deposit insurance fund

Filial

- bank branch bank, multiple office bank

- bankensystem branch banking

- kostenrechnung branch costing

- netz branch network

- prokura authority to act for the branch of a company

- steuerung branch control

Finanz

- anlagen investments; financial assets

- anzeige financial advertisement

- ausstattung financial (capital) resources available; availability of capital resources

- bedarf borrowing (finance) requirements

- bewegung source and application of funds

- disposition treasury (financial) management

- flußrechnung funds statement, financial flow statement

82

- gebaren   financial management (policy)

finanziell   financial
- e Belastung   financial strain (burden)
- e Beteiligung   financial interest (stake)
- es Engagement   financial commitment (exposure)
- er Engpaß   financial straits (squeeze)
- e Gesundung   financial revitalisation (reconstruction)
- e Lage   financial condition (position)
- e Mittel   financial resources (funds)
- e Schwierigkeiten   financial difficulties (woes)
  in finanziellen Schwierigkeiten befindliches Unternehmen   financially distressed (strapped) company
- er Spielraum   financial elbow room (leeway)
- e Unterstützung   financial backing (support)
- e Verpflichtungen   financial obligations
  das Projekt - absichern   to ensure the provision of funds for a project, to provide financial backing for a project
  auf eine gesunde -e Grundlage stellen   to put on a sound financial footing

finanzieren   to finance, to fund

Finanzierung   financing, funding
- durch Aktien   stock financing
- durch Bankkredite   financing through borrowings with banks (through bank loans)
- außerhalb der Bilanz bei Projektfinanzierungen: financing off the balance sheet
- aus Eigenmitteln   financing from funds generated internally (from internal earnings)
- durch Forderungsabtretung   accounts receivable financing
- durch Fremdmittel   financing with outside capital (borrowed funds)
- langlebiger Gebrauchsgüter   financing consumer durables
- aus einer Hand   one-stop financing package
- von Investitionen   capital investment financing
- der Mehrkosten bei Projektfinanzierungen: overrun financing, funding overruns
- durch Pensionsgeschäfte   financing with repurchase agreements
- mit eingeschränktem Rückgriff bei Projektfinanzierungen: limited recourse financing
- mit vollem Rückgriff bei Projektfinanzierungen: full recourse financing
- von Vorratsvermögen   inventory financing; financing inventories

Kredite zur - von Firmenübernahmen   loans to finance corporate take-overs

Finanzierungs
- aufwand   finance expenditure (charges)
- bedarf   borrowing requirements, funding needs
- bedarf der Emittenten   issuers' borrowing requirements, issuers' capital needs
- bedarf der öffentlichen Hand   public borrowing requirements
- bedarf auf dem Kreditmarkt befriedigen   to meet (to cover) borrowing requirements in the financial markets
- bedingungen   financing terms, terms of finance
- bilanz   statement of sources and application of funds

Finanzierungs
- form   method of financing, funding arrangement
- gesellschaft   finance company
- konditionen   financing terms, terms of finance
- konzept   financing (funding) blueprint
- kosten   finance charge (expenditure), finance costs
- leasing   finance leasing
- mittel   financial resources, finance capital, funds required to finance
- mittel bereitstellen   to provide funds (loans,finance capital)
- modell   financing (funding) model
- möglichkeiten   (a) financing (funding) options; (b) funding capabilities (opportunities)
- paket   financing (funding) package, loan package
- papiere   financing (funding) instruments (money market paper issued by local authorities to cover their borrowing requirements)
- plan   financial planning statement
- programm   financing (funding) scheme
- quelle   funding source, source of financing
- rückhalt   financial backing (support)
- schätze   finance bonds (interest is paid by way of a discount from the purchase price)
- schwierigkeiten   funding difficulties, difficulties in providing the necessary funds (finance)
- technik   finance (financial) engineering; financing techniques; mechanics of finance

- träger   financing (funding) institution, organisation providing the funds for ..
- verbund   financing pool
- vereinbarung   financing arrangement
- wechsel   finance (credit) bill
- zusage   undertaking (commitment) to finance, commitment to fund, finance (funding) commitment
- zusageprovision   finance commitment commission

Finanz
- interessen   financial interests
- intermediäre   financial intermediaries
- kapital   finance capital; im bilanziellen Kontext: equity and long-term borrowings
- klemme   financial straits (squeeze)
- konsortium   finance syndicate
- kraft   financial muscle, funding capabilities
- kredit   finance loan, loan to finance (e.g. the takeover of a company)
- kreditbürgschaft   loan guarantee
- kreditdeckung des Bundes   government loan guarantee
- kreise   financial community
- lage   financial position
- leistungen   financial services
- makler   finance broker
- management   financial management
- markt   financial market
- papiere   financial securities
- plan   financial planning statement
- planung   financial (budget) planning
- platz   financial centre

84

Finanz
- schulden borrowings; indebtedness
- schwaches Unternehmen financially weak company
- schwierigkeiten financial difficulties, shortage of funds, funding difficulties
- spritze capital injection, infusion of capital, fresh funding
- starkes Unternehmen financially strong (sound) company
- termingeschäfte financial futures
- terminkontrakte financial futures contracts
- terminmarkt financial futures market
- titel financial securities
- wechsel finance bill
- wirtschaft finance

Firmenbürgschaft corporate guarantee

Firmenkredit corporate loan (lending)

- engagements (Gesamtsumme) total corporate lendings, total lendings to corporate customers
- geschäft corporate lending business (activities)

Firmenkunde corporate (company) customer

Firmenkunden
- bereich corporate banking sector (area, side)
  im Firmenkundenbereich on the corporate banking side, in the corporate banking market
- betreuung servicing corporate customers
- geschäft corporate banking, firm banking, wholesale banking
  Konditionen im Firmenkundengeschäft: corporate banking terms; corporate lending terms
- kredit corporate (business)loan
- termineinlagen corporate time deposits

fixen to sell short

Fixer short seller

Fixgeschäft Leerverkauf: short sale; Termingeschäft: time bargain

Fixkostenbelastung fixed cost charge

flau Börsenumsätze: dull, slow, slack

Flaute am Aktien -(Renten-)Markt stalemate in the equity (bond) market

flexible Konditionengestaltung flexible pricing

flexibler Wechselkurs flexible exchange rate

Floatgewinn float, float profit, profit from varying value dates

floatinduzierter Zinsverlust float-induced loss of interest

flotierender Zinssatz floating interest rate

flottantes Material freely tradeable stock

flüssige Mittel liquid funds (resources), liquidity

flüssig sein to hold ample liquid resources (funds)

Folgeaufträge Börse: follow-up orders, follow-through support

Fonds fund, investment fund; mutual fund (US),unit trust (Br)
- anlagen fund investments
- anlageziel investment objective of a fund
- anteil investment fund share; unit, share

Fonds
- anteile zum Inventarwert zurückkaufen   to repurchase units at the net asset value
- anteilseigner   unitholder, shareholder
- depotbank   depository (trustee, custodian) of a fund
- gebundene Lebensversicherung   unit-linked life assurance
- vermögenswerte   assets of a fund
- verwaltungsgesellschaft   management company of a fund

Forderungen   Ansprüche: claims;
Kredite: lendings, loans;
Warenforderungen: receivables, accounts receivable
- aus Aktienzeichnungen   stock subscriptions receivable
- an Banken   due from banks, lendings to banks
- gegen die Bank   claims on (against) the bank
- der bevorrechtigten Gläubiger   claims by priority creditors
- an öffentliche Haushalte   lendings to local authorities
- aus Inkassogeschäften   collections due
- aus Kapitalzeichnungen   receivables from equity subscriptions due
- gegenüber Konzerngesellschaften   due from group companies
- aus Kreditgeschäften   receivables from lending transactions
- an Kreditinstitute   due from banks, lendings to banks
- an Kunden   loans and advances to non-bank customers
- an staatliche Schuldner   lendings to sovereign borrowers
- an verbundene Unternehmen   due from affiliated companies
- und sonstige Vermögensgegenstände   receivables and miscellaneous assets
- aus Warenlieferungen   accounts receivable, trade
- aus Wertpapiergeschäften   receivables from securities transactions
- aus Zeichnungen   subscription receivables

Forderungs
- abtretung   assignment of receivables
- anmeldung   im Konkursverfahren: proving of a debt
- ausfälle   bei Krediten: loan charge-offs, loan losses
- ausfallverhältnis   loan charge-off ratio
- beitreibung   collection of receivables, collection (recovery) of a debt
- einzug ⟶ Forderungsbeitreibung
- recht   claim to ownership, proprietary interest
- verkauf   sale of accounts receivable
- verzicht   einer Bank: write-off of loans

Förderungsmaßnahmen   measures designed to promote ...

Forfaitierer   forfaiter, forfaiting house

Forfaitierung   forfaiting; non--recourse financing; provision of medium-term refinancing of suppliers' credits without recourse to the supplier

Forfaitierungs
- geschäft   forfaiting transaction
- marge   forfaiting margin
- markt   à forfait market
- material   à forfait paper

Forfaitierungs
- prämie   forfaiting premium
- volumen   forfaiting portfolio
- zusage   undertaking to forfait

fortlaufende Notierung   variable-price quotation

fortsetzen   Bankaktien setzten ihre Aufwärtsbewegung fort   bank stocks continued to advance, bank stocks continued on their upward trend

frei
- e Aktionäre   outside shareholders
- e Berufe   als Kreditnehmergruppe: professional firms
- er Goldmarkt   free-tier gold market
- er Kapitalverkehr   free flow of capital, freedom of capital movements
- e Liquiditätsreserven   free liquidity reserves
- er Makler   unofficial broker
- er Markt   (a) open market; (b) Börse: off-floor trading
- e Rücklagen   unallocated reserves; retained earnings
- es Spiel der Marktkräfte   free play of market forces
- e Stücke   Börse: freely marketable stock
- konvertierbare Währungen   freely convertible currencies
- schwankende Wechselkurse   freely fluctuating exchange rates

Freiaktien   bonus shares; capitalisation (scrip) issue

freibleibend   subject to confirmation; bei einem Anleiheangebot: subject to prior sale
- e Konditionen   bei einem Kredit: terms (interest rates) subject to change

- er Verkaufskurs   einer Emission: selling price subject to changes

freifinanzierter Wohnungsbau   privately financed housebuilding (housing construction)

Freigabe
- einer Garantie   release of a guarantee, releasing a guarantee
- von Geldern   unblocking (of) funds
- des Wechselkurses   floating (of) the exchange rate

freigeben   (a) to release; (b) to unblock; (c) to float

freihändig
- erworbene Stücke   securities purchased in the open market
- er Ankauf   purchase at market rates
- er Rückkauf   repurchase in the open market
- er Verkauf   einer Emission   selling an issue privately to a number of investors
- e Verwertung   sale in the open market

Freijahre   bei einer Anleihe: redemption-free years, grace period, capital repayment holiday

Freisetzung   von Kapital: release of capital (of equity resources)

Freiverkehr   geregelter Freiverkehr: unlisted securities market (USM) (Br); over-the-counter market (OTC) (US)

ungeregelter Freiverkehr: off-board trading, unofficial market

Freiverkehrs
- ausschuß   Quotations Committee (for securities traded on the unlisted securities market)
- händler   unlisted dealer (Br), over-the-counter dealer (US)

Freiverkehrs

- kurse prices on the unlisted securities market; over-the-counter quotations
- markt unlisted securities market (Br), over-the-counter market (US)
- usancen customs and practice governing the unlisted securities market (over-the-counter market)
- werte unlisted securities, securities traded on the unlisted securities market; over-the-counter stocks

freiwillige Rücklagen retained earnings

Freizeichnungsklausel non-liability clause

fremd outside, external, third-party; foreign

- e Gelder einer Bank: deposits
- e Währung foreign currency

für -e Rechnung on behalf of a third party, for third-party account

Fremd

- besitz, Anteile im - minority interests
- emission offering through an issuing house, issue through an investment bank
- finanzieren to finance with outside capital (with borrowed funds)
- finanzierung external financing (funding), financing with borrowed (outside) funds
- finanzierungsbedarf borrowing requirements, external fund requirements
- grundschuld land charge registered in favour of a third party

Fremdkapital outside capital, external funds

Beschaffung von - generation (procurement) of outside capital

mit einem hohen -anteil arbeiten to operate with a high degree of financial leverage

Fremdleistungen outside services

Fremdmittel outside funds, external funds, borrowed funds, external resources; einer Bank: deposits

- bedarf borrowing requirements, external fund requirements
- bedienung servicing outside capital
- beschaffung generation (procurement) of external funds
- kosten cost of external funds
- zufluß inflow of deposits
- zuwachs increase (growth) in deposits

Fremdvaluta foreign currency

Fremdvalutakäufe foreign currency buying

Fremdwährungs

- anleihe foreign currency bond (loan)
- engagement (a) Devisen: currency exposure; (b) Kredit: foreign currency loan (lending)
- ertrags- und Aufwandskonten currency income and expense accounts
- forderungen (a) foreign currency lendings; (b) receivables in foreign currencies
- guthaben foreign currency balances
- konto foreign currency account
- kreditaufnahme foreign currency borrowing, currency loan
- verbindlichkeiten (a) foreign currency borrowings; (b) payables in foreign currencies
- wechsel foreign currency bill

freundlich Börse: cheerful, bright

- e Grundstimmung cheerful undertone (sentiment)

Frist term, period set (given); deadline

die - für die Rückzahlung des Kredites verlängern to grant an extension of time for the repayment of the loan

eine letzte - für die Rückzahlung des Kredites setzen to set a deadline for the repayment of the loan

die - für die Zeichnung der neuen Stücke the period set for subscribing to the new securities

Fristen

- asymmetrie mismatched maturities; mismatching of maturities

- entsprechung matching maturities; matching of maturities

- gerecht → fristenkongruent

- gliederung breakdown according to maturities; maturity spacing

fristenkongruent (at) matching maturities

- abdecken to hedge a transaction at matching maturities

- e Refinanzierung unserer Ausleihungen im Hypothekenbereich funding (refinancing) of our mortgage lendings at matching maturities

Fristen

- kongruenz matching maturities; matching of maturities

- raum maturity range

- struktur des Kreditgeschäftes maturity pattern of lendings

- symmetrie matching maturities

- transformation maturity transformation

fristgerechte Vorlage der Dokumente presenting the documents on the date (within the period) agreed upon

Fristigkeit maturity; period, term

- en der zu verzinsenden Gelder maturities (maturity pattern) of interest-bearing deposits

Fristigkeitstabelle maturity ladder

Fristverlängerung extension of time (for payment of a debt); extension of maturity; extending the period set (for payment, for subscribing to the new shares)

Fristwahrung observing the deadline set for ...

Front die Aktienkurse zogen auf breiter Front an equity prices firmed broadly, stock prices moved higher across the board (across a broad front)

führen Emission/Konsortium: to lead, to lead-manage, to manage Konto/Bücher: to keep, to maintain; Unternehmen: to run, to manage

führend

- e Börsenwerte leading shares (stocks), leaders, Blue Chips

- e Chemiewerte (Industriewerte) leading chemicals (industrials)

Führung (a) management, lead-management; (b) maintenance

ein Konsortium unter - der .. Bank a syndicate led by ..

eine Neuemission unter - der .. a new issue lead-managed by ..

kostenlose - des Kontos maintaining an account free of charge

ordnungsgemäße - des Kontos proper conduct (maintenance) of the account

die Konsortial- liegt bei .. (Bank) .. (Bank) is running the books

Führungsbank   lead bank, leading
  bank, lead manager, managing
  bank, bank running the books

Führungsgruppe   management group,
  lead-management group

Führungsprovision   management fee,
  manager's commission

Fundierungsanleihe   consolidation
  (funding) loan

fungible Wertpapiere   fungible
  securities

G

G → Geld

-G → gestrichen, Geld

GAA → Geldausgabeautomat

galoppierende Inflation runaway inflation

gängige Emissionen seasoned securities

Garantie guarantee (Br), guaranty (US); für Waren: warranty

  Erlöschen der - determination of the guarantee

  Erstellung der - drawing up the guarantee

  Inanspruchnahme unter der - calling upon the guarantor, enforcing the guarantee

  Stellung einer - furnishing a guarantee

  Zahlungsverpflichtungen aus einer - payment commitments under a guarantee

  wenn die Bank aus ihrer - in Anspruch genommen wird if the bank is called upon under its guarantee

  die - bleibt in Kraft bis the guarantee shall remain operative (shall continue in force) until

garantieähnliche Erklärung letter of intent similar to a guarantee

Garantie
- begünstigter guarantee
- beschränkungen restrictive provisions of a guarantee
- betrag amount guaranteed, amount of a guarantee
- deckung guarantee cover
- deckungskonto guarantee cover account
- erklärung guarantee (surety)bond
- fall bei Eintritt des Garantiefalles: when the debtor has defaulted
- frist life (term) of a guarantee; bei Waren: warranty period

Garantiegeber guarantor, surety

  die Ansprüche der Bank gegen den - the bank's claims (rights) against the guarantor

  den - aus seiner Garantie in Anspruch nehmen to call upon the guarantor, to call in the guarantee, to enforce the guarantee

  den - aus seiner Haftung entlassen to discharge (to release) the guarantor from liability

Garantie
- geschäft der Bank the bank's guarantee operations
- gruppe bei einer Emission: stand-by group (syndicate)
- haftung liability on (under) a guarantee
- hinterlegung bei der Bank depositing (lodging) a guarantee with the bank
- höhe amount guaranteed
- inanspruchnahme enforcing a guarantee, calling upon the guarantor
- kapital share capital plus reserves
- konsortium stand-by syndicate
- kosten guarantee charges
- laufzeit term (life, currency) of a guarantee
- leistung furnishing a guarantee
- mittel guarantee funds
- nehmer guarantee
- provision guarantee commission; Emission: underwriting commission

Garantie
- rahmenvertrag   guarantee override agreement

garantieren   (a) to guarantee, to warrant, to furnish a guarantee; (b) to ensure, to warrant

wir - hiermit Ihnen gegenüber die ordnungsgemäße und pünktliche Rückzahlung des genannten Kredites   we hereby guarantee to you the due and prompt repayment of said loan

gegenüber dem Kreditgeber die Erfüllung aller Verbindlichkeiten -   to guarantee (to warrant) to the lender the fulfillment of all obligations and liabilities

garantierende Bank   guaranteeing bank

Garantie
- rückstellungen   guarantee reserves

- schreiben   guarantee undertaking (commitment)

- summe   amount guaranteed, amount of the guarantee

- übernahme   furnishing (accepting) a guarantee

- verband   der Genossenschaftsbanken: deposit insurance fund (operated by cooperative banks)

- verpflichtungen   guarantee (warranty) commitments, liabilities under guarantee arrangements; im Hinblick auf den Garantieverband der Genossenschaftsbanken: payments to be made into the deposit insurance fund

- versprechen   guarantee undertaking (commitment), undertaking to guarantee

- versicherung   guarantee (suretyship) insurance

- vertrag   contract of guarantee, guarantee agreement

- wert   value of a guarantee

- zeit   life of a guarantee, guarantee (warranty) period

Gattung   (a) Aktien: stock category, class of shares; (b) Renten: bond category

geben   im Geldhandel: to sell, to lend

 Tagesgeld -   to sell (to lend) overnight funds

Geberbank   selling (lending) bank

gebietsansässige Kreditinstitute   resident financial institutions

gebietsfremde Anleger   non-resident investors

geborene Orderpapiere   registered securities endorsable by nature

Gebote der Anleger   investors' bids

Gebrauchsgüterfinanzierung   financing consumer durables

gebremst gefahrene Bilanzsumme   curbed increase in total assets

Gebühr   charge, fee
Bearbeitungsgebühren: service charge, handling fee; Kontoführungsgebühr: account-maintenance charges

Gebühren
- belastung /-berechnung   charging fees, debiting charges, debit of charges

- gestaltung   einer Bank: pricing

- modell   pricing model

- politik   einer Bank: pricing policy

- struktur   pricing pattern

- tabelle   schedule (tariff) of charges

gebunden
- e Aktie   vinculated share

- e Mittel   blocked (frozen)funds, funds allocated for a particular purpose gebunden langfristig - tied up for a longer period

gedeckter Kredit secured loan, secured borrowing

gedrückte Stimmung subdued sentiment (tone)

gefährdeter Kredit risky loan; stark gefährdeter Kredit: high-risk loan (exposure)

Gefälle differential

Gefälligkeitswechsel accommodation bill, non-value bill

gefragt

Bankwerte waren weiterhin - banks remained in demand (in support), banks continued to find support

Fahrzeugwerte waren lebhaft - motors encountered lively interest

Maschinenbauwerte waren kaum - engineerings found little support

Gegen
- akkreditiv countervailing credit
- buchung counterentry, offsetting entry
- forderung counterclaim
- posten counteritem; offsetting item
- seite Wertpapiergeschäft: counterparty

Gegenwert proceeds; equivalent

wir bitten um Anschaffung des -s auf Konto ... please remit the proceeds to account ...

- der Dokumente proceeds of the documents
- eines Wechsels bill proceeds
- der gehandelten Wertpapiere purchase or selling price of securities traded

Gegenwertverrechnung settling the proceeds, settlement of the proceeds

Gehaltskonto payroll account

gekorene Orderpapiere securities made endorsable by a special clause

gekündigt
- er Betrag amount for which notice has been given
- es Sparguthaben savings deposits for which notice of withdrawal has been given
- e Stücke securities called for redemption, securities for which notice of redemption has been given

Geld money; Gelder: funds, capital, financial resources (means)

Geld (Sortenankaufskurs der Banken) buying rate

Geld (Kurszusatz bei amtlich notierten Devisenkursen) bid, buyers

Geld (Kurszusatz bei Wertpapieren) buyers over; quotation at which stocks were sought for purchase but not offered for sale

Geld
- abgänge outflow of funds (of deposits)
- angebot money supply
- angebotsmultiplikator money supply multiplier
- anlage investment; investment of funds
- anlageformen types of investment, investment vehicles

Geldanlagen im Geldhandel: placing of deposits, lendings in the interbank market
- bei anderen Kreditinstituten deposits placed with other banks
- von Gebietsfremden non-resident

deposits (investments)

Geldaufnahmen (a) borrowings;
(b) im Geldhandel: taking
deposits, overnight borrowings
- am Euromarkt   borrowing in the
  Euromarket
- im Interbankgeschäft   borrowing
  overnight or term money in the
  interbank market

Geldausgabeautomat   cash dispenser

Geldausleihungen   lendings
- im Interbankgeschäft   overnight
  and term lendings in the interbank market

Geldbeschaffung   procurement of
funds, raising (generating)
funds

Geldbeschaffungs
- kosten   (a) cost of funds,
  fund-raising cost; (b) cost of
  obtaining credit
- kosten der Bank   cost of funds
  to the bank, funding costs of
  the banking credit
- papiere   fund-raising instruments

Geld
- deckung prüfen   to check the
  availability of adequate funds,
  to check the cover
- defizit in der täglichen Gelddisposition   day-to-day shortage of funds
- disponent   chief money dealer;
  cash manager; treasurer
- disposition   money dealings;
  cash management; treasury
  management
- durchhandel   im Interbanken-
  handel: borrowing and relend-
  ing funds at an interest markup; hard arbitrage, round tripping
- eingänge   inflow of funds (of
  deposits)
- einstandskosten   cost of money

- einzahlungsautomat   automated
  (auto) depositor
- entwertung   inflation

geldgebende Bank   selling (lending)
bank

Geldhandel   dealings in the money
market, money dealings, money-
broking, borrowing and lending
in the money market

Geldhandels
- abteilung   money market division,
  money dealing operation, money
  desk
- forderungen   overnight and term
  money lendings, due from money
  market operators
- geschäft   money market deal
- linie   money market line
- verbindlichkeiten   overnight
  and term money borrowings,
  due to money market operators

Geldhändler   money dealer

Geld
- institut   financial institution
- kapitalbildung   monetary
  capital formation
- knappheit   monetary tightness,
  shortage of funds
- kurs   → Geld
- leihe   interbank lending

Geldmarkt   money market
- abschlüsse   money market
  transactions
- adresse   operator in the money
  market, money market member
- adresse, erste   prime borrower
  (seltener: lender) in the
  money market
- alimentierung   feeding the money
  market
- anlagen   money market investments
- anspannung   tightness in the
  money market

Geldmarkt
- betätigung   dealing (operating) in the money market
- empfindlich   sensitive to rate fluctuations in the money market
- fälligkeiten   money market maturities, money market commitments
- fonds   money market fund
- forderungen an ausländische Banken   lendings to foreign banks in the money market
- geschehen   money market activities, trading in the money market
- intervention   intervention in the money market
- mittel   money market funds
- papiere   money market securities (instruments)
- satz   money market rate
- sätze unter Banken   interbank money market rates
- teilnehmer   money market operator
- titel   money market securities
- verschuldung   money market indebtedness
- wechsel   money market bill

Geldmenge   money supply (stock)
- in ihrer weitesten Abgrenzung   broad money supply
- in der engeren Definition   narrow money supply
  M 1   cash and demand deposits
  M 2   cash, demand deposits, time deposits with terms of less than four years
  M 3   M 2 plus savings deposits subject to a three months' withdrawal notice

Geldmengen
- kontrolle   money supply control
- zahlen   monetary aggregates
- ziele   monetary aggregate targets

Geldmittelfluß, den notwendigen - gewährleisten   to ensure the necessary flow of funds

geldnehmende Bank   im Geldhandel: borrowing (buying) bank

Geldpolitik, restriktive   tight (restrictive) monetary policy

geldpolitisches Instrumentarium   instruments of monetary policy

Geld
- repartierung   Effektenhandel: scale-down of purchase orders
- schöpfung   money creation
- schwemme   money surge
- spritze   money infusion
- stelle   money desk; dealing operation
- steuerung   money supply regulation
- tausch   money swap, swap of interbank commitments
- überschüsse in der täglichen Gelddisposition   day-to-day surplus of funds
- umlauf   notes and coins in circulation
- umlaufgeschwindigkeit   velocity of monetary circulation
- verknappung   monetary tightness, monetary contraction
- verknappungspolitik   policy of monetary contraction
- vermögensneubildung   new capital formation
- vermögenswerte   cash (liquid) assets
- verrechnung   settlement of the proceeds
- volumen   money supply
- wertstabilität   monetary stability
- zuflüsse   inflow of funds (of deposits)

geleistete Anzahlungen   advances
paid

gelten
  die Gebührenneuregelung gilt
  nicht für Depotkonten   the new
  tariff of charges does not
  apply to custody accounts

  unsere Kreditzusage gilt weiterhin   our loan undertaking
  shall continue in force (shall
  remain operative)

  das gleiche gilt für den Privatkundenbereich   the same holds
  true for the retail banking
  sector

  der Wechsel gilt als nicht eingelöst   the bill will be deemed
  non-paid

  die neuen Zinssätze gelten ab ..
  the new interest rates will
  apply from ..

geltende Bestimmungen   provisions
in force

geltend machen   to enforce (a
claim);to assert (a right)

gemeiner Wert   current value

Gemeinkosten   overheads, over-
head costs

gemeinsam zeichnen   to sign
jointly

gemeinschaftliche Verfügungsberechtigung   joint authority
to draw, joint authority to
operate an account

gemeinschaftlich zeichnungsberechtigt   authorised to sign
jointly

Gemeinschafts

- emission   joint issue

- konto   joint account

- kredit   joint (syndicate) loan;
  joint loan extension (accommodation)

- unternehmen   joint venture

Gemeinschuldner   bankrupt; debtor
adjudicated bankrupt

gemessen   am Eigenkapital   measured
by capital and reserves

gemischte Hypothekenbank   mixed-type
mortgage bank

genehmigen   die Begebung neuer
Emissionen -   to authorise the
floating of new issues

genehmigtes Kapital   authorised
capital

Genehmigung   authorisation; approval

- einer Geldhandelslinie in Höhe
  von ..   authorising a money market
  line in the amount of ..

- des Kreditantrages   approval of
  the loan application

Genehmigungsbefugnisse   approval
powers

genehmigungspflichtige Termingeschäfte   forward deals subject
to approval

genossenschaftliche Zentralbank
central cooperative bank

Genossenschaftsbank   cooperative
bank

Genossenschaftsring   giro network
operated by the cooperative banks

Genußschein   profit-sharing certificate, participation certificate(US)

- inhaber   holder of a profit-
  sharing certificate

- kapital   equity represented by
  profit-sharing certificates,
  profit-sharing certificate stock

- recht   profit-sharing right

- umlauf   profit-sharing certificates
  outstanding

geordneter Markt   regular (organised) market

geparkte Gelder   funds temporarily
invested (deposited), parked funds

geregelter Wertpapiermarkt
organised stock exchange

geringes Anlegerinteresse little investor interest

geringfügig
- fester slightly firmer
- schwächer nach Gewinnmitnahmen slightly off (lower) on profit-taking
- e Umsätze sparse (thin)trading

Gesamt
- ausleihungen aggregate loan portfolio, total lendings
- bestand aggregate holdings
- bestand an langfristigen Ausleihungen total long-term lendings
- betrag total (aggregate) amount;total
- börsenkapitalisierung aggregate market capitalisation
- engagement aggregate credit exposure, aggregate (total) loan commitments
- ermittlungsverfahren global valuation
- ertrag aggregate (total) earnings; total return
- ertrag des Kreditgeschäftes aggregate earnings from lending operations

gesamtfällige Schuldverschreibungen bonds repayable in full

Gesamt
- haftungsverpflichtung unconditional liability undertaking
- hypothek blanket mortgage
- kapitalbetrag aggregate principal amount
- kreditlinie aggregate credit line; overall borrowing arrangement
- kündigung einer Anleihe:calling in all outstanding bonds
- laufzeit total life
- leistung aggregate operating performance

- linie aggregate line
- liquidität einer Bank: total liquid assets (means), i.e. cash, cheques, bills eligible for rediscount with Bundesbank, due from banks, bonds and marketable shares
- nennbetrag einer Anleihe: aggregate principal amount, aggregate face value
- obligo total exposure, total commitments; aggregate liability
- prokura authority to act jointly for a company
- rendite aggregate yield
- schuld joint and several debt
- schuldner joint and several debtor

gesamtschuldnerisch
- e Bürgschaft joint and several guarantee
- haften to be jointly and severally liable

Gesamt
- sparleistung net growth in savings deposits and savings bond sales
- summe aller liquiden Mittel cash float
- umsatz Börse: aggregate turnover
- verschuldung total borrowings (debts), aggregate indebtedness
- vollmacht general power of attorney
- volumen balance sheet total plus endorsement liabilities and credits by way of guarantee

gesamtwirtschaftlich
- e Nachfrage aggregate economy-wide demand
- e Sparquote overall savings ratio

Gesamt
- zinsbelastung total interest charge, aggregate interest payments

Gesamtzinsspannenrechnung establishment of the overall interest margin

Geschäft deal, bargain, transaction; Börsenumsätze: trading, dealings, activity, turnover

das - in Auslandswerten hat sich belebt trading in foreign issues went up

bei geringem - notierten Bankwerte etwas fester with trading remaining at a low ebb, bank stocks turned slightly higher

ein lebhaftes - entwickelte sich in Fahrzeugwerten motors saw active trading

Maschinenbauwerte gaben bei ruhigem - nach engineerings drifted lower in quiet dealings

das - konzentrierte sich auf spekulative Werte trading centred on speculative counters

Geschäfts
- abschluß (a) bargain, transaction, deal; (b) striking a deal; (c) performance, results for the year, annual accounts
- abschlüsse an der Börse dealings (transactions) on the stock exchange
- anteil share (interest, stake) in a business
- bank commercial bank
- belebung an der Börse: upturn in trading (dealings)
- bereich line of business; Abteilung: division; Zuständigkeit: competence, province
- bericht annual (business) report
- besorgungsvertrag contract of agency, agency contract (agreement)
- entwicklung development of business, business trend

Geschäftsergebnis performance, business performance; results, trading results

ein ausgezeichnetes - a strong business performance

das - der Bank im abgelaufenen Geschäftsjahr the bank's performance over the past twelve months

Hinweis auf das 84er - indications of the 84 performance

Verbesserung des -es improvement in performance; improved results

zuversichtlich im Hinblick auf das - des laufenden Jahres confident about this year's results

1983 wurde mit einem wesentlich verbesserten - abgeschlossen the company came out of 1983 with noticeably improved figures

Geschäftserweiterung expanding operations, expansion of business (of capacities)

geschäftsfähig voll geschäftsfähig sein to be of full contractual capacity

Geschäfts
- fähigkeit contractual capacity
- gewinn trading profit
- interessen business (financial) interests
- kapital business (working) capital
- kredit business loan
- losigkeit Börse: dullness, stagnation, inactivity
- möglichkeiten business opportunities
- stelle branch, office
- stellennetz branch network
- umfang size of a transaction, magnitude of a deal; Börse: trading volume, volume of dealings

Geschäfts
- verlust   trading loss
- volumen einer Bank: business volume, i.e. balance sheet total plus endorsement liabilities
- vorfall   transaction

Geschehen am Rentenmarkt   trading (turnover, dealings) in the bond market

geschlossener
- Immobilienfonds   closed-end real property fund
- Investmentfonds   closed-end fund

Gesellschaft   company; Kapitalgesellschaft: public company, corporation; Personengesellschaft: partnership
- mit beschränkter Haftung   private limited company

Gesellschafter   partner
- anteile   partners' interests
- darlehen   loan made by a partner (shareholder) to the company
- einlagen   partners' investments
- versammlung   partners' meeting

Gesellschafts
- anteil   share (stake, interest) in a company; partnership interest
- blätter   newspapers authorised to publish company announcements
- kapital   company's capital (equity)
- mittel   corporate funds; company's financial resources
- recht   company law
- schulden   Kapitalgesellschaft: corporate debts; Personengesellschaft: partnership debts
- vermögen   corporate assets; partnership property
- vertrag   deed of partnership, partnership agreement

Gesetzgebungsumfeld für Banken   regulatory environment for banks

gesetzlich
- e Bestimmungen, die von den Banken zu beachten sind   legal provisions (statutory regulations) to be observed by banks
- e Kündigungsfrist bei Spareinlagen: legal (statutory) withdrawal notice
- e Rücklage   legal (statutory) reserve

gesicherter Kredit   secured loan

gespalten
- er Goldmarkt   two-tier gold market
- er Kurs   two-way price
- er Wechselkurs   multiple exchange rate

gespannter Wechselkurs   mean spread of the fixing

gesperrte Guthaben   blocked assets (balances), frozen funds

gestaffelter Zinssatz   sliding rate of interest, staggered interest rate

Gestehungskosten   cost of acquisition, cost price

gestreute Anlagen   diversified (scattered) investments

gestrichen   no dealings, no quotation
- Brief (Geld)   no quotation for lack of buying (selling) orders

gestückelt   issued in denominations of ..

gestützter Wechselkurs pegged rate of exchange

gesucht

Fahrzeugwerte blieben - motors attracted renewed demand (fresh support)

Kaufhauswerte waren gegen Ende der Börsensitzung - stores attracted late support

... wurden zu 125 DM gesucht
... were wanted at 125 DM

gesunde finanzielle Lage strong (sound) financial position

Gesundungskonzept financial reconstruction scheme

getrennt notiert quoted separately

gewähren einen Kredit: to grant (to extend, to accommodate) a loan

gewährleisten Zahlung bei Fälligkeit - to guarantee (to warrant) payment upon maturity

Gewährleistung guarantee, warranty; guaranteeing, ensuring

Gewährleistungs
- aval guarantee
- frist guarantee (warranty) period
- garantie performance bond
- vertrag indemnity agreement

Gewährträger /Gewährträgerverband guarantor, guaranteeing local authority

Gewährträgerhaftung guarantor's liability

gewerblich
- e Beleihungen lendings against (loans granted on)commercial properties
- e Beteiligungen trade and commercial interests
- es Finanzierungsinstitut commercial finance company

- e Hypothek industrial mortgage
- es Kreditgeschäft business (corporate) lendings
- er Kreditnehmer industrial (corporate) borrower
- es Kreditneugeschäft new business lendings

gewichteter Durchschnitt weighted average

gewillkürte Orderpapiere registered securities made endorsable by a special clause

Gewinn profit, profit figures; gain; earnings
- je Aktie earnings per share
- aus dem Eigenhandel profit from trading for own account
- aus der Einlösung von Wertpapieren gain on redemption of securities
- aus Neubewertungen surplus on revaluations
- vor (nach) Steuern pre-tax (after-tax) profits, profits before (after) taxation
- aus der Veräußerung von Beteiligungen gain on sale of investments
- aus der Veräußerung von Gegenständen des Anlagevermögens gain on disposal of assets
- aus Wechselkursschwankungen gain (surplus) on exchange rate fluctuations
- aus Wechselkursumrechnungen translation gains

Gewinn
- abführungsvertrag profit transfer agreement
- anteil share in profits
- anteil der Minderheitsaktionäre profit applicable to minorities
- anteilschein coupon
- anteilscheinbogen coupon sheet
- ausschüttung distribution of profits

- ausweis statement of income
- belassungserklärung profit retention undertaking

gewinnberechtigt (a) participating, entitled to a share in the profits; (b) ranking for dividend
- ab 1. Juli 19.. ranking for dividend as from July 1,19..
- für das laufende Geschäftsjahr carrying dividend rights for the current business year

Gewinn
- beteiligung profit-sharing, share in the profits
- beteiligungsplan profit-sharing scheme

gewinnbringend profitable, gainful, income-producing
- e Dienstleistungen income-producing services

gewinnen to win, to gain
... (Aktien) gewannen einige Punkte hinzu ... put on a few points
neue Kunden - to win new accounts

Gewinn
- entwicklung earnings history (records)
- ermittlung profit recognition, determination of profits
- gemeinschaft profit pooling agreement
- mitnahmen des Berufshandels profit-taking by professional traders
- mitnahmen gegen Schluß der Börsensitzung late profit-taking
- optimierung /-maximierung profit maximisation, maximising the return on (the profit from)
- prognose profit forecast
- realisierung realising (realisation of) stock price gains

- rücklagen retained (unappropriated) profits
- schuldverschreibung participating bond
- spannen der Unternehmen corporate profit margins
- thesaurierung profit retention
- und Verlustrechnung profit and loss account, statement of income
- verwendung profit appropriation
- verwendungsvorschlag proposed appropriation of profits
- vortrag profit brought forward
- zone in die Gewinnzone zurückkehren to be back in the black, to return to profitability
- zunahme im Eigenhandel increase in profits from security trading for own account
- zuschlag profit markup

gewogener Anschaffungspreis weighted purchase price

Giralgeld cheque (bank) money, checkbook money, deposit money

Girant endorser

Giratar endorsee

girieren to endorse

Giro (a) endorsement; (b) money transmission, giro
- 'giro' bezieht sich in Großbritannien entweder auf den Banküberweisungsverkehr (bank giro system) oder auf den Postscheckverkehr (National Giro) -

Giro
- abteilung money transmission service
- ausgang payments made
- eingang payments received
- einlagen sight deposits, current account deposits
- guthaben current account balance

Giro
- kette chain of endorsements
- konto current account, chequing account (Br), checking account (US)
- kunde current account customer
- netz giro network
- organisation giro organisation

Girosammel
- anteil share in a collective custody account
- bestand portfolio of securities held collectively
- depot collective custody account
- depotermächtigung authorisation to hold securities under a collective custody account
- depotstücke securities held under collective custody accounts

girosammelverwahrfähig eligible for collective custody (safekeeping)

girosammelverwahrte Aktien stocks held under collective custody accounts

Giro
- stelle clearing agency
- system giro system, bank giro system (Br)
- verkehr giro transactions (system), money transmission
- zentrale Central Savings Bank (acting as clearing house and liquidity manager to the savings banks)

glattstellen

Bestände - to square (to liquidate) positions, to sell off, to shake out

ein Konto - to settle (to balance)an account ; to repay the debit balance, to settle an overdraft

Glattstellung (a) squaring positions, book squaring, liquidation; (b) settlement, repayment
- durch den Berufshandel professional liquidation
- von Spitzenbeträgen settlement of (settling) fractions

Gläubiger creditor
- bank creditor bank
- begünstigung preference of a creditor
- kündigungsrecht creditor's call privilege; creditor's right to call in a loan
- position im Geldhandel: selling (lending) position, to be sellers
- versammlung creditors' meeting
- verzicht foregiveness of indebtedness, waiver on the part of the creditor

gleichbleibende Belastung invariable interest and redemption payments

gleichgerichtete Kursbildung parallel pricing

Gleichgewichtswechselkurs equilibrium rate of exchange

gleichrangig of equal rank, ranking pari passu, equal-ranking
- e Lasten charges ranking equally amongst themselves
- e Sicherheit security (collateral) ranking pari passu

gleitende Bandbreiten gliding bands

Gleitklausel escalator clause

Gleitparität crawling peg

Global
- aktie multishare certificate
- finanzierung block financing

Global
- urkunde   global bond certificate (→reine,→technische Globalurkunde)
- vorschuß   global advance
- zession   global assignment

Gold   gold, bullion
- agio   gold premium
- aktien   gold shares (stocks), gold equities (mines)
- ausfuhrpunkt   export gold point
- bestände   gold holdings
- devisenstandard   gold exchange standard

goldene Bankregel   principle of matching the maturities of assets and liabilities ; if you borrow short, don't lend long

Gold
- handel   dealing in gold bullion, gold trading
- händler   bullion dealer
- kernwährung   gold bullion standard
- markt   gold market
- münzen   bullion coins
- notiz   gold quote
- preis   gold price Festsetzung des Goldpreises gold fixing
- standard   gold standard
- termingeschäfte   gold futures, gold forward contracts
- umlaufwährung   gold specie standard
- und Devisenreserven   gold and foreign currency reserves
- verkäufe am freien Markt gold sales in the open market

Gradmesser für das Verhalten der Anleger   gauge of investor attitude

Gratisaktien   bonus shares, capitalisation (scrip) issue

Grenz
- ertragswert der Investitionen marginal earnings value of investments
- kostenrechnung   marginal costing
- leistungsfähigkeit des Kapitals efficiency of capital

grenzüberschreitende Kreditvergabe cross-frontier lending (loan extension)

Griff   die steigenden Personalkosten in den - bekommen   to get a handle on mounting staff expenditure

Groß
- aktionär   principal (major) shareholder; heavy stockholder
- anleger   large-scale investor
- bank   big (large) bank die drei Großbanken   the Big Three
- emission   jumbo deal (offering)

Größenordnung   eine Neuemission dieser -   a new issue deal of this magnitude

großer Kupontermin   major coupon payment date

großer Steuertermin   major tax payment date, i.e. date on which big tax bills fall due

große Stücke   fixed-income securities with a nominal value of DM 1,000 or more

Großhandelswerte   big volume stock, big ticket stock

Großkredit   large-scale loan
- geschäft   large-scale lendings

Großkundengeschäft   wholesale banking

Grund für die Nichteinlösung des Schecks   reason for dishonouring the cheque

Grundakkreditiv   basic letter of credit

Grundbesitz   real (landed) property, realty (US)

Grundbuch   land register (Br), land records (US)
- abschrift, beglaubigte   certified land certificate
- amt   Land Registry (Br), Land Records Office (US)
- auszug   land certificate, abstract of title
- berichtigung   amendment of the entry at the Land Registry
- einsicht   inspection (search) of the land register; searching the land register
- eintragung   registration at (with) the Land Registry, entry at the Land Registry, recording in the Land Records Office

grundbuchlich gesichert   protected (secured) by registration at the Land Registry

Grund
- eigentum   landed property, real property (estate), realty
- erwerbssteuer   realty transfer tax
- geschäft   underlying transaction
- interventionspreis   basic intervention price
- kapital   equity, share capital, capital stock
- kredit   land credit, mortgage loan, lending on real property
- pfandgläubiger   holder of a real estate lien; lienor
- pfandrecht   real estate lien, lien on landed property

grundpfandrechtliche Absicherung   putting up (provision of) a real estate lien

Grundpfandrechtsbestellung   creation of (creating) a real estate lien

Grundsatz I (KWG)   Principle I of the German Banking Act (stipulates that lendings of a banking organisation must not exceed 18 times share capital and reserves)
- belastende Aktiva (Ausleihungen)   lendings falling under Principle I of the German Banking Act
- neutrale Aktiva   lendings not falling under Principle I of the German Banking Act

Grundsatz der Fristenentsprechung   principle of matching maturities

Grundsätze über das Eigenkapital   capital adequacy regulations

Grundschuld   land charge, real estate lien

  die durch die - gesicherten Ansprüche der Bank   the bank's claims protected (secured) by the land charge

Grundschuld
- abtretung   assignment of a land charge
- bestellung   creation of a land charge; creating a lien on landed property
- bestellungsurkunde   document creating the charge
- brief   land charge deed, charge certificate
- gläubiger   holder of a land charge
- kapital   principal represented by the charge
- kredit   real estate lending
- umschreibung   transferring (conveying) a land charge

Grundsicherheit   security by real property, real estate collateral

Grundstück   piece of land, land, landed property

Beleihung eines -s   lending against land, advancing money on land

nachrangige Beleihung eines -s   lending against land on the security of a second or later mortgage

- e zu Anschaffungskosten   land valued at cost

- e und grundstücksgleiche Rechte   landed property and equivalent titles to land

Grundstücks

- belastung   encumbrances (charges) on land, encumbrances affecting the land; encumbrancing (mortgaging) land

- eigentümer   proprietor of the land, landowner

- lasten   land charges

- übertragung   conveyance of land, conveying (conveyancing, transferring) land

- wert   land value

Grundton   Börse: basic tone

grüne Effektenschecks   instructions to pledge the share in a collective custody account

Gruppen

- engagement   group exposure, loans extended (total lendings) to a group

- floating   joint (block) floating, common float

- umsatz   group turnover

Gültigkeit   validity

bei Börsenaufträgen:

- nur heute   day order

- bis Ultimo   good this month

- bis auf Widerruf   good till cancel order, GTC order

gut abschneiden am Markt: to show up well, to fare well, to have a good record

gut behauptete Aktienkurse   well--maintained equity prices

gutbringen   einem Konto: to place in an account, to credit an account with

Guthaben   (a) credit, credit balance; (b) balances, deposits

das - auf Ihrem Konto beläuft sich auf ..   the credit balance in your account amounts to ..; the amount standing to your credit totals ..

- bei der Bundesbank   balances (deposits) with Bundesbank

- auf Kontokorrentkonten   balances (deposits) in current accounts

Guthabenbasis   das Konto wird ausschließlich auf - geführt   the account is exclusively kept in the credit (on a non-borrowing basis)

Guthabensaldo   credit balance

Guthabenzinsen   credit (creditor) interest

gutschreiben   to credit to an account, to enter (to pass) to the credit of an account

Gutschrift   credit, credit entry

wir haben den Scheck zur - hereingenommen   we have accepted the cheque for credit to your account

Gutschriftsanzeige   credit advice, credit note

H

Habenbuchung credit entry

Habenzinssatz creditor interest rate

Haftbarmachung der Bank holding the bank liable

haften (a) to be liable (responsible); (b) to serve as security

gegenüber der Bank - to be liable to the bank

aus einer Bürgschaft - to be liable on a guarantee

gemeinsam für die Rückzahlung des Kredites - to be jointly liable for the repayment of the loan

voll für die Verbindlichkeiten der Gesellschaft - to be fully liable for the company's debts

die hinterlegten Wertpapiere - für alle Ansprüche der Bank aus dem Kredit the securities deposited serve as security for all claims of the bank arising from the loan

haftendes Eigenkapital share capital and reserves

haftende Mittel share capital and reserves plus general loan loss provisions

Haftsummenzuschlag addition of members' uncalled liabilities to capital and reserves

Haftung liability, responsibility

- gegenüber dem Kunden liability to the customer

- der Muttergesellschaft parental liability, parent company's liability

gesamtschuldnerische - aus einer Bürgschaft joint and several liability on a guarantee

die - ist auf die Kapitaleinlage begrenzt the liability is limited to the amount of capital contributed

Haftungs

- ausschluß disclaimer of responsibility (liability)

- ausschlußklausel non-warranty clause, clause disclaiming liability

- erklärung liability bond

- übernahme gegenüber dem Kreditgeber accepting (assuming) liability to the lender

- verhältnisse Bilanz: contingent liabilities

- zuschlag liability markup

Halbjahresdollar six-month dollar

Halbjahresgeld six-month money

Hand Finanzierung aus einer - one-stop financing package

Handel Börse: (a) trading, dealings; (b) dealers, traders, dealer community

- per Erscheinen trading (dealings) on terms of issue

- in Freiverkehrswerten trading in unlisted securities, over-the-counter trading

- in Kurz- bzw. Langläufern dealings in shorts (longs)

- im Sekundärmarkt secondary market dealings

handelbar tradeable, marketable, negotiable

handeln to trade, to deal

mit einem Abschlag von 1 % - to trade at a discount of 1 per cent

außerbörslich - to trade off the floor (off the board)

nachbörslich - to trade after hours

auf eigene Rechnung - to trade for own account

im Telefonverkehr - to trade over the telephone, to trade in the unofficial market

per Termin - to trade for future delivery

vorbörslich - to trade before hours (in the pre-market hours)

die Anleihe wurde mit einem Aufschlag gegenüber ihrem Emissionskurs gehandelt the bond traded at a premium to its issue price

Chemieaktien wurden lebhaft gehandelt chemicals were actively traded, chemicals encountered lively interest

die Emission wurde mit einem Abschlag von ca. 1 % gehandelt the issue traded at a discount of around 1 p.c.

handelsbedingter Personal- und Sachaufwand dealing-related staff and operating expenditure

Handels
- bestand trading portfolio
- bilanz (a) trade balance; (b) financial statements
- effekten marketable debt
- gewinne einer Bank: earnings from trading for own account
- kredit trade credit
- kreditbrief commercial letter of credit
- register Register of Companies
- registerauszug certificate of incorporation
- währung dealing currency
- wechsel trade bill

Händler dealer, trader
- bestände dealer holding of securities, dealers' holdings
- bonifikation dealer's concession
- geschäft dealer transaction, dealing transaction
- gewinn dealer's turn, dealing spread
- kauf dealer purchase
- kreise dealer community
- provision dealer allowance, dealing commission
- spanne dealing spread

Hartwährungsländer hard currency countries

Haupt
- aktionär majority (principal) shareholder
- kommissionär principal agent
- versammlung general meeting
- zahlstelle principal paying agent
- zinstermin principal coupon date

Hausbank principal banker, principal (main) banking connection

Haussammelverwahrung in-house collective custody

Hausse bull market, boom, sharp rise, rocketing (zooming) prices
- in Elektrowerten bull run in electricals
auf - kaufen to buy (to go) for a rise, to bull the market

Hausse
- bedingungen boom conditions
- position bull account
- spekulation speculation for a rise, buying long
- stimmung den Aktienmarkt in - versetzen to trigger off a bull run in equities
- tendenz strong upward trend

Haussier bull, bull operator

haussieren to rise sharply, to rocket, to soar

107

heftige Kursausschläge   erratic price swings

herabsetzen Diskontsatz,Zinsen: to lower, to cut back, to bring down, to reduce; Kapital: to write down

Herabsetzungsverhältnis bei einer Kapitalherabsetzung: write-down ratio

heraufsetzen Diskontsatz,Zinsen: to lift, to increase, to raise; Kurse: to mark up

Herausgabeansprüche gegen Dritte   restitution claims against third parties

herauskommendes Material   stocks (securities) offered

herauslegen Kredit: to extend, to grant

herausragen Banken ragten mit einem deutlichen Kurssprung heraus banks featured (stood out) with a sharp rise

Hereinnahme accepting, acceptance; taking on deposit

- zum Inkasso   accepting for collection

bei - des Schecks   upon accepting the cheque

- von Termineinlagen accepting (acceptance of) time deposits

- der Transportdokumente acceptance of the forwarding documents

hereinnehmen to accept, to take on (to accept) deposits

hereingenommene Dividendenscheine coupons accepted for encashment

hereingenommene befristete Mittel   term funds taken on deposit

zum Diskont hereingenommene Wechsel   bills accepted for discount

Kaufaufträge in Höhe von DM 5 Mio wurden in den letzten drei Wochen hereingenommen   new buying orders worth DM 5m were booked over the past three weeks

Hergabe von Eigenkapital: provision of capital (equity)

heute gültig Wertpapierauftrag: good this day

hier abtrennen bei Kupons: tear along this line

hinauslegen / hinausreichen

ein Aval - to furnish a guarantee

ein Dokumentenakkreditiv - to open (to issue) a documentary credit

einen Kredit - to grant (to extend) a credit

Hindernis ein echtes - für einen weiteren Rückgang der Zinssätze a real hindrance (impediment) to a further downturn in interest rates

Hintergrund vor dem - eines sich abschwächenden Pfund-Kurses against the background of a weakening Pound

hinterlegen to deposit, to lodge

bei einer Bank - to deposit at a bank, to lodge with a bank

als Sicherheit hinterlegte Wertpapiere   securities deposited as collateral (security)

zur Verwahrung - to place for safekeeping

Hinterleger depositor

Hinterlegung deposit, depositing; lodging, lodgement

Hinterlegungs

- bestätigung custody receipt
- stelle depository agent, custodian
- tag date (day) of deposit
- vertrag deposit (safekeeping, custody) agreement

hinweghelfen über die gegenwärtigen Liquiditätsschwierigkeiten to tide over the current liquidity squeeze

historischer Anschaffungswert historical cost

hochkarätiges Team von Finanzexperten high-powered team of financial experts

Hochrisikoengagement im Kreditgeschäft: high-risk loan exposure

hochspekulative Wertpapiere wildcat securities

Höchstbetragsbürgschaft limited guarantee (i.e. the guarantor's liability is limited to the principal of a loan plus interest and charges)

Höchstbetragshypothek limited mortgage (i.e. the liability on the mortgage is limited to the debt recorded at the Land Registry plus interest and charges)

Höchstkurs / Höchststand peak price (rate), high

absoluter - all-time high

auf einen neuen - klettern to surge to a new high (to a new record level)

hochverzinslich

- e Anleihe high-coupon loan

- e Langläufer high-coupon longs

Hochzins

- phase period of high interest rates

- politik high interest-rate (dear-money) policy

Höhe Kurse, Zinsen: level

Importe in - von DM 400 Mio imports worth DM 400m

die restriktiven Maßnahmen könnten die Zinssätze weiter in die - treiben the restrictive measures could well push the interest rates further up

Höhenflug die Aktienkurse setzten ihren Höhenflug weiter fort equity prices continued on their record-breaking run

höher bewerten (notieren) to mark up, to trade higher

höher rentierliche Anleihen higher-yielding bonds

höher verzinsliche Anlagen investments offering a higher (better) interest rate

Höherverzinsung paying a higher interest rate

Holgeld borrowed funds, borrowings

honorieren Dokumente, Wechsel, Schecks: to honour, to pay, to meet

Hyperinflation hyperinflation, runaway inflation

Hypothek mortgage

- mit fester Verzinsung fixed-rate mortgage

- mit fünfjähriger Zinsfestschreibung mortgage carrying a fixed interest rate for five years

- mit variabler Verzinsung variable-rate mortgage, floating-rate mortgage

hypothekarisch

- belastbar mortgageable

- belasten to mortgage

- gesicherte Forderung mortgage claim

- gesicherter Schuldschein mortgage note

- gesicherte Schuldverschreibung mortgage-secured debenture

- e Sicherheit mortgage collateral, security by mortgage

Hypothekarkredit   mortgage loan, real estate loan

Hypothekarkreditgeschäft   mortgage lending business

Hypotheken
- ablösung   mortgage redemption (repayment), satisfaction of mortgage, mortgage retirement
- aufnahme   taking out a mortgage
- auszahlung   mortgage payment, disbursement of a mortgage
- auszahlung erfolgt auf Konto ...   the mortgage proceeds will be credited to account ...
- bank   mortgage bank, mortgage credit institution
- bedienung   mortgage servicing, servicing a mortgage, principal and interest payments on a mortgage
- bedingungen   mortgage terms
- begründung   creation of a mortgage
- belastung   mortgage encumbrance, mortgage charge
- bestand   einer Bank: mortgage loan portfolio
- bestellung   creation of a mortgage, taking out a mortgage
- brief   mortgage deed
- damnum   mortgage discount
- darlehen   mortgage advance (loan)
- eintragung   registration of a mortgage, recording a mortgage
- fälligkeit   mortgage maturity
- finanzierung   mortgage financing, financing through mortgage borrowing
- forderung   mortgage claim; mortgage lending
- gelder   mortgage funds; mortgage loans
- geschäft   mortgage lending business

- gewährung   extending (granting) a mortgage
- gläubiger   mortgage creditor, mortgagee, creditor on mortgage
- konditionen   mortgage loan terms, mortgage rates
- kosten   mortgage cost
- kostenanstieg   increase in the cost of mortgages

Hypothekenkredit   mortgage loan, real estate loan, mortgage credit
- aufnahme   mortgage borrowing
- geschäft   mortgage lending business
- gewährung   extending a mortgage loan, mortgage loan accommodation
- nachfrage   demand for mortgage credit; Begrenzung der - mortgage squeeze
- summe   mortgage loan principal
- versicherung   mortgage protection insurance, mortgage guarantee insurance
- volumen   mortgage loan portfolio, mortgages book
- zusage   mortgage loan undertaking, undertaking to extend a mortgage loan

Hypotheken
- kündigung   calling in a mortgage
- laufzeit   mortgage term (period)
- löschung   mortgage release (US), satisfaction of mortgage (Br)
- mittel   mortgage finance, mortgage funds
- nachfrage   demand for mortgage credit
- neugeschäft / - neuzusagen   new mortgage lendings
- pfandbrief   mortgage bond
- rang   mortgage rank
- rangordnung   ranking of mortgages

Hypotheken

- register   register of mortgages serving as cover for mortgage bonds issued
- rückzahlung   mortgage repayment (redemption, retirement)
- schuld   mortgage debt
- schuldner   mortgage debtor
- schuldverschreibung   collateral mortgage bond
- summe   mortgage principal
- tilgung   mortgage redemption, mortgage amortization (US)
- titel   (a) mortgage instruments (paper); (b) mortgage bank stocks
- übernahme   assuming a mortgage, mortgage assumption
- übertragung   transferring (assignment of) a mortgage
- urkunde   mortgage deed (certificate)
- valuta   mortgage proceeds
- verschuldung   mortgage indebtedness
- versicherung   mortgage protection insurance
- vertrag   mortgage agreement, mortgage indenture
- volumen   mortgage portfolio
- vorrang   mortgage priority
- zinsen   mortgage interest
- zinssatz   mortgage lending rate, mortgage rate
- zusage   mortgage loan undertaking, mortgage lending commitment, mortgage commitment
- zusagen Gesamtsumme: mortgage loan exposure, total mortgage lendings
- zusagen für den Wohnungsbau   residential mortgage lendings
- zusammenlegung   consolidation of mortgages
- zwangsvollstreckung   foreclosing a mortgage, mortgage foreclosure

I

Ib-Hypothek subsequent mortgage loan guaranteed by an official agency

Immobilien
- anlage property investment
- fonds property fund, real estate investment trust (US)
- fondsanteil property fund share
- kredit real estate loan, credit on landed property
- werte property shares, properties
- zertifikat property fund share

Importerstfinanzierung initial import financing

Impuls stimulus, impellent, incentive

dem stagnierenden Aktienmarkt neue -e verleihen to reinvigorate (to liven up) the sluggish stock market

Inanspruchnahme (a) drawing on (under), tapping; (b) amount drawn upon; (c) availment of, recourse to; (d) calling, call

- eines Akkreditivs drawing under a documentary credit
- von Bankdienstleistungen availment of bank services
- eines Bürgen calling upon a guarantor
- von billigeren Finanzierungsmöglichkeiten availment of cheaper funding opportunities
- aus einer Garantie call to pay up under a guarantee
- des Kapitalmarktes call on the capital market, tapping the capital market
- auf Konto ... drawdowns to be effected against account ...
- eines Kredites drawing on a loan, availment of a credit facility
  in Anspruch genommener Betrag: amount drawn upon, drawdown effected
- von Nachfristen recourse to grace periods
- der Rücklagen drawing on reserves

die Berechnung der Zinsen erfolgt auf die tatsächliche - interest will be charged on the amount drawn upon

Indeckungnahme von Exportkrediten providing cover (providing guarantees) for export credits

Index index; Börse: share (stock) price index (Aktien), average; fixed securities index (Rentenwerte)

Indexanleihe indexed loan

indexgebundener Hypothekenzins index-linked mortgage rate

indexgesicherte Verzinsung index-linked (indexed) interest payments

Index
- terminkontrakte index-linked futures contracts
- währung index-based currency
- werte average stocks
- zahlen (a) index figures; (b) financial ratios

indifferentes Geschäft non-lending transactions

indirekt
- e Devisenarbitrage   indirect (compound) arbitrage
- es Hypothekengeschäft   mortgage lending (with the bank holding the title to land but not entering into its ownership)
- e Parität   cross rate

Individualkundschaft einer Bank: high-income customers

individuelle Konditionengestaltung   individually negotiated terms and rates; tailoring the loan terms to the borrower's specific requirements

individuelle Kundenbetreuung   personal banking service, personal contact with the customer

Indossament   endorsement

Indossaments
- provision   endorsement commission
- reihe   order of endorsers
- verbindlichkeiten   endorsement liabilities

Indossant   endorser

indossierbar   endorsable

indossieren   to endorse

Industrie
- adresse   am Emissionsmarkt: industrial borrower
- aktien   industrial equities (shares, stocks)
- clearing   (Geldhandel zwischen Industriebetrieben) intercompany money dealings
- kredit   industrial loan (lending), corporate loan
- kreditgeschäft   corporate lending business
- kreditnachfrage   corporate demand for credit

- schuldverschreibung   corporate debenture, industrial (corporate) bond
- werte   industrials, industrial issues
- werte, führende   blue chip industrials, top-quality industrials

inflationär
- er Druck   inflationary pressure
- er Preisauftrieb   inflationary price upsurge

inflationsbedingter Kreditbedarf   inflation-fed (inflation-induced) borrowing requirements

inflationsbereinigte Erträge   inflation-adjusted earnings

inflationsbereinigte Bilanzierung   inflation accounting

Inflations
- eindämmung   curb on inflation
- gefälle   inflation differential
- schutz / - sicherung   hedge against inflation
- tempo   inflationary pace

Infrastrukturkredit   infrastructure--financing loan

Inhaber   Konto: holder; Wertpapiere: owner, bearer
- aktie   bearer share
- grundschuld   bearer land charge
- indossament   bearer endorsement
- konnossement   bearer bill of lading
- papiere   bearer instruments
- scheck   bearer cheque
- schuldverschreibung   bearer debenture
- teilschuldverschreibung   bearer bond
- Vorzugsaktien ohne Stimmrechte   bearer preference shares without voting rights

Inhaberwechsel   bearer bill

Inkasso   collection
- von Forderungen   collection of accounts receivable, debt collection, collecting debts
- von Lastschriften   presenting direct debits for payment; claiming payment (debiting a customer's account) under the preauthorized payments system
- von Schecks (Kupons)   collection of cheques (coupons)

Inkasso
- anweisung / - auftrag   collection order, collection instructions
- bank   collecting banker
- basis   auf Inkassobasis übersandte Schecks   cheques sent (remitted) for collection
- beauftragter   collection agent
- bedingungen   terms of collection
- benachrichtigung   advice of fate
- büro   debt-collecting agency
- erlös   collection proceeds
- ermächtigung   collection authority
- gebühren   collection charges
- geschäft   collection business
- indossament   collection endorsement
- konto   collection account
- provision   collection commission
- scheck   cheque (remitted) for collection
- spesen   collection charges
- stelle   collecting agent; debt-collecting agency
- tage   collection days
- tarif   terms (rates) of collection
- vollmacht   collection authority, power of collection (collecting)
- währung   collection currency
- wechsel   bill (remitted) for collection

inkongruent refinanziertes Kreditgeschäft   lendings funded at mismatched maturities

Inkongruenz der Ausleihungen   mismatched lendings; mismatching of lending maturities

Inländerkonvertibilität   resident convertibility

Inlands
- anleihe   domestic bond (loan)
- aval   domestic guarantee
- beteiligungen   domestic trade investments, domestic participations (interests)
- geschäft   einer Bank: domestic banking, domestic operations
- kreditgewährung   domestic lending
- valuta   domestic (national) currency
- werte   domestic (home) securities
- zahlungsverkehr   domestic payments

Innenfinanzierung   internal financing

innovative Kreditpolitik   innovative approach towards lending, innovative lending policy

instabiler Markt   jumpy market

Instrument für die Inanspruchnahme im Dokumentengeschäft: operative credit instrument

Instrumentarium der Kreditpolitik   credit policy instruments

Intakthalteerklärung   commitment not to alter (e.g. the subsidiary's equity), support agreement (US)

Interbank (Interbanken-)
- aktiva   interbank lendings, lendings in the interbank market, due from banks
- forderungen ⟶ Interbankaktiva
- geschäft   interbank dealings (business, transactions)
- handel   interbank dealings
- markt   interbank market
- passiva   interbank borrowings, borrowings in the interbank market, due to banks
- rate (-satz)   interbank rate
- verbindlichkeiten ⟶ Interbankpassiva
- zahlungsverkehr   interbank payments

Interesse
- der privaten Anleger   retail investment interest, retail buying interest

großes - bestand für Hochtechnologiewerte   high technology stocks found strong support

Kaufhauswerte standen im Mittelpunkt des -s   investment (buying) interest centered on stores

für die neue Emission bestand kaum -   the new issue was poorly received in the market

Interessenkäufe   (a) speculative buying, special-purpose buying; (b) stock purchases designed to acquire a majority

interessewahrend   bei Wertpapieraufträgen: safeguarding the investor's interests

interimistische Globalurkunde   interim global certificate

Interimsschein   scrip, interim certificate

intervenieren   to intervene in, to operate on

die Bundesbank intervenierte nur in einem geringen Umfang   the Bundesbank kept a low profile on (e.g. the foreign exchange market)

die Bundesbank intervenierte sowohl am Kassa- als auch am Terminmarkt   the Bundesbank operated on both the spot and forward markets

Intervention   intervention, support
- am Devisenmarkt   foreign exchange market intervention
- am freien Markt   intervention in the open market

Interventions
- bestände   intervention holdings (stock)
- käufe   support buying, supporting purchases
- kurs   intervention rate (price)
- mechanismus   intervention mechanism
- politik   intervention policy, policy of support points
- punkt / - schwelle   intervention (support) point
- salden   intervention balances
- währung   intervention currency

Inventarwert eines Fondsanteils   net asset value of a share (of a unit)

inverse Zinsstruktur   reverse interest rate pattern (i.e. short-term lending rates are higher than those charged for long-term funds or short-term securities offer a higher yield than long-term securities)

Investitionen   investments, capital spending (expenditure)

Investitions
- anreiz   investment incentive, inducement to invest
- aufwand   capital expenditure
- beihilfe   capital investment grant

Investitions
- bereitschaft   propensity to invest
- bewertung   capital expenditure rating, evaluating capital investment projects
- budget   capital spending budget
- darlehen   development loan, investment credit (loan)
- drosselung   investment curb
- entscheidung   capital expenditure decision
- finanzierung   financing capital expenditures
- genehmigung   authorising capital expenditures
- güter   capital goods
- güterfinanzierung   financing capital goods
- kraft   capital spending potential
- kredit   investment credit, development loan
- kürzungen   capital spending cuts
- lenkung   capital investment control, channelling of investments
- mittel   funds for capital expenditures (investments)
- nachweis   capital expenditure performance report
- planung   capital expenditure planning
- programm   capital investment scheme
- projekt   capital investment project, proposed capital expenditure
- rechnung   capital budgeting
- rentabilität   investment profitability
- tätigkeit   investment activity
- umfang   size of capital expenditures
- volumen   investment total
- vorhaben   capital expenditure project
- vorschläge   capital expenditure proposals

Investment
- anlage   investing in investment company shares, investing in mutual funds
- anteil   investment fund share, unit (Br), share (US)
- ausschüttung   fund payout, income distributed by a fund
- fonds   investment fund, unit trust (Br), mutual fund (US)
- gedanke   investment company idea
- gesellschaft   investment company
- konto   investment account
- papiere   investment company securities
- plan   investment accumulation plan
- sparen   investment fund saving
- zertifikat   investment fund share

J

Jahres
- abschluß (a) Bilanz: annual accounts; (b) eines Kontos: year-end balancing (closing) of an account
- abschlußprüfung   annual audit
- bilanz   annual financial statements, annual statement of condition
- endabrechnung   year-end settlement
- ergebnis   profit (loss) for the year
- geld   one-year funds, twelve-months money
- hoch   annual high
- leistung   annual principal and interest payments
- rendite   annual yield
- tief   annual low
- tilgungsquote   annual redemption rate
- überschuß   net income for the year
- ultimoglattstellung   year-end position squaring
- verzinsung   annual interest return

jährlich
- e Ertragsausschüttung   annual distribution of income
- er Schuldendienst   annual debt service
- er Zinsendienst   annual interest payments

Jumbo-Operation   Emission: jumbo deal

Jumbo-Stückelungen   large denominations

junge Aktien   new shares

Jungschein   scrip, provisional bond (stock) certificate
- guthaben   scrip balances, scrips receivable
- konto   scrip account
- verkehr   scrip transactions, dealings in scrips

juristische Person   body corporate

K

kaduzierte Aktien forfeited shares

Kalender bei Emissionen:issuing calendar (timetable)

Kapazitätsausnutzungsgrad capacity utilisation rate, capacity usage ratio

Kapital capital, equity; Kapitalien: financial resources; Darlehens-, Anleihekapital: principal

- abfluß outflow of capital, capital efflux

- abwanderung capital drain (exodus)

- anbieter suppliers of capital (of funds)

- angebot supply of capital

- anlage investment

- anlageberatung investment counseling

- anlagegesellschaft capital investment company

- anleger investor

- anteil equity share (interest)

- aufbringung putting up (raising) capital

- aufnahme durch eine Anleiheemission raising capital through a bond issue

- aufstockung capital increase

- aufwand capital expenditure, capital spending

- ausfallrisiko Darlehen: loan loss risk

- ausfuhr capital export

- ausstattung capital resources available; availability of funds

- auszahlung capital paid out

- bedarf capital needs (requirements), funds required

- belassungserklärung undertaking not to sell or assign an equity interest; support agreement

- bereitstellung provision of capital, providing funds, commitment of capital

- berichtigung capital adjustment

- berichtigung im Verhältnis 6:1 one-for-six capitalisation issue

- berichtigungsaktie bonus share

- beschaffung generation (procurement) of capital, equity (fund) raising

- beschaffungskosten cost of equity raising, cost of funds

- beteiligung equity stake, share in the capital, capital interest

- beteiligungsgesellschaft (a) equity investment company; (b) venture capital company

- betrag principal; capital sum

- bewertung capital rating

- bilanz capital account

- bildung capital formation, accumulation of capital

- bindung tying up funds, commitment of capital

- budget capital budget

- decke capital (equity) base

- decke erweitern to broaden the equity base

- dienst debt service

- diensthilfe debt service subsidies

Kapital

- dividende   dividend (paid on the amount of capital invested)
- eigner   shareholder, equity holder
- einbuße   loss of capital
- einfuhr   capital imports
- einlage   capital (equity) contribution, amount of capital invested (contributed), capital brought into the business
- einsatz   employment of capital, capital employed
- emission   capital issue
- entnahme   withdrawal (drawing) of funds
- erhaltung   preservation of capital
- erhöhung   capital increase, increase in capital
- erhöhung aus Gesellschaftsmitteln   capital increase out of company reserves
- erhöhung im Verhältnis 6:1   one-for-six capital increase
- erträge   investment income
- ertragssteuer   withholding tax
- ertragszahl   return on investment
- erweiterung   capital widening
- fälligkeiten   principal maturities, repayments of principal falling due
- flucht   capital exodus (flight)
- fluß   capital flow, flow of funds
- flußrechnung   funds statement, flow-of-funds analysis
- fonds eines Unternehmens: capital resources
- forderungen   equity claims
- geber   investor, lender, supplier of capital (of funds)
- gesellschaft   public and/or private limited company (Br), corporation, joint stock corporation (US)
- gewinn   capital gain
- gewinnsteuer   capital gains tax
- herabsetzung   capital reduction, capital write-down
- hergabe   provision of capital, providing funds
- hunger   heavy equity requirements, heavy capital needs
- intakthalteerklärung   undertaking not to sell or assign an equity interest; support agreement

kapitalintensiv   capital-intensive

kapitalisieren   to capitalise

die Kreditkosten -   to capitalise the finance charge, to add on the total finance charge to the amount borrowed

die Rücklagen -   to capitalise reserves, i.e. to convert reserves into share capital

kapitalisierter Marktwert   capitalised market value

Kapitalisierung   capitalisation

- eines Unternehmens   company's capitalisation (i.e. shares, debentures and loan capital, capital reserves, bank borrowings); Börsenkapitalisierung: market capitalisation

die Börsenkapitalisierung beläuft sich auf ungefähr ...   capitalised on the market at around ...

Kapital

- knappheit   shortage of funds (of capital)
- koeffizient   capital output ratio
- kosten   cost of capital
- lenkung   capital investment control

119

Kapitalmarkt   capital market
Emittenten am -   issuers operating on the capital market
- adresse   capital market operator
- adresse, erste   prime borrower in the capital market
- anspannung   tightness in the capital market
- ausschuß   capital issues committee
- entspannung   easing of the situation in the capital market

kapitalmarktgerecht
- e Ausstattung einer Anleihe bond features (interest coupon) in line with capital market conditions
- e Verzinsung   interest payments in accordance with the rates ruling in the capital market

Kapitalmarkt
- konditionen   capital market rates, terms and rates in the capital market
- lage   state of the capital market, conditions (situation) in the capital market
- lenkung   capital market control
- mittel   capital market funds
- orientierung   capital market orientation, gearing (tailoring) to capital market rates
- papiere   capital market instruments
- renditen   capital market yields
- situation   state of the capital market, conditions (situation) in the capital market
- teilnehmer   operators in the capital market, capital market participants
- verhältnisse   conditions in the capital market

- zins   capital market rate

Kapital
- mehrheit   majority of shares, majority shareholding
- mittel   funds, financial resources
- nachfrage   demand for capital
- nachfrager   demanders of capital
- nehmer   borrower
- nutzungskosten   capital user costs
- polster   equity cushion
- quellen   capital (equity) resources
- rendite   return on investment
- risiko   capital risk
- rückflußdauer   payback period
- rücklagen   capital surplus
- rückwanderung   reflux (reflow) of capital
- rückzahlung   capital repayment; repayment of principal
- sammelstellen   institutional investors
- sanierung   capital (financial) reconstruction, capital overhaul
- sanierungsprogramm   capital reconstruction scheme
- schnitt   capital write-down
- schöpfung   creation of capital
- schwund   shrinkage of funds
- situation   capital position
- spritze   capital infusion, equity injection, financial pump priming
- steuerung   capital control
- ströme   capital flows
- struktur   (a) capital structure; (b) leverage ratio, ratio of debt to equity

kapitalsuchende Emittenten
capital-seeking issuers

Kapital
- überschuß capital surplus, surplus of funds
- übertragung transfer of capital
- umschichtung regrouping of capital (of funds)
- umschlag capital turnover, ratio of sales to net worth
- und Zinsendienst debt service
- verflechtung equity (capital) links, financial interdependence
- verhältnisse capital situation (position), capital structure
  Neuordnung der Kapitalverhältnisse capital reorganisation
- verkehr capital movements
- verkehrsbilanz capital account
- verkehrssteuer capital transfer tax
- verminderung capital reduction, capital write-down
- vermittler financial intermediary
- vermögen capital assets
- verwässerung equity dilution, stock watering
- verwendung application of capital, appropriation of funds
- verzinsung return on capital
- wachstumsrate capital growth rate
- wert capital value
- wertpapiere stocks and bonds
- wertzuwachs capital appreciation
- zinsen interest on capital
- zufluß inflow of capital
- zusammenlegung capital consolidation (merger), regrouping of capital

Karenzfrist (a) qualifying period (b) grace period, period of grace

Kassa
- devisen spot exchange, exchange for spot delivery
- dollar spot dollar
- geschäft Devisen: spot deal (transaction); Wertpapiere: cash bargain, dealing for cash, transaction against cash settlement
- kurs Devisen: spot rate; Wertpapiere: cash settlement price, cash quotation
- markt cash (spot) market
- papiere securities traded for cash, cash securities
- positionen spot commitments (positions)
- regulierung cash settlement

Kasseliquidität cash liquidity (i.e. cash and central bank balances, bills and securities eligible as collateral for borrowings with Bundesbank)

Kassen
- haltung cash management
- kredit Federal Government's loan facility with the Central Bank
- kredite short-term lendings to public bodies
- obligation fixed-rate medium-term note
- quittung bei Wertpapieren: scrip, provisional certificate
- terminal teller (POS) terminal
- verein securities clearing and deposit bank

Kaufabrechnung bei Wertpapieren: bought note

Kaufauftrag buy order

Käufe Börse: buying
- des Berufshandels professional buying
- auf ermäßigter Basis buying at a reduced price level

121

Kaufempfehlung buy advice (recommendation)

kaufen

für den eigenen Bestand - to buy for own account

an der Börse - to buy in the market

auf Hausse - to buy for a rise

gegen den Markttrend - to buy anti-marketwise

Käufer buyer, purchaser

- abruf buyer's call
- bank buying bank
- interesse Börse: buying interest
- mangel lack of buying orders
- markt buyer's market
- publikum buyers, investing public

Kaufhauswerte stores

Kaufhedge long hedge

Kaufinteresse buying interest, buying attention

das - konzentrierte sich auf spekulative Werte buying interest centered on speculative counters, speculative counters stood in the limelight

Hoffnungen auf eine Dividendenerhöhung belebten das - hopes on a dividend rise spurred buying interest

Kaufoption Prämiengeschäft: call option

Erwerb einer - buying a call, purchase of a call option

Erwerber einer - buyer of a call option, call buyer

Inhaber einer - call holder

Stillhalter einer - writer (seller) of a call option

Verkäufer einer - seller of a call option

verkaufte -en calls written

Kaufwelle Börse: welter of buying, buying surge, spate of new buying

Kautionseffekten stocks held as security

Kautionswechsel guarantee bill

Kellerwechsel windmill, kite

Kernleistungen einer Bank: mainstream banking, traditional banking services

kleine Stücke odd lots, fixed-interest securities with a nominal value of DM 500 or less

kleine Stückelungen small denominations

Kleinigkeiten Börse: odd lots

Kleinkredit small loan

Kleinsparer small saver

Kleinzeichner small subscriber

klettern to climb, to move up

Fahrzeugwerte kletterten kräftig nach oben motors moved up sharply

XYZ kletterten um 6 auf 140DM XYZ jumped (rose) 6 to 140DM

Bankwerte kletterten auf einen absoluten Höchststand bank stocks surged to an all-time high

Kollektivzeichnung signing jointly

kombiniertes Transportdokument combined transport bill of lading

Kommanditeinlagen equity contributions by the limited partners, amount of capital put up by the limited partners

Kommanditgesellschaft limited partnership

Kommanditist limited partner

kommerziell
- e Ausleihungen corporate lendings
- es Bankgeschäft corporate banking
- e Kunden corporate customers

Kommissionsbasis nur auf - tätig werden to operate purely on a commission basis

Kommissionsgeschäft agency transaction

kommissionsweise Übernahme einer Emission selling on a best efforts basis; taking up and selling an issue on a commission basis

Kommittent principal

Kommunal
- anleihe municipal bond, local authority bond
- darlehen local authority loan
- darlehensgeschäft lendings to local authorities
- kredit local authority loan
- obligationen municipal bonds, local authority bonds

Kompensationskurs settlement price

Kompensationsschlußnote settlement note

kompensieren to compensate, to balance, to set off, to match

Kauf-und Verkaufsaufträge - to match buy and sell orders, to set off buy orders against sell orders

XYZ kompensierte die Verluste des Vortages XYZ recovered from yesterday's losses

kompensierte Valuta value compensated (i.e. identical value date)

Kompetenz province, authority; im Kreditgeschäft: approval powers

unter die - des Kreditausschusses fallen to come within the province of the loan committee

Kompetenzliste list of approval powers

Kompetenzträger officer holding powers of approval

kompetenzüberschreitende Darlehensausreichungen loan extensions exceeding the approval powers of the officer concerned

Komplementär general partner

Komptantgeschäft cash deal

Konditionen Kredite: terms, interest rate charged; Bankdienstleistungen im allgemeinen: fees and commission rates; Oberbegriff: pricing

- im Aktivgeschäft lending rates
- einer Anleihe bond terms, bond features, loan terms
- für Festgeldanlagen interest rates paid on time (term) deposits
- für Hypothekenkredite mortgage loan rates; mortgage rates and discounts deducted from the principal
- für Konsumentenkredite consumer loan terms, consumer loan pricing
- eines Kredites loan terms, interest rate and commission charged

Anpassung der - an die veränderte Marktlage adjusting the terms (the interest rate charged) to the changed conditions in the market

Festsetzung der - im langfristigen Kreditgeschäft pricing of long-term lendings

Festsetzung der - für Überziehungskredite overdraft pricing

Neufestsetzung der - in Übereinstimmung mit dem Diskontsatz der Deutschen Bundesbank renegotiation (refixing) of the interest rate in keeping with the Bundesbank's discount rate

Überprüfung der - im langfristigen Hypothekengeschäft reviewing the terms (interest rates) for long-term mortgage lendings

Konditionen

- angebot   terms (interest rates) offered

- anpassung   adjustment of the loan terms, adjusting the interest rate to (e.g. the new money market rates); pricing adjustment

- bindung   establishment of a fixed interest rate (of fixed loan terms); locking in the interest rate

- druck   competitive pressure on terms and rates offered

- festlegung   im Kreditgeschäft: fixing (establishing) the terms for (e.g. borrowings in the Euromarket, overdraft facilities, etc.); pricing of loans
für Bankdienstleistungen im allgemeinen: pricing of banking services

- festschreibung ⟶ Konditionenbindung

- frage zur Sprache bringen   to bring the pricing issue up for discussion

- gefälle   interest rate differential

- gestaltung   im Kreditgeschäft: pricing of loans; Bankdienstleistungen im allgemeinen: pricing of banking services

- politik   pricing policy

- regelung → Konditionenfestlegung, - gestaltung

- wettbewerb   pricing competition

- zugeständnisse   rate concessions

kongruent

- e Ausleihungen   lendings at matching maturities

- e Deckung   matching cover

- e Laufzeit   matching maturity (life, term)

- e Refinanzierung   funding at matching maturities

- e Währungsdeckung   matching currency cover

- refinanzieren   to fund at matching maturities

- refinanziertes Kreditgeschäft   lendings funded at matching maturities

Grundsatz der -en Deckung   principle of matching cover

Kongruenz   im Laufzeitenbereich: matching maturities; im Währungsbereich: matching currencies

Konjunktur   business activity, economic activity; state of economic activity

- abkühlung   economic slowdown

- abschwung   downturn in business activity, economic downswing

- anreiz   stimulus to economic activity

- aufschwung   economic upswing, upturn in business

- belebung   economic revival

- einbruch   sharp setback in business activity

- förderung   stimulation of economic activity

- lage   economic situation, state of economic activity

- motor   primary mover of economic activity

- phase   business cycle

- prognose   economic forecast, business outlook

- rückgang   downturn in business

- rückschlag setback in economic activity
- spritzen government measures (e.g. tax reliefs) designed to stimulate economic activity
- umschwung turnaround in economic activity, break in the economic trend
- verlauf economic trend, development of business activity
- zyklus business cycle

Konkurrenz im Privatkundengeschäft: competition in the retail banking sector

Konkurs bankruptcy; im Sinne von Unternehmenszusammenbrüchen: company failure, insolvency

den - über das Vermögen des Schuldners eröffnen to adjudicate the debtor bankrupt

Konkurs
- abwicklung administration of the bankrupt's estate, liquidating the bankrupt's estate
- antrag petition in bankruptcy, bankruptcy petition
- bilanz debtor's statement of affairs
- delikt bankruptcy offence
- eröffnung adjudication in bankruptcy, opening of bankruptcy proceedings
- eröffnungsbeschluß adjudication order, receiving order

Konkursforderung claim against the bankrupt's estate, creditor's claim

anmeldbare - provable debt, debt provable in bankruptcy

Anmeldung einer - proving a debt; proof

- en anmelden to prove debts, to make claims against the bankrupt's estate

Konkurs
- gericht bankruptcy court
- gläubiger creditor in bankruptcy
- handlung act of bankruptcy
- masse bankrupt's estate, assets of the bankrupt
- ordnung bankruptcy rules
- quote dividend in bankruptcy, dividend distributed to the creditors
- schuldner bankrupt, debtor adjudicated bankrupt
- verfahren bankruptcy proceedings, bankruptcy procedure
- verwalter gerichtlich bestellter: receiver, official receiver; von den Gläubigern bestellter: trustee in bankruptcy(Br) bankruptcy commissioner (US)

Konnossement bill of lading, B/L

Konnossements-Ausfertigung B/L copy

Konnossements-Garantie B/L letter of indemnity

konsolidieren to consolidate

konsolidierte Bilanz consolidated balance sheet (statement of condition)

konsolidierte G+V consolidated statement of income

Konsolidierung consolidation
- von Baudarlehen conversion of short-term building loans into long-term lendings
- von Verbindlichkeiten debt consolidation

Konsolidierungs
- anleihe consolidation loan
- kreis scope of consolidation
- phase Börse: period (process) of consolidation

Konsorte syndicate member, underwriter

Konsortial
- abteilung new issues department

125

Konsortial
- anteil   syndicate (underwriting) share
- banken   syndicate banks, underwriting banks
- beteiligung   syndicate interest

Konsortialführer / konsortialführende Bank   lead bank, lead manager, managing bank, syndicate leader (manager)

Konsortialführung   lead management

unter der - von   led by ..

mit der - betrauen   to award the lead management to, to entrust with the management

die - innehaben   to run the books

Konsortial
- geschäft   syndicate (underwriting) business
- konto   new issue account
- kredit   syndicated loan, consortium loan
- kreditgeschäft   syndicated loan business
- mitglied   syndicate member, underwriter
- nutzen   underwriting commission, spread
- quote   underwriting share
- rechnung   syndicate account; syndicate accounting
- sitzung   meeting of the syndicate members
- spanne   underwriting (overriding) commission
- vermögen   syndicate assets
- vertrag   syndicate (syndication) agreement, underwriting agreement

Konsortium   syndicate, management group

ein von der ... Bank geführtes - a syndicate led by ...

Bildung eines -s   forming a syndicate; syndication

Zusammenstellung eines -s   arranging (assembling) a syndicate

Konsumenten
- bankgeschäft   consumer banking
- kredit   consumer loan
- kreditgeschäft   consumer lending
- kreditvolumen   total consumer lendings

Kontensparen   deposit account saving

Kontensparer   account depositor

Konto   account
- abschluß   balancing an account (e.g. quarterly, half-yearly account balancing), periodical closing up of an account; im Sinne von Auflösung: closing out an account
- abstimmung   account reconciliation
- akte   account file
- angaben   account information (data)
- auflösung   closing out an account
- ausgleich   settling the debit balance of (in) an account; repayment of the amount overdrawn
- auszug   statement of account, bank statement
- belastung   debiting the account, debit to the account; account debit, amount debited to the account
- bewegungen   account movements, movements (transactions) routed through the account
- bezeichnung   title of an account, account heading
- deckung   account cover

vorbehaltlich entsprechender Kontodeckung   provided that there is sufficient credit in the account

Konto

- einrichtung   opening of an account
- einzahlung   payment (paying) into an account, deposit
- eröffnung   opening of an account
- eröffnungsantrag   account-opening application
- eröffnungsschreiben   account-opening confirmation, letter confirming the opening of an account
- führende Filiale   account-maintaining branch (office)
- führer /-in   accounts officer
- führung   (a) account maintenance, account-keeping, maintaining (running) an account; (b) conduct of an account
- führung auf Guthabenbasis   keeping an account in the credit, maintaining an account on a non-borrowing basis
- führungsgebühren   account maintenance charges, account-keeping fees, charges for running an account
- guthaben   credit balance of (in) an account, credit in an account
- gutschrift   crediting an account, credit to an account; account credit, amount credited to an account
- inhaber   account holder

Kontokorrent

- einlagen   demand (checking) deposits, deposits on current accounts
- guthaben   current account balance
- kapitalschuld   principal debt
- konto   current account, chequing account (Br), checking account (US)
- kredit   advance on current account, overdraft facility, drawing credit
- verhältnis   current account relationship

Konto

- saldo   account balance
- sparvertrag   investment account savings scheme
- sperre   blocking an account
- sperrvermerk   account-blocking notice
- stand   account balance, balance in (of) an account
- tasche   account envelope
- übertrag   transfer to account ...
- überziehung   (a) account overdraft, sum overdrawn; (b) overdrawing an account
- überziehungskredit   overdraft facility, personal credit line
- umsatz   account movements, turnover on the account, transactions routed through the account
- umschreibung   transferring the account to the name of ..
- unterlagen   account records
- verbindung   (a) banking connection, account maintained (kept) with; (b) account relationship
- verfügung   drawing on an account, signing on an account
- verfügungsberechtigung   authority (power) to draw on an account, authority to sign on an account
- vollmacht   account mandate, authority to draw on an account, authority to operate an account

Kontrahent   contracting party

kontraktive Geldpolitik   tight monetary policy

Kontrolle der Ausleihungen   controlling (monitoring) lendings

Konvertibilität   convertibility

Konvertierungsanleihe   conversion loan

Konzern group

- abschluß consolidated financial statements, consolidated (group) accounts

- bilanz consolidated balance sheet, consolidated statement of condition (US)

- engagement group exposure, loans extended to a group

- finanzgesellschaft group finance company, captive finance company (US)

konzernfremden Gesellschaftern zustehender Gewinn minority interest in income

konzerngebundene Hypothekenbank captive mortgage bank

Konzern

- gesellschaft group company
- gewinn consolidated profit
- hintergrund des Kreditnehmers the borrower's (the borrowing company's) parentage
- stab central staff management
- umsatz group sales

konzertierte Aktion auf den Devisenmärkten concerted action in the foreign exchange markets

Konzertzeichner stag

Konzertzeichnung stagging

koordinieren mit anderen Banken to act in concert (to coordinate) with other banks

Kopffiliale regional head office, main branch

koppeln to tie, to link, to peg
 an den Diskontsatz der Bundesbank - to tie (to link) to the Bundesbank's discount rate
 an den jeweils gültigen Marktsatz - to link to the prevailing market rate

die Zinssätze für Ausleihungen sind an den Diskontsatz gekoppelt lending rates are pegged to the discount rate

Kopplung tying (linking, pegging) to

Kopplungsgeschäft tie-in transaction

Kopplungsklausel tie-in clause

Korbwährung basket currency

Körperschaftssteuer corporation tax

Körperschaftssteuer-Anrechnungsbetrag corporation tax credit

Korrealhypothek consolidated (collective) mortgage

Korrespondenzbank correspondent, correspondent bank

 Guthaben bei -en correspondent balances, due from correspondent banks

Kosten cost, expenses, charges

- der Mittelbeschaffung für kurz- und langfristige Kredite cost of funds for short and long-term loans

- der umgesetzten Leistung cost of sales

Kosten

- abgrenzung cost deferment
- beitrag contribution towards costs
- deckend covering the costs of .., cost-covering
- einsparung cost saving
- empfindlichkeit sensitiveness to costs
- ersparnisse cost savings
- gesichtspunkt, unter - en from a cost point of view
- gliederung cost breakdown
- intensive Zahlungen cost-intensive payments
- inflation cost inflation, cost-push inflation

- minimierung minimising costs
- Nutzen-Analyse cost-benefit analysis
- rechnung cost accounting
- stelle cost centre
- stellenrechnung cost centre accounting
- struktur cost pattern

Kostgeschäft take-in transaction

Kraftfahrzeugwerte motors

kräftige Erholung Börse: sharp (strong) rally

kräftig vorrücken (zulegen) to move up strongly

Kraftloserklärung von Wertpapieren invalidation of securities

Kredit loan, credit, facility, advance, lending; im Sinne von Engagement: exposure
- mit gebundener Kondition fixed-rate loan (lending)
- mit fester Laufzeit fixed-term loan
- mit Zinsbindung fixed-rate loan
- mit variablem Zinssatz variable-interest (floating-rate) loan

Kredit
- abdeckung repayment of a loan
- abkommen loan agreement
- abteilung loan department, lending division
- abwicklung loan processing, loan administration
- akte loan file, loan envelope
- anbieter lender
- angebot loan offer
- annahme accepting (acceptance of) the loan offer

Kreditantrag loan application (request)
  Bearbeitung des -es processing the loan application
  Überprüfung des -es examining (checking) the loan application
- stellen to make a loan application

Kredit
- antragsteller loan applicant, applicant for the loan
- apparat banking (credit) system
- art type of a loan
- auflagen restrictive loan provisions, credit carrying specific conditions

Kreditaufnahme borrowing, raising a loan, taking out a loan
- im Ausland overseas borrowing, borrowing abroad
- am Eurodollarmarkt Eurodollar borrowing
- durch die öffentliche Hand borrowing by public authorities
- am Kapitalmarkt borrowing in the capital market, tapping the capital market
- beschränken to tighten up on credit
  vorübergehende - in Form eines Überziehungskredites temporary borrowing by way of an overdraft
  Zweck der - ist die Deckung der Projektmehrkosten purpose of the borrowing is to defray overruns

Kredit
- ausfall loan loss (charge-off)
- ausfallverhältnis /-quote loan loss ratio, charge-off rate, default (delinquency) rate (US)
- auskunft credit position report, credit information, banker's reference
- ausreichende Stelle lending bank (office)

Kredit
- ausreichung extending (granting) a loan, loan extension (accommodation)
- ausschuß loans committee
- ausweitung credit expansion
- auszahlung loan disbursement, disbursement of the loan proceeds, crediting the loan proceeds to the customer's account
- auszahlung zu 100 % with loan proceeds being paid in full
- banken private commercial banks
- bearbeitung loan processing, loan administration
- bearbeitungsgebühr loan processing charge

Kreditbedarf borrowing requirements (needs)
- der öffentlichen Haushalte public borrowing requirements
- der Unternehmungen corporate borrowing requirements

Kredit
- bedingungen loan terms, terms of a credit
- befugnis borrowing authority, borrowing powers

Kreditbereitstellung extension (granting) of a loan, making a loan available

für die Dauer der - as long as the facility is available
- zu Vorzugskonditionen making loans available at preferential terms

Kreditbeschränkungen lending restrictions (constraints), lending squeeze

Kreditbesicherung provision of security for a loan, putting up (providing)security for a loan
- erfolgt durch die Abtretung von Forderungen security will be provided by an assignment of accounts receivable
- durch die Belastung von Immobilienwerten providing security by a charge on real property

Kredit
- besicherungsgarantie stand-by letter of credit
- bestand loan portfolio, loan book, total lendings
- beteiligung loan participation, interest (stake) in a loan commitment
- beurteilung loan (credit) assessment
- bewerber loan applicant
- bewilligung loan approval, credit sanction
- bewilligungsausschuß sanctioning committee
- bewilligungsgrenze sanctioning limit
- bilanz financial statements
- bodensatz hard core lendings
- bremsen credit brakes
- brief letter of credit
- bürgschaft loan guarantee
- büro loan department, loan office
- disagio discount on a loan
- drosselung credit crunch (squeeze), credit contraction
- einräumende Stelle lending office (branch)
- einräumung extension (granting) of a loan, loan accommodation
- einräumungsschreiben loan undertaking
- einweisung loan approval (undertaking),loan commitment
- erleichterungen (a) der Kreditpolitik: easing of the tight credit policy; (b) bei einem Engagement: easing (tempering) of the loan terms
- ermächtigung borrowing authorisation

Kredit
- erneuerung loan renewal, renewal of a credit line
- expansion credit expansion, growth in lendings
- fähigkeit (a) credit-worthiness (b) capacity to borrow
- fälligkeit loan maturity
- fazilität credit (borrowing) facility
- finanzierung borrowing, financing on credits
- finanzierungsquote borrowing ratio
- forderungen lendings
- fristen der Aktiv- und Passivseite maturities of lendings and deposits
- garantiegemeinschaft credit guarantee society
- gebaren lending policy, lending practice
- gebende Bank lending bank, lender
- gebühren loan charges
- gefährdung damage to credit-worthiness
- genehmigung loan approval, loan (credit) sanction
    der Kredit muß zuvor durch unsere zuständigen Kreditausschüsse genehmigt werden the loan must have the prior approval of our senior loan committees
- genossenschaft credit cooperative

Kreditgeschäft insgesamt: lendings, lending business, lending operations
- mit Firmen-(Privat-)kunden lendings to corporate (private) customers
- mit mittelständischen Kunden small business lendings

Kredit
- gesuch loan application
- gewährung extension (granting) of a loan, loan (credit) accommodation
- gewährungsspielraum lending leeway
- gewährungszusage loan undertaking, loan commitment
- gewerbe banking industry, banks, banking business
- grenze borrowing (loan) limit
- hergabe (a) loan extension, granting a loan; (b) crediting
- höchstgrenze credit (lending) ceiling

kreditieren (a) to lend, to extend (to grant) a loan; (b) to credit

kreditierende Bank lending bank

Kreditierung (a) lending, loan accommodation; (b) crediting
- der erforderlichen Vorauszahlungen providing the funds for the advance payments to be made

Kredit
- inanspruchnahme drawing on a loan, drawing against a credit, availment of a credit facility
- inflation credit-induced inflation
- institut financial institution, banking organisation
- kapazität lending capacity (power)
- kauf instalment buying, purchase on credit, credit sale
- knappheit credit stringency
- kompetenz loan approval powers
- konditionen loan terms, terms of a credit, lending rates
- konsortium loan syndicate
- konto loan account
- kontrolle credit (loan) control
- kosten cost of borrowing, cost of credit, finance charge

Kredit
- kunde borrowing customer
- kündigung   calling in a loan, termination of a loan agreement

Kreditlaufzeit term (life)of a credit, loan maturity (period)

Kredite mit festen Laufzeiten von ein bis vier Jahren loans for fixed periods of one to four years

während der vereinbarten Laufzeit des Kredites over the agreed life (period)of the loan

Kredit
- leihe guarantee credit, credit by way of guarantee
- leihgeschäft lending business
- lenkung   credit control

Kreditlinie credit line

Aufstockung einer -   increase in a credit line, providing fresh (additional) funds

Einräumung einer - extending (granting) a credit line

Erneuerung einer - line renewal (replacement), renewing a credit line

Verlängerung einer - extending the maturity of a credit line, line renewal

Kredit
- lockerung → Krediterleichterungen
- markt financial (credit)market
- marktverschuldung des Bundes government borrowings in the financial markets
- mäßig unterstützen to support by way of a loan, to back up by lendings
- mittel borrowed funds, loan funds
- möglichkeiten   borrowing sources, sources of finance

- nachfrage   demand for credit, loan demand
- nachfrage im Baubereich demand for building loans
- nachfrager borrower, loan applicant
- nebenkosten loan-related cost, non-interest charges
- nehmer borrower
- nehmerbonität credit-worthiness (solvency) of the borrower
- nehmerstaat   sovereign borrower
- neugeschäft new lendings
- neuzusagen   new loan commitments
- offerte   loan offer

Kreditoren   einer Bank: deposits; eines Industrieunternehmens: accounts payable

Kreditorenzuwachs growth in deposits

kreditorisch
- es Konto creditor account, account kept in the credit, account maintained on a non--borrowing basis
- er Saldo   credit balance

Kredit
- plafond   lending (credit) ceiling, asset ceiling
- plafondierung setting a limit for lendings, setting an asset ceiling
- politik   credit (lending) policy

kreditpolitisch
- e Beschlüsse zur Konjunkturankurbelung   credit policy measures designed to stimulate economic activity
- e Lenkungsmittel (Instrumentarium) credit policy instruments

Kredit
- portefeuille loan portfolio, total lendings, loan book

Kredit
- potential   lending power, lending capacities
- preis   cost of borrowing, loan cost
- preispolitik   loan pricing policy
- programm   lending (loan) scheme
- prolongation   extending the maturity of a loan, renewal of a loan commitment
- provision   loan commission
- punktbewertungssystem   credit scoring system
- pyramiden im Bankgewerbe   shifting of loans extended by the parent to subsidiaries and associated companies
- quelle   source of borrowing, source of funds
- rahmen   credit line, credit availability, open-to-borrow arrangement
  gesamter Kreditrahmen   total credit availability
- rahmenvertrag   credit override agreement, open-to-borrow arrangement
- restriktionen   credit (lending) restrictions, credit squeeze, loan curbs
- richtsätze   (a) loan directives, lending guidelines; (b) principles relating to the equity and liquidity ratio of banking organisations
- risiko   credit risk, loan risk
- rückflüsse   repayments on loans (lendings), loans repaid

Kreditrückführung   (a) reduction of a loan; (b) repayment of a loan
  Rückführung des Kredites in bestimmten Zeitabständen   reduction of the loan at agreed intervals

Kreditrücklauf   repayments on loans (lendings)

Kreditrückzahlung   repayment of a loan
  falls eine monatliche Zahlung nicht pünktlich erfolgt, wird der gesamte Kredit sofort zur Rückzahlung fällig   if any monthly payment is not made on time, the entire loan becomes repayable immediately
  wir stellen hiermit den Kredit zur sofortigen Rückzahlung fällig   we hereby call in the loan for immediate repayment
  der Kreditnehmer kann den Kredit mit dreimonatiger Kündigungsfrist jederzeit zurückzahlen   the borrower has the option to give three months' notice of repayment at any time

Kredit
- sachbearbeiter   loan (lending) officer
- schädigung   damage to credit-worthiness
- schöpfung   credit creation
- schraube   credit screw
- schrumpfung   credit crunch
- schutzverein   credit interchange service
- sekretariat   loan office
- sicherheit   loan collateral, security for a loan
  eine erstklassige Sicherheit in Höhe des Kredites zur Verfügung stellen   to put up first-rate security (collateral) to the amount of the loan
- sicherung   providing security for a loan, putting up security for a loan
- sicherungsvertrag   loan security agreement, loan collateral agreement
- spielraum   margin (leeway) for lendings
- status   financial statements

Kredit
- stopp ban on new lendings, credit (lending) freeze
- streuung loan diversification, diversification of lendings
- struktur lending pattern, set-up of borrowing customers
- stundung loan respite, debt deferral
- suchender loan-seeking company, loan applicant
- summe loan amount (principal), principal of a loan
- syndizierungen loan syndication business
- tilgung repayment of a loan
- tranche loan instalment
- transparenz transparency in lending transactions
- überschreitung exceeding a borrowing limit (a credit line)
- überwachung policing (monitoring) loan commitments, credit control, supervision of loan commitments
- überziehung overdrawing a credit; overdraft
- überziehungsprovision overdraft commission
- umschuldung rescheduling (refunding) of a loan
- unterlagen loan records, loan documents
- valuta (a) loan proceeds, loan amount (principal); (b) loan (lending) currency
- valutierung commitment of funds, allowing drawings against a credit
- verbilligung (a) lowering (easing) of lending rates; (b) interest rate subsidies
- vereinbarung loan agreement, loan (credit) arrangement
- verfügbarkeit availability of loans, credit availability

- vergabe loan extension, granting a loan (a facility)

Kreditverhältnis loan agreement, loan arrangement

Kündigung des -ses calling in the loan, terminating the loan agreement

nach Beendigung des -ses upon repayment of the loan, upon termination of the loan agreement

Kredit
- verkehr lending operations (transactions)
- verknappung credit squeeze, shortage of loan funds
- verlagerung shift of lendings
- verlängerung extending the maturity of a loan, renewal of a credit line
- verlust loan loss (charge-off)
- verlustquote loan loss ratio, charge-off rate, default (delinquency) rate (US)
- vermittler finance broker, loan broker
- vermittlung loan (credit) brokerage
- versicherung credit (loan) insurance, payment default policy
- versprechen loan undertaking, commitment (undertaking) to extend a loan
- vertrag loan agreement (contract), facility letter
- verwendung application of the loan funds
- volumen loan portfolio, total lendings, loan book, aggregate lendings
- vorlage loan application, loan under consideration
- wesen banking industry, banking business
- wesengesetz German Banking Act

Kredit

- wertberichtigungen charges for bad debt provisions, provisions for bad and doubtful debts
- wirtschaft banking industry, banking business, banks
- wünsche borrowing requirements, loans applied for
- würdigkeit credit-worthiness
- würdigkeit prüfen to assess the credit-worthiness
- würdigkeitsprüfung credit assessment (investigation)
- zinsen loan interest, interest charged on the loan
- zins /-zinssatz lending rate
- zusage loan undertaking, commitment to extend a loan, lending (loan) commitment; IWF: stand-by arrangement
- zusageschreiben facility letter, loan undertaking
- zusagevolumen total loan commitments

Kreuzparität cross rate

krisenfeste Anlage crisis-proof investment

krummer Betrag odd amount

KT-Risiko conversion and transfer risk

Kulisse professional traders, unofficial market

Kulissenwerte securities traded in the unofficial market

kumulative stimmrechtslose Vorzugsaktien non-voting cumulative preferred stock

kündbar (a) callable; (b) subject to notice; (c) terminable, cancellable
- e Anleihe callable loan
- e Einlagen deposits subject to a withdrawal notice
- e Vereinbarung terminable (cancellable) agreement

Kunden

- abwerbung customer poaching
- akquisition soliciting customers, seeking out new business (new accounts)
- bediente Terminals customer-operated terminals
- beratung counselling of customers, advisory services for customers
- betreuung servicing and counselling of customers
- beurteilung customer rating
- beziehungen connections, contacts
  Ausbau der bestehenden - developing the portfolio of existing clients
- debitoren lendings to customers
- depot securities held for third-party account
- einlagen customer deposits
- ertrags-Ergebnis aus der Sicht der Bank: earnings from an account
- forderungen lendings to customers
- geschäfte im Effektenhandel: transactions for customer accounts
- kreditbank instalment credit company
- kreditgeschäft lendings to customers
- kreditnachfrage customer loan demand
- kreditvolumen total lendings to customers
- pflege cultivating existing accounts (connections)
- profil customer profile
- stamm customer portfolio, customer base

Kunden

- termingelder customer term
  (time) deposits

- verbindlichkeiten customer
  deposits

- verhalten customer behaviour

- wechsel trade bill

kündigen to give notice; to
call in; to cancel, to terminate

  eine Anleihe - to call in a
  loan, to give notice of redemption

  einen Kredit - to call in a loan

  zur sofortigen Rückzahlung - to
  call in for immediate repayment

  den Vertrag unter Beachtung einer
  sechsmonatigen Kündigungsfrist
  - to terminate (to cancel)
  the agreement on a six months'
  notice

Kündigung notice; giving notice;
Anleihe/Kredit:call,calling in
Spareinlagen: giving notice
of withdrawal; Vertrag: termination, cancellation

  die vollständige oder teilweise -
  der Emission calling in the
  issue in part or in its entirety

  nur nach vorheriger - rückzahlbar
  repayable only after the specified period of notice has been
  given

Kündigungs

- aufgeld call premium

- bestimmung call provision,
  call feature

- freijahre call deferment
  period

Kündigungsfrist notice period,
period of notice; bei Spareinlagen: withdrawal notice

  Tilgungen sind unter Beachtung
  einer sechsmonatigen - möglich
  redemptions are permitted on
  a six months' notice

Spareinlagen mit einjähriger -
savings deposits subject to a
twelve months' withdrawal notice

Kündigungs

- gelder notice deposits, deposits
  at notice

- geldkonten notice deposit
  accounts

- grundschuld / -hypothek land
  charge/mortgage subject to a
  calling notice

- kontrolle bei Anleihen: loan
  redemption control

- kurs call price

- möglichkeit /-option call
  facility, call privilege (option)

- recht Anleihe/Kredit: call
  right (privilege)

- sperrfrist Spareinlagen:period
  during which no withdrawal notice
  can be given

- termin Anleihe: call date; Spareinlagen: date on which notice of
  withdrawal must be given

Kupon coupon

- ausgang   coupon payments made

- bogen   coupon sheet

- eingang   coupon payments received

- einlösung   collection (encashment) of coupons

- fälligkeit   coupon date

- inhaber   coupon holder

- kasse   coupon paying agency

- steuer   coupon tax

- termin   coupon date, coupon
  payment date

Kurs Wertpapiere: price, quotation; Devisen: exchange rate,
rate

- abschlag price markdown, quotation ex; Disagio: discount

- abschwächung am Aktienmarkt
  easing (sagging) of prices in
  the equity market

Kurs
- absicherung →Kurssicherung
- abstriche   price markdowns
- abwärtsbewegung   downward trend (drift) in prices
- angabe   price indication, quotation
- anpassung   price adjustment; rate adjustment

Kursanstieg   price increase (rise, run-up), advance in prices
- des Dollar gegenüber dem Yen   dollar rise against the yen
- auf breiter Front   buoyancy of prices across the board, broad equity advance
- durch Übernahmegerüchte   bid-inspired rise

  starker - bei Aktien   upsurge in equities, sharp rise in share (stock) prices

Kurs
- anzeigetafel   quotations board
- aufschwung am Rentenmarkt   upturn in bond prices
- ausschläge bei Aktienwerten   erratic price swings (fluctuations) in equities
- aussetzung   suspension of a quotation
- befestigung   strengthening (stiffening) of prices, price advance
- befestigung der DM gegenüber den meisten anderen Währungen   firming up of the D-mark against most other major currencies
- befestigung bei lebhaften Umsätzen   advance in active trading
- bewegungen   price movements

  keine nennenswerten Kursbewegungen bei Aktienwerten   featureless trading in equities

  geringe Kursbewegungen bei den Hauptwährungen   the major currencies moved within a fairly narrow range
- bildung   price making, price determination
- bildungsfaktoren   price determinants
- blatt   quotations list, stock exchange list
- chancen   stock appreciation potential, upward price potential
- druck im Bankenbereich   pressure on bank stocks
- druck auf das Pfund   pressure coming to bear on the pound
- einbruch bei Aktienwerten   downslide in equity prices, sharp setback in stock prices
- einbußen   Devisen: loss on exchange; Wertpapiere: price losses
- entwicklung an den Wertpapiermärkten   price trends in the securities markets, stock (bond) market trend
- erholung am Aktienmarkt   stock price recovery, rally in equities
- erholung der Mark gegenüber dem Dollar   recovery (improvement) of the D-mark against the dollar
- explosion   sharp upsurge in stock prices, rocketing (zooming) equity prices
- festsetzung bei Wertpapieren: price making, price determination, establishment of prices

  des amtlichen Wechselkurses: fixing
- findung im Freiverkehr   price making in the unlisted market
- freigabe des Wechselkurses   floating of the exchange rate
- garantie   Devisen: forward exchange guarantee (cover, protection)

137

kursgesichert   rate-hedged, covered forward

- e Dollars   dollars hedged forward, dollars covered forward
- e Währungsanleihe   rate-hedged currency loan

Kurs

- gestrichen   no dealings, no quotation, non-quoted
- gewinn   Wertpapiere: price gain; Devisen: exchange profit, gain on exchange
- gewinnchancen   appreciation potential, price potential
- Gewinn-Verhältnis   price earnings ratio, P/E ratio
- höhe   price level, rate level
- index   share (stock) price index, market average
- korrektur nach oben (unten)   upward (downward) price correction
- limit   price limit
- makler   official broker
- manipulation   rigging a price (rate), market rigging
- niveau   price level, rate level
- notiz   quote, quotation
- pflege   price support, price-supporting purchases, price-regulating intervention
- pflege für eine Emission   stabilising the price of an issue by buying and selling in the open market
- pflegemittel   funds for price-supporting purchases
- regulierung   price intervention (support)
- regulierungskonsortium   price support syndicate
- risiko   price risk; exchange risk
- risiko nach unten   downside risk

- rückgang am Aktienmarkt   fall (drop, decline) in equity prices, price slippage
- rückgang des Dollar gegenüber der DM   dollar fall against the D-mark
- rückgänge auf breiter Front   fall in prices across the board
- rückgänge bei geringen Umsätzen   prices turning lower in thin trading
- rücknahmen zu Beginn der Börsensitzung   opening markdowns
- rückschlag am Rentenmarkt   setback in bond prices
- rutsch am Aktienmarkt   slide in equity prices
- schnitt   price fraud
- schwäche des Pfundes   weakness of the pound
- schwankungen   price swings (fluctuations); rate fluctuations; ups and downs of the market

kurssichernd

- e Abschlüsse   rate-hedging deals
- e Interventionen   Devisen: rate-supporting interventions

Kurssicherung   Devisen: rate-hedging, forward exchange guarantee (protection); Wertpapiere: hedge against price risks

Kurssicherungs

- geschäft   rate-hedging transaction
- gewinn   gain on forward exchange
- kosten   hedging cost, forward exchange guarantee costs
- möglichkeiten   hedging options
- programm   rate-hedging scheme
- strategie   hedging strategy
- technik   hedging techniques
- verhalten   hedging policy, exposure management
- verlust   loss on forward exchange

Kurs
- spanne   price range; trading range
- spekulation   speculation on the stock exchange, market jobbery; currency speculation
- spielraum nach oben   Aktien: stock appreciation potential, upside price potential; Wechselkurs: rate appreciation potential
- sprünge am Aktienmarkt   jumps in equity prices
- stabilisierung   price (rate) stabilisation, steadying of the market
- steigerung am Aktienmarkt   increase (advance) in prices, firming up of prices
- sturz am Rentenmarkt   heavy drop (nosedive) of prices
- stützung   price support, price-supporting purchases
- stützung der DM   intervening in support of the D-mark
- tafel   quotations board
- tendenz   trend in stock (bond) prices, stock (bond) market trend
- über dem Nennwert   premium price (rate), price above par
- umschwung   rebound (turnaround) in prices
- unter dem Nennwert   discount price, price below par
- veränderungen   price swings (changes); rate changes
- verfall am Rentenmarkt   collapse (heavy fall) in bond prices
- verlust   Devisen: exchange loss; Wertpapiere: price loss
- vor Aussetzung der Notierung   pre-suspension price
- wert   market value, value quoted
- wertberichtigungen von Wertpapierbeständen   write-downs of the securities portfolio
- wert-Milliardär   corporation the shares of which have reached a market value of more than DM 1 billion
- zettel   list of quotations, quotations (stock exchange) list
- ziel   upside price objective, upside target

kurz
- e Laufzeit   short life, short maturity
- e Zinsbindung   fixed interest rate for a short period, locking in the interest rate for a short term

  im - en Bereich   at the short end of the market

kurzfristig
- e Ausleihungen   short-term lendings
- e Finanzierungsmittel   short-term finance
- er Fremdwährungskredit   short-term currency credit
- es Geschäft   short-term lendings
- e Kapitalanlage   short-dated investment, investing for the short term
- er Kredit   short-term loan (credit), short loan
- e Kreditaufnahme   short-term borrowing
- er Kreditbedarf   short-term borrowing requirements
- es Kundengeschäft   short-term lendings to customers
- er Schuldschein   short note
- e Titel   shorts, short-dated securities
- aufgenommene Gelder   short-term borrowings
- aufnehmen   (a) to raise at short notice; (b) to borrow for the short term
- fällige Teile der langfristigen Verbindlichkeiten   current

139

portion of long-term debt
- zwischenfinanzieren to raise a short-term bridge-over loan

<u>kurzlaufende Bankschuldverschreibungen</u> short-term bank debentures

<u>Kurzläufer</u> shorts, short-dated securities

<u>Kurzläufer-Rendite</u> yield on shorts

<u>KWG</u> German Banking Act

<u>KWG-Novelle</u> amendment of the German Banking Act

L

Ladenkassen-Terminal point-of-sales terminal, POS terminal

Lagerhalter-Konnossement custody bill of lading

Lagerort / Lagerstelle bei Wertpapieren: place of custody (of deposit), depositary

Länderengagement country exposure, country commitment

Länderkredit country debt, sovereign loan

Umschuldung von -en country debt rescheduling

Länderobligo country exposure

Länderrisiko country risk

Bewertung des -s country risk assessment

Landesbank Central Savings Bank (acting as clearing house and liquidity manager to the savings banks; jointly owned by a Federal State and the savings bank associations in that state)

Landeswährung national currency

Landeszentralbank Regional Bundesbank Office

lang im langen Bereich at the long end of the market

langfristig long-term, long-dated

- e Ausleihungen long-term lendings

- e Emission long-dated issue

- e Finanzierungsmittel long-term finance

- es Geschäft long-term lendings

- er Kredit long-term loan, long credit

- es Kreditportefeuille long-term loan book, long-term loan portfolio

- e Kundenforderungen long-term lendings to customers

- e Verbindlichkeiten long-term debts, non-current liabilities

- er Wechsel long-dated bill, long bill

- aufgenommene Gelder long-term borrowings

- belegt das Kreditvolumen war zu 60 % langfristig belegt long-term lendings accounted for 60 p.c. of the loan portfolio

- investieren to invest for the long term

Langfristzins long-term interest rate, interest rate for long-term lendings

langlaufende Terminkonten long-term time deposits

Langläufer longs, long-dated stocks, long maturities

Langläufer-Rendite yield on longs, long-term bond yield

Lasten Grundstückslasten:charges (encumbrances) on real property

zu - Ihres Kontos einlösen to pay (to honour) to the debit of your account

die Eintragungsgebühren gehen zu - des Kreditnehmers the registration fees will be debited to the borrower's account

lastenfrei unencumbered, clear of encumbrances, unmortgaged

Lastschrift (a) debit, debit entry; (b) debit advice, debit voucher; (c) direct debit

141

Lastschrift
- bearbeitung   processing direct debits
- einlösung   honouring direct debits
- einreichung   presenting a direct debit for payment
- inkasso   collection of a direct debit
- retoure   direct debit returned unpaid, dishonoured direct debit
- rückgabe   returning a direct debit unpaid, dishonouring a direct debit
- valutierung   fixing the value dates of direct debits
- verfahren / - verkehr   direct debiting system (Br), pre-authorised payments system (US)
- vordruck   direct debit form

laufend
- e Emission   tap issue
- e Erträge aus festverzinslichen Wertpapieren   current income from fixed-interest securities
- es Konto   current account, chequing account (Br), checking account (US)
- er Kupon   current coupon
- e Zinsen   (a) interest accrued; (b) interest accruing

Laufzeit   term, life, maturity, duration

Anleihen mit zehnjähriger -   ten-year bonds

eine variabel verzinsliche Anleihe mit vierjähriger -   a four-year floater

Einlagen mit fester -   fixed-term deposits

die Emission hat eine - von acht Jahren   the issue has an eight-year maturity (life)

die - des Kredites ist zunächst bis ... begrenzt   the initial term of the credit expires on ...

Laufzeiten
- bereich   life range
- gliederung   maturity breakdown
- staffelung   staggering of maturities
- struktur   maturity pattern
- struktur beim Erstabsatz   maturity pattern of new offerings
- transformation   maturity transformation

laufzeitkongruent   (at)matching maturities
- refinanziertes Kreditgeschäft   lendings funded at matching maturities
- e Deckung der Aktiv- und Passivpositionen   matching maturities of lendings and deposits

Laufzeit
- kongruenz   matching (of) maturities
- verkürzung   shortening the maturity, maturity reduction
- verlängerung   extending the maturity

lauten   auf DM lautend   denominated (issued) in D-mark

auf den Inhaber lautend   made out to bearer

Leasing
- Geber   lessor
- Gesellschaft   leasing company
- Nehmer   lessee

lebhaft
- gehandelte Aktien   equities (shares) actively traded, active (high-volume) stocks
- e Umsätze in Bankaktien   brisk (active) trading in banks
 bei -en Umsätzen anziehen   to advance (to move ahead) in active trading

leere Stücke   stripped securities (bonds), securities ex subscription rights or ex warrants

Leerverkauf   short sale (selling)
Leerverkäufe vornehmen to sell short

Leerverkäufer   short seller

leicht
- abgeschwächt slightly lower
- anziehen to edge higher
- nachgeben to turn slightly lower, to turn (to drift) a shade easier
- realisierbare Vermögenswerte quick assets, assets easily convertible into cash
- e Kurserholung bei Aktien slight rally in equities
- e Papiere low-priced securities

leichter
 auf breiter Front - lower across the board
 geringfügig - slightly (marginally) lower
- nach anfänglichen Kursgewinnen easier after a firm start, lower after early gains
- nach Glattstellungen durch den Berufshandel lower on professional liquidation
- eröffnen to open lower, lower at the start of trading
- schließen to close lower, to close on retreating prices
- tendieren to ease, to slither, to turn lower, to lose ground

Leihdevisen short-term currency borrowings by banks

Leihgeld funds borrowed in the money market

Leihgeldlinie short-term credit line

Leihkapital borrowings

Leiste renewal coupon

leisten to perform, to pay; to provide, to furnish, to put up
 eine Anzahlung - to pay down a deposit, to make a downpayment
 eine Bürgschaft (Sicherheit) - to furnish a guarantee, to put up security
 Rembours - to provide reimbursement
 Zahlung - to make (to effect) payment

Leistungsschein renewal coupon

Leistung
 Ergebnis: performance, achievement, results
 Dienstleistung: service, facility
 Gegenleistung: consideration
 Lieferung bzw. Zahlung: delivery and/or payment
 Wertschöpfung: output

 die für den Kredit anfallenden -en interest and principal payments to be made on the loan
- en im Privatkundenbereich (a) performance in retail banking; (b) services offered in the retail banking sector
- en für die Risikovorsorge bad debt provisioning
- en einer Versicherung (a) insurance benefits; (b) claims paid

Leistungs
- angebot einer Bank: range of services (facilities) offered; spectrum of services
- aufgabe im Rahmen des Zins- und Tilgungsdienstes: statement of interest and principal payments
- aval performance guarantee
- bewertung performance appraisal
- bilanz (a) current account; (b) Erfolgsrechnung: income account (statement)

143

Leistungs
- bilanzdefizit   current account deficit
- bilanzüberschuß   current acount surplus
- garantie   performance bond
- kontrolle   performance control
- rate   bei Krediten: (monthly, quarterly, etc.) interest and principal payments
- schein   renewal coupon
- schuldverschreibungen depositary receipts; bearer certificates representing foreign stocks
- termin   date of payment
- verpflichtung   (a) payment undertaking; (b) undertaking to deliver

Leitkurs   EWS: central rate

Leitwährung   key currency

Leitzinsen   key lending rates
Senkung der - lowering of (cut in) the key lending rates

lenken   in den Kapitalmarkt - to channel into the capital market

LIBOR-Aufschlag   spread over Libor (London Interbank Offered Rate)

Lieferansprüche   delivery claims, deliveries receivable
- aus Wertpapierkäufen   delivery claims under securities purchased

Lieferantenkredit   supplier credit

Lieferantenwechsel   supplier bill

lieferbare Aktien   good delivery stock

Lieferbarkeitsbescheinigung
Wertpapiere: good delivery certificate

Liefergarantie   delivery (performance) guarantee

liefergebundener Finanzkredit
finance tied to a specific delivery

Lieferung   delivery

Lieferungs
- anspruch   right (claim) to a delivery
- sperre   blocking period (relating to securities subscribed)
- verkehr   delivery operations
- verzug   default

Lieferverpflichtung   delivery commitment
- en aus Wertpapierverkäufen   deliveries to be made under securities sold

liegen
Neuaufträge lagen bei knapp DM 14Mrd   new orders were close to DM 14billion
das Neuemissionsvolumen wird bei ungefähr DM 20 Mio - the volume of new issues will be in the range (in the region) of DM 20m

Limitauftrag / limitierter Auftrag
limit order, buying and/or selling order at limit

Limitkurs   limit price

linear
- e Abschreibung   depreciation on a straight-line basis
- e Zinsberechnungsmethode   straight-line interest computation

Linie   credit line

Linien
- absicherung   providing (putting up) security for a credit line
- absprache   credit line agreed upon, credit line agreement

- aufstockung increase in a credit line
- streichung line cancellation
- verlängerung line renewal; extending the maturity of a credit line

Linksunterzeichner signatory to the left

Liquidation einer Gesellschaft: winding-up (dissolution) of a company; eines Wertpapiergeschäftes: settlement of a deal

Liquidations
- bilanz statement of affairs
- kurs settlement price
- vergleich scheme of composition
- verkauf winding-up sale
- wert break-up value

liquide Anlagen investments (or lendings) which can easily be turned into cash

liquide Mittel liquid funds
- erster Ordnung cash and central bank balances
- zweiter Ordnung bills eligible for rediscount plus securities eligible as collateral for Bundesbank borrowings

liquide Sicherheiten liquid security (e.g. savings deposits, securities accounts)

liquidierbar / liquidisierbar convertible into cash

kurzfristig -e Aktiva assets which can easily be turned into cash

Liquidierbarkeit possibility to turn assets into ready cash

liquidieren (a) to turn (to convert) into cash, to realise; (b) to wind up, to dissolve; (c) to sell off, to square the books

Liquidierungen des Berufshandels book squaring by professional traders

Liquidität liquidity, liquid funds
- des Bankenapparates liquidity in (of) the banking system
- der Unternehmen corporate liquidity

Liquidität I (ersten Grades)
Banken: ratio of cash and central bank balances to short-term deposits

Industrieunternehmen: ratio of liquid assets to current liabilities

Liquidität II (zweiten Grades)
Banken: ratio of cash, central bank balances, rediscountable bills, securities eligible as collateral for Bundesbank borrowings, and short-term lendings to banks to total deposits

Industrieunternehmen: ratio of liquid assets plus short-term receivables to current liabilities

Liquiditäts
- abfluß efflux (outflow) of liquidity
- abschöpfung skimming off liquidity, draining liquidity (e.g. from the banking system)
- abzüge liquidity drain
- angebot liquidity supply, supply of liquid funds
- anreicherung measures designed to increase liquidity
- anspannung strains on liquidity, tightness of liquidity, liquidity squeeze
- ausstattung liquidity position, availability of liquid resources
- ausweis liquidity return
- ausweitung liquidity expansion
- auswirkungen effects (repercussions) on liquidity

Liquiditäts
- bedarf   liquidity requirements
- bereitstellung   supply of liquidity
- beschaffer   provider of liquidity (of liquid funds)
- beschaffung   provision of liquidity, liquidity procurement
- beurteilung   liquidity assessment (rating)
- bodensatz   liquidity base
- defizit   shortfall of liquidity, liquidity shortage
- disposition   liquidity management
- engpaß   liquidity squeeze, tight liquidity position
- entzug   drain on liquidity
- erfordernisse   liquidity requirements
- freigabe /-freisetzung   release of liquidity
- garantie   debt service guarantee (issued by a parent company to assist a subsidiary in raising funds)
- grad   liquidity ratio
- grundsätze   liquidity directives (laid down by the Banking Supervisory Authority to safeguard bank liquidity)
- hilfe   liquidity support, liquidity aid, measures designed to increase liquidity
- hilfe im Wege eines Offenmarktgeschäftes offerieren   to provide liquidity by way of open-market transactions
- kennzahlen   liquid asset ratios
- koeffizient   liquidity ratio
- kontingent   liquidity quota
- kosten   cost of liquidity
- lage   liquidity position (situation)
- neigung der Anleger   investors' preference for liquid funds
- papiere   liquidity instruments
- planung   liquidity planning
- politik   liquidity policy (management)
- relationen   liquidity ratios
- reservehaltung   liquidity reserve management
- reserven   liquid reserve assets
- richtsätze ⟶ Liquiditätsgrundsätze
- rückhalt   liquidity back-ups (support)
- schöpfung   liquidity creation
- schraube   liquidity screw
- schwemme   surge (welter) of liquidity
- sicherung   measures designed to safeguard liquidity
- spanne   liquidity margin
- spritze   injection of fresh funds, infusion of liquidity
- steuerung   liquidity control, liquidity management
- stützen   liquidity back-ups
- überhang   surplus liquidity
- umschichtung   liquidity switching, shifting of liquid assets
- verknappung   liquidity squeeze
- verlust   loss of liquidity
- vorsorge   liquidity provision
- vorsorge betreiben   to provide for adequate liquidity
- zufuhr   supply of fresh liquid funds, inflow of liquidity
- zusage   liquidity undertaking

Lockerung   easing, relaxation
- der Kreditbremsen /der kreditpolitischen Zügel   loosening of the credit reins, easing of the credit squeeze

Lohnkosteninflation   wage-push inflation

Lohnpfändung   attachment of wages

Lohn- und Gehaltskonto   payroll account

Lokalmarkt   local stocks, market in local securities

Loko
- geschäfte   spot dealings (in commodities)
- markt   spot market
- preis   spot rate (price)

Lombard
- ausnutzung   drawing on Lombard facilities
- effekten   securities serving as collateral for a loan, pledged securities
- fähige Wertpapiere   securities eligible as collateral for borrowings from Bundesbank
- fenster   special Lombard facility   in etwa vergleichbar mit: discount window (Br), Fed window (US)
- forderungen   Lombard lendings

lombardieren   to lend against securities (or commodities)

Lombardierung   lending (advancing money) against securities or commodities

Lombard
- inanspruchnahme   Lombard borrowing, drawing on Lombard facilities
- kredit   loan (advance) against securities or commodities
  Darlehen der Bundesbank an ein Kreditinstitut: Lombard facility (loan)
  Bedarfsspitzen über den Lombardkredit ausgleichen   to draw on the Lombard facility to meet peak borrowing requirements
- kreditgeschäft   lending against securities or commodities
- satz   Lombard rate, rate for advances against securities
- schulden   Lombard debt
- spielraum   scope (leeway) for drawing on Lombard facilities, Lombard leeway
- verbilligung   lowering of the Lombard rate
- verschuldung   total borrowings against securities or commodities
- verzeichnis   list of securities eligible as collateral for borrowings from Bundesbank

Londoner Interbanken-Angebotssatz   Libor rate

Loro-Effekten   loro securities, securities held by one bank for account of another bank

Loro-Valuta-Konto   loro currency account

löschen   to cancel, to delete

eine Grundschuld -   to release a real estate lien (land charge)

eine Hypothek -   to enter a satisfaction of mortgage, to discharge a mortgage, to release a mortgage

ein Konto -   to close out an account

eine Vollmacht -   to revoke (to cancel) a power of attorney

Löschung   cancellation; revocation
- einer Hypothek   satisfaction of mortgage, discharge of mortgage, mortgage release
- aller bei Ihnen geführten Konten   closing out all accounts maintained with you

Löschungs
- anspruch   right to discharge (to release) of mortgage
- anzeige   notice of satisfaction, mortgage release notice

147

Löschungs

- auftrag Hypothek: instructions to enter a satisfaction of mortgage; mortgage release instructions
  Konto: instructions to close out an account

- bewilligung memorandum of satisfaction, mortgage release authority

- fähige Quittung certificate issued by the creditor to the effect that a mortgage has been wholly satisfied

- vermerk entry of satisfaction

Luftfahrtwerte aviation stocks, aircrafts

lustloser Aktienmarkt dull (listless) equity market

lustlose Stimmung dull (flat) sentiment

M

MABILA automated balance sheet analysis

Majoritätskäufe Börse: buying designed to acquire or to increase a majority shareholding

Makler broker
- gebühr brokerage
- kammer brokers' association
- ordnung brokers' conduct code
- tafel marking board

Mandat bei Emissionen: das Mandat erhalten to be awarded the mandate

mangelhaftes Akkreditiv faulty letter of credit

mangels
- Annahme for lack of acceptance
- Deckung (Guthaben) zurückgeben to return for lack of funds
- Zahlung failing payment, in default of payment
- Zahlung protestieren to protest for non-payment

manipulieren Kurse: to rig the market

Mantel bei Wertpapieren: share (bond) certificate; einer Kapitalgesellschaft: corporate shell, shares of a company

Mantelzession blanket assignment of receivables

Marathonläufer securities carrying extremely long maturities

Marge margin, spread

Margen im Neugeschäft spreads for new lendings

Margen
- aufschlag spread mark-up
- geschäft margin transaction
- verengung narrowing of spreads
- verfall sharp drop in margins

Markt market

die auf den - kommende Neuemission the new issue coming onto the market

die Emission kam zu 102 % auf den - the issue entered the market at 102%

am - gut eingeführt sein to be well entrenched in the market

aus dem - nehmen to buy up, to repurchase securities offered

am - sein to intervene in the market, to tap the market

- für Kurzläufer short end of the market
- für Neuemissionen primary market
- für im Umlauf befindliche Papiere secondary market
- für Zentralbankgeld central bank funds market, federal funds market (US)

Markt
- abschwächung weakening of the market
- anspannung market strains (tightness)
- aussichten market prospects (outlook)
- bedingte Aufwertung revaluation brought about by the market development
- befestigung market consolidation, stabilisation of the market
- beherrschend controlling the market

149

Markt
- breite breadth of the market
- durchdringung market penetration
- einschätzung analysis of market prospects
- enge tightness of the market, market constraints, tight market conditions
- entwicklung market trend, development of the market
- erholung market recovery, market rally
- fähigkeit am Geldmarkt marketability (negotiability) in the money market
- finanzierung financing through borrowings in the market, raising of funds in the market
- flexibilität market resilience

marktgängig
- e Konditionen current terms, prevailing market rates
- er Satz fair market rate

marktgerecht
- e Ausstattung bond terms (bond features) in line with general market conditions
- e Konditionengestaltung market-oriented pricing, fixing the lending rates in accordance with the prevailing market rates

Markt
- geschehen market activity, activity (operations) in the market
- instrumentarium market instruments
- intervention market intervention, intervention in the market
- kennziffern market indices
- klima tone (sentiment) of the market
- konditionen market terms, rates and terms ruling in the market
- konstellation market set-up (configuration)
- korrektur market correction
- kräfte market forces
- kreise market community, market operators
- lage state of the market, situation in the market
- mechanismus mechanics of the market
- mittel market funds
- notierung market quotation
- pflege stabilising a price by buying and selling in the market, market support
  zur Marktpflege reservieren to set aside for market support
- preis market price, current (ruling) price
- schwäche market softness (weakness)
- schwankungen market fluctuations (swings), ups and downs in the market
- standort market position
- stützung market support
- technische Erholung nach überdurchschnittlichen Abgaben technical rally from oversold positions
- teilnehmer market operator, participant in the market
- trend market trend, development of (in) the market
  gegen den Markttrend anti--marketwise
- umschwung break in the market, turn of the market, rebound in prices
- usancen market customs, market practice
- verfassung state of the market, market sentiment
- wert market value (price)
- zins market (current) interest rate

maschinelle Bilanzanalyse automated balance sheet analysis

maschinelles Übertragungsverfahren cash pooling system

Maschinenbauwerte engineering stocks, engineerings

maschinenlesbar machine-readable

Massedarlehen loan extended after the opening of composition proceedings

Massengeschäft retail banking

maßgeschneidertes Finanzierungskonzept tailor-made financing blueprint

mäßige Umsätze Börse: moderate trading (turnover)

massive Abgaben Börse: heavy selling

Material securities, securities (stocks) on offer
- abgaben selling of securities
- aufnahmen buying (taking) up securities
- mangel shortage of offerings

materielle Kreditwürdigkeit loan repayment capacity, borrower's financial ability to repay the loan

maximale Laufzeit maximum maturity

Medio
- gelder funds repayable (loans due) at mid-month
- geschäft transaction for mid-month settlement
- liquidation mid-month settlement

Mehrerlös surplus proceeds

Mehrfacharbitrage compound arbitrage

Mehrfunktionsterminal multi-purpose terminal

Mehrheitsaktionär controlling shareholder

Mehrheitsbesitz /-beteiligung majority holding (stake)

Mehrkosten bei Projektfinanzierungen: cost overruns

Mehrstimmrechtsaktie plural (multiple) voting share

Mehrwährungsklausel multi-currency clause

Meinungskäufe speculative buying

meistgehandelte Aktie volume leader

Melde
- pflicht duty to report (to notify)
- termin reporting date
- system reporting system
- vorschriften reporting requirements (provisions)

Meldungen zur Außenwirtschaftsverordnung reports to be filed in accordance with foreign trade regulations

Mengengeschäft retail banking, retail business

Mengentender volume-linked tender (relating to repurchase agreements)

Merkmale einer Anleihe: bond features

Metageschäft transaction on joint account (with profit and loss sharing)

Metakredit joint loan extension

Metisten parties to a joint transaction

Mietaval rent guarantee

151

mildern die Kreditrestriktionen - to alleviate the credit squeeze

Minder
- einnahmen shortfall in receipts
- heitsbeteiligung minority interest (holding)
- konditionen concessional rates, lending rates below market rates

Mindest
- bietkurs minimum bidding price
- bietsatz minimum bidding rate
- einlage minimum deposit
- einschußpflicht minimum margin requirements
- gewinnspanne bottom-line profit margin
- kapital minimum capital (equity)
- kapitalausstattung minimum capital resources
- kapitalerfordernisse minimum capital required, minimum equity level requirement, capital adequacy requirements
- kurs floor price
- laufzeit minimum term (life)
- marge über Libor minimum spread above Libor
- rendite minimum yield

Mindestreserve minimum reserve
- anforderungen minimum reserve requirements
- berechnung calculation of the minimum reserve requirement
- disposition minimum reserve management
- erhöhung increase in the minimum reserve ratios

mindestreservefrei
- e Beschaffung von Geldern reserve-exempt procurement of funds
- e Refinanzierung reserve-exempt funding

Mindestreserve
- freiheit exemption from minimum reserves, reserve exemption
- guthaben minimum reserve balances
- haltung maintenance of (maintaining) minimum reserves
- kosten minimum reserve cost

mindestreservepflichtig
- e Einlagen reserve-carrying deposits
- es Kreditinstitut financial institution subject to reserve requirements

Mindestreserve
- politik minimum reserve policy
- sätze minimum reserve ratios
- senkung lowering of (cut in) in the minimum reserve ratios
- soll minimum reserve requirements
- tagesüberschuß daily minimum reserve surplus
- vorsorge provision of minimum reserves

Mindestschluß Börse: minimum lot

Minus mit - ankündigen to mark down, to trade sharply lower, to downgrade
- ankündigung sharp markdown
- korrektur downward adjustment, markdown
- position (a) oversold position; (b) shortage of cover
- stückzinsen accrued interest deducted
- zeichen markdown

Mischfinanzierung joint financing (e.g. by Federal and Land governments); hybrid financing

Mitbürgschaft co-guarantee

Miteigentum co-ownership

- am Sammelbestand co-ownership in (of) collective holdings, co-ownership share

mitfinanzieren to co-finance

Mitfinanzierung co-financing

mitführen Emission: to co-manage

Mitführung co-management

Mitgliedsquote IWF: members' quota subscription

Mithaftung joint liability

Mitkonsorte co-underwriter

Mitnahme von Kursgewinnen: profit-taking

mitnehmen Kursgewinne: to cash in on profits, to take profits

Mitschuldner co-debtor, joint debtor

Mittel (a) funds, financial resources (means); (b) mean, average

- aus der Kapitalerhöhung funds stemming from the capital increase; funds available as a result of the capital increase

Mittel
- abflüsse outflow of funds
- abschöpfung draining (skimming off) liquidity
- aufkommen funds accrued; Investmentfonds: fund share sales
- aufnahme borrowing, raising of funds
- aufnahme am Kapitalmarkt borrowing in the capital market
- ausstattung financial (equity) resources available, availability of funds

Mittelbeschaffung procurement of funds, raising (generating) funds

Kosten der - cost of funds
- im Ausland borrowings abroad; funds (loans) raised abroad

mittelfristig
- e Anlage medium-term investment, investing for the medium term
- e Anleihen medium-dated bonds
- er Kredit term loan, intermediate credit, medium-term credit

Mittelkurs Devisen: mean rate of exchange, middle rate, median bid and ask quotation

Mittelpunkt

Fahrzeugwerte standen im - des Interesses motors held the limelight throughout the session

Nebenwerte standen wieder im - des Interesses secondary counters returned to the centre of the stage

Mittel
- rückfluß bei Investmentfonds: fund share redemptions, units (shares) repurchased
- rückfluß aus dem Kreditportefeuille repayments on lendings
- standskredit small business loan (lending)
- standskreditprogramm lending scheme for medium-sized business
- umlenkung shifting of funds
- valuta mean value date
- zufluß inflow of funds; bei Investmentfonds: fund share sales, shares(units) sold
- zuweisung appropriation (allocation) of funds

mittlerer Verfalltag mean value date

mitziehen Bankwerte wurden mitgezogen banks rose (dropped) in sympathy

Mobilisierung des in Effekten angelegten Kapitals mobilisation of capital invested in stocks

Mobilisierungspapiere mobilisation instruments (treasury bills and notes sold by Bundesbank to banks)

Modalitäten einer Anleihe: loan terms, bond features

Modernisierungsdarlehen home improvement loan

Möglichkeit der vorzeitigen Verfügung early withdrawal facility

monatlich
- e Belastung monthly interest and redemption payments
- e Erfolgsrechnung monthly income account (statement)

Monats
- abschluß Abrechnung: monthly settlement
- ausweis monthly return
- bilanz monthly statement of condition
- dollar one-month dollar
- gattung month-linked stock (bond) category
- geld one-month money (funds), funds borrowed for one month
- leistung monthly interest and redemption payments

Montanwerte steels ; mining and steel shares (stocks)

Moratorium standstill agreement

Motorenwerte motors

Multifunktions-Kreditkarte all-purpose credit card

multiple
- Giralgeldschöpfung multiple bank deposit creation
- r Wechselkurs multiple exchange rate

mündelsichere Wertpapiere gilt-edged securities (Br), trustee stock (US)

Mündelsicherheit eligibility as trustee stock

mündlich adj.: verbal, oral; adv. verbally, by word of mouth

mündliche Vereinbarung verbal agreement

Börse: Abschlüsse erfolgen mündlich und werden schriftlich bestätigt deals are made by word of mouth and confirmed in writing

N

Nachbelastung der Zinsen   subsequent debit of interest

Nachbörse   after-hours market

nachbörslich

- fest   strong in after-hours trading
- es Interesse für Bankaktien   after-hours support for bank stocks
- er Kurs   price after hours

Nachdeckungspflicht   duty to provide additional cover (to furnish additional guarantees)

Nachemission   follow-up issue

nachfällige Posten   post-maturity debit or credit entries

Nachfolge-Kreditnehmer   successor borrower

Nachforderung   calling in additional funds

Nachfrage   demand

- nach Firmenkundenkrediten   corporate loan demand
- nach Wohnungsbaukrediten   demand for housing loans

die neue Emission stieß auf geringe -   the new issue found little support

die - nach Bankwerten war gering   interest in banks was at a low ebb

nachfragebedingte Inflation   demand-induced inflation

nachgeben   to turn easier, to drift lower, to slip

Bankaktien gaben bei geringen Umsätzen nach   banks turned lower in thin trading

Fahrzeugwerte gaben bei fehlenden Anschlußaufträgen nach   motors drifted easier on lack of follow-through support

gegen Schluß der Börsensitzung -   to skid late in the session

... (Aktien) gaben um 2 auf 110DM nach   ... fell (slipped) 2 to 110DM

nachgeordnetes Darlehen   subordinated loan

nachgestellt   ⟶ nachrangig

nachgesuchte Kredite   loans applied for

Nachindossament   post-maturity endorsement

nachkommen   Verpflichtungen -   to meet obligations

Nachlaßguthaben   balance in the estate account

Nachlaßkonto   estate account

Nachmann   subsequent endorser

nach oben (unten) engagiert   speculation on a rise (fall)

nachordnen   to subordinate

nachrangig   ranking after, secondary, junior in right of payment

- er Gläubiger   secondary creditor
- e Grundschuld   subordinated land charge
- e Hypothek   secondary (junior, subordinated) mortgage
- es Hypothekendarlehen   junior mortgage loan

155

Nachrangvereinbarung   subordination agreement

Nachschußpflicht   liability to assessments

nachschußpflichtig
- e Aktien   assessable stock
- er Gesellschafter   contributory partner

Nachschußverbindlichkeiten   assessments payable

Nachschußzahlungen auf Aktien   stock assessments

Nach-Sicht
- Frist   grace period
- Tratte   usance draft
- Wechsel   after-sight bill

nachstellen   to subordinate

nachstellig ⟶ nachrangig

Nachstellung   subordination

Nachsteuer-Gewinn   profit after taxes, post-tax profits

nach unten drücken   to drive lower, to push (to force) down

Nachvaluten   back values

Nachweis   proof, evidence
- für die Nichteinlösung   proof of dishonour
- für die Hinterlegung bei einer Bank   evidence of deposit with a bank

Nachzugsaktien   deferred shares

Namens
- aktie   registered share (stock)
- kassenobligationen   registered medium-term notes
- pfandbrief   registered mortgage bond
- schuldverschreibung   registered debenture

Neben
- leistungen einer Bank: related banking services
- markt Börse: side-line market, market in second-line stocks
- papier   coupon sheet
- platz   secondary bank place
- werte   second-line stocks, second-tier stocks, secondary stocks (issues)
- zahlstelle   sub-paying agent

negativer Zinssaldo   net interest loss

Negativklausel   negative pledge clause

Negativzins   negative interest

negoziieren   to negotiate
ohne Regreß auf den Aussteller - to negotiate without recourse to drawer

negoziierende Bank   negotiating banker

Negoziierungs
- akkreditiv   authority to negotiate
- erlös   negotiation proceeds
- kredit   negotiation credit
- linie   negotiation line (indicates the bank's willingness to purchase documentary drafts)
- provision   negotiating commission
- verpflichtung   undertaking to negotiate

nehmen Tagesgeld: to buy, to borrow
aus dem Markt - to take up, to buy up, to absorb, to drain from the market

Nehmer   borrower
- im kurzfristigen Bereich   borrower at the short end of the market

<u>Nehmer</u> am Geldmarkt: buyer (borrower) of funds

<u>Nehmerbank</u> buying (borrowing)bank

<u>Nennwert</u> face amount, nominal (face) value

über (unter, zum) - above (below, at) par

<u>nennwertlose Aktie</u> no-par stock

<u>Netto</u>
- abrechnung   net settlement
- absatz von Wertpapieren   net security sales (sales less redemptions and repurchases)
- aktivposition im Geldhandel:net sellers (lenders), net selling position
- anlagevermögen net fixed assets
- aufnahme von Wertpapieren: net take-up
- auslandsverschuldung   net external indebtedness
- ausleihungen   net lendings
- barausschüttung   net cash distribution
- bestand   net holdings, net position
- betriebsgewinn   net operating (trading) profit
- erlös   net proceeds, net avails
- ersparnisbildung der privaten Haushalte   net personal savings
- erträge aus dem Dienstleistungsgeschäft   net income from service transactions
- erträge aus Wertpapiergeschäften net security gains
- forderungsausfall bei Krediten: net loan charge-offs
- geldvermögen bei der Kapitalflußrechnung: net current position
- geschäft   net price transaction, transaction without deduction for commission and/or charges
- gewinn aus Devisentermingeschäften net gains on forward exchange contracts
- gewinn nach Steuern   net after-tax profits
- gläubigerposition im Geldhandel: net selling (lending) position, to be net sellers
- kapitalbildung   net capital formation
- kreditaufnahme am Kapitalmarkt net borrowings in the capital market
- kreditgewährungen   net lendings
- kurs   net price
- liquiditätszufluß   net liquidity inflow
- neugeschäft   net new advances
- passivposition im Geldhandel: net buyers, net borrowers, net borrowing position
- position (a) net position, net holdings; (b) net profit (loss)
- rendite   net yield, after-tax yield
- schuldnerstellung im Geldhandel: to be net buyers (borrowers), net buying (borrowing) position
- tilgung am Kapitalmarkt   net redemptions in the capital market
- umsatzerlöse   net sales
- vermögen je Stammaktie   net assets per ordinary share

<u>neu</u> auf neue Rechnung   relating to the new accounting period, for the new accounting period, for new account

<u>Neu</u>
- abschlüsse im Kreditgeschäft: new loans extended, new lendings
- abschlüsse sind mit fünfjähriger Bindungsfrist ausgestattet   new lendings carry fixed rates for five years

Neu
- absprache (a) re-arrangement; (b) fixing a new lending rate
- bestellung Hypothek: taking out a new mortgage
- bewertung revaluation, reassessment
- einschätzung der Kreditrisiken reassessment of the loan risks
- einstufung regrading, new rating
- emission new (fresh) issue Festsetzung der Kurse für Neuemissionen new issue pricing
- emissionsbereich, im - on the new issuing side
- emissionsmarkt new issue market, primary market
- emittierte Papiere newly issued securities
- engagements Börse: fresh orders (buying); im Kreditgeschäft: new lendings

Neufestsetzung resetting, reestablishment, renegotiation
- der Hypothekenzinsen alle fünf Jahre the mortgage rate will be renegotiated every five years
- der Kreditkonditionen gemäß den Geldmarktbedingungen resetting the loan terms in line with the general conditions in the money market

Neugeschäft new lendings, new loan accommodations
- im Hypothekenbereich new mortgage lendings, new mortgage commitment activity

  Rückgang des -s bei Krediten für Privatkunden decline in new credits extended to private customers

  Wachstum des -s growth in net new lendings

Neu
- kredit new loan, new advance, new facility, fresh funds
- kreditbedarf new borrowing requirements
- ordnung der Kapitalverhältnisse capital reconstruction (reorganisation)
- ordnung der Währungsparitäten realignment of exchange rates
- strukturierung des Kreditgeschäftes restructuring of the lending business, reorganisation of lending operations
- valutierungen new loan extensions
- verschuldung new borrowing
- verschuldung der Unternehmen new corporate borrowings
- zusagen new lendings (commitments), new loans extended
- zusagen an Festzinshypotheken new fixed-rate mortgage lendings

neutrale Leistungen einer Bank: non-banking services

NE-Werte non-ferrous metals stock

nicht
- abgeschriebene Agiobeträge unamortised premiums
- abgesprochene Überziehungen unauthorised overdrafts
- amtlicher Handel unofficial trading (dealings)
- ausgewiesene Gewinne undisclosed profits
- bankfähig unbankable
- beleihbar not qualifying as collateral
- börsenfähig non-marketable
- deckungspflichtige Titel securities not requiring cover
- dokumentäre Zahlungen clean payments

nicht

- eingefordertes Kapital uncalled capital
- eingelöste Kupons unclaimed coupons
- eingelöste Lastschriften dishonoured direct debits
- eingezahltes Kapital unpaid capital
- emissionsfähiges Unternehmen company not qualifying for security offerings
- gezeichnete Aktien unsubscribed shares, shares not subscribed
- gewandelte Schuldverschreibung bond not converted
- girosammelverwahrfähig not qualifying for collective safe-keeping
- in Anspruch genommener Kredit undrawn credit (loan)facilities
- in der Bilanz ausgewiesen unaccounted, not reported (stated) in the balance sheet
- kündbar non-callable, irredeemable
- lombardfähige Wertpapiere securities not qualifying as collateral (e.g. for borrowings from Bundesbank)
- nachschußpflichtig non-assessable
- notierte Aktie unlisted (unquoted) share
- notifiziertes Factoring undisclosed factoring
- realisierter Wertzuwachs unrealised capital appreciation
- rediskontfähiger Wechsel ineligible bill
- testierter Abschluß unaudited accounts
- übertragbares Akkreditiv non--assignable documentary credit
- vertretbare Wertpapiere non-fungible securities
- voll in Anspruch genommen not fully drawn
- vollständig gezeichnete Emission undersubscribed issue
- zugeschriebene Disagiobeträge unamortised discounts
- zweckgebundene Ausleihungen uncommitted lendings

Nicht

- abnahmeentschädigung bei einer Kreditbereitstellung: compensation for non-availment of a credit line
- ausführung von Zahlungsanweisungen non-execution of payment instructions
- banken non-financial corporations, non-banks, non-bank customers
- bankensektor non-banks, non-bank sector
- bezahltmeldung advice of non-payment, notice of dishonour
- einlösung des Wechsels non-payment of a bill, dishonouring a bill
- erfüllung der Akkreditivbedingungen non-compliance with the terms and conditions of the documentary credit
- firmengeschäft retail banking
- inanspruchnahme einer Kreditlinie: non-availment of a credit line
- leistung non-performance, non-feasance
- valutierung non-extension of a loan, refusal to extend a loan
- veranlagungsbescheinigung non--assessment certificate
- zahlungsrisiko risk of default

Niederlassung branch

Niederlassungskompetenz branch approval powers

159

Niederstwertprinzip   nach dem -
bewerteter Wertpapierbestand
securities portfolio valued at
the lower of cost or market

niedrig
- bewertete Aktie   low-priced
  share
- verzinst werden   to carry a low
  rate of interest
- e Anfangsbelastung   low initial
  debt service (starting with
  low interest and redemption
  payments)
  zum -eren Börsen- oder Marktwert
  ausweisen   to state at cost or
  market value whichever is lower
- er notieren   to trade lower,
  to mark down, to downgrade

Niedrigstkurs   bottom price (rate)
absoluter -   all-time low,
rock-bottom price

niedrigverzinslich
- er Kredit   low-interest loan
  (credit)
- e Kurzläufer   low-coupon shorts
- e Papiere   low-coupon securities

Niedrigzinspolitik   policy of
low interest rates, cheap-
-money policy

Niveau   dieses - konnte nicht
gehalten werden   this level
proved unsustainable

Noch / Nochgeschäft   call of more

Nominalkapital   nominal share
capital

Nominalverzinsung   nominal
interest return

Normalkonditionen   usual terms
and conditions

normiertes Kreditgeschäft
standardised lendings, standard lending schemes

Nostro
- effekten   nostro securities,
  securities owned by the bank
- guthaben   nostro balances,
  balances with other financial
  institutions, due from banks
- konto   nostro account
- verpflichtungen   nostro commitments, funds borrowed

Notadressat   referee in case
of need

Notanzeige   advice of dishonour

notarielle Urkunde   document given
by a notary public (solicitor)

Notenausgaberecht   note-issuing
privilege (power)

Notenbank
- ausweis   Central Bank return
- fähig   eligible for rediscount
  with the Central Bank
- guthaben   Central Bank balances
- kredit   Central Bank lending,
  Central Bank facility (loan)
- politik   Central Bank policy
- zinssätze   official interest
  rates, key interest rates

Notendeckung   reserves held to
cover a note issue

Notenumlauf   notes in circulation

notieren   to quote, to list
  Bankaktien notierten geringfügig
  schwächer   banks were a fraction
  easier
  Chemieaktien notierten weiterhin
  fest   chemicals remained firm
  ...(Aktien) notierten per Saldo
  minus 5DM .. settled 5DM cheaper
  on balance
  ... notierten plus 15DM   ... put
  on 15DM

notierte Wertpapiere   quoted (listed) securities

Notierung   quotation, listing

- en im kurzfristigen Bereich
  quotations at the short end

- en gaben auf breiter Front nach
  quotations went into a broad
  retreat

- en zogen an, vor allem bei Bankwerten quotations edged higher
  with the emphasis on banks

- im Freiverkehr USM quote (Br),
  over-the-counter quotation

- im Telefonverkehr off-board
  (unofficial) quotation

aus der - nehmen to suspend the
  quotation, to delist

Notierungstag   quotation day

notifiziertes Factoring   disclosed factoring

Notiz quote, quotation

notleidend in default, non-
-performing

- es Engagement →notleidender
  Kredit

- e Inkassi dishonoured collections

- er Kredit non-performing loan

- er Wechsel overdue bill, bill
  in suspense

Notlimit Wertpapiere: stop

N-Papiere discounted treasury
notes (not callable prior to
maturity)

Nummern

- buch   securities code ledger

- konto   numbered account

- skontrierung updating of
  security code numbers

- verzeichnis   list of securities
  deposited

nur zur Verrechnung 'and company'
'account payee only'

nutzen   eine Kreditlinie voll -
  to make full use of a credit
  line

Nutzenschwelle   break-even point

Nutzung einer Kreditlinie: availment of a credit line, drawing
on a credit line

O

<u>oben</u>

Ausleihungen von - nach unten lendings by a central banking organisation to its member banks

nach - berichtigte Schätzung upward-revised estimate

der nach - verfügbare Spielraum upside potential

nach - zeigender Trend upward trend

<u>oberer Interventionspunkt</u> upper intervention point

<u>Obergrenze</u> upper limit, ceiling

- für Ausleihungen lending ceiling

- für Postengebühren ceiling for entry fees

<u>Obligation</u> debenture, bond

<u>Obligationär</u> debenture holder, bondholder

<u>Obligo</u> liability, exposure, commitment

- aus angekauften Wechseln liability on bills purchased

- der deutschen Banken exposure (loan commitments) of the German banks

- aus unter unserer Haftung hinausgelegten Krediten liability on loans extended against guarantees furnished by us

wir befinden uns mit DM .. im - our exposure (liability) totals DM ..

<u>Obligo</u>

- begrenzung limitation of liability

- buch /-kartei commitment ledger

- kontrolle monitoring the liabilities (e.g. on bills)

- übernahme assumption of liability

<u>Oder-Konto</u> joint account with individual drawing powers

<u>offen</u> open

- es Depot standard custody account (the administration of the securities deposited is handled by the custodian, e.g. the bank)

- es Factoring notification factoring

- es Indossament blank endorsement

- er Investmentfonds open-end investment fund, mutual fund

- er Kredit open credit

- e Positionen (a) open commitments (contracts); (b) uncleared (unsettled) items

- e Rücklagen general reserves, surplus

- e Verschuldungsmöglichkeiten open-to-borrow arrangements

- e Zession disclosed assignment, assignment on a notification basis

am -en Markt kaufen to buy in the open market

<u>offenlegen</u> to disclose

<u>Offenlegung</u> disclosure

<u>Offenlegungs</u>

- pflicht duty to disclose

- richtlinien / - vorschriften disclosure requirements (provisions)

<u>Offenmarkt-Geschäfte</u> open-market transactions (operations)

<u>Offenmarkt-Käufe</u> buying in the open market, open-market purchases

Offenmarkt-Papiere (Titel)
open-market securities

öffentlich   public
- e Anleihen   public bonds, public sector securities
- es Baudarlehen   public housing loan
- e Begebung   public offering, public floatation
- e Bekanntmachung   gazetting, public advertisement
- geförderte Darlehen zur Existenzgründung   government--subsidised business start-up loans; business start-up scheme
- e Kredite   (a) lendings by public authorities; (b) public borrowings, loans raised by public authorities
- e Kreditprogramme   public (government) lending schemes
- e Plazierung   public placing, market floatation
- rechtliches Kreditinstitut   public financial institution
- rechtlicher Träger   public guarantor
- es Zeichnungsangebot   public offering (offer for sale), public issue by prospectus

Offerte   Kreditofferte: loan offer; Zeichnungsangebot: offer, offering

ohne
- Kosten   bei Wechseln: no protest
- Notiz   no quotation
- Rückgriff   bei Wechseln: no (without) recourse

Opposition   stop, stop order
 mit - belegte Wertpapiere   stopped securities

Oppositionsliste   list of securities invalidated or stopped

optimistisch Börsenkreise bleiben -   the stock exchange community remains bullish

Option   (a) im Optionsgeschäft: option; (b) bei Optionsanleihen: warrant

Options
- aktien   optioned shares (stocks)
- anleihe   bond with warrants; warrant issue
- ausübung   (a) exercising an option; (b) exercising a warrant
- börse   options exchange, options market
- erwerb   (a) buying an option, option purchase; (b) warrant purchase
- frist   (a) option period; (b) warrant exercise period
- geschäft   option contract, option bargain
- handel   (a) options trading; (b) trading in warrants
- inhaber   (a) option holder; (b) warrant holder
- käufer   (a) option buyer; (b) buyer of a warrant
- kontrakt   option deal
- papiere   (a) optioned securities; (b) securities with warrants
- prämie   option money
- preis   (a) option money; (b) warrant exercise price
- recht   (a) option right; (b) warrant
- schein   warrant
- scheininhaber   warrant holder
- schuldverschreibung → Optionsanleihe
- stelle   warrant agent
- verkäufer   option writer, writer (seller) of an option

ordentliches Betriebsergebnis
ordinary trading profit (loss)

ordentliche Hauptversammlung
ordinary general meeting

Order
- aufbereitung   order documentation
- eingang   order intake, incoming orders, intake of orders
- konnossement   order bill of lading
- mangel   Börse: shortage of buying orders
- papiere   instruments made out to order, registered securities
- scheck   cheque to order
- schuldverschreibung   bond payable to order
- volumen   Börse: total buying orders

ordnungsgemäße Dokumente   documents in accordance with the terms and conditions of the documentary credit

ordnungsgemäß zur Zahlung vorgelegt   duly presented for payment

Ordnungsmäßigkeit   die - des Akkreditivs feststellen   to note (to be satisfied) that the terms and conditions stipulated in the documentary credit have been complied with

Organ   body
- ertrag   income from affiliated companies
- gesellschaft   affiliated company, subsidiary
- kredite   loans extended by a corporation to its officers
- schaft   pooling of interests; profit and loss transfer agreement
- träger   parent company
- verlust   loss incurred by a subsidiary

orientieren

die Zinssätze - sich an den Geldmarktsätzen   interest rates take their lead from money market rates

kapitalmarktorientierte Anleiheausstattung   bond pricing orientated at (geared to) the prevailing capital market rates

Orientierung   orientation at, gearing to

zu Ihrer -   for your guidance

Ortsausschuß   im Freiverkehr: supervisory body for the unlisted securities market

Ortszahlungsverkehr   town payments

P

Paket   share block, block of shares
- angebot   block offer
- besitz   shareholding exceeding 25 p.c. of a company's capital
- handel   block trading, large-block transactions
- zuschlag   share block premium; premium paid on the market price of a share block

Panikverkäufe   panic (distress) selling

Papiere erster Adressen   securities issued by prime (first-rate) borrowers

Parallel
- anleihen   parallel loans (identical loans floated by the issuer in several countries)
- finanzierung   parallel financing
- markt   parallel market
- währung   parallel standard

Pari
- Bezugsrecht   par rights issue
- Emission   issue at par, par issue
- Kurs   par rate (price)

Parität   parity

Paritäten-Gitter (-Netz)   EWS: parity grid

Paritätsklausel   parity clause

parken   to invest (to deposit) temporarily, to park

Parkett   Börse: floor

Parkplatz   temporary investment, temporary home (deposit), outlet for funds
Gelder, die einen Parkplatz suchen   funds which are looking for a temporary home

partiarisches Darlehen   loan linked to an equity kicker (instead of interest the lender is given a share in the borrower's capital, profit or sales)

Passiva   liabilities; Bilanz: liabilities and shareholders' equity

passiv
- er Rechnungsabgrenzungsposten   deferred liability item
- e Scheckfähigkeit   capacity to have cheques drawn on oneself

Passiv
- devisenposition   foreign currency liabilities
- gelder   deposits
- geschäft der Banken   deposit banking, deposit operations, deposit-taking business

passivieren   to expense, to carry (to report) as liabilities, to state on the liabilities side

Passivierung   carrying (reporting) as liabilities

Passiv
- konditionen   deposit rates, interest rates paid on deposits
- kundschaft   depositors, savers
- management   liabilities management
- saldo   adverse (debit) balance, deficit
- seite   liabilities side

Passiv
- steuerung   liabilities management
- überhang   surplus of deposits; im Geldhandel: net borrowing (buying) position
- wechsel   bills payable
- zins   (a) deposit interest rate, interest paid on deposits (b) interest payable

Patronatserklärung   letter of comfort, letter of awareness

Patronin   guarantor

Pauschalbetrag   lump sum

Pauschaldeckung   blanket cover

Pauschalwertberichtigung   general charge for bad and doubtful debt provisions

Pension
 in - geben   to pledge (or to sell) under a repurchase agreement

 Wertpapiere in - nehmen   to lend against securities

Pensionsgeber   pledgor, borrower

Pensionsgeschäft   sale and repurchase agreement; in der Regel nur: repurchase agreement, repos (US)   (i.e. the borrower pledges or sells securities to the lender but simultaneously contracts to repurchase the same securities at a later date)

Pensionskasse   staff pension scheme, pension fund

Pensionsnehmer   pledgee, lender

Pensionswechsel   bill pledged (or sold) under a repurchase agreement

periodengerechte Rechnungslegung   accrual basis of accounting

Personal   staff, personnel
- bedarfsplanung   staff resourcing
- bestand   total staff, labour force
- beurteilung   staff (personnel) rating, merit rating, performance appraisal
- fluktuation   staff turnover
- intensiv   labour-intensive
- kosten   personnel expenditure, staff costs
- kredit   personal loan, personal drawing credit
- sicherheiten   personal securities
- stärke   staff level, labour force
- union   director and/or staff sharing
- wirtschaft   personnel management

Personendepotbuch   personal custody ledger

persönlich
- es Anschaffungsdarlehen   consumer loan
- er Dispositionskredit   personal drawing credit, personal loan overdraft facility
- e Kennummer   personal identification code (number) PIC/PIN
- e Kreditwürdigkeit   credit-worthiness, borrower's reputation (in terms of his reliability in repaying the loan)
- e Kundenbetreuung   personal banking service, individual professional counselling of customers
- er Kundenkontakt   personal contact with the customer
- er Ratenkredit   personal instalment loan

Pfandbestellung   taking out a lien, creation of a lien

Pfandbrief   mortgage bond
- absatz   mortgage bond sale
- anstalt   public mortgage credit bank
- ausstattung   mortgage bond terms
- deckung   mortgage bond cover
- disagio   mortgage bond discount
- emission   mortgage bond issue
- gegenwert   mortgage bond proceeds
- geschäft   mortgage bond business (operations)
- inhaber   mortgage bondholder
- institut   mortgage bank
- markt   mortgage bond market
- umlauf   mortgage bonds outstanding
- zins   mortgage bond rate

Pfanddepot   pledged securities account; securities account under which pledged securities are held

Pfandeffekten   pledged securities

pfänden   to seize, to attach

Pfand
- freigabe   release (discharge) of a pledge
- geber   pledgor
- gegenstand   pledged property, property subject to a lien
  Befriedigung aus dem Pfandgegenstand   selling pledged property in satisfaction of a debt
- gläubiger   pledgee
- indossament   pledging endorsement
- kredit / -leihe   loan against a pledge of chattels
- nehmer   pledgee

Pfandrecht   lien
- an Wertpapieren (Forderungen)   lien over securities (receivables)
  kraft Gesetz entstehendes -   lien arising by operation of law
  durch Vertrag begründetes -   lien by agreement
  Bestellung eines -s   creation of a lien, taking out a lien
  Inhaber eines -s   lienholder, lienor
  das - erlischt mit der Rückzahlung des Kredites   the lien is extinguished by (on) repayment of the loan

Pfandschuldner   pledgor

Pfändung   attachment, seizure

Pfändungs
- ankündigung   notice of attachment (seizure)
- beschluß   attachment order
- pfandrecht   lien by enforcement

Pfand
- vertrag   deed of pledge
- verwahrung   safekeeping of pledged property
- verwertung   realisation of pledged property, selling pledged property

Pflege der Kundenbeziehungen   cultivating existing accounts

pflegen den persönlichen Kontakt mit dem Kunden - to cultivate the personal contact with the customer

Pflichtbekanntmachung   (a) statutory company notice; (b) statutory public advertisement

Pflichtblatt   journal for statutory stock market notices

Pflichtmitteilungen   statutory company statements

Pflicht
- prüfung   statutory audit
- reserven   statutory reserves
- reservesatz   statutory reserve ratio

Phantasie   bei Aktienkursen: upside potential

Phantasiewerte   bazaar securities, cats and dogs

Plafond   ceiling, line, upper limit

plafondieren   to set (to impose) a limit

Plankostenrechnung   budget accounting

planmäßig   scheduled, regular
- e Abschreibungen   regular depreciation
- e Rückführung   repayment as agreed upon
- e Tilgung   scheduled redemption

Platzakkreditiv   local documentary credit

platzen lassen   to return unpaid, to dishonour

Platz
- giroverkehr   town clearing
- institut   local bank
- scheck   town (local) cheque, locally drawn cheque
- spesen   local charges
- überweisung   local transfer, transfer between local banks
- usancen   local (town) practices
- verlust   local charges
- wechsel   town (local) bill

plazieren   to place
 mit einem Agio (Disagio) -   to place at a premium (discount)
 beim Publikum -   to place with the public

Plazierung   placing, selling

Plazierungs
- konsortium   selling group
- kraft   placing power
- provision   selling (placing) commission
- vertrag   selling (placing) agreement

Plus
- Stückzinsen   plus interest accrued; accrued interest added

 Bankaktien wurden mit - angekündigt   banks were marked up, banks improved sharply

 XYZ erzielten ein - von 5DM   XYZ registered a gain of 5DM

Plusankündigung   sharp price markup

Pluskorrektur   upward adjustment, markup
- en überwogen   markups predominated

 kräftige -en wurden bei Fahrzeugwerten vorgenommen   motors moved up strongly

Politik
- des billigen Geldes   cheap (easy) money policy
- des knappen Geldes   tight money policy
- des teuren Geldes   dear money policy, policy of high interest rates

Poolkonsortium   pool syndicate

Portefeuille   portfolio, holdings
- bewertung   portfolio valuation
- investitionen   portfolio investments
- umschichtung   portfolio switching (restructuring)
- zugänge   additions to a portfolio

Position   position, commitment,
interest
- en unter dem Strich   off-
  -balance sheet items

Positionsbereinigung (-glatt-
stellung)   position squaring,
liquidating positions

positiv die erste Reaktion auf
die Ausstattung der neuen Anleihe war - initial response
to the coupon of the new loan
has been positive(favourable)

positiver Zinssaldo   net
interest income

Posten   entry

Postengebühr   entry fee

Postscheck   postal cheque, giro
cheque (Br)
- guthaben   postal giro balances
- konto   postal giro account,
  Giro account (Br)
- verkehr   postal giro payments,
  National Giro (Br)

Prämie   premium, bonus; beim
Optionsgeschäft: option
money

prämienbegünstigter Sparvertrag
bonus-carrying savings scheme

Prämienguthaben   scheme-linked
deposits (balances)

Preis   price
- auftrieb   price upsurge
- bildung   pricing, price determination, fixing prices
- bildung im kurzfristigen Kreditgeschäft   pricing of
  short-term lendings
- bildung im Mengengeschäft
  pricing of retail banking
  transactions
- bindung der zweiten Hand   resale price maintenance
- einbruch   sharp drop in prices

- entwicklung, unterschiedliche
  disparities in the price trend
- erhöhungsspielraum   leeway for
  price increases
- gestaltung, gleichgerichtete
  parallel pricing
- gestaltung im langfristigen Kreditgeschäft   pricing of long-
  -term lendings
- kartell   restrictive agreement
  on prices
- kostenschere   price-cost gap
- mechanismus des Marktes   market
  price mechanism
- obergrenze   ceiling price, price
  limit
- politik im Einlagengeschäft
  pricing of deposit transactions
- politik im Kreditgeschäft   loan
  pricing policy
- steigerungsrate   price increase
  rate

Prima
- bankscheck   prime banker's draft
- nota   day book
- papiere   prime (first-rate)
  acceptances
- wechsel   first of exchange

primäre internationale Liquidität
currency reserves held by the
Central Banks

Primär
- geschäft   new issue business,
  dealings in newly issued securities
- liquidität   primary liquidity,
  → Liquidität ersten Grades
- markt   primary market, new issue
  market

Prinzip der kongruenten Deckung
principle of matching cover

Prioritätsaktien   preference
(preferential) shares, privileged
stock

Prioritätsobligationen
preference bonds

privat
- e Anleger   private (individual) investors
- e Geschäftsbanken   private commercial banks
- e Hypothekenbanken   private mortgage banks
- es Investitionsvolumen   total private investments
- e Sparkapitalbildung   formation of private savings
- er Wohnungsbau   private housebuilding sector

Privat
- anleger   private (retail) investors
- banken   private banks
- bankier   private banking house
- darlehen   personal loan
- diskont   (buying or selling) rate for prime bankers' acceptances
- diskonten   prime bankers' acceptances
- diskontfähig   qualifying as prime bankers' acceptances
- diskontmarkt   zum Privatdiskontmarkt zugelassen   admitted to dealings in the prime bankers' acceptance market
- diskontsatznotierungen   rates quoted for prime bankers' acceptances
- entnahmen   personal drawings

Privatisierung   putting into private ownership (into private hands), privatisation
- der Währungsreserven   increasing shift of currency reserves to the private sector

Privatkunde   retail customer, private customer, retail banking customer

Privatkunden
- abteilung   retail banking department (division)
- beratung   advising (counselling) private customers
- bereich   retail area (operations), personal market
  das Ergebnis im Privatkundenbereich   performance on the retail banking side (in the personal market)
- betreuung   servicing and counselling of private customers
- einlagen   retail deposits, private non-bank deposits
- geschäft   retail banking, retail banking business, retail operations, personal banking
- kredit   retail lending, personal loan
  Nachfrage nach Privatkundenkrediten   retail lending demand, demand for personal loans
- kreditgeschäft   retail (personal) lending business
- markt   retail banking market, personal market

Privat
- kundschaft   retail customers, private (personal) customers
- plazierung   private placement
- publikum   private (retail) investors
- satz   rate for prime bankers' acceptances
- sektor   private sector
- vermögen   private property, private means

privatwirtschaftliche Adresse
private sector borrower

Problemengagement / Problemkredit
problem exposure

produktbezogene Gebührenberechnung
product-related pricing (e.g. of banking services)

profitieren to profit (to benefit) from

XYZ profitierten von Börsendienstempfehlungen XYZ were stimulated by newsletter recommendations

von unserer langjährigen Erfahrung im Emissionsgeschäft - to draw on our long-standing experience in the new issue business

Goldwerte profitierten von spekulativer Nachfrage golds profited from speculative support

die Umsätze profitierten von Hoffnungen auf eine Dividendenerhöhung turnover was helped by hopes on a dividend rise

Prognose forecast

- hinsichtlich der Gewinnentwicklung profit forecast

- über die weitere Zinsentwicklung forecast of the future trend in interest rates

Programmkredite standardised lendings, loans extended under special lending schemes

Programmsparen scheme-linked saving

progressive Abschreibung depreciation on a rising scale

Projektfinanzierung project financing

projektgebunden

- e Ausleihungen project-tied (project-linked) lendings

- e Investitionsfinanzierung project-linked investment financing

Projektmehrkosten project overruns

Finanzierung der - overrun financing

Projektmittel project finance

Projektträger project sponsor

Prokura power of attorney (to act for the company); signing authority

Prokura-Indossament collection endorsement

Prokurist executive holding a general power of attorney (to act for the company)

Kurzform: assistant manager, authorised signatory, signing officer

Prolongation extension, renewal; Börse: carry-over, contango, extending a contract until the next settlement date

- eines Wechsels (a) renewal of a bill; (b) extension of time for payment of a bill

Prolongations

- abschnitt renewal bill

- gebühren commission on contangoes

- satz carry-over (contango) rate

- wechsel renewal bill

- zusage commitment (undertaking) to extend; renewal undertaking

prolongieren to renew, to extend the time for payment; Börse: to carry over

Promptgeschäfte dealings for cash (for immediate settlement)

Properhandel dealings for own account, own account trading

Prospekt prospectus, issuing prospectus

- für die Zulassung zum Börsenhandel listing prospectus

Prospekt

- angaben information given in the prospectus, statements made in the prospectus

- befreiung exemption from the prospectus requirements

prospektfreie Einführung
  prospectus-exempt listing

Prospekt
- haftung   liability for statements made in the prospectus
- inhalt⟶Prospektangaben
- veröffentlichung   publication of a prospectus
- zwang   duty to publish a prospectus, prospectus requirement

Protest   protest (nicht zu verwechseln mit 'noting', dem in Großbritannien üblichen Vorprotest)
- mangels Annahme   protest for non-acceptance
- mangels Zahlung   protest for non-payment
  zu - gehen lassen   to protest a bill, to have a bill protested

Protestat   defaulting drawee, defaulting party

Protest
- anzeige   advice of protest, advice of dishonour
- aufnahmegebühr   protest recording fee
- beamter   protesting official
- erhebung   protesting, levying the protest against the defaulting drawee
  Rückgriff nach Protesterhebung nehmen   to take recourse once the bill has been protested
- erlaß   waiver of protest
- erlaßklausel   protest waiver clause
- frist   time allowed for protesting a bill
- gebühr   protest fee

protestieren   to protest, to have a bill protested

Protestierung   protesting, protest of a dishonoured bill

Protest
- liste   list of bills protested
- lokal   place of protest
- ort   place of protest (i.e. the drawee's premises)
- urkunde   certificate of protest, protest certificate
- zeit   protesting hours

Protokoll   minutes, official record of proceedings

protokollieren   (a) to take down on record, to put on record, to put on record before a notary public; (b) to enter in the minutes

Provision   commission

Provisions
- aufteilung   commission splitting
- aufwendungen   commissions paid
- basis   Verkauf auf Provisionsbasis   selling on a commission basis, commission selling
- berechnung   (a) charging a commission ; (b) calculation of the commission, calculating the commission
- einnahmen   commission income, commissions earned
- forderungen   commissions receivable
- saldo   net commission income or loss
- satz   commission rate
- überschuß einer Bank: net commission income
- tabelle   commission scale, table of commissions charged

Prozenter   Zehn-Prozenter   bond carrying a 10 p.c. coupon

Prozentnotierung   percentage quotation

prozentualer Anteil   percentage share

prüfen   to examine, to check; to audit

Prüfer   examiner; auditor

Prüfung   examination, check; audit

- der Bücher   audit of the books and accounts of ..
- der Dokumente   examination of the documents, checking the documents
- der Eigentumsrechte   examination of title, investigating a person's claim to be the owner of
- der Kreditinstitute   checking and monitoring the banks' operations; auditing the banks' business records
- der finanziellen Lage   making an investigation into the financial affairs of ..
- der Unterschrift des Scheckausstellers   checking the genuineness of the writer's signature

Prüfungs

- bericht   audit report
- kosten   auditing charges
- pflicht   duty to have the books audited; duty to inspect (examine) the books
- richtlinien   auditing standards
- stelle   auditing agency
- verband   auditing body
- vermerk   audit certificate, audit opinion

Publikationsorgane   newspapers or journals publishing statutory company or stock exchange notices

Publikum   investors, investing public

das - blieb vorsichtig   investors continued to take a cautious view, investors remained steadfastly cautious

das - verhielt sich abwartend   investors remained on the sidelines, investors waited to see (e.g. how the market would respond to the interest rate cut)

Publikums

- fonds   retail fund
- geschäft   einer Bank: retail banking
- gesellschaft   public company
- interesse   investor interest, retail interest
- käufe   public buying
- nachfrage   investor demand
- papiere   securities offered for public subscription
- werte   leaders, leading shares, popular stocks

Publizitätspflicht   duty to disclose

Publizitätsvorschriften   disclosure requirements

Punkt   point

der Index gab um zwei -e nach   the index edged two points down

der Index stieg um drei -e   the index gained (advanced, put on) three points

per Saldo einen halben - höher   a net half a point higher on the day

um einige -e schwächer schließen   to close a couple of points cheaper

Punktebewertungssystem   bei Krediten: scoring system

Q

qualifizierte Minderheit   minority representing at least 25 p.c. of the equity

Qualitätseinstufung   bei einer Emission: rating

Qualitätswerte   top-quality stocks, blue chips

Quasigeld   near-money

Quellenbesteuerung   taxation at source

Quellensteuer   withholding tax, tax levied at source

quellensteuerfrei   exempt from withholding tax

Quittung   für die Hinterlegung: custody receipt

Quote   Internationaler Währungsfonds: quota; im Emissionsgeschäft: underwriting share, share allocated to an underwriter (member of a selling group)

Quoten

- aktie   no-par value share
- erhöhung   IWF: increase in quotas
- kartell   commodity restriction scheme, quota ring
- rest   im Emissionsgeschäft: securities not placed by an underwriter
- schlüssel   allocation formula

R

Rahmen

in einem geordneten - within a well-ordered scope

in einem globalen - on a global scale

im - der vereinbarten Fazilität erfolgende Inanspruchnahmen drawings under the agreed facility

im - der üblichen Geschäftstätigkeit within the ordinary course of business

der für Neuanschaffungen gesetzte - the ceiling set on new equipment spending

im - des Vertrages under the terms of the contract

im - eines normalen Gewinnzuwachses given a normal growth in profits

Rahmen

- aval guarantee credit line
- bedingungen der Wirtschaftspolitik general setting (lay) of economic policy
- kredit overall credit facility, credit line
- kreditvereinbarung loan agreement, open-to-borrow arrangement, facility letter
- kreditzusage credit line undertaking; loan agreement up to a given amount for the financing (e.g. of new capital spending projects)
- limit borrowing (credit) limit; maximum amount up to which the company may borrow by way of cash loans, Euromarket loans, bill credits or any other facilities
- vertrag basic agreement; bei einem Kreditgeschäft: credit override agreement
- wechsel master (override) note
- zusage general undertaking, basic commitment

Raiffeisenbank agricultural credit co-operative

Rang rank

im - gleichgestellte Sicherheiten securities ranking equally (concurrently, pari passu)

im - nachgehende Forderung subordinated claim

im - nachgeordnete Sicherheiten subordinated (junior) securities, subordinated collateral

im - nachgestellte Verbindlichkeiten liabilities ranking after, subordinated liabilities (debts)

im - vorgehende Forderung prior claim, claim ranking ahead (before)

im - vorgehende Hypothek senior (prior) mortgage

Rang

- änderung amending the rank (priority) of.., change of priority
- folge ranking, rank order, priority, order of priority
- folge der Gläubiger ranking of creditors
- folge der Hypotheken mortgage ranking
- folge der Konkursforderungen arrangement of claims (proofs)
- gleichheit equal rank, equality of rank
- gleichstellung (a) accommodating

175

an equal rank, putting on an equal footing; (b) enjoying the same rights (rank)

- gleichstellungsklausel equally (rateably) secured clause

ranghöher higher-ranking, senior, prior

- e Belastung prior charge

Rang

- ordnung ranking, rank order, order of priority
- rücktritt subordination
- rücktrittserklärung letter of subordination
- stelle rank
- verhältnis ändern to change the priority (ranking)
- vermerk rank-related entry in the land registry
- vorbehalt proviso relating to the rank of a charge

rasende Inflation rocketing (runaway) inflation

Rate instalment

Raten

- anleihe instalment bond
- finanzierung instalment financing
- hypothek instalment mortgage
- kauf buying on hire purchase, buying by instalments
- kredit instalment credit
- kreditversicherung instalment credit insurance
- kreditvolumen instalment credit portfolio
- rückstand instalments in arrears
- sparen instalment-based saving
- sparvertrag instalment-based savings scheme
- zahlung (a) instalment, instalment payment; (b) payment by instalments

rationieren Börse: to scale down

Raumsicherungsvertrag assignment of goods stored at a specific place

real Anstieg um real 5 % a 5 p.c. increase (growth) in real terms

Realdarlehen mortgage loan

Realisationswert realisation (liquidation) value, realisable value

realisieren to sell, to realise, to liquidate Kursgewinne: to cash in on profits, to realise gains, to take profits

Realisierung sale, selling, realisation; von Kursgewinnen: cashing in on profits, realising price gains, profit-taking

Realisierungswelle Börse: welter (surge) of selling

Real

- kapital tangible fixed assets
- kredit real estate loan, lending (loan) against real estate, land credit
- kreditinstitut mortgage bank, land credit bank, mortgage loan company
- lasten real servitudes
- verzinsung effective (real) interest return

Realzins effective (real) interest rate

- anhebung raising (lifting) the effective interest rate
- auf Dollarbasis dollar-based effective interest rate
- niveau effective interest rate level
- reduktion cut in (lowering of) the effective interest rate

176

rechnerischer Gewinn   book
(paper) profit

rechnerischer Wert eines Bezugsrechtes   theoretical value of
a subscription right

Rechnung   (a) invoice; (b)account

für - unseres Kunden   for
account of our customer

für neue -   for (on) new
account

Kontoführungsgebühren in -
stellen   to charge account-
-maintenance fees

Vortrag auf neue -   account
carried forward

Rechnungs

- abgrenzung   deferment

- abgrenzungsposten   Aktivseite:
deferred charges; Passivseite:
deferred income

- einheit   unit of account

- legung der Unternehmen   corporate accounting

- periode   accounting period

- prüfung   audit

- wesen   accounting, accountancy

Rechts

- anspruch   legal claim, title

- gutachten   legal opinion

- kraft   legal force, validity

- mittel   remedy

- nachfolger   successor in
title, legal successor

- titel   title, title to property

- unterzeichner   signatory to
the right

rechtsverbindlich   legally binding

eine Gesellschaft - vertreten
to act in the name of a company,
to bind a company by deed

- für den Kreditnehmer   legally binding on the borrower

- e Verpflichtung   legally binding
undertaking

Rediskont   rediscount

rediskontfähig

- bei der Bundesbank   eligible
for rediscount at the Bundesbank

- es Material (-e Wechsel)   bills
eligible for rediscount, eligible paper, rediscountable bills

Rediskontfähigkeit   eligibility
for rediscount

Rediskontfazilität   rediscount
facility (line)

rediskontieren   to rediscount

Wechsel - lassen   to have bills
rediscounted at (with, by)

Rediskontierung   rediscounting,
rediscount

Rediskontierungskosten   cost of
rediscount funds

Rediskont

- kontingent   rediscount quota

Festlegung der Rediskont-Kontin-
gente   fixing the rediscount
quotas

- kredit   rediscount credit (facility)

- obligo   liability on rediscounts

- papiere   paper(bills) eligible
for rediscount, rediscountable
paper

- plafond   rediscount limit (line)

- politik   rediscount policy

- rahmen   rediscount line

- satz   rediscount rate

- zusage   rediscount undertaking,
undertaking (commitment) to rediscount

Referenzzeitraum   reference period

refinanzierbar   refinanceable

177

refinanzieren to fund, to refinance

sich bei der Bundesbank - to fund lendings through Bundesbank borrowings (⟶ Refinanzierungsmöglichkeiten)

Exportkredite bei .. - lassen to have export credits refinanced with ..

mit kurzfristigem Geld - to fund with short-term money

über den Kapitalmarkt - to refinance in the capital market

Kredite am Interbankenmarkt - to fund (to refinance) lendings in the interbank market

durch die Emission von Pfandbriefen - to fund lendings through the issue of mortgage bonds

laufzeitgerecht am Geldmarkt - to fund (to refinance) at matching maturities in the money market

währungskongruent - to refinance at matching currencies

XYZ (Bank) konnte sich weiterhin zu günstigen Konditionen - XYZ kept funding itself on favourable terms

Refinanzierung funding, refinancing

- des Aktivgeschäftes funding lending activities

- des Anpassungsgeschäfts funding loans to be renewed (renegotiated)

- des kurzfristigen Kreditgeschäftes funding of short--term lending operations

- auf dem freien Markt funding in the open market

Refinanzierungs

- bedarf der Banken banks' funding requirements

- geschäft funding operations, refinancing transactions

- konditionen funding (refinancing) terms

- kosten funding cost, cost of refinance

- kredit refinance credit, funding loan

- mittel funding capital, refinance, refinancing funds

- möglichkeiten funding (refinancing) facilities (e.g. rediscounting of eligible bills with Bundesbank, pledging securities and/or bills under repurchase agreements)

- plafond refinancing limit

- quellen funding sources, sources of refinance

- schwierigkeiten funding difficulties, difficulties in providing the necessary refinance

- spielraum refinancing leeway

- verbindlichkeiten liabilities under funding operations, refinancing liabilities

- vereinbarung funding (refinancing) arrangement

- zusage refinancing undertaking, undertaking (commitment) to refinance

regelmäßig

- gehandelt werden to have a steady market

- e Dividendenzahlungen unbroken dividend record

registrieren to register, to record

Registrierung registration, recording

Registrierungsvorschriften registration (filing) requirements

reglementierter Markt controlled market

Regreß recourse

- mangels Annahme recourse for want of acceptance

Regreß mangels Zahlung   recourse in default of payment

Regreß
- anspruch   right of recourse
- forderung   recourse claim
- freier Forderungsverkauf   non-recourse sale of receivables
- pflichtig   liable to recourse
- recht   right of recourse
- schuldner   recourse debtor
- verzichtserklärung   waiver of recourse

reguläres Bankgeschäft   mainstream banking

regulieren   to settle, to pay

Regulierung   settlement, payment
- des Gegenwertes   settlement of the proceeds (equivalent)
- am gleichen Tag   same-day settlement

Regulierungskurs   settlement price (rate)

Reihenrückgriff   recourse in order of endorsers

rein
- e Globalurkunde   global bond certificate which cannot be replaced by individual certificates
- es Konnossement   clean bill of lading
- e Stücke   good delivery stock
- e Verschiffungsdokumente   clean shipping documents
- e Zahlung   clean payment

Rein
- erlös   net proceeds
- ertrag   net earnings (surplus)
- gewinn je Aktie   net profit (net income) per share
- vermögen   net assets (property)

reinvestieren   to reinvest, to plough (to plow) back

Reitwechsel   windmill, kite

Rekta
- grundschuldbrief   registered land charge certificate
- konnossement   straight bill of lading
- papiere   registered (non-negotiable) stock
- rentenschuldbrief   registered annuity bond
- wechsel   non-negotiable bill

Rembours   reimbursement
- auf erstes Anfordern   to provide reimbursement on first call

Rembours
- bank   reimbursing bank (banker)
- benachrichtigung   documentary payment advice
- berechtigte Bank   bank entitled to claim reimbursement
- ermächtigung   reimbursement authority
- fazilitäten   documentary acceptance facilities
- geschäft   documentary payment transactions
- kredit   documentary acceptance credit
- leistung   providing reimbursement
- linie   acceptance credit line
- rückgriff   reimbursement recourse
- schreiben   reimbursement instructions
- schuldner   documentary credit debtor
- schutzbrief   reimbursement covering letter
- stelle   reimbursing bank, reimbursing office
- zusage   agreement to reimburse

179

Remittent   eines Wechsels: payee of a bill

Rendite   yield
- einer Anlage   yield on an investment
- am Kapitalmarkt   yield in the capital market
- bei Kurz- (Lang-)Läufern   yield on shorts (longs), short-dated (long-dated) bond yield
- vor (nach) Steuern   pretax (post-tax) yield

Rendite
- angleichung   yield adjustment
- anstieg im kurzen Bereich   yield increase at the short end of the market
- berechnung   yield calculation, computation of the yield
- differenz   yield gap
- erwägungen   Käufe aufgrund von Renditeerwägungen   buying on yield considerations
- erwartungen   yield expectations
- gefälle   yield differential
- niveau   yield level
- objekte im Immobilienbereich: investment properties
- papiere   high-yield securities
- schwankungen   yield (yield-rate) fluctuations
- spanne   yield spread

Rentabilität   profitability
Rentabilitäts
- bewußtsein   profit awareness
- rechnung   profitability accounting
- schwelle   break-even point

Renten   bonds, fixed-interest (fixed-income) securities
- anleger   bond investor
- baisse   sharp drop in bond prices, slump in the bond market
- bestand   bond holdings (portfolio)
- depot   bond portfolio
- flaute   stalemate in the bond market, sagging (sluggish)bond market
- fonds   bond fund, fixed-interest securities fund
- handel   bond trading (dealings)
- händler   bond dealer
- hausse   bull run in the bond market, strong upsurge in bond prices
- index   bond market average
- käufer   bond buyers
- kurse   bond prices
- markt   bond market, fixed-income securities market
- markt in Anspruch nehmen   to tap the bond market
- notierungen   bond prices (quotations)
- parkett   bond trading floor
- portefeuille   bond portfolio, portfolio of fixed-income securities
- schwäche   weakness in bond prices
- umlauf   total bonds outstanding
- umsätze   turnover (dealings) in bonds, bond dealings
- werte   fixed-interest (fixed-income securities), bonds

rentieren   to yield

repartieren   Wertpapiere: to scale down

Repartierung   scaling down

repatriieren   to repatriate, to transfer back

Repatriierung   der ins Ausland abgeflossenen Gelder   repatriation of funds transferred abroad

Report   contango, continuation, carry-over

Reportgeschäft   carry-over (contango) transaction

reportieren   to carry over to the next settlement

Report
- nehmer   giver
- satz   contango (carry-over) rate
- tag   contango (continuation) day

Repräsentanz   representative office

reprivatisieren   to put back into private ownership

Reprivatisierung   putting back into private ownership, privatisation

Reserve
- einheit   IWF: reserve unit
- entnahmen   drawing on reserves
- haltung   reserve management
- mittel   IWF: reserve facility, reserve funds
- pflichtige Verbindlichkeiten   reserve-carrying liabilities
- sätze   reserve ratios
- soll   reserve requirements
- währung   reserve currency
- währungsguthaben   reserve currency balances
- zuweisung   allocation to reserves

reserviert   die Anleger verhielten sich -   investors remained on the sidelines

Resonanz   die Emission fand eine geringe -   the issue received a poor reception in the market

Restanten/Restantenliste   (a) unclaimed securities (relating to securities drawn or called for redemption); (b) unsettled securities transactions

Rest
- forderung   residual claim
- laufzeit   time to maturity, residual life (term)
- risiko   residual exposure
- schuld   residual debt
- tilgung   residual payment (redemption)

Restriktions
- erleichterungen   easing of (alleviating) restrictions
- kurs   restrictive course (policy)
- maßnahmen   restrictive measures

restriktiv   restrictive, tight
- e Geldpolitik   tight monetary policy
- e Kreditpolitik   restrictive credit policy

Retouren   cheques and bills returned unpaid

Retourscheck   returned cheque

Reugeld   Termingeschäft: premium to be paid upon rescission of a futures contract

Revision   audit

Revisionspflicht   duty to have the books audited; duty to audit

revolvierend   revolving
- es Akkreditiv   revolving documentary credit
- er Kredit   revolving credit

rezessionsanfällig   recession--prone

rezessionsbedingte Insolvenzen   recession-induced company failures (insolvencies)

Ricambiowechsel   redraft

Richtsatz   für Kontokorrentkredite   target rate for current account credits

Rimesse (a) remittance; (b) bill, draft

Rimessebrief   letter of remittances

Ringhauptstelle   main clearing agency (within the giro network operated by the cooperative banks)

Ringstelle   clearing agency

Risiko   risk, exposure

das - durch Devisentermingeschäfte abdecken   to hedge the risk by selling and buying forward

das nicht gedeckte finanzielle -   the unhedged financial risk

das mit einem Geschäft verbundene - risk inherent in a transaction, transaction exposure

das - war zur Hälfte abgedeckt   50 per cent of the risk had been covered

mit einem hohen - behafteter Kredit   high-risk loan, high-risk exposure

dem - im Kreditgeschäft Rechnung tragen   to set up loan loss provisions, to provide for the risks inherent in lending, to provide for non-performing loans

das - bei der Umrechnung ausländischer Vermögenswerte in die Inlandswährung   the risk when foreign assets are translated into the national currency

Risiko

- absicherung   risk hedging, hedging (covering) the risk
- aktiva   problem loans (lendings)
- arme Anlage   low-risk investment, defensive investment
- belastung   risk burden, degree of risk involved
- bereitschaft   willingness to assume (incur) risks
- bereitschaft der Anleger   the risk investors are prepared to incur
- berichtigt   risk-adjusted
- bewertung   risk measuring (measurement), risk rating (appraisal)
- deckung   risk hedging, covering (hedging) a risk
- engagement   problem exposure, problem loan
- freudiger Anleger   risk lover, risk-loving investor
- gehalt eines Kreditengagements   risk inherent in a lending transaction, exposure risk
- kapital   risk capital, venture capital
- kredit   problem loan (lending), problem exposure
- management   risk management
- mäßig verhaftet   to be liable for the risks (involved in ..)
- minderung   risk reduction, lowering (alleviating) the risk
- politik   risk management policy
- prämie   risk premium
- scheue Anleger   risk-averse (risk-averting) investors
- schuldnerland   problem debtor country
- streuung   risk spreading
- teilung   risk sharing
- tragendes Kapital   risk capital, venture capital
- transformation   shift in risk spreading
- übernahme   assuming a risk, risk assumption
- überwachung   monitoring a risk, risk control
- umfang   degree of risk incurred
- vorsorge   bad debt provisioning, providing for risks
- vorsorge im Kreditgeschäft   setting up loan loss provisions, providing for possible loan losses, providing for non-performing loans

- vorsorge treffen to provide for bad and doubtful debts (for non-performing loans),to set up loan loss provisions
- zuschlag   risk markup

Roh-, Hilfs- und Betriebsstoffe raw materials and supplies

Rollover-Kreditvertrag rollover loan agreement

rote Effektenschecks instructions to transfer securities held under a collective securities account to another account

rote Zahlen

in die roten Zahlen geraten to plunge (to slide)into the red

Rückbildung der Sparquote decline in the savings ratio

rückbuchen to transfer back, to retransfer; im Sinne von stornieren: to reverse

Rückbuchung retransfer; reversing, reversing entry

Rückbürge counter-guarantor

Rückbürgschaft counter-guarantee

Rückbürgschaftsprovision counter-guarantee commission

Rückdisponierung retransfer

rückerstatten to refund, to reimburse; to restitute

Rückerstattung refund, reimbursement; restitution

- zuviel gezahlter Depotgebühren refund of custodian charges paid in excess

Rückfluß reflux, reflow

- der ins Ausland abgeflossenen Gelder reflux of funds transferred abroad

Rückflüsse aus dem Aktivgeschäft repayments on lendings

Rückflüsse von Fondsanteilen units (investment fund shares) offered for repurchase

rückführen to transfer back, to repatriate;Kredit: to reduce,to repay

Rückführung retransfer, repatriation; Kredit: reduction,repayment

- von Kapital repatriation of capital

- in den vereinbarten Kreditrahmen reducing the overdraft to the limit agreed upon

Rückgabe return, returning

- der Papiere vor Fälligkeit returning the securities prior to maturity

- der als Sicherheit hinterlegten Vermögenswerte restitution of property deposited as collateral

Rückgang decline, fall, drop, plunge

- der Eigenhandelsgewinne fall in own-account-trading income

- der Kurse auf breiter Front drop in prices across the board, retreat of prices over a broad front, widespread decline

- des Zins- und Provisionsüberschusses decline in net interest and commission income

Rückgewähr refund, reimbursement
Rückgriff recourse

- auf den Aussteller nehmen to call on the drawer (writer), to have recourse against the issuer (drawer)

- gegenüber Dritten recourse against third parties

- auf den Kapitalmarkt tapping the capital market, borrowing in the capital market

- auf die Rücklagen drawing on the reserves

- auf fällige Guthaben aus Sparverträgen drawing on scheme-linked savings

Rückgriff
- mangels Zahlung recourse in default of payment

 der Indossant hat den - ausdrücklich ausgeschlossen the endorser has expressly negatived the recourse

 auf einen Indossanten - nehmen to call upon (to have recourse against) an endorser

Rückgriffsforderungen recourse claims

rückgriffslose Finanzierung bei Projektfinanzierungen: non-recourse financing

Rückgriffsrecht right of recourse
 ein - gegenüber jeder Wechselpartei besitzen to have a right of recourse against any party to the bill

Rückgriffsschuldner recourse debtor

Rückkauf repurchase, redemption; eigener Aktien:buying in

rückkaufen to repurchase, to redeem; to buy in

Rückkaufs
- angebot repurchase offer, offer of redemption
- disagio repurchase (redemption) discount
- kurs repurchase (redemption) price, buy-back price
- möglichkeit repurchase privilege (feature, facility)
- recht repurchase option, right of repurchase (redemption)

Rückkaufsvereinbarung repurchase agreement
 Verkauf von Wechseln mit - sale of bills concurrent with an agreement to repurchase the same bills at a later date

Rückkaufsverlust loss on repurchase

Rückkehr return
- in die Gewinnzone return to the black, recovery into profit
- zu festen Wechselkursen return to fixed parities

Rückkredit back-to-back credit

Rücklage reserve, surplus
- für Ersatzbeschaffung reserve for replacements
- für Tilgungsverpflichtungen reserve for redemption commitments

Rücklagen
- auflösung writing back reserves
- bildung setting up reserves, build-up of reserves
- dotierung (-bedienung) allocation (transfer) to reserves
- fonds reserve (surplus) fund
- konto surplus account
- polster reserve cushion
- stärkung strengthening reserves
- zuweisung allocation to reserves, reserve appropriation

Rücklastschrift dishonoured (returned) direct debit

rückläufig sagging, softening, weakening, flagging
- e Aktienkurse softening (weakening) equity prices
- e Konjunktur sagging economic activity
 Bankaktien waren weiterhin - bank stocks crumbled (wilted) further

Rücklaufstücke securities repurchased

Rücknahme Wertpapiere: repurchase, redemption
- zum Inventarwert repurchase (redemption) at net asset value
- der Leitzinsen lowering of key lending rates

Rücknahme
- garantie repurchase (redemption) guarantee
- gebühr repurchase (surrender) charge
- kurs (-preis) redemption price
  Fondsanteile: bid (call) price, cash-in price
- satz repurchase rate
- verpflichtungen aus Pensionsgeschäften repurchase commitments under sale and repurchase agreements
- wert von Fondsanteilen: bid value; Police: surrender value
- zusage der Bundesbank Bundesbank's commitment to repurchase, Bundesbank's repurchase undertaking

Rückrechnung return (back) account, reaccount

Rückrufgebühren Wechsel: recall charges

Rückscheck returned (rubber) cheque

Rückstand arrears

im - sein to be in arrears

mit den Zins- und Tilgungszahlungen in - geraten to fall behind with interest and redemption payments

rückständig

- e Dividenden arrearages in dividends, arrears of dividend
- e Tilgungszahlungen redemption arrears

Rückstellungen provisions
- für Avale guarantee provisions
- für Eventualverbindlichkeiten provisions for contingencies
- für dubiose Forderungen bad and doubtful debt provisions
- im Kreditgeschäft loan loss provisions
- für notleidende Kredite provisions for non-performing loans
- für Länderrisiken country risk provisioning, provisions for country debts
- für Minderung des Marktwertes provisions for diminution in market value
- für Substanzverluste provisions for depletion

Auflösung von - writing back provisions

Bildung von - setting up provisions, provisioning

Rückstellungsbedarf im Kreditgeschäft loan loss provisions required, provisioning required for lendings

Rückübertragung an den ursprünglichen Eigentümer reconveyance (transferring back) to the original owner

Rückvalutierung backvaluation

Rückvergütung refund, reimbursement

Rückverlagerung repatriation

Rückwechsel re-exchange, redraft

rückzahlbar repayable; Wertpapiere: redeemable, repayable
- zum Nennwert zuzüglich Stückzinsen redeemable at par plus interest accrued
- in monatlichen Raten in Höhe von .. to be repaid (repayable) in monthly instalments of ..

Rückzahlung repayment; Anleihe: repayment, redemption
- mit einem Aufschlag repayment at a premium
- vor Fälligkeit redemption (repayment) prior to maturity
- in voller Höhe redemption (repayment) in full
- über (unter) dem Nennwert redemption above (below) par

- in gleichen Tilgungsraten straight-line redemption, repayment in equal instalments

bis zur vollständigen - des Kredites until repayment in full of the loan

zur - fällig stellen Kredit: to call in a loan

zur - fällig werden to fall due, to mature

der gesamte Kredit wird sofort zur - fällig the whole of the loan accommodation becomes instantly repayable

Rückzahlungs

- agio   redemption premium

- anspruch   right to repayment (redemption), redemption claim

- aufforderung   call for repayment

- disagio   redemption discount

- fähigkeit   ability to repay

- garantie   return-of-money bond

- gewinn   gain on redemption

- kurs   redemption (repayment) price

- mittel   funds for repayment, redemption funds

- modalitäten   terms of repayment, redemption terms

- plan   repayment (redemption) schedule

- rate   instalment, redemption instalment

- rendite   yield to maturity (redemption)

- sperrfrist   repayment-free years, redemption holiday, grace period

- verlust   loss on repayment (on redemption)

- wert   value upon redemption, redemption price

ruhiges Geschäft   Börse: quiet (thin) trading

Run auf kurzfristige Anleihen   stampede into shorts

Rüstungswerte   Börse: defence stocks

S

Sach
- anlagen   fixed assets; Bilanzposten: property, plant and equipment
- anlagenzugänge   fixed asset additions, additions to fixed assets
- aufwand einer Bank: operating expenditure
- bearbeiter   junior bank officer (official)

  der zuständige Sachbearbeiter the officer handling (processing) this matter, the officer in charge of this matter
- depotbuch   securities custody ledger
- dividende   dividend payable in kind, commodity dividend
- einlagen   contributions in kind
- investitionen   equipment spending, fixed asset investments
- kapital   real capital
- kosten   operating expenditure, personnel and material costs
- kredit   loan against collateral, secured loan
- leistungen   benefits in kind
- sicherheiten   impersonal securities
- vermögensbildung   fixed capital formation
- wert einer Aktie: intrinsic value
- werte   real properties
- wert-Investmentfonds   property fund

saisonbedingter Kreditbedarf   seasonal borrowing requirements

saisonbereinigt   seasonally adjusted

Saisonkredit   seasonal loan

Salden
- abstimmung   balance reconciliation
- anerkenntnis   (a) acknowledgement of a debit balance; (b) confirmation of balance
- ausgleich   settlement of a debit balance
- berichtigung   rectifying a balance, adjustment of account
- bestätigung   confirmation of balance, confirming an account balance
- bilanz   trial balance sheet
- ermittlung   determining the balance
- feststellung   (a) determining (ascertaining) the balance; (b) confirmation of balance
- mäßige Aufrechnung   offsetting account balances
- mitteilung   account statement, statement of account

saldieren   (a) ein Konto: to balance, to strike the balance, to close up; (b) verrechnen: to set off (to net) against

Saldierung   balancing, closing up an account; setting off

tägliche -   daily balancing (closing up of accounts)

- der Forderungen an Kreditinstitute mit den Verbindlichkeiten gegenüber Kreditinstituten setting off due from banks against due to banks
- eines Kontos   balancing an account

187

Saldo balance, account balance
- per - 10DM fester schließen to close 10DM higher on balance
- aus Konsolidierung balance arising from consolidation

Saldo
- ausgleich settlement of a balance
- guthaben account balance, balance in the account
- übertrag balance to be carried forward
- vortrag balance brought forward

Sammel
- abschreibungen global write--downs (depreciation)
- aktie global share
- bestand collective holdings
- bestandteil share in collective holdings
- depot collective custody (securities) account
- depotermächtigung authorisation for collective safekeeping
- formular summary slip(voucher)
- inkassosystem collective collection system
- konnossement omnibus (combined) bill of lading
- liste mit Opposition belegter Wertpapiere list of invalidated securities
- schuldbuchforderungen collective government-inscribed debt
- urkunde global certificate
- verrechnung consolidated billing

sammelverwahrfähige Wertpapiere securities eligible for collective safekeeping (collective safe custody)

sammelverwahrte Aktienzertifikate share certificates held collectively (in collective safekeeping)

Sammelverwahrung collective safekeeping (safe custody) of securities

Einlieferung von Wertpapieren in die - depositing securities for collective safekeeping

Hereinnahme zur - accepting for collective safekeeping

sammelwertberichtigte Forderungen lendings for which general loan loss provisions have been made

Sammelwertberichtigung general provisions for bad and doubtful debts, general loan loss provisions, bad loan charge
- für nicht erkennbare Risiken general loss provisions for undiscernible risks

Sammler summary slip (voucher)

sanieren to reconstruct, to reorganize, to revitalise, to revamp

Sanierung reconstruction, restructuring (Br), reorganization (US), revitalisation
- der Kapitalverhältnisse capital reconstruction
- durch Kapitalherabsetzung reconstruction based on a capital write-down
- durch Veränderung der Gesellschaftsmittel external reconstruction
- durch Zufuhr neuer Mittel putting the company back on its feet through the infusion of fresh funds

Sanierungs
- bilanz reconstruction accounts, reorganization statement (US)
- gewinn surplus on reconstruction
- konsortium reconstruction (reorganization) syndicate, rescue group

- kredit reconstruction loan
- programm financial reconstruction scheme, reorganization scheme
- übersicht reconstruction accounts
- vergleich reconstruction based on an arrangement (a compromise) with creditors

Satz rate

Sätze im kurzfristigen Bereich short-term lending rates

Sätze für Spareinlagen saving deposit rates

Satznennungen rates quoted

Satzung bye-laws, memorandum and articles of association

säumig defaulting, in default
- er Schuldner defaulting debtor
- er Vertragsteil defaulting party

SB-Bankterminal customer-operated terminal, automated teller terminal

Schachtel / Schachtelbeteiligung controlling interest (equity stake amounting to at least 25 per cent of the capital)

Schachtelgesellschaft affiliated company (with interlocking equity holdings)

Schachtelprivileg preferential tax treatment of profits made by affiliated companies (to avoid double taxation)

Schalter counter

am - in bar auszahlen to pay in cash across the counter

am - einlösen to cash over the counter

am - zur Zahlung vorlegen to present for payment over the counter

Schalterauslieferung delivery across the counter

Schaltergeschäft Wertpapiere: counter transaction, teller transaction, delivery of securities against cash payment

Kredite: cash advance, counter lending, loan taken out at the counter

Sätze für Schaltergeschäfte counter lending rates

Schalter
- kredit cash advance, counter lending, loan taken out at the counter
- nutzen placing (selling) commission
- personal counter staff
- provision placing (selling) commission
- raum banking hall
- stücke counter stock
- terminal counter terminal
- vergütung placing (selling) commission
- verkehr counter transactions

Schatz
- anweisung treasury note
- brief (Federal) savings bond
- schein treasury certificate
- wechsel treasury bill
- wechselkredit treasury bill credit

Schätze ⟶ Schatzanweisungen

schätzen to estimate; taxieren: to appraise, to value

Schätzung estimate; appraisal, valuation

Schaukelbörse seesaw market

Scheck cheque (Br), check (US)

Scheck

auf andere Banken gezogene -s
cheques drawn on other banks

Bestätigung eines -s durch die
Bundesbank veranlassen to have
a cheque certified by Bundesbank

die Einlösung eines -s mangels
Deckung verweigern   to dishonour (to refuse payment of)
a cheque for lack of cover

die Einlösung eines -s bei Vorlage garantieren to guarantee
payment of a cheque upon presentation, to undertake that a
cheque will be met (paid,
honoured) upon presentation

einen - am Schalter einlösen to
cash a cheque across the counter

Einreichung eines -s zur Gutschrift auf Konto .. paying in
(presenting) a cheque for
credit to account ..

einen - zum Einzug hereinnehmen
to take (to accept) a cheque
for collection

auf Fremdwährung lautende - s
foreign currency cheques, cheques
written in foreign currencies

den Gegenwert des -s haben wir
Ihrem Konto gutgeschrieben the
proceeds of the cheque have
been credited to your account

Grund für die Nichteinlösung
eines -s   reason for dishonouring a cheque

durch -s über ein Konto verfügen
to draw on an account by cheques

die Sperrung des -s wurde tele-
fonisch vorgenommen und schriftlich bestätigt   countermand of
payment was given over the telephone and confirmed in writing

der - wurde vom Aussteller gesperrt the drawer (writer) of
the cheque has instructed the
bank to stop (to refuse) payment of the cheque

faksimilierte Unterschrift auf -s
facsimile signature on cheques

einen - unbezahlt zurückgeben
to return a cheque unpaid

Scheck

- abrechnung (a) cheque clearing; (b) cheque settlement note

- abrechnungsverkehr cheque clearing

- aussteller writer (drawer) of
  a cheque

- ausstellung   writing (drawing)
  a cheque

- auszahlung paying a cheque (e.g.
  across the counter)

- bearbeitung processing of
  cheques

- begebung   negotiating a cheque

- berechtigter person entitled to
  payment under a cheque

- bestand   cheques in hand

- bestätigung certification of
  a cheque, undertaking to pay
  (to meet) a cheque upon presentation

- betrag   amount of a cheque,
  cheque amount

- betrug   cheque fraud

- bezahltmeldung   advice (notification) of payment

- bezogener   drawee of (under) a
  cheque

- bürgschaft cheque guarantee

- buch   cheque book

- deckung cheque cover, cover for
  a cheque

- disposition   drawing by cheque

- einlieferung paying in (depositing) cheques

- einlieferungsbeleg   paying-in
  slip, credit slip

- einlösung paying (meeting,
  honouring) a cheque, durch den
  Kunden: cashing a cheque

- einlösungsgarantie cheque
  guarantee, undertaking to pay
  (to meet) a cheque upon presentation

- einlösungsgebühr   cheque cashing
  fee

Scheck
- einreicher   presenter of a cheque, person paying in (presenting) a cheque
- einreichung   paying in (presenting) a cheque; presentation of a cheque for payment
- einreichung am Schalter   paying in (presenting) a cheque over the counter
- einreichungsformular   paying-in slip, credit (inpayment) slip
- einzug   cheque collection, collecting a cheque
- einzugsverfahren   cheque clearing
- fähigkeit   capacity to draw (to write) cheques
- gegenwert   cheque proceeds, proceeds of a cheque
- gesetz   German Cheques Act
- gesperrt (Vermerk)   orders not to pay, payment countermanded
- gutschrift   cheque credit, crediting the cheque to an account
- haftung   liability on a cheque
- heft   cheque book
- honorierung   paying (honouring, meeting) a cheque
- inhaber   holder of a cheque
- inkasso   cheque collection
- karte   cheque card
- kartenbetrug   cheque card fraud
- karteninhaber   holder of a cheque card
- konto   current account, chequing account (Br), checking account (US)
- kreuzung   crossing of a cheque
- nehmer   person accepting a cheque for payment
- prüfung   inspecting (examining) a cheque
- reiterei   kiting, kite flying, cheque kiting
- retoure   returned (dishonoured) cheque
- retouren   returns, cheques returned unpaid
- rückgabe   return of an unpaid (dishonoured) cheque
- rückgriffsrecht   right of recourse under a cheque
- rückrechnung   cheque return bill, banker's ticket
- rückseite   reverse of a cheque
- sperre   stopping a cheque, countermanding payment of a cheque
- sperre veranlassen   to give instructions to stop (to refuse) payment of a cheque
- summe   amount of a cheque, cheque amount
- unterschrift prüfen   to check the genuineness of the drawer's (writer's) signature
- unterschriftenmaschine   cheque signer
- verpflichteter   party liable on a cheque
- vorlage   presenting a cheque, cheque presentation
- vorleger   presenter of a cheque, person paying (presenting) a cheque
- vorlegungsfrist   presentation period for cheques
- weitergabe   negotiating a cheque, negotiation of cheques
- widerruf   countermanding payment of a cheque, countermand of payment, stopping a cheque
- zahlung   payment by cheque
- zeichnungsmaschine   cheque signer

Schere   zwischen Kassa- und Terminkursen   gap (differential) between spot and forward rates

Scheingebot rigged (straw) bid

Scheinkurs fictitious price

Schichtenbilanz statement of loan and interest maturities

Schiffahrtswerte shippings, shipping shares (stocks)

Schiffs

- beleihungsgeschäft lendings against ships
- beleihungsgrundsätze principles for lendings against ships
- hypothek ship mortgage
- hypothekarkredit ship mortgage loan
- hypothekenbank ship mortgage bank
- pfandbrief ship mortgage bond

Schlange currency snake

schleichende Inflation latent (creeping) inflation

schleppendes Aktiengeschäft sluggish market in equities

schließen to close, to finish

die Börse schloß geringfügig schwächer the stock market closed a shade lower

Maschinenbauwerte schlossen fester engineerings finished on a firmer note

zu Tageshöchstkursen - to close at the day's best

unverändert bei .. - to close unchanged at ..

.. schlossen um .. DM höher
.. closed ..DM up, settled .. DM dearer

Schließfach safe deposit box, strongbox

Schluß (a) close, closing; (b) Handelseinheit: minimum trading lot

- der Börsensitzung close of the session
- der Zeichnung closing of the application (subscription) list

Schluß

- basis auf Schlußbasis sprechen to quote at the day's close
- einheit minimum trading lot
- geschäft business at the close of the session
- kurs closing price (quotation, rate)
- note contract note, settlement note
- notierung / -notiz closing quotation
- rechnung Konkursverfahren: receiver's account
- schein contract note
- tag Börse: trading (settlement) day; bei einer Ausschreibung/Zeichnung: closing date
- termin Konkursverfahren: last meeting of the creditors
- verteilung distribution of the bankrupt's estate

schmälern die Gewinne - to clip profits

schmutziges Floaten dirty floating

schnell greifbare Mittel quick assets (i.e. cash in hand, cheques and bills eligible for rediscount with Bundesbank, securities eligible as collateral for Bundesbank borrowings,and interbank deposits running for less than three months)

schnell realisierbare Vermögenswerte quickly realisable assets, assets quickly convertible into cash

Schrankfachvermietung renting safe deposits (strongboxes)

Schrankfachvertrag safe deposit agreement

schrumpfen to shrink, to dwindle, to contract

schrumpfende Gewinnspannen der Unternehmen shrinking corporate profit margins

Schrumpfung der Zinsspannen contraction in (narrowing of) interest margins

Schrumpfungsprozeß process of contraction

Schufa credit information agency

Schuld debt, amount owed

bestehende -en über einen langfristigen Zeitraum refinanzieren to refinance existing debt over a long period

- en halbjährlich bedienen to service debts every six months

- en des öffentlichen Sektors neu strukturieren to restructure public sector borrowings

Schuld

- ablösung repayment (liquidation) of a debt, debt retirement, discharge of a debt

- anerkenntnis acknowledgement of debt, debt acknowledgement

- bedienung debt servicing

- befreiende Wirkung debt-discharging effect

- beitritt bei einem Kredit: co-signing for a loan

- buch government debt register

- buchforderungen government-inscribed debt

schulden to owe

$ 60 Mio, die internationalen Banken aus Umschuldungskrediten geschuldet werden $ 60m owed to international banks on rescheduling loans

die im Rahmen der Kreditvereinbarungen geschuldeten Gelder money owed under the loan (lending) agreements, debt outstanding under the facilities granted

Schuldendienst debt service, debt servicing, interest and redemption payments

Aufrechterhaltung des -es keeping the debt service going

Bereitstellung der für den - benötigten Mittel provision of funds for servicing the debt

Einstellung des -es suspension of debt service payments

Rückstände im - arrears in debt service payments, debt service arrears

Schuldendienst

- abkommen debt service agreement (accord)

- erfordernisse debt service requirements

- finanzierung financing (funding) debt service payments

- last debt servicing burden, debt service load, burden of debt service payments

- leistung servicing a debt, effecting debt service payments, debt servicing

- mittel debt service funds

- relation debt service ratio, ratio of debt service payments to foreign exchange income

- verpflichtungen debt service commitments

seinen Schuldendienstverpflichtungen nicht nachkommen to default on one's debt service commitments

- zahlungen debt service payments, interest and redemption payments

Schulden

- erlaß remission of a debt, foregiveness of indebtedness

- frei unindebted; Grundbesitz: unmortgaged, unencumbered

193

Schulden
- haftung   liability on (for)debts
- krise, internationale   international debt crisis
- last   debt burden (load), total debt (liabilities); bei Grundbesitz: encumbrances, property charges
- management   debt management
- rahmen   debt ceiling, borrowing limit, borrowing ceiling
- refinanzierung   refinancing debts, debt refinancing
- regelung   debt settlement, loan repayment
- stand   debt level, level of indebtedness
- tilgung   debt retirement, discharge (liquidation) of a debt
- umstrukturierung   debt rescheduling, restructuring (rescheduling) the outstanding debt
- verpflichtungen   debt repayment commitments
- verringerung   debt reduction
  Möglichkeiten der Schuldenverringerung   ways to reduce the debt
- verwaltung   debt management

Schuldmitübernahme   bei einem Kredit: cosigning for a loan

Schuldner   debtor, borrower
- adresse, erstklassige   prime (top-quality, first-rate) borrower
- land   debtor country (nation)
- position   im Geldhandel: buying (borrowing) position, to be buyers
- qualität   borrower's standing
- verzug   default of the debtor (of the borrower)

Schuldsaldo   debit balance
Schuldschein   note

Schuldschein
- darlehen   note loan
- forderungen   notes receivable
- geschäft   note business
- markt   note loan market
- offerte   note tender, note offering
- verbindlichkeiten   notes payable

Schuld
- summe   (a) amount owed, amount due; (b) Kredit, Hypothek: principal
- teile   Bilanz: liabilities
- titel   debt issue(s)
- übernahme   assuming a debt, assumption (take-over) of a debt
- umwandlung   debt conversion; im Sinne von Umschuldung: rescheduling
- urkunde   debt instrument
- verschreibung   debenture, bond
- verschreibungen im Umlauf   debentures outstanding
- wechsel   bills payable
- zinsen   interest charges, debt interest, debit interest, interest payable

schwach
- e Verfassung des Marktes   weak (depressed) state of the market
  sehr - tendieren   to turn sharply lower, to be marked sharply lower

Schwäche der DM gegenüber dem Dollar   weakness of the D-mark against the dollar

schwächer
  auf breiter Front -   lower across the board
  erneut - tendieren   to weaken afresh, to continue to weaken
- bei geringen Umsätzen   lower in light (thin) trading

- nach Gewinnmitnahmen   lower on profit-taking

Schwachwährungsländer   soft currency countries

schwanken   to fluctuate, to vary
 die Wechselkurse schwankten stark   exchange rates varied greatly

Schwankungen   fluctuations, variations, swings
 starke -   sharp fluctuations, erratic swings
- der Aktienkurse   fluctuations in equity prices, ups and downs of share prices (in the stock market)
- am Devisenmarkt   fluctuations in the foreign exchange market, vagaries of the foreign exchange market

Schwankungs
- breite   band (margin) of fluctuation, variation range
- kurs   variable price
- markt   variable-price market
- werte   variable-price securities

Schwänze   corner

schwänzen   to corner, to cause a corner situation, to buy up all securities offered in the market

schwarze Zahlen
- schreiben   to operate in the black, to operate at a profit
 wieder - schreiben   to return to the black

Schwebedepot   suspense securities account

Schwebedepotabstimmung   reconciliation of securities accounts

schwebend
- es Engagement   pending commitment
- e Schulden   floating debt

- e Verrechnungen   float

schwere Papiere   heavy-priced shares (stocks)

Schwierigkeiten   difficulties
 in finanziellen - befindliches Unternehmen   financially distressed company
 das Unternehmen geriet in ernste finanzielle -   the company ran into serious financial difficulties

Sechsmonats-Libor   six-month Libor

sehr feste Börse   bull market, strong market

sekundäre internationale Liquidität   foreign exchange held by the private sector

Sekundärgeschäfte   trading in secondary market securities

Sekundärliquidität   secondary liquidity, ⟶ Liquidität zweiten Grades

Sekundärmarkt   secondary market, market for outstanding securities

Sekundawechsel   second of exchange

Selbst
- bedienungs-Terminal   bei einer Bank: customer-operated terminal, automated teller terminal
- behalt / - beteiligung   einer Bank: bank's franchise
- diskontierung   discounting of own acceptances
- eintritt eines Maklers: trading (dealing) for own account
- eintrittsrecht   right to trade for own account
- emission   issue by the company itself (without calling on an issuing house), direct offering, direct placement

Selbst
- finanzierung   self-financing, financing (funding) out of retained profits
- finanzierung der Unternehmen   corporate self-financing
- finanzierungsquote   self--financing ratio
- käufer   underwriter, buyer of an issue (i.e. the underwriter buys the whole of the issue from the company and itself offers it to the investors)

Selbstkostenpreis   cost price
zum - ausweisen   to state (to show) at cost

selbstschuldnerische Bürgschaft   directly enforceable guarantee (i.e. the bank (lender) may claim payment directly from the guarantor)

Selbststeuerungskräfte des Marktes   self-regulating forces of the market

selbsttragend   sich -er Aufschwung am Aktienmarkt   a self-sustaining (self-sufficient) upturn in the equity market

senken   to lower, to reduce, to cut down
Senkung   lowering, reduction, cutting down
- der Kreditzinsen   lowering of lending rates

sichere Anlage   safe investment

Sicherheit   Kreditsicherheit: security, collateral, loan collateral, security for a loan; allgemein: safety, security
 eine für die Bank annehmbare -   a security (collateral) acceptable to the bank
 als annehmbare - ansehen   to regard as reasonably good security

die häufigste -   the most common type of security (collateral)
die bei der Bank als - hinterlegten Wertpapiere   the securities deposited (lodged) with the bank as collateral
die für einen Kredit hinterlegte -   security provided (deposited) in support of a loan, collateral provided for a loan
der Kurswert der als - verwahrten Wertpapiere   the market value of the securities held as collateral
als - für einen Kredit abtreten   to assign as security for a loan
die - verbleibt im Besitz des Kreditnehmers   the collateral remains in possession of the borrower
den Kredit gegen Stellung einer erstklassigen - gewähren   to extend the loan against a first--rate security
die - bei Zahlungsverzug des Kreditnehmers verwerten   to liquidate (to sell) the collateral in the event that the borrower defaults
- einer Anlage (des investierten Kapitals)   safety of an investment (of the capital invested)
- in Form von Immobilien   real estate security (collateral)
- in Form von börsenfähigen Wertpapieren   stock market collateral

Sicherheiten
- bewertung   evaluating the security offered by the borrower, evaluation of a collateral
- form   type of collateral
- geberin   guarantor; party providing security (a collateral)
- nehmerin   guarantee; party accepting a collateral
- prüfung   checking a collateral, evaluation of a collateral

Sicherheiten
- stellung providing (putting up) security for a loan, provision of security (of a collateral)
- verwaltung administration of securities (collaterals)
- verwertung realisation (liquidation) of a collateral
- wert value of a collateral

Sicherheits
- depot securities account serving as collateral
- form security device, type of collateral
- grad degree of security
- gründen, aus for safety reasons
- hinterlegung depositing (lodging) a security
- leistung (a) security (collateral) provided for a loan; (b) providing (putting up) security for a loan, provision of security (of a collateral)
- wechsel collateral bill
- zuschlag safety margin

sichern (a) to secure; (b) to protect, to safeguard; (c) to guarantee; (d) to hedge

den Devisenkurs durch Termingeschäfte - to hedge the exchange rate by forward covering

durch eine Grundbucheintragung gesichert secured by an entry in the land registry

hypothekarisch - to secure by way of mortgage (e.g. by a first-rate mortgage)

Kundeninteressen - to safeguard customer interests

sicherstellen (a) to secure; (b) to ensure, to guarantee, to make sure

Sicherstellungsvertrag security agreement, deed of assignment

Sicherung (a) security; (b) providing security; (c) safeguarding, protection; (d) ensuring, guaranteeing; (e) hedging

zur - aller bestehenden und künftigen Ansprüche as security for all current and future claims; serving as security for and in consideration of all claims to which XYZ is now or may hereafter be entitled

Namensschuldverschreibungen zur - aufgenommener Darlehen begeben to float registered debentures as security for borrowings

Sicherungsabtretung assignment (of claims as security for a loan)
- von Forderungen aus Warenlieferungen assignment of accounts receivable (of trade receivables)

die - offenlegen (den Schuldner über die - informieren) to notify the assignment to the debtor

Sicherungs
- beschlagnahme seizure for security
- form security device, type of collateral
- geber assignor; borrower
- gegenstand ⟶ Sicherungsgut
- geschäft hedge, hedging transaction
- grundschuld land charge registered as security for a loan

Sicherungsgut collateral, property subject to a security interest, property assigned (or pledged or deposited) as security

Übereignung eines -es assignment of a collateral

Verwertung des -es liquidation of the collateral, sale of the property assigned as security

197

Sicherungsgut

Wert des -es   value of the collateral

wirtschaftliche Nutzungsdauer des -es   life of the collateral

Sicherungs

- klausel   security clause; negative pledge clause (i.e. the borrower undertakes not to pledge its assets elsewhere / or: not to grant another lender a higher-ranking security)

- marge   safety margin

- mittel / - möglichkeit   security device

- nehmer   assignee; lender

- pfändung   seizure for security

- recht   security interest

- übereignen   to assign as security (collateral)

- übereignung   assignment (of movables as security for a loan)

- übereignung des Lagerbestandes   assignment of the inventory

- übereignungsvertrag   deed of assignment

- vereinbarung   security agreement (arrangement)

- verkauf   (a) sale (liquidation) of a collateral;(b) hedge (hedging) sale

- vertrag   security agreement

sicherungsweise   as security for, security-wise

- bestellte Grundschuld   land charge registered as security

- abgetretene Warenforderungen   trade receivables assigned as security

Sicherungswert   collateral value

Sicherungszession   →Sicherungsabtretung

Sicht

- einlagen   demand (sight) deposits

- kurs   sight rate

- negoziationskredit   sight negotiation credit

- tratte   sight draft

- verbindlichkeiten   sight liabilities

- wechsel   sight bill

signalisieren   eine Zinssenkung - to herald a cut in interest rates

sinken   der Index für Industriewerte sank um 14 Punkte   the industrial average plunged (dropped, fell) 14 points

Sitz   einer Gesellschaft:registered seat, head office

Sitzung   Börse: session

Sitzungsbeginn /-schluß   Börse: opening (close) of the session

Skontration /Skontrierung   settlement

skontrieren   to settle

Skontro   auxiliary ledger

sofort

- fällig stellen   to call for immediate repayment

- kündbar   immediately callable

- verfügbare Gelder   immediately available funds

Sofort-Abbuchungssystem   on-line debit system

Solawechsel   promissory note

Solidarhaftung   joint and several liability

Soll   debit

- buchung   debit entry

- ertrag   budgeted (projected) earnings

Soll
- kosten   budgeted (projected) expenditure
- kostenrechnung   budget accounting
- posten   debit entry (item)
- saldo   debit balance
- seite   debit side
- zinsen   debit interest
- zinssatz   lending rate

Solvenz   solvency

Sonder
- abschreibung   additional capital allowance
- ausschüttung   special distribution, surplus dividend, superdividend
- ausstattung   von Wertpapieren: special terms, special features
- depot   special securities account
- einlage   special deposit
- finanzierung   special financing facility
- genehmigung   special clearance
- konditionen   special (preferential) terms, preferential (concessional) interest rate
- kontingent   special quota
- konto   special account
- kredit   special facility, special-purpose loan, project-tied facility
- kreditprogramm   special lending scheme
- kündigungsrecht   bei einer Anleihe: special call right
- Lombardkredit   special Lombard facility
- plafond   special line, special facility
- posten mit Rücklagenanteil   special reserves
- posten aus Währungsumrechnung   unrealised gain (loss) from currency translations
- prüfung   special audit
- rechte   special rights
- rücklage   special contingency reserve, surplus reserve, appropriated reserve
- verwahrung   individual safekeeping (custody) of securities, jacket custody
- vollmacht   special power of attorney, special proxy
- wertberichtigung   special allowance, special charge for bad and doubtful debts
- wertberichtigung auf Kredite   special charge for bad loans

Sorgfaltspflicht der Bank   banker's duty of care

Sorten   currency, foreign notes and coin
- ankaufskurs   currency buying rate
- bestand   currency in bank vaults
- handel   dealings in foreign notes and coin, currency dealings
- kurs   exchange rate (i.e. buying or selling rate)
- verkaufskurs   currency selling rate

Sortiment   einer Bank: range of services offered, bank's product line (range)

Sortimentserweiterung   increase in the range of services offered

Spanne   spread, margin
- zwischen Ausgabe- und Rücknahmekurs bei Fondsanteilen: bid/offer spread
- zwischen Geld- und Briefkurs Aktien: bid/offer spread, spread between bids and offers
  Devisen: bid/ask spread, spread between buying and selling rates

Spannen   spreads, margins

- im traditionellen Kreditgeschäft   spreads (margins)
on the traditional forms of
lending

Erweiterung der -   widening of
spreads

Verringerung der -   narrowing
of spreads

Spannenpreis   spread price

Spannenrechnung   margin costing

Spannkurs   mean spread of the
fixing

Spar

- anreiz   incentives for saving,
stimulus to savings, savings
incentive

- aufkommen   volume of saving,
net savings

- betrag   amount saved, amount
paid into a savings account

- bildung   formation of savings

- brief   savings certificate

ein 8%iger - mit vierjähriger
Laufzeit   a four-year savings
certificate paying 7 per cent
interest

- buch   passbook

Auszahlungen gegen Vorlage des
-es   withdrawals (payments)
against presentation of the
passbook

- dauerauftrag   standing savings
order

- eckzins   basic savings rate

Spareinlagen   savings deposits,
savings; niedrigverzinsliche
Spareinlagen: passbook deposits
(US), Oberbegriff für Spareinlagen: thrift deposits (US)

- mit einjähriger Kündigungsfrist
savings deposits subject to a
12 months' withdrawal notice

- mit gesetzlicher Kündigungsfrist
savings deposits subject to the
statutory withdrawal notice
(i.e. three months); ninety-day
notice deposits

Abfluß von -   savings outflow, outflow of savings deposits

Abzug von -   drain on savings
deposits, withdrawal of savings

höherverzinsliche -   savings
deposits carrying a higher rate
of interest

Kündigung von -   giving notice
of the intended withdrawal of
savings

Kündigungsvorschriften für -
notice requirements for savings
deposits

Rückgang der -   decline (drop)
in savings deposits

Verzinsung der -   interest rate
paid (earned) on savings deposits,
return on savings

Vorschußzinsen für eine vorzeitige
Verfügung über -   interest
penalty for an early withdrawal
of savings (i.e. prior to expiration of the agreed notice period)

für einen bestimmten Zeitraum
festgelegte -   savings committed
for a specific period (length)
of time

Zinssätze auf -   savings deposit
rates

Zufluß von -   savings inflow, inflow of savings deposits (of new
savings funds)

sparen / Sparen   to save / saving

Sparer   saver, depositor, savings
depositor

- schutz   assuring the safety
of depositors' funds

Spar

- ergebnis   net savings

- förderung   encouraging savings,
promoting thrift, promoting the
idea of thrift in the popula-
tion

Spar

- förderungsmaßnahmen measures designed to promote saving (thrift), ways to encourage thrift
- form type of savings, savings facility (vehicle)
- freudigkeit saving propensity, propensity to save
- funktion saving function
- gelder savings funds, savers' funds, savings deposits
- geldstrom savings flow
- geschäft savings business, deposit-taking operations (activities), thrift business
- girokonto current account (kept with a savings bank)
- gironetz giro network operated by the savings banks
- guthaben (a) balance in a savings account;(b) insgesamt: deposits (balances) on savings accounts
- kapitalbildung formation of savings capital

Sparkasse savings bank (institution); Trustee Savings Bank (Br); USA - in der Reihenfolge ihrer Bedeutung: savings and loan association, mutual savings bank, credit union -Oberbegriff für diese Institute in den USA: thrift institutions, thrifts

Aktivgeschäft der -n savings bank lending, thrift institution lending

Hypothekengeschäft der -n savings banks' mortgage operations, thrifts' mortgage credit activities

Passivgeschäft der -n savings banks' deposit operations, thrifts' deposit-taking business

Refinanzierungskosten der -n cost of funds to savings banks, thrift institutions' cost of funds

Sparkassen

- brief savings bank certificate
- buch passbook
- einlagen deposits with savings banks, deposits with thrifts
- girozentrale Central Savings Bank
- obligation savings bank bond
- prüfung savings bank audit
- sektor savings bank sector, savings banks; thrifts, thrift institutions
- stelle savings bank office
- verband Savings Bank Association
- verwaltungsrat Board of Directors of a savings bank, Savings Bank Board
- vorstand Board of Management of a savings bank
- wesen savings bank system, thrift institution system,thrifts

Sparkonto savings account; USA: savings and loan account(bei savings and loan associations); passbook savings account -Oberbegriff: thrift account

Abhebung vom - withdrawal of funds from a savings account

Beträge automatisch auf ein - überweisen lassen to have funds automatically transferred to a savings account

Verfügung über ein - gegen Vorlage des Sparbuches drawing on a savings account against presentation of the passbook

auf ein - einzahlen to pay into a savings account, to put (to place, to deposit) in a savings account

das - wird mit einer vereinbarten Kündigungsfrist geführt the savings account is kept under an agreed period of notice

Spar
- kontoinhaber savings account holder, thrift account holder
- leistung (a) amount saved, amount paid into a savings account; (b) insgesamt: net savings, new deposits less withdrawals
- mittel savings funds, savers' funds
- motive reasons for saving
- obligation savings bond
- plan savings scheme
- prämie savings bonus
- quote savings ratio (rate)
- rate savings instalment
- schuldverschreibung savings bond
- summe amount saved, amount paid into a savings account
- tätigkeit savings activity
- verhalten savings behaviour
- vertrag savings scheme
- vertragskonto savings scheme account
- volumen total savings
- willen propensity to save
- zinsen (a) interest on savings deposits, interest paid (earned) on savings deposits; (b) saving deposit rates

Spektrum range, spectrum
- an Anlagemöglichkeiten spectrum of investment vehicles (opportunities)
- an Dienstleistungen range of services offered

Spekulation speculation

spekulationsbedingt speculative, speculation-induced
- e Kursschwankungen speculative price swings
- e leichte Kurserholung speculative flurry
- e Pluskorrekturen speculative mark-ups

Spekulations
- druck speculative pressure
- gelder speculative (hot) funds
- geschäft speculative bargain (deal)
- gewinn speculative gain
- käufe speculative buying
- steuer capital gains tax
- verkäufe speculative selling
- welle speculative surge in the market, welter of speculative buying
- werte speculative counters, speculatives, hot issues

spekulativ speculative
- e Anlage speculative investment
- e Kapitalbewegungen speculative flows of capital
- e Nachfrage bei geringen Umsätzen speculative demand in a thin market

spekulieren to speculate, to play the market, to trade in and out of the market

Sperre (a) blocking, locking in; (b) ban, freeze, immobilisation; (c) blocking period

sperren to block, to immobilise, to lock in, to stop

ein Konto - to block (to stop) an account

einen Scheck - to stop payment on a cheque, to stop a cheque

Sperr
- frist (a) blocking period; (b) Karenzzeit: waiting (qualifying) period
- guthaben blocked deposits (balances)
- konto blocked account

Sperr
- liste   black list
- minorität   blocking minority (minority representing at least 25 per cent of the equity)
- stücke / - titel   blocked (earmarked) securities
- vermerk   (a) blocking notice; (b) non-negotiability clause
- verpflichtung   undertaking not to sell the securities prior to a fixed period

Spezialitätenhausse   Börse: upsurge in specialties

Spezialwerte   specialties

Spielraum
geringer - für ein Nachgeben der Zinssätze   little scope for a fall in interest rates

jmd. - zur Durchführung der notwendigen Veränderungen geben   to give s.o. elbowroom to make the necessary changes

der verfügbare fiskalpolitische -   the fiscal leeway available

Spitze   (a) residual amount; (b) bei Wertpapieren: fraction, fractional share

Spitzen
- ausgleich   settlement of fractions, settling fractions
- bedarf   im Kreditgeschäft: peak borrowing requirements
- beträge   fractions, fractional (residual) amounts
- ergebnis   record performance
- gruppe   top bracket
- inanspruchnahmen   im Kreditgeschäft: peak borrowings
- institut   top (umbrella) organisation
- konto   fractions account
- regulierung   settlement of fractions
- verband   top (head, parent) organisation

sprunghaft steigende Aktienkurse
zooming (rocketing) equity prices

Sprungregreß   recourse to prior endorsers

staatlich
- subventioniert   government-subsidised, aided by the government
- e Bürgschaften für Exportkredite   government guarantees for export credits
- e Förderungsmaßnahmen   government (state) incentives
- e Kapitalmarktbeanspruchung   government borrowings in the capital market
- es Konjunkturprogramm   government measures designed to stimulate economic activity
- e Kreditaufnahme   government borrowing
- er Schuldner   bei Länderkrediten: sovereign borrower
- e Wohnungsbauförderung   government aid to housing
- e Zuschüsse   government (state) subsidies, government grants

Staatspapiere / Staatstitel
government securities, governments (US), gilt-edged securities, gilts (Br)

Stadtanleihe   local authority bond

Staffel   scale, table

Staffelanleihe   graduated-interest loan

staffeln   to graduate, to grade, to stagger

Staffelzins   graduated interest rate

Stagnation   stagnation, stalemate, sluggishness, dullness

stagnierende Börse   stale (dull,
stagnant) market

Stahlaktien   steels

Stämme / Stammaktien   ordinary
shares (Br), common shares,
common stock (US)

Bezugsrechtsscheine auf -
common stock warrants

Kaufoption auf -   common stock
purchase privilege

Stammaktien
- dividende   dividend on ordinary shares, common stock
  dividend
- emission   ordinary share issue,
  common stock issue
- inhaber   ordinary shareholder,
  common stockholder
- kapital   ordinary share capital,
  common stockholders' equity

Stand   (a) Kurs, Zinssätze: level;
Konto, Wertpapierbestand:
balance, position
- per Jahresende   (a) year-end
  level; (b) balance (position)
  as of December 31st
den höchsten - erreichen   to
reach an absolute high
den tiefsten - erreichen   to
touch rock bottom, to reach
an absolute low

Standardaktien   equity leaders,
leading (first-line) equities,
Blue Chips

standardisierte Kreditprogramme
standardised lending schemes

standardisierter Privatkredit
standardised personal loan

Stand-by Kredit   stand-by loan
(facility)

stark
- er Anstieg der Aktienkurse
  strong advance in equities,
  sharp rise of stock prices
- er Kursrückgang   heavy drop in
  prices, sharp slump (plunge) in
  prices
- e Kursschwankungen   wildly
  erratic price swings
- variabler Kurs   wide quotation

stärken   to strengthen, to re-
inforce
die Eigenkapitalbasis -   to
strengthen the equity base
die Ankündigung stärkte das Ver-
trauen der Anleger in einen Kursaufschwung   the announcement
buttressed the investors' confi-
dence in an upturn in prices

Stärkung   strenghtening, reinforcement

Starthilfekredit   business set-up
loan

Status   (a) status, position;
(b) Vermögensaufstellung:finan-
cial statements, statement of
condition

Statuten   articles of association,
statutes

steigen   to rise, to increase
steigende Kreditnachfrage   rising
credit (loan) demand
Hoffnungen auf eine Wiederaufnahme
der Dividendenzahlungen ließen
XYZ um 5 auf 130DM steigen   hopes
on a resumption of dividend payments lifted XYZ 5 to 130DM
die Nettoerträge stiegen gegenüber
dem Vorjahreszeitraum um das vierfache   net earnings were four
times those of the same period
last year
der Provisionsüberschuß stieg gegenüber dem Vorjahr um .. DM Mio
net commission income was DM .. m
ahead of the results achieved a
year earlier

Maschinenbauwerte stiegen weiter engineerings continued to advance

der Zinsüberschuß stieg auf .. net interest income rose to ..

steigern to increase, to raise, to lift; verbessern: to improve; verstärken: to intensify, to step up

XYZ konnten sich um 5 auf 80DM - XYZ firmed (hardened) 5 to 80DM

Steigerung increase, rise, growth; improvement; intensification, stepping up; Wertsteigerung: appreciation

eine achtprozentige - gegenüber dem Vorjahr an 8 per cent increase over last year's level

eine beträchtliche - des Neuemissionsgeschäftes a noticeable growth in new issue activities

eine vierfache - des Absatzes von Sparobligationen a fourfold increase in savings bond sales

- des Ergebnisses im Hypothekenbereich improving the performance in the mortgage banking sector

steile

- Abwärtsbewegung downhill slide, sharp downward trend, nosedive

- Aufwärtsbewegung strong upturn (upward trend)

Stellage put and call transaction, straddle

Stelle (a) position, place; (b) rank; (c) office

von der Bilanzsumme her an zweiter - stehen to rank second in total assets

an zwölfter - unter den ersten 100 stehen to rank 12th in the top 100

bei anderen -n aufgenommene Kredite loans raised from other sources

kreditgebende -n lenders, lending offices (sources)

zuständige -n bodies (offices, agencies) concerned

stellen

ein Akkreditiv - to open a documentary credit

das Geschäftsvolumen stellte sich auf DM .. volume of business totalled DM ..

der vom Kreditnehmer zu stellende Antrag the application to be filed by the borrower

einen Kurs - im Devisenhandel: to quote a rate

eine Sicherheit - to put up security, to provide (to furnish) a collateral

der Wechsel ist bei .. zahlbar gestellt the bill of exchange is made payable at ..

der durch die Zahlungsanweisung zur Verfügung gestellte Betrag the sum being made available by the payment order

Stellgeschäft → Stellage

Stellkurs put and call price

Stellung position, standing, rating; putting up

- am Kapitalmarkt position (rating) in the money market

- dinglicher Sicherheiten provision of real security

- liquider Sicherheiten putting up liquid security (e.g. savings deposits)

Stellvertretung in offener Stellvertretung verkaufen Emission: to sell in the name and for account of the issuer

Steuer tax

- aufwand tax charge (expenditure)

- aval tax payment guarantee

- befreiung tax exemption

steuerbegünstigt
- e Anlagen tax-privileged investments
- e Investitionen capital expenditure carrying tax reliefs

Steuer
- belastung tax burden (load)
- belastung der Ausschüttungen tax levied on payouts
- erhebung levying a tax, taxation
- erklärung tax return
- erleichterung tax relief
- ersparnis tax saving

steuerfrei tax-exempt, tax-free, tax-sheltered
- e Wertpapiere tax-exempt (tax-sheltered) securities

Steuer
- freijahre tax break (holiday)
- gutschrift tax credit
- kurswert tax-related stock price
- lastquote tax load ratio
- lich absetzbar tax-deductible
- oase tax haven

steuerpflichtig taxable, subject to tax
- e Kapitalerträge taxable investment income

Steuer
- rückerstattung tax refund
- rückstellungen tax provisions, taxation provisions
- schraube tax load (push)
- schuld tax liability
- termin tax payment date, date on which major tax payments fall due
- verbindlichkeiten taxes payable, tax liabilities

- vergünstigung tax relief

Stichkupon renewal coupon

Stichtag record (cut-off) date; accounting (balance sheet) date; settlement date

Stichwort-Akkreditiv proposed letter of credit

still
- e Beteiligung dormant holding
- es Factoring undisclosed (non-notification) factoring
- er Gesellschafter dormant (sleeping) partner
- e Rücklagen hidden (undisclosed) reserves
- e Zession undisclosed (non-notification) assignment

Stillhalter writer (seller) of an option
- in Aktien (einer Kaufoption) writer (seller) of a call option
- in Geld (einer Verkaufsoption) writer (seller) of a put option, put writer

stillegen (a) to shut down, to close down;(b) to immobilise

stimmberechtigt carrying voting rights, voting
- er Aktionär voting shareholder
- e Stammaktien ordinary voting shares

Stimmenliste voting list, list of shareholders represented in a general meeting

Stimm-Material voting shares

Stimmrecht voting right (power)

Stimmrechts
- ausübung voting, exercising the voting right
- ausübung durch einen Bevollmächtigten voting by proxy

- bevollmächtigter   proxy
- kontrolle   voting control
- lose Aktie   non-voting share
- treuhänder   voting trustee
- verwässerung   dilution of voting power
- übertragung   transfer of voting rights, voting right transfer
- vertreter   proxy
- vollmacht   voting proxy
- weisung   voting instructions

Stimmung   Börse: sentiment, tone of the market

Stimmungsbesserung   improvement in market sentiment

stimulieren
die Entwicklung am Rentenmarkt stimulierte Anleger   investors were encouraged by the bond market trend

gute Konjunkturnachrichten stimulierten   favourable economic news propelled the stock market

Presseberichte stimulierten   press comment lifted stock prices, equity prices were buoyed by press comment

stoppen   to stop, to halt
den Zinsauftrieb -   to halt the upsurge in interest rates

Zinszahlungen -   to halt interest payments

Stoppkurs   stop (ceiling) price

Stopp-Loss-Auftrag   stop-loss order, cutting limit order

Stopp-Tag   record date

stornieren   to cancel, to reverse an entry

Stornierung   cancellation, reversal, reversing an entry

stoßen
auf spekulative Nachfrage -   to meet with speculative demand

XYZ stießen bei 130DM auf Interesse   XYZ encountered support at 130DM

straffe Haushaltsführung   stringent budget policy

Strategie im Privatkundenbereich   retail banking strategy

Strazze   jacket

strecken
ein Darlehen -   to extend the maturity of a loan, to stretch out a loan repayment

Streckung   extending the loan maturity, maturity extension, stretching out a loan repayment
- der Kapitalfälligkeiten   extending the maturity of principal repayments

Streckungsdarlehen   (a) advance granted to cover the discount deducted from a loan; (b) bridge-over loan

Streifband
- depot   individual securities account, allocated custody account
- depotstücke   securities held under individual securities accounts
- gebühr   individual custody fee
- verwahrung   individual safekeeping of securities, jacket custody

Streubesitz   widely spread holdings

streuen   to spread, to diversify

Streuung   spread(ing), diversification
- von Anlagen   spreading of investments, asset diversification

Strich   Positionen unter dem -   off-balance sheet items

Strukturanpassungskredit structural adjustment loan

stückbezogene Erträge unit-related earnings

Stückdividende dividend per share

Stücke securities

zur Rückzahlung fällige - securities (bonds) due for redemption

Übergabe effektiver - delivery (surrender) of physical securities

Stücke
- aussonderung segregating securities
- bewegungen securities transactions, transactions (turnover) in securities
- bilanz statement of securities transactions

stückeln (a) to fix denominations of, to denominate; (b) to split up

stückelos
- e Abwicklung paperless settlement; settlement not involving the transfer of physical securities
- e Anleihen paperless bonds
- e Lieferung paperless delivery
- er Wertpapierverkehr paperless securities transactions

Stückelung denomination

in - en von DM 1000 emittieren to issue in denominations of DM 1,000

in - en von DM 1000 oder einem Mehrfachen davon in denominations of DM 1,000 or multiples thereof

Wertpapiere in großen -en large--denomination securities

Stückelungsanweisungen denomination instructions

Stückemangel shortage of offerings

stückemäßiger Verkehr securities transactions involving transfer of the underlying certificates

Stücke
- nummer security code number
- regulierung delivery of the securities involved, delivery of the underlying certificates
- verzeichnis list of securities
- zuteilung allotment of securities

Stückgebühren unit charges

Stück
- leistungen einer Bank: technical banking services (e.g. money transmission service)
- notierung unit quotation
- nummer share (bond) certificate number
- wertaktie share quoted per unit
- zinsen interest accrued, running interest
- zinsenberechnung calculation of interest accrued

Stufen
- flexibilität crawling peg
- kauf Wertpapiere: scale buying
- preise staggered prices

stunden to grant an extension of time for payment, to defer

Stundung deferral, deferment
- von Krediten debt deferral
- der Tilgungszahlungen deferring repayments on loans
- von Zinszahlungen deferral of interest rate payments

stützen Kurs, Währung: to support, to peg; finanziell: to back, to support

Stützung   support, backing, pegging

Intervention zur - der amerikanischen Währung   intervention in support of the US currency

Maßnahmen zur - der Zinspolitik   measures designed to prop up the interest rate policy

Stützungs
- aktion   (a) support operation (measures); (b) zur Rettung eines finanziell angeschlagenen Unternehmens: rescue operation, lifeboat

  die an der Stützungsaktion beteiligten Banken   lifeboat banks

- fonds   support (stand-by) fund; guarantee fund

- konsortium   support group, backing syndicate; rescue group

- kredit   standby credit

- kurs   pegged rate (price)

- maßnahmen   support measures; rescue measures

- maßnahmen, konjunkturelle   measures designed to support economic activity

- programm   support scheme; rescue scheme

- verpflichtungen   support commitments

Submissionsverfahren   Emissionsgeschäft: public tender

subsidiäres Akkreditiv   secondary credit

Substanz   material assets, value
- erhaltung   maintenance of value
- gesicherte Aktie   stock backed by material assets
- steuern   property taxes
- verlust   loss of material assets

- wert   Investmentfonds: net asset value; Wertpapiere: intrinsic value; Unternehmung: net asset value

- werte   Wertpapiere: top-quality (first-line) industrials; einer Unternehmung: fixed assets

- zuwachs   (a) growth in assets; (b) capital appreciation, increase in value

Substitutionskonto   substitution account

subventionieren   to subsidise, to support, to grant subsidies

subventioniertes Kreditprogramm   government-supported loan (lending) scheme

Subventionierung   subsidising, subsidisation, granting subsidies

- durch zinsgünstige Kredite   subsidising through low-interest loans

Subventionsprogramm   subsidising scheme

Summenaktie   share issued for a specific amount

Superdividende   superdividend, surplus dividend

Swapgeschäft   swap transaction

Swapkonditionen   swap terms

Swapkurs / - satz   swap rate

Switch-Geschäft   switch

Switch-Prämie   switch premium

Syndikatsführung   lead management

mit der - betrauen   to award the lead management to

syndizieren   to syndicate

syndiziert
- e Anleihe   syndicated loan
- e Bankfinanzierung   syndicated bank financing

<u>syndizierter Eurowährungskredit</u>
  <u>syndicated Eurocurrency credit</u>

<u>Syndizierung</u>   syndication

<u>Syndizierungstechnik</u>   syndication
  techniques

<u>System</u>
- fester Wechselkurse   system of
  fixed exchange rates
- gleitender Wechselkurse   system
  of floating exchange rates
- multipler Wechselkurse   multiple
  exchange rate system

T

T Kurszusatz: estimated price (no official quotation)

Tafelgeschäft ⟶ Schaltergeschäft

Tagesauszug daily statement of account

Tagesdefizit/Tagesfehlbetrag im Geldhandel: day-to-day deficit (shortage), deficit at the close of trading

Tagesgeld overnight money (funds) (Br), Federal (Fed) funds (US); in beiden Sprachräumen auch bekannt: call money

- unter Banken overnight interbank money

Tagesgeld
- abschlüsse overnight contracts (deals), transactions in Fed funds, call money deals
- ausleihung overnight loan (lending)
- forderungen overnight money sold, overnight loans (lendings), Fed funds sold
- handel dealings in overnight money, trading in Fed funds
- hergaben overnight loans (lendings)
- markt overnight money market, Fed funds market, call money market
- positionen overnight money commitments, call money commitments
- satz overnight rate, Fed funds rate, call money rate
- verbindlichkeiten overnight money bought (borrowed), overnight borrowings, Fed funds bought

Tages
- höchstkurs day's high (peak, best)
- kurs daily price (quotation), current rate
- order bei Börsenaufträgen: day order
- saldo daily balance
- spitze unbalanced position (surplus or deficit) at the close of trading
- überschuß im Geldhandel: day-to-day surplus, surplus at the close of trading
- umsätze Börse: daily turnover, daily volume of business
- wert market price (value)

taggleiche Verbuchung same-day settlement (accounting)

täglich fällige Gelder sight (demand) deposits

täglich kündbar subject to call

Tagwechsel bill due on a specified date

Talfahrt
- der Aktienkurse nosedive of stock prices, sharp slide in equities
- der Konjunktur sharp economic downswing (downturn), plunge into a recession

Talon renewal coupon
- einreichung presentation of a renewal coupon

Tarif Gebührenordnung: scale (schedule) of charges; Gehaltstarif: agreed pay scale

tarifbesteuerte Wertpapiere fully taxed securities

Tarif
- partner   management and unions, employers and employed
- vertrag   collective pay agreement
- werte   Börse: utilities

tätig   im Eurokreditgeschäft -e Banken   banks operating in the Eurolending business

tätigen   Abschlüsse - to trade contracts, to make (to conclude) deals

Tätigkeit   activity, operations

tatsächlich
- e Kosten der Inanspruchnahme   true cost of borrowing
- e Kreditaufnahme   actual borrowings
- e Verzinsung   effective (true) interest return
- er Zinssatz   effective interest rate

Tausch
- depot   exchangeable securities account
- transaktion   bei Aktien: switching, equity switching
- verwahrung   exchangeable custody

Taxe/Taxkurs   estimated price

technisch
- e Globalurkunde   global bond certificate (certificate which may be replaced by individual certificates)
- e Kurserholung   technical rally, technical markups
- e Reaktion   technical rebound
- e Reaktion auf die Kurssteigerungen der vergangenen Woche   the market entered a correction phase in reaction to last week's widespread advance

Technologiebereich/Technologiewerte   technology stocks

Teil
- akzept   partial acceptance
- amortisationsvertrag   partial pay-out (non-fully-pay-out) agreement
- annahme   partial acceptance
- ausnutzung eines Akkreditivs   partial drawdown (drawing) on a documentary credit
- betrag   partial amount
- betriebsergebnis   partial operating results (figures excluding securities and foreign exchange trading income as well as loan loss provisions and write-offs)
- briefbildung   taking out (executing) a partial land charge deed
- emission   partial issue, part of an issue
- habereffekten   equities
- inanspruchnahme   partial drawing (drawdown), drawing in part
- indossament   partial endorsement
- kündigung einer Emission   partial redemption notice, calling in part of an issue, partial call
- löschung   partial discharge (release, satisfaction)
- rechte   fractions, fractional interests
- reproduktionswert einer Unternehmung: net asset value
- schuldschein   short-term note
- schuldverschreibung   bond, debenture
- übertragung des Akkreditivs   partial assignment of the documentary credit
- wertmethode   discount value method

Teilzahlung   instalment, payment on account, partial payment

Teilzahlungs
- bank   instalment credit bank, personal finance company (US), hire purchase finance house (Br)
- basis   auf - on an instalment basis
- finanzierung   instalment financing, hire purchase financing
- forderungen   instalment debtors
- geschäft   (a) instalment credit transaction; (b) insgesamt: instalment credit operations
- institut → Teilzahlungsbank
- kauf   instalment buying, hire purchase, credit purchase (sale)
- kredit   instalment credit, hire purchase loan
- kreditgeschäft   instalment lending, instalment credit operations
- kreditinstitut → Teilzahlungsbank
- kreditkosten   instalment credit costs
- vertrag   instalment credit agreement, hire purchase agreement
- wechsel   instalment credit bill

Telefon
- handel   over-the-telephone dealings, unofficial market
- papiere   securities traded in the unofficial market
- verkehr   unofficial market, market over the telephone

telegrafische Anschaffung   remittance by cable

Tendenz   tendency, trend
- umschwung   trend reversal, turnaround, break

Tenderverfahren   Börse: Angebot im Tenderverfahren   offer for sale by tender

tendieren
Bankaktien tendierten uneinheitlich bei geringen Umsätzen   bank stocks were mixed in light (thin) trading

Chemieaktien tendierten nach Glattstellungen des Berufshandels rückläufig   chemicals trended downward on professional profit-taking

Termin   per - kaufen (verkaufen)   to buy (to sell) for forward delivery

Termin
- abschlag   forward discount
- abschluß   forward contract (deal), futures contract
- aufgeld   forward premium
- börse   futures (forward) exchange
- devisen   forward exchange, exchange for forward (future) delivery
- dollar   forward dollar
- einlage   time (term) deposit investment, term money placed
- einlagen   time (term) deposits

termingebunden   tied (linked) to a specific date

Termingeld   im Geldhandel: term money; im Privatkundengeschäft: time (term) deposits

- abschlüsse   term money contracts (deals), term money dealings
- anlage   im Geldhandel: term money placed; im Privatkundengeschäft: time (term) deposit investment
- aufnahmen   term money borrowings
- bestand   term money holdings; time deposit volume

Termingeld
- geschäfte   term money transactions, time deposit operations
- hergaben   term money lendings
- konto   term money account, time deposit account
- mit einer Laufzeit von mehr als zwei Monaten   term money (time deposits) running for more than two months
- satz   term money rate, time deposit rate

Termingeschäft
Devisentermingeschäft: forward currency transaction (deal); Finanztermingeschäft: financial futures contract; Warentermingeschäft: commodity futures contract; Zinstermingeschäft: interest rate futures contract

Terminhandel   forward dealings, futures trading, trading (dealings) in futures
- in Aktienindizes   stock-index futures trading
- in Devisen   forward currency dealings (trading)
- in Zinspapieren   interest rate futures trading

terminiertes Tagesgeld   term money (running for more than thirty days)

Termin
- kauf   forward purchase, purchase for future delivery, buying (e.g. foreign currency) forward
- käufer   forward buyer
- kaufs-Deckungsgeschäft   long hedge
- kommissionär   futures commission broker
- kontrakt   futures contract, forward deal
- kurs   forward rate (price)
- kursbildung   determination of the forward rate
- markt   forward market, futures market
- markt für Finanzpapiere   financial futures market
- markt für Zinspapiere   interest rate futures market
- notierung   forward quotation, futures quotation, quotation for forward delivery
- papiere   forward securities, securities traded for forward (future) delivery, futures instruments
- positionen   forward commitments (interests), commitments for forward (future) delivery
- sicherung   forward cover, futures hedge
- spekulation   forward speculation, speculation in futures
- überwachung   monitoring (control) of maturities
- überwachungsliste   maturity control list
- verbindlichkeiten   time liabilities, liabilities under futures contracts
- verkauf   sale for future delivery, forward sale, selling (e.g. foreign currency) forward
- verkaufs-Deckungsgeschäft   short hedge
- ware   future commodity

tertiärer Sektor   tertiary industry (sector)

Testat des Buchprüfers: auditor's (audit) opinion

thesaurieren   to reinvest, to retain

thesaurierte Anlageerträge   reinvested investment income

thesaurierter Gewinn   retained profit (income)

Thesaurierungsfonds   growth fund

Thesaurierungspolitik   profit retention policy

Ticker-Notierung   tape quotation

Tiefpunkt   low, bottom

absoluter -   all-time low, rock-bottom, lowest-ever level

- der Baisse   bottom of the bear market

- der Rezession   bottom of the recession (of the trough)

den - erreichen   to bottom, to touch bottom

auf einen - fallen   to drop (to plummet) to a new low

tilgen   Anleihe: to redeem; Hypothek: to clear (to pay) off; Kredit: to repay, to pay back (off)

Tilgung   redemption, repayment

- durch jährliche Auslosungen redemption by annual drawings

- mit einem Aufgeld   redemption at a premium

- zum (über, unter dem) Nennwert redemption at (above, below) par

Tilgungs

- ankündigung   redemption (call) notice

- anleihe   redemption bond, callable bond (loan)

- aufforderung   call for redemption (repayment)

- aufgeld   premium on redemption, call (redemption) premium

- aufschub   deferral of redemption payments, deferring repayments (e.g. on a loan)

- aussetzung   suspension (halt) of redemption payments, redemption break (holiday)

- belastung   redemption requirements, redemption charge, loan payments required

- betrag, jährlicher   annual redemption payment

- darlehen   annuity loan (i.e. the loan is repaid in equal instalments or at redemption rates increasing over the life of the loan)

- dauer   redemption period, period of repayment

- dienst   redemption service, loan payment service

- erfordernisse   redemption requirements, repayments (redemption payments) required

- fonds   sinking (redemption) fund

- freie Jahre   redemption-free years, grace period, redemption holiday

- gewinn   gain on redemption

- hypothek   redemption mortgage

- kongruente Refinanzierungstitel funding instruments at matching redemption rates

- kurs   redemption (repayment) price

- lebensversicherung   mortgage protection insurance

Tilgungsleistungen   repayments, redemptions, redemption payments, repayments on a loan, loan payments

gleichbleibende monatliche - während der vereinbarten Laufzeit des Kredites   equal monthly repayments (loan payments) over the life of the loan

falls der Kreditnehmer mit den - in Verzug geraten ist   if the borrower has defaulted on his payment schedule (on his loan payment commitments)

Tilgungs

- mittel   redemption funds, funds available for redemptions (repayments)

- modalitäten   repayment terms, terms of redemption (repayment)

Tilgungs
- plan   redemption (repayment) schedule, loan repayment schedule (plan)
- quote   repayment (redemption) rate
- rate   (a) repayment (redemption) rate; (b) loan instalment payment, redemption instalment
- recht   right of redemption, call right
- rückflüsse   repayments on loans
- rücklage   sinking fund reserve
- rückstände   redemption (repayment) arrears
- satz   repayment (redemption) rate
- streckung   (a) extending the redemption period, extending the period of repayment; (b) bei Hypothekendarlehen:adding the mortgage discount to the loan principal (thus extending the repayment period)
- streckungsdarlehen   loan to cover the discount deducted from the loan principal
- stücke   securities repurchased by the issuer or the underwriter
- überhang   excess of redemptions, net repayments (e.g. on loans)
- verpflichtungen   redemption (repayment) commitments
- volumen   total of securities redeemed, total redemptions
- wert   redemption value, value upon redemption (repayment)
- zahlung   repayment (on a loan), redemption payment
- zeitraum   period of repayment, redemption period

totes Kapital   idle funds

totes Konto   gesperrtes Konto: blocked account; umsatzloses Konto: dormant (inactive)account

tote Papiere   inactive stock

totes Portefeuille   blocked portfolio

traditionelles Bankgeschäft   mainstream banking

Traditionspapiere   title documents

Tranche   tranche

Transaktions-Nummer   beim Bildschirmtext: TAN (transaction number)

Transfer
- abkommen   transfer agreement
- einkommen   transfer income
- risiko   transfer risk
- stelle   transfer agent
- zahlungen   transfer payments

transitorisch
- e Aufwendungen   deferred charges
- e Buchung   suspense entry
- e Diskonterträge   unearned discounts
- e Forderungen   suspense receivables
- er Posten   deferred item

Trassant   drawer

Trassat   drawee

Trassierungskredit   documentary acceptance credit, reimbursement credit

Tratte   draft

Trattengegenwert / -erlös   proceeds of a draft

treiben in die Höhe -   to drive (to force, to push) up

Trend zu niedrigeren Konditionen   downward movement in pricing

Treppenkredit   graduated-interest loan

Treppenkupon interest rate (coupon rate) increasing over the life of a loan

Tresor strongroom, vault
- fach strongbox, safe deposit box
- räume vaults

Treugeber trustor, donor of a trust

Treuhand
- anlagen trustee investments
- bank trust bank company, trustee bank
- einlagen trustee deposits

Treuhänder trustee, fiduciary

als - tätig sein to act as trustee, to trustee, to act in a fiduciary capacity

Treuhänderdepot securities trust account, third-party custody account

treuhänderisch verwahren to hold on trust

Treuhänderschaft trusteeship

Treuhand
- gelder trustee funds
- geschäfte, Erträge aus -n trust (fiduciary) investment income
- gesellschaft trust company
- konto trust account
- kredite loans extended under public lending schemes (the lending bank does not assume the loan risk); credits extended for third-party account
- stelle trust agency (office)
- urkunde trust deed
- verhältnis trusteeship
- vermögen trust property, trust assets (fund)
- vertrag trust indenture, trust agreement
- verwaltung trusteeship, fiduciary management

Treunehmer trustee

trockene Stücke mortgage bonds in circulation

trockener Wechsel promissory note

U

überbeanspruchen die steigende Zahl von Neuemissionen hat den Markt überbeansprucht the growing number of new issues has overstretched the market

Überbesicherung der eingeräumten Fazilitäten providing excess security for facilities granted

überbewerten to overvalue, to overprice; in der Bilanz: to overstate

überbewertete Aktie overpriced stock, top-heavy share

überbewertete Anlagen overvalued (overstated) assets

überbewertete Währung overvalued currency

Überbewertung overvaluation, overpricing, overstating

Überbringerklausel bearer clause

Überbringerscheck bearer cheque

überbrücken to bridge over, to fill a gap

Überbrückungs

- finanzierung bridge-over (interim) financing

- kredit bridge-over loan, bridging facilities

Überdeckung surplus cover

überdenken die Konditionengestaltung überdenken to re-evaluate (to review) the pricing policy

Überdividende superdividend, surplus dividend

Übereinstimmung mit den Akkreditivbedingungen compliance with the terms and conditions of the documentary credit

Übergabe delivery, surrender

- am Schalter delivery across (over) the counter

- der effektiven Stücke constructive (actual) delivery

Übergang der Eigentumsrechte auf den Kreditgeber passing of ownership to the lender

übergehen auf den neuen Eigentümer übergehen to pass into the hands of the new owner

Überhang surplus, overhang, excess, backlog

- an Aufträgen backlog of orders in hand

- an alten langfristigen Festsatzkrediten overhang of old fixed-rate loans

überhängige Emission issue not fully subscribed or sold

überkapitalisiertes Unternehmen top-heavy (overcapitalised) company

Überkapitalisierung overcapitalisation

Überkreuzkompensation cross compensation

Überkreuzverflechtung intercorporate relationship

überladener Markt top-heavy market

überlassen im Geldhandel: to sell, to lend

überlassende Bank selling (lending) bank

Überlassung
- der Dokumente handing over the documents, delivery of the documents
- von Tagesgeld selling overnight funds, lending overnight money, lending in the interbank market

Übernahme taking over (up); take-over; assumption; underwriting
- einer Emission underwriting (taking up) an issue
- amerikanischer Emissionsverfahren adaptation of US investment banking techniques
- einer Garantie furnishing a guarantee, guarantee undertaking
- der Haftung accepting (assuming) the liability, assumption of liability
- der Kosten accepting the costs, cost acceptance
- eines Unternehmens taking over a company, take-over of a company

Übernahme
- angebot take-over bid, tender offer
- garantie underwriting commitment (guarantee), undertaking to underwrite (to take up) an issue
- gerüchte take-over (acquisition) rumours, bid talk
- gewinn gain on take-over
- kandidaten shares of bid-for companies
- konsortium underwriting syndicate (group)
- kurs (a) underwriting price; (b) take-over price
- provision underwriting commission
- strategie take-over (acquisition) strategy
- verlust loss on take-over
- verpflichtung (a) ⟶ Übernahmegarantie; (b) firm bid
- vertrag (a) underwriting agreement; (b) take-over agreement

übernehmen Emission: to underwrite, to take up, to sponsor; Haftung, Kosten: to assume; Unternehmen: to take over, to acquire

   übernehmende Bank underwriting (sponsoring) bank

   übernehmende Gesellschaft acquiring company

   zu übernehmende Gesellschaft company sought to be taken over

Überpari-Emission issue above par, issue at a premium

Überschreitung der vereinbarten Kreditgrenze exceeding the credit limit (ceiling) agreed upon

Überschuldung excess indebtedness, liabilities exceeding assets

überschüssige Kassenmittel surplus funds

Überschuß surplus, excess
- der Erträge aus dem Dienstleistungsgeschäft net income from service transactions
- aus Zinsen und Provisionen net interest and commission income
- aus dem Eigenhandel net income from trading for own account

Überschuß
- gelder surplus funds

   Rückführung der Überschußgelder recycling of surplus funds

- positionen net income items
- rechnung statement of income
- reserven surplus reserves
- sparen transferring surplus cash (i.e. from a customer's chequing

account automatically to an interest-bearing savings account

übersendende Bank   remitting bank

übersetzte Zinsen   excessive interest rates

Übersicherung → Überbesicherung

Übertrag   (a) carryover, amount carried over, amount brought forward; (b) transfer to another account

übertragbares Akkreditiv   transferable (assignable) documentary credit

Übertragbarkeit einer Aktie   transferability of a share

übertragen   to transfer; to assign; to convey; to confer

auf die Bank -   to transfer (to assign) to the bank

dem neuen Eigentümer alle Rechte - to vest in the new owner all rights

vom Kontokorrentkonto auf das neueröffnete Sparkonto -   to transfer from the current account to the newly opened savings account

auf den Namen von XYZ -   to transfer into the name of XYZ

die dem Bevollmächtigten übertragenen Vollmachten   the powers vested in (conferred on) the donee

übertragende Gesellschaft   transferor company

Übertragender   transferor

Übertragung   transfer; assignment; conveyance; conferring, delegation

- der Eigentumsrechte   transfer of title (ownership)

- von Grundbesitz   conveyance of (conveying) real property, real estate transfer

- durch Indossament   transfer by endorsement

- von Vollmachten   conferring (delegation of) powers

zum Zeitpunkt der -   at the time of transfer

Übertragungs

- anspruch   right of (to) transfer

- anzeige   notice of transfer (assignment)

- bilanz   transfer payments account

- empfänger   transferee

- gebühr   transfer fee (charges)

- genehmigung   authority to transfer

- stelle   transfer agent (office)

- urkunde   deed of conveyance (of transfer), transfer deed (instrument)

- vollmacht   power to transfer

- wert   value upon transfer, transfer value

überwachen   to control, to supervise, to monitor

Überwachung   control, supervision, monitoring

- eines Kreditengagements   monitoring a loan commitment (an exposure)

- des Kreditgeschäfts   control (supervision) of lending activities

überwälzen   to pass on, to shift

überweisen   to transfer, to remit

Überweisung   transfer, funds transfer, remittance, money transmission, bank credit transfer (Br)

Überweisungs

- auftrag   payment order, instructions to transfer funds, money transmission order

- auftraggeber   remitter, principal

Überweisungs
- betrag amount transferred, principal amount
- empfänger beneficiary, remittee
- formular transfer form (slip)
- gebühren transfer (remittance) charges, money transmission charges
- träger transfer slip (voucher)
- verkehr funds transfer, money transmission, bank credit transfer system, bank giro system (Br)

überwiegen Kursrückgänge überwogen falls predominated, declines led advances

überwiegend
- fester bei lebhaften Umsätzen mainly higher in active trading
- schwächer predominantly lower

überzeichnen to oversubscribe
überzeichnete Emission oversubscribed issue

Überzeichnung oversubscription, surplus of applications for an issue

überziehen (a) to overdraw an account; (b) to exceed a credit line

Überziehung overdraft; overdrawing an account; exceeding a credit line

Überziehungs
- kredit overdraft facility, advance on current account
- möglichkeit bis zum dreifachen Nettogehalt overdraft line of up to three times net monthly salary
- provision overdraft commission

übliche Bankpraxis established banking practice

Ultimo end-of-month oder year-end
- ausschläge end-of-month fluctuations (swings)
- differenz difference between settlement and forward rate
- dispositionen end-of-month trading arrangements
- geld short-term loan repayable on the last trading day of a month
- geschäft transaction for end-of-month settlement
- glattstellungen end-of-month position squaring
- handel dealings (trading) for end-of-month settlement
- kurs end-of-month quotation
- regulierung end-of-month settlement
- vorbereitungen auf der kurzen Seite end-of-month dealings at the short end
- wechsel bill maturing at the end of the month

umbuchen auf ein anderes Konto: to transfer to another account; stornieren: to reverse an entry

Umbuchung transfer to another account; reversal, reversing an entry
- aus (in) Rücklagen transfer from (to) reserves

Umdisposition von Anlagen regrouping (rearrangement) of investments; switching over into (e.g. shares, bonds)

Umfeld für Banken operating environment for banks, banking climate

Umfinanzierung debt rescheduling, restructuring a debt

Umgang im Umgang mit Privatkunden when dealing with private (retail) customers

Umkehrzins   interest rate marking a turn of the market

Umlage von Kosten   allocation of expenses, cost allocation

Umlageschlüssel   cost allocation formula

Umlauf   circulation
- an Hypothekenpfandbriefen   mortgage bonds outstanding

im - befindliche Banknoten   bank notes in circulation

Umlauf
- grenze   bond issuing ceiling
- intensiver Betrieb   company with a high proportion of current assets
- kapital   current capital
- kredit   operating loan

Umlaufs
- markt   secondary market, market for outstanding securities
- rendite   current (running) yield

Umlauf
- vermögen   current assets
- volumen festverzinslicher Wertpapiere   total bonds outstanding

umrechnen   to convert, to translate

Umrechnung   conversion, translation

Umrechnungs
- gewinn   gain on conversion (translation), currency translation gain
- kurs   exchange rate, conversion rate (price)
- risiko   exchange rate risk, translation exposure
- verlust   loss on conversion (translation), currency translation loss

Umsatz   turnover

Umsätze   Börse: trading, dealings, turnover, activity in the stock market; Konto: turnover, movements
- in Autoaktien blieben gering   activity in motors remained at a low ebb
- in Kurzläufern   dealings in shorts
- in Rentenwerten   bond dealings (sales)
- gegen Schluß der Börsensitzung   late trading (dealings)

die über das Konto geleiteten -   the movements (transactions) routed through the account

Umsatz
- erlöse   Bilanzposten: sales
- kredit   business loan
- loses Konto   dormant (inactive) account
- provision   turnover commission
- rentabilität   profit/sales ratio
- rückgang   drop in turnover; Börse: decline in trading, contraction in market volume, volume shrinkage
- spitzenreiter   Börse: volume leader
- starkes Konto   high-activity account, large-volume account
- stärkste Werte   volume leaders
- steigerung   increase in turnover; Börse: upturn in trading (in dealings), increase in market volume
- volumen   transaction volume, volume of turnover, volume of trading

umschichten   to regroup, to rearrange, to shift to (into)

Anlagen von Aktien in Rentenwerte -   to shift investments from stocks into bonds

in andere Währungen -   to switch into other currencies

umschichten
    das Wertpapierportefeuille - to regroup the securities portfolio

Umschichtung regrouping, rearrangement, shifting into, switching into

umschreiben Grundbesitz: to transfer, to convey

Umschreibung transfer, conveyance

umschulden to reschedule, to restructure;Anleihe: to refund

Umschuldung rescheduling, restructuring, debt rescheduling (restructuring); refunding

Umschuldungs

- abkommen rescheduling agreement (accord)

- anleihe refunding bond

- bedarf debt restructuring requirements

- engagements rescheduling commitments (exposure)

- kredit rescheduling loan

- land rescheduling country

- paket rescheduling package

- vereinbarung rescheduling agreement

- welle welter of debt restructuring

- zeitraum rescheduling period

Umschwung an der Börse: turn for the better in the market; der Konjunktur: turnaround in economic activity

umsetzen mehr als ... Aktien wurden umgesetzt more than ... shares were traded
    ... Optionen wurden umgesetzt ... options were transacted

umsteigen to switch into
    von Renten in Aktien - to switch out of the bond market into stocks
    auf höher verzinsliche Festgeldanlagen - to switch into time deposits bearing a higher rate of interest

umstellen (a) to convert; (b) to reorganise

Umstellung conversion; reorganisation

umstrukturieren to restructure, to reconstruct, to reorganise

Umtausch exchange, conversion

- in Aktien exchange for shares, conversion into shares

- von Aktien exchange of shares, stock swap

Umtausch

- aktionen swap transactions

- angebot exchange offering (offer), conversion offer

- aufforderung conversion call

- frist conversion period, period for exchanging

- recht exchange (conversion) privilege, conversion option

- stelle exchange agent, conversion agent

- verhältnis exchange ratio, conversion ratio

umtauschen to exchange, to convert, to swap

umwandeln to convert, to change

Umwandlung conversion, change

- der bestehenden Fazilitäten in langfristige Kredite conversion of the existing facilities into long-term loans

- in Namensschuldverschreibungen converting into registered debentures

- von Rücklagen capitalisation of reserves

- langfristiger Schulden in Eigenkapital conversion of long--term debt into equity

223

- eines Unternehmens change in the legal form of a company
- von Wandelschuldverschreibungen in Aktien converting bonds into shares

Umwidmung von Wertpapieren in der Bilanz: regrouping of securities

unbare Zahlung cashless payment

unbelasteter Grundbesitz uncharged (unencumbered) property

unbesicherter Kredit unsecured (uncollateralised) loan

unbestätigtes Akkreditiv unconfirmed documentary credit

unbewegliche Anlagegüter immovable property

unbeweglicher Kurs sticky price

Und-Konto joint account (all account-holders must sign on any relevant documents, e.g. cheques, etc.)

unechtes Durchkonnossement unclean through bill of lading

uneinbringliche Forderung uncollectible (irrecoverable) debt

uneingeschränkt
- es Akzept unconditional (unqualified) acceptance
- er Bestätigungsvermerk unqualified audit certificate

uneinheitlich
- bei geringen Umsätzen irregular in light (thin) trading
- bei ruhigen Umsätzen quietly mixed
- bis schwächer schließen to close mixed to lower

unerfahrene Marktteilnehmer unseasoned market (stock) operators

unfertig
- e Erzeugnisse work in progress
- e Leistungen unfilled orders

unfundierte Schuld floating charge (debt)

ungedeckt
- er Kredit unsecured loan, uncovered advance
- er Scheck dud cheque
- er Wechsel uncovered bill

ungefähr approximately, in the range (region) of

die Anlage beläuft sich auf ungefähr .. DM Mio the investment will be in the range of DM ..m

ungenutzte Kreditlinie unused (undrawn) credit line

ungeregelter Freiverkehr off-board (off-floor) trading, unofficial market

ungesichert
- er Kredit unsecured loan (credit)
- es Wechselkursrisiko unhedged exchange rate risk, unhedged currency exposure

Universalbank universal bank, all-purpose (multi-purpose) bank

Universalkarte multi-purpose card

unkündbare Wertpapiere uncallable (irredeemable) securities, undated stocks

Unkündbarkeitsfrist (a) non--redemption period; (b) period of non-callability

unmittelbar im Ergebnis verrechnen to charge (oder: to credit) to operations as incurred

unrentabel uneconomical, unprofitable

unsichere Börsenstimmung unsteady tone of the market, jumpy market

Unsicherheit hinsichtlich der Entwicklung der Zinssätze uncertainty over the direction (the further trend of) in interest rates

unstimmige Dokumente inaccurate documents

unten Tagesgelder nach - abgeben to lend overnight funds to member banks

Unterbesicherung collateral shortage, shortage of security (of cover)

Unterbeteiligung sub-interest; an einer Emission: sub-underwriting share

unterbewerten Aktie: to undervalue, to underprice

Unterbilanz negative net worth

unterbreiten Angebot: to submit an offer (a quotation), to tender for

unterbringen Emission: to place; Gelder, Zahlungen: to apply

nicht unterzubringende Gelder funds which cannot be applied

im freihändigen Verkauf - to place privately with investors

wir können Ihre Zahlung nicht - we feel unable to apply your payment

Unterbringung (a) placing; (b) applying, application

- einer Emission beim Publikum placing an issue with the public

- der Zahlungseingänge application of payments received

Unterbringungsrisiko placing risk

unter
- er Interventionspunkt bottom (lower, floor) support point

- e Kursgrenze bottom rate (price)

- e Preisgrenze price floor

- e Renditegrenze yield floor

Unterdeckung shortage of cover

Unterfinanzierung financing shortage, inadequate financial resources, underfunding

unterhalten to maintain

ein Guthaben von DM .. auf dem Kontokorrentkonto - to maintain a balance of DM .. in the checking account

Unterhaltung maintenance

- von Mindestreserven maintenance of minimum reserves

Unterkapitalisierung undercapitalisation

Unterkonsorte sub-underwriter

Unterkonsortium sub-syndicate

Unterkonto sub-account, subsidiary account

Unterlagen records, documents

unterlegen to secure, to provide security, to support, to guarantee

unterlegt durch Dokumente supported by documents

unterlegt durch gesperrtes Festgeld secured (guaranteed) by blocked time deposits

der Kredit wird durch eine Garantie unterlegt the facility is supported by a guarantee

das Projekt mit Eigenmitteln - to secure the project with own capital resources

durch eine dingliche Sicherheit unterlegter Kredit loan secured by a collateral (guaranteed by real security)

Unterlegung provision of security, putting up security, support

225

Unterlegung

- einer Bürgschaft   provision of security for a guarantee

- eines Kredites   putting up security in support of a loan, provision of security (providing security)for a loan

  zur - der Kreditlinie   as security (collateral) for the credit line

unterliegen

  den Schwankungen des Aktienmarktes -   to be subject to the ups and downs (to the vagaries) of the stock market

  der Vertrag unterliegt deutschem Recht   the agreement shall be governed by and construed in accordance with the law of the Federal Republic of Germany

Unternehmen   company, corporation

  Finanzierungsbedarf der -   corporate finance (borrowing) requirements

  Gewinnspannen der -   corporate profit margins

Unternehmens

- abschluß   company's annual accounts (financial statements)

- bereich   division, corporate sector

- beteiligung   interest (stake, share) in a company

- finanzierung   corporate financing

- führung durch Delegierung von Befugnissen   management by delegation

- führung durch Erfolgsmessung   management by results

- führung durch Systematisierung   management by system

- führung durch Zielvorgabe   management by objectives

- kundschaft einer Bank: corporate customers

- leitung   management, Board (of Managing Directors)

- liquidität   corporate liquidity

- politik   corporate (business) policy

• sanierung   company reconstruction

- verschuldung   corporate indebtedness

- vertrag   inter-company agreement, profit and loss pooling agreement

- zusammenschluß   merger of companies

Unternehmer

- einkommen   entrepreneurial income

- gewinne   corporate profits

- risiko   entrepreneurial risk

Unternehmungslust   Börse: activity in the market, buying interest

  die - wurde durch die Unsicherheit über die weitere Zinsentwicklung gebremst   investment enterprise was inhibited by interest rate uncertainties

Unter-Pari-Emission   issue below par, issue at a discount

Unterschreitung der Mindestsätze   falling (dropping) below the minimum rates

Unterschrift   signature

  Unterschriften im Kreditgeschäft   underwritings

unterschriftsberechtigt

  für ein Konto: authorised to sign on an account

  für eine Gesellschaft: authorised to sign for and on behalf of a company

Unterschrifts

- berechtigung   signing authority, authority to sign

- bestätigung   confirming the genuineness of a signature

- bevollmächtigter authorised signatory, authorised signing officer
- karte signature card
- probe specimen signature
- probenblatt specimen signature card
- prüfung signature verification, checking the genuineness of a signature
- träger authorised signatory, authorised signing officer
- verzeichnis signature book (index), list of persons given authority to sign on an account
- vollmacht authority to sign, signing authority

unterstützen (a) to support, to back; (b) billigen: to endorse

unverändert bei .. schließen to close unchanged at ..

unverrechnete Lieferungen und Leistungen unbilled contracts

unverzinslich
- e Einlagen non-interest-bearing deposits
- e Guthaben non-earning balances
- e Schatzanweisungen discounted treasury notes (interest is paid by way of a discount from the purchase price)

unwiderruflich
- es Akkreditiv irrevocable letter of credit
- e Kreditzusage irrevocable loan undertaking
- e Refinanzierungszusage irrevocable undertaking to fund (to refinance); Weltbank: unqualified agreement to reimburse

unzureichende Kapitalausstattung inadequate equity base

unzweifelhafte Bonität undoubted credit-worthiness

Urkunde deed, instrument, document

ursprünglich eine Hypothek zu den -en Konditionen übernehmen to assume a mortgage on the same rate and conditions as were originally granted

Ursprungskapital bei einer Hypothek: original principal

Usancen des Marktes: market customs, market practice, established practice in the market

Usancenhandel cross dealings

U-Schätze ⟶ unverzinsliche Schatzanweisung

V

vagabundierende Gelder erring funds

Valoren (a) valuables; (b) securities

Valuta (a) Währung: currency; (b) Darlehenserlös: loan proceeds; (c) Wertstellung: value date

- akzept foreign currency acceptance
- anleihe foreign currency bond (loan)
- forderungen foreign currency receivables
- geschäft foreign currency transaction, exchange transaction (deal)
- klausel (a) foreign currency clause; (b) value given clause
- kompensiert identical value date (for buyer and seller)
- konto foreign currency account
- kredit foreign currency loan (lending)
- papiere foreign currency stock (securities)
- politik monetary policy
- rischer Saldo available balance
- risiko exchange (currency) risk
- schuld foreign currency debt
- schuldschein foreign currency note
- tag value date
- trassierungskredit currency acceptance credit
- wechsel currency bill

Valuten (a) foreign currencies; (b) foreign currency coupons

Valutenarbitrage currency arbitrage

valutengleiche Abrechnung settlement under identical value dates

valutieren to fix the value date; to make a loan available

der valutierte Kredit the loan made available

die Kreditlinie valutiert noch mit DM .. DM .. are still outstanding under the credit line extended to you

der Kredit valutiert mit .. the loan amounts to ..

Valutierung (a) fixing the value date; (b) Kreditgeschäft: making a loan available, permitting drawdowns on a loan; (c) Wertpapiergeschäft: debiting the amount subscribed to the subscriber's account

bei - in Abzug bringen to deduct when the loan is made available to the borrower

die - des Kredites erfolgt nach Genehmigung durch unsere zuständigen Kreditausschüsse the loan will be made available (drawdowns will be possible) once our senior loan committees have given their approval

Valutierungserlös float profit

Valutierungstag / - termin (a) Wertstellung: value date; (b) Kreditgeschäft: date on which the loan is made available; (c) Wertpapiergeschäft: date on which the loan amount subscribed will be debited to the subscriber's account

variabel
- verzinsliche Anleihe floater, floating-rate bond
- verzinsliche Anleihe mit achtjähriger Laufzeit, die zu Sechsmonats-Libor plus 1/8% verzinst wird eight-year floater paying 1/8 point over six-month London Interbank Offered Rate (LIBOR)
- verzinsliche Hypothek variable-rate mortgage
- verzinslicher Schuldschein floating-rate note

variabler Handel floating-price (floating-rate)dealings

variabler Kurs floating price, variable rate (price)

variabler Markt variable-rate market

variable Notierung variable-price quotation, floating quotation

variable Werte floaters, floating-price securities

Kredit mit variabler Verzinsung variable-interest loan, floating-rate loan

veranlagen to assess

Veranlagung assessment

veranschlagen die Kosten wurden mit nahezu DM .. veranschlagt the cost was estimated to be almost DM ..

verarbeitende Industrie manufacturing sector

veräußern to sell, to dispose (e.g. of assets)

Veräußerung sale, disposal
- von Anlagen disposal of assets, asset disposal
- von Werten aus dem Deckungsbestand selling assets from the holdings maintained as cover

Veräußerungswert realisable value

verbessern to improve; Börse: to improve, to pick up, to put on

die Kurse konnten sich nach schwachem Beginn - following losses in early trade, most quotations picked up

XYZ verbesserten sich um 8 auf 130DM XYZ put on 8 to 130DM

Verbesserung der Ertragslage improvement in earnings

verbilligen to lower (e.g. a rate, price), to cheapen; Börse: to fall, to drop, to drift lower

XYZ verbilligten sich um 3 auf 150DM XYZ slipped (fell) 3 to 150DM

die Hypothekenkreditaufnahme - (a) to lower mortgage lending rates; (b) to subsidise mortgage interest payments

Verbilligung lowering (a price, rate), cheapening
- der Dispositionskredite lowering of personal lending rates, lowering the interest rates for drawing credits
- der Refinanzierung der Banken lowering the cost of funds to banks, decrease in funding costs

verbilligungsfähig eligible for an interest-rate subsidy

verbindlich binding; firm

nach Billigung ist der Vorschlag für alle Parteien - the proposal, if sanctioned, becomes binding on all concerned

- es Angebot binding (firm) offer

Verbindlichkeiten liabilities, debts, due to, amounts (accounts) payable
- gegenüber Banken due to banks
- aus der Begebung und Übertragung von Wechseln liabilities from the drawing and endorsement of bills
- aus Bürgschaften liabilities on guarantees furnished

Verbindlichkeiten

- aus Einlagen   liabilities to depositors
- aus zweckgebundenen Geldern liabilities on earmarked funds
- gegenüber Konzerngesellschaften due to group companies
- aus Pensionsansprüchen liabilities on vested benefits
- aus Sichteinlagen demand deposit liabilities
- aus Währungstermingeschäften liabilities on forward exchange contracts
- aus Warenlieferungen accounts payable, trade
- aus diskontierten Wechseln liabilities on bills discounted
- aus Wertpapiergeschäften amounts payable for securities traded
- aus Wertpapierpensionsgeschäften   liabilities on repurchase agreements

Verbraucherkredit consumer credit

verbriefen to secure (by bond), to vest, to evidence the ownership

in einer Globalurkunde verbrieft secured (evidenced) by a global certificate

verbrieftes Recht   vested right

Verbriefung securing, vesting

- von Spareinlagen   shifting savings deposits into savings bonds, issuing savings bonds

verbuchen

auf ein Konto - to post to an account, to enter into an account

Kursgewinne - to score (to register) price gains

Verbuchung (a) entering, posting, entry;(b) scoring, registering

Verbund

- darlehen   joint loan extension (accommodation) (e.g. by a commercial and a mortgage bank)
- direktorium   interlocking directorate
- finanzierung   joint financing
- geschäfte einer Bank: cross selling
- wirtschaft vertical integration

verdecktes Factoring   non-notification factoring

verdoppeln der Gewinn verdoppelte sich praktisch auf DM .. profits virtually doubled to DM ..

verdrängen vom Kapitalmarkt - to squeeze out of the capital market

vereinbarte Kündigungsfrist agreed period of notice

Vereinbarung über die Rückführung des Krédites agreement on the repayment of the loan

vereinnahmen to receive, to collect, to cash

vereinzelt

- geringfügige Abgaben scattered small selling
- e Kursgewinne scattered gains

Verengung tightening, narrowing, contraction, squeeze

- des Geldmarktes tigthening up of the money market, squeeze in the money market
- der Gewinnspannen narrowing of profit margins

Verfall

Ablauf: expiration, lapse
Fälligkeit: maturity, due date
der Kurse: collapse (nosedive, sharp drop) of prices
Verwirkung: forfeiture

verfallen (a) to expire, to lapse; (b) to fall due, to mature; (c) to cease to be valid

verfallener Scheck stale cheque

alle Zinsen verfallen, wenn all interest is forfeited if

Verfallklausel forfeiture clause

Verfalltag /-termin due date, maturity date; im Optionsgeschäft: expiry date

Verfassung Börse: tone of the market, market sentiment

verflachen to slacken, to level off

Verflechtung der Kapitalmärkte interpenetration (interdependence) of capital markets

verflüssigen to realise, to turn into cash, to sell

Verflüssigung realisation, turning into cash, sale

- des Marktes increasing the liquidity in the market

- des Wertpapierbestandes realisation (sale) of the securities portfolio

Verflüssigungspolitik policy designed to increase liquidity

verfügbar

- es Einkommen der privaten Haushalte disposable personal income

- es Kontoguthaben balance available in the account

- e Mittel liquid funds

Verfügbarkeitsklausel availability clause

verfügen
über große Bestände (z.B. Wertpapiere)- to carry large positions, to carry large inventories

über ein Konto - to draw on an account, to operate an account

durch Scheck - to draw by cheque

Verfügung (a) drawing (e.g. on an account); (b) sale; (c) provision; (d) regulation, decree, ruling

- nach Ablauf der vereinbarten Kündigungsfrist withdrawal of the funds upon expiration of the notice period agreed upon

- en über ein Konto drawings on an account

- über den eingeräumten Kredit drawings on the loan extended

diese Emissionen stehen nicht mehr zur - these issues are no longer on offer

eine kurzfristige - über die Gelder drawing on the funds (withdrawing the funds) at short notice

dem Zeichner zur - stellen to make available to the subscriber

verfügungsberechtigt über ein Konto: authorised to draw on an account

Verfügungs

- berechtigter person authorised to draw (to sign) on an account

- berechtigung authority to draw (to sign) on an account, drawing authorisation, authority to operate an account

- beschränkungen drawing restrictions, restrictions imposed on the authority to draw, restrictions on the power of attorney

- möglichkeit drawing facility

Vergabe

- eines Auftrages placing of an order, awarding a contract

- eines Kredites extension (granting) of a loan, loan accommodation

vergeben to place, to award; to extend, to grant

231

Vergleich (a) composition, arrangement, settlement; (b) comparison

im internationalen - by international standards

im - zum Vorjahr compared with the same period last year

die Bedingungen des -s ausarbeiten to draw up the terms of the composition (settlement)

der - wird einer Gläubigerversammlung zur Billigung vorgelegt the scheme of arrangement goes before a creditors' meeting for sanction

einen - mit den Gläubigern schließen to come to an arrangement with the creditors

der - muß von der Mehrheit der Gläubiger gebilligt werden the arrangement must be agreed to by a majority in value and number of the creditors

vergleichen to compare with (to), to put against

wenn man diese Bank mit wesentlich größeren Konkurrenten vergleicht if this bank is put against much larger rivals

Vergleichs

- bedingungen terms of composition (of arrangement)
- bilanz statement of affairs
- eröffnung opening of composition proceedings
- gläubiger creditor in composition proceedings
- ordnung composition code
- quote dividend in composition
- status statement of affairs
- vereinbarung deed of arrangement
- verfahren composition proceedings
- verwalter trustee in composition proceedings, trustee under a scheme of arrangement

- vorschlag proposal for an arrangement, scheme of arrangement (Br), reorganization scheme (US)

vergrößern to increase, to enhance; to expand, to enlarge, to widen

vergüten to pay (e.g. interest, commission, etc.); to remunerate (e.g. services)

Vergütung (a) payment; (b) Gehalt, Honorar: remuneration; (c) im Emissionsgeschäft: commission (e.g. selling commission)

- eines Sonderzinssatzes payment of (paying) a special interest rate

Verhältnis ratio; proportion

im - zur Kapitaleinlage in proportion of the capital contribution

- von Eigenkapital zu Fremdkapital equity/debt ratio

Kapitalerhöhung im - 6:1 one-for-six capital increase

verjähren to become statute--barred, to fall under the statute of limitations

die Forderungen gegen den Garantiegeber - nach sechs Jahren the claims against the guarantor become statute-barred after six years

verjährte Forderung statute-barred claim

Verjährung barring by limitation, limitation, falling under the statute of limitations

Verjährungsbestimmungen statute of limitations, statute of repose

Verjährungsfrist limitation period

nach Ablauf der - after the limitation period has elapsed

Verkauf sale, selling

Verkauf

eine Anleihe zum - stellen to offer a bond (loan) for sale

- in offener Stellvertretung einer Emission: selling on a best efforts basis
- auf dem Submissionsweg sale by tender

verkaufen

bestens - to sell at best (at the market)

mit einem Abschlag von 1 % - to sell at a 1 % discount

einschließlich der Bezugsrechte - to sell rights on, to sell cum rights

einschließlich (ausschließlich) aller Rechte - to sell cum (ex) all rights

die Emission verkaufte sich gut the issue traded well in the market

im Freiverkehr - to sell over the counter, to sell in the unlisted securities market

am freien Markt - to sell in the open market

gegen den Markttrend - to sell anti-marketwise

mit einer Rendite von durchschnittlich 8 % - to sell at an average yield of 8 %

per Termin - to sell for future delivery

Verkäufer

- abruf seller's call
- bank selling bank
- markt seller's market
- option seller's option

Verkaufs

im Zusammenhang mit Emissionen und sonstigen Wertpapier- bzw. Börsengeschäften

- abrechnung sold note, contract note
- angebot offer for sale
- auftrag selling (sell) order
- beschränkungen selling restrictions, issue not for sale in ..
- druck selling pressure
- empfehlung sell advice, sell recommendation
- erlös sales proceeds
- finanzierung sales financing
- frist selling (subscription) period
- gruppe selling group
- hedge short hedge
- kommission selling commission
- kommissionär selling agent
- kommissionsbank agency bank
- konditionen selling terms (rates)
- konsortium selling group
- kurs offering (selling) price

Verkaufsoption put option

Erwerber einer - buyer (purchaser) of a put option

Inhaber einer - put holder

Stillhalter einer - put writer, seller (writer) of a put option

Verkaufs

- order selling (sell) order
- prospekt offering prospectus
- provision selling commission
- stelle selling (subscription, issuing) agent
- vermittlung eine Emission zur Verkaufsvermittlung übernehmen to take up an issue (to undertake to sell an issue) on a best efforts basis
- vertrag selling agreement
- welle spate (welter) of selling
- zinssatz discount deducted from the par value

Verkehrs
- aktien transportation stocks
- fähige Forderungen marketable receivables
- fähigkeit von Wertpapieren marketability of securities
- hypothek conventional mortgage
- wert market (current) value
- werte transportation stocks

Verknappung am Geldmarkt tightening up of (contraction in) the money market

verlagern Gelder in Aktienwerte
- to shift funds into equities

verlängern to extend; Wechsel: to renew

verlängerter Eigentumsvorbehalt extended reservation of title (ownership)

die Laufzeit auf zehn Jahre - to extend the maturity to ten years

die Laufzeit wurde von fünf auf acht Jahre verlängert the life has been extended from five to eight years

das Zahlungsziel - to grant an extension of time for payment

Verlängerung extension, renewal
- einer Kreditlinie extension to (renewal of) a credit line
- eines Kreditverhältnisses renewal of a loan accommodation
- der Laufzeit extending the maturity (life)
- eines Wechsels renewal of a bill

eine - der Zeichnungsfrist beantragen to seek an extension to the subscription deadline

Verlängerungsklausel renewal clause

Verlängerungsprovision renewal fee (commission)

verlieren an eine Konkurrenzbank - to lose out to a rival bank

verlosbare Wertpapiere securities redeemable by drawings

verlosen to draw (by lots)

Verlosung drawing (by lots)

Verlosungs
- anzeige notice of drawing
- kontrolle monitoring (supervision) of drawings
- liste list of bonds drawn
- termin date of drawing

Verlust loss

Kreditverlust: loan loss, loan charge-off

Abschreibung als -e writing off as losses

- e aus dem Abgang von Gegenständen des Anlagevermögens loss on disposal (sale) of fixed assets
- e aus Darlehen und Währungsabwertungen losses on loans and from currency devaluations
- e aus der Veräußerung von Beteiligungen loss on sale of trade investments
- e aus Wertminderung valuation adjustments on current assets
- e aus Wertpapiergeschäften losses on securities traded

Verlust
- abzug offsetting losses from previous years against current earnings
- ausgleich loss offsetting (settlement), setting off a loss against, compensation (compensating) for the loss incurred
- bilanz adverse annual accounts, annual accounts showing a loss
- risiko exposure to loss
- rücktrag loss carryback
- übernahme loss takeover, assuming (accepting) a loss

Verlust
- umlage loss apportionment, allocating a loss
- vortrag loss carried forward, loss carryover
- zone in die Verlustzone geraten to plunge into the red

vermietete Erzeugnisse goods on lease

vermittelte Darlehen loans extended through our agency

Vermittler intermediary, middleman
die als - tätige Bank hat .. the bank, acting as middleman, has

Vermittlung durch die Vermittlung der Bank through the agency of the bank, through the good offices of the bank

Vermittlungsgebühr agency fee; bei Krediten: procuration fee

Vermittlungsgeschäft einer Bank: agency business (operations)

Vermögen property, assets

Vermögens
- anlagen investments, investment (asset) portfolio
- aufstellung property statement, statement of assets held; eines Investmentfonds: investment portfolio
- beratung investment counseling
- bilanz statement of assets and liabilities
- bildung capital-building, capital formation, build-up of capital
- bildungsprogramm capital-building scheme
- einbußen, inflationsbedingte inflation-induced loss of income
- einkommen der privaten Haushalte private property income
- neubewertung property revaluation
- steuer property tax
- streuung asset diversification, investment spreading
- übernahme acquisition of assets
- übersicht asset and liability statement
- übertragung transfer of assets (property), property transfer; bei einer Fusion: asset-acquisition merger
- umschichtung regrouping (rearrangement) of assets, portfolio shift
- verwalter investment (portfolio) manager

Vermögensverwaltung investment (portfolio) management, management service
- mit Dispositionsbefugnis für den Vermögensverwalter (bzw. Anlageberater) discretionary management services (Br), full management agency (US)
- ohne Dispositionsbefugnis des Anlageberaters account management services (Br), limited management agency (US)
Gebühren für die - investment management fee, agency fee (US)

Vermögenswerte assets, property

vermögenswirksam
- e Leistungen des Arbeitgebers capital-building fringe benefits
- er Sparvertrag capital-building savings scheme

Vermögenszuwachs growth in assets, capital appreciation

vernachlässigen Bankwerte wurden weiterhin vernachlässigt bank stocks remained out of favour

veröffentlichen to publish; Bilanzen, etc. to disclose

Veröffentlichung publication; disclosure, disclosing

Veröffentlichungsvorschriften
disclosure provisions (requirements)

verpfänden to pledge

der Bank als Sicherheit - to pledge to the bank as security (collateral)

Verpfändung von Forderungen pledging accounts receivable

Verpfändungs

- erklärung memorandum of pledge
- ermächtigung authority to pledge

verpflichten

wir - uns unwiderruflich und uneingeschränkt zur Leistung einer Bürgschaft in Höhe von we irrevocably and unconditionally undertake to furnish a guarantee in the amount of

Bestimmungen, die den Kreditnehmer - provisions which obligate the borrower to ..

die Gesellschaft durch eine Garantie - to bind the firm in a guarantee

Verpflichtung obligation, commitment, undertaking

- der Bank gegenüber dem Begünstigten commitment (engagement) of the bank to the beneficiary

- der eröffnenden Bank undertaking on the part of the issuing (opening) bank

- en gegenüber der Bank obligations (commitments) toward the bank

- zur Bereitstellung eines erstrangigen Hypothekendarlehens undertaking to extend a first-rank mortgage loan

- en aus dem Kreditvertrag commitments under the loan agreement

- zur hinausgeschobenen Zahlung deferred payment undertaking

Verpflichtungserklärung undertaking, letter of undertaking

verrechnen to settle, to clear; ausgleichen mit: to net (to set off) against

Verrechnung (a) clearing, settlement; (b) netting (setting off) against, offsetting, set off

unter - von Stückzinsen plus (less) interest accrued

- der Kontokorrentschuld mit den Sparguthaben setting off the debit balance in the current account against the savings deposits

Verrechnungs

- dollar clearing (offset) dollar
- einheit unit of account
- guthaben clearing balances
- konto clearing (offset) account
- kurs settlement price
- scheck crossed cheque
- spitze clearing fraction
- stelle clearing office
- tage settlement days
- währung clearing currency

Versand

- bereitstellungskredit packing credit
- hauswerte mail orders
- scheck out-of-town cheque
- wechsel bill sent for collection, out-of-town bill

Verschärfung increase; tightening; stiffening

- der restriktiven Kreditpolitik tightening the credit screw
- des Wettbewerbs stiffening of competition

Verschiebebahnhof subsidiary or associated company taking over a loan commitment from the parent verschieben to put off, to defer, to postpone, to shelve

Neuanlagen bis nächstes Jahr - to put off new investments until next year

die Pläne zur Eröffnung einer neuen Repräsentanz wurden verschoben plans to set up a new representative office have been shelved

verschiffen to ship

Verschiffung shipping, shipment

Verschiffungsdokumente shipping documents

Verschnaufpause einlegen Börse: to take a breather

verschulden, sich to raise a loan, to incur (to contract) a debt

sich im Verhältnis 4:1 verschulden (Verhältnis zwischen Eigenleistung und Kreditaufnahme bei einem Hauskauf) to leverage at a ratio of four to one

sich in Dollar - to contract a dollar debt

die am stärksten verschuldeten Länder the most heavily indebted countries

Verschuldung indebtedness; contracting (incurring) a debt, contraction of debts

Verschuldungs

- bereitschaft propensity to borrow, propensity to contract debts

- grad degree of indebtedness

- koeffizient debt/equity ratio, leverage, leverage ratio

- krise debt crisis

- problem debt problem

- rahmen debt ceiling, borrowing limit (ceiling)

- wünsche borrowing requirements

Verschwiegenheitspflicht der Kreditinstitute banks' duty of secrecy, banking secrecy

Versorgung des Bankensystems mit Liquidität supplying banks with liquidity

Versorgungsbereich/Versorgungswerte utilities, utility stocks

verstärken

die Aktienkurse gerieten verstärkt unter Druck equity prices came under increasing pressure

die Auslosungen für diese Anleihen - to accelerate drawings for these bonds

die Befürchtungen der Anleger - to fuel investor fears, to heighten investor concern

die Bemühungen - to step up efforts

der Liquiditätsdruck wurde durch die hohen Zinssätze verstärkt strain on liquidity has been accentuated by high interest rates

die Sanierungsmaßnahmen - to speed up (to intensify) the restructuring measures

der Trend wurde durch die hohen Zinssätze im Ausland verstärkt the trend was reinforced by high interest rates abroad

Verstärkung increase; reinforcement, intensification; stepping up; speeding up, acceleration

Versteifung am Geldmarkt contraction (constraint) in the money market

verstimmen die Börse - to unsettle the market

vertagen to adjourn, to postpone

<u>verteilen</u> to divide, to spread

das Risiko auf viele Papiere - to spread the risk across (over) a wide range of securities

<u>verteuern</u> to increase (to rise) in price, to become dearer

XYZ verteuerten sich um 3 auf 110DM XYZ firmed (hardened, rose) 3 to 110DM

die neue Zinsanhebung wird die Kreditaufnahme weiter - the new interest hike is bound to add to the cost of borrowing

<u>Verteuerung</u> increase in price

- der Kredite increase in the cost of borrowing

- der Refinanzierung increase in the cost of refinancing, increase in the cost of funds

<u>vertikal</u>

- e Diversifikation vertical diversification

- e Preisbindung vertical price-fixing, resale price maintenance

- er Zusammenschluß vertical amalgamation

<u>Vertikalverbund</u> vertical integration

<u>Vertrag</u> contract, agreement
<u>vertraglich</u>

- ausschließen to contract out

- binden to bind by contract

- festlegen to stipulate by contract

- vereinbaren to agree by contract

<u>Vertrags</u>

- abschluß conclusion of contract, entering into an agreement

- änderung amendment of contract, amending an agreement

- aufhebung rescission of contract

- auflösung termination (discharge) of contract

- bedingungen contract terms, terms of contract

- bruch breach of contract

- dauer life of contract, life (term, duration) of an agreement

- entwurf draft agreement

- erfüllung performance of contract

- fähigkeit capacity to contract, contractual capacity

- gegenstand subject matter of a contract

- gemäße Bedienung eines Kredites debt service as agreed upon (as stipulated in the relevant loan agreement)

- gültigkeit validity of contract, validity of an agreement

- haftung contractual liability, liability under a contract

- klausel contract clause, covenant

- leistung contractual consideration

- partei contracting party

- pflichten contractual duties, duties under a contract

- rechte contractual rights

- sparen scheme-linked saving, contractual saving

- summe amount contracted

- text wording of a contract, contract terms

- unfähigkeit contractual incapacity

- verhältnis contractual relationship

- verlängerung extension to (renewal of) an agreement

- verletzung breach of contract, infringement of contract terms

<u>vertretbare Wertpapiere</u> fungible securities

Vertreter representative, agent;
Stellvertreter: deputy; Stimm-
rechtsbevollmächtigter: proxy

ordnungsgemäß bevollmächtigter -
properly (duly) appointed representative

Vertretung representation; agency

Vertretungsauftrag (a) proxy,
proxy statement (instructions);
(b) instructions to represent
(to act as agent)

Vertretungsaufträge anderer
Banken proxies given by other
banks (i.e. to exercise voting
rights on behalf of other banks)

vertretungsberechtigt für eine
Gesellschaft: authorised to act
for a company

allein - authorised to act
singly for a company

gemeinsam - authorised to act
jointly for a company

Vertretungs

- berechtigter für eine Gesellschaft: person authorised to
act for a company

  für ein Konto: person authorised to draw on an account

- berechtigung ⟶ Vertretungsvollmacht

- vertrag agency contract, contract of agency

- vollmacht (a) authority to
act; (b) power of attorney;
(c) proxy (i.e. for voting
shares)

Vertrieb sale, distribution

Vertriebs

- anstrengungen sales efforts

- gemeinkosten selling overheads

- gesellschaft distributor,
marketing company

- intensivierung stepping up
sales efforts

- konsortium bei einer Emission:
selling group (syndicate)

- kosten selling cost

- mitarbeiter sales staff

- steuerung der Filialen control of branch sales

verunsichern Anleger wurden
durch widersprüchliche Prognosen
verunsichert investors have
been puzzled by conflicting
forecasts

verwahren to hold (in safe custody,
in safekeeping)

verwahrende Bank custodian bank,
depositary bank

Verwahrer/Verwahrstelle custodian,
depository

Verwahrpflichten custodial duties

Verwahrung holding (in safe
custody, in safekeeping); custody, deposit

- bis zur Fälligkeit holding
until maturity

in - geben to place (to deposit)
into safe custody

in - nehmen to receive in (for)
safe custody, to take into safekeeping

zur - hinterlegt placed for safekeeping

Verwahrungs

- art type of safekeeping (custody), safekeeping device

- buch custody ledger

- gebühren custodian fees, safekeeping charges

- geschäft custody (safekeeping)
transactions

- ort place of deposit

- quittung custody receipt

- stücke custody items, property
held in custody (in safekeeping)

- vertrag custody (safekeeping)
agreement

verwalten Vermögen: to manage

Verwaltung administration; management

- eines Nachlasses administration of an estate
- eines Wertpapierportefeuilles management of a securities portfolio, investment management

Verwaltungs

- aktien stock held in treasury
- aufwand einer Bank: staff and operating expenditure
- beirat advisory board
- gebühr management fee
- gemeinkosten administration (management) overheads
- gesellschaft management company, manager
- kosten administration cost, management expenses
- kosten je Produktionseinheit administration cost per unit of output
- kredite loans extended on behalf of third parties
- mehrheit majority of shares held by the Board
- vertrag management agreement, investment management contract

Verwässerung dilution

Verwässerungsschutz antidilutive provisions

verweigern to refuse, to decline

die Aufnahme der Dokumente - to refuse acceptance of the documents, to dishonour the documents

die Einlösung des Schecks - to dishonour a cheque

Verwendung use, employment, application

Verwendungszweck intended use; bei Überweisungen: reason for transfer

verwerten to sell, to realise, to liquidate

Verwertung sale, realisation, liquidation

- von Ansprüchen realising claims
- von Bezugsrechten sale of subscription rights
- von Grundsicherheiten realisation of real estate liens
- des Sicherungsgutes realisation (sale) of the collateral

Verwertungs

- aktien stock held in treasury
- erlös sales proceeds
- fall, im - in case of realisation
- konsortium Emission: selling syndicate
- schwierigkeiten difficulties in liquidating a collateral

verwirken to forfeit (e.g. a right)

Verwirkung forfeiture

Verwirkungsklausel forfeiture clause

verzeichnen to record, to register, to post

der Fahrzeugbereich verzeichnete starke Gewinne (Verluste) motors recorded heavy gains (losses)

die Gesellschaft verzeichnete höhere Gewinne the company posted higher earnings

verzichten to waive, to disclaim (e.g. a right)

Verzicht / Verzichterklärung waiver, disclaimer, dispensing notice

verzinsen (a) to pay interest; (b) to attract interest

die Anleihe wird mit 8% verzinst the bond pays (carries) an 8 per cent coupon ab Ausstellungsdatum mit 6 % verzinst werden   to attract (to bear, to carry) 6 per cent interest from the date of issue

Einlagen auf Sparkonten werden nicht verzinst   funds in checking accounts earn no interest

höher verzinst werden   to carry a higher rate of interest

zu Sechsmonats-Libor plus 1/8% verzinst werden   paying 1/8 point over six-month Libor

Verzinsung   (a) Zinssatz: interest rate; (b) Zinszahlung: payment of interest, interest payment; (c) Rendite: yield, return

- einer Anlage   return on an investment, yield of an investment

- zu Dreimonats-Libor   interest at three-month Libor

- von Kontokorrenteinlagen   interest paid on balances in current accounts

- von Spareinlagen   interest paid on savings deposits

die bestmögliche -   the highest rate of interest (return) available

die - richtet sich nach den Kapitalmarktsätzen   payment of interest is geared to the prevailing capital market rates

Verzug   default

der in - geratene Kreditnehmer   the defaulting borrower

mit der Rückzahlung des Kredites in - geraten   to default on a loan

Verzugs

- erklärung   statement of default
- schaden   loss incurred as a result of the default, default-induced loss
- zinsen   interest on arrears

Vielfach

Wertpapiere mit Stückelungen von DM 1.000 oder einem -en davon   securities in denominations of DM 1,000 or multiples thereof

Vinkulationsgeschäft   lending on goods carried by rail

vinkulierte Aktien   registered shares transferable only with the issuer's consent

Volksbank   entspricht in etwa einer: commercial credit cooperative, credit union

voll

- in Anspruch genommener Kredit   fully drawn loan
- eingezahltes Aktienkapital   fully paid share capital

Voll

- amortisationsvertrag   full--pay-out agreement
- finanzierung   financing exclusively based on borrowed funds
- indossament   unqualified endorsement
- kostenrechnung   absorption costing

Vollmacht   power, power of attorney, mandate, authority; Kontovollmacht: authority to draw on an account, account mandate; Stimmrechtsvollmacht: proxy

- zur Aufnahme von Krediten   borrowing authority
- eine Gesellschaft rechtsverbindlich zu vertreten   power to bind a company (to act on behalf of a company)

die ihm übertragenen -en   the powers vested in him

Vollmachtgeber   donor (of the power)

Vollmachts

- aktionär   proxy shareholder
- beschränkungen   restrictions (imposed) on a power of attorney

241

Vollmachts
- erteilung granting a power, vesting powers in s.o., conferring powers on s.o.
- geber donor
- inhaber holder of a power of attorney, proxy, donee
- stimmrecht proxy voting right
- vertrag discretionary investment management contract
- widerruf revocation of a power of attorney

vollständig
- ausgezahlter Kredit loan amount paid in full
- gezeichnete Anleihe fully subscribed bond
- e Rückzahlung repayment in full

Verbindlichkeiten - begleichen to repay debts (to discharge liabilities) in full
- ersetzen to replace in its entirety

vollstreckbarer Titel enforceable title, foreclosure ruling

Volumen Börse: turnover, volume, activity, trading, dealings; Kreditvolumen: loan portfolio, total lendings
- an Neuemissionen new issue volume, volume of new issue activity
- an niedrig verzinslichen Krediten low-yield loan portfolio

Volumen
- steuerung volumes control
- veränderungen changes in terms of volume
- wachstum increase in terms of volume

Vorabausschüttung advance distribution

Vorausabtretung advance assignment

Vorausplazierung advance selling

Vorauszahlung advance payment

Vorbehalt reservation, reserve

unter den üblichen -en under the usual reservations, under the usual reserve

Regulierung unter - settlement under reserve

vorbehalten to reserve

sich das Recht auf Zinsänderungen - to reserve the right to change the interest rate

vorbehaltlich
- des Eingangs gutschreiben to credit due payment provided (e.g. of the cheque)
- gegenteiliger Bestimmungen save as otherwise provided, unless expressly otherwise stated herein
- anderslautender Vereinbarungen unless otherwise agreed

Vorbehalts
- gutschrift credit subject to reservations
- klausel saving (reservations) clause
- rechte rights reserved

Vorbörse market before hours, pre-market

vorbörslich
- er Kurs pre-market price

die Anleihe wurde - mit einem Abschlag von ca. 1% gehandelt the bond traded at a discount of around 1 per cent in the pre-market

vordatierter Scheck postdated cheque

Vordergrund Kaufhauswerte standen im - des Interesses stores held the limelight throughout the session

Vordermann previous endorser

Vorfälligkeitsentschädigung early repayment penalty, prepayment penalty (indemnity)

vorfinanzieren to lend against future proceeds, to finance provisionally, to extend a bridge-over loan, to pre-finance

Vorfinanzierung lending against future proceeds, pre-financing, bridge-over financing

Vorfinanzierungskredit pre-financing loan

Vorgabekalkulation budget accounting

Vorgabekosten budgeted expense

vorgegebener Kurs specified price level

vorgehen im Rang - to rank prior to, to rank ahead (before)

vorhandenes Guthaben funds available, balance in the account

Vorkaufsrecht preemption right, right of first refusal

vorkehren für Risikokredite: to set up loan loss provisions, to make bad debt provisions

Vorkommen bei - des Schecks upon presentation of the cheque

Vorlage presentation, presentment, production; submission

  zahlbar bei - payable upon presentation

  in - treten to advance

  - der Dokumente presentation of the documents

  - zum Inkasso presentation for collection

  - des Sparbuches production of the passbook

vorläufiger Abschluß provisional accounts

vorlegen to present, to produce; to submit

  den Bericht der Hauptversammlung - to present the report to the general meeting

  zum Inkasso (zur Zahlung) - to present for collection (payment)

vorlegende Bank presenting bank

Vorlegung → Vorlage

Vorlegungs

  - frist presentation period, period allowed for presentation

  - gebot instructions to present

  - ort place of presentation

  - verbot instructions not to present

Vorleistung advance contribution

Vormann previous endorser

vormerken to note

  wir haben Ihre Aufträge vorgemerkt we have duly noted your orders

  einen Kredit - to make a loan available to

  vorgemerkter Kreditrahmen credit line made available, credit line arranged, bank accommodation

Vormerkung (a) making a loan available; (b) taking due note of; (c) provisional registration

Vorrang priority

  - gegenüber anderen Forderungen priority to other claims

vorrangig

  - e Belastung prior charge (encumbrance)

  - e Hypothek senior (prior) mortgage, prior-ranking mortgage

  - es Pfandrecht senior (prior-ranking) lien

vorrangig beglichen werden to be paid in priority

Vorrat stock, inventory

Vorrats
- aktien stock held in treasury
- emission issue the proceeds of which will not be required immediately
- haltung stockpiling
- kredit inventory-financing loan
- stellenwechsel storage agency bill

Vorschaltdarlehen bridge-over loan

Vorschaltgesellschaft holding company

Vorschau
- bilanz projected balance sheet
- ergebnisrechnung projected income statement
- finanzflußrechnung projected working capital funds statement

vorschießen to advance

vorschreiben to stipulate; to set, to lay down

die vorgeschriebenen Tilgungsraten the repayments (instalments) laid down in the loan agreement

der vorgeschriebene Zeitraum the period (deadline) set for , the period stipulated

Vorschrift regulation, rule; provision, stipulation

Vorschuß advance

Vorschüsse deposits repaid prior to maturity

Vorschußwechsel bill deposited as security

Vorschußzinsen early withdrawal penalty, interest penalty for an early withdrawal, pre-withdrawal penalty

vorschußzinsfreie Verfügung withdrawing funds without an early withdrawal penalty being charged

vorsehen to provide for, to call for

die vorgesehenen Gebührenerhöhungen the price increases scheduled

im Kreditvertrag sind halbjährliche Tilgungszahlungen vorgesehen the loan agreement calls for semi-annual repayments

vorsichtig
- e Anleger risk-averting investors, conservative investors
- e Dispositionen des Handels guarded selling and buying by professional traders
- eröffnen to open cautiously
- optimistische Börsenstimmung cautiously (guardedly) optimistic market sentiment

Anleger wurden -er investors turned increasingly cautious

Vorsitz chairmanship
den - führen to be in the chair, to preside over

Vorsorge (a) provision, providing for; (b) bad debt provisioning
- für Risiken im Kreditgeschäft (zur Absicherung von Kreditrisiken)treffen to set up loan loss provisions, to make bad and doubtful debt provisions

in die - gehen to be used for setting up loan loss provisions

Vorsorgelast burden of providing for bad and doubtful debts

Vorsorgemaßnahmen der Banken banks' bad debt provisioning

vorsorgen to provide for (e.g. for loan risks)

Vorsorgepolitik bad debt provisioning policy

Vorsorgesparen precautionary saving, nest-egg saving

Vorstand Board of Managing Directors, Board of Directors

Vorstands
- mitglied Member of the Board of Managing Directors, Board member
- sitzung Board meeting
- vorsitzender Chairman of the Board of Managing Directors, Chief General Manager (Br), Chief Executive Officer (US)

Vorsteuer-Gewinn (Verlust) pre-tax profit (loss)

Vortagesnotiz previous quotation

Vortagesschluß previous close

Vorteil advantage, benefit
die Vor- und Nachteile der neuen zinspolitischen Maßnahmen abwägen to weigh the pros and cons of the new interest policy measures

Vortrag
- auf neue Rechnung account (balance) carried forward
- aus letzter Rechnung balance brought forward

vortragen to carry (to bring) forward, to carry over

Vorvaluten forward value

Vorverkauf einer Emission: pre-issue selling

vorverlegen Fälligkeitstermin: to accelerate the maturity

Vorvertrag preliminary contract

Vorwegkompensation advance netting

vorwegnehmen die Börse hat die Zinssenkung vorweggenommen the stock market has already discounted the effects of the cut in interest rates

vorzeichnen der von der Bundesbank vorgezeichnete Kurs the course charted by Bundesbank

vorzeitig
der Kredit kann - abgelöst werden the loan may be retired ahead of schedule
- es Kündigungsrecht right to call in a loan prior to maturity
- er Rückkauf repurchase prior to maturity (ahead of schedule)
- zur Rückzahlung fällig gestellter Kredit loan called in prior to maturity
- e Tilgung aus Steuergründen premature redemption on tax grounds
- e Verfügung premature withdrawal
- zurückzahlen to repay ahead of schedule

Vorzinsen bond interest payable from deposit of the subscription money until the first coupon date

Vorzüge preferred shares (stocks)

Vorzugs
- aktien preferred (privileged) stock, preferred (preferential) shares, priority shares
- aktien aus der Kapitalerhöhung preference shares stemming from the capital increase
- aktienkapital preference share capital
- aktionär preference shareholder, preferred stockholder
- dividende preference dividend, dividend on preferred stock
- dividendendeckung times preferred dividend earned

Vorzugs
- gewinnanteil (a) preferred share in profits; (b) preferred dividend
- konditionen preferential terms
- kurs preferential price, price below market conditions
- obligationen preference (priority) bonds
- recht preference right
- stammaktien preferred ordinary shares, privileged common stock
- zeichnungsrecht preferential right of subscription
- zinssatz preferential rate of interest

Vostro-Konto   vostro account

W

wachsen der wachsende Druck auf die Zinssätze the growing (mounting) pressure on interest rates

Wachstum growth

Wachstums
- fonds growth fund
- impulse growth incentives
- industrie growth industry
- korridor growth target range
- werte growth stocks

Wagnisfinanzierung venture financing

Wagniskapital venture capital

Wahrung der Vertraulichkeit maintenance of confidentiality

Währung currency

Währungs
- abkommen currency (monetary) agreement
- abschnitt foreign currency bill
- abwertung currency devaluation, currency depreciation
- akzept foreign currency acceptance
- anleihe external bond (loan), currency bond
- aufwertung currency revaluation, currency appreciation
- ausgleich exchange equalisation
- bandbreiten currency bands
- beistand currency support
- deckung currency cover
- diversifikation currency diversification
- einheit currency unit
- einlagen foreign currency deposits
- fonds (a) currency fund; (b) Internationaler: International Monetary Fund
- forderungen currency receivables, receivables in foreign currencies
- gewinn (a) exchange profit, currency translation gain; (b) im Sinne von Wertsteigerung: currency appreciation
- gold monetary (currency) gold
- guthaben foreign currency balances (funds)
- hüter monetary (currency) watchdogs

währungskongruent
- e Deckung der aktivischen und passivischen Positionen matching currencies of lendings and deposits
- e Refinanzierung funding (refinancing) at matching currencies; matching the currency of the funding transaction against the currency of the loan

Währungs
- kongruenz das Prinzip der Währungskongruenz beachten to observe the principle of matching currencies
- konto currency account
- konvertibilität currency convertibility
- korb basket of currencies
- kredit foreign currency loan, currency borrowing

Währungs
- mix   currency mix
- option   currency option
- ordnung   currency system
- parität   currency parity
- politisches Instrumentarium   monetary policy instruments
- rechnungseinheit   currency unit
- reserven   currency (monetary) reserves
- risiko   currency (exchange) risk
- scheck   foreign currency cheque
- schlange   currency snake
- titel   currency securities
- umrechnung   exchange, translation
- umrechnungsrisiko   exchange risk, currency translation risk
- umstellung   currency conversion
- union   monetary union
- verbindlichkeiten   currency debts, payables in foreign currencies
- verbund   currency bloc
- verfall   monetary erosion
- verluste   currency (exchange) losses
- vorschuß   currency advance
- zuschlag   currency (exchange) markup

Wandelanleihe   convertible bond
wandelbar   convertible
- er Schuldschein   convertible capital note
- in Stammaktien   convertible into common stock

Wandelgeschäft   callable forward transaction

wandeln   to convert (into)
Wandel
- obligation   convertible bond

- prämie   conversion premium
- recht   conversion privilege (option), right of conversion
- schuldverschreibung   convertible bond (debenture)
- vorzugsaktien   convertible preferred stock

Wandlung   conversion
Wandlungs
- aufgeld   conversion premium
- bedingungen   conversion terms
- frist   conversion period
- möglichkeit   conversion feature (privilege)
- recht   conversion privilege (option), right
- verhältnis   conversion rate (ratio)

Wandprotest   protest in the drawee's absence

Waren
- beleihung   lending on (against) goods
- bestandsfinanzierung   inventory financing
- börse   commodity exchange
- delkredere-Versicherung   accounts receivable insurance
- fonds   commodity fund
- geld   commodity money
- korb   basket of commodities
- kredit   advance (lending) on goods
- lombard   lending on (against) goods
- pensionsgeschäfte   sale and repurchase agreements in commodities
- terminbörse   commodity futures exchange
- terminhandel   commodity futures trading, commodity forward dealings
- wechsel   trade bill

248

<u>Warrantlombard</u> lending on goods

<u>Wartezimmerverfahren</u> deferment of payment orders until receipt of cover funds

<u>Wasseraktien</u> heavily diluted stock

<u>Wechsel</u> bill of exchange, bill

den - zum Akzept vorlegen lassen to have the bill presented for acceptance

- mit mehreren Ausfertigungen bill drawn in several copies

im Ausland zahlbar gestellter - bill payable abroad

- mit einem Bankindossament bill bearing a bank endorsement

blanko indossierter - bill endorsed in blank

Deckung für den fällig werdenden - anschaffen to provide funds to meet the maturing bill

bis zum Eingang des Gegenwertes des -s until the proceeds of the bill are received

- mit einer Laufzeit von drei Monaten three months' bill, bill having a usance of three months

nicht rediskontfähiger - bill which does not qualify for rediscount (e.g. at the Bundesbank)

Verfahren bei Nichteinlösung des -s proceedings on dishonour of the bill

<u>Wechsel</u>
- abrechnung bill discount note
- adresse name on a bill
- agent bill broker
- akzept bill acceptance, accepting a bill
- anhang allonge, rider
- ankauf bill purchase, buying bills, accepting bills for discount
- ankauf mit Rücknahmeverpflichtung accepting bills for rediscount under repurchase agreements
- ankaufskonditionen bill purchase terms, bill dealing rates
- annahme bill acceptance, accepting a bill
- ausfertigung copy of a bill; first, second or third of exchange
- aussteller drawer of a bill
- ausstellung drawing a bill
- bearbeitung processing bills of exchange
- bestand bill holdings (portfolio)
- beteiligte parties to a bill
- betrag amount (face value) of a bill
- bezogener drawee on a bill
- bürge guarantor on a bill
- bürgschaft bill guarantee
- deckung provision of (providing) cover for a bill, bill cover
- debitoren bills receivable
- diskontierung bill discounting, discounting bills (a bill)
- diskontkredit discount credit
- diskontlinie discount line
- diskontsatz bill rate
- drittausfertigung third of exchange
- einlösung payment of a bill, meeting (honouring) a bill
- einreicher presenter of a bill, person (party) presenting a bill
- einreichung presenting a bill (e.g. for discount)
- einreichungsmöglichkeiten bill discounting facilities
- einzug bill collection, collecting a bill
- einzugsspesen bill collection charges

Wechsel

- erstausfertigung first of exchange
- fähigkeit capacity to contract by bill of exchange, capacity to draw bills or to become liable on bills
- forderung claim based on a bill, claim under a bill
- forderungen Bilanz: bills (notes) receivable
- gegenwert proceeds of a bill
- geschäft bill operations, bill brokerage business
- gesetz German Bill of Exchange Act
- girant endorser of a bill
- giro endorsement of a bill
- gläubiger creditor on a bill
- hereinnahme accepting bills (e.g. for discount)
- inhaber holder of a bill
- inkasso bill collection, collection of a bill
- intervention intervention for honour
- klage suit upon a bill
- klage erheben to sue on a bill
- kommission billbroking

Wechselkurs exchange rate

- änderung change in the exchange rate, parity change
- arbitrage arbitration of exchange, cross exchange
- bereinigt exchange-rate-adjusted
- berichtigung exchange rate adjustment
- bewegungen exchange rate movements, movements in the exchange rate
- festsetzung fixing of the exchange rate, rate-fixing
- freigabe floating of the exchange rate

- garantie exchange rate cover
- gewinn exchange rate gain, exchange profit (surplus), gain on exchange
- klausel exchange clause
- korrektur exchange rate adjustment
- nehmer taker of a bill
- neuordnung currency realignment
- notierung exchange rate quotation
- parität exchange rate parity
- politik exchange rate policy
- prognose foreign exchange forecast, forecasting the further development of exchange rates

Wechselkursrisiko exchange rate risk, currency exposure, exchange rate exposure

gedecktes (ungedecktes) - hedged (unhedged) currency exposure

das - durch Termingeschäfte abdecken to hedge the currency exposure by selling or buying currencies forward

Wechselkursschwankungen fluctuations in the exchange rate, exchange variations, currency fluctuations

Rücklage für - currency fluctuations reserve

starke - wild swings (sharp fluctuations) in exchange rates, currency gyrations

Wechselkurs

- sicherung hedging the exchange (currency) risk, rate-hedging
- stabilität, größere improved exchange rate stability
- system exchange rate system
- umrechnung conversion, translation
- verlust exchange loss, loss on exchange

Wechsel
- laufzeit   usance (term) of a bill
- makler   bill broker
- mäßig haften   to be liable on a bill
- mäßige Haftung   liability on a bill
- material   (a) bills; (b) bills presented for discount
- obligo   liabilities on bills discounted, bill commitments
- pensionsgeschäfte   repurchase agreements on bills
- portefeuille   bill portfolio, bill case (book)
- prolongation   renewal of a bill
- protest   protesting a bill
  - nicht zu verwechseln mit 'noting', dem in Großbritannien üblichen Vorprotest, d.h. Feststellung der Nichteinlösung durch einen Notar -
- protestanzeige   notice of protest
- protestgrund   reason for protesting a bill
- protestkosten   protest charges (fees)
- protesturkunde   deed of protest
- provision   bill brokerage
- rechtliche Haftung   liability on a bill
- rediskontierung   rediscounting a bill
- regreß   recourse to a party liable on a bill
- reiterei   kiting, kite flying, drawing of kites
- rückgabe   return of an unpaid bill
- rückgriff → Wechselregreß
- rückrechnung   reaccount, banker's ticket
- schuldner   debtor on a bill, bill debtor
- sekunda   second of exchange
- skontro   bill ledger
- steuer   bill stamp duty
- strenge   stringent bill of exchange provisions
- triplikat   third of exchange
- übertragung   transfer of a bill
- umlauf   bills in circulation
- verbindlichkeiten   bill commitments; Bilanz: bills (notes) payable
- verkehr   bill of exchange operations; payments by bill of exchange
- verpflichteter   party liable on a bill, bill debtor, drawee
- zahlung   payment by bill of exchange
- zinsen   interest paid on a bill
- zweitschrift   second of exchange

Weg   den - für eine neue Zinssenkung ebnen   to clear (to pave) the way for a new cut in interest rates

weiche Währung   soft currency

Weichwährungsländer   soft currency countries

weiße Effektenschecks   instructions to deliver securities held under collective securities accounts

weiterleiten   to pass on, to transfer; Kreditmittel: to on-lend

Weiterleitungskredite   loans extended under public lending schemes

Weltwährungsfonds   International Monetary Fund

Weltwährungssystem   international monetary system

werbend angelegte Aktiva   einer Bank: interest-bearing loans

251

Wert   value; worth

Portefeuille im - von DM .. portfolio worth DM ..

der Scheck wurde Ihrem Konto - 3. Mai belastet   the cheque was debited to your account value May 3rd

- erhalten (in Rechnung)   value received

wertabhängige Positionen   transaction-linked commissions

Wertansatz   carrying value, amount stated

Wertaufholung   increase in the carrying value

wertberichtigen   (a) to write down (off); (b) to provide for possible losses; (c) to adjust the value

um DM ... wertberichtigen   to write down by DM ..

das Volumen der wertberichtigten Kredite   the total of lendings for which loan loss provisions have been made

Wertberichtigung   (a) write-down, write-off; (b) provision (charge) for bad and doubtful debts; (c) value adjustment

der Aufwand für -en fiel niedriger als erwartet aus   charges for bad and doubtful debts turned out to be lower than expected

- en auf Beteiligungen   provisions against trade investments

- en auf Darlehen und Kredite   charges for bad and doubtful debts, loan loss provisions

- en auf Wertpapiere   securities write-offs

- en auf zweifelhafte Forderungen   provisions for doubtful accounts, bad debts allowance

Wertberichtigungsbedarf im Kreditgeschäft   bad loan charge, loan loss provisions required

Wert
- bestimmung   valuation
- erhöhung   increase in value, appreciation
- erlöse   einer Bank: interest and interest-related income
- ermittlung   valuation
- freie Aushändigung der Dokumente   delivery of the documents without corresponding payment
- haltige Garantie   valuable guarantee
- klausel   valuation clause
- kosten   einer Bank: interest and interest-related expenses
- leistungen   deposit and lending services
- los   eine Garantie wertlos machen   to render a guarantee valueless
- mäßig   in terms of value
- minderung   decrease in value, depreciation

Wertpapier/e   security/securities
- des Anlagevermögens   investment securities
- zum Einstandspreis oder darunter   securities, at cost or less
- zum Marktwert   securities, at current value
- in großen Stückelungen   large-denomination securities
- des Umlaufvermögens   marketable securities
- und Schuldscheine   marketable securities and notes

Wertpapier
- abrechnung   bought (sold) note
- abschreibungen   securities write-offs, write-down on securities
- abteilung   securities department (division)
- analyse   security (stock) analysis

Wertpapier
- angebot   (a) securities currently being offered (e.g. by banks, investment houses); (b) supply of securities
- anlage   securities investment, investment (investing) in securities
- anleger   securities investor
- arbitrage   arbitrage in securities
- aufstellung   statement of securities
- ausgang   securities sold, outgoing securities
- auslieferung   delivery of securities
- aussteller   issuer of securities
- beleihung   lending against (on) securities
- beratung   investment counselling
- bereich   securities sector
- bereinigung   securities validation
- besitz   security ownership, holding of securities
- besitzer   owner (holder) of securities
- bestand   security (securities) holdings
- bewertung   (a) steuerrechtlich: valuation of securities; (b) als Anlagepapiere: rating of securities
- börse   security (stock) exchange
- deckung   securities cover
- depot   securities portfolio
- depotbank   depositary bank, custodian, depository
- eigengeschäfte   securities transactions for own account
- eigenhandel   securities trading for own account, own-account trading
- eigenhandelsgewinne   own-account trading income
- emission   security issue, securities offering
- ergebnis   securities trading result
- erträge   security income, income from securities
- fernscheck   securities transfer order
- finanzierung   financing through securities, raising capital through a security issue
- gattung   type (class) of security, security category
- geschäft   einzelnes: security transaction, transaction in securities, bargain, deal insgesamt: securities business, securities trading operations, trading in securities
- gesetzgebung   securities regulation, regulation of the securities business
- gewinne   gains on securities, security gains, stock market profits
- giroverkehr   securities clearing transactions
- handel   securities trading (dealings), trading in securities
- handelsgewinne   securities trading income
- händler   security (securities) dealer
- hinterlegung   depositing (lodging) securities with, deposit of securities
- inhaber   owner (holder) of securities
- kauf   security purchase, buying securities
- kaufabrechnung   bought note
- kaufpreis   security purchase price
- kennummer   security code number
- kommissionsgeschäft   securities

253

Wertpapier (Fortsetzung) agency business, securities transactions completed on a commission basis
- konto   securities account
- kosten   charges on securities transactions
- kredit   (a) loan (lending) against securities; (b) loan to purchase stock, securities market credit, margin credit
- kurs   price, security price, quotation
- lombard   loan (lending) against securities
- markt   securities market
- mitteilungen   Securities Business Journal
- nachfrage   demand for securities
- nennbetrag   face value (of securities)
- notierung   (a) listing of securities (on the exchange); (b) quotation, security price
- numerierung   security numbering, numbering securities
- paket   block of securities
- pensionen   im Rahmen von Wertpapierpensionen erworbene Wertpapiere   securities purchased under agreements to resell
- pensionsgeschäft   sale and repurchase agreement (in securities); in der Regel nur: repurchase agreement
- plazierung   placing of securities
- portefeuille   securities portfolio
- rechnung   (a) bei Auslands--Wertpapiergeschäften: safekeeping of securities abroad; (b) establishment of the rights value; (c) yield computation
- rendite   yield on securities (e.g. bond or stock yield)

- rückkauf   repurchase of securities
- sammelbank   securities clearing and deposit bank
- sammelverwahrung   collective safekeeping of securities
- scheck   securities transfer order
- skontro   security transactions ledger
- sparen   saving through securities, investment saving
- sparvertrag   security savings scheme
- spitze   fraction
- stückelung   security denomination
- tausch   exchange of securities, stock swap
- termingeschäft   forward transaction in securities
- übertragung   transfer of securities, securities (stock) transfer
- urkunde   certificate, stock (bond) certificate
- verkauf   (a) security sale; (b) selling securities
- verkaufsabrechnung   sold note
- verlust   loss on securities, security loss, stock market loss
- vermögen   securities portfolio (holdings)
- verpfändung   pledging securities
- verrechnungskonto   securities clearing account
- verschuldung   security debts
- verwahrung   safekeeping (safe custody) of securities
- verwaltung   (a) investment (portfolio) management; (b) administration of securities
- verzinsung   return on securities
- wesen   securities business
- zuteilung   allotment of securities; Repartierung: scaling down

Wert
- rechte loan stock rights (not evidenced by certificates)
- rechtsanleihe government-inscribed debt
- rechtsemission issue of government loan stock rights
- schöpfung value added; contribution
- schriftenclearing securities clearing
- steigerung increase in value, appreciation, increment
- steigerung durch Neubewertung valuation surplus
- steigerungsklausel appreciation (escalation) clause
- stellung value, value date

  mit alter Wertstellung with (under) good value
- stellungsberichtigung value correction, value adjustment
- stellungsgewinne float profits
- verringerung diminution (decrease) in value
- zuwachs increase in value, appreciation, increment
- zuwachssteuer increment tax

Wettbewerb competition

wettbewerbsfähige Konditionen
competitive lending rates (terms), competitive loan pricing

wettmachen im Bankenbereich konnten Anfangsverluste wettgemacht werden bank stocks recouped early losses

Widerruf revocation

widerruflich revocable
- es Akkreditiv revocable letter of credit
- e Refinanzierungszusage qualified agreement to reimburse

Widerspruch die Entwicklung steht im - zu früheren Gewinnerwartungen the development contrasts with earlier profit expectations

Widerstand die Zinssenkungspläne sind auf - gestoßen plans for a cut in interest rates have run into opposition from..

Wiederanlage reinvestment
- der Ausschüttungen reinvestment of income distributed (of distributions, of payouts)
- der angefallenen Erträge reinvestment of income accrued

zur - zur Verfügung stehen to be available for reinvestment

Wiederanlagerabatt reinvestment discount

Wiederbeschaffungswert replacement value, cost of replacement

Wiederverkäuferrabatt Emission: re-allowance

Wirkung effect

die Kapitalerhöhung hat die gleiche - wie .. the capital increase is equivalent in its effect to a ..

mit rückwirkender - with retroactive effect

mit sofortiger - effective immediately, with immediate effect

Wirkungsbereich sphere of influence, province

Wochenausweis weekly return

Wochengeld seven-days' money

Wochengewinn einen - von 8 Punkten verzeichnen to record (to register) a gain on the week of 8 points

Wohlwollenserklärung letter of comfort (of awareness)

<u>Wohnungsbau</u> house-building, housing

privater - residential building, house-building in the private sector

<u>Wohnungsbau</u>

- beleihungen lendings to the housing sector, residential lendings

- darlehen home (housing) loan, house-building loan

- finanzierung house-building finance, housing finance

- kredit ⟶ Wohnungsbaudarlehen

- kreditgeschäft residential lendings

- mittel residential (housing) finance

<u>Wuchswerte</u> growth stocks

Z

- Z gestrichen Ziehung   no quotation prior to drawing

zahlbar   payable, due
- stellen   to make payable, to domiciliate
- bei Fälligkeit   payable upon maturity, payable when due
- bei Sicht   payable at sight, payable on demand
- an Order (Überbringer)   payable to order (bearer)
- bei Vorlage   payable upon presentation
- bei Zeichnung   payable upon application (subscription)

Zahlbarkeitstag   maturity, maturity date, due date

Zahlbarstellung   domiciliation, making payable

zahlen   aus einem Akkreditiv - to pay under a documentary credit

Zahlstelle   paying agent; für den Anleihedienst: loan servicing agent

Zahlstellen
- bank   paying bank
- dienst   paying agency services, settlement of redemption and interest payments
- geschäft   paying agency operations
- provision   paying agency commission
- vereinbarung   paying agency agreement
- verzeichnis   list of paying agents
- wechsel   domiciled bill

Zahlung   payment
- auf erste Anforderung   bei einer Garantie: payment upon first call (demand)
- gegen Dokumente   payment against documents
- bei Vorlage   payment upon presentation
- bei Zuteilung der Wertpapiere   payment upon allotment of the securities

Zahlungs
- abwicklung   (a) making (effecting) payment; (b) handling (processing) payments
- anweisungen   payment instructions
- aufforderung   request for payment, reminder; gerichtliche: summons to pay
- aufschub   deferring payment, payment deferral; extension of maturity, extension of the period (time) stipulated for payment
- auftrag   payment order
- bedingungen   terms of payment
- begünstigter   beneficiary of a payment
- bilanzdefizit   deficit in the balance of payments
- bilanzüberschuß   balance of payments surplus
- bilanzungleichgewicht   payments imbalance, disequilibrium in the balance of payments
- eingänge   payments received, receipts
- einstellung   suspension of payments
- empfänger   recipient of a payment, payee

257

Zahlungs
- ermächtigung authority to pay
- fähigkeit solvency
- garantie payment guarantee
- gepflogenheiten customary terms of payment, payment practices
- leistung payment, making (effecting) payment
- mittel means of payment; gesetzliches: legal tender
- mittelumlauf money supply, notes and coin in circulation
- modalitäten terms of payment
- moratorium payment standstill, standstill agreement
- nachweis evidence of payment
- papiere im Dokumentengeschäft: financial documents
- rückstände payment arrears, payments in arrear
- sicherung securing payment, payment guarantee
- sperre payment stop, countermand of payment
- unfähigkeit insolvency, default
- termin date of payment
- verkehr payments, payment transactions
- verkehrsautomation automation of payments, automating payments
- verpflichtung payment commitment
- versprechen payment undertaking, undertaking to pay
- verzug default
    im Falle eines -s des Kreditnehmers in the event of default by the borrower
- verzugszinsen default interest, interest on arrears
- vollmacht authority to pay
- weise mode of payment
- ziel period (time) allowed for payment

Zedent assignor

zedieren to assign

Zehnerklub Group of Ten

zeichnen to subscribe (to apply) for shares

Zeichner subscriber, applicant
- bank subscribing bank
- liste list of applicants (subscribers)

Zeichnung subscription, application
- von Aktien subscription to (for) shares, application for shares

Zeichnungs
- angebot subscription offer, offer for sale, offer for subscription
- aufforderung invitation for subscription, invitation to subscribe
- aufkommen total amount of securities subscribed
- bedingungen terms of subscription
- berechtigt authorised to sign
- berechtigter authorised signatory
- betrag subscription (application) money, amount subscribed
- einladung invitation (offer) for subscription
- formular subscription blank, application blank
- frist subscription (exercise) period, offering period
- gebühr subscription (application) charges
- kurs subscription price
- liste application list, subscription book
- prospekt issuing (offering) prospectus
- rendite yield upon subscription

258

Zeichnungs
- schein subscription (application) form
- schluß closing of the subscription book (application list), closing of an issue
- stelle subscription agent
- termin subscription day
- verpflichtung undertaking to subscribe
- vollmacht signing authority, authority to sign (e.g. on an account)

Zeitgeschäfte forward dealings

zeitkongruent
das Darlehensgeschäft - refinanzieren to fund new lendings at matching maturities
- e Refinanzierung refinancing (funding) at matching maturities

Zeitraum der Inanspruchnahme period of the drawdown

Zeittratte sight draft

Zeitwert zum - bilanzieren to carry (to state) at the market price

zentralbankfähig (a) eligible for rediscount at the Central Bank; (b) eligible as security for Central Bank borrowings

Zentralbank
- geldmenge central bank money stock
- guthaben central bank balances

Zentraler Kapitalmarktausschuß Central Capital Market Committee

zerstreuen Anlegerbefürchtungen- to diffuse investors' concern

Zertifikat (a) certificate; (b) Fondsanteil: unit, share

Zession assignment

Zessionar assignee

Zessions
- kredit loan against assignment of receivables, advance on receivables
- liste statement of receivables
- urkunde deed of assignment

ziehen Scheck, Wechsel: to draw

Ziehung drawing

Ziehungs
- avis Scheck: draft advice
- ermächtigung authority to pay (to draw), drawing authorisation
- liste list of drawings
- rechte drawing rights

zielgruppenorientierte Beratung und Betreuung counseling and servicing geared to specific target groups

Zielkorridor target range

Zielwechsel time bill

Zielzahlungsakkreditiv deferred payment credit

Zins (a) interest; (b) interest rate
- en auf die Darlehenssumme interest on the principal
- en am kurzen (langen) Ende short-term (long-term) interest rates
- en und zinsähnliche Aufwendungen interest and interest-related expenditure
- en und zinsähnliche Erträge aus Kredit- und Geldmarktgeschäften interest and interest-related income from credit and money market transactions
- en abwerfen to generate interest
  die fälligen -en errechnen to compute the interest due

Zins

bis zu 10 % -en zahlen to pay as much as 10 per cent interest

die -en dem Kapital zuschlagen to add the interest to the capital

zinsabhängig

- es Geschäft interest-related business
- e Werte securities dependent on the interest rate level

Zins

- abschlag interest discount
- abwärtstrend downward trend in interest rates
- änderung change in interest rates (in the interest rate)
- anpassung interest rate adjustment, adjusting the interest rate, adaptation of the interest rate to the market situation
- arbitrage interest rate arbitrage
- aufschlag interest markup; bei Libor: spread over Libor
- auftrieb upturn (upsurge) in interest rates
- aufwand interest charge (expenditure, expense), interest paid
  Berechnung des -es für den Kredit computing the interest charge on the loan
- ausfall interest loss, loss of interest
- ausfallrisiko interest loss risk
- ausgleichssteuer interest equalisation tax
- ausschläge sharp interest rate fluctuations, erratic interest rate swings
- außenstände interest arrears
- ausstattung interest terms, einer Anleihe: coupon, coupon (interest) rate

- band interest rate spread (range)
- bedingte Kapitalströme interest-induced capital flows
- begünstigte Programmkredite interest-subsidised loans extended under (public) lending schemes
- beihilfen interest subsidies
- belastung (a) charging interest; (b) interest load (charge, burden); (c) entry representing interest charged
- berechnung (a) computation of interest, computing (calculating) the interest due; (b) charging interest
- berechnungsmethode method of computing interest
- bewußte Anleger rate-conscious investors, interest-rate-sensitive investors
- bindung (a) Festschreibung: establishment of a fixed interest rate, locking in the interest rate; (b) an den Diskontsatz: linking the interest rate to the discount rate
- bindungsfrist fixed-interest period
- bogen coupon sheet
- bonifikation additional interest, granting a special interest rate; granting an interest bonus
- buckel interest hump
- differenz interest rate gap, interest differential
- druck interest rate pressure
- entlastungen im industriellen Bereich lowering corporate lending rates
- entspannung easing of interest rates
- ergebnis net interest income
- erhöhung interest rate hike, increase in the interest rate
- ermäßigung interest rate cut, lowering of interest rates
- erneuerungsschein renewal coupon

Zins

- ersparnis   interest saved, interest saving
- erträge   interest income, interest earned (received)
- ertragsbilanz   interest income statement

Zinseszins   compound interest

- berechnung   computation of compound interest
- formel   compound interest formula

Zins

- explosion   sharp upsurge in interest rates, rocketing (soaring) interest rates
- fächer   interest rate spread (range)
- faktor   interest factor
- fälligkeit   interest payment date; coupon date
- festschreibung   establishment of a fixed interest rate, locking in the interest rate
- festsetzung   fixing an interest rate
- fluktuation   fluctuations (swings) in interest rates
- forderungen   interest receivable
- formel   interest formula
- freigabe   decontrol (deregulation) of interest rates
- fuß   interest rate, rate of interest
- garantie   interest rate guarantee, guaranteeing a fixed interest rate
- gebundener Kredit   fixed-rate loan
- gefälle   interest rate differential
- gipfel   interest peak
- gleitklausel   interest escalator clause

zinsgünstig   carrying a low rate of interest; at a favourable rate of interest, favourable in terms of interest rates

- e Anlage   investment at a favourable rate of interest
- e Konditionen   favourable lending terms, keenly priced lending terms (rates)
- er Kredit   low-interest loan, loan carrying a low interest rate
- beschaffte Mittel   funds raised at a low rate of interest
- es Wohnungsbaudarlehen   (a) low-interest housing loan; (b) interest-subsidised housing loan

Zins

- gutschrift   (a) interest credited; (b) crediting interest, credit of interest; (c) entry representing interest credited
- höhe   interest rate level
- kalkulation   computation (calculation) of interest, interest calculation, computing interest
- kartel   interest rate cartel
- konditionen   interest rates; interest terms

zinskongruent

- e Ausleihungen   lendings at matching interest rates
- refinanzieren   to refinance (to fund) at matching interest rates

Zins

- konstellation   interest rate pattern
- kosten   interest charges, interest cost (expenditure)
- kupon   interest coupon
- last   interest load (charge, burden)
- lastschrift   (a) interest debited; (b) debiting interest, debit of interest; (c) entry representing interest debited

Zins
- leiste   renewal coupon
- leistungen   interest payments
- liberalisierung   decontrol of interest rates

zinslos
- es Darlehen   interest-free loan
- e Guthaben   non-interest-bearing deposits, interest-free balances
- unterhalten   to maintain free of interest

Zins
- marge   interest margin
- mäßige Kompensation   interest netting, netting (compensation of) interest accrued
- mehraufwand   surplus interest expenditure
- mehrertrag   surplus interest income
- nachlaß   interest rate rebate
- niedriger Festkredit   low fixed-rate loan
- niveau   interest rate level
- note   statement of interest
- notierung   quotation of interest rates
- obergrenze   interest rate ceiling
- politik   interest rate policy
- reagible Aktien   interest-sensitive stocks
- reagibles Kreditgeschäft   interest-sensitive lendings
- rechnung   interest calculation
- reduktion   lowering of interest rates, interest rate cut (reduction)
- regulierung   interest settlement, settling interest accrued
- regulierungsklausel   interest settlement clause
- rückstände   overdue interest, interest in arrears
- rutsch   downslide (sharp drop) in interest rates
- saldo   net interest income (oder: net interest loss)

Zinssatz   interest rate; bei einer Anleihe auch: coupon

mit einem festen (variablen) - carrying a fixed (floating) rate of interest

den - von Zeit zu Zeit den Geldmarktsätzen anpassen   to alter the interest rate from time to time to accord with money market rates

- ermittlung   determination of the interest rate
- sicherung   hedging the interest rate, interest rate hedge
- zusage   fixed-rate undertaking; granting (guaranteeing) a fixed rate of interest

Zinssätze
- im kurzfristigen Bereich   short-term interest rates
- für Euro-Dollareinlagen   Eurodollar deposit rates
- für Festgeldeinlagen   time deposit rates
- für Hypothekenkredite   mortgage lending rates
- am Kapitalmarkt   interest rates in (on) the capital market
- für Kredite an erste Adressen   prime lending rates, blue chip rates
- für Kredite an die Firmenkundschaft (Privatkundschaft)   corporate (personal) lending rates
- für Kurzläufer   short rates
- für Langläufer   long rates
- für Privatkundeneinlagen   retail deposit rates
- am Rentenmarkt   interest rates (coupons) in the bond market

Zinssätze
- für Spareinlagen saving deposit rates
- für Termingelder term money rates
- für Wohnungsbaudarlehen home (housing) loan rates

Zins
- schein interest coupon
- scheineinlösung cashing (of) interest coupons, coupon payment
- scheineinlösungsdienst coupon service
- schwankungen interest rate fluctuations (swings), ups and downs in interest rates
- senkung interest rate cut, lowering of interest rates
- senkungen an Kunden weitergeben to pass interest rate cuts on to customers
- senkungsrunde round of interest rate cuts
- senkungsspielraum leeway for interest rate cuts
- senkungstrend downward trend (course) of interest rates
- spanne interest margin, interest rate spread
- spannenerweiterung widening of the interest margin
- spannenrechnung interest margin costing
- spannenverengung narrowing of the interest margin
- sprung jump in interest rates, sharp rise in interest rates
- stabilisierung stabilisation (steadying) of interest rates
- stabilität interest rate stability
- staffel interest table
- stopp interest freeze
- struktur interest rate pattern
- stundung interest payment deferral, respite for interest payments, deferral of interest payments
- subvention interest payment subsidy
- subventionierung subsidising interest payments
- swap interest rate swap
- tabelle interest statement (table)
- tage interest days
- talfahrt nosedive of interest rates
- tender interest-rate-linked tender (relating to repurchase agreements)
- termin interest due date, interest payment date, coupon date
- Terminkontrakt interest rate futures contract
- Terminmarkt interest rate futures market
- treibende Faktoren factors driving (forcing, pushing) up interest rates
- überschuß net interest income
- umschwung turnaround in interest rates, interest rebound
- und Dienstleistungsgeschäft interest and service transactions
- und Tilgungsbelastung debt service load
- und Tilgungsleistungen /-zahlungen interest and redemption payments, payments of interest and principal
- unsicherheit uncertainty over the direction (further trend) of interest rates
- untergrenze interest floor
- variables Darlehen floating--rate loan, interest-variable loan
- verbilligter Kredit interest--subsidised loan

zinsverbilligte Kredite aus
öffentlichen Förderprogrammen
interest-subsidised loans extended under public lending schemes

Zins
- verbilligung (a) lowering (easing) of interest rates; (b) subsidising interest payments
- verbilligungsprogramm interest subsidy scheme
- verbindlichkeiten interest payable, interest due
- vergütung payment (allowance, credit) of interest, interest payment
- verteuerung increase in interest rates, interest rate hike
- verzicht interest waiver, foregiveness of interest
- wende turnaround in interest rates, interest rebound
- zahlen interest product
- zahlung interest payment, payment of interest

  gleichmäßige (regelmäßige) -en equal (periodic) interest payments

  - en bleiben während der Laufzeit des Kredites gleich interest payments remain constant over the life of the loan
- zahlungsverpflichtungen interest payment commitments
- zugeständnisse interest rate concessions
- zyklus interest rate cycle

Zirkaauftrag order at an approximate limit (i.e.slight deviations from the limit given by the customer are permissible)

Zirka-Kurs approximate price

ZKMA-Unterausschuß central capital market sub-committee

Zollbürgschaft customs guarantee

Zufluß ausländischer Gelder
inflow (influx) of foreign funds

zuführen to allocate; to supply; to invest

dem Anlagevermögen - to invest in fixed assets

neue Mittel - to supply (to provide, to invest) fresh funds

den Rücklagen - to allocate (to transfer) to reserves

Zugang access; Zugänge (z.B. Portefeuillezugänge) additions
- zum Kapitalmarkt access to the capital market
- zum Notenbankkredit über das Lombardfenster access to Bundesbank (overnight) funds through the Lombard facility (Lombard window)

Zugeständnisse in der Konditionengestaltung rate (pricing) concessions

zugrunde legen

die gegenwärtigen Kurse bei der Portefeuillebewertung - to base the portfolio valuation on market prices (on the prices prevailing in the market)

das zugrunde liegende Wertpapiergeschäft the underlying securities transaction

zukaufen to buy in addition

Zukauf additional purchase; buying in addition, fresh buying

Zukäufe von Bezugsrechten buying additional subscription rights

Zukäufe durch institutionelle Anleger fresh buying by institutional investors zulassen zum Börsenhandel to admit to dealings on the stock exchange

zulässige Bandbreite permitted band of fluctuation

zulässiges Fremdwährungsengagement allowable exposure in foreign currencies

Zulassung zur Börsennotierung admission to listing (to official quotation) on the stock exchange

Zulassungs
- antrag application for listing
- ausschuß Listing Committee
- bescheid listing notice
- beschluß listing approval
- stelle Listing Board
- verfahren listing procedure
- vorschriften listing requirements

Zunahme increase, rise, growth; addition
- des Geschäftsvolumens increase in the volume of business
- des Kreditbestandes growth in total lendings, loan portfolio growth
- im kurz- und mittelfristigen Bereich increase in short and medium-term lendings

zunehmen to increase, to rise, to grow; to move up (ahead), to advance

Zurückbehaltungsrecht (a) retaining lien; (b) right of retention

zurückbelasten dem Kunden - to redebit to the customer's account

Zurückbildung der Zinssätze downward course (gradual lowering) of interest rates

zurückbleiben hinter dem Index - to lag behind the index

zurückdisponieren to retransfer, to repatriate

zurückfahren das Interbankgeschäft - to curtail interbank transactions, to cut down on interbank transactions

zurückfallen to drop, to fall, to slump, to turn lower

Chemiewerte fielen stark zurück chemicals fell sharply

der Kurs fiel auf den Vorjahresstand zurück the price slipped to last year's level

die Umsätze fielen auf unter DM .. zurück turnover dropped below DM ..

XYZ fielen um 2 Punkte zurück XYZ shed (eased) 2 points

zurückführen (a) to reduce; (b) to repatriate; (c) to attribute (to ascribe) to

Kapital - to repatriate capital

den Kredit in den vereinbarten Rahmen - to reduce the loan to the limit (line) agreed upon

der Gewinnanstieg wurde auf die Erweiterung der Zinsspannen zurückgeführt the increase in profits was attributed to the widening of interest margins

zurückgeben to return

den Scheck mangels Deckung unbezahlt - to return the cheque unpaid for lack of cover

zurückgehen to fall, to slip, to drift lower, to ease, to slump

die Kurse gingen um durchschnittlich 10 % zurück prices slumped an average of 10 per cent

Zinsunsicherheiten ließen die Aktienkurse - interest rate uncertainties sent stock (equity) prices lower

Zurückhaltung restraint
- der Anleger investor restraint

die Anleihe wurde mit - aufgenommen the loan received a tepid reception zurückkaufen am Markt - to repurchase in the market

zurücknehmen eine Aktie im Kurs - to mark down a stock

zurückrufen vor Verfall - to retire (to call in) prior to maturity

zurückstellen to defer, to postpone; to set aside

eine Emission - to shelve an issue

eine Zahlung - to defer a payment

zurückstufen to downgrade, to mark down

die Anleihen - to downgrade the bonds, to lower the bonds' rating

zurückzahlen to repay

die Anleihe kann vorzeitig zurückgezahlt werden the bond may be repaid (called in) prior to maturity (ahead of schedule)

zurückziehen to withdraw, to revoke, to cancel

die Garantiezusage - to withdraw (to revoke) the guarantee undertaking

Zurverfügungstellung des Krediets making the loan available (to the borrower)

Zusage commitment, undertaking

Zusagen für langfristige Kredite (im langfristigen Bereich) long-term loan commitments

unsere - , den Kredit bei Fälligkeit zu verlängern our undertaking to extend the loan upon its maturity

Zusage

- provision commitment commission

- schreiben bei einem Kredit: facility letter, commitment letter

- volumen total loan commitments

zusagen den Kredit fest - to give a binding (firm) loan undertaking

Zusammenbruch collapse, breakdown

zusammenfallen to coincide

die Zinssenkung fiel mit einer Reihe von Neuemissionen zusammen the interest rate cut coincided with a host of new issues

Zusammenfallen coincidence, coinciding; cumulation

durch das - von Steuer- und Kuponterminen with tax and coupon payment dates coinciding, the ..., as a result of the cumulation of tax and coupon payment dates

zusammenfassen (a) to sum up, to summarise; (b) to consolidate, to combine

Zusammenfassung eine - über die Kursentwicklung an den verschiedenen Börsen geben to give a rundown (summary) on the developments in the various stock markets

zusammenlegen (a) to merge, to amalgamate; (b) to consolidate, to combine

die verschiedenen Aktiengattungen - to consolidate the various classes of shares

Unternehmensbereiche - to merge divisions

zusammenschließen, sich (a) to join forces, to unite; (b) to merge, to amalgamate

Zusammenschluß (a) union, uniting; (b) merger, amalgamation

es werden keine ernsthaften Einwände gegen den - erwartet no serious objections to the merger are expected

- mehrerer kleiner Banken amalgamation of several small banks

zusammenstellen

einen neuen Großkredit - to arrange a new jumbo loan

ein Konsortium - to assemble a syndicate

Zusatz supplement, addition; Anhang: annex, rider, supplemental instrument

- aktien bonus shares

- dividende superdividend, surplus dividend

- finanzierung supplementary financing

zusätzlich additional, supplementary

- e Gelder bereitstellen to provide further capital

- e Sicherheiten stellen to deposit further security

Zuschlag (a) surcharge, markup; (b) award; (c) Aufschlag auf Libor: spread (margin) over Libor

den - erteilen to award the contract

zuschlagen dem Kapitalbetrag - to add on to the principal

Zuschlagserteilung award of contract

Zuschreibungen zu Gegenständen des Anlagevermögens additions to fixed assets, property additions

Zuschuß (a) subsidy, grant; (b) contribution, allowance

- bewilligung granting a subsidy

- unternehmen loss-making company (depending on subsidies)

zusichern weitere finanzielle Unterstützung - to guarantee continued financial backing

zuständige Abteilung department concerned

Zuständigkeitsbereich Neuengagements fallen unter seinen - new loan commitments come within his province

zustehen jedem Zeichner stehen zwei Aktien zu each subscriber (applicant) is entitled to two shares

Zustimmung agreement, consent, approval

die ausdrückliche - des Kunden the customer's express consent

die offizielle - zu dem neuen Großkredit the formal approval of the new jumbo loan

Zustrom von Auslandskapital inflow of foreign capital

zuteilen to allot, to allocate; Aufgabe: to assign; repartieren: to scale down

einen Bausparvertrag - to allow drawdowns on a savings and loan contract; to extend a building society loan under a savings and loan contract

die den Konsorten durch die Konsortialführerin zugeteilten Beträge amounts allotted to the syndicate members by the lead manager

die Neuemission konnte nicht voll zugeteilt werden the new issue had to be scaled down

Zeichnungen bis zu DM 1.000 werden voll zugeteilt subscriptions up to DM 1,000 will be allotted in full

Zuteilung allotment, allocation; assignment; scaling down

die - der gezeichneten Aktien allotment of shares subscribed

- neuer Aufgaben im Kreditbereich assignment of new duties in the loan division

der Aktionär kann auf seine - verzichten the shareholder may renounce his allotment

267

Zuteilung
- eines Bausparvertrages allowing drawdowns on a savings and loan contract; granting a building society loan under a savings and loan contract

die - beläuft sich auf 60 % 60 per cent of the amount subscribed will be allotted to the applicant

Zuteilungs
- anzeige   allotment letter
- betrag   allotment money; amount allotted
- empfänger   allottee
- kurs   allotment price
- rechte   rights to a collective securities account

zuversichtlich die Börse zeigte sich zuversichtlich   the stock market remained confident

Zuwachs   growth, increase
- im kurzfristigen Bereich   growth in short-term lendings
- bei Spareinlagen   growth (increase) in savings deposits

Zuwachs
- aktivreserven   surplus lending reserves
- mindestreserven   surplus minimum reserves
- rate   growth rate
- steuer   increment tax

zuweisen   to allocate

Zuweisung an die Rücklagen   allocation to reserves

Zuzahlung   additional cash payment

zuzüglich aufgelaufener Zinsen   plus any accrued interest

Zwangs
- anleihe   forced loan
- einziehung   forced retirement
- hypothek   forced registration of a mortgage
- liquidation   forced liquidation
- regulierung   forced settlement
- vergleich   composition in bankruptcy
- versteigerung   foreclosure sale, forced sale
- verwaltung   receivership

Zwangsvollstreckung   foreclosure proceedings
- in eine Hypothekenforderung   foreclosure on a mortgage (on a mortgage loan)
- in das Vermögen des Schuldners betreiben   to levy execution against a debtor by seizure of his goods
- betreiben   to foreclose

Zweckbindung   earmarking, tying to

zweckgebunden
- es Darlehen   loan tied (linked) to .., project-tied loan
- e Gelder   earmarked funds
- e Rücklagen   appropriated reserves, appropriated retained earnings

zweifelhafte Forderungen   bad and doubtful debts, doubtful accounts receivable

zweigeteilter Markt   two-tier market

Zweigstelle   branch
Zweigstellendichte   branch density
Zweigstellennetz   branch network

Zweitbegünstigter   second beneficiary

zweite Hypothek   second (junior) mortgage

Zweitmarkt   secondary market
- titel   secondary market securities

zweitrangiges Grundpfandrecht
second real estate lien

Zwischen
- ausweis   interim return
- bericht   interim report
- betriebliche Forderungen   intercompany receivables
- betrieblicher Vergleich   interfirm comparison
- bilanz   interim accounts, interim statement of condition
- dividende   interim dividend

zwischenfinanzieren   to extend a bridge-over loan (a bridging advance)

einen Bausparvertrag -   to extend a bridge-over loan pending receipt of a building society loan

die zwischenfinanzierende Bank the bank extending the bridge-over loan

Zwischen
- finanzierungskredit   bridging advance, bridge-over loan
- gewinn   (a) mid-way profit, profit at midway; (b) innerhalb eines Konzerns: intergroup profits
- schein   scrip, interim certificate

zwischenzeitliche Abdeckung eines Kredites   temporary repayment (cleanup) of a loan

DICTIONARY
OF BANKING AND STOCK TRADING

ENGLISH – GERMAN

A

Aaa beste Anleiheklassifizierung

Aa / A zweit- bzw. drittbeste Anleiheklassifizierung

ability to turn assets into ready cash Liquidisierbarkeit, Realisierbarkeit

ABS → Automated Bond System

abstract of title Grundbuchauszug, Eigentumsnachweis

accelerated depreciation Sonderabschreibung, erhöhte Abschreibung

accelerated payments Sonderrückzahlungen

acceleration clause Vorfälligkeitsklausel

acceleration of maturity Vorverlegung des Fälligkeitstermines

accept v. annehmen, akzeptieren

to - deposits Einlagen hereinnehmen

to - documents Dokumente aufnehmen

to - the liability die Haftung übernehmen

acceptance Annahme; Akzept, Akzeptleistung; Hereinnahme; Aufnahme; Übernahme

- credit Akzeptkredit, Rembourskredit

- facility Akzeptkredit

- fee Grundgebühr einer Bank für die Bearbeitung eines Nachlasses (Br)

- for honour Ehrenakzept, Ehrenannahme

- level → minimum acceptance level

- liabilities Akzeptverbindlichkeiten

accepting bank akzeptgebende (akzeptierende) Bank

Accepting House → Merchant Bank

accommodate v. bereitstellen, gewähren (Kredit); entgegenkommen

accommodation Gewährung, Kreditbereitstellung

- bill Gefälligkeitswechsel

- taken aufgenommener (in Anspruch genommener) Kredit

account (a) Konto, Rechnung, Abrechnung; (b) Kunde; (c) Börsenhandelsperiode (jeweils zwei oder drei Wochen - Br)

for - of für Rechnung von

for the - zur Verrechnung am nächsten Erfüllungs- bzw. Liquidationstermin

accountant (a) Bilanzbuchhalter; (b) Abschlußprüfer, Wirtschaftsprüfer

accountant's opinion Prüfungsvermerk des Abschlußprüfers

account

- balance Kontoguthaben; Kontostand

- balancing (a) Kontoausgleich; (b) Kontoabschluß

- carried forward Vortrag auf neue Rechnung

- day Erfüllungstermin, Liquidationstermin

- envelope Kontotasche

- heading Kontobezeichnung

accounting (a) Bilanzierung; (b) Rechnungslegung; (c) Rechnungswesen

- period Abrechnungszeitraum, Geschäftsjahr

account
- keeping charges → account-maintenance charges
- maintaining branch kontoführende Stelle
- maintenance Kontoführung
- maintenance charges Kontoführungsgebühren
- management (a) im weiteren Sinne: Betreuung von Großkunden; (b) im engeren Sinne: Kontoführung
- manager (a) für eine Gruppe von Großkunden zuständiger Mitarbeiter einer Bank; (b) Kontoführer
- mandate Kontovollmacht
- opening application Kontoeröffnungsantrag
- payee only nur zur Verrechnung
- period Börsenhandelsperiode
- reconciliation Kontoabstimmung

accounts (a) Konten; (b) Kunden; (c) Abschluß, Bilanzziffern
- officer Kontoführer
- payable Verbindlichkeiten, Kreditoren
- receivable Forderungen, Debitoren
- receivable financing Finanzierung durch Forderungsabtretung, Factoring

accredited dealer zugelassener Händler

accreditee Akkreditivbegünstigter, Akkreditierter

accrual basis of accounting periodengerechte Rechnungslegung

accrued interest aufgelaufene Zinsen, Stückzinsen

accumulated loss aufgelaufener Verlust, Bilanzverlust

accumulating ordinary shares Aktien, bei denen Dividenden in Form von Gratisaktien ausgeschüttet werden

accumulation of interest Auflaufen von Zinsen

accumulation plan Sparvertrag, Anlageplan

accumulative dividend kumulative Dividende

ACH → Automated Clearing House

acid-test-ratio Liquiditätsgrad

acquisition (a) Anschaffung, Erwerb, Kauf; (b) Übernahme einer Firma
- cost (a) Einstandskosten, Gestehungskosten; (b) Abschlußkosten

active
- bids and asks Geld- und Briefkurse für lebhaft gehandelte Aktien
- stocks lebhaft gehandelte Papiere
- trading lebhafte Umsätze

activity (a) Tätigkeit; (b) Börsenumsätze
- in motors remained at a low ebb Umsätze in Autoaktien blieben gering
- of the collateral Zeitraum, der für die Verwertung einer Sicherheit benötigt wird

actual cost Ist-Kosten, tatsächliche Kosten, Gestehungskosten

actual delivery effektive Übergabe, Übergabe (Lieferung, Aushändigung) der effektiven Stücke

acute stock shortage developed Käufer stießen auf einen leeren Markt

additions Zugänge, Zuschreibungen

- to fixed assets Zuschreibungen zu Gegenständen des Anlagevermögens
- to working capital Erhöhung des Betriebskapitals

addressed bill Domizilwechsel

address in case of need Notadresse

adjudication order Konkurseröffnungsbeschluß

adjust v. (a) berichtigen, anpassen; (b) bereinigen; (c) einen Vergleich schließen, sanieren, umschulden (US)

adjusted capital ratio Indexzahl zu den haftenden Eigenmitteln (Kapital und Rücklagen abzüglich voraussichtlicher Kreditausfälle - US)

adjusted eligible net income Anteil des steuerfreien Einkommens einer ⟶ International Banking Facility

adjusted for reserves mindestreservebereinigt

adjusted for seasonal fluctuations saisonbereinigt

adjustable
- mortgage loan variabel verzinsliches Hypothekendarlehen
- rate mortgage variabel verzinsliche Hypothek

adjustment Berichtigung, Anpassung; Bereinigung; Vergleich, Sanierung (US)

obtaining a voluntary - Schließung eines außergerichtlichen Vergleichs

- of an entry Berichtigung einer Buchung
- on a bond Umschuldung einer notleidenden Anleihe

administration of securities Depotverwahrung, Verwahrung und Verwaltung von Wertpapieren

admission to listing Zulassung zur Börsennotierung

admission to the trading floor Zulassung zum Börsenhandel

ADRs ⟶ American Depositary Receipts

advance (a) Darlehen, Kredit; (b) Bevorschussung; (c) Anziehen, Kursbefestigung

advance v. (a) einen Kredit gewähren, bevorschussen; (b) anziehen, sich befestigen (Kurse)

advance
- assignment Vorausabtretung
- decline-index Index der Kurssteigerungen und Kursrückgänge
- in active trading Kursbefestigung bei lebhaften Umsätzen
- netting Vorwegkompensation
- on current account Kontokorrentkredit, Überziehungskredit, Dispositionskredit
- on securities Wertpapierkredit, Effektenlombard(ierung)
- payment guarantee Anzahlungsaval, Vorauszahlungsgarantie
- refunding Umschuldung bzw. Refinanzierung einer Anleihe zwei oder drei Jahre vor ihrer Fälligkeit
- selling Vorausplazierung einer Emission

adverse defizitär; nachteilig
- balance (a) Verlustbilanz, Unterbilanz; (b) Passivsaldo, Sollsaldo
- market Baissemarkt
- opinion eingeschränkter Bestätigungsvermerk des Abschlußprüfers

advice Aufgabe, Anzeige, Ankündigung
- of deal Ausführungsanzeige
- of dishonour Nichtbezahltmeldung; Protestanzeige

advice
- of fate   (a) Inkassobenachrichtigung; (b) Bezahltmeldung, Scheckdeckungsanzeige
- of non-payment   Nichtbezahltmeldung

advising the credit to the beneficiary   Avisierung des Akkreditivs an den Begünstigten

advisory management services   Vermögensverwaltung ohne Dispositionsbefugnisse des Anlageberaters

after-date bill   Datowechsel

after-hours support for bank stocks   nachbörsliches Interesse für Bankaktien

after-market   (a) Nachbörse; (b) Sekundärmarkt, Markt für im Umlauf befindliche Papiere

after-sight bill   Nachsichtwechsel

à forfait market (paper)   Forfaitierungsmarkt (-material)

against the box ⟶ short sale against the box

agency   (a) Vertretung, Vollmacht; (b) Behörde; (c) Zahlstelle; (d) Niederlassung einer Auslandsbank in den USA; agencies können Ausleihungen vornehmen und Devisengeschäfte abwickeln; das Einlagengeschäft ist ihnen jedoch verwehrt

through our agency   durch unsere Vermittlung

agency
- account   Treuhandkonto; Depotkonto (US)
- bonds   öffentliche Anleihen
- commission   Zahlstellenprovision; Provision der⟶ agent bank
- contract   (a) Geschäftsbesorgungsvertrag, Vertretungsvertrag; (b) Zahlstellenvereinbarung
- fee   (a) Abwicklungsgebühr; (b) Vermögensverwaltungsgebühr; (c) Zahlstellenprovision
- marketing (selling)   Vertrieb einer Anleihe (Übernahme zur Verkaufsvermittlung)

agent   (a) Agent; (b) Bevollmächtigter, Beauftragter, Vertreter

agent bank   Agent, Zahlstelle; in Verbindung mit variabel verzinslichen Wertpapieren: Bank, die den jeweiligen Zinssatz für diese Papiere festlegt

aggregate   Gesamtsumme
- credit exposure   Gesamtengagement, Gesamtkreditrahmen
- face value   Gesamtnennwert
- loan commitments (loan portfolio)   Gesamtausleihungen, Kreditvolumen
- principal amount   Gesamtkapitalbetrag, Gesamtnennbetrag

aggressive investment   stark spekulative Anlage, mit einem hohen Risiko behaftete Anlage

agreed period of notice   vereinbarte Kündigungsfrist

agreement corporation   Finanzierungsgesellschaft, die nur internationale Bankgeschäfte abwickeln darf (US)

agreement to reimburse   Remboursermächtigung

agreement to (purchase and) sell   Emissionsvertrag, Übernahmevertrag

aircrafts   Luftfahrtwerte

all-in   einschließlich aller Rechte

allocation to reserves Zuweisung (Zuführung) an die Rücklagen, Bedienung der Rücklagen

allotment (a) Zuteilung; (b) Zuteilungsquote
- account Zuteilungskonto
- letter Zuteilungsanzeige, Zuteilungsbescheinigung
- money Zuteilungsbetrag
- of shares Zuteilung von Aktien; Zuteilungsquote
- price Zuteilungskurs

allottee Zuteilungsempfänger

allowance for depreciation Abschreibungsbetrag

allowance for possible loan losses Wertberichtigungen auf Kredite

all-purpose credit card Multifunktions-Kreditkarte

American Depositary Receipts Namenszertifikate, die von US-Banken für erstklassige ausländische Aktien ausgegeben werden

American Stock Exchange zweitgrößte US-Börse

AML → adjustable mortgage loan

amortisation (a) Tilgung; (b) Abschreibung
- features Tilgungsmodalitäten, Tilgungsbestimmungen

amortise v. (a) tilgen; (b) abschreiben

amortised cost Buchwert

amortising mortgage Tilgungshypothek, Amortisationshypothek

amortized note Tilgungsschuldschein (US)

and company nur zur Verrechnung

and interest plus Stückzinsen

annual
- accounts Jahresabschluß, Jahresbilanz
- cleanup feature Klausel eines Kreditvertrages, derzufolge der Kredit einmal pro Jahr vollständig zurückgeführt werden muß
- debt service jährlicher Schuldendienst
- general meeting Jahreshauptversammlung
- interest payments jährlicher Zinsendienst, jährliche Zinszahlungen
- percentage rate Gesamtprozentsatz der pro Jahr für einen Kredit aufzubringenden Zinsen und Gebühren, Effektivzinssatz (US)
- principal and interest payments jährliche Belastung (Zins- und Tilgungszahlungen), jährlicher Schuldendienst
- redemption rate Jahrestilgungsquote
- yield Jahresrendite

annuity Annuität, jährliche Zahlung, jährliche Zins- und Tilgungszahlungen

annuity bond Annuitätenanleihe

anticipated redemption vorzeitige Tilgung, vorzeitiger Rückkauf

anticipatory credit Akkreditivbevorschussung

anti-marketwise operations Wertpapiergeschäfte gegen den Markttrend

applicant for the credit (a) Kreditantragsteller; (b) Akkreditivauftraggeber, Akkreditivsteller

application (a) Antrag; (b) Zeichnung (von Wertpapieren);(c)Unterbringung (Verbuchung) von Geldern
- account Zeichnungskonto
- blank Zeichnungsformular
- charges Zeichnungsgebühren

275

application
- for listing   Antrag auf Börseneinführung
- form   Zeichnungsformular
- for shares   Zeichnung von Aktien
- list   Zeichnungsliste
- money   Zeichnungsbetrag
- of payments received   Verwendung (Unterbringung) der Zahlungseingänge
- rights   Zeichnungsrechte

apply v. (a) beantragen; (b) zeichnen (Wertpapiere); (c) verwenden, unterbringen, verbuchen (Gelder)

apportion v. (a) verteilen, aufteilen, umlegen (Kosten); (b) zuteilen, repartieren (Wertpapiere)

apportionment of applications   Zuteilung (Repartierung) der gezeichneten Wertpapiere

apportionment of costs   Aufteilung (Umlegung) der Kosten

appraise v. (a) bewerten, analysieren; (b) schätzen

appraised value   Schätzwert

appreciate v. im Wert (Kurs) steigen, den Wert erhöhen

appreciation (a) Wertzuwachs, Kapitalgewinn, Kapitalzuwachs; (b) Kursgewinn, Kurssteigerung
- potential   Kurschancen, Wertsteigerungspotential

appropriate v. (a) bereitstellen, bewilligen; (b) zuweisen, zuführen; (c) anrechnen auf

appropriated from the reserves   aus den Rücklagen bereitgestellt, den Rücklagen entnommen

appropriated funds   bereitgestellte Mittel

appropriated retained earnings   zweckgebundene Rücklagen

appropriated surplus   Sonderrücklage

appropriated to the amount outstanding   mit dem offenstehenden Betrag verrechnet

appropriated to the reserves   den Rücklagen zugeführt, in die Rücklagen eingestellt

appropriation (a) Bereitstellung, Bewilligung; (b) Zuweisung, Zuführung; (c) Anrechnung auf
- account   Aufstellung über die Verwendung des Bilanzgewinnes
- of fresh funds   Bereitstellung neuer Kredite (Mittel)
- of payments   Verwendung (Verrechnung) von Zahlungen
- of the net income   Verteilung (Verwendung) des Nettogewinnes
- power   Bewilligungsrecht
- to the reserve   Einstellung in die Rücklage
- to the sinking fund   Zuweisung an den Tilgungsfonds

appropriations (a) bereitgestellte Gelder, bewilligte Investitionen; (b) Rücklagen
- committee   Bewilligungsausschuß, Investitionsgenehmigungsausschuß

approval   Genehmigung, Billigung, Bewilligung
- powers   Bewilligungskompetenz (für Kredite), Dispositionsbefugnisse, Kreditkompetenz

approve v. genehmigen, billigen, bewilligen

approved depository   zugelassene Hinterlegungsstelle

approved securities   lombardfähige Wertpapiere

approximate price   Zirkakurs

APR → annual percentage rate

arbitrage in securities   Effektenarbitrage

arbitrage stocks   Arbitragewerte

arbitration of exchange   Devisenarbitrage, Wechselkursarbitrage

ARIEL → automated real-time investments exchange

arm's length principle   Prinzip der Selbständigkeit

arrangement   (a) Vereinbarung; (b) Vergleich; (c) Anordnung, Rangfolge

- fee   (a) Bearbeitungsgebühr, Koordinierungsgebühr; (b) Bereitstellungsprovision

- of claims   Rangfolge der Konkursforderungen

- of a loan   (a) Aufnahme eines Kredites; (b) Zusammenstellung einer Finanzierung

arrears   Rückstände, rückständige Zahlungen

arrears certificate   Zahlungsverpflichtung im Hinblick auf rückständige Zinsen

ASE → American Stock Exchange

A shares   dividendenberechtigte, aber stimmrechtslose Aktien

asked   Brief, Briefkurs, Verkaufskurs

asked discount   Abschlag auf den Verkaufskurs

assemble v.   zusammenstellen (ein Konsortium)

assess v.   (a) prüfen, beurteilen (Bonität, Kreditwürdigkeit); (b) veranlagen (zur Einkommensteuer); (c) zu Nachschußzahlungen auffordern

assessable stock   nachschußpflichtige Aktien

assessment   Beurteilung, Prüfung; Veranlagung; Zahlungsaufforderung

assessment bond   Kommunalobligation (gesichert durch das kommunale Steueraufkommen)(US)

asset   (a) Vermögenswert; (b) Aktivposten

assets   Aktiva, Ausleihungen einer Bank

asset

- additions   Anlagenzugänge

- ceiling   Kreditplafond, Höchstgrenze für Ausleihungen einer Bank

- cost   Anschaffungswert der Anlagegüter

- disposal   Veräußerung von Gegenständen des Anlagevermögens, Anlagenabgänge

- diversification   Vermögensstreuung, Anlagenstreuung

- exposure   Gesamtausleihungen, Kreditvolumen

- growth   (a) Zunahme der Ausleihungen; (b) Bilanzwachstum; (c) Vermögenszuwachs

- lock-up arrangement   Anlagen-Übernahmeoption, Vorkaufsrecht auf Betriebsanlagen

- maintenance requirements   Verpflichtung für US-Banken ein bestimmtes Verhältnis zwischen Forderungen und Verbindlichkeiten zu gewährleisten

- management   Aktivmanagement, Aktivsteuerung

- portfolio   (a) Kreditvolumen; (b) Vermögensanlagen

- replacements   Anlagenerneuerungen

- sales surplus   Gewinn aus dem Verkauf von Anlagen

- shifting   Umschichtung von Vermögensanlagen

assign v.   abtreten, übertragen

assignable credit   übertragbares Akkreditiv

assignee   Zessionar, Rechtsnachfolger, Übertragungsempfänger

assignment   Abtretung, Übertragung, Zession

- of receivables   Abtretung von Forderungen

assignor   Zedent, Abtretender

associated company   Beteiligungsgesellschaft

assumed bond   Anleihe, deren Bedienung durch einen Drittschuldner gewährleistet wird

at a premium   mit einem Aufgeld

at best   bestens, billigst

at limit   mit Limit, limitierter Wertpapierauftrag

ATM → automated teller machine

at par   zum Nennwert, zu pari

ATS → automated transfer service

at the lower of cost or market   zum Niederstwertprinzip

at the market   bestens

at the net realisable value   zum Nettoveräußerungswert

attracted deposits   akquirierte Einlagen, Kundeneinlagen (US)

attracting interest at call money rates   Verzinsung zum Tagesgeldsatz

attributable profit   ausschüttungsfähiger Gewinn

audit   (a) Abschlußprüfung, Buchprüfung; (b) Revision
- certificate   Prüfungsvermerk, Bestätigungsvermerk des Abschlußprüfers
- qualification   Einschränkung des Bestätigungsvermerks

authorise v.   genehmigen; bewilligen (Kredit)

authorised capital   autorisiertes Kapital, Nominalkapital

authorised depository   zugelassene Hinterlegungsstelle

authorised signing officer   Unterschriftsträger, Unterschriftsbevollmächtigter

authorised to sign jointly   gemeinschaftlich zeichnungsberechtigt

authorised to sign on an account   zeichnungsberechtigt für ein Konto, über ein Konto verfügungsberechtigt

authority   Genehmigung; Bewilligung; Vollmacht, Berechtigung
- to contract   Abschlußvollmacht
- to draw   (a) Verfügungsberechtigung (über ein Konto); (b) Ziehungsermächtigung (Akkreditiv)
- to operate an account   Verfügungsberechtigung (über ein Konto), Kontovollmacht
- to pay   Zahlungsermächtigung, Einlösungsermächtigung

auto depositor   (Geld-)Einzahlungsautomat

Automated Bond System   computergestützter Handel in Rentenwerten der New Yorker Börse

Automated Clearing Houses   Clearing-Zentralen, denen nicht nur Banken sondern auch Industrieunternehmen angeschlossen sind

Automated Real-Time Investments Exchange   Computersystem für die Abwicklung von Börsengeschäften unter Umgehung der Londoner Börse

automated servicing of bank customers   automatisiertes Schaltergeschäft, automatisierte Kundenbedienung

automated teller machine   Mehrfunktions-Bankautomat, SB-Bankautomat

automated transfer service   automatisierter Überweisungsverkehr

automation in banking   Bankautomation, Automatisierung in Bankgeschäft

automation of payments Zahlungs-
verkehrsautomation

automobile shares (stocks) Automobilaktien, Fahrzeugwerte

availability clause Verfügbarkeitsklausel

availability fee → commitment
commission

available balance (a) verfügbarer
Saldo; (b) valutarischer Saldo

available funds liquide
(flüssige) Mittel, verfügbare
Gelder

availment of a credit line Inanspruchnahme einer Kreditlinie

average (a) Durchschnitt; (b)
Börsenindex

- asset maturity durchschnittliche Laufzeit der Kredite

- deposit maturity durchschnittliche Laufzeit der Einlagen

- due date mittlerer Verfalltag

averaging (a) Nachkauf einer
Aktie bei rückläufigem Kurs, um
einen besseren Durchschnittskurs zu erzielen;(b) regelmäßige Anlage eines gleichblei-
benden Betrages in den gleichen
Papieren

average

- life durchschnittliche Laufzeit

- linked investments an einen
  Kursindex gebundene Anlagen

- price Durchschnittskurs

- stocks durch einen Index er-
  faßte Aktien

- yield Durchschnittsrendite

aviation stocks Luftfahrtwerte,
Aktien von Luftverkehrsgesell-
schaften

B

Baa/Ba/B Klassifizierungskennzeichen für Anleihen von durchschnittlicher bis unterdurchschnittlicher Qualität

back v. stützen, unterstützen; auffangen

backdoor transaction Ankauf von Schatzwechseln durch die Bank von England

backing Unterstützung, Stützung

backing syndicate Stützungskonsortium

back interest Zinsrückstände

backstop by a bank line Absicherung durch die Kreditlinie einer Bank

back-to-back credit (loan) (a) Gegenakkreditiv; (b) Auffangkredit

back-up for commercial paper Deckungslinie für kurzfristige Schuldtitel, die von Industrieunternehmen emittiert werden

back-up line Deckungslinie, Auffanglinie

back-up support Börse: Anschlußaufträge

backvaluation Rückvalutierung

backwardation Deport
- rate Deportsatz
- transaction Deportgeschäft

BACS → bankers' automated clearing services

bad debt provisioning Risikovorsorge im Kreditgeschäft, Vorsorge für Risikokredite

bad debt provisioning policy Vorsorgepolitik

bad debt provisions (a) Rückstellungen für Risikokredite (für notleidende Kredite); (b) Rückstellungen für zweifelhafte Forderungen

bad debts allowance Wertberichtigungen auf Kredite (auf zweifelhafte Forderungen)

bad loan notleidender Kredit; Risikokredit

bad loan charge Wertberichtigungsbedarf im Kreditgeschäft

B/A facility Akzeptkredit

balance (a) Bilanz; (b) Saldo; (c) Kontostand; (d) Guthaben

balances with other banks Guthaben bei anderen Banken

balanced fund Investmentfonds, dessen Anlagevermögen zu gleichen Teilen in Aktien und festverzinslichen Papieren investiert wird

balance
- brought forward Saldovortrag, vorgetragener Saldo
- in the account Kontostand, Saldo
- on current account (a) Leistungsbilanz; (b) Kontokorrentsaldo
- reporting Form des Cash Management; gibt Firmenkunden die Möglichkeit, schnell und durch Zugriff auf ein EDV-System, genaue und aktuelle Informationen über Kontostände und Währungsrisiken weltweit abzurufen

balance
- requirements → compensating balances
- sheet   Bilanz
- sheet date   Bilanzstichtag
- sheet evaluation   (a) Bilanzbewertung; (b) Bilanzansatz
- ticket   Bestätigung, daß die zur Übertragung bestimmten Aktien bei der emittierenden Gesellschaft hinterlegt wurden
- to be carried forward   Saldoübertrag

balloon payment   überdurchschnittlich hohe (oft auch einzige) Tilgungszahlung bei Fälligkeit des Kredites

band 1/2/3/4   Fälligkeiten bis zu 14 Tagen /von 15-33/ von 34-63/ von 64-84 Tagen

band of fluctuation   Schwankungsbreite

bankable bill   diskontfähiger Wechsel

bankable security   bankmäßige (bankübliche) Sicherheit

bank
- accounting rules   Bankbilanzierungsrichtlinien
- advance   Bankkredit, Bankdarlehen
- and cash balances   Kassenbestand und Bankguthaben
- base rate   Eckzins der Londoner Clearing-Banken für Ausleihungen
- bill   Bankwechsel
- bond   Bankschuldverschreibung, Bankobligation
- book   Sparbuch
- charges   Bankgebühren
- chartering authority   Bankenzulassungsbehörde (US)
- code   Bankleitzahl

- collateral   Banksicherheit, bankmäßige Sicherheit
- commissioner   Vertreter der Bankenaufsichtsbehörde eines US-Bundesstaates
- credit   Bankkredit
- credit transfer   Banküberweisung
- deposit insurance   Bankeinlagenversicherung
- deposit rates   Zinssätze auf Spareinlagen, Sparzinsen
- deposits   Bankeinlagen
- documentary credit   Bankrembours
- endorsed   bankgiriert

banker's
- bond   Bankgarantie
- buying rate   Ankaufskurs (Geldkurs) einer Bank
- call rate   Tagesgeldsatz
- card   Scheckkarte
- draft   Bankscheck, Bankwechsel
- duty of care   Sorgfaltspflicht der Bank
- duty of secrecy   Bankgeheimnis, Geheimhaltungspflicht der Bank
- franchise   Selbstbehalt der Bank
- lien   Bankenpfandrecht
- opinion   Bankauskunft, Kreditauskunft
- ratio   der von einer Bank erwartete Liquiditätsgrad eines Industrieunternehmens
- reference   Bankauskunft, Bankreferenz
- right of set-off   Verrechnungsrecht der Bank
- ticket   Scheckrückrechnung, Wechselrückrechnung

bankers'
- automated clearing services   EDV-Abwicklung von Kundenüberweisungen
- clearing house   zentrale Abrechnungsstelle der Geschäftsbanken

281

bankers'
- deposit rate Zinssatz für Einlagen mit siebentägiger Kündigungsfrist (Br)
- deposits Guthaben der Geschäftsbanken bei der Bank von England

bank
- examiner Vertreter einer Bankenaufsichtsbehörde (US)
- giro Banküberweisung, bargeldlose Zahlung (Br)
- giro credit Überweisungsauftrag
- giro network Gironetz, Giroorganisation
- giro system Giroverkehr
- group (a) Bankenkonsortium; (b) Bankenkette (US)
- guarantee Bankgarantie, Bankaval
- holiday Bankfeiertag

banking Bankwesen, Bankgewerbe, Bankgeschäfte
- aggregates Geldmengenzahlen
- authority Bankenaufsichtsbehörde
- commissioner Vertreter einer Bankenaufsichtsbehörde (US)
- community Bankkreise
- connection Bankverbindung
- customs Bankpraxis, Bankgepflogenheiten
- density Bankstellendichte
- department Abteilung der Bank of England (zuständig für die Abwicklung der üblichen Bankgeschäfte)
- facilities Dienstleistungsangebot einer Bank
- hall Schalterhalle
- hours Schalterstunden
- industry Bankgewerbe, Kreditwirtschaft
- interests Bankbeteiligungen
- organisation Bank, Bankbetrieb; Bankenorganisation
- package Bank-Servicepaket
- product Bankprodukt, Bankdienstleistung
- regulation Bankengesetzgebung
- regulator Bankengesetzgeber
- sector Bankgewerbe, Bankensektor
- security bankübliche Sicherheit
- services Bankdienstleistungen, Dienstleistungspalette einer Bank
- supervision Bankenaufsicht
- syndicate Bankenkonsortium, Bankengruppe
- system Kreditwesen, Bankenapparat

bank
- lending (a) Bankkredit; (b) Ausleihungen der Banken
- lending policy Kreditpolitik der Banken
- lending rate Kreditzinssatz
- line Kreditlinie einer Bank
- liquidity Bankenliquidität
- liquidity ratio Liquiditätsgrad einer Bank
- loan Bankkredit
- merger Bankenfusion
- money Buchgeld, Giralgeld
- name Bankadresse (z.B. auf dem Anleihemarkt)
- note (a) Banknote; (b) Schuldschein
- official Bankangestellter, Bankkaufmann
- of issue Notenbank
- overdraft Überziehungskredit
- product Bankprodukt, Bankdienstleistung
- rate (a) frühere Bezeichnung für den Diskontsatz der Bank of England; (b) umgangssprachlich für Kreditzinssatz

bank
- reference Bankauskunft
- regulation Bankengesetzgebung
- regulatory agency Bankenaufsichtsbehörde
- related paper Geldmarktpapiere, die von Banken oder mit Banken verbundenen Unternehmen ausgegeben werden
- related services Banknebenleistungen
- reserves Liquiditätsreserven einer Bank
- return Bankausweis

banks Bankaktien, Bankwerte
bank
- stamp Bankgiro
- statement Kontoauszug
- statement printer Kontoauszugsdrucker
- stock (a) Bankaktien; (b) Kapital einer Bank
- superintendent Vertreter einer Bankenaufsichtsbehörde
- term credit mittelfristiger Bankkredit
- valuables Bankvaloren
- wire Clearingnetz der US-Banken

bar Geldhandelsgeschäft über 1 Mio Pfund-Sterling

bargain Geschäft, Abschluß

bargain for account Termingeschäft

BAS → Block Automation System

base
- lending rate Eckzins der Londoner Clearing-Banken für Ausleihungen
- period Bezugszeitraum
- rate → base lending rate
- related money an die → base lending rate gekoppelte Ausleihungen

basic sentiment Grundton (Börse)

basic yield Ausgangsrendite, Grundrendite

basis Warentermingeschäft: Unterschied zwischen Kassa- und Terminpreis

basis point Treasury bill rates fell 35 basis points Schatzwechselsätze fielen um 0,35 %

basket of currencies Währungskorb

basket purchase Erwerb verschiedener Wertpapiere zum gleichen Kurs

bazaar securities Phantasiewerte

bear Baissier, Baissespekulant
- closing Rückkauf von leerverkauften Aktien
- commitment Baisseposition, Baisseengagement
- covering Deckungskäufe von Baissespekulanten

bearer (a) Inhaber; (b) Überbringer
- bond Inhaberobligation
- certificate Inhaberzertifikat
- cheque Überbringerscheck
- debenture Inhaberschuldverschreibung
- share Inhaberaktie

bearish mood Baissestimmung, Baissetendenz

bear
- market Baisse, starker Kursrückgang, Kurseinbruch
- position Baisseengagement
- raid Baissemanöver
- raiding Leerverkäufe, um einen Kurs nach unten zu drücken
- sale Verkauf auf Baisse, Leerverkauf

bear
- seller Leerverkäufer
- speculator Baissier, Baisse-spekulant
- squeeze Druck auf Baissiers (Kursanstieg der leerverkauften Aktien)

bed and breakfast deal Wertpapiergeschäft zur Umgehung der Kapitalgewinnsteuer (nachbörslicher Verkauf mit Verlust und Rückkauf am folgenden Tag -Br)

before hours Vorbörse

below par unter dem Nennwert, unter pari

beneficiary Begünstigter, Anspruchsberechtigter

best efforts selling Übernahme des Vertriebs einer Anleihe

beta coefficient Kurskoeffizient (zeigt an, wie schnell eine Aktie oder ein Depot während eines bestimmten Zeitraumes im Vergleich zur Marktentwicklung gestiegen oder gefallen ist)

beverages Aktien der Getränkeindustrie

bid (a) Geld, Geldkurs; (b) Angebot, Gebot (c) Übernahmeversuch, Übernahmeangebot

bid v. bieten, ein Angebot unterbreiten

to - on an issue ein Übernahmeangebot (Plazierungsangebot) unterbreiten

bid-ask spread Spanne zwischen Geld- und Briefkurs

bid bond Bietungsgarantie

bidding syndicate Bietungskonsortium

bid-for candidates (companies) Übernahmekandidaten

bid-inspired rise Kursanstieg durch Übernahmegerüchte

bid-offer spread Spanne zwischen (a) Ausgabe- und Rücknahmepreis von Fondsanteilen; (b) Geld- und Briefkurs

bid price (a) Angebotspreis; (b) Ankaufskurs (Rücknahmepreis) von Fondsanteilen; (c) Geldkurs

bid value → bid price (b)

big block Aktienpaket

big block trading Pakethandel

Big Board listing Notierung an der New Yorker Börse

Big Board volume Umsätze an der New Yorker Börse

Big Buyer Bezeichnung für die Fed bei Kursstützungskäufen (US)

big-ticket lending Vergabe von Großkrediten, Konsortialkreditgeschäft

big-ticket stocks Großhandelswerte

bill (a) bill of exchange Wechsel; (b) Rechnung; (c) Banknote (US)

bill v. in Rechnung stellen

bill
- broker Wechselmakler
- brokerage Wechselprovision
- business Wechselgeschäft
- case Wechselportefeuille
- collection Wechselinkasso, Wechseleinzug
- collection charges Wechselinkassospesen
- commitments Wechselobligo, Wechselverbindlichkeiten
- copy Wechselausfertigung
- currency (a) Wechsellaufzeit; (b) Wechselwährung
- dealing rates Wechselankaufssätze, Wechselankaufskonditionen

284

bill
- discounting   Wechseldiskontierung
- discounting facilities   Diskontkredit
- drawn in a foreign currency   Auslandswechsel
- drawn on a foreign customer   auf einen ausländischen Kunden gezogener Wechsel
- due   fälliger Wechsel
- eligible for rediscount   rediskontfähiger Wechsel
- guarantee   Wechselbürgschaft
- holdings   Wechselbestand
- in suspense   notleidender Wechsel
- jobbing   Wechselreiterei
- line   Diskontierungslinie, Diskontkreditlinie
- maturing shortly   kurzfristig fällig werdender Wechsel
- offering   Schatzwechselemission (im Tenderverfahren)
- of lading   Konnossement
- of lading to bearer   Inhaberkonnossement
- of sale   Sicherungs-Übereignungsvertrag
- payable abroad   im Ausland zahlbar gestellter Wechsel
- payable after sight   Nachsicht-Wechsel
- portfolio   Wechselportefeuille, Wechselbestand
- presented for acceptance (discount)   zum Akzept (Diskont) vorgelegter Wechsel
- proceeds   Wechselerlös, Wechselgegenwert
- rate   (a) Wechseldiskontsatz; (b) Schatzwechselzinssatz

bills
- discounted   diskontierte Wechsel
- in circulation   Wechselumlauf
- of Exchange Act   Wechselgesetz
- payable   Wechselverbindlichkeiten, Passivwechsel, Wechselobligo
- presented for discount   zum Diskont eingereichte Wechsel, Wechselmaterial
- receivable   Wechselforderungen, Aktivwechsel

bind   v. verpflichten, binden
  to - in a guarantee   durch eine Bürgschaft verpflichten
  to - jointly and severally   gesamtschuldnerisch verpflichten
  to - by contract   vertraglich verpflichten

binding offer   verbindliches Angebot

black   to operate in the black   schwarze Zahlen schreiben

blank cheque   Blankoscheck

blanket bond   Vertrauensschadenversicherung

blanket mortgage   Gesamthypothek

block   v. sperren, einfrieren
  blocked assets (balances)   gesperrte (eingefrorene) Guthaben
  blocked securities   Sperrstücke

Block Automation System   computergestütztes Informationssystem der New Yorker Börse für den Handel in Aktienpaketen

block floating   Gruppenfloating

blocking   Sperren, Einfrieren
- minority   Sperrminorität
- notice   Sperrvermerk
- period   Sperrfrist, Bindungsfrist

block of shares   Aktienpaket

block positioner Wertpapierhändler, der Aktienpakete auf eigene Rechnung kauft (US)

block trading (a) Handel in Aktienpaketen; (b) Handel in großen Stückelungen

Blue Chip investment erstklassige (sichere) Wertpapieranlage

Blue Chip rate Zinssatz für Kredite an erste Adressen

Blue List Verzeichnis der von Wertpapierhändlern angebotenen öffentlichen Anleihen

Blue Sky Laws Gesetze gegen Emissionsbetrug

board lot volle 100 Aktien, Hunderter-Einheit

body corporate juristische Person

bond (a) Anleihe, Schuldverschreibung, Obligation (in den USA ist ein bond in der Regel besichert, in Großbritannien hingegen unbesichert); (b) Kaution, Bürgschaft

bonds im weiteren Sinne: festverzinsliche Wertpapiere, Renten, Rentenwerte

bond
- borrowing requirements Anleihebedarf
- broker auf Rentenwerte spezialisierter Wertpapiermakler
- called ahead of schedule vorzeitig gekündigte (zur Tilgung aufgerufene) Anleihe
- capital Anleihekapital
- carrying an 8 per cent coupon 8 %ige Anleihe
- certificate Anleihemantel
- collateral Sicherheit für eine Anleiheemission
- contract features Anleihevertragsbedingungen
- conversion Wandlung einer Anleihe
- counsel Fachanwalt für Emissionsfragen
- coupon Anleihekupon, Anleiheverzinsung, Anleihezinssatz
- creditor Anleihegläubiger
- dealer Rentenhändler
- dealings Rentenhandel, Umsätze (Abschlüsse) in Rentenwerten
- debtor Anleiheschuldner
- default Zahlungsverzug des Anleiheschuldners
- denominated in US dollar auf US $ lautende Anleihe, $-Anleihe
- denomination Anleihestückelung
- discount Anleihedisagio
- drawn ausgeloste Anleihe
- exposure Engagement in Rentenwerten (im Rentenbereich)
- features Anleiheausstattung, Anleihekonditionen, Anleihemodalitäten
- financing Anleihefinanzierung
- flotation (floataation) Anleihebegebung
- fund Rentenfonds
- holder Anleiheinhaber, Anleihebesitzer, Obligationär
- house auf Festverzinsliche spezialisierter Broker (und/oder Emissionsfirma)
- indebtedness Anleiheverschuldung
- indenture Anleihevertrag
- instrument Anleihevertrag
- interest Anleihezinsen
- interest rate Anleihekupon, Anleihezinssatz
- investments Anlagen in Anleihen (Festverzinslichen), Rentenanlagen
- investor Anleihekäufer
- issue Anleiheemission

bond
- issuer   Anleiheemittent
- launching   Anleihebegebung
- listing   Anleihenotierung, Notierung einer Anleihe an der Börse
- market   Anleihemarkt, Rentenmarkt
- market average   Renten-Index
- maturity   (a) Fälligkeitstermin einer Anleihe, Anleihefälligkeit; (b) Laufzeit einer Anleihe
- offering   Anleiheangebot, Zeichnungsangebot für eine Anleihe
- of short (long) maturity   Kurzläufer (Langläufer)
- placed directly with private investors   direkt bei privaten Anlegern untergebrachte Anleihe
- placement   Anleiheplazierung
- portfolio   Bestand an festverzinslichen Wertpapieren, Anleihedepot, Rentendepot
- premium   Anleiheagio
- price   Anleihekurs
- price average   Renten-Index
- prices   Rentenkurse, Notierungen für Festverzinsliche
- pricing   Festsetzung des Anleihezinssatzes
- principal   Anleihenennwert, Anleihekapital
- proceeds   Anleiheerlös
- quotations → bond prices
- rating   Anleihebewertung, Bonitätseinstufung (Klassifizierung) einer Anleihe
- redeemable by drawings   Auslosungsanleihe
- redemption   Anleihetilgung
- redemption notice   Anleihekündigung
- redemption schedule   Anleihetilgungsplan
- refunding   Anleiheumschuldung
- retirement   Anleihetilgung, Rückzahlung einer Anleihe
- risk   Anleiherisiko

bonds
- calendar   Emissionsfahrplan, Emissionskalender
- called in for redemption   zur Tilgung aufgerufene Anleihen, gekündigte Anleihen
- floated in the Eurobond market   am Eurobond-Markt aufgelegte Anleihen
- in denominations of $ 100 or multiples thereof   Anleihen in Stückelungen von $ 100 oder einem Vielfachen davon
- in face amounts of $ 1,000   Anleihen mit einem Nennwert von $ 1000
- offered for subscription   zur Zeichnung aufgelegte Anleihen
- payable   Anleiheverbindlichkeiten, Verbindlichkeiten aus Anleiheemissionen
- traded in the secondary market   am Sekundärmarkt gehandelte Anleihen
- with maturities of 5 to 8 years   Anleihen mit Laufzeiten von 5 - 8 Jahren

bond
- terms   Anleihebedingungen, Anleiheausstattung
- trading   Rentenhandel, Handel in festverzinslichen Wertpapieren
- trading at a 1 per cent discount   mit einem Abschlag von 1 % gehandelte Anleihe
- underwriting   Übernahme einer Anleihe
- valuation   Anleihebewertung
- value   Wert (Marktpreis) einer Anleihe

bond
- washing Verkauf einer Anleihe und anschließender Rückkauf zu einem niedrigeren Kurs
- with warrants Optionsanleihe
- write-offs Abschreibungen auf den Rentenbestand
- yield Anleiherendite

bonus-carrying savings deposits bonifizierte Spareinlagen

bonus issue Ausgabe (Emission) von Gratisaktien

bonus share Gratisaktie

book
- entry to hold in book-entry form buchmäßig verwahren
- squaring by professional traders Glattstellungen (Liquidierungen) des Berufshandels
- value Buchwert, Bilanzwert
- value per share ausgewiesenes Eigenkapital je Aktie
- yield Buchrendite (auf der Grundlage des Buchwertes und nicht des Kurswertes errechnete Umlaufsrendite)

boot als Bonus zugeteilte Stammaktien

borrow v. einen Kredit aufnehmen

borrowed capital (funds) Fremdmittel, aufgenommene Gelder (Mittel)

if you borrow short, don't lend long goldene Bankregel in Großbritannien

to - in the capital market am Kapitalmarkt aufnehmen

to - on securities (goods) Wertpapiere (Waren) beleihen lassen, einen Lombardkredit aufnehmen

to - short-term einen kurzfristigen Kredit aufnehmen

borrower Kreditnehmer, Darlehensnehmer
- in the bond market Adresse (Kreditnehmer) am Anleihemarkt, Anleiheadresse
- of funds (in the money market) Nehmer (auf dem Geldmarkt)

borrowing Kreditaufnahme, Aufnahme von Geldern

  borrowings aufgenommene Kredite, Verbindlichkeiten, Fremdkapital
- agreement Kreditvertrag
- arrangement Kreditvereinbarung
- authority Kreditbefugnis, Vollmacht zur Aufnahme von Krediten
- bank Nehmerbank
- by public authorities Kreditaufnahme durch die öffentliche Hand
- ceiling (limit) Schuldenrahmen, Verschuldungsrahmen
- country Schuldnerland
- covenants Kreditauflagen, Kreditbeschränkungen
- customer Kreditkunde
- facilities Kreditfazilitäten
- limit Kreditobergrenze, Kreditlinie
- power Kreditbefugnis, Kreditfähigkeit
- ratio Kreditfinanzierungsrate
- requirements Kreditbedarf
- term money Aufnahme von Termingeld

bottom Tiefpunkt, Tiefstand

bottom v. einen Tiefpunkt erreichen

bottom price niedrigster Kurs

bottom support point unterer Interventionspunkt

bought note Effektenkaufabrechnung

bought position Hausse-Engagement

branch Filiale, Zweigstelle
- banking Filialbankensystem
- costing Filialkostenrechnung
- density Zweigstellendichte
- network Filialnetz

breadth of the market Marktbreite

break-even point Nutzenschwelle, Rentabilitätsschwelle

break-up value Liquidationswert

breweries Brauereiaktien

bridge-over loan / bridging advance Überbrückungskredit, Zwischenfinanzierungskredit

brisk market (trading) lebhafte Umsatztätigkeit

broad equity advance Anstieg der Aktienkurse auf breiter Front

broad money supply Geldmenge in ihrer weitesten Abgrenzung

broken amount nicht handelsübliche Stückzahl

broken interest Bruchzins

broker Makler, Broker

brokerage statement Courtagerechnung

broker-dealer Brokerfirma, die auch Händlerfunktionen wahrnimmt (US)

broker's deposit rate Broker-Zinssatz für Tagesgeld bzw. Einlagen mit kurzfristiger Kündigungsfrist (Br)

brought forward Vortrag aus letzter Rechnung

budget accounting Plankostenrechnung, Sollkostenrechnung

budgeted income statement budgetierte Erfolgsrechnung

budget estimates Ansätze in der Plankostenrechnung, Haushaltsansätze

building and loan association Bausparkasse (US)

buildings Bauwerte, Bauaktien

building society Bausparkasse (Br)
- deposits Bausparkasseneinlagen
- funds Bausparkassenmittel
- loan Bausparkassendarlehen
- rates Zinsen auf Bausparkasseneinlagen
- shares Bausparkassenanteile

build-up of reserves Rücklagenbildung

bull Haussier, Haussespekulant
- buying Kauf auf Hausse
- commitments Hausse-Engagements

bulldogs ₤-Sterling-Auslandsanleihen

bullet Anleihe ohne Tilgungsfonds

bullet loan Kredit, bei dem in den ersten Jahren nur Zins- und keine Tilgungszahlungen zu leisten sind

bulling Kauf auf Hausse

bullion Gold, Silber
- coins Gold-(Silber-)münzen
- price Goldnotiz
- trade Edelmetallhandel

bullish haussierend

bull market (run) Hausse

buoyancy Kursanstieg (Aufwärtsbewegung) auf breiter Front

buoyant fest

business
- activity Konjunktur, Wirtschaftstätigkeit
- advisory service Unternehmensberatung durch eine Bank (Br)
- development loan Investitionskredit
- disclosure Offenlegung der finanziellen Verhältnisse
- downturn Konjunkturrückgang
- lendings gewerbliches Kreditgeschäft
- loan Betriebsmittelkredit, gewerblicher Kredit
- property loan gewerblicher Immobilienkredit
- start-up loan Existenzgründungskredit
- start-up scheme Existenzgründungs-Kreditprogramm (Br)
- upswing Konjunkturaufschwung

butt Talon

buy advice Kaufempfehlung

buy-back price Rückkaufpreis

buyer Käufer, Erwerber
- credit Käuferkredit
- of a call option Erwerber einer Kaufoption
- of funds Nehmer auf dem Geldmarkt

buyer's
- bank Akkreditivbank
- call Käuferabruf (Warentermingeschäft)
- market Käufermarkt

buyers Käuferpublikum
- only (over) Kurszusatz: Geld

buy-in Deckungskauf; Rückkauf

buying a call Erwerb einer Kaufoption

buying
- ahead Deckungskäufe, Käufe in Erwartung von Kurssteigerungen
- at a reduced price level Käufe auf ermäßigter Basis
- bank (a) Nehmerbank (bei Interbankgeschäften); (b) Käuferbank
- currencies forward Devisenterminkäufe
- for a rise Kauf auf Hausse
- for own account Käufe für den eigenen Bestand
- in stock (a) Rückkauf eigener Aktien (z.B. für den Eigenbestand); (b) Deckungskäufe
- interest Anlegerinteresse, Käuferinteresse
- in the Fed funds market Aufnahme von Tagesgeld (US)
- long Haussespekulation
- of DM-securities Engagements in DM-Titeln
- on close (on opening) zum Schlußkurs (Eröffnungskurs) erwerben
- on margin Effektenkredit, Kauf von Wertpapieren gegen Kredit
- order Kaufauftrag, Effektenkaufauftrag
- outright Kassekauf
- price (a) Kaufpreis; (b) Ausgabekurs; (c) Rücknahmepreis (für Fondsanteile)
- public Anlagepublikum
- rate Ankaufskurs, Sortenankaufskurs
- rates for eligible bills Ankaufssätze für rediskontfähige Wechsel
- surge Kaufwelle

buy or cancel Gültigkeit nur heute (Effektenkaufauftrag, der nur für einen Tag gilt)

buy-out Aufkauf einer Kapitalgesellschaft durch Mitglieder der Geschäftsleitung und Umwandlung in eine Personengesellschaft

C

Caa/Ca/C Klassifizierungskennzeichen für Anleihen von unterdurchschnittlicher Qualität bzw. für Papiere mit stark spekulativem Charakter

calculation of interest accrued Berechnung (Errechnung) der aufgelaufenen Zinsen, Stückzinsenkalkulation

call (a) Zahlungsaufforderung, Einforderung von Geldern; (b) Kaufoption

call v. (a) kündigen (Anleihe, Kredit); (b) einfordern, abrufen (Gelder)

to - for semi-annual repayments halbjährliche Tilgungszahlungen vorsehen

to - in for immediate repayment zur sofortigen Rückzahlung fällig stellen

to - in the guarantee →to call upon the guarantor

to - on the capital market den Kapitalmarkt in Anspruch nehmen

to - up an account balance den Kontostand abrufen (abfragen)

to - upon the guarantor den Garantiegeber aus seiner Garantie in Anspruch nehmen

callable (a) kündbar; (b) abrufbar

call
- buyer Erwerber einer Kaufoption
- date Kündigungstermin
- deferment / call deferment period Kündigungsfreijahre
- expiration date Verfalltermin einer Kaufoption
- facility / call feature Kündigungsmöglichkeit, Kündigungsklausel
- holder Inhaber einer Kaufoption
- ing in a guarantee Garantieinanspruchnahme, Inanspruchnahme aus einer Garantie
- ing in the issue in part or in its entirety vollständige oder teilweise Kündigung einer Emission
- letter Einzahlungsaufforderung
- loan (a) jederzeit kündbarer Kredit, kurzfristiges Darlehen; (b) Überlassung von Tagesgeld
- money Tagesgeld
- money deals Tagesgeldabschlüsse
- money market Tagesgeldmarkt
- money rate Tagesgeldsatz
- notice Tilgungsankündigung
- on minimum reserves Einforderung von Mindestreserven
- option Kaufoption
- option trading Abschlüsse (Handel) in Kaufoptionen
- option writer Verkäufer einer Kaufoption
- premium Tilgungsaufgeld, Aufgeld für vorzeitige Kündigung
- price (a) Rücknahmekurs (von Investmentfondsanteilen); (b) Kündigungskurs, Kurs zu dem eine Anleihe gekündigt werden kann
- privilege Kündigungsrecht
- protection (a) Anzahl der tilgungsfreien Jahre;(b) Kündigungsschutz
- provision Kündigungsbestimmung

call
- right Kündigungsrecht
- risk Risiko der vorzeitigen Kündigung (Anleihe oder Kredit)
- schedule Tilgungsplan
- to statutory reserves Einforderung von Mindestreserven
- writer Verkäufer einer Kaufoption, Stillhalter einer Kaufoption, Stillhalter in Aktien
- written verkaufte Kaufoption

CAMEL capital, asset quality, management, earnings, liquidity Prüfungsschema der Aufsichtsbehörden bei der Überwachung der Geschäftsbanken (US)

capacity (a) Fähigkeit; (b) Kapazität; (c) materielle Kreditwürdigkeit(⟶ three Cs of credit)
- to borrow Kreditfähigkeit
- to charge assets Hypothekenfähigkeit
- to contract Geschäftsfähigkeit, Vertragsfähigkeit
- to contract by bill of exchange Wechselgeschäftsfähigkeit
- to create mortgages Hypothekenfähigkeit
- to draw cheques Scheckfähigkeit
- to guarantee Garantiefähigkeit
- utilisation ratio Kapazitätsausnutzungsgrad, Auslastungsgrad

capital Kapital
- account (a) Kapitalkonto; (b) Kapitalverkehrsbilanz
- accumulation (a) Kapitalbildung; (b) Vermögensbildung
- adequacy erforderliche Kapitaldecke; von US-Banken zu beachtende Eigenkapitalgrundsätze
- adequacy ratios Eigenmittelrelationen
- adjustment Kapitalsanierung(US)
- allowance Abschreibung
- appreciation Kapitalwertsteigerung, Vermögenszuwachs, Wertzuwachs
- appropriation Bewilligung von Investitionsmitteln, Kapitalbereitstellung
- base Kapitaldecke, Kapitalbasis
- budgeting Investitionsrechnung
- building Vermögensbildung
- charges Kapitalkosten
- commitment (a) Kapitalbindung; (b) Investitionsvorhaben; (c) Kapitalbeteiligung; (d) Kapitalbereitstellung
- contribution (a) Kapitaleinlage; (b) Eigenkapital, Eigenleistung (z.B. bei Erwerb von Immobilien)
- contributions by the limited partners Kommanditeinlagen
- cost (a) Kapitalkosten; (b) Kaufpreis; (c) Investitionskosten
- depreciation Eigenkapitalverzehr
- dilution Kapitalverwässerung
- efflux Kapitalabfluß, Kapitalabwanderung
- employed investiertes Kapital (Summe von Eigenkapital und langfristigen Fremdmitteln); Kapitaleinsatz
- equipment spending Anlageinvestitionen
- expenditure Investitionen, Kapitalaufwand
- expenditure budget Investitionsrechnung
- flow Kapitalfluß
- flows Kapitalströme, Kapitalbewegungen

capital
- formation   Kapitalbildung
- funds   Eigenmittel einer Bank (US)
- gain   Kapitalgewinn
- gain fund   Wachstumsfonds (Aktienfonds, der die ihm zufließenden Mittel in Aktien mit einem hohen Wachstumspotential investiert)
- gains tax   Kapitalgewinnsteuer
- gearing   Kapitalstruktur; Verhältnis zwischen Eigen- und Fremdkapital
- goods   Investitionsgüter
- inadequacy   Eigenkapitalschwäche
- increase   Kapitalerhöhung, Kapitalaufstockung
- increase on the basis of a one for ten rights issue   Kapitalerhöhung bei Einräumung eines Bezugsrechtes im Verhältnis 10:1
- increase out of company reserves   Kapitalerhöhung aus Gesellschaftsmitteln
- infusion   Kapitalspritze
- interest   Kapitalbeteiligung
- invested   eingebrachtes Kapital, Kapitaleinlage
- investment company   Kapitalanlagegesellschaft
- investment financing   Investitionsfinanzierung

capitalisation   (a) Kapitalisierung, Aktivierung, Umwandlung in Aktienkapital; (b) Börsenkapitalisierung
- issue   Ausgabe von Gratisaktien (Berichtigungsaktien)
- Issues Committee   Kapitalmarktausschuß (Br)
- of a company   Kapitalisierung eines Unternehmens (Aktienkapital, Anleihekapital, Rücklagen, Fremdkapital)
- of interest on outstanding capital   Aktivierung von Fremdkapitalzinsen
- of reserves   Kapitalisierung von Rücklagen, Umwandlung der Rücklagen in Kapital
- share   Berichtigungsaktie

capitalise v.   kapitalisieren, aktivieren

capitalised market value   kapitalisierter Marktwert

capitalised on the market at around ..   die Börsenkapitalisierung beläuft sich auf ungefähr ..

capital
- issue   Emission
- liabilities   langfristige Verbindlichkeiten
- links   Kapitalverflechtung
- loss   Kapitalverlust
- market   Kapitalmarkt
- market instruments   Kapitalmarktpapiere
- market operator   Kapitalmarktteilnehmer, Kapitalmarktadresse
- market rate   Kapitalmarktzins
- movements   Kapitalverkehr, Kapitalbewegungen
- net worth   Eigenkapital
- note   Schuldschein
- output ratio   Kapitalkoeffizient
- procurement / -raising   Kapitalbeschaffung, Kapitalaufbringung
- profit   Kapitalgewinn
- ratios   Indexzahlen, die die Angemessenheit des Eigenkapitals bestimmen
- reconstruction   Kapitalsanierung
- redemption reserve fund   Tilgungsfonds
- reorganisation   Kapitalsanierung, Neuordnung der Kapitalverhältnisse

capital
- repayment Rückzahlung des Kapitalbetrages; Tilgung des Anleihebetrages
- repayment holiday tilgungsfreie Jahre
- reserves Sonderrücklagen
- resources Eigenmittel, Kapitalausstattung, Kapitalfonds eines Unternehmens
- return Kapitalverzinsung
- seeking issuers kapitalsuchende Emittenten
- shares (a) von einem →split trust ausgegebene Anteile, die im Wert gegebenenfalls stark steigen, auf die aber keine Erträge ausgeschüttet werden; (b) Aktien,auf die Dividenden in Form von Gratisaktien ausgeschüttet werden
- spending Investitionen, Kapitaufwand
- standards Eigenkapitalgrundsätze (US)
- stock and surplus Eigenkapital, Eigenmittel (US)
- supply Kapitalangebot; Verfügbarkeit von Kapital
- surplus Rücklagen (US)
- write-down Kapitalschnitt, Kapitalverminderung

captive finance company konzerneigene Finanzierungsgesellschaft

card account Kreditkartenkonto

card authorisation (verification) terminals Prüfterminals zur Überprüfung der Identität bzw. Kreditwürdigkeit des Karteninhabers

carry v.
  to - dividend rights dividendenberechtigt (gewinnberechtigt) sein
  to - forward (a) vortragen; (b) prolongieren

  to - a high coupon (rate of interest) hoch verzinst werden
  to - at the market price zum Marktwert ausweisen
  to - large positions über große Bestände verfügen
  to - tax reliefs steuerbegünstigt sein
  to - over to the next settlement date reportieren
  to - a spread mit einem Aufschlag ausgestattet sein

carrying value Wertansatz, Bilanzwert, Buchwert

carry-over (a) Übertrag; (b) Report, Prolongation
- facilities Reportfazilitäten
- rate Reportsatz

cash v. (a) einlösen (Scheck, Kupon); (b) zurückgeben (Fondsanteile)

cash Bargeld; Kasse
- adapter vom Schalterpersonal bedienter Geldausgabeautomat
- against documents Barzahlung (Kasse) gegen Dokumente
- and due from banks Kassenstand und Bankguthaben
- and new Form des Reportgeschäftes (Wertpapiere werden am letzten Tag einer→ account period verkauft und per Termin für die neue account period zurückgekauft)
- assets (a) flüssige Mittel, Kassenbestand; (b) Primärliquidität
- bargain Kassageschäft, Promptgeschäft
- bid (offer) Übernahmeangebot gegen Barzahlung
- bonus Sonderausschüttung in bar
- call Bareinforderung
- card Geldausgabeautomaten-Karte, GAA-Karte

cash
- contribution Bareinlage
- control Liquiditätskontrolle
- credit Überziehungskredit, Blankokredit
- credit line Barkreditlinie
- deposit Bareinzahlung
- dispenser Geldausgabeautomat
- distribution Barausschüttung, Bardividende
- documentary credit Barakkreditiv
- drawdown Barinanspruchnahme eines Krediftes
- drawings Barabhebungen, Entnahmen in bar
- float Kassenbestand, Gesamtsumme der liquiden Mittel
- flow Cash-flow; Summe aus Reingewinn, Zuführungen an Rücklagen und Abschreibungen
- flow financing Finanzierung, bei der der künftige cash flow und das Gewinnpotential des zu finanzierenden Projektes die Höhe des Zins-und Tilgungsdienstes bestimmen
- funds Barmittel
- ing banker einlösende Bank
- ing charge Einlösungsgebühr (für Schecks, Kupons)
- ing commission Einlösungsprovision
- in hand Kassenbestand, Barguthaben
- -in price Rücknahmepreis (bei Fondsanteilen)
- in tills Kassenbestand
- less payment bargeldlose (unbare) Zahlung
- less payments bargeldloser Zahlungsverkehr
- liquidity Kasseliquidität
- management (a) Gelddisposition, Liquiditätssteuerung, Kassenhaltung, Cash Management; (b) maschinelles Übertragsverfahren von Bankguthaben bzw. Kompensation von Konten bei verschiedenen Filialen der gleichen Bank (Ziel ist eine straffe und gewinnorientierte Steuerung der flüssigen Mittel und des Währungsrisikos)
- management account services von Brokern angebotene Kontokorrentfazilitäten (US)
- payment (a) Barzahlung; (b) Auszahlung in bar, Kassenausgang
- payout Barausschüttung, Bardividende
- payout and capital appreciation Anlageerfolg
- position (a) verfügbare Barmittel, Kassenbestand;(b) Liquiditätskoeffizient
- price Barpreis, Kassakurs
- quotation Kassakurs
- ratio Liquiditätsgrad, Liquiditätskoeffizient
- receipts (a) Kasseneingänge; (b) Liquiditätszuflüsse
- reserve /cash reserve assets Barreserve
- settlement Barregulierung, Kassaregulierung; Promptgeschäft
- settlement price Kassakurs
- subscriber Barzeichner
- withdrawal Barabhebung, Barauszahlung

cats and dogs Spekulationspapiere

CBCT → customer-bank-communications-terminals

ceiling Obergrenze, Höchstgrenze

ceiling price (a) Stopp-Kurs, äußerster Kurs; (b) Preisobergrenze

ceiling rate of interest Zinsobergrenze

central paying agency Zentralzahlstelle

central rate Leitkurs (EWS)

certificate (a) Bescheinigung, Bestätigung; (b) Zertifikat, Anteilschein

- account Sparkonto (US)
- holder Zertifikatsinhaber
- of charge (Grund-)Schuldurkunde
- of compliance Bestätigung der Ordnungsmäßigkeit der Dokumente
- of debt Schuldtitel
- of deposit (a) CD, Einlagenzertifikat (Inhaberschuldschein, der ein Bankguthaben für eine bestimmte Zeit zu einem vereinbarten Zinssatz bestätigt); (b) Hinterlegungsschein; (c) gelegentlich:Sparbrief (US)
- of incorporation Gründungsurkunde (US)
- of incumbency Bestätigung der Funktion eines leitenden Angestellten
- of indebtedness (a) Schuldscheinzertifikat; (b) Schatzanweisung, Kassenobligation(US)
- of intent Absichtserklärung
- of origin Ursprungszeugnis
- of satisfaction Löschungsbestätigung
- of search Grundbuchauszug
- savings account Sparkonto(US)

certification of transfer Bestätigung, daß die zur Übertragung bestimmten Aktien bei der emittierenden Gesellschaft hinterlegt wurden

certified cheque von einer Bank bestätigter Scheck

certified public accountant Wirtschaftsprüfer

chain of title lückenloser Nachweis der Eigentumsrechte

CHAPS → clearing house automated payments system

CHAPS settlement banks Banken, die dem CHAPS System angeschlossen sind

character persönliche Kreditwürdigkeit (→ three Cs of credit)

character analysis Prüfung des Leumundes des Kreditnehmers

charge (a) Gebühr; (b) Belastung

charge v. berechnen, in Rechnung stellen; belasten

to - against profits zu Lasten der Gewinne verbuchen

to - to operations as incurred im Ergebnis verrechnen

chargeable gains steuerpflichtige Gewinne

charge certificate Grundschuldbrief

charge-off (a) Abbuchung, Ausbuchung; (b) Kreditverlust, Ausfall

charge-off rate Ausfallquote im Kreditgeschäft, Forderungsausfallverhältnis

charging order Pfändungsbeschluß

charging power Vollmacht zur Belastung des Anlagevermögens

chattels bewegliche Sachen

cheapen v. verbilligen (Kredite); nachgeben, schwächer tendieren (Kurse)

cheap-money policy Niedrigzinspolitik, Politik des billigen Geldes

checkable demand deposits Kontokorrenteinlagen (US)

checkbook money Giralgeld (US)

checking account Kontokorrentkonto (US)

checking deposits Kontokorrenteinlagen, Sichteinlagen (US)

checking for good delivery Prüfung der Lieferbarkeit der Wertpapiere

checkless payments scheckloser Zahlungsverkehr

check verification terminal Scheckprüfterminal

check- writing privilege Möglichkeit über ein Sparkonto per Scheck zu verfügen (US)

cheerful freundlich (Börse)

chemicals Chemiewerte, Chemieaktien

cheque Scheck (Br)

cheques paid in across the counter am Schalter eingereichte Schecks

cheques returned unpaid nicht eingelöste (unbezahlte) Schecks, Scheckretouren

cheques written ausgestellte Schecks

cheque
- book Scheckheft, Scheckbuch
- book facility (a) Kontokorrentkredit; (b) ⟶ check-writing privilege
- cashing fee Scheckeinlösungsgebühr
- clearing Scheckabrechnung, Scheckverrechnung
- collection Scheckeinzug, Scheckinkasso
- cover Scheckdeckung
- encashment Scheckeinlösung
- for collection Inkassoscheck
- money Buchgeld, Giralgeld
- proceeds Scheckerlös, Scheckgegenwert
- return bill Scheckrückrechnung
- signer Scheckzeichnungsmaschine, Scheckunterschriftenmaschine
- to order Orderscheck
- without cover ungedeckter Scheck

chief dealer / chief money dealer Chefhändler, Chefgeldhändler

CHIPS ⟶ Clearing House Interbank Payments System

circulating capital Betriebskapital

civil bond Kommunalanleihe (US)

claim under a guarantee Anspruch aus einer Garantie

class (a) Aktienkategorie, Aktiengattung; (b) Aktionärsgruppe; (c) Interessengruppe

classified loan von einer Bankenaufsichtsbehörde beanstandetes Kreditengagement (US)

class meeting Hauptversammlung, zu der nur die Aktionäre einer bestimmten Kategorie einberufen werden

class rights mit einer Aktiengattung verbundene Rechte

claused bill of lading einschränkendes Indossament

clean
- acceptance vorbehaltloses Akzept
- bill of lading reines Seekonnossement
- collection einfaches Inkasso
- credit Blankokredit
- payment (a) nicht dokumentäre Zahlung; (b) ordnungsgemäße Zahlung
- payments Zahlungen, die im computergestützten Abrechnungsverkehr der Banken(CHAPS)abgerechnet werden

clean red clause Akkreditivbevorschussungsklausel

cleanup of a loan Rückführung eines Kredites (einer Kreditlinie), Rückzahlung eines Kredites (US - oft nur vorübergehend)

clear v. (a) abrechnen, verrechnen (Schecks); (b) tilgen, ablösen (Schuld, Hypothek); (c) verzollen

to clear the market alle Kauf- und Verkaufsaufträge abwickeln

clearance (a) Ablösung, Tilgung; (b) Genehmigung; (c) Verzollung

clearance loan Darlehen zur Ablösung anderer Verbindlichkeiten

clearer Geschäftsbank (Br)

clear estate lastenfreier Grundbesitz

clearing Abrechnung, Verrechnung, Clearing

clearings Abrechnungspapiere, Schecks und sonstige zur Verrechnung eingereichte Papiere

clearing
- balances Clearing-Guthaben, Verrechnungsguthaben; Abrechnungssalden
- bank Geschäftsbank (Br)
- bank base rate Eckzins der Geschäftsbanken für Ausleihungen
- currency Verrechnungswährung
- dollar Clearing-Dollar
- fractions Verrechnungsspitzen
- house Abrechnungsstelle, Clearing-Stelle
- House Automated Payments System computergestützter Abrechnungsverkehr der Banken untereinander (CHAPS)
- House Interbank Payments System Clearing-Netz der New Yorker Banken (CHIPS)

- house members Abrechnungsmitglieder
- instruments Abrechnungspapiere
- receivables Clearing-Forderungen
- system Clearing-System, Abrechnungssystem
- transactions Clearing-Verkehr, Abrechnungsverkehr

clear of encumbrances lastenfrei

clear profit Reingewinn

client account (Notar-) Anderkonto (Br)

closed-end fund geschlossener Investmentfonds (Investmentfonds mit im voraus festgelegter Emissionshöhe)

closed-end mortgage Hypothek, die eine weitere hypothekarische Belastung der in Frage kommenden Liegenschaft ausschließt

closed indenture Anleihevertrag, der eine weitere Anleihebegebung ausschließt

close price enge Spanne zwischen Geld- und Briefkurs

closing
- balance Abschlußsaldo
- cost (a) Kreditbereitstellungskosten; (b) Kosten für die Bearbeitung eines Kreditantrages (US)
- entry Abschlußbuchung
- of the application list (of the offer) Zeichnungsschluß
- of an issue after closing of the issue nach Zeichnungsschluß
- price (quotation) Schlußkurs, Schlußnotiz
- purchase Rückkauf einer Kaufoption durch den Stillhalter

co-finance mitfinanzieren

co-financing Mitfinanzierung, Ko-Finanzierung

cold calling   Ausleihungen ausländischer Banken an britische Unternehmen zu Konditionen,die unter der →base rate liegen

collate v.   abstimmen, vergleichen (Buchungen)

collateral   (a) (dingliche) Sicherheit, Deckung, Sicherungsgut; (b) zusätzliche Sicherheit (im Sinne des Stamp Act-Br)
- agreement   Sicherheitenvereinbarung
- bill   Sicherheitswechsel
- charge form   Sicherungsübereignungsformular
- evaluation   Bewertung einer Sicherheit

collateralise v.   besichern

collateral
- loan   Lombardkredit, dinglich gesicherter Kredit
- mortgage bond   Hypothekenschuldverschreibung
- security   dingliche Sicherheit
- shortage   Unterbesicherung
- trust bond (note)   durch die Verpfändung von Wertpapieren besicherte Anleihe (Schuldschein)
- value   Beleihungswert, Sicherheitenwert, Wert des Sicherungsgutes, Sicherungswert

collect v.   (a) einziehen (Forderungen, Schecks); (b) erheben, berechnen (Steuern, Zinsen)

collecting banker   Inkassobank

collection   Inkasso, Einzug; Erhebung
- agent   Inkassobeauftragter, Inkassostelle
- authority   Inkassovollmacht
- charges   Inkassogebühren
- currency   Inkassowährung
- fee   Inkassogebühr
- items   Inkassopapiere
- of receivables   Forderungseinzug
- order   Inkassoauftrag, Inkassoweisung
- proceeds   Inkassoerlös
- terms   Inkassotarif

co-manage v.   mitführen (bei einem Konsortium)

co-management   Mitführung, Co-Management

combination covenants   Auflagen, die ein Kreditnehmer bei der möglichen Fusion seines Unternehmens beachten muß (US)

combined bill of lading   Konnossement des kombinierten Transports

comfort letter   Kreditbesicherungsgarantie

coming-out price   Emissionskurs, Ausgabekurs

commercial
- bank   Geschäftsbank
- bill   Handelswechsel
- credit   Handelskredit, Warenkredit
- credit company   Finanzierungsinstitut
- dealer   auf Firmenkunden spezialisierter Geldhändler
- loan portfolio   Gesamtausleihungen an Firmenkunden
- paper   von Industrieunternehmen emittierte kurzfristige Schuldtitel (Laufzeit in der Regel 30-180 Tage - US)
- paper support facility /commercial paper support line   Deckungslinie für →commercial paper
- prime   →prime rate
- properties   Industrieimmobilien, gewerblich genutzte Grundstücke und Gebäude
- real estate loan   gewerblicher Immobilienkredit

commission (a) Provision; (b) Kommission

commissions paid Provisionsaufwendungen

commissions receivable Provisionsforderungen

commission
- basis on a commission basis auf Provisionsbasis, kommissionsweise
- income Provisionseinnahmen
- on guarantee Avalprovision
- rate Provisionssatz, Courtage
- revenue Provisionseinnahmen, Provisionserträge
- scale Gebührentabelle

commit v. (a) bereitstellen, zusagen; (b) festlegen; (c) verpflichten (sich)

the bank is committed with $ ... die Bank ist mit $ .. exponiert

to - funds (a) Kapital (finanzielle Mittel) bereitstellen; (b) Gelder festlegen

to - funds to new issues Gelder in Neuemissionen anlegen

to - a loan einen Kredit bereitstellen, einen Kredit zusagen

commitment (a) Bereitstellung, Zusage (an Krediten); (b) Engagement (in Wertpapieren, Devisen); (c) Verpflichtung; (d) Konsortialquote

commitments for future delivery Terminengagements, Terminpositionen

commitments under the loan agreement (under documentary credits) Verpflichtungen aus dem Kreditvertrag (aus Akkreditiven)

commitment
- commission Zusageprovision
- fee Bereitstellungsprovision
- fee clawback zusätzliche Bereitstellungsprovision
- fee on the unused amount Bereitstellungsprovision auf den nicht in Anspruch genommenen Betrag
- fee pricing Festlegung der Bereitstellungsprovision
- interest Bereitstellungszinsen
- letter Zusageschreiben, Kreditzusage

common float (floating) Gruppenfloating, Blockfloating

common stock Stammaktien, Stämme
- appraisal ➔ common stock valuation
- dividend Dividende auf Stammaktien
- holder Inhaber von Stammaktien
- holders' equity Stammaktienkapital
- in treasury Stammaktien im Eigenbesitz
- issue Stammaktienemission
- load fund Aktienfonds, der auf seine Anteile einen Ausgabeaufschlag erhebt
- purchase privilege Kaufoption für Stammaktien
- valuation Bewertung von Stammaktien
- warrants Bezugsrechtsscheine auf Stammaktien

common trust fund Gemeinschafts-Treuhandfonds (zur Erzielung höherer Kapitalerträge werden kleinere Treuhandfonds von Banken zu einem zentralen common trust fund zusammengelegt - US)

Commonwealth Bonds australische Staatspapiere

company equity Gesellschaftskapital

company reconstruction Unternehmenssanierung

comparison ticket Bestätigung eines Wertpapiergeschäftes (US)

compensating balances Deckungs-
    guthaben (bestimmter Prozent-
    satz eines Krediten, der beim
    Kreditgeber als unverzinsliches
    Guthaben zu hinterlegen ist)
    (US)

competition in lending rates
    Konditionenwettbewerb

competitive bidding Ausschrei-
    bung bzw. Versteigerung einer
    Emission

composite fee zusätzliche Bear-
    beitungsgebühr, die der Dar-
    lehenssumme hinzugerechnet wird

composite quotations ⟶ NYSE com-
    posite quotations

composites Aktien der Universal-
    -Versicherungsgesellschaften

composition Vergleich

composition deed Vergleichsver-
    einbarung

compound v. (a) einen Vergleich
    schließen; (b) aufgelaufene
    Zinsen wiederverzinsen

compound arbitrage indirekte
    Devisenarbitrage, Mehrfacharbi-
    trage

compounding bond account Renten-
    portefeuille, bei dem Zinser-
    träge reinvestiert werden

compound interest Zinseszins

compound yield Gesamtrendite,
    Ausschüttungen plus Kurssteig-
    erungen

comprehensive short-term guarantee
    Exportkreditversicherung, die
    für einen kurzfristigen Zeit-
    raum oder für einen bestimmten
    Markt abgeschlossen wird (Br)

compromise Vergleich

compromise v. einen Vergleich
    schließen

Comptroller of the Currency eine
    der verschiedenen US-Bankenauf-
    sichtsbehörden

compulsion rule Bestimmung des
    ⟶ Take-over Code: Wenn die In-
    haber von 90 % des stimmberechtig-
    ten Kapitals einem Übernahmeange-
    bot zugestimmt haben, kann das
    übernehmende Unternehmen die rest-
    lichen 10 % zur Annahme seines
    Angebotes zwingen

compulsory cross default clause
    Klausel in parallelen Kreditver-
    trägen, die ein Entwicklungsland
    gleichzeitig mit der Weltbank
    und einem privaten Bankenkon-
    sortium abschließt (wird der Kre-
    ditvertrag mit dem Konsortium ver-
    letzt, hat die Weltbank die Pflicht,
    ihrerseits ihren Kredit zur Rück-
    zahlung fällig zu stellen oder
    weitere Auszahlungen auszusetzen;
    ⟶ optional cross default clause)

compulsory disclosure Offenlegungs-
    pflicht, Publizitätspflicht

compulsory intervention system
    Pflichtinterventionssystem

compute v. errechnen, kalkulieren

computing interest / computation
    of interest Zinsberechnung,
    Zinskalkulation

concentration account Hauptkonto
    im Rahmen eines ⟶ Cash Manage-
    ment Systems

concentrations Gesamtausleihungen
    aufgegliedert nach Großkredit-
    kunden, Industriezweigen, etc. (US)

concession bei einer Emission:
    Schalternutzen, Bonifikation

concessional rates (terms) Aus-
    nahmesätze, Vorzugskonditionen

conditional
- endorsement bedingtes Indossament
- payment Zahlung 'Eingang vorbe-
    halten', bedingte Zahlung

conditional sales contract Kaufvertrag, bei dem das Eigentum erst nach Entrichtung des vollen Kaufpreises auf den Käufer übergeht

conduct of an account Kontoführung

confession of judgment clause Klausel, die bei Zahlungsverzug des Kreditnehmers dem Kreditgeber das Recht zur sofortigen Zwangsvollstreckung gibt (US)

confirm v. bestätigen

confirmed documentary credit bestätigtes Akkreditiv

confirming bank bestätigende Bank

confirmation Bestätigung

confirmation note Wertpapierabrechnung

consideration Gegenwert, Entgelt, Kaufpreis

consolidate v. (a) konsolidieren, fundieren (Abschlüsse, Verbindlichkeiten); (b) zusammenlegen (Hypotheken, Wertpapiere)

consolidated
- accounts Konzernabschluß
- annuities Staatsanleihen
- mortgage Einheitshypothek, Korrealhypothek
- mortgage bond nachrangiger Pfandbrief
- statement of income konsolidierte Gewinn- und Verlustrechnung
- ticker tape Ticker, der die Notierungen von zwei oder mehr Börsen erfaßt

consolidation Konsolidierung; Zusammenlegung

consols Staatsanleihen

constant dollar accounting inflationsbereinigte Bilanzierung (US)

constraints on the borrower Auflagen für den Kreditnehmer

construction loan Baudarlehen, Baufinanzierungskredit

constructions Bauwerte, Bauaktien

constructive delivery Übergabe der effektiven Stücke, effektive Übergabe

consumer
- banking Konsumentenbankgeschäft
- credit (loan) persönliches Anschaffungsdarlehen, Konsumentenkredit
- installment credit Ratenkredit
- lending Konsumentenkreditgeschäft
- loan company Teilzahlungskreditinstitut
- loan terms Konditionen für Konsumentenkredite

contango Report, Verlängerung

contango rate of interest Reportsatz

contingent commitment Eventualobligo

contingent liabilities Eventualverbindlichkeiten

contingent obligation option bedingte Beteiligungsoption (falls der Schuldendienst für einen Kredit an ein Entwicklungsland eine bestimmte Obergrenze überschreitet, übernimmt die Weltbank den Differenzbetrag)

continuation day Prolongationstag

continuity of dividend payments Dividendenkontinuität

contra account Gegenkonto

contract (a) Vertrag; (b) Abschluß; (c) Mindeststückzahl von Papieren bei Abschluß eines Börsengeschäftes contract v. (a) sich vertraglich verpflichten, einen Vertrag abschließen; (b) kontrahieren (Börse); (c) aufnehmen (einen Kredit)

contract broker   Ringmakler

contracting bank   kontrahierendes Kreditinstitut

contracting party   Vertragspartei

contraction   Anspannung, Verengung, Verknappung
- of debts   Verschuldung, Übernahme von Verbindlichkeiten
- of fund availability   Liquiditätsverknappung

contract note   Effektenkauf- bzw. Verkaufsabrechnung, Ausführungsanzeige

contractual
- capacity   Geschäftsfähigkeit, Vertragsfähigkeit
- consideration   Vertragsleistung
- investments   Anlagen in festverzinslichen Wertpapieren
- plan   Anlageplan eines Investmentfonds
- power   Abschlußvollmacht
- saving   Vertragssparen

controlled company   beherrschtes (abhängiges) Unternehmen

controlling interest   (a) Mehrheitsbeteiligung; (b) Sperrminorität

controlling shareholder   Mehrheitsaktionär

control
- of borrowing   Regulierung der Kreditaufnahme
- of lending transactions   Überwachung des Kreditgeschäftes
- of the money supply   Geldmengensteuerung

convening notice   Einberufungsbekanntmachung

conventional mortgage   Verkehrshypothek

conventional mortgage loan   Hypothekendarlehen, das nicht durch die Garantie einer staatlichen Organisation unterlegt ist (US)

convention values   Bilanzansätze für Wertpapiere (US)

conversion   (a) Wandlung, Konversion; (b) Umrechnung, Umtausch
- agent   Umtauschstelle
- call   Umtauschaufforderung
- cut   Ermäßigung des Wandlungspreises
- feature   Wandlungsmöglichkeit, Wandlungsoption
- into shares   Umtausch in Aktien
- loan   Wandelanleihe
- offer   Wandelangebot, Wandlungsangebot
- of long-term debt into equity   Umwandlung von langfristigen Verbindlichkeiten in Aktienkapital
- of reserves   Umwandlung von Rücklagen
- of the one-year facility into a three-year evergreen   Umwandlung des auf ein Jahr befristeten Kredites in eine automatisch verlängerbare Fazilität
- option   Wandeloption, Umtauschoption, Umtauschrecht
- period   Wandlungsfrist, Umtauschfrist
- premium   Wandlungsaufgeld, Wandelprämie
- price   (a) Wandlungskurs, Konvertierungskurs; (b) Umrechnungskurs
- privilege   Umtauschrecht, Wandlungsrecht
- rate   (a) Wandlungsverhältnis; (b) Umrechnungskurs

303

conversion
- ratio Wandlungsverhältnis; Umtauschverhältnis
- stock Wertpapiere mit Umtauschrechten
- terms Wandlungsbedingungen

convert v. wandeln, umwandeln; umtauschen, konvertieren

convertibility Konvertibilität; Konvertierbarkeit

convertible (a) wandelbar; (b) konvertierbar
- bond Wandelschuldverschreibung, Wandelanleihe
- currency konvertierbare Währung
- debenture Wandelschuldverschreibung
- into cash liquidisierbar
- into common stock wandelbar in Stammaktien
- preferred stock wandelbare Vorzugsaktien

Cooke Committee Internationaler Ausschuß, der sich mit Fragen der Bankenaufsicht beschäftigt (setzt sich aus Vertretern der Bankenaufsichtsbehörden und der Notenbanken zusammen)

core deposits Bodensatz einer Bank

corner v. den Markt aufkaufen, schwänzen, aufschwänzen

corporate
- AAA erstklassige Industrieschuldverschreibung
- account (a) Firmenkonto; (b) Firmenkunde
- adjustment Unternehmenssanierung (US)
- advisory service Firmenkundenberatung (durch die Bank)
- banking Firmenkundengeschäft
- banking sector (side) Firmenkundenbereich
- banking terms Konditionen im Firmenkundengeschäft
- bond Industrieschuldverschreibung
- bond fund auf Industrieobligationen spezialisierter Investmentfonds
- borrowing Industriekredit, Kreditaufnahme der Unternehmen
- buying in of stock Rückkauf eigener Aktien
- cash requirements Liquiditätsbedarf der Unternehmen
- customer Firmenkunde
- debt instruments (debt securities) Industrieschuldtitel
- deposits Einlagen von Firmenkunden
- guarantee Firmenbürgschaft
- lending Industriekredit, Firmenkredit
- lending business Firmenkreditgeschäft
- lending rates Zinsen für Firmenkredite
- loan (a) Industriekredit, Firmenkredit;(b) Industrieobligation
- loan demand Nachfrage nach Firmenkrediten
- market Firmenkundenmarkt
- name Emittent von Industrieobligationen
- note Schuldschein eines Unternehmens
- profits Unternehmergewinne
- reconstruction Unternehmenssanierung
- services Dienstleistungen einer Bank für Firmenkunden
- stock (a) Aktien einer Kapitalgesellschaft; (b) langfristige Schuldverschreibungen einiger großer Städte (US)

corporate

- time deposits Termineinlagen von Firmenkunden
- underwriting Übernahme bzw. Plazierung von Industrieobligationen

corporation Aktiengesellschaft, Kapitalgesellschaft

corporation loan prospectus Emissionsprospekt

correspondent Korrespondenzbank

- balances Guthaben bei Korrespondenzbanken
- banking Geschäfte mit Korrespondenzbanken

co-signing Schuldbeitritt, Schuldmitübernahme (bei einem Kredit - US)

cost Kosten

- accounting Kostenrechnung
- benefit-analysis Kosten--Nutzen-Analyse
- centre Kostenstelle
- of borrowing Kreditkosten, Kreditpreis
- of credit Kreditkosten
- of external funds Fremdmittelkosten, Beschaffungskosten für Fremdmittel
- of funds (a) Kosten der Mittelbeschaffung; Refinanzierungskosten; (b) Geldbeschaffungskosten
- of funds pricing Ausrichtung der Kreditkonditionen an den Kosten der Mittelbeschaffung
- of funds to the bank Geldbeschaffungskosten (Refinanzierungskosten) der Bank
- of money Geldeinstandskosten, Kreditkosten
- of mortgages / cost of mortgage finance Hypothekenkosten
- of payments traffic Zahlungsverkehrskosten
- overruns Projektmehrkosten

Council of the Stock Exchange Börsenvorstand

Council for the Securities Industry Aufsichts- und Koordinierungsorgan der Londoner City für den Wertpapiersektor

co-underwriter Mitkonsorte

counter Schalter

across (over) the - am Schalter

counter

- staff Schalterpersonal
- stock Schalterstücke
- terminal / counter teller terminal Schalterterminal

counterentry Gegenbuchung

counterfoil Scheckabschnitt

counterguarantee Rückbürgschaft

- commission Rückbürgschaftsprovision

countermand of payment Schecksperre, Scheckwiderruf; Zahlungsstopp, Zahlungswiderruf

countervailing credit Gegenakkreditiv

country exposure Länderengagement, Länderobligo, Ausleihungen an ein Land

country risk Länderrisiko

coupon (a) Kupon, Zinsschein, Ertragsschein; (b) Zinssatz einer Anleihe

couponed securities festverzinsliche Wertpapiere

coupons accepted for encashment hereingenommene Kupons (Dividendenscheine)

coupons on the bond market Zinssätze am Rentenmarkt

coupon bond Inhaberschuldverschreibung

coupon
- cut   (Anleihe-) Zinssenkung
- date   Kupontermin, Kuponfälligkeit
- detached   ex Kupon (Dividende)
- holder   Kuponinhaber
- payment date   Kupontermin
- rate   Anleihezins
- sheet   Kuponbogen

cover   Deckung

cover   v. decken
  to - positions   Deckungskäufe vornehmen
  covered forward   kursgesichert (durch ein Termingeschäft)

coverage ratio   Deckungsverhältnis; bei Projektfinanzierungen: Höchstbetrag der Fremdmittelaufnahmen für ein Projekt

cover
- for cheques written   Deckung für ausgestellte Schecks
- funds   Deckungsmittel, Deckung
- note   Deckungszusage

creation of a mortgage charge   Hypothekenbestellung

credit   (a) Kredit; (b) Kreditwürdigkeit; (c) Akkreditiv
 provided that there is sufficient credit in the account   vorbehaltlich entsprechender Kontodeckung

credit
- accommodation   (a) Kreditgewährung, Hinauslegung eines Kredites, Kreditausreichung; (b) Akkreditivhinauslegung
- administration   Kreditbearbeitung
- advice   Gutschriftsanzeige
- analysis   Kreditwürdigkeitsprüfung, Bonitätsprüfung
- application   (a) Kreditantrag; (b) Akkreditivauftrag
- approval   Kreditbewilligung, Kreditgenehmigung, Kreditzusage
- approval powers   Kreditkompetenz, Kreditbewilligungsbefugnisse
- assessment   Beurteilung der Kreditwürdigkeit, Bonitätsprüfung
- at the bank   Bankguthaben
- authorisation   Kreditbewilligung, Genehmigung eines Kreditantrages
- availability   Verfügbarkeit eines Kredites(einer Kreditlinie);Kreditrahmen
- balance   Guthabensaldo,kreditorischer Saldo
- bill   Finanzierungswechsel
- broker   Finanzmakler, Kreditvermittler
- brokerage   Kreditvermittlung
- bureau   Auskunftei
- buying   Kreditkauf, Ratenkauf
- ceiling   Kredithöchstgrenze
- commitment   Kreditengagement; Kreditzusage
- confirmation   Kreditbestätigung; Akkreditivbestätigung
- contraction   Beschränkung der Kreditaufnahme, Kreditkontraktion, Kreditdrosselung
- control   (a) Kreditüberwachung, Kreditkontrolle; (b) Kreditlenkung
- cost   Kreditkosten
- creation   Kreditschöpfung
- crunch   scharfe Kreditrestriktionen
- entry   Gutschrift; Habenbuchung
- evaluation   Kreditprüfung
- expansion   Kreditausweitung, Kreditexpansion
- facility   Kreditfazilität, Darlehen
- guarantee society   Kreditgarantiegemeinschaft
- information   Kreditauskunft
- insurance   Kreditversicherung

credit
- interchange service Kreditschutzverein
- interest Habenzinsen, Guthabenzinsen
- investigation Prüfung der Kreditwürdigkeit, Bonitätsprüfung
- line Kreditlinie, Kreditrahmen
- markets Finanzmärkte
- note Gutschriftsanzeige
- officer Kreditsachbearbeiter
- on goods Beleihung von Waren, Warenlombard
- on securities Effektenkredit, Beleihung von Wertpapieren, Wertpapierlombard

creditor Gläubiger
- account kreditorisches Konto, auf Guthabenbasis geführtes Konto
- bank Gläubigerbank
- in composition proceedings Vergleichsgläubiger
- interest rate Habenzinssatz
- on mortgage Hypothekengläubiger

creditor's call privilege Kündigungsrecht des Gläubigers

credit
- override agreement Kreditrahmenvertrag
- policy (a) Kreditpolitik; (b) Kreditversicherungspolice
- position finanzielle Lage
- proxy Mittel, die einer Bank für Ausleihungen zur Verfügung stehen
- purchase Teilzahlungskauf, Ratenkauf
- rating (a) Kreditwürdigkeit, Bonität; (b) Bonitätseinstufung
- rating agency Auskunftei
- ratio Verhältnis der Ausleihungen zu den Einlagen einer Bank
- reins kreditpolitische Zügel
- report Kreditauskunft
- reporting agency Evidenzzentrale
- reporting system Evidenzsystem
- restraint Kreditbeschränkungen, Kreditdrosselung
- risk Kreditrisiko, Bonitätsrisiko
- risk score Maßstab zur Beurteilung des Kreditrisikos
- sale Teilzahlungskauf, Ratenkauf
- sanction Kreditbewilligung, Kreditgenehmigung
- sanctioning limit Kreditbewilligungsgrenze
- scoring Kreditbeurteilung, Beurteilung des Kreditrisikos
- screw Kreditschraube
- slip (a) Einzahlungsbeleg; (b) Gutschriftsanzeige; (c) Überweisungsformular
- squeeze Beschränkung der Kreditaufnahme, Kreditdrosselung, Kreditverknappung
- standards Kreditrichtlinien, Grundsätze der Kreditgewährung
- standing (status) Kreditwürdigkeit, Bonität
- stringency Kreditknappheit
- terms (a) Kreditkonditionen; (b) Akkreditivbedingungen
- to capital reserve Einstellung in die Sonderrücklage
- transfer Banküberweisung (Br)
- transfer slip Überweisungsträger (Br)
- transfer system Giroverkehr, Girosystem, bargeldloser Zahlungsverkehr (Br)
- undertaking Kreditzusage
- union genossenschaftliches Kreditinstitut (US)

credit
- verification Überprüfung der Kreditwürdigkeit, Bonitätsprüfung
- voucher (a) Überweisungsträger; (b) Gutschriftsbeleg
- worthiness Kreditwürdigkeit, Bonität

criticised loan von einer Bankenaufsichtsbehörde beanstandetes Kreditengagement (US)

cross
- border lending Auslandsausleihungen
- default clause reziproke Verzugsklausel
- ed cheque Verrechnungsscheck
- holding gegenseitige (Kapital-) Beteiligung
- rate Usance-Kurs, indirekte Parität
- selling Angebotspaket, ergänzende Dienstleistungen, Verbundgeschäfte

CRS → creditor reporting system

CSI levy Abgabe, die auf Wertpapierverkäufe über ₤ 5.000 erhoben und an den → Council for the Securities Industry abgeführt wird

cum
- all einschließlich aller Rechte
- dividend mit Dividende
- interest mit Stückzinsen
- new (rights) einschließlich Bezugsrechte

cumulative dividend kumulative (nachzahlungspflichtige) Dividende

currency (a) Währung, Fremdwährung (FW), Valuta, Sorten; (b) Laufzeit (z.B. bei einem Wechsel), Gültigkeitsdauer

currency
- acceptance Valutaakzept
- acceptance credit Valutatrassierungskredit
- account Währungskonto, FW-Konto
- appreciation Wechselkurssteigerung, Wertsteigerung einer Währung
- arbitrage Devisenarbitrage, Wechselkursarbitrage
- assets Devisenguthaben, FW--Bestände
- bands Währungsbandbreiten
- basket Währungskorb
- bill Fremdwährungswechsel, Valutawechsel
- bond Fremdwährungsanleihe
- borrowing Fremdwährungskredit, Valutakredit
- buying (a) Devisenankauf, Sortenankauf; (b) (Fremd-)Valutakäufe
- buying rate Sortenankaufskurs
- clause Valutaklausel
- coupons Fremdwährungskupons, Valuten
- cover Währungsdeckung
- debt Fremdwährungsverbindlichkeiten, Valutaschuld
- diversification Währungsdiversifikation, Streuung von Fremdwährungsengagements
- exposure (a) Fremdwährungsengagement(s), Fremdwährungspositionen, Devisenbestände; (b) Währungsrisiko, Wechselkursrisiko
- fluctuations reserve Rücklage für Wechselkursschwankungen
- futures contract Devisentermingeschäft
- futures trading Devisenterminhandel
- gains Währungsgewinne, Wechselkursgewinne
- in bank vaults Sortenbestände

currency
- inflow Deviseneingänge, Devisenzuflüsse
- intervention Intervention am Devisenmarkt
- loan Fremdwährungskredit, Valutakredit
- losses Währungsverluste, Wechselkursverluste
- misalignments Währungsungleichgewichte
- mix Währungsmix
- netting Devisen-Netting (Form des Cash Management; Devisenaufrechnung - Möglichkeit, den grenzüberschreitenden Zahlungsverkehr entsprechend den jeweiligen Gegebenheiten konzernintern durchzuführen)
- note Valutaschuldschein
- outflow Devisenabflüsse
- parity Währungsparität
- payables Fremdwährungsverbindlichkeiten, Valutaverbindlichkeiten
- quotations list Devisenkurszettel
- realignment Neuordnung der Währungsparitäten
- receivables Fremdwährungsforderungen, Valutaforderungen
- regulations Devisenbestimmungen
- repurchase agreement Devisenpensionsgeschäft
- reserves Währungsreserven, Devisenreserven
- risk Währungsrisiko, Wechselkursrisiko, Valutarisiko
- risk management Devisenkurssicherung, Kurssicherungsmaßnahmen
- securities Währungstitel, Fremdwährungspapiere, Valutapapiere
- selling (a) Devisenverkauf, Sortenverkauf;(b) (Fremd-) Valutaverkäufe
- snake Währungsschlange
- support Stützung einer Währung
- surplus Devisenüberschuß
- swap transaction Devisen-Swapgeschäft
- swings Wechselkursschwankungen
- syndicated loan syndizierter Fremdwährungskredit
- system Währungssystem, Währungsordnung
- trading desk Devisenhandelsabteilung
- translation gains (losses) Gewinne (Verluste) aus der Umrechnung von Fremdwährungen
- translation risk Währungsumrechnungsrisiko
- unit Währungsrechnungseinheit
- watchdogs Währungshüter

current
- account (a) Kontokorrentkonto, Girokonto; (b) Leistungsbilanz; (c) laufende Rechnung
- account balances Guthaben auf Kontokorrentkonten
- account deposit base Bodensatz an Kontokorrentkonten
- account loan Kontokorrentkredit, Dispositionskredit
- assets Umlaufvermögen
- cost accounting inflationsbereinigte Bilanzierung
- coupon derzeitiger Anleihezins, laufende Verzinsung
- interest Marktzins, gegenwärtiger Zinssatz
- liabilities kurzfristige Verbindlichkeiten
- market value Marktwert
- price Marktkurs, Tageskurs
- ratio Liquiditätskennzahl (Verhältnis zwischen gesamtem Umlaufvermögen und kurzfristigen Verbindlichkeiten)

current

- securities   Wertpapiere, die Teil des Umlaufvermögens bilden
- value   Verkaufswert, Marktwert
- yield   Umlaufsrendite

cushion bond   Anleihe, die über ihrem Rücknahme- bzw. Tilgungskurs notiert wird

cushion of equity   Kapitalpolster

custodial
- duties   Verwahrpflichten
- services   (a) Depotverwaltung; (b) Depotabteilung

custodian   (a) Depotbank, Hinterlegungsstelle; (b) Verwalter, Verwahrer
- bank   Depotbank
- fees   Depotgebühren, Verwahrungsgebühren

custody   Verwahrung, Depotverwahrung
- account   Depotkonto
- account statement   Depotauszug
- agreement   Depotvertrag, Verwahrungsvertrag
- business   Depotgeschäft, Verwahrungstätigkeit
- charges   Depotgebühren, Verwahrgebühren
- items   Depotgüter, Verwahrungsstücke
- operations   Depotgeschäft
- receipt   Depotbescheinigung, Verwahrungsquittung, Hinterlegungsbestätigung
- services ⟶ custodial services

custodyship   (a) Verwahrung, Depotverwahrung; (b) Verwaltung

customer   Kunde
- bank-communications-terminals   kundenbediente Zahlungsverkehrsterminals
- behaviour   Kundenverhalten
- counselling   Kundenberatung
- deposits   Kundeneinlagen
- lendings   Kundenkreditgeschäft, Ausleihungen an Kunden
- orientated pricing   kundenorientierte Gebührenberechnung
- rating   Kundenbeurteilung
- servicing   Kundenbetreuung

cut in lending rates   Senkung der Kreditzinsen

cut-off date   Stichtag

cut-off score   Punkt, an dem ein Kreditengagement zu risikoreich erscheint

D

Daily Official List   amtliches Börsenkursblatt (Br)

daily volume of business (turnover)   Tagesumsätze (Börse)

date   Datum, Termin

  dated date   Tag, an dem die Verzinsung beginnt
- of accounts   Bilanzstichtag, Bilanztermin
- of maturity   Fälligkeitstermin

day order   Tagesauftrag (limitierter Wertpapierauftrag, der nur einen Tag gültig ist)

days of grace   Nachfrist, Respekttage

day's best (high)   Tageshöchstkurs

day's spread   Spanne zwischen dem höchsten und niedrigsten Kurs eines Tages

days' sight   Tage nach Sicht

day-to-day money   Tagesgeld

day-to-day shortages (surpluses)   Tagesdefizite (Tagesüberschüsse) im Geldhandel

DDA-account → demand deposit account

dead
- account   umsatzloses Konto
- loan   uneinbringlicher Kredit
- money   Gelder, die nur zu einem hohen Zinssatz aufgenommen werden können
- weights   (a) unverzinsliche Wertpapiere; (b) schwierig zu plazierende Emissionen

deal   Abschluß, Geschäft

deal v.   handeln
  to - off the floor   außerbörslich handeln

dealer   Händler
- allowance   Händlerprovision
- community   Händlerkreise
- corporate repurchase agreement   Pensionsgeschäft zwischen einem Wertpapierhändler und einem Industrieunternehmen
- holding of securities   Händlerbestände
- in the unlisted market   Freiverkehrshändler
- inventories   Händlerbestände, Händlerpositionen
- margin   Händlerspanne
- purchase   Händlerkauf
- secondary market   auf Händler beschränkter Sekundärmarkt (US)
- transaction   Händlergeschäft

dealer's concession   Händlerbonifikation

dealer's spread (turn)   Händlerspanne, Händlergewinn

dealing
- currency   Handelswährung
- for new time   Abschlüsse für die nächste → account period
- in the money market   Geldmarktbetätigung
- operation   Geldhandel, Geldhandelsabteilung
- price   Abschlußkurs, Abrechnungskurs
- spread   Händlerspanne
- within the account   Abschlüsse in der laufenden → account period

dealings   Handel, Abschlüsse; Börsenumsätze
- for cash   Kassageschäfte
- in futures   Terminhandel
- in overnight money   Tagesgeldabschlüsse
- in shorts (longs)   Abschlüsse in Kurz- (Langläufern)
- in the secondary market   Sekundärmarktumsätze
- on terms of issue   Handel per Erscheinen

dear-money policy   Hochzinspolitik

debenture   Schuldverschreibung, Obligation, Anleihe (in den USA ist eine debenture normalerweise unbesichert, in Großbritannien hingegen besichert; in der Regel Langläufer)
- capital   Anleihekapital
- financing   Anleihefinanzierung
- holder   Obligationär

debit   (a) Belastung, Lastschrift; (b) Soll, Debet
- to the account   Kontobelastung
debit   v. belasten
debit
- advice   Belastungsanzeige
- authorisation   Belastungsermächtigung
- balance   Sollsaldo, Debetsaldo
- card   Kreditkarte; genauer: Lastschriftkarte zur direkten Abbuchung von Einzelhandelskäufen
- entry   Sollbuchung, Sollposten
- interest   Sollzinsen, Schuldzinsen
- note   Belastungsanzeige
- slip   Lastschrift

debt   Schuld, Verbindlichkeit; Forderung

debt
- burden   Schuldenlast
- capital   (a) Fremdkapital; (b) Anleihekapital
- ceiling   Schuldenrahmen, Verschuldungsrahmen
- certificate   Schuldtitel
- collection   Forderungseinzug
- collection agency   Inkassobüro, Inkassostelle
- consolidation   Konsolidierung von Verbindlichkeiten
- conversion   Umschuldung
- counselling   Finanzierungsberatung
- crisis   Verschuldungskrise
- deferral   Stundung von Krediten
- discharge   Ablösung einer Schuld (Verbindlichkeit)
- equity ratio   Verschuldungskoeffizient
- instrument   (a) Schuldurkunde; (b) Schuldtitel
- issue   Schuldtitel
- level   Schuldenstand
- limiting covenants   Bestimmungen eines Anleihe- oder Kreditvertrages, durch die eine weitere Verschuldung des Kreditnehmers bzw. Anleiheschuldners eingeschränkt wird
- management   Schuldenmanagement

debtor   (a) Schuldner; (b) Kreditnehmer
- account   debitorisches Konto
- country   Schuldnerland
- on mortgage   Hypothekenschuldner
- reporting system   Evidenzsystem (z.B. der Weltbank)

debt
- provisioning   Risikovorsorge, Rücklagenbildung im Kreditgeschäft
- ratio   Verschuldungsgrad

debt
- recovery Forderungseinzug
- recovery agency Inkassobüro
- reduction Schuldenverringerung, Rückführung von Verbindlichkeiten
- refunding Refinanzierung, Umschuldung
- rescheduling Umschuldung
- retirement Ablösung einer Schuld, Schuldentilgung
- service Schuldendienst
- service arrears Schuldendienstrückstände
- service commitments Schuldendienstverpflichtungen
- service funds Schuldendienstmittel
- service load Schuldendienstlast
- service payment Schuldendienstzahlung
- service ratio Schuldendienstrelation; Verhältnis des Schuldendienstes zu den Deviseneinnahmen
- service subsidies Kapitaldiensthilfe, Schuldendienstzuschüsse
- servicing Bedienung einer Schuld (Anleihe oder Kredit), Schuldendienstleistung
- servicing bill (burden) Schuldendienstlast
- settlement Schuldenregelung

declaration Erklärung
- of assignment Abtretungserklärung
- of suretyship Bürgschaftserklärung

decline in equity prices Rückgang der Aktienkurse

decontrol of interest rates Freigabe der Zinssätze

deed Urkunde; Vertrag
- of arrangement Vergleichsvereinbarung
- of assignment Abtretungsurkunde
- of conveyance (Grundstücks-) Übertragungsurkunde
- of postponement Rangrücktrittserklärung
- of protest Protesturkunde
- of reconveyance Löschungsbewilligung (US)
- of trust (a) Treuhandvertrag; (b) Hypothekenbrief
- stock Inhaberwertpapiere

deep discounts / discount bonds stark abgezinste Papiere; mit einem hohen Abschlag vom Nennwert gehandelte Papiere

default (a) Zahlungsverzug, Nichtzahlung; (b) Vertragsverletzung

default v. (a) in Verzug geraten, nicht zahlen; (b) nicht erfüllen (vertragliche Verpflichtungen)
  to - on a loan mit der Rückzahlung eines Kredites in Verzug geraten

defaulting
- borrower in Zahlungsverzug geratener Kreditnehmer
- shareholder Aktionär, der einer Einzahlungsaufforderung nicht nachgekommen ist

default
- interest Verzugszinsen
- of payment Zahlungsverzug, Nichtzahlung
- of the borrower (debtor) Verzug des Kreditnehmers, Schuldnerverzug
- rate Ausfallquote im Kreditgeschäft
- risk Ausfallrisiko, Debitorenrisiko

defective title anfechtbarer Anspruch (Rechtstitel)

defence stocks Rüstungswerte

defensive
- investment risikoarme Anlage
- investment policy vorsichtige (konservative) Anlagepolitik
- securities risikoarme Wertpapiere

defer v. (a) aufschieben; (b) stunden; (c) abgrenzen

deferred charges (income) abgegrenzte Kosten (Erträge), Rechnungsabgrenzungsposten

deferred interest Abgrenzungszinsen

deferred interest warrant Zahlungsverpflichtung im Hinblick auf rückständige Zinsen

deferred payment credit Zielzahlungsakkreditiv

deferred payment undertaking Verpflichtung zur hinausgeschobenen Zahlung

deferred revenue Ertragsabgrenzung

deferred share Nachzugsaktie

deferment Aufschub; Stundung; Abgrenzung
- of debt repayments Moratorium, Zahlungsaufschub
- of income Ertragsabgrenzung
- of interest rate payments Zinsstundung

deferral ⟶ deferment

deficit Defizit, Fehlbetrag, Ausfall
- at the close of trading Tagesfehlbeträge (z.B. im Geldhandel)
- on current account Leistungsbilanzdefizit

delinquency rate Ausfallquote bei Krediten (US)

delinquency risk Ausfallrisiko

delinquent loan notleidender Kredit (US)

delist v. von der Börsennotierung streichen

delivery across the counter Auslieferung (Übergabe, Aushändigung) am Schalter

demand (a) Nachfrage; (b) Forderung
- balances Sichtguthaben
- bill Sichtwechsel
- deposit account Kontokorrentkonto
- deposit liabilities Verbindlichkeiten aus Sichteinlagen
- deposits Sichteinlagen
- for mortgage funds Hypothekenkreditnachfrage
- liabilities Sichtverbindlichkeiten
- note Schuldschein
- rate Sichtkurs

denominate v. (a) bezeichnen; (b) stückeln

dollar-denominated floater variabel verzinsliche $-Anleihe

denomination Stückelung

in -s of $ 500 or multiples thereof in Stückelungen von $ 500 oder einem Vielfachen davon

Department of Stock Lists Börsenzulassungsausschuß (US)

deposit (a) Einzahlung; (b) Einlage; (c) Einlieferung;(d) Hinterlegung

deposit v. (a) einzahlen; (b) einliefern; (c) hinterlegen

deposit
- account (a) Einlagenkonto; (b) niedrigverzinsliches Sparkonto
- ary bank Depotbank, Hinterlegungsstelle
- banking Einlagengeschäft (Passivgeschäft) einer Bank
- base (a) Bodensatz; (b) Einlagenvolumen
- dealer Geldhändler
- drain Abzug von Einlagen, Einlagenabfluß
- insurance Einlagensicherung
- insurance fund Einlagensicherungsfonds
- ledger Depotverzeichnis
- leverage Verhältnis zwischen Einlagen und Eigenkapital
- mix Einlagen-Mix
- money Giralgeld, Buchgeld
- operations Einlagengeschäft

depositor Einleger, Einlagenkunde; Hinterleger

depository Depotbank, Hinterlegungsstelle
- agent Hinterlegungsstelle
- bond Garantie einer Depotbank

deposit
- portfolio Einlagenvolumen
- protection Einlagenschutz
- protection board staatliche Einlagenschutz-Versicherung (Br)
- protection fund Einlagensicherungsfonds
- protection scheme Einlagensicherungsprogramm
- rate Einlagenzins, Zinssatz auf Spareinlagen
- receipt Einlieferungsbestätigung
- slip (a) Einzahlungsbestätigung; (b) Hinterlegungsbestätigung
- taking activities Passivgeschäft, Einlagengeschäft

depreciate v. (a) abschreiben; (b) im Wert mindern

depreciation (a) Abschreibung; (b) Wertminderung

depressant belastender Faktor

depressed sentiment Baissestimmung

designated order turnaround System, das einem Mitglied der New Yorker Börse die Möglichkeit gibt, seine Aufträge ohne Einschaltung eines Ringmaklers direkt an einen ⟶ specialist weiterzuleiten

detachable warrants abtrennbare Options- oder Wandlungsrechte (Bezugsrechtsscheine)

determination (a) Festsetzung, Ermittlung; (b) Ablauf, Erlöschen, Verfall
- clause Verfallklausel
- date Verfalltag
- of the forward rate Terminkursbildung
- of the guarantee Verfall (Erlöschen) der Garantie
- of the interest rate Festsetzung des Zinssatzes

devaluation Abwertung
- rate Abwertungssatz

devalue v. abwerten

development (a) Entwicklung; (b) Erschließung; Bau
- finance Existenzgründungs-Darlehen, Projektfinanzierungsmittel, Investitionsmittel
- guarantee Erschließungsgarantie

development loan Investitionskredit

difficulties in funding Finanzierungsschwierigkeiten

dilute v. verwässern
 diluted unter Einbeziehung des
 bedingten Kapitals, unter Einbeziehung aller Umtauschrechte

dilution of voting power Stimm-
rechtsverwässerung

direct
- arbitrage einfache Devisenarbitrage
- debit Abbuchung (im Last-
 schrift- bzw. Einzugsverfahren);
 Lastschrift, Abbuchungsbeleg
- debits from bank accounts Ab-
 buchungen vom Bankkonto
- debiting Abbuchungsverfahren,
 Lastschriftverfahren
- debit returned unpaid nicht
 eingelöste Lastschrift, Last-
 schriftretoure
- negotiation Privatplazierung
- offering freihändiger Verkauf, Direktemission
- placing Direktplazierung
- reduction mortgage Tilgungshypothek

dirty
- bill of lading unreines
 Konnossement
- floating schmutziges Floaten

disband v. auflösen (z.B. ein
Konsortium)

disburse v. auszahlen (Darlehen)
ausschütten (Dividende)

disbursement Auszahlung; Ausschüttung
- commitments Auszahlungsver-
 pflichtungen
- rate Auszahlungskurs

disbursements
- on committed loans Auszahlungen
 auf zugesagte Darlehen
- under the loan agreement Auszahlungen aus dem Kredit

discharge Ablösung, Tilgung,
Begleichung
- of a debt Tilgung (Ablösung)
 einer Schuld
- of a contract Vertragserfüllung,
 Vertragsauflösung
- of the guarantor Entlassung
 des Garantienehmers aus der
 Haftung
- of a loan Ablösung (Rückzahlung)
 eines Darlehens
- of a mortgage Löschung einer
 Hypothek
- of a pledge Pfandfreigabe

disclaim v. ablehnen, verzichten;
ausschließen
 to - an opinion den Bestätigungsvermerk versagen
 to - property von der Konkurs-
 masse aussondern

disclaimer Verzicht, Verzichterklärung, Ablehnung; Ausschluß
- of responsibility Haftungs-
 ausschluß

disclose (a) offenlegen; (b) ausweisen

disclosure Offenlegung, Ausweis
- requirements Publizitätsvorschriften, Ausweisvorschriften

discount (a) Diskont; (b) Disagio,
Abschlag; (c) Abzinsungsbetrag
 discounts allowed Diskontauf-
 wendungen
 discounts earned (received) Diskonterträge
 discount on the mortgage principal
 Damnum, Hypothekendisagio
 discount from the offering price
 Abschlag vom Emissionskurs

discount v. (a) diskontieren;
(b) vorwegnehmen; (c) abzinsen

discounted bond Abzinsungsanleihe, Abzinsungspapier

discounted certificate of deposit abgezinstes Einlagenzertifikat

discounted receivables abgetretene Forderungen

discountable diskontfähig, diskontierbar

discount
- bank   diskontierende Bank, Diskontbank
- broker   Wechselmakler
- ceiling   Diskontlinie
- charges   Diskontspesen
- contract note   Diskontnota
- credit   Diskontkredit
- credit line   Diskontkreditlinie
- commission   Diskontprovision

discounter   Diskontgeber

discount
- facility   Diskontkredit, Diskontierungsphase
- holdings   Wechseldiskont--Portefeuille
- house buying rate   Wechsel--Ankaufssatz der Diskonthäuser (Br)
- ing banker   diskontierende Bank, Diskontbank
- ing proceeds   Diskonterlös
- market   Diskontmarkt
- method   Abzinsungsverfahren
- policy   Diskontpolitik
- rate   (a) Diskontsatz; (b) Abzinsungssatz
- undertaking   Diskontzusage
- window   Lombardfenster

discretionary account   Portefeuille (Depotkonto), bei dem der Vermögensverwalter Dispositionsvollmacht besitzt

discretionary limits   Kreditkompetenz eines Bankfilialleiters (Br)

discretionary powers   Dispositionsvollmacht, Ermessensbefugnisse

dishonour v.   nicht einlösen, nicht bezahlen, die Annahme verweigern

dishonoured bill   nicht eingelöster Wechsel, Wechselrückgabe

dishonoured cheque   nicht eingelöster Scheck, Scheckretoure

dishonoured collections   notleidende Inkassi

to - the documents   die Aufnahme der Dokumente verweigern

disintermediation   Abzug von Bankeinlagen und Wiederanlage in höher rentierlichen Festverzinslichen

dispensing notice   Verzichtserklärung

displacements   Papiere, deren Emission aufgrund ungünstiger Marktverhältnisse annulliert oder verschoben werden mußte

disposable funds   verfügbare Mittel

disposal   (a) Verfügung, Veräußerung; (b) Abgang (z.B. von Sachanlagen)

distress borrowing   zusätzliche Kreditaufnahme (zur Finanzierung von Zinszahlungen auf bereits aufgenommene Kredite)

distress selling   (a) Panikverkäufe an der Börse; (b) Versteigerung

distributable profit   ausschüttungsfähiger Gewinn

distribution   (a) Ausschüttung; (b) Verteilung; (c) Vertrieb

Ditchley Group   Informations- und Arbeitsgruppe von 35 im internationalen Geschäft besonders aktiven Banken

dive to be in a - eine Baisse durchlaufen

divergence
- indicator Abweichungsindikator (Europäisches Währungssystem)
- margin Abweichungsspanne
- threshold Abweichungsschwelle

diversification of investments Anlagenstreuung

diversified common stock fund Aktienfonds mit breiter Anlagenstreuung

divest v. veräußern, ausgliedern (Unternehmensbereich)

dividend (a) Dividende; (b) Konkursquote
 dividends paid Dividendenaufwand
 dividends received Dividendenerträge, Dividendenaufkommen

dividend
- announcement Dividendenankündigung, Dividendenerklärung
- arrears Dividendenrückstände
- collection Dividendeninkasso
- counterfoil Dividendenabrechnungsschein
- coupon Dividendenschein, Dividendenabschnitt
- cover Dividendendeckung
- cut Dividendenkürzung
- disbursement Dividendenausschüttung, Auszahlung der Dividende
- disbursing agent Dividendenzahlstelle
- distribution Dividendenausschüttung
- due fällige Dividende
- due date Dividendentermin
- freeze Dividendenstopp
- guarantee Dividendengarantie

- in arrears Dividendenrückstände
- income Dividendenerträge
- increase Dividendenerhöhung, Dividendenaufstockung
- limiting covenants Bestimmungen eines Kredit- oder Anleihevertrages, durch die dem Schuldner Auflagen hinsichtlich der Ausschüttung von Dividenden gemacht werden
- list to return to the dividend list die Dividendenzahlungen wiederaufnehmen
- mandate Dividendenüberweisungsauftrag
- markdown Abschlag ex Dividende
- note Dividendenabrechnung
- off ex Dividende
- omission Dividendenausfall
- on einschließlich Dividende
- on account Abschlagsdividende
- paying agent Dividendenzahlstelle
- payment Dividendenzahlung
- payout Dividendenausschüttung
- payout ratio Dividendensatz
- per ordinary share Dividende je Stammaktie
- rate Dividendensatz
- reinvestment Wiederanlage der Dividende
- restrictions Auflagen, die ein Kreditnehmer bei seinen Dividendenausschüttungen beachten muß
- rights Dividendenrechte
- statement Dividendenerklärung, Dividendenankündigung
- warrant Dividendenberechtigungsschein

documentary
- acceptance credit Rembourskredit, Akzeptakkreditiv
- business Dokumentengeschäft

documentary
- collection dokumentäres Inkasso, Dokumenteninkasso
- credit   Akkreditiv
- credit operations   Akkreditivgeschäft
- draft   Dokumententratte
- payment   dokumentäre Zahlung
- term credit   Nach-Sicht-Akkreditiv

documents   Dokumente
- against discretion of collecting bank   Dokumentendisposition steht der Inkassobank zu
- against payment (acceptance) / (D/P - D/A)   Dokumente gegen Zahlung (Akzept)
- in accordance with the terms and conditions of the credit   akkreditivgemäße Dokumente

dollar
- acceptance credit   Dollarrembours
- cost averaging   regelmäßige Dollarkäufe während eines längeren Zeitraumes zur Erzielung eines günstigen Durchschnittskurses
- debt   (a) Dollartitel, Dollaremission; (b) Dollarschuld
- denominated issues / dollar issues   Dollar-Emissionen, Emissionen im Dollarbereich, Dollar-Schuldtitel
- drain   Dollarabfluß
- exchange   (a) in US $ zahlbar gestellter Wechsel;(b) Summe der im Umlauf befindlichen US-Wechsel
- premium   Betrag, um den die Kurse von US-Wertpapieren an der Londoner Börse über den entsprechenden Kursen von New York liegen
- proceeds   (a) Dollarerlös; (b) Dollargegenwert

- secondary market   Dollar-Sekundärmarkt, Sekundärmarkt in Dollar-Titeln
- securities   Dollar-Titel

domestic
- assets einer Bank: Inlandsausleihungen
- banking einer Bank: Inlandsgeschäft
- currency   Inlandsvaluta
- lending   Inlandsausleihungen, inländisches Kreditgeschäft
- margin   Zinsspanne im Inlandsgeschäft
- priced loan   Kredit zu Inlandskonditionen
- retail operations   Privatkundengeschäft im Inland
- wholesale operations   Großkundengeschäft im Inland

domiciled bill   Domizilwechsel

domiciliation   Domizilierung

donee   Bevollmächtigter

donor   Vollmachtgeber

dormant account   umsatzloses Konto

dormant funds   unverzinsliche Gelder

DOT → Designated Order Turnaround

double leverage   Bezeichnung für eine Situation, in der Kreditaufnahmen der Muttergesellschaft der Tochtergesellschaft als Aktienkapital zur Verfügung gestellt werden (US)

Dow Jones Industrial Average   Dow Jones Industrie-Aktienindex

downpayment guarantee   Anzahlungsgarantie

downside risk   Kursrisiko nach unten

downslide in interest rates
Zinsrutsch

downstairs members Kursmakler der New Yorker Börse

downstream loan Kredit der Muttergesellschaft an ein Tochterunternehmen (⟶ upstream loan)

downticks Kursabschläge (US)

downward course of interest rates Zinssenkungstrend

downward movement in pricing Trend zu niedrigeren Konditionen

downward price correction Kurskorrektur nach unten

draft (a) Tratte; (b) Scheck, Bankscheck; (c) Debitorenziehung (von einer Bank auf einen Kreditnehmer gezogener Wechsel); (d) Entwurf
- advice Ziehungsavis

drain Abfluß, Abzug, Entzug
- on liquidity Liquiditätsentzug

draw v. (a) ausstellen, ziehen (Schecks,Wechsel);(b)auslosen; (c) in Anspruch nehmen

amount drawn upon in Anspruch genommener Betrag

bill drawn upon XY auf XY gezogener Wechsel

bonds drawn ausgeloste Anleihen

numbers drawn Auslosungsnummern

to - down a mortgage eine Hypothek aufnehmen

to - down the second tranche die zweite Tranche in Anspruch nehmen

to - on an account über ein Konto verfügen

to - on a credit line eine Kreditlinie in Anspruch nehmen

drawdown Inanspruchnahme
- currency Währung, in der ein Kredit in Anspruch genommen wird
- period Zeitraum der Inanspruchnahme

drawee Bezogener

drawee banker bezogene Bank

drawee's liability Bezogenenobligo, Haftung des Bezogenen

drawer Aussteller

drawer's liability Ausstellerobligo, Haftung des Ausstellers

drawing (a) Ausstellung, Ziehung; (b) Auslosung (einer Anleihe); (c) Inanspruchnahme (eines Kredites); (d) Verfügung (über ein Konto)
- account Kontokorrentkonto
- authorisation (a) Kontovollmacht; (b) Verfügungsberechtigung; (c) Ziehungsermächtigung (Akkreditiv)
- credit Dispositionskredit, Kontokorrentkredit
- notice Auslosungsanzeige
- of a bill Wechselziehung
- of funds Abhebung von Geldern
- on an account Verfügung über ein Konto
- on reserves Inanspruchnahme der Rücklagen, Reserveentnahmen
- price Auslosungskurs
- restrictions Verfügungsbeschränkungen
- rights Ziehungsrechte
- under a documentary credit Inanspruchnahme eines Akkreditivs

drive-in window Autoschalter

droplock Bankkredit, der in eine langfristige Schuldverschreibung umgewandelt werden kann

droplock issue variabel verzinslicher Schuldschein, der bei Erreichen eines bestimmten Index-

punktes (trigger rate) in ein
festverzinsliches Wertpapier
umgewandelt werden kann

DRS ⟶ debtor reporting system

dual currency convertibles   inländische Wandelschuldverschreibungen, die in Aktien einer ausländischen Gesellschaft umgewandelt werden können

dual currency issue   auf zwei Währungen lautende Emission

dud check   ungedeckter Scheck

due   fällig
- bill   Nachweis über die Abtretung von Dividenden- oder Bezugsrechten
- date   Fälligkeitstermin
- from banks   Guthaben bei Banken, Forderungen gegenüber Banken
- on sale clause   Klausel, die die sofortige Fälligstellung einer Hypothek bei Verkauf der entsprechenden Liegenschaft vorsieht (US)
- payment provided   Zahlung 'Eingang vorbehalten'
- to banks   Verbindlichkeiten gegenüber Banken

duly presented for payment
ordnungsgemäß zur Zahlung vorgelegt

duration   Dauer der Zins- und Tilgungszahlungen bei einer Anleihe (muß nicht mit der Laufzeit identisch sein - US)

duty of care   Sorgfaltspflicht (der Bank)

duty of disclosure   Anzeigepflicht, Offenlegungspflicht, Publizitätspflicht

duty of secrecy   Geheimhaltungspflicht (der Bank)

E

early
- call provision   Bestimmung hinsichtlich der vorzeitigen Kündigung (in einem Anleihe- oder Kreditvertrag)
- redemption   vorzeitige Tilgung
- withdrawal facility   Möglichkeit der vorzeitigen Verfügung
- withdrawal penalty   Vorschußzinsen

earmarked funds (reserves)   zweckgebundene Gelder (Rücklagen)

earned surplus   erwirtschaftetes Eigenkapital; einbehaltene Gewinne

earnest money   Angeld, Draufgeld

earning assets   einer Bank: Ausleihungen, Kredite

earnings   Ertrag, Erträge, Gewinn; Einkünfte
- control   Ertragssteuerung
- gain   Ertragszuwachs
- orientated pricing   ertragsorientierte Konditionengestaltung (Gebührenpolitik)
- per diluted ordinary share   Gewinn je Stammaktie unter Einbeziehung aller Umtauschrechte
- position   Ertragslage
- power   Ertragskraft
- ratios   Gewinnkennzahlen
- statement   Gewinn- und Verlustrechnung

easily convertible into cash   leicht liquidisierbar

easing of equity prices   Nachgeben (Abbröckeln) der Aktienkurse

easing of interest rates   Zinsverbilligung, Nachgeben der Zinssätze, Lockerung der Kreditpolitik

ECP → Eurocommercial Paper

Edge Act Corporations   Institute (Tochtergesellschaften von US-Banken oder Niederlassungen ausländischer Banken in den USA), die nur Auslandsgeschäfte abwickeln dürfen

Edge Acts → Edge Act Corporations

EDRs → European Depositary Receipts

effective
- interest load   effektive Zinsbelastung
- interest rate   Effektivzinssatz, tatsächlicher Zinssatz
- interest return   Effektivverzinsung

EFTPOS → electronic funds transfer at the point of sale

EFTS → electronic funds transfer system

electrical majors   führende Elektrowerte

electricals/electrical stocks   Elektropapiere, Elektrowerte

electronic
- banking   elektronische Bankdienstleistungen, elektronische Abwicklung von Bankgeschäften
- delivery system   elektronisches Übertragungssystem
- funds transfer at the point of sale   elektronischer Zahlungsverkehr in Verbindung mit einem POS-System

electronic
- funds transfer system elektronisches Zahlungsverkehrssystem
- money   elektronisches Geld
- point-of-sale system elektronisches POS-System (elektronische, beleglose Abbuchung)

eligibility for rediscount   Rediskontfähigkeit

eligible
- assets   liquide Mittel und erstklassige Ausleihungen (gemäß den US-Liquiditätsrichtlinien müssen diese eligible assets die Fremdverpflichtungen der Banken mit einem bestimmten Prozentsatz überdecken - US)
- banks   Banken, die Wechsel bei der Bank von England rediskontieren können (Br)
- bill   rediskontfähiger Wechsel
- liabilities   Bankeinlagen mit Laufzeiten von weniger als zwei Jahren (Br)
- reserve assets   Liquiditätsreserven
- security   (a) beleihungsfähige Sicherheit; (b) mündelsicheres Wertpapier
- status   Status einer→ eligible bank

embarrassed corporation   in Liquiditätsschwierigkeiten befindliches Unternehmen

employed capital   investiertes Kapital

employees stock ownership plan   Belegschaftsaktien-Programm

encash v.   einlösen, einziehen

encashment   Einlösung (von Schecks); Einzug (von Kupons)
- commission   Einlösungsprovision

encumbrance   Belastung
- limit   Belastungsgrenze

end-of-month
- settlement   Ultimoregulierung
- trading arrangements   Ultimodispositionen

endorse v.   (a) indossieren; (b) genehmigen, billigen

endorsement   (a) Indossament, Giro, Indossierung; (b) Billigung
- in blank   Blankoindossament
- liabilities   Indossamentsverbindlichkeiten

endorser   Girant, Indossant

enfranchisement   Übertragung von Stimmrechten auf zuvor nicht stimmberechtigte Aktien

entitled
- to current dividend   mit laufender Gewinnberechtigung
- to draw on an account (to operate an account)   Verfügungsberechtigung über ein Konto besitzen

entitlement issue   Bezugsrechtsemission

entry   Buchung, Buchungsposten
- fee   Postengebühr
- of satisfaction of mortgage   Hypothekenlöschung, Löschungsvermerk

equal interest payments   gleichmäßige Zinszahlungen

equal lien   gleichrangiges Pfandrecht

equally secured clause   Klausel hinsichtlich der Ranggleichstellung

equilibrium rate of exchange   Gleichgewichtswechselkurs

equipment investment loan Investitionskredit

equities (a) Aktien, Dividendenpapiere; (b) Beteiligungsrechte
- fund   Aktienfonds

equity   Kapital, Aktienkapital
- contribution   Kapitaleinlage
- conversion option   Möglichkeit der Umwandlung in Aktienkapital
- finance   Beteiligungskapital; Kapitalmittel
- financing   (a) Beteiligungsfinanzierung; (b) Aktienfinanzierung, Mittelaufnahme am Aktienmarkt
- fund   (a) Aktienfonds; (b) Beteiligungsfonds
- funding   Eigenkapitalkonsolidierung
- holder   Kapitaleigner
- holding (interest)   Kapitalbeteiligung, Aktienbeteiligung
- investment   (a) Aktienanlage; (b) Kapitalbeteiligung
- investment company   Kapitalbeteiligungsgesellschaft
- investment service   Beteiligungsvermittlung
- issue   Aktienemission
- kicker   Beteiligung des Kreditgebers am Kapital oder Gewinn des Kreditnehmers (im Rahmen eines partiarischen Darlehens)
- leaders   führende Aktienwerte
- links   Kapitalverflechtung
- market   Aktienmarkt
- market capitalisation   Börsenkapitalisierung
- offering   Aktienemission
- offering premium   Aktienemissionsagio
- option   Anspruch auf Umwandlung eines Darlehens in eine Kapitalbeteiligung

- participation mortgage   Hypothekenvereinbarung, nach der der Hypothekengläubiger an der Wertsteigerung einer belasteten Liegenschaft partizipiert (US)
- portfolio   Aktienportefeuille
- price   Aktienkurs
- requirements   Kapitalbedarf
- securities   Aktien, Dividendenpapiere
- share (stake)   Kapitalanteil, Kapitalbeteiligung
- switching   Aktientausch
- trading   Aktienhandel
- turnover   Börsenumsätze in Aktien
- warrant   Aktienbezugsrechtsschein

erring funds   vagabundierende Gelder

escalation clause   (a) Gleitklausel; (b) Zinserhöhungsklausel

escrow
- account   Treuhandkonto, Anderkonto
- agreement   Treuhandvertrag
- bond   bei einem Treuhänder hinterlegte Anleihe

established banking practice   übliche Bankpraxis

establishment commission ⟶ commitment fee

estimated price   Taxkurs

Eurobond market   Euro-Anleihemarkt, Eurobond-Markt

Eurocapital market   Euro-Kapitalmarkt

Eurocommercial paper   am Euro-Dollarmarkt aufgelegte Schuldtitel

Eurocredit
- market   Euro-Kreditmarkt
- syndication   Euro-Kreditsyndizierung

Eurocurrency
- loan   Euro-Währungskredit
- market   Euro-Währungsmarkt

Eurodollar
- bond issue   Euro-Dollartitel, Emission einer Euro-Dollaranleihe
- borrowing   Euro-Dollarkredit, Kreditaufnahme am Euro-Dollarmarkt
- deposit rates   Zinssätze für Euro-Dollareinlagen
- deposits   Euro-Dollareinlagen
- straights   Euro-Dollaranleihen ohne Wandlungsrechte

Euroissue   Euro-Emission
- currency   Euro-Emissionswährung

Eurolending business (operations)   Euro-Kreditgeschäft

Euromoney market   Euro-Geldmarkt

European
- Currency Unit   Europäische Währungseinheit
- Depositary Receipts   Inhaberzertifikate, die bei Emissionen ausländischer AGs auf den europäischen Kapitalmärkten durch die die Emissionen besorgenden Inlandsbanken ausgegeben werden
- Monetary System   Europäisches Währungssystem
- Unit of Account   Europäische Rechnungseinheit

evaluation of a collateral   Sicherheitenbewertung, Sicherheitenprüfung

evening out accounts   Glattstellung von Positionen

evergreen clause   Kreditvertragsklausel, die eine automatische Vertragsverlängerung (in der Regel um 1 Jahr) vorsieht, falls keine Kündigung durch einen der Vertragspartner erfolgt

evergreen commitment   revolvierender Kredit

evidence of payment   Zahlungsnachweis

ex all   ausschließlich aller Rechte

ex allotment   ex Bezugsrecht, exB

ex capitalisation   ausschließlich Gratisaktien

exceptions to title   Eigentumsvorbehalte

excess shares   Spitzen, nicht gezeichnete junge Aktien (Bezugsrechte)

exchange   (a) Devisen, Währung; (b) Börse; (c) Umtausch, Austausch
- arrangement   Angebot eines Investmentfonds: Kostenloser Umtausch von Aktienbeständen in Fondsanteile
- board   Börsenvorstand
- broker   Devisenmakler
- clause   Währungsklausel, Wechselkursklausel
- contract note   (a) Devisenabrechnung; (b) Effektenkauf- bzw. Verkaufsabrechnung
- control   Devisenbewirtschaftung
- dealing network   Händlernetz
- dealings   Börsenhandel, Börsenumsätze
- distribution   (a) Umtauschangebot; (b) Zeichnungsangebot für bereits im Umlauf befindliche Wertpapiere
- facility   Umtauschmöglichkeit
- floor   Börsenparkett
- for forward delivery   Termindevisen
- for (into) shares   Umtausch in Aktien
- for spot delivery   Kassadevisen
- futures   Devisentermingeschäfte
- futures contract   Devisentermingeschäft

325

exchange
- guarantee Wechselkursgarantie, Wechselkurssicherung
- intervention Intervention am Devisenmarkt
- listing Börsennotierung
- loss Wechselkursverlust
- market Devisenmarkt
- membership Börsenmitgliedschaft
- offering Umtauschangebot (bei Wertpapieren)
- offset agreement Devisenausgleichsabkommen
- of shares Aktientausch
- premium Devisenaufgeld
- privilege Umtauschrecht
- rate Wechselkurs
- rate adjustment Wechselkursberichtigung
- rate cover Wechselkursgarantie
- rate exposure Wechselkursrisiko
- rate guarantee Wechselkursgarantie
- rate hedging Wechselkurssicherung
- ratio Umtauschverhältnis
- regulations (a) Devisenbestimmungen; (b) Börsenordnung
- reserves Devisenreserven
- risk Wechselkursrisiko
- risk guarantee Wechselkurssicherung
- rules Börsenordnung
- seat Börsenmitgliedschaft, Börsensitz
- stabilisation fund Währungsausgleichsfonds
- surplus (a) Wechselkursgewinn; (b) Devisenüberschuß
- traded stock Börsenpapiere

Exchequer Bill Schatzwechsel (Br)

Exchequer Bond Schatzanweisung(Br)

ex claims ex Bezugsrechte

ex dividend ex Dividende

ex drawing ex (ausschließlich) Ziehung

executive warrants Optionsrechte leitender Angestellter

exempted dealer Wertpapierhändler, der Wertpapiere auf eigene Rechnung kaufen und verkaufen kann

exempt from disclosure requirements nicht den Publizitätsvorschriften unterliegen

exemption from minimum reserves Mindestreservefreiheit

exempt securities Staatspapiere, deren Erträge steuerfrei sind

exercise price Abnahme- bzw. Lieferungskurs

exercising subscription rights Ausübung von Bezugsrechten

ex interest ohne Stückzinsen

ex new ex Bezugsrechte

expansion of the loan portfolio Ausweitung des Kreditvolumens

expense accounts Aufwandskonten

expiry date im Optionsgeschäft: Verfalltag, d.h. der letzte Tag, an dem ein Optionsrecht ausgeübt werden kann

export credit insurance Exportkreditversicherung

Export Credits Guarantee Department staatliche Exportkreditversicherungsgesellschaft (Br)

export finance facilities Exportkredite, Exportfinanzierungsmöglichkeiten exposure (a) Engagement (Devisen, Kredite, Wertpapiere); (b) Obligo, Risiko

our - totals DM .. wir sind mit DM .. engagiert (exponiert)

to increase the loan - sich mit neuen Krediten engagieren

exposure

- in foreign currencies Engagement in Fremdwährungen

- in stocks Engagement in Aktien, Aktienbestand

- management (a) Kurssicherung, Kurssicherungsverhalten; (b) Risikomanagement; (c) Bearbeitung eines Engagements

- risk Risikogehalt

- to loss Verlustrisiko

ex rights ex Bezugsrechte

ex scrip issue ex Gratisaktien

extend v. (a) verlängern (Laufzeit); (b) strecken (Darlehen); (c) erweitern (Dienstleistungsangebot); (d) hinauslegen, gewähren, bereitstellen (Kredit)

extended access to the Fund's resources (IMF) erweiterter Zugang zu den Fondsmitteln

extended bond Anleihe, deren Laufzeit verlängert wurde

extendable maturity verlängerbare Fälligkeit; Fälligkeit eines Wertpapiers, die nach Wahl des Emittenten oder Käufers verlängert werden kann

extension (a) Verlängerung; (b) Streckung; (c) Erweiterung; (d) Gewährung

- of a bridge-over loan Gewährung eines Überbrückungskredites, Zwischenfinanzierung

- of fresh money Gewährung (Bereitstellung) neuer Kredite

- of a loan Kreditgewährung, Hinauslegung (Hinausreichung) eines Kredites

- of maturity Verlängerung der Laufzeit, Zahlungsaufschub, Fristverlängerung

- of payments Zahlungsaufschub

- of time for payment Verlängerung des Zahlungsziels

- of time for payment of a bill Prolongation eines Wechsels

- to the cover Erweiterung der Deckungszusage

- to the subscription deadline Verlängerung der Zeichnungsfrist

external

- account Ausländerkonto

- bill Auslandswechsel

- debt Auslandsverschuldung

- finance Fremdkapital

- financing (funding) Außenfinanzierung, Fremdfinanzierung

- fund requirements Fremdfinanzierungsbedarf, benötigte Fremdmittel

- loan Auslandsanleihe

extra interest deposit account bonifiziertes Sparkonto

F

f → flat

face amount   Nennbetrag, Nennwert

facility   Kredit, Fazilität, Kreditlinie
- approval   Kreditgenehmigung, Krediteinweisung
- letter   Kreditzusageschreiben, Kreditbestätigung
- pricing   Festsetzung der Kreditkonditionen, Konditionengestaltung

factorage   Factoring-Gebühr

factoring   Factoring, Ankauf und Bevorschussung von Forderungen aus Waren- und Dienstleistungsgeschäften

fad-oriented stocks   Aktien von Unternehmen, deren Erträge vom Verbraucherverhalten abhängig sind (US)

failing payment   mangels Zahlung

Fair Credit Reporting Act   gesetzliche Regelung der Einholung und Erteilung von Auskünften (Br)

fall   v. to fall due for payment zur Zahlung fällig werden

Fannie Mae securities   Wertpapiere der → Federal National Mortgage Association

farming credit   Agrarkredit

faulty letter of credit   mangelhaftes Akkreditiv

FCIA → Foreign Credit Insurance Association

FDIC → Federal Deposit Insurance Corporation

featureless trading   keine nennenswerten Kursbewegungen

federal agency notes   von US-Bundesbehörden emittierte kurzfristige Schuldscheine bzw. Kassenobligationen

federal agency securities   Bundespapiere, Staatstitel (US)

Federal Deposit Insurance Corporation   Einlagensicherungs-Institut (Pflichtmitgliedschaft für alle dem Federal Reserve System angeschlossenen Banken)

Federal Discount Window   Lombardfenster der → Federal Reserve Banks

Federal Financing Bank   US-Bundesfinanzierungsbank

Federal funds   Tagesgeld (US)
- bought   aufgenommenes Tagesgeld
- market   Tagesgeldmarkt
- rate   Tagesgeldsatz (Leitzins des US-Geldmarktes)
- sold   überlassenes Tagesgeld

Federal Home Loan Banks   Zentral- bzw. Refinanzierungsbanken (insgesamt 12) der US-Spar- und Bausparkassen

Federal National Mortgage Association   US-Bundes-Hypothekenbank (inzwischen privatisiert)

Federal Open Market Committee   Ausschuß für Offenmarkt-Politik des → Federal Reserve System

Federal Reserve Bank US-Noten-
bank (insgesamt 12)
- balances Guthaben bei einer
  Federal Reserve Bank
- credit Gesamtsumme der Ausleihungen der Federal Reserve
  Banks an die Mitgliedsbanken

Federal Reserve margin requirements Vorschriften der Federal
Reserve Banks hinsichtlich der
Mindestdeckung bei Effektenkrediten

Federal Reserve System US-Zen-
tralbankensystem

Federal Savings and Loan Insurance Corporation Einlagensicherungs-Institut der Sparkassen

federal securities US-Staats-
papiere

Fed funds ⟶ federal funds

Fed window ⟶ Federal Discount
Window

Fed Wire Clearingnetz der
Federal Reserve Banken, dem
auch Großbanken und Behörden
sowie Scheckverrechnungszen-
tralen angeschlossen sind

fee income Provisionseinnahmen

fee pricing Gebührenfestsetzung

FFB ⟶ Federal Financing Bank

FHLB⟶ Federal Home Loan Banks

fiduciary
- agent Treuhänder
- income Erträge aus Treuhand-
  geschäften
- loan ungedeckter Kredit,
  Blankokredit

filing requirements Registrierungsvorschriften

fill or kill limitierter Wertpapierauftrag, der zu annullieren
ist, falls er nicht sofort ausge-
führt werden kann

filter rules Anlagegrundsätze
(z.B. Kauf einer Aktie nachdem sie
sich 10 % von ihrem Tiefstand
erholt hat, oder Verkauf, wenn sie
sich bis auf 10 % ihrem Höchstkurs genähert hat)

final
- call letzte Einforderung
- dividend Schlußdividende
- tone Stimmung gegen Schluß der
  Börsensitzung

finance Finanzierungsmittel,
finanzielle Mittel

finance v. finanzieren

finance
- bill Finanzwechsel
- charge Finanzierungskosten,
  Finanzierungsaufwand; Kreditkosten
- company Finanzierungsgesellschaft;
  Teilzahlungskreditinstitut (US)
- engineering Finanzierungs-
  technik
- house base rate Eckzins der
  Finance Houses (Finanzierungs- bzw.
  Teilzahlungskreditinstitute) für
  Ausleihungen (Br)
- requirements Finanzbedarf

financial finanziell
- advertisement Finanzanzeige
- assets Finanzanlagen
- backing finanzielle Unterstützung, Finanzierungsrückhalt
- engineering Finanzierungs-
  technik, Entwicklung eines Finan-
  zierungskonzeptes
- exposure finanzielles Engagement
- futures contract Finanztermin-
  kontrakt

financial
- futures market   Terminmarkt für Finanztitel
- institution   Kreditinstitut
- intermediary   Kapitalsammelstelle, Finanzintermediär
- leeway   finanzieller Spielraum
- leverage   Verhältnis zwischen Eigen- und Fremdkapital; einer Bank: Verhältnis von Einlagen und Verbindlichkeiten zum Eigenkapital
- muscle   Finanzkraft
- planning statement   Finanzierungsbilanz, Finanzplan
- record   Bilanzergebnisse
- resources   (a) finanzielle Mittel; (b) Kapitalausstattung
- restructuring   Sanierung
- securities   Finanztitel
- services   Finanzleistungen
- standing   (a) Kreditwürdigkeit; (b) finanzielle Lage
- straits   finanzielle Schwierigkeiten

financing
- arrangement   Finanzierungsvereinbarung
- blueprint   Finanzierungskonzept
- capital goods   Investitionsgüterfinanzierung
- consumer durables   Finanzierung langlebiger Gebrauchsgüter
- cost   Finanzierungskosten, Finanzierungsaufwand
- deficiency   Finanzierungslücke
- options   Finanzierungsmöglichkeiten
- pool   Finanzierungsverbund
- statement   (a) Finanzierungserklärung; (b) Vertrag, durch den eine Sicherheit gegen Ansprüche Dritter geschützt wird (US)
- terms   Finanzierungsbedingungen

- vehicle   Finanzierungsform
- with funds generated internally   Eigenfinanzierung, Finanzierung aus Eigenmitteln
- with outside capital   Fremdfinanzierung

finders of private placements   Vermittler von Privatplazierungen

fine rate   →prime rate

fine trade bill   erstklassiger Handelswechsel

firm   v. sich befestigen, anziehen

firm
- banking   Firmenkundengeschäft
- bargain   Festgeschäft, Fixgeschäft
- closing   fester Börsenschluß
- underlying sentiment   feste Grundstimmung
- underwriting   feste Übernahme (einer Emission)

first
- call on shares   erste Einforderung auf Aktien
- checking   Dauersparauftrag (regelmäßiger Übertrag vom Kontokorrent- auf Sparkonto - US)
- class name   erstklassige Adresse
- line equities   erstklassige Aktien, Standardaktien
- mortgage   erststellige Hypothek
- of exchange   Erstausfertigung eines Wechsels
- priority lien   erstrangiges Pfandrecht
- rate borrower   erstklassige Schuldneradresse
- rate name in the bond market   erstklassige Anleiheadresse

fixed
- asset restrictions   Auflagen, die der Kreditnehmer bei Verkauf, Erwerb oder Belastung von Anlagen beachten muß

fixed
- asset support   Besicherung durch Sachanlagen
- capital spending (investments)   Anlageinvestitionen
- ceiling certificate   festverzinslicher Sparbrief
- cost charge   Fixkostenbelastung
- coupon bond   festverzinsliche Anleihe
- deposits   Festgeldeinlagen
- income fund   Rentenfonds
- income securities   Festverzinsliche, Rentenwerte, festverzinsliche Wertpapiere
- interest market   Rentenmarkt
- interest portfolio   Rentenportefeuille, Bestand an Festverzinslichen
- interest rate   Festzinssatz, festgeschriebener Zinssatz
- interest securities   festverzinsliche Wertpapiere, Festverzinsliche
- interest securities fund   Rentenfonds
- parities   feste Paritäten
- period of investment   Festlegungsdauer
- period rates   Zinsen auf Festgeldeinlagen
- rate lendings   Festzinskredite, Festzinsaktiva einer Bank
- rate lending sector   Festsatzbereich
- rate loan   Festzinskredit, Festsatzkredit, Festdarlehen
- rate loan portfolio   Festzinskreditportefeuille, Volumen der Festzinskredite
- rate mortgage   Festzinshypothek
- rate period   Festschreibungsfrist, Bindungsfrist
- term   Festlaufzeit
- terms   Festkonditionen

fixing   (a) Festsetzung, Feststellung (z.B. des amtlichen Mittelkurses; (b) Ermittlung des Goldpreises
- of the loan terms   Festlegung der Anleihemodalitäten (der Kreditkonditionen), Benehmen herstellen

fixture   Darlehen mit einer festgeschriebenen Laufzeit und Festzinssatz
- period   Festschreibungszeitraum

flat / flat quotation   Notierung einschließlich Stückzinsen

flat
- commitment fee   pauschale Bereitstellungsprovision
- market   lustlose Börse
- selling commission   pauschale Vertriebsprovision
- yield   Umlaufsrendite

flexible pricing policy   flexible Konditionengestaltung

flexirate (flexible-rate) mortgage   variabel verzinsliche Hypothek

float   Valutierungserlös, Wertstellungsgewinn (Zinsertrag, der durch den Unterschied zwischen der wertmäßigen Belastung des Kontos des Zahlenden und der wertstellungsmäßigen Gutschrift auf dem Konto des Zahlungsempfängers entsteht)

float v.   (a) auflegen, begeben (Anleihe, Emission); (b) freigeben (Wechselkurs)
 to - a loan   eine Anleihe begeben
 to - in the Eurobond market   am Eurobond-Markt auflegen
 to - the exchange rate   den Wechselkurs freigeben, floaten

floater   variabel verzinsliche Anleihe, variabel verzinslicher Schuldschein floater market Markt in variabel verzinslichen Anleihen (Schuldscheinen)

floating-rate
- bond variabel verzinsliche Anleihe
- certificates of deposit variabel verzinsliche Einlagenzertifikate
- dollar debt variabel verzinsliche Dollaranleihe
- loan zinsvariables Darlehen
- mortgage zinsvariable Hypothek
- notes variabel verzinsliche Kassenobligationen (Schuldscheine)

float profit Wertstellungsgewinn, Valutierungserlös

floor (a) Börsenparkett; (b) Untergrenze, Mindestpreis
- brokerage Händlergebühr
- member Börsenmitglied
- plan accommodation (arrangement) Form der Warenbestandsfinanzierung (US)
- price Mindestpreis
- support point unterer Interventionspunkt

FNMA → Federal National Mortgage Association

follow-on financing Anschlußfinanzierung

follow-through support Kursbefestigung durch Anschlußaufträge

follow-up loan Anschlußkredit

FOMC → Federal Open Market Committee

foreclose v. die Zwangsvollstreckung betreiben

foreclosure Zwangsvollstreckung
- on a mortgage (on a mortgage loan) Zwangsvollstreckung in eine Hypothekenforderung
- proceedings Zwangsvollstreckungsverfahren
- rate Anzahl der Zwangsvollstreckungen
- sale Zwangsversteigerung

Foreign Credit Insurance Association US-Export-Kreditversicherungsgesellschaft

foreign currency Fremdwährung, FW
- balances Devisenguthaben, FW-Guthaben
- bill Fremdwährungswechsel, FW-Wechsel
- bond Fremdwährungsanleihe
- borrowing FW-Kreditaufnahme
- exposure FW-Engagement
- lendings Ausleihungen in Fremdwährungen, FW-Kredite

foreign exchange Devisen
- dealer Devisenhändler
- earnings Deviseneinnahmen, Erträge aus Devisengeschäften
- exposure Fremdwährungsengagement; eingegangene Kursrisiken; Fremdwährungsverbindlichkeiten
- forecast Wechselkursprognose
- futures Devisentermingeschäfte
- guarantee Kurssicherung
- holdings Devisenbestände, Devisenreserven
- market Devisenmarkt
- positions Devisenbestände, Fremdwährungsengagements
- risk Wechselkursrisiko
- risk management Devisenkurssicherung, Kurssicherungsmaßnahmen
- trading income Erträge aus dem Devisenhandel

foreign stocks (sector, issues) Auslandsaktien, Auslandswerte

forfaiting Forfaitierung
- house Forfaitierer
- portfolio Forfaitierungsvolumen
- premium Forfaitierungsprämie
- transaction Forfaitierungsgeschäft

forfeit v. verwirken
forfeited shares kaduzierte Aktien
all interest is forfeited if alle Zinsen verfallen, wenn

forgiveness of interest Zinsverzicht

formula plan Anlageplan (US)

forward
- buyer Terminkäufer
- commitments Terminengagements, Terminpositionen
- cover Terminsicherung
- currency dealings (trading) Devisenterminhandel
- deal Termingeschäft
- dealings Terminhandel
- discount Terminabschlag
- dollar Termindollar

forward exchange (a) Termindevisen; (b) Terminbörse
- dealings Devisenterminhandel
- exposure Terminengagements in Fremdwährungen
- guarantee costs Kurssicherungskosten
- loss Kurssicherungsverlust
- market Devisenterminmarkt
- profit Kurssicherungsgewinn

forward
- option Terminoption

- outright Devisenkauf bzw. -verkauf zu einem bestimmten Termin
- premium Terminaufgeld
- purchase Terminkauf
- quotation (rate) Terminkurs, Terminnotierung
- sale Terminverkauf
- securities Terminpapiere

fourth market computergestützter Interbankenmarkt für Wertpapiere

fractional
- amounts Spitzenbeträge
- rise in equities geringfügiger Anstieg der Aktienkurse
- shares Aktienspitzen
- units Anteilsbruchteile

fractions Spitzen
- account Spitzenkonto
- settlement Spitzenregulierung

franchise Selbstbehalt

franked investment income steuerfreie (bereits versteuerte) Kapitalerträge

FRB →Federal Reserve Bank

FRCDs → floating-rate certificates of deposit

free banking kostenlose Führung eines Bankkontos

free market quotation außerbörsliche Notierung

fresh
- buying Zukäufe (von Wertpapieren)
- funding Finanzspritze, Kapitalspritze
- issue Neuemission
- money neue (zusätzliche) Kredite
- orders Neuengagements (in Wertpapieren)

fringe banking   Teilzahlungskreditgeschäfte, sekundäre Bankdienstleistungen

FRNs → floating rate notes

front-door transaction   Kreditaufnahme der Diskonthäuser bei der Bank of England

front-end finance   zusätzlicher Kredit, ergänzende Finanzierung

front-end loading   (a) Aufzinsung (d.h. die bei einem Kredit anfallenden Zinsen werden der Darlehenssumme hinzugeschlagen oder sind in einem Betrag zu Beginn der Laufzeit zu entrichten); (b) zusätzliche Bearbeitungsgebühr, die der Darlehenssumme hinzugeschlagen wird; (c) Erhebung eines Ausgabeaufschlages auf Fondsanteile

front-end load plan   Anlageprogramm eines Investmentfonds, bei dem in den ersten Jahren ein besonders hoher Ausgabeaufschlag auf Fondsanteile erhoben wird

front loading → front-end loading

frozen balances   gesperrte (festliegende) Guthaben

FRS → Federal Reserve System

FSLIC → Federal Savings and Loan Insurance Corporation

full faith and credit bond   Kommunalobligation bzw. Bundesanleihe, die nur durch die Kreditwürdigkeit bzw. Finanzhoheit der emittierenden Regierungsstelle gedeckt ist(US)

full management agency   Vermögensverwaltung, bei der dem Vermögensverwalter Dispositionsbefugnis eingeräumt wird

full recourse financing   Finanzierung mit uneingeschränktem Rückgriff

full set clean on board bills of lading   voller Satz reiner Seekonnossemente

full stock   Aktien mit einem Nennwert von $ 100

fully
- depreciated assets   voll abgeschriebene Vermögenswerte
- diluted earnings per share   Gewinn je Aktie unter Berücksichtigung aller Umtauschrechte
- drawn loan   voll in Anspruch genommener Kredit
- paid share   voll eingezahlte Aktie
- subscribed issue   vollständig gezeichnete Emission
- tax-supported obligations   Kommunalobligationen, die durch die Finanzhoheit der emittierenden Gebietskörperschaft gedeckt sind (US)

fund   Fonds

fund   v. (a) finanzieren; (b) refinanzieren; (c) fundieren

to - an account   ein Konto auffüllen

to - at matching currencies   währungskongruent refinanzieren

to - at matching maturities   laufzeitkongruent refinanzieren

to - its lendings in the interbank market   sich am Interbankenmarkt refinanzieren

to - itself on favourable terms   sich zu günstigen Konditionen refinanzieren

to - new advances   neue Ausreichungen finanzieren

funder   Kreditgeber, Kapitalgeber

funding   (a) Finanzierung; (b) Refinanzierung; (c) Fundierung
- capital   Refinanzierungsmittel
- costs   Finanzierungskosten, Refinanzierungskosten

funding
- costs of the banking system Refinanzierungskosten (Geldbeschaffungskosten) der Banken
- difficulties Finanzierungsschwierigkeiten; Schwierigkeiten bei der Refinanzierung
- in the open market Refinanzierung am freien Markt
- loan Fundierungsanleihe
- of lending operations Refinanzierung des Aktivgeschäftes
- of loans requiring renewal Refinanzierung des Anpassungsgeschäftes
- option Finanzierungsoption (die Weltbank übernimmt einen Anteil an einem Konsortialkredit, den Geschäftsbanken einem Entwicklungsland gewähren)
- requirements Finanzierungsbedarf, Refinanzierungserfordernisse
- scheme Finanzierungsprogramm
- sources Finanzierungsquellen; Refinanzierungsquellen

fund manager Verwaltungsgesellschaft eines Investmentfonds

fund of funds Dachfonds

fund-raising Kapitalbeschaffung, Mittelbeschaffung
- cost Geldbeschaffungskosten
- instruments Geldbeschaffungspapiere

funds (a) Gelder, Mittel, Kapital; (b) Staatstitel (Br)
- generated internally Eigenmittel
- transfer Überweisungsverkehr

fund share redemptions Mittelrückflüsse, Rücknahmen von Fondsanteilen

fund share sales Mittelzuflüsse, Verkäufe von Fondsanteilen

fungible securities vertretbare (fungible) Wertpapiere

futures Termingeschäfte
- contract Terminkontrakt
- exchange Terminbörse
- hedge Terminsicherung
- market Terminmarkt
- trading Terminhandel

FX → foreign exchange

G

<u>gain</u>   Gewinn, Überschuß

- on redemption   Rückzahlungsgewinn
- on retirement of debts   Überschuß aus der Ablösung von Verbindlichkeiten
- on securities   Wertpapiergewinne

<u>gaming stocks</u>   Aktien von Unternehmen der Unterhaltungsindustrie

<u>gang</u> v.to - up   sich zum Erwerb oder Verkauf eines Aktienpaketes zusammenschließen

<u>gazette entry</u>   Veröffentlichung im Amtsblatt

<u>gear</u> v. to - up   Kapital (Kredite) aufnehmen

<u>gearing ratio</u>   Verschuldungsgrad, Verhältnis zwischen Eigen- und Fremdkapital

<u>general</u>
- charge for bad and doubtful debt provisions   Sammelwertberichtigung
- common stock fund   Aktienfonds
- endorsement   Blankoindossament
- loan loss provisions   Sammelwertberichtigung auf Kredite
- loss provisions for undiscernible risks   Sammelwertberichtigung für nicht erkennbare Risiken
- meeting   Hauptversammlung
- mortgage bond   nachrangiger Pfandbrief
- obligations   Kommunalobligationen, die nur durch die Kreditwürdigkeit bzw. Finanzhoheit der emittierenden Gebietskörperschaft gedeckt sind (US)
- power of attorney   Gesamtvollmacht
- warranty deed   Kaufvertrag, bei dem sich der Verkäufer verpflichtet, den Käufer gegen mögliche Eigentumsansprüche Dritter schadlos zu halten (US)

<u>generate</u> v.   beschaffen, aufbringen

to - interest   Zinsen abwerfen

to - new business   neue Kunden akquirieren

<u>Gensaki</u>   Pensionsgeschäft in Yen

<u>gilt-edged</u>
- investment   (a) Anlage in Staatspapieren; (b) erstklassige (mündelsichere) Anlage
- market   Markt für Staatstitel (Br)
- portfolio   Bestand an Staatstiteln
- securities   Staatstitel (Br)

<u>gilts</u> → gilt-edged securities

<u>Ginnie Mae mortgages</u>   Hypotheken der Government National Mortgage Association

<u>giro system</u>   Giroverkehr, bargeldloser Zahlungsverkehr

<u>giro transfer</u>   Banküberweisung

<u>give</u> v. to - first call   einen erstrangigen Anspruch einräumen

<u>givers-on</u>   Reportnehmer

<u>Glass-Steagall Act</u>   US-Kreditwesengesetz, das die Trennung zwischen Einlagen- und Kreditgeschäft auf der einen und dem Wertpapiergeschäft auf der anderen Seite bzw.

die Trennung zwischen Geschäftsbanken und Emissionshäusern vorsieht

gliding bands   gleitende Bandbreiten

GNMA ⟶ Government National Mortgage Association

go
- to - into default on the loan terms   mit der Rückzahlung eines Kredites in Verzug geraten
- to - to a discount   mit einem Disagio notiert werden

going
- concern   tätiges Unternehmen
- concern value   Unternehmenswert, Substanzwert
- ex dividend   ex Dividende notiert werden
- non-recourse   in ein Engagement ohne Rückgriffsmöglichkeit umgewandelt werden
- public   an der Börse notiert werden; in eine Aktiengesellschaft umgewandelt werden

gold   Gold
- actual   Goldbarren; Anlagen in Goldbarren
- bullion   Goldbarren
- bullion standard   Goldkernwährung
- equities   Goldaktien
- forward contracts (futures)   Goldterminkontrakte
- indexed bonds   an die Goldnotiz gebundene Anleihen
- premium   Goldagio
- trading   Goldhandel

gone-concern value   Liquidationswert

good commercial paper   (a) diskontfähiges Wechselmaterial;
(b) beleihbare kurzfristige Industrieschuldtitel (US)

good this week (month)   für eine Woche (Monat) gültiges Börsenlimit

good till cancel order   Auf-Widerruf-Auftrag; bis zur ausdrücklichen Annullierung gültiger Börsenauftrag

good title   einwandfreier Rechtsanspruch

good value   (a) sofort realisierbar (verfügbar); (b) Barmittel

government bond   Staatsanleihe, öffentliche Anleihe

government borrowings in the capital market   staatliche Kapitalmarktbeanspruchung

Government National Mortgage Association (Ginnie Mae)   staatliche Hypothekenkredit- und Pfandbriefanstalt (US)

government security dealer   Händler in Staatstiteln

governments   Staatstitel

grace period   (a) Nachfrist, Respekttage; (b) tilgungsfreie Jahre

graduated-interest loan   Staffelanleihe

graduated-payment mortgage   Hypothek mit gestaffelten Tilgungsleistungen

grandfathering   Verschachtelung zur Besitzstandswahrung (US)

grantee   Käufer (US)

grantor   Verkäufer (US)

grantor's title   Eigentumsrechte des Verkäufers

green clause   Farbklausel; im Akkreditivgeschäft: Gewährung von Vorschüssen gegen dingliche Sicherheit grossed-up dividend Dividende einschließlich Steuergutschrift

gross interest income Zinsertrag vor Steuern

gross return Bruttoverzinsung

group Gruppe, Konzern
- accounts Konzernabschluß
- collection Sammelinkasso
- division Konzernbereich
- exposure Konzernengagement, Gruppenengagement
- of banks Bankenkonsortium, Bankengruppe
- of Ten Zehnerklub (Gruppierung der zehn wichtigsten Industrieländer)
- of Thirty Beratungsgremium für wirtschafts- und währungspolitische Fragen (setzt sich aus Zentralbankiers, Unternehmern und Wissenschaftlern zusammen)

growth Wachstum
- fund Wachstumsfonds
- in deposits Einlagenzuwachs
- target range Wachstumskorridor

GTC order ⟶ good till cancel order

guarantee (a) Garantie, Bürgschaft, Sicherheit, Aval; (b) Garantienehmer, Garantiebegünstigter

guarantee v. garantieren, gewährleisten, avalieren

guaranteed coupon garantierte Verzinsung

guaranteed stocks Aktien, bei denen Dividendenzahlungen durch eine dritte Partei garantiert werden

guarantee
- acceptance Avalakzept
- accommodation Avalhinauslegung
- agreement Garantievertrag
- bond Garantieurkunde, Garantieerklärung, Bürgschaftserklärung
- commission Garantieprovision, Avalnutzen, Avalprovision
- commitments Garantieverpflichtungen, Avalobligo
- credit Avalkredit
- deed Garantieurkunde, Bürgschaftsurkunde
- limit (line) Avallinie, Bürgschaftsplafond
- option Garantieoption (die Weltbank übernimmt die Garantie für einen längerfristigen Kredit, den Geschäftsbanken einem Entwicklungsland gewähren)
- period Garantiefrist, Gewährleistungsfrist
- policy Garantieversicherungspolice
- society Garantieversicherungsgesellschaft

guarantor Garantiegeber, Bürge, Avalkreditgeber

guarantor bank avalkreditgebendes Institut

guarantor's liability Haftung des Garantiegebers (des Bürgen)

H

half a bar   Abschluß über
£ 500.000

half stock   Aktien mit einem
Nennwert von $ 50

hard arbitrage   im Geldhandel:
Durchhandeln (Aufnahme von
Geldern und anschließende
Weitergabe zu einem höheren
Zinssatz)

hard-currency country   Hartwährungsland

head mortgage   Rahmenhypothek

heavy industrials   Aktien der
Schwerindustrie

heavy stockholder   Großaktionär

hedge   (a) Schutz, Absicherung;
(b) Sicherungsgeschäft, Deckungsgeschäft

hedge v.   absichern, decken; ein
Kurssicherungsgeschäft abschließen

dollars hedged forward   kursgesicherte Dollars

to - the exchange (currency)
risk   das Wechselkursrisiko abdecken

to - the exposure to loss   das
Verlustrisiko abdecken

to - at matching maturities
fristenkongruent sichern

hedging   Absicherung, Deckung;
Kurssicherung; Abschluß eines
Deckungs-(Kurssicherungs-)Geschäftes

- cost   Kurssicherungskosten

- facilities (options)   Kurssicherungsmöglichkeiten

- policy   Kurssicherungspolitik

- techniques   Kurssicherungsverfahren

HH/H bond   staatlicher Sparbrief (US)

high   Höchstkurs, Höchststand

high-activity account   umsatzstarkes Konto

high-coupon loan   hochverzinsliche
Anleihe

highly-geared company (Br)/ highly
leveraged corporation (US)   Gesellschaft, die mit einem hohen
Fremdkapitalanteil arbeitet

high market   Hausse

high operating leverage   hoher
Fremdkapitalanteil

high-percentage mortgage loan
Hypothek im Rahmen einer Eigenheimfinanzierung, bei der der
Schuldner nur eine geringe Eigenleistung erbracht hat

high-risk exposure   stark gefährdetes Kreditengagement,
Hochrisikoengagement

high-risk investment   mit einem
hohen Risiko behaftete Anlage

highway revenue bonds → turnpike
bonds

hire purchase   Ratenkauf, Teilzahlungskauf

hire purchase financing   Ratenfinanzierung, Teilzahlungsfinanzierung

hire purchases   Aktien von Teilzahlungskreditinstituten

historical cost   Anschaffungswert

historical interest rate   Einstandszins

holding of securities   Wertpapierbesitz, Wertpapierbestand

holding over Zahlungsaufschub bis zum nächsten →settlement day

holding the bank liable Haftbarmachung der Bank

home
- banking terminals Terminals in privaten Haushalten zur Abwicklung von Bankgeschäften
- improvement loan Modernisierungsdarlehen
- loan Wohnungsbaudarlehen
- loan operations Wohnungsbaukreditgeschäft
- loan rates Zinssätze für Wohnungsbaudarlehen

homestead association Bausparkasse (US)

honour v. einlösen, bezahlen

hot issues Spekulationswerte

house umgangssprachlich für das Parkett der Londoner Börse
- bill Eigenwechsel
- call Aufforderung eines Brokers an einen Kunden, zusätzliche Sicherheiten für einen Effektenkredit zu hinterlegen

householder's protest Bestätigung der Nichteinlösung eines Wechsels durch zwei geschäftsfähige Personen (wenn ein Notar nicht verfügbar ist)

housing finance Wohnungsbaugelder; Wohnungsbaufinanzierung

housing loan Wohnungsbaudarlehen

hybrid financing Mischfinanzierung

hypothecation Verpfändung; Belastung
- value Beleihungswert

I

IBFs → International Banking Facilities

IDRs → International Depositary Receipts

immediate order   Tagesauftrag; für einen Tag gültiges Börsenlimit

immediately available funds   sofort verfügbare Gelder

immediately callable   sofort kündbar

impersonal security   Sachsicherheit

improved figures   verbessertes Geschäftsergebnis

inaccurate documents   unstimmige Dokumente

inadequate capital base   unzureichende Kapitalausstattung

income   Ertrag, Gewinn
- account   Erfolgskonto
- for the year   Jahresüberschuß
- from investment securities   Erträge aus Wertpapieren des Anlagevermögens
- from service transactions   Erträge aus Dienstleistungsgeschäften
- fund   Investmentfonds, dessen Anlageziel auf die Erzielung hoher Ausschüttungen ausgerichtet ist
- gearing   Verhältnis von Finanzaufwendungen zum Gewinn nach Steuern
- shares   von einem → split trust ausgegebene Anteile, auf die nur die Fondserträge ausgeschüttet werden; in der Regel keine Wertsteigerung der Anteile selbst (Gegensatz: → capital shares)

inchoate instrument   unvollständiges Wertpapier

incoming cash letters   eingehende Fernschecks (US)

inconvertible securities   (a) nicht wandelbare Wertpapiere; (b) Wertpapiere, die nur schwer zu realisieren sind

increment   (a) Aufschlag (z.B. auf die Prime Rate); (b) (Wert-) Zuwachs, Steigerung

incremental borrowing   zusätzliche Kreditaufnahme

incumbrance   Belastung

indenture   (a) Vertrag, Urkunde; (b) Anleihevertrag

indenture terms   Anleihemodalitäten

indexed home loan   indexgebundenes Wohnungsbaudarlehen

indexed return   indexgebundene Verzinsung

index fund   Investmentfonds, der seine Mittel in die von einem Börsenindex erfaßten Wertpapiere anlegt

indexing a portfolio → portfolio indexing

index-linked futures   Index-Terminkontrakte

indirect arbitrage (exchange)   indirekte Devisenarbitrage, Mehrfacharbitrage

individual loan   Personaldarlehen

341

individually negotiated terms
and rates individuelle Konditionengestaltung

individual retirement account(IRA)
steuerbegünstigtes Spar- bzw.
Depotkonto (im Rahmen der privaten Altersvorsorge - US)

individual shareholder Einzelaktionär

industrial
- aid bonds kapitalertragssteuerfreie Kommunalobligationen (zur Finanzierung von Industrieprojekten)
- bond Industrieschuldverschreibung, Industrieobligation
- demand for credit Kreditnachfrage der Unternehmen
- equities Industrieaktien
- issues Industriewerte
- loan Industriekredit; Betriebsmittelkredit
- revenue bonds projektgebundene Industrieobligationen (werden von kommunalen Stellen in Zusammenarbeit mit Banken oder gegen Bankbürgschaften emittiert) (US)

industrials Industrieaktien; Industriewerte

ineligible bill nicht rediskontfähiger Wechsel

inflation-fed borrowing requirements inflationsbedingter Kreditbedarf

inflation hedge Inflationsschutz

in-hall ATMs Bankautomaten in der Schalterhalle

initial
- coupon Anfangsverzinsung
- debt service Anfangsbelastung, Zins- und Tilgungszahlungen zu Beginn der Laufzeit

- dividend Abschlagsdividende
- margin percentage Mindestdeckung, die bei einem Effektenkredit vorhanden sein muß
- maturity Anfangslaufzeit
- offering price Ausgabekurs, Erstausgabepreis
- public offerings Erstemissionen, Neuemissionen (US)
- rate Tilgungsrate (Tilgungshöhe) zu Beginn der Laufzeit

inpayment slip Einzahlungsbeleg

inscribed shares Namensaktien

instalment Rate
- credit Teilzahlungskredit, Ratenkredit
- credit bank Teilzahlungsbank
- lendings Teilzahlungsgeschäft

institutional
- buying Käufe durch institutionelle Anleger
- dominance Marktbeherrschung durch institutionelle Anleger
- investors / institutions institutionelle Anleger
- placing Plazierung bei institutionellen Anlegern

instruments of monetary policy
geldpolitisches Instrumentarium

insurance money Gewinn eines jobber bei einem →bed and breakfast deal (Br)

insurances / insurance shares
Versicherungsaktien, Versicherungswerte

insured bank Bank, deren Einlagen durch die→ Federal Deposit Insurance Corporation versichert sind (US)

intensive care unit Bankabteilung, die für die Sanierung in Zahlungsschwierigkeiten geratener Kunden zuständig ist (Br)

<u>interbank</u>
- cost of money Refinanzierungskosten am Interbanken-Markt
- dealings Interbanken-Handel
- facility Interbanken-Fazilität
- lendings Bank-an-Bank Kredite, Interbanken-Forderungen
- market Interbanken-Markt
- money Bankengelder
- money market Bankengeldmarkt
- money market rates Geldmarktsätze unter Banken
- payments Interbanken-Zahlungsverkehr
- rate Interbanken-Rate
- spreads Margen im Interbanken--Markt (Zinsdifferenz, zu der die Banken untereinander Gelder anbieten und hereinnehmen)

<u>interchangeable bond</u> Anleihe, die jederzeit gegen eine andere Anleihe ausgetauscht werden kann

<u>intercompany money dealings</u> Industrie-Clearing, Geldhandelsgeschäfte zwischen Industrieunternehmen

<u>interest</u> (a) Zinsen, Zinssatz; (b) Anteil, Beteiligung
- accrued angefallene Zinsen, Stückzinsen
- and fees on loans Zinsen und zinsähnliche Erträge im Kreditgeschäft
- and redemption payments Zins- und Tilgungszahlungen, Schuldendienst
- at 1/4 % over six-month LIBOR Verzinsung mit einem Aufschlag von 1/4% auf Sechsmonats-LIBOR
- at the short (long) end of the market Zinsen im kurz- (lang-)fristigen Bereich
- bearing verzinslich
- burden Zinsbelastung, Zinslast

- ceiling Zinsobergrenze, Höchstzins
- charges Zinsaufwand, Schuldzinsen
- credit Zinsgutschrift
- expenditure Zinsaufwand, Zinskosten
- for equities was in low key die Nachfrage nach Aktien hielt sich in engen Grenzen
- forgiveness Zinsverzicht
- forgiveness programme eine Bank erhält anstelle von Zinszahlungen Stammaktien des Kreditnehmers
- free zinslos
- hike Zinserhöhung, Zinssteigerung
- income net of interest expense Nettozinsertrag
- increment above prime Zinsaufschlag auf die Prime Rate
- level Zinshöhe, Zinsniveau
- load charge Zinslast
- loss Zinsverlust, Zinsausfall
- margin Zinsspanne
- netting zinsmäßige Kompensation
- omission Ausfall der Zinszahlungen
- on arrears Verzugszinsen
- on the principal Zinsen auf die Darlehenssumme
- payment (a) Zinszahlung; (b) Verzinsung
- payment deferral Zinsstundung
- penalty Strafzins, Negativzins
- penalty for early withdrawal Vorschußzinsen
- premium Zinsaufschlag

<u>interest rate</u> Zinssatz, Zinsfuß
- anticipation switch Portefeuilleumschichtung in Erwartung von Zinssatzänderungen
- cartel Zinskartell

interest rate
- concessions Zinszugeständnisse
- cut Zinssenkung, Zinsermäßigung
- cycle Zinszyklus
- futures contract Zinsterminkontrakt
- futures trading Terminhandel in Zinspapieren
- hedging Zinssatzsicherung
- level Zinsniveau, Zinshöhe
- pattern Zinsstruktur, Zinskonstellation
- peak Zinsgipfel
- range Zinsfächer
- spread Zinsspanne
- swap Zins-Swap (bei dem ein Schuldner die variabel verzinsliche Anleihe eines anderen Schuldners übernimmt)
- swings Zinsschwankungen, Zinsausschläge
- uncertainty Zinsunsicherheit
- volatility Zinsschwankungen

interest
- revenue Zinserträge
- sensitive stock zinsreagible Aktien
- subsidies Zinszuschüsse, Zinsbeihilfen
- subsidised loans zinsverbilligte Kredite
- terms Zinskonditionen
- warrant Zinsschein, Kupon

interim dividend Zwischendividende, Abschlagsdividende

interim loan Zwischenkredit, Überbrückungskredit

Intermarket Trading System elektronisches Kursanzeigesystem, durch das die wichtigsten US-Börsen miteinander verbunden sind

intermediate days die letzten drei Börsentage vor dem → account day

intermediate holding company Zwischenholding-Gesellschaft

intermediate maturities mittelfristige Laufzeiten

internal financing Eigenfinanzierung; Innenfinanzierung

internal funds / internally generated funds eigene Mittel, Eigenmittel

International Banking Facilities Bankniederlassungen (oft ausgegliederte Geschäftsbereiche einer Bank) in den USA, die in erster Linie auf das Eurowährungsgeschäft spezialisiert sind und nicht den üblichen Reservevorschriften unterliegen

international cash management grenzüberschreitendes Management der liquiden Mittel und Kursrisiken (→ cash management)

international dealer / dealership Wertpapierhändler, der Geschäfte ausschließlich in Auslandswerten abwickelt

International Depositary Receipts Inhaberzertifikate, die bei Parallelemissionen ausländischer Kapitalgesellschaften durch die konsortialführenden Inlandsbanken aufgelegt werden

international lending operations (activities) Auslandskreditgeschäft

international margin Zinsspanne im Auslandsgeschäft

International Monetary Fund Weltwährungsfonds

inter-office trading Telefonverkehr

interstate banking   Eröffnung von Bankfilialen in verschiedenen Bundesstaaten (US)

intervention   Intervention
- currency   Interventionswährung
- in the foreign exchange market   Intervention am Devisenmarkt
- rate   Interventionskurs

in the money   Bezeichnung für eine Situation, in der der Options-Basiskurs unter dem Tageskurs der zugrunde liegenden Papiere liegt

introduction on the stock exchange   Börseneinführung

introduction syndicate   Einführungskonsortium

invariable interest and redemption payments   gleichbleibende Zins- und Tilgungszahlungen

inventory financing   Warenbestandsfinanzierung, Finanzierung des Vorratsvermögens

inventory lending   Beleihung des Warenbestandes

investment   (a) Investition; (b) Kapitalanlage; (c) Beteiligung
- account   Sparkonto; Festgeldkonto
- advisor   Anlageberater
- bank   Emissionsbank
- Bankers Association   Verband der Emissionshäuser (US)
- banking   Emissionsgeschäft
- banking techniques   Emissionstechniken
- buying   Anlagekäufe
- certificate   Anteilschein, Investmentzertifikat
- company   Kapitalanlagegesellschaft, Investmentgesellschaft
- income   Kapitalerträge, Erträge aus Beteiligungen

- interest   Anlegerinteresse
- fund share   Investmentfondsanteil
- management   Vermögensverwaltung
- management company   (a) Anlageberatungsgesellschaft; (b) Verwaltungsgesellschaft eines Investmentfonds
- outlet   Anlagemöglichkeit; Parkmöglichkeit
- performance   Anlageergebnis, Anlageerfolg
- rating   Anlagebewertung
- securities   Anlagepapiere, Beteiligungswerte
- shift   Depotumschichtung, Portefeuilleumschichtung
- spread   Anlagestreuung
- supervision in connection with trust functions   Vermögensverwaltung durch eine Bank, die gleichzeitig als Treuhänder fungiert (US)
- trust   Investmentfonds (mit festgelegter Emissionshöhe)

investor   Anleger

investors' imagination   Börsenphantasie

invitation for subscription (to subscribe)   Zeichnungsaufforderung, Bezugsaufforderung

invitation telex   Fernschreiben, mit dem ein Konsortialführer zur Zeichnung von Quoten einlädt

invite v.   to - subscriptions for   zur Zeichnung auflegen

invoice discounting   Bevorschussung von Forderungen

IPOs → initial public offerings

IRA → individual retirement account

IRBs → industrial revenue bonds

irrevocable documentary credit   unwiderrufliches Akkreditiv

345

issue (a) Emission, Ausgabe
(Wertpapiere); (b) Ausstellung
(Schecks, Wechsel)

the - has a seven-year life
(maturity) and pays (carries)
a 9 p.c. coupon die Emission
hat eine Laufzeit von sieben
Jahren und wird mit 9 % verzinst

taking up an - and selling it on
a best efforts basis Übernahme
einer Emission zur Verkaufsvermittlung

issue v. (a) emittieren, ausgeben; (b) ausstellen

to - through the tap im Wege
der Daueremission begeben

issue

- at a discount Unterpari--Emission, Emission mit einem
  Abschlag (Disagio)

- at a premium Überpari-Emission,
  Emission mit einem Aufschlag
  (Agio)

- at par Emission zum Nennwert,
  Pari-Emission

- calendar Emissionskalender,
  Emissionsfahrplan

- manager Konsortialführer

- market Emissionsmarkt

- price Emissionskurs, Ausgabekurs

issuing

- activity Emissionstätigkeit

- agency emittierende Stelle
  (Behörde)

- approval Emissionsgenehmigung

- bank (a) Emissionsbank; (b)
  Akkreditivbank, eröffnende Bank

- cost Emissionskosten

- currency Emissionswährung

- discount Emissionsdisagio,
  Emissionsabschlag

- freeze Emissionsstopp

- house Emissionsinstitut,
  Emissionsunternehmen

- premium Emissionsagio,
  Emissionsaufgeld

- prospectus Emissionsprospekt

- share Konsortialquote

- syndicate Emissionskonsortium

- yield Emissionsrendite

items in transit   Inkassopapiere

ITS ⟶ Intermarket Trading System

J

jacket custody Sonderverwahrung, Streifbandverwahrung

jobber Eigenhändler; Händler, der für eigene Rechnung kauft und verkauft

jobber's turn Händlerspanne

jobbing in and out spekulative Käufe und Verkäufe von Wertpapieren

joint
- account Gemeinschaftskonto
- and several debtor Gesamtschuldner
- and several guarantee gesamtschuldnerische Bürgschaft
- authority to draw (to operate an account) gemeinschaftliche Verfügungsberechtigung
- debtor Mitschuldner
- financing Verbundfinanzierung, Gemeinschaftsfinanzierung
- floating Gruppenfloating, Blockfloating
- issue Gemeinschaftsemission
- loan extension Gemeinschaftskredit
- venture Gemeinschaftsunternehmen

jumbo
- deal Großemission, Jumbogeschäft
- floater große Emission variabel verzinslicher Schuldscheine
- loans umfangreiche syndizierte Eurokredite

junior mortgage loan nachrangiges Hypothekendarlehen

K

kaffirs Sammelname für südafrikanische Werte an der Londoner Börse

key lending rates Leitzinsen

kicker (a) Vergünstigung, die ein emittierendes Unternehmen oder ein Kreditnehmer dem Kreditgeber gewährt (in der Regel eine zusätzliche Provision oder Stammaktien der Gesellschaft); (b)→equity kicker

kite Kellerwechsel

L

lack of fresh support Börse: Mangel an Anschlußaufträgen

lack of funds fehlende Deckung

lag v. to - behind the index hinter dem Index zurückbleiben

lagging Verzögerung bei der Begleichung von Fremdwährungsverbindlichkeiten (→leading)

land
- charge Grundstücksbelastung, Grundschuld
- charge deed Grundschuldurkunde, Grundschuldbrief
- credit Hypothekenkredit
- credit bank Hypothekenkreditbank, Realkreditinstitut
- Records Office Grundbuchamt (US)
- Registry Grundbuch; Grundbuchamt (Br)

large-block transactions Pakethandel

large-denomination
- money-market securities Geldmarktpapiere in großen Stükkelungen
- securities Jumbo-Stücke, Wertpapiere in großen Stückelungen

large loan Großkredit

large-scale
- investor Großanleger
- lendings Großkreditgeschäft

large-volume account umsatzstarkes Konto

late dealings Abschlüsse gegen Schluß der Börsensitzung

late quotation Schlußnotierung

launch v. begeben, auflegen, einführen
to - a bond issue eine Anleihe auflegen
to - dollar-denominated issues Emissionen im Dollarbereich begeben
to - a fund einen Fonds auflegen

launch / launching Auflegung, Begebung, Einführung

lead v. ein Konsortium führen, als Konsortialführer fungieren

lead bank Führungsbank, Konsortialführerin

leaders Standardaktien, Spitzenwerte

leading vorgezogene Begleichung von Fremdwährungsverbindlichkeiten (→lagging)

leading bank → lead bank

lead-manage v. → to lead
lead-managed (led) by XYZ bank unter Führung der XYZ Bank

lead-management group Führungsgruppe

lead manager Konsortialführer(in)

legal
- lending limit Kreditobergrenze; Höchstgrenze für die Ausleihungen einer Bank (US)
- list Verzeichnis mündelsicherer Wertpapiere (US)
- opinion Rechtsgutachten
- placements mündelsichere Anlagen (US)

- reserves gesetzliche Rücklagen
- securities mündelsichere Wertpapiere (US)

legals ⟶ legal securities

lend v. ausleihen, ausreichen; kreditieren, beleihen

lender Kreditgeber, Geldgeber

lender of funds im Geldhandel: Geber auf dem Geldmarkt

lending (a) Kredit, Ausleihung; (b) Kreditgewährung, Kreditierung; (c) Beleihung

lending against a second or later mortgage nachrangige Beleihung

lending on goods Warenlombardgeschäft, Beleihung von Waren

lending on securities Effektenlombardgeschäft, Effektenkredit, Wertpapierbeleihung

lendings at matching maturities fristenkongruente (laufzeitkongruente) Ausleihungen

lendings in the interbank market Ausleihungen im Interbanken-Markt, Interbanken-Forderungen

lendings to corporate/private customers Firmen-/Privatkundenkredite, Ausleihungen an die Firmen-/Privatkundschaft

lending
- activities Kreditgeschäft, Aktivgeschäft einer Bank, Kreditverkehr
- authority Kreditkompetenz
- bank kreditgebende (kreditausreichende, kreditierende) Bank
- business ⟶ lending activities
- capacity Kreditkapazität, Kreditpotential
- ceiling Kreditplafond; Höchstgrenze für die Ausleihungen einer Bank
- charges Kreditkosten
- commitment (a) Kreditengagement; (b) Kreditzusage
- constraints Kreditbeschränkungen
- currency Kreditvaluta
- interest Kreditzinsen, Aktivzinsen
- interest margin Aktivzinsmarge
- limit (a) ⟶ lending ceiling; (b) Beleihungsgrenze
- operations ⟶ lending activities
- pattern Struktur des Aktivgeschäftes (der Ausleihungen)
- policy Kreditpolitik
- portfolio Kreditportefeuille, Ausleihvolumen
- potential Kreditpotential
- power (a) Kreditkompetenz; (b) Kreditpotential, Kreditkapazität
- rate Kreditzins, Zinssatz für Ausleihungen
- scheme Kreditprogramm
- squeeze Kreditbeschränkungen
- terms Kreditkonditionen, Kreditsätze, Konditionen im Aktivgeschäft, Aktivkonditionen
- undertaking Kreditzusage
- value Beleihungswert

letter of
- allocation (allotment) Zuteilungsanzeige
- awareness Patronatserklärung
- comfort Wohlwollenserklärung, Kreditbesicherungsgarantie
- indemnity Schadlosbürgschaft, Entschädigungsgarantie
- intent Absichtserklärung
- responsibility Verpflichtungserklärung, Patronatserklärung
- rights Bezugsrechtsangebot
- set-off Vereinbarung, durch die ein Kunde die Bank zur Verrechnung von Haben- und Sollsalden ermächtigt

letter of subordination Rangrücktrittserklärung

letter stock fund Aktienfonds,
der die ihm zufließenden Mittel
in erster Linie in privat plazierten bzw. spekulativen Papieren investiert

level earnings gleichbleibende
Erträge

leverage Verschuldungsgrad,
Verhältnis zwischen Fremdkapital
und Eigenkapital, Kapitalstruktur; bei einem Hauskauf: Verhältnis zwischen aufgenommenen
Krediten bzw. Hypotheken und
Eigenleistung

leverage v. the company has
leveraged at a ratio of 4:1
die Gesellschaft hat sich im
Verhältnis von 4:1 verschuldet

leveraged buy-out Aufkauf einer
Kapitalgesellschaft durch das
Firmenmanagement

leverage fund Investment-Fonds,
der das Fondsvermögen auch durch
Kredite finanziert

leverage ratio Verschuldungs-
kennzahl

leverage risk Kapitalstruktur-
risiko

liabilities Verbindlichkeiten

- and stockholders' equity
  Passiva; Verbindlichkeiten
  und Eigenkapital

- from the drawing and endorsement
  of bills Verbindlichkeiten aus
  der Begebung und Übertragung
  von Wechseln

- management Passivsteuerung,
  Passivmanagement

- on forward exchange contracts
  Verbindlichkeiten aus Devisentermingeschäften

- on guarantees furnished Verbindlichkeiten aus Bürgschaften

- on repurchase agreements Verbindlichkeiten aus Pensionsgeschäften

- to banks Verbindlichkeiten
  gegenüber Kreditinstituten

- to depositors Verbindlichkeiten
  aus Einlagen

liability (a) Haftung, Obligo;
(b) Verbindlichkeit, Verpflichtung

- bond Haftungserklärung

- on bills purchased Obligo aus
  angekauften Wechseln

- on a guarantee Garantiehaftung,
  Haftung aus einer Garantie

- on loans extended against guarantees furnished by us Obligo
  aus unter unserer Haftung hinausgelegten Krediten

- structure Passivstruktur; Struktur des Passivgeschäftes

- to the customer Haftung gegenüber dem Kunden

LIBOR rate Londoner Interbanken-
-Angebotssatz

licensed dealer Wertpapierhändler, der Geschäfte auf eigene
Rechnung vornehmen kann

licensed deposit taker Kreditinstitut, das nach dem Banking Act
1979 durch die Bank of England
zur Hereinnahme von Einlagen ermächtigt wurde

lien Pfandrecht, Sicherungsrecht

- arising by operation of law
  kraft Gesetz entstehendes Pfandrecht, gesetzliches Pfandrecht

- by agreement vertragliches
  Pfandrecht

- by enforcement Pfändungspfand-
  recht

- letter Vereinbarung, durch die
  ein Kunde die Bank zur Verrechnung von Soll- und Habensalden
  ermächtigt

- over movables (personalty) Pfandrecht an beweglichen Sachen

life-boat Sanierungskonsortium, Auffangkonsortium

- issue Emission eines Sanierungskonsortiums

life issues Aktien von Lebensversicherungsgesellschaften

life range Laufzeitpalette

life-to-call Restlaufzeit (bis zur Kündigung)

life-to-maturity Restlaufzeit (bis zur Endfälligkeit)

LIFFE ➞ London International Financial Futures Exchange

light selling geringfügige Abgaben

light share billige Aktie

limitation period Verjährungsfrist

limited
- management agency Vermögensverwaltung ohne Dispositionsbefugnis des Anlageberaters
- market enger (begrenzter) Markt
- order limitierter Börsenauftrag
- recourse financing bei Projektfinanzierungen: Finanzierung mit begrenzter Möglichkeit des Rückgriffs
- service brokerage houses Broker, die nur Kundenaufträge ausführen und keine Anlageberatung offerieren

line bank kreditgebende Bank

line of credit Kreditlinie

line of deposit durchschnittlicher Guthabensaldo eines Kontos

line replacement Erneuerung einer Kreditlinie bzw. Ablösung eines Kredites durch eine neue Kreditvereinbarung

liquid assets flüssige Mittel, Barvermögen

liquidate v. (a) glattstellen (Wertpapierpositionen); (b) verwerten (Sicherheit); (c) tilgen, zurückführen (Kredit)

liquidation (a) Glattstellung, Positionsbereinigung, Positionsglattstellung; (b) Verwertung, Sicherheitenverwertung, Realisierung; (c) Tilgung

liquidation value Realisationswert

liquidity Liquidität, flüssige Mittel
- backups Liquiditätsstützen
- base Liquiditätsbodensatz
- drain Liquiditätsentzug
- in the banking sector Bankenliquidität
- management Liquiditätssteuerung, Liquiditätsdisposition
- margin requirements Liquiditätsvorschriften (z.B. für Mitglieder der Londoner Börse)
- procurement Liquiditätsbeschaffung
- ratio Liquiditätskoeffizient, Liquiditätsgrad
- reserve management Liquiditätsreservehaltung

liquid security liquide Sicherheit (z.B. Spareinlagen, Wertpapierdepots)

list Zeichnungsliste

list closed Zeichnungsschluß

list v. zum Börsenhandel zulassen, an der Börse notieren

listed company börsennotiertes Unternehmen

listed shares (stocks) Börsenwerte, notierte Aktien

listing   Börsennotierung; Börsenzulassung, Zulassung zum Börsenhandel

- approval   Zulassungsbeschluß
- board   Zulassungsstelle
- commission   Börseneinführungsprovision
- committee   Börsenzulassungsausschuß
- notice   Börsenzulassungsbescheid

listless market   lustlose Börse

list of
- applications   Zeichnerliste (bei einer Emission)
- drawings   Auslosungsliste
- quotations   Kursblatt

load charge / loading fee
(a) Ausgabeaufschlag, Ausgabeaufgeld (bei Investmentfondsanteilen); (b) zusätzliche Provision (Bearbeitungsgebühr)

load fund   Investmentfonds, der einen Ausgabeaufschlag auf seine Anteile erhebt

loan   (a) Kredit, Darlehen; (b) Anleihe

loan in default   notleidendes Engagement, notleidender Kredit

loan guaranteed by real security   durch eine dingliche Sicherheit unterlegter Kredit

loans and advances   Ausleihungen, Debitoren einer Bank

loans approved   bewilligte Kredite, Bewilligungsvolumen

loans on preferential terms   Kredite zu Vorzugskonditionen

loans outstanding   Kreditvolumen, Gesamtausleihungen

loans repaid   Kreditrückflüsse, abgelöste (getilgte) Darlehen

loans secured by stock exchange collateral   durch börsenfähige Wertpapiere besicherte (unterlegte) Kredite

loans stated at cost   zum Auszahlungsbetrag ausgewiesene Kredite

loanable funds   Kreditmittel, Darlehensmittel, Darlehensgelder

loan
- accommodation   Kreditgewährung, Kreditausreichung
- account   Darlehenskonto
- administration   Kreditabwicklung
- agreement   (a) Kreditvertrag, Darlehensvertrag; (b) Anleihevertrag
- applicant   Kreditantragsteller, Kreditbewerber
- application   Kreditantrag, Darlehensantrag, Kreditvorlage
- approval   Kreditzusage, Kreditbewilligung
- approval powers   Kreditkompetenz
- book   Kreditportefeuille, Kreditvolumen
- brokerage   Kreditvermittlung
- charge-off   Kreditausfall, Kreditverlust
- charge-offs   Ausfälle im Kreditgeschäft, Debitorenausfälle
- charge-off ratio   Ausfallquote im Kreditgeschäft
- charges   Darlehenskosten, Kreditgebühren
- collateral   Darlehenssicherheit, Kreditsicherheit
- collateral agreement   Kreditsicherungsvertrag
- commitment   Kreditengagement, Darlehenszusage
- committee   Kreditbewilligungsausschuß
- company   Teilzahlungskreditinstitut
- cost   Kreditkosten
- creditor   (a) Kreditgeber; (b) Anleihegläubiger

loan
- curbs Kreditrestriktionen
- debt Darlehensschuld; Anleiheschuld
- debtor Darlehensschuldner; Anleiheschuldner
- demand Kreditnachfrage
- deposit ratio Verhältnis von Ausleihungen zu Einlagen
- disbursement Kreditauszahlung, Darlehensauszahlung, Darlehensvalutierung
- diversification Kreditstreuung, Streuung der Ausleihungen
- documents Kreditunterlagen
- envelope Kreditleitkarte
- exposure Kreditengagement, Gesamtsumme der gewährten Kredite, Ausleihvolumen; Obligo aus einem Kreditengagement
- extension Kreditausreichung, Kreditvergabe, Kreditbereitstellung
- facilities Kreditfazilitäten
- finance (funds) Darlehensmittel, Fremdmittel
- guarantee Kreditbürgschaft
- guarantee scheme Kreditbürgschafts-Programm für die mittelständische Wirtschaft(Br)
- instalment Kredittranche
- interest (a) Kreditzinsen, Darlehenszinsen; (b) Anleihezinsen
- interest rate (a) Kreditzinssatz; (b) Anleihezinssatz
- loss Kreditausfall, Kreditverlust, Forderungsausfall
- loss experience Ausfallerfahrungswerte, Entwicklung der Wertberichtigungen auf Kredite
- loss provisions Rückstellungen im Kreditgeschäft, Wertberichtigungen auf Kredite

  to set up loan loss provisions Risikovorsorge im Kreditgeschäft treffen

- loss provisions required Rückstellungsbedarf im Kreditgeschäft
- loss ratio Ausfallquote im Kreditgeschäft, Kreditausfallverhältnis, Kreditverlustquote
- maturity Kreditfälligkeit, Darlehensfälligkeit; Laufzeit eines Kredites, Darlehenslaufzeit
- offer Kreditangebot, Kreditofferte
- officer Kreditsachbearbeiter
- origination Kreditbereitstellung
- origination fees einmalige Kreditbearbeitungsgebühr
- package Finanzierungspaket
- participation Kreditbeteiligung, Kreditanteil
- payment Kreditrückzahlung, Darlehenstilgung; Tilgungsleistung, Tilgungszahlung
- payment frequency Häufigkeit der Tilgungsleistungen
- percentage Beleihungswert, Beleihungsgrenze (US)
- portfolio (a) Kreditvolumen; (b) Anleiheportefeuille
- pricing (a) Konditionengestaltung, Festsetzung der Kreditkonditionen; (b) Festsetzung des Anleihezinssatzes (der Anleihemodalitäten)
- pricing policy Konditionenpolitik, Kreditpreispolitik
- principal (a) Kreditbetrag, Darlehensbetrag; (b) Anleihebetrag
- production office Kreditvermittlungsbüro (in der Regel die Zweigstelle einer Geschäftsbank)
- rejection Ablehnung eines Kreditantrages
- related costs Kreditnebenkosten
- renewal Krediterneuerung, Darlehensverlängerung, Darlehensprolongation
- repayment Rückzahlung (Abdeckung) eines Kredites, Darlehenstilgung, Kreditrückführung

loan
- repayment capacity materielle Kreditwürdigkeit (US)
- repayment holiday tilgungsfreie Jahre
- repayment schedule Tilgungsplan für einen Kredit
- replacement →line replacement
- respite Darlehensstundung, Stundung der Tilgungsleistungen
- restrictions (a) Kreditrestriktionen; (b) Auflagen für den Kreditnehmer
- risk Kreditrisiko, Darlehensrisiko
- sanction Kreditgenehmigung, Kreditbewilligung
- sanctioning limit Kreditbewilligungsgrenze
- scheme Kreditprogramm
- security agreement Kreditsicherungsvertrag
- service Anleihedienst
- stock Schuldverschreibungen
- syndicate Kreditkonsortium; Anleihekonsortium
- syndication business Kreditsyndizierungen
- terms Kreditkonditionen
- to-value ratio Beleihungsgrenze, Beleihungswert (US)
- undertaking Kreditzusage, Kreditversprechen, Krediteinräumungsschreiben
- write-offs (a) Kreditverluste; (b) Forderungsverzicht von Banken

local
- acceptance Platzakzept
- authority bonds Kommunalobligationen
- bill Platzwechsel
- charges Platzgebühren, Platzverlust
- cheque Platzscheck

lock v.
  to - in an interest rate einen Zinssatz festschreiben
  to - in (up) a loan einen Festsatzkredit vereinbaren, den Zinssatz für einen Kredit festschreiben
  to - into fixed-rate bonds Gelder in Festverzinslichen für einen längeren Zeitraum anlegen
  to - in a profit einen Gewinn sichern

lock-box arrangement (system) Einzug von Forderungen bzw. Verrechnungspapieren durch die Bank im Auftrag eines Firmenkunden (Form des US-Cash Managements)

lock-in arrangement Festsatz-/Festzinsvereinbarung

lock-up arrangement Vorkaufsrecht, Übernahmeoption (im Hinblick auf Aktien oder Betriebsanlagen)

lock-up period (a) Festschreibungszeitraum, Bindungsfrist; (b) Zeitraum zwischen Zeichnungsschluß und Ausgabe der effektiven Stücke

lodge v. hinterlegen; anmelden
  to - a collateral with the bank eine Sicherheit bei der Bank hinterlegen
  to - a proof eine Konkursforderung anmelden

London Interbank Offered Rate Londoner Interbanken-Angebotssatz

London International Financial Futures Exchange Londoner Börse für Finanz-Terminkontrakte

London parity £-Sterling Äquivalent einer Auslandsaktie

long (a) Langläufer; (b) Haussier
- bill Wechsel mit einer Laufzeit von mehr als drei Monaten
- dated issue langfristige Emission
- end of the capital market langes Ende des Kapitalmarktes
- exchange Fremdwährungswechsel mit einer Laufzeit von mehr als drei Monaten
- hedge Terminkauf-Deckungsgeschäft
- maturities Langläufer
- term bond yield Langläufer--Rendite
- term lendings langfristige Ausleihungen (Kredite)
- term loan book langfristiges Kreditportefeuille, Gesamtsumme der langfristigen Ausleihungen
- term loan exposure langfristiges Kreditengagement

loosening the credit reins Lockerung der kreditpolitischen Zügel

loss Verlust
- experience on loans →loss rate
- from operations Betriebsverlust
- on currency fluctuations (on foreign exchange) Wechselkursverluste
- rate Ausfallquote im Kreditgeschäft

low Tiefstand

low-activity account Konto, das nur geringe Umsätze aufweist

low-cost
- funds (a) zinsgünstige Gelder; (b) billige Refinanzierungsmittel
- loan niedrigverzinslicher Kredit; zinsgünstiges Darlehen

lower
- across the board auf breiter Front schwächer
- in light trading schwächer bei geringen Umsätzen

lowering Senkung, Ermäßigung
- the cost of funds Verbilligung der Refinanzierungskosten
- of interest rates Senkung der Zinssätze, Zinsverbilligung

low-geared company (Br) / low-leveraged corporation (US) Gesellschaft, die mit einem niedrigen Fremdkapitalanteil arbeitet

low-priced securities leichte Papiere

low-rated share niedrig bewertete Aktie

low-start mortgage Hypothek, bei der zu Beginn der Laufzeit nur geringe Zins- und Tilgungszahlungen zu leisten sind

low-yield loan portfolio Volumen an niedrig verzinslichen Krediten

LTD → licensed deposit-taker

lump größere Anzahl von Aktien bzw. Aktienpaket

lump sum Pauschalbetrag

lump-sum mortgage maturity in einem Betrag fälliges Hypothekendarlehen

M

M1, M1A, M1B, M2, M3 money supply

magnetic data carrier exchange belegloser Datenträgeraustausch

mail credit Postlaufkredit

mainstream banking Kernleistungen einer Bank

mainstream retail banking das traditionelle Privatkundengeschäft

maintenance (a) Führung (eines Kontos); (b) Aufrechterhaltung (Deckung, Guthaben)
- fee Kontoführungsgebühr
- margin Mindestdeckung, die bei einem Effekten-Kreditkonto vorhanden sein muß

majority holding Mehrheitsbeteiligung

major-swing trading auf die Ausnutzung von Kursschwankungen ausgerichtete Anlagepolitik

making-up price (a) Abrechnungskurs; (b) Prolongationskurs

management (a) Konsortialführung; (b) Unternehmensführung; (c) Verwaltung
- fee (a) Führungsprovision; (b) Verwaltungsgebühr
- group bei einer Emission: Führungsgruppe

manager (a) Konsortialführer; (b) Verwaltungsgesellschaft

manager's commission Führungsprovision

managers' discretionary limits Kreditkompetenz bzw. Dispositionsbefugnisse der leitenden Mitarbeiter

managing bank Führungsbank

mandate to be awarded the - bei Syndizierungen: das Mandat erhalten

margin (a) Spanne, Marge; (b) Aufschlag; (c) Sicherheitsleistung, Deckung
- of 1/2 per cent over six-month Libor Aufschlag von 0,5 % auf Sechsmonats-Libor
- of loading Prozentsatz der Abschlußkosten bzw. Verwaltungsgebühren

marginable securities beleihbare Wertpapiere

margin
- account Effekten-Kreditkonto
- buying Kauf von Wertpapieren unter Inanspruchnahme eines Kredites
- credit Effektenkredit
- loan value Beleihungsgrenze bei Wertpapieren
- regulations Fed-Bestimmungen im Hinblick auf Effekten-Kredite
- requirements Deckungserfordernisse, Einschußsätze, erforderliche Sicherheitsleistung
- rules Vorschriften für die Aufnahme von Effektenkrediten
- securities unter Inanspruchnahme von Krediten erworbene Wertpapiere

mark v. to - down (up) niedriger (höher) notieren, mit Minus (Plus) ankündigen

marketable marktgängig, verkehrsfähig; handelsüblich
- amount handelsübliche Stückzahl bei Wertpapieren

marketable
- debt Handelseffekten
- quantity handelbare Menge
- securities (a) (börsen-)gängige Titel; (b) leicht realisierbare Wertpapiere

market
- activity Marktgeschehen
- advance Kursanstieg, Kursbefestigung
- appreciation Wertzuwachs, Kurssteigerung
- bid price (a) Geldkurs; (b) marktgängiger Rücknahmekurs
- capitalisation Börsenkapitalisierung einer Unternehmung
- close Börsenschluß, Schluß der Börsensitzung
- community Marktkreise
- correction Marktkorrektur, Kurskorrektur
- customs Marktusancen
- days Börsentage
- decline Kursrückgang
- for outstanding securities Sekundärmarkt
- funds Marktmittel
- hours Börsensitzung
- ing fee (a) Ausgabeaufschlag; (b) Verkaufsprovision
- leaders führende Börsenwerte
- makers Wertpapierhändler bzw. Banken, die Abschlüsse zustande bringen
- operator Marktteilnehmer
- order Bestensauftrag
- orientated pricing marktorientierte Konditionengestaltung
- price Marktkurs, Börsenkurs, Tageskurs
- price display service elektronische Börsenkursanzeige, Ticker
- profits Kursgewinne
- quantity handelsübliche Stückzahl (Stückelung) bei Wertpapieren
- quotation Börsennotierung
- rate Marktkurs, Tageskurs, marktgängiger Satz
- receptivity Aufnahmefähigkeit des Marktes
- risk Kursrisiko
- sentiment Börsenstimmung
- slide Kursrückgang
- stabilisation Marktbefestigung
- terms Marktkonditionen, Marktbedingungen
- unease unsichere Börsenstimmung

marking Kurszusatz, Kurskennzeichen

marking board Maklertafel

markup (a) Heraufsetzung eines Kurses, Plusankündigung; (b) Aufschlag

marrying Zusammenlegung eines gleichlautenden Kauf- und Verkaufsauftrages

matching

fundings at - maturities laufzeitkongruente (fristenkongruente) Refinanzierungen

lendings at - interest rates zinskongruente Ausleihungen

- of lendings and deposits Deckung der Laufzeiten auf der Aktiv- und Passivseite, laufzeitkongruente Deckung des Aktiv- und Passivgeschäftes (des Kredit- und Einlagengeschäftes)
- maturities (a) gleiche Laufzeiten; (b) Fristenentsprechung, Fristenkongruenz, Fristensymmetrie

mature v. fällig werden

maturity (a) Fälligkeit, Fälligkeitstermin, Verfalltag; (b) Laufzeit; (c) Fristigkeit

maturity
- breakdown Laufzeitengliederung, Fristengliederung
- dated obligations Schuldtitel mit fester Laufzeit
- extension Streckung eines Darlehens
- factoring Fälligkeitsfactoring, Ankauf von Forderungen Valuta Verfalltag
- hedging Fristenschutz, Absicherung der Fälligkeitsstruktur
- ladder Fristigkeitstabelle
- linked fälligkeitsgebunden
- pattern of lendings Fristenstruktur des Kreditgeschäftes
- pattern of new offerings Laufzeitenstruktur beim Erstabsatz
- range Fristenraum, Fälligkeitsfächer
- schedule Fälligkeitsliste
- spacing Fristengliederung
- transformation Fristentransformation
- value Wert per Fälligkeit

maximum loan value Beleihungsgrenze bei Wertpapieren

MDLs → managers' discretionary limits

mean
- due (value) date mittlerer Verfalltag, Mittelvaluta
- rate of exchange Mittelkurs
- spread of the fixing Spannkurs

mechanics of the market Marktmechanismus

medium-term commercial lendings mittelfristiges Firmenkreditgeschäft

member bank reserve requirements Mindestreservevorschriften für Banken, die dem → Federal Reserve System angeschlossen sind

members' quota subscriptions Mitgliedsquoten (IWF)

memorandum of
- deposit (a) Hinterlegungsbestätigung; (b) Abtretungserklärung
- pledge Verpfändungserklärung
- satisfaction Löschungsbewilligung

Merchant Bank auf das Emissions- und Akzeptgeschäft spezialisierte Bank(Br)

minimising costs Kostenminimierung

minimum
- acceptance level Mindestprozentsatz des stimmberechtigten Kapitals, dessen Inhaber einem Übernahmeangebot zugestimmt haben müssen
- contract Mindestschluß (Börse)
- deal → minimum contract
- life Mindestlaufzeit
- lot → minimum contract
- margin requirements Mindesteinschußpflicht
- reserve ratios Mindestreservesätze
- term → minimum life

minority interests in income konzernfremden Gesellschaftern zustehender Gewinn

MINTS → Mutual Institutions National Transfer System Inc.

mismatched asset and liability maturities fehlende Kongruenz der Fälligkeiten im Aktiv- und Passivgeschäft (bei Ausleihungen und Einlagen)

mismatched maturities Fristenasymmetrie

moderate-leverage companies Unternehmen, die mit einem begrenzten Einsatz von Fremdkapital arbeiten (US)

MON Geldmenge in der engeren Abgrenzung (Br)

monetary
- aggregates Geldmengenzahlen
- aggregate targets Geldmengenziele
- contraction Geldverknappung
- control provisions Verordnungen der Bank von England zur Sicherung der Geldversorgung bzw. Geldmengensteuerung
- realignment Neuordnung der Währungsparitäten

money
- at call Tagesgeld
- at short notice kurzfristig kündbare Gelder
- center banks Geschäftsbanken (US)
- dealer Geldhändler
- dealing Geldhandel, Gelddispositionen
- desk Geldhandelsabteilung
- infusion Kapitalspritze

money market Geldmarkt
- activities Geldmarktgeschäfte, Geldmarktgeschehen
- certificate (a) im weiteren Sinne: Geldmarktpapier; (b) im engeren Sinne: von Geschäftsbanken emittierte Sparbriefe (US)
- division Geldhandelsabteilung
- fund Geldmarktfonds (durch Zeichnung von Anteilen investiert der Anleger in Einlagenzertifikaten, Schuldscheinen und Geldmarktpapieren, die sonst nur in großen Stükkelungen verfügbar sind - US)
- funds (a) Geldmarktmittel;(b) Geldmarktpapiere, Geldmarkttitel
- line Geldhandelslinie
- offering Emission am Geldmarkt
- operator Geldmarktteilnehmer
- rate Geldmarktsatz
- securities Geldmarkttitel, Geldmarktpapiere
- transactions Geldmarktabschlüsse, Geldmarktgeschäfte

money
- on seven days' call Einlagen mit siebentägiger Kündigungsfrist
- stock (a) Geldmenge;(b) kurzfristig fällig werdende Titel
- stock targets Geldmengenziele

money supply Geldmenge, Geldvolumen

M1 Geldmenge in der engeren Abgrenzung; in der Regel: Bargeldumlauf und Sichteinlagen

Unterteilung in den USA:

M1A Bargeldumlauf und Sichteinlagen bei den Geschäftsbanken

M1B M1A plus Sichteinlagen bei sonstigen Spar- und Kreditinstituten

M2 Geldmenge in der weiteren Abgrenzung; in der Regel: M1 unter Einbeziehung von Termingeldern und Quasi-Geld

in den USA: M1A und M1B sowie Termin- und Spareinlagen bis $ 100.000, Investmentfondsanteile

M3 M2 plus Termin- und Spareinlagen über $ 100.000

money
- surge Geldschwemme
- swap Geldtausch
- trading Geldhandel
- trading department (desk) Geldhandelsabteilung, Geldstelle
- transfer Überweisung
- transfer charges Überweisungsgebühren

money
- transfer system Form des →Cash Management; durch Einschaltung der an das System angeschlossenen ausländischen Filialen seiner inländischen Hausbank kann der Firmenkunde weltweit Geldtransaktionen ohne Zeitverzögerung abwickeln

- transmission service Überweisungsverkehr

monitoring
- a loan commitment Überwachung eines Kreditengagements, Kreditkontrolle
- maturities Fälligkeitskontrolle, Terminüberwachung

monthly
- banking make-up day Stichtag für die Erstellung der Monatsausweise der Kreditinstitute
- income account monatliche Erfolgsrechnung
- interest and redemption payments monatliche Zins- und Tilgungszahlungen, monatliche Belastung

moral obligation bonds bundesstaatliche Anleihen (gesichert durch die Kreditwürdigkeit des emittierenden Bundesstaates-US)

more one-way Hinweis eines Brokers oder Jobbers, daß bei einer Aktie noch weitere Kauf- oder Verkaufsaufträge vorliegen

Morris Plan banks Finanzierungsgesellschaften, die in erster Linie auf Teilzahlungsgeschäfte spezialisiert sind (US)

mortgage Hypothek

mortgage v. hypothekarisch belasten

mortgage
- amortisation payment Hypotheken-Tilgungsrate, Hypothekentilgung

- assumption Übernahme einer Hypothek
- backed pass-through securities Pfandbriefe, auf die monatliche Zinszahlungen erfolgen
- bond Pfandbrief
- book Hypothekenkreditvolumen
- borrowing Hypothekenkredit, Aufnahme eines Hypothekenkredites
- charge hypothekarische Belastung, Hypothek
- claim hypothekarisch gesicherte Forderung, Hypothekenforderung
- collateral hypothekarische Sicherheit
- commitment Hypothekenzusage
- consolidation Zusammenlegung von Hypotheken
- credit Hypothekenkredit
- creditor Hypothekengläubiger
- debenture Hypothekenschuldverschreibung
- debt Hypothekenschuld
- deed Hypothekenbrief, Hypothekenurkunde
- defaults Ausfälle im Hypothekenkreditgeschäft
- discount Hypothekendamnum
- encumbrance Hypothekenbelastung
- exposure (a) Hypothekenzusagen; (b) Hypothekenkredit
- finance Hypothekenmittel
- financing Hypothekenfinanzierung
- foreclosure Hypothekenzwangsvollstreckung
- funds Hypothekengelder
- guarantee insurance Hypothekenversicherung, Hypothekenkreditversicherung
- Guaranty Insurance Corporation Hypothekenkredit-Versicherungsgesellschaft (US)
- indenture Hypothekenvertrag
- interest Hypothekenzinsen

mortgage
- lending Hypothekenkredit, Gewährung eines Hypothekenkredites
- lending business Hypothekenkreditgeschäft
- lending commitment Hypothekenkreditzusage
- lending rate Hypothekenzinssatz
- lien Grundpfandrecht
- loan Hypothekendarlehen, Realdarlehen
- loan accommodation → mortgage lending
- loan portfolio Hypothekenkreditvolumen
- loan proceeds Hypothekenvaluta, Hypothekenerlös, ausgezahltes Hypothekendarlehen
- loan servicing Bedienung eines Hypothekendarlehens
- loan terms Hypothekenkonditionen
- loan undertaking Hypothekenkreditzusage
- maturity Hypothekenfälligkeit
- participation certificate Hypothekengenußrecht (im Hinblick auf zusammengelegte langfristige Hypotheken - US)
- portfolio Hypothekenkreditvolumen
- principal Hypothekensumme, Hypothekenbetrag
- proceeds Hypothekenerlös, Hypothekenvaluta
- protection insurance Hypothekenversicherung
- purchase bond Hypothekenpfandbrief
- rank Hypothekenrang
- rates Hypothekenzinsen, Hypothekenkonditionen
- redemption Hypothekentilgung
- release Hypothekenlöschung
- retirement Hypothekenablösung
- security hypothekarische Sicherheit
- servicing Hypothekenbedienung, Bedienung eines Hypothekendarlehens
- squeeze Begrenzung der Hypothekenkreditaufnahme
- terms Hypothekenbedingungen, Hypothekenkonditionen

mortgagor Hypothekenschuldner

motors Kraftfahrzeugwerte, Automobiltitel

movement charge Hinterlegungs- bzw. Übertragungsgebühr

MOW Geldmenge in der weiteren Abgrenzung (Br)

MPDS → Market Price Display Service (Br)

MSRB → Municipal Securities Rulemaking Board

multi-currency clause (a) Mehrwährungsklausel; (b) Währungsänderungsklausel

multiple
- branch banking Filialbankensystem
- exchange rate gespaltener Wechselkurs
- voting share Mehrstimmrechtsaktie

multi-purpose bank Universalbank

multi-share certificate Globalaktie

municipal bond Kommunalobligation

municipal bond fund Investmentfonds, dessen Vermögen in Kommunalobligationen angelegt ist

municipals → municipal securities

municipal securities   Kommunalobligationen (US - Begriff
schließt oft auch bundesstaatliche Anleihen ein)

Municipal Securities Rulemaking
Board   Organisation zur Überwachung des Handels in Kommunalobligationen (mit quasi-ge-
setzgeberischen Befugnissen)

mutual fund   (offener) Investmentfonds   (US)

Mutual Institutions National
Transfer System Inc.   elektronisches Zahlungsverkehrssystem der Sparkassen (US)

N

NACHA → National Automated Clearing House Association

naked option   Option, bei der der Stillhalter nicht im Besitz der entsprechenden Papiere ist

naked writer   Stillhalter, der nicht über die entsprechenden Papiere verfügt

name   Adresse, Kreditnehmer

  first-rate name in the bond market   erstklassige Anleiheadresse

  name on a bill   Wechseladresse

name day   Aufgabetag

narrowing of spreads   Margenverengung

narrow market   enger (begrenzter) Markt

narrow money supply   Geldmenge in der engeren Definition

National Association of Securities Dealers Automated Quotation System (NASDAQ)   elektronisches Kursnotierungssystem der Händler am → over-the-counter market (US)

National Automated Clearing House Association (US)   Dachverband der Clearing-Zentralen, denen Banken und Industrieunternehmen angeschlossen sind

National Bank   durch Bundesbehörden zugelassene Bank (US)

national charter   Bundeszulassung

National Giro   Postschecksystem (Br)

natural deposits   Bareinlagen

NAV per share → net asset value per share

near-banking sector   bankverwandter Sektor

negative interest   Strafzins

negative net worth   Unterbilanz

negative pledge clause (covenant)   Negativklausel

negotiable   begebbar, marktfähig, girierbar

negotiable order of withdrawal account → NOW account

negotiate v.   negoziieren, begeben

  to - without recourse to drawer   ohne Regreß auf den Aussteller negoziieren

  negotiated brokerage rates   Courtagesätze, die zwischen Broker und Kunde ausgehandelt werden

negotiating

- banker   negoziierende Bank
- commission   Negoziierungsprovision

negotiation   Negoziierung, Begebung

- credit   Negoziationskredit
- fee   (a) Negoziierungsgebühr; (b) Konsortialprovision
- line   Negoziationslinie

363

nest-egg account   Kleinstsparkonto

nest-egg saving   Vorsorgesparen

net   (a) netto; (b) net of abzüglich

net v. aufrechnen, kompensieren

  netting interest income against interest payable   Aufrechnung von Guthaben- und Schuldzinsen

net
- asset value per share   (a) Buchwert je Aktie; (b) Inventarwert je Anteil (bei Investmentfonds)
- borrowers → net borrowing position
- borrowing position   im Geldhandel: Nettoschuldnerposition, Nettopassivposition, Passivüberhang
- borrowing requirements   Nettokreditbedarf
- borrowings in the capital market   Nettokreditaufnahme am Kapitalmarkt
- buyers → net borrowers
- capital ratio   Indexzahl zur Bewertung des haftenden Eigenkapitals (d.h. Kapital plus Rücklagen abzüglich aller notleidenden Kredite sowie der als unterdurchschnittlich einzustufenden Ausleihungen)
- charge-offs   Nettokreditausfälle, Nettoforderungsverlust im Kreditgeschäft
- commission income (revenue)   Provisionsüberschuß
- funds generated from operations   Mittelherkunft aus der betrieblichen Leistungserstellung
- gearing   Nettoverschuldung in % des Eigenkapitals
- income for the year   Jahresüberschuß
- income from service transactions   Überschuß der Erträge aus dem Dienstleistungsgeschäft
- interest income   Zinsüberschuß, positiver Zinssaldo, positives Zinsergebnis
- interest loss   negativer Zinssaldo, negatives Zinsergebnis
- interest margin   Nettozinsspanne
- lenders → net selling position
- lendings   Nettoausleihungen, Nettoausreichungen
- loan position   Nettokreditaufnahme
- new advances   Nettoneugeschäft (im Kreditbereich)
- price transaction   Nettogeschäft (bei Wertpapieren)
- savings   Sparergebnis
- sellers (net selling position)   Nettogläubigerposition, Nettoaktivposition, Aktivüberhang
- surplus   Reingewinn
- take-up   Nettoaufnahme, Nettoübernahme (von Schuldtiteln)
- worth   Eigenkapital

new
- business lendings   gewerbliches Kreditneugeschäft
- credit extended to private customers   Neugeschäft im Privatkundenbereich
- facility   Neukredit

newgo   Börsengeschäfte, die erst in der folgenden → account period abgerechnet werden

new issue   Neuemission
- business   Neuemissionsgeschäft, Primärgeschäft, Erstabsatz
- market   Neuemissionsmarkt, Primärmarkt
- project   Emissionsvorhaben
- requirements   Emissionsbedarf

new
- lendings (loan accommodations) Neuabschlüsse im Kreditgeschäft, Neuzusagen, Neuvalutierungen, Neugeschäft
- money im Zusammenhang mit Umschuldungen: Neukredit, zusätzlicher Kredit
- mortgage lendings Hypothekenneugeschäft
- offering Neuemission
- shares junge Aktien

New York Interbank Offered Rate New Yorker Interbanken-Angebotssatz

next day funds Valutierung bzw. Kreditierung am nächsten Tag

next time ⟶ newgo

ninety-day notice account (passbook account, deposits) Sparkonto mit dreimonatiger Kündigungsfrist

N.L. ⟶ no-load fund

no dealings Kurs gestrichen

no funds keine Deckung

no-load contracts Verträge, auf die keine Abschlußgebühr erhoben wird

no-load fund Investmentfonds, der beim Verkauf von Anteilen keinen Ausgabeaufschlag erhebt

nominated bank im Dokumentengeschäft: benannte Bank

nomination of stock (a) Benennung eines Nominee; (b) Erbeinsetzung im Hinblick auf Wertpapierbesitz

nominative security Namenspapier

nominee Brokerfirma oder Treuhandgesellschaft, auf deren Namen die Aktien von Bankkunden registriert werden

non
- acceptance Annahmeverweigerung, Nichtannahme
- assessable stock nicht nachschußpflichtige Aktie
- assignable documentary credit nicht übertragbares Akkreditiv
- availment of a credit line Nichtinanspruchnahme einer Kreditlinie
- bank-customers ⟶ non-banks
- bank deposits Nichtbankeneinlagen
- banking services neutrale Leistungen einer Bank
- bank retail investors private Anleger
- banks Nichtbanken; Nichtbankensektor
- callable nicht kündbar
- call provision Unkündbarkeitsklausel
- commercial banks Sparkassen und Kundenkreditbanken
- compliance with the terms and conditions of the documentary credit Nichterfüllung der Akkreditivbedingungen
- conventional loan Hypothekendarlehen, das durch die Garantie einer staatlichen Organisation unterlegt ist
- coupon securities abgezinste Wertpapiere
- cumulative dividend nicht nachzahlungspflichtige Dividende
- current maturities Wertpapiere, die nicht dem Umlaufvermögen zugerechnet werden
- domestic business Auslandsgeschäft einer Bank
- earning assets Passivgeschäft einer Bank

non
- earning balances unverzinsliche Guthaben
- ferrous metals stock NE-Werte
- financial corporations ⟶ non-banks
- fungible securities nicht vertretbare Wertpapiere
- guaranteed agency bonds unbesicherte Anleihen halböffentlicher Stellen (z.B. Export-Import-Bank - US)
- interest charges Kreditnebenkosten
- leverage companies Unternehmen, die ohne Fremdkapital arbeiten
- listed securities amtlich nicht notierte Werte
- local cheque Distanzscheck, Fernscheck
- marketable debt nicht börsengängige Schuldtitel
- par bank Bank, die bei den auf sie gezogenen Schecks nicht den vollen Betrag vergütet(US)
- payment of a bill Nichteinlösung eines Wechsels
- performing assets (loans) notleidende Kredite
- performing bonds notleidende Anleihen
- personal time deposits Festgeldeinlagen von Firmenkunden
- quoted investments Beteiligungen an nicht börsennotierten Unternehmen
- recoursefinancing rückgriffslose Finanzierung; Forfaitierung
- resident Gebietsfremder
- risk assets Einlagen einer Bank
- value bill Gefälligkeitswechsel
- voting share stimmrechtslose Aktie

normal market quantity handelsübliche Schlußeinheit (US)

notation on a bill Nichteinlösungsvermerk auf einem Wechsel

note (a) Schuldschein, Kassenobligation; (b) Wechsel

notes am Euromarkt: Schuldtitel mit kurzen und mittleren Laufzeiten bis zu 7 Jahren (fest und variabel verzinslich)

notes payable (a) Schuldscheinverbindlichkeiten; (b) Wechselverbindlichkeiten

notes receivable (a) Forderungen aus Schuldscheinen; (b) Wechselforderungen

note v. die Nichteinlösung eines Wechsels feststellen (Wechselvorprotest)

note loan Schuldscheindarlehen

note tender Schuldscheinofferte

notice (a) Anzeige; (b) Kündigung

notice deposits Kündigungsgelder

notice of
- assignment Abtretungsanzeige
- determination of guarantee Garantieaufkündigungs-Anzeige
- dishonour Wechselprotestanzeige, Notanzeige, Nichtbezahltmeldung
- dividend Dividendenankündigung
- drawing Auslosungsanzeige
- meeting Einberufungsbekanntmachung (zu einer Hauptversammlung)
- redemption Tilgungsanzeige, Rückzahlungsankündigung
- rights Bezugsrechtsangebot
- satisfaction Löschungsanzeige
- withdrawal Kündigungsfrist bei Einlagen

notification of credit Akkreditivanzeige

notification of payment Bezahltmeldung, Einlösungsanzeige

notification provisions Anzeigevorschriften

not to press Vermerk auf Effekten-
 abrechnungen: Auslieferung der
 Titel muß vorerst nicht erfolgen

NOW account verzinsliches
 Kontokorrentkonto (US)

NPV shares nennwertlose Aktien,
 Quotenaktien

NTP ⟶ not to press

NYBOR ⟶ New York Interbank
 Offered Rate

NYSE New Yorker Börse

NYSE-Composite quotations NYSE-
 Verbundnotierungen (basieren
 auf den Umsätzen an den Börsen
 New York, Midwest, Pacific,
 Philadelphia, Boston und Cin-
 cinnati sowie den Freiverkehrs-
 bzw. NASDAQ-Umsätzen)

nucleus group bei Syndizierungen:
 Führungsgruppe

numbered account Nummernkonto

O

obligations   Schuldtitel

OCC → Options Clearing Corporation

odd lot(s)   weniger als 100 Aktien oder weniger als 5 Anleihen; Sammelbegriff: Kleinigkeiten

odd-lot index   Verhältnis zwischen Käufen und Verkäufen bei → odd lots

off-balance sheet items   Positionen unter dem Strich

off-balance sheet reserves   nicht in der Bilanz ausgewiesene Rücklagen

off-board market   Freiverkehr

offer   Angebot, Offerte
- document   (a) Zeichnungsunterlagen; (b) Übernahmeangebot
- for sale   Zeichnungsangebot
- for sale by tender   Angebot im Tenderverfahren

offering   Emission
- cost   Emissionskosten
- currency   Emissionswährung
- memorandum   Emissionsprospekt
- price   Emissionskurs, Ausgabekurs; bei Fondsanteilen: Ausgabepreis
- prospectus   Emissionsprospekt
- rate   Briefkurs
- sheet   Angebotsliste eines Wertpapierhändlers
- terms   Emissionsbedingungen

official   amtlich
- buying-in   Stützungskäufe durch die Bank of England
- exchange rate   amtlicher Wechselkurs
- list   amtliches Kursblatt
- quotation   amtliche Notierung
- support   Stützungskäufe
- support point   Interventionspunkt

off-line system   bei Geldautomaten: keine Verbindung zwischen Automat und zentralem Computer

off-shore bank   Bank in einem exterritorialen Finanzmarkt

off-shore banking   Bankgeschäfte außerhalb der nationalen Grenzen bzw. der Währungsgesetzgebung eines Landes

off-shore centre   exterritorialer Finanzmarkt

off-shore unit   Tochtergesellschaft in einem exterritorialen Finanzmarkt

old bonds   alte Sterling-Anleihen ausländischer Emittenten (Br)

OLTTS → on-line teller terminals

omnibus bill of lading   Sammelkonnossement

one-month
- dollar   Monatsdollar
- maturities   Monatsgelder

one-off payment   einmalige Zahlung

one-stop financing package   Finanzierung aus einer Hand

one-way
- market   Wertpapier, das nur angeboten oder nur gesucht wird
- only   Hinweis, daß nur Käufe oder nur Verkäufe möglich sind

ongoing financing Anschlußfinanzierung

on-line debit system Sofortab-
buchungssystem

on-line system bei Geldautomaten: ständige Verbindung
zwischen Automat und Computer

on-line teller terminals
on-line Schalterterminals

on-margin purchase Kauf von
Wertpapieren gegen Kredit

open
- cheque Barscheck
- commitments offene Positionen
- credit Blankokredit

open-end
- loan agreement Kreditvertrag,
  bei dem über die Art der zu er-
  bringenden Sicherheit noch
  nicht entschieden ist
- mutual fund offener Investmentfonds
- note Schuldschein in Form
  einer Kreditlinie

open indenture Anleihevertrag,
in dem die Möglichkeit weiterer
Anleihen vorgesehen ist

opening
- bank Akkreditivbank, Eröff-
  nungsbank
- markdowns Kursabschläge zu
  Beginn der Börsensitzung

open
- interests offene (noch nicht
  abgewickelte Terminengagements)
- line of credit ungedeckte
  Kreditlinie
- market operations Offenmarkt-
  Geschäfte
- market securities Offenmarkt-
  Papiere (Titel)

- order Effektenauftrag, bei dem
  wohl ein Kurs- aber kein Zeit-
  limit angegeben wurde
- to-borrow arrangement Rahmen-
  kreditvertrag, Kreditlinie

operating
- facility Betriebsmittelkredit
- funds Betriebsmittel
- loan → operating facility
- profit Betriebsgewinn
- ratio Relation zwischen Be-
  triebsaufwand und Umsatz
- statement Gewinn- und Verlustrechnung, Betriebsergebnisrech-
  nung

operative credit instrument Instrument für die Inanspruchnahme
des Akkreditivs

operator in the money market
Geldmarktteilnehmer

option Option

optional
- cross default clause Klausel
  in parallelen Kreditverträgen,
  die ein Entwicklungsland zum
  einen mit der Weltbank und zum
  anderen mit einem privaten Bank-
  konsortium abschließt (wird
  der Kreditvertrag mit dem Konsortium verletzt, hat die Weltbank die Möglichkeit, aber
  nicht die Pflicht, ihrerseits
  ihren Kredit zur Rückzahlung
  fällig zu stellen oder weitere
  Auszahlungen im Rahmen dieser
  Fazilität auszusetzen (→
  compulsory cross default clause)
- redemption mögliche Tilgung;
  Option des Anleiheschuldners,
  die Anleihe vorzeitig zurück-
  zuzahlen

option
- buyer Optionskäufer, Optionser-
  werber
- contract Optionsgeschäft,
  Optionskontrakt
- deal → option contract

optioned
- securities Optionspapiere
- shares (stocks) Optionsaktien

option
- holder Optionsinhaber
- income fund Investmentfonds, der in Dividendenpapieren investiert und in diesen Papieren Optionsgeschäfte abschließt
- money Optionspreis, Optionsprämie
- period Optionsfrist
- premium → option money

Options Clearing Corporation zentrale Abrechnungsstelle aller Optionsbörsen (US)

Options Exchange Optionsbörse

option
- trading Optionshandel
- warrant Optionsschein
- writer Optionsverkäufer

ordinary
- account niedrigverzinsliches Sparkonto (Br)
- creditor nicht bevorrechtigter Gläubiger
- dividend Dividende auf Stammaktien
- share issue Stammaktienemission

organised resale market geregelter Sekundärmarkt

original subscriber Erstzeichner

originate v. (a) emittieren (eine Anleihe); (b) Kreditvertrag ausfertigen

originating house Konsortialführerin, Emissionshaus

originating party Auftraggeber

OTC quotation Freiverkehrskurs

OTC quotation sheet Freiverkehrskurszettel

outlet for funds Parkmöglichkeit, Anlagemöglichkeit

out-of-state municipals Kommunalobligationen, die in Bundesstaaten gehalten bzw. verwahrt werden, in denen sie nicht emittiert wurden (US)

out-of-the money Bezeichnung für eine Situation, in der der Optionsbasiskurs über dem Tageskurs der zugrunde liegenden Papiere liegt

out-of-town cheque Distanzscheck, Fernscheck

outright cash take-over Firmenübernahme gegen Barzahlung

outside capital Fremdkapital

outside financing Fremdfinanzierung

outstanding
- debt aufgenommene Kredite, bestehende Kredite (Verbindlichkeiten)
- shares emittierte (im Umlauf befindliche) Aktien
- short interests offenstehende Baisseengagements

outward investment in securities Anlagen in ausländischen Wertpapieren

overall borrowing arrangement Gesamtkreditlinie

overdraft Kontoüberziehung
- commission Überziehungsprovision
- facility Dispositionskredit, Überziehungskredit
- line Dispositionslinie, Überziehungsmöglichkeit

overdraft
- pricing   Festsetzung der Konditionen für Überziehungskredite
- rate   Zinssatz für Dispositions-(Überziehungs-)Kredite

overdue bill   notleidender Wechsel

overdue loan   notleidendes Kreditengagement

overgeared company (Br) / overleveraged corporation (US)   Gesellschaft, die mit einem sehr hohen Fremdkapitalanteil arbeitet

overheads   Betriebskosten; Gemeinkosten

overnight
- contracts   Tagesgeldabschlüsse
- borrowing   Aufnahme von Tagesgeld
- borrowings   Tagesgeldverbindlichkeiten
- deals → overnight contracts
- funds   Tagesgeld
- interbank money   Tagesgeld unter Banken
- lendings → overnight loans
- loan   Tagesgeldausleihung, Überlassung von Tagesgeld
- loans   Tagesgeldhergaben, Tagesgeldforderungen
- money   Tagesgeld
- money commitments   Tagesgeldpositionen
- money market   Tagesgeldmarkt
- rate   Tagesgeldsatz

override agreement   Rahmenvertrag

overriding commission   Konsortialspanne, Führungsprovision

overseas buying   Käufe ausländischer Anleger

oversold positions   Baisseengagements, Minusposition

overstocked positions   Hausseengagements

oversubscribed issue   überzeichnete Emission

oversupply of new issues   Emissionsüberhang

over-the-counter   (US)
- market   Freiverkehr
- quotation   Freiverkehrskurs, Notierung im Freiverkehr
- resale market   Freiverkehrs-Sekundärmarkt
- securities (stocks)   Freiverkehrswerte

over the turn   Gültigkeit über Monats- bzw. Jahresultimo hinaus

owe v. to - on rescheduling loans   aus Umschuldungskrediten schulden

own-account trading   Eigenhandel, Properhandel

P

P → provisional rating

packaging a loan syndicate Zusammenstellung eines Kreditkonsortiums

packing credit (a) Akkreditivbevorschussung; (b) Versandbereitstellungskredit

paid cheque eingelöster Scheck

paid-up share capital eingezahltes Aktienkapital

pair v. to - stock exchange orders gleichlautende Effektenkauf- und -verkaufsaufträge miteinander verrechnen

PAN → personal account number

panic sales (selling) Angstverkäufe

paper-based transmission services bargeldloser Überweisungsverkehr

paperless entries beleglose Buchungen

paperless payments belegloser Zahlungsverkehr

parallel
- financing Parallelfinanzierung
- loan Parallelanleihe

par bank Bank, die bei den auf sie gezogenen Schecks den vollen Betrag vergütet

parental guarantee (liability) Garantie (Haftung) der Muttergesellschaft

pari passu mortgage gleichrangige Hypothek

par issue Pari-Emission

parity Parität
- grid Paritätengitter

par rights issue Pari-Bezugsrecht

partial
- call teilweise Kündigung, Teilkündigung
- discharge Teillöschung; Teilfreigabe; Teilentlastung
- drawdown on a credit line Teilausnutzung (teilweise Inanspruchnahme) einer Kreditlinie
- release clause Klausel hinsichtlich der Teillöschung eines Grundpfandrechtes

participating
- bond Anleihe, bei der neben den Zinszahlungen eine zusätzliche Gewinnausschüttung erfolgt
- preference share Vorzugsaktie mit einem zusätzlichen Gewinnanspruch

participation Beteiligung; Anteil
- certificate Genußschein; Gewinnschuldverschreibung
- rights Gewinnbeteiligungsrechte, Dividendenansprüche

partly paid-up share teileingezahlte Aktie

party liable on a cheque (bill) Scheck-(Wechsel-)verpflichteter

par value Nennwert

passbook Sparbuch
- account Sparkonto

passbook deposits   niedrigverzinsliche Spareinlagen (in der Regel ohne Kündigungsfrist US)

passthrough instruments   Pfandbriefe, auf die monatliche Zinszahlungen erfolgen (US)

pattern of deposits   Einlagenstruktur

pattern of maturities   Fristenstruktur, Fälligkeitsstruktur

pay v.   zahlen; auszahlen; entrichten

to - across the counter   am Schalter auszahlen

to - a cheque   einen Scheck einlösen

to - in a cheque   einen Scheck (zur Gutschrift auf ein Konto) einreichen

to - down a deposit   eine Anzahlung leisten

to - up under a guarantee   einer Garantieverpflichtung nachkommen

payable   zahlbar

- at sight   zahlbar bei Sicht

- to bearer (order)   zahlbar an Überbringer (Order)

- upon application   zahlbar bei Zeichnung

pay day   Börse: Erfüllungstermin, Liquidationstermin

payee   Zahlungsempfänger

paying

- agency agreement   Zahlstellenvereinbarung

- agency commission   Zahlstellenprovision

- agency operations   Zahlstellengeschäft

- agent   Zahlstelle; Zahlstellenbank

- bank   (a) (scheck-) einlösende Bank; (b) mit der Zahlung beauftragte Bank, Zahlstellenbank

- in slip   Einzahlungsbeleg

payment   (a) Zahlung, Zahlungsleistung; (b) Auszahlung

- by automated credit transfer   bargeldlose Zahlung

- by bill of exchange   Wechselzahlung

- commitments under a guarantee   Zahlungsverpflichtungen aus einer Garantie

- countermanded   Scheckvermerk: Scheck gesperrt

- default policy   Kreditversicherung

- on allotment   Zahlung bei Zuteilung der Wertpapiere

- order   Zahlungsauftrag

- record   Zahlungsverhalten, Zahlungsmoral

payments   Zahlungsverkehr

- system   Zahlungsverkehrssystem

payment undertaking   Zahlungsversprechen

pay-off period   Kapitalrückflußdauer

payout   Ausschüttung

payroll credits   Lohn- und Gehaltsgutschriften

pay-up   (a) Börse: Paketzuschlag; (b) zusätzliche Kosten, Aufgeld

PC → participation certificate

peak

- borrowing requirements   Bedarfsspitzen, Spitzenkreditbedarf

- borrowings   Spitzeninanspruchnahmen

- price   Höchststand, Höchstkurs

peg v. (a) koppeln (z.B. an den Diskontsatz);(b)stützen (Kurs)

peg point Interventionspunkt

penal interest Strafzinsen, Negativzinsen

penalty Konventionalstrafe

penalty-free repayment privilege Anrecht auf vorzeitige und entschädigungsfreie Rückzahlung eines Darlehens

percentage advance (percentage advanced) Beleihungsquote

performance (a) Leistung, Erfüllung; (b) Ergebnis (z.B. im Kreditgeschäft); (c) Anlageerfolg (eines Investmentfonds)

performance bond Gewährleistungsgarantie, Erfüllungsgarantie

periodic interest payments regelmäßige Zinszahlungen

period of
- consolidation Konsolidierungsphase
- credit Zahlungsziel, Zahlungsfrist
- grace (a) Nachfrist, Respekttage; (b) tilgungsfreie Jahre
- high interest rates (of tight money) Hochzinsphase
- non-callability Unkündbarkeitsfrist

period rates Terminsätze

permanent deposits Bodensatz (einer Bank)

per share
- asset value (a) Buchwert je Aktie; (b) Inventarwert je Fondsanteil
- earnings Gewinn je Aktie

personal
- account number (PAN) persönliche Kontonummer
- banker service individuelle Kundenbetreuung
- banking Privatkundengeschäft
- credit (a) persönliches Anschaffungsdarlehen, Personalkredit; (b) Kreditwürdigkeit
- customers Privatkunden (einer Bank)
- deposits Einlagen (der Privatkunden)
- finance company Teilzahlungsbank (US)
- identification code (PIC) / personal identification number (PIN) persönliche Kennummer
- lending business Privatkundenkreditgeschäft
- loan Privatkredit, Dispositionskredit
- market Privatkundenbereich
- security Personalsicherheit

personalty bewegliche Sachen

physical delivery of securities effektive Lieferung (Auslieferung) von Wertpapieren

PIC/PIN → personal identification code / number

pick-up (a) Kurserholung; (b) Renditegewinn (bei einem Tausch von Aktienpaketen)

pink form issue Emission, bei der vorhandenen Aktionären ein Vorzugskurs eingeräumt wird

pink sheets NASDAQ-Kursblätter

pitch Börsenstand

place v. plazieren, unterbringen
 to - privately with investors im freihändigen Verkauf unterbringen

placement Plazierung, Unterbringung

placement ratio Verhältnis zwischen dem wöchentlichen Emissionsvolumen und dem Verkauf neuer Papiere

placing
- agreement Plazierungsvertrag
- backlog Emissionsüberhang
- memorandum informeller Prospekt bei einer Privatplazierung
- power Plazierungskraft
- price Plazierungskurs, Emissionskurs
- risk Unterbringungsrisiko

plague v. to - the market den Markt (die Börse) belasten

playing the pattern of rates Zinsschwankungen zu Tauschoperationen bei Festverzinslichen nutzen

PLC →public limited company

pledge v. verpfänden
 pledged securities Lombardeffekten, Pfandeffekten
 to - to the bank as security der Bank als Sicherheit verpfänden
 to - under a repurchase agreement in Pension geben

pledgee Pfandgläubiger, Pfandnehmer; bei Pensionsgeschäften: Pensionsnehmer

pledgor Pfandgeber, Pfandschuldner; bei Pensionsgeschäften: Pensionsgeber

plunge in equity prices (Aktien-)Kurssturz

plus interest accrued zuzüglich aufgelaufener Zinsen (Stückzinsen)

point ein Prozent
 three points taken on a mortgage ein 3 %iges Disagio (Damnum)
 paying 1/8 point over six-month LIBOR zu Sechsmonats-LIBOR plus 1/8% verzinst werden

policy of support points Interventionspolitik

policy on bad debt provisions Risikovorsorgepolitik (im Kreditgeschäft)

pollution control bonds kapitalertragssteuerfreie Kommunalobligationen zur Finanzierung von Projekten des Umweltschutzes

portfolio Portefeuille, Bestand
- additions Portefeuillezugänge
- appreciation Wertzuwachs des Portefeuilles
- company Beteiligungsgesellschaft
- improvement switch wertsteigernde Portefeuilleumschichtung
- indexing Bindung des Portefeuilles an einen Börsenindex (d.h. das Portefeuille setzt sich aus jenen Aktien zusammen, auf denen der Index basiert)
- makeup Zusammensetzung eines Portefeuilles
- of non-performing loans Gesamtsumme der notleidenden Kreditengagements
- of services Dienstleistungspalette
- restructuring Portefeuilleumschichtung
- securities Anlagepapiere
- switch (switching) Portefeuilleumschichtung
- valuation Portefeuillebewertung

position in futures Terminengagements

POS terminal Kassenterminal

post-tax yield   Rendite nach Steuern

pound averaging   regelmäßige Pfund-Sterling Käufe zur Erzielung eines günstigen Durchschnittskurses

power of attorney   Vollmacht, Vertretungsvollmacht

power to contract   Abschlußvollmacht

power to draw   Verfügungsberechtigung

precautionary saving   Vorsorgesparen

preemption right   Vorkaufsrecht

preference

- dividend   Vorzugsdividende, Dividende auf Vorzugsaktien

- share   Vorzugsaktie

preferential

- creditor   bevorrechtigter Gläubiger

- debts   bevorrechtigte Konkursforderungen

- loan   Kredit zu Vorzugskonditionen

- rates (terms)   Vorzugskonditionen, Ausnahmesätze

pre-financing loan   Vorfinanzierungskredit

pre-market   Vorbörse

- price   (a) vorbörslicher Kurs; (b) informeller Kurs für eine Anleihe vor ihrer Plazierung

- trading   vorbörslicher Handel

premium   (a) Prämie; (b) Agio, Aufgeld

- on early redemption   Aufgeld für vorzeitige Tilgung

- on redemption   Tilgungsagio

- price   Kurs über dem Nennwert (Emissionswert)

prepayment   Vorauszahlung; vorzeitige Rückzahlung

- clause   Klausel hinsichtlich der vorzeitigen Darlehensrückzahlung

- penalty   Vorfälligkeitsentschädigung

pre-scrip note   Kurs vor Ausgabe der Bezugsrechte

presentation   Vorlage, Einreichung

- period   Einreichungsfrist

presenting bank   einreichende Bank

pressure on earnings   Ertragsdruck

Prestel   britisches Bildschirmtext-System

pre-suspension price   Kurs vor Aussetzung der Notierung

pre-tax return   Rendite vor Steuern

prevailing rate   Marktkurs

price   (a) Kurs; (b) Preis

price   v. berechnen, in Rechnung stellen

the facility is priced at prime   für den Kredit wird die Prime Rate in Rechnung gestellt

the loan is presently priced at 9 %p.a.   der Zinssatz für den Kredit beträgt zur Zeit 9 % p.a.

price

- after hours   nachbörslicher Kurs

- appreciation   (a) Kurssteigerung; (b) Wertzuwachs

- behaviour in the unlisted market   Kursentwicklung im Freiverkehr

- changes   Kursveränderungen

- determination   Kursfeststellung, Kursfestsetzung

- earnings ratio   Kurs-Gewinn-Verhältnis

- for the settlement   Terminkurs

price
- gains Kursgewinne
- indication Kursangabe
- level Kursniveau, Preisniveau
- level hedging (a) Kurssicherung; (b) Vermögenssicherung, Inflationsschutz
- losses Kursverluste
- making Kursbildung, Kursfindung
- markdown Kursabschlag, Kursrücknahme, Minuszeichen
- markup Kursheraufsetzung, Pluszeichen
- offered Briefkurs
- pegging Kursstützung, Kurspflege
- potential Kurspotential, Kurschancen
- propping Kursstützung
- rally Kurserholung
- range Kursspanne (Hoch/Tief)
- rigging Kursmanipulation
- risk Kursrisiko
- slump Kursrückgang
- spread → price range
- stabilisation (a) Kursbefestigung; (b) Kursstützung
- supporting purchases Kursstützungskäufe
- trends in the securities markets Kursentwicklung an den Wertpapiermärkten

pricing (a) Festlegung der Konditionen, Konditionengestaltung; (b) Festsetzung der Gebühren
- advantage Konditionenvorteil
- issue (a) Konditionenproblem; (b) Gebührenfrage
- meeting Konsortialsitzung
- of a bond Festlegung der Anleihemodalitäten
- of deposit transactions Preisgestaltung im Einlagengeschäft
- of long-term lendings Konditionengestaltung im langfristigen Kreditgeschäft
- policy Konditionenpolitik, Gebührenpolitik, Preispolitik

primarily liable selbstschuldnerisch haftbar

primary
- capital primäres Eigenkapital (d.h. Stammaktien, Rücklagen, Rückstellungen) US; → secondary capital
- dealer von der Federal Reserve Bank New York anerkannter Händler in Staatstiteln
- earnings per share Gewinn je Aktie unter Berücksichtigung des bedingten Kapitals
- liquidity Primärliquidität, liquide Mittel erster Ordnung
- market Primärmarkt, Markt für Neuemissionen
- market issue Erstemission, Neuemission
- trend Grundtendenz

prime
- banker's draft Primabankscheck
- bill erstklassiger (bankgirierter) Wechsel
- borrower erstklassiger Kreditnehmer, erste Schuldneradresse
- borrower in the money market erste Geldmarktadresse
- paper erstklassige Geldmarkttitel, Primapapiere
- rate Kreditzins für erstklassige Kunden (US)

principal (a) Auftraggeber; (b) Kapital, Kapitalbetrag
- amount (a) Kapitalbetrag; (b) Darlehenssumme; (c) Nennwert; (d) Überweisungsbetrag

principal
- debtor Hauptschuldner
- maturity Kapitalfälligkeit
- repayment Kapitalrückzahlung
- repayment rate Tilgungssatz
- shareholder Hauptaktionär

principle of
- matching cover Prinzip der kongruenten Deckung; goldene Bankregel
- single capacity Grundsatz der Trennung von Broker- und Jobber-Funktionen

prior
- charge vorrangige Belastung
- endorser Vormann

priority shares Vorzugsaktien

prior-ranking charge vorrangige Belastung

private
- banking services Dienstleistungen für die Privatkundschaft
- credit demand private Kreditnachfrage
- customer lendings Kreditgeschäft mit Privatkunden, Ausleihungen an Privatkunden
- investors private Anleger
- non-bank deposits Einlagen der Privatkunden
- placement Privatplazierung

private sector Privatsektor, Privatwirtschaft
- banks Privatbanken
- borrowing Kreditaufnahme durch die Privatwirtschaft
- issues Emissionen des Privatsektors
- market Privatkundengeschäft der Banken

privately financed housebuilding freifinanzierter Wohnungsbau

privatized agency bonds Anleihen halbstaatlicher Organisationen (z.B. Federal Home Loan Banks, Federal National Mortgage Association)

privileged stock Vorzugsaktien

privileged subscription Bezugsrecht

probate advance Bevorschussung eines Nachlasses

problem
- debtor country Risikoschuldnerland
- exposure Problemkredit(e), Problemengagement(s)
- lendings Risikoausleihungen, Risikoaktiva
- loan Risikokredit, Problemkredit

proceeds Erlös; Gegenwert

proceeds of
- a bill Wechselgegenwert
- the credit (a) Darlehenserlös, Kreditvaluta; (b) Akkreditiverlös
- debt security sales Emissionserlöse
- the documents Gegenwert der Dokumente

processing fee Bearbeitungsgebühr

procuration fee bei Krediten: Vermittlungsgebühr (US)

procurement of capital Kapitalbeschaffung

procuring deposits in the market Einlagenbeschaffung am Markt

production of the passbook Vorlage des Sparbuches

production payment financing Projektfinanzierung

product-related pricing of banking services produktbezogene Gebührenberechnung für Bankdienstleistungen

professional liquidation Glattstellungen durch den Berufshandel

professional profit-taking Gewinnmitnahmen durch den Berufshandel

profit Gewinn
- available to shareholders ausschüttungsfähiger Gewinn
- before taxes Gewinn vor Steuern
- brought forward Gewinnvortrag
- center Sparte; Unternehmensbereich, der Erträge und Aufwendungen eigenverantwortlich steuert
- center analysis Spartenergebnisrechnung
- contribution Deckungsbeitrag, Gewinnbeitrag
- from operations Betriebsgewinn
- from trading for own account Gewinn aus dem Eigenhandel
- margin Gewinnspanne
- maximisation Gewinnmaximierung
- performance Gewinnergebnis, Abschluß
- retention Einbehaltung der Gewinne, Gewinnthesaurierung
- retention policy Thesaurierungspolitik
- sales ratio Umsatzrentabilität
- sharing Gewinnbeteiligung
- sharing certificate Genußschein
- taking Börse: Gewinnmitnahmen

project
- finance Projektmittel
- financing Projektfinanzierung
- overruns Projektmehrkosten
- tied lendings projektgebundene Ausleihungen

promissory note (a) Schuldschein; (b) Solawechsel

property (a) Vermögen; (b) Grundbesitz
- bond fund →property fund
- charges Grundstückslasten
- fund (a) Sachwertfonds; (b) Immobilienfonds
- lending Realkreditgeschäft
- shares Immobilienwerte
- tax Vermögenssteuer
- unit trust → property fund

proposed letter of credit Stichwortakkreditiv

prospectus Emissionsprospekt
- vetting Prüfung des Emissionsprospektes

protection Schutz; Absicherung, Sicherung
- by registration at the Land Registry grundbuchamtliche Absicherung
- of a bill Einlösung eines Wechsels
- of deposits Einlagensicherung, Einlagenschutz

protective committee Schutzvereinigung von Aktionären eines in Zahlungsschwierigkeiten geratenen Unternehmens

protective covenants Schutzbestimmungen

protest Protest
- certificate Protesturkunde
- fee Protestgebühr

protest for non-acceptance (non-payment) Protest mangels Annahme (Zahlung)

protest v. protestieren

to have a bill protested einen Wechsel zu Protest gehen lassen

provable debt anmeldbare Konkursforderung

provide v. bereitstellen, zur Verfügung stellen

to - adequately against lending risks angemessene Risikovorsorge treffen

to - for loan losses Rückstellungen (Wertberichtigungen) für Verluste im Kreditgeschäft vornehmen

to - security for a loan einen Kredit unterlegen, eine Sicherheit für einen Kredit bereitstellen, besichern

provision (a) Bereitstellung, Zurverfügungstellung; (b) Vorschrift, Bestimmung; (c) Rückstellung

- of capital Bereitstellung von Kapital
- of cover Indeckungnahme; Anschaffung der Deckung
- of real security dingliche Absicherung

provisional vorläufig

- accounts vorläufiger Abschluß
- allotment letter Bezugsrechtsangebot
- bond Interimsschein
- rating vorläufige Anleihebewertung

provisioning Bildung von Rückstellungen, Risikovorsorge (im Kreditgeschäft)

- policy Vorsorgepolitik, Wertberichtigungspolitik
- requirements Rückstellungsbedarf

provisions Rückstellungen, Wertberichtigungen

- against sovereign risks Rückstellungen für Länderrisiken
- for bad and doubtful debts (for doubtful accounts) Rückstellungen für (Wertberichtigungen auf) zweifelhafte Forderungen
- for country debts →provisions against sovereign risks
- for diminution in market value Rückstellungen für Minderung des Marktwertes
- for loan losses Rückstellungen (Wertberichtigungen) für Verluste im Kreditgeschäft, Verlustrückstellungen
- written back aufgelöste Rückstellungen

proxy (a) Vollmacht, Stimmrechtsvollmacht, Vertretungsvollmacht; (b) Stimmrechts-Bevollmächtigter, Vollmachtsinhaber

- card Vollmachtsformular
- shareholder Vollmachtsaktionär
- statement (a) Vollmachtsformular; (b) Vertretungs- (Stimmrechts-) Anweisungen
- voting right Vollmachtsstimmrecht

prudent man rule Grundsatz, nach dem Treuhänder die ihnen anvertrauten Gelder in Papieren anlegen können, die sie mit der Sorgfalt eines ordentlichen Kaufmannes ausgewählt haben

public

- bond öffentliche Anleihe
- borrowing requirements Kreditbedarf der öffentlichen Hand
- buying Publikumskäufe, Käufe des Anlagepublikums
- company Publikumsgesellschaft
- debt offering öffentliches Zeichnungsangebot, zur öffentlichen Zeichnung aufgelegte Emission

public
- floatation öffentliche Plazierung, Unterbringung beim Publikum
- lending schemes öffentliche Kreditprogramme
- limited company Aktiengesellschaft (Br)
- offering ⟶ public debt offering

purchase for future delivery Terminkauf

purchase on margin Wertpapierkauf gegen Kredit

purchasing syndicate Übernahmekonsortium

pure bond value Wert einer Anleihe ohne Umtausch- bzw. Wandlungsrechte

put Verkaufsoption

put v.

to - on Börse: sich befestigen, anziehen

to - up capital Kapital aufbringen (bereitstellen)

to - up a mortgage lien eine hypothekarische (grundpfandrechtliche) Sicherheit stellen

to - up security for a loan einen Kredit besichern (unterlegen), eine Kreditsicherheit bereitstellen

put holder Inhaber einer Verkaufsoption

put option Verkaufsoption

putting up security Sicherheitsleistung, Besicherung, Unterlegung

put writer Stillhalter einer Verkaufsoption, Stillhalter in Geld

Q

qualification shares Pflichtaktien der Mitglieder des Verwaltungsrates

qualified
- agreement to reimburse eingeschränkte Remboursermächtigung
- audit certificate eingeschränkter Bestätigungsvermerk
- for dividend dividendenberechtigt

quarter stock Aktien mit einem Nennwert von $ 25

quick assets leicht realisierbare Aktiva, schnell greifbare Mittel

quiescent stocks Aktien ohne nennenswerte Kursbewegungen bzw. Umsätze

quorum beschlußfähige Mehrheit

quotation Notierung, Kurs

quotations
- at the short end Notierungen im kurzfristigen Bereich
- for future delivery Terminnotierungen
- sheet Kursblatt, Kurszettel

quote v. notieren; einen Kurs stellen (im Devisenhandel)

to - in the USM im Freiverkehr notieren (Br)

quoted company börsennotiertes Unternehmen

R

R/R/R Begriff im Zusammenhang mit Umschuldungen: restructuring / rescheduling / refinancing Sanierung / Umschuldung / Refinanzierung

raising funds in the capital market Mittelbeschaffung am Kapitalmarkt, Inanspruchnahme des Kapitalmarktes

rally in equities Kurserholung am Aktienmarkt

range Spanne, Bandbreite
- of investment vehicles Anlagepalette, Spektrum der Anlagemöglichkeiten
- of maturities Fälligkeitsfächer
- of services offered Dienstleistungspalette, Leistungsangebot

rank Rang, Rangstelle
to - ahead (after) im Rang vorgehen (nachgehen)
to - pari passu im Rang gleichgestellt sein
to - preferentially bevorrechtigt sein

ranking (a) Rangfolge, Rangordnung; (b) Rangstelle
- of mortgages Hypothekenrangordnung, Hypothekenrangfolge

rate (a) Kurs, Wechselkurs; (b) Satz, Zinssatz
rates at the short end of the market Sätze (Notierungen) im kurzfristigen Bereich
rates offered Konditionenangebot

rate v. bewerten, klassifizieren, beurteilen (Anleihe, Kreditnehmer)

rateably secured clause Ranggleichstellungsklausel

rate
- adjustment Zinsanpassung, Konditionenanpassung
- anticipation switch Portefeuilleumschichtung (in Erwartung einer Kurs- bzw. Zinssatzänderung)
- ceiling Zinsobergrenze
- concessions Zugeständnisse bei den Konditionen
- fixing Kursfestsetzung
- fluctuations Kursschwankungen

rate-hedged currency transactions kursgesicherte Währungsgeschäfte

rate-hedging Kurssicherung
- cost Kurssicherungskosten
- deal Kurssicherungsgeschäft
- facility Kurssicherungsoption, Kurssicherungsmöglichkeit
- scheme Kurssicherungsprogramm
- transaction → rate-hedging deal

rate-supporting
- interventions kurssichernde (kursstützende) Interventionen
- purchases Kursstützungskäufe

rating Bewertung, Klassifizierung, Bonitätseinstufung, Stellung
- in the money market Bewertung (Stellung) am Geldmarkt
- of a bond issue Anleiheklassifizierung
- of the issuer Bonität des Emittenten, Emissionskredit
- ratios Bewertungskennziffern (z.B. für Emissionen)
- table Bonitätsskala

ratio (a) Verhältnis; (b) betriebswirtschaftliche (finanzielle) Kennzahl
- analysis Kennzahlanalyse
- of allotment Zuteilungsverhältnis, Zuteilungsquote (bei Neuemissionen)
- of loans to deposits Verhältnis zwischen Ausleihungen und Einlagen

readily convertible into cash leicht liquidisierbar

ready market aufnahmefähiger Markt

real estate Grundbesitz, Immobilien
- appreciation Immobilienwertsteigerung
- collateral Grundsicherheit, Sicherheit in Form von Grundstücken bzw. Gebäuden
- investment trust Immobilienfonds
- lien Grundpfandrecht, Grundschuld
- loan Realkredit, Hypothekarkredit
- security →real estate collateral

realignment
- of exchange rates Wechselkursneuordnung
- of lending rates Neuausrichtung der Konditionen im Kreditgeschäft

real
- interest rate Realzinssatz, Effektivzinssatz
- interest return Effektivverzinsung

realisable value Veräußerungswert, Realisationswert

realisation Veräußerung, Verwertung; Verflüssigung; Realisierung
- of a collateral (security) Verwertung einer Sicherheit
- of price gains Realisierung von Kursgewinnen
- of the securities portfolio Verflüssigung des Wertpapierdepots

reallowance bei einer Emission: Bonifikation, Wiederverkäuferrabatt

real security dingliche Sicherheit

reassessment of the loan risks Neueinschätzung der Kreditrisiken

receivables Forderungen, Außenstände
- from lending transactions Forderungen aus Kreditgeschäften

receiver Konkursverwalter

receiving agent bei einer Emission: Annahmestelle

receiving order Konkurseröffnungsbeschluß

receptive market aufnahmefähiger Markt

recognised bank nach dem Banking Act von 1979 zugelassene Bank

reconciliation of accounts Kontoabstimmung

reconstruct v. sanieren

record date Stichtag (z.B. für die Feststellung der dividendenberechtigten Aktionäre)

record of stockholders Aktionärsregister

recourse Rückgriff, Regreß
to have - against the drawer Rückgriff auf den Aussteller nehmen

recourse
- claim   Regreßforderung
- debtor   Rückgriffsschuldner
- in default of payment   Regreß mangels Zahlung
- in order of endorsers   Reihenrückgriff
- to a party liable on a bill   Wechselregreß

recover (a) beitreiben, einziehen; (b) sich erholen

to - in after-hours trading sich nachbörslich erholen

to - a loan by legal process eine Darlehensforderung gerichtlich beitreiben

recovery (a) Beitreibung, Einzug; (b) Erholung

recoveries on loans previously charged off   Einbringung von bereits abgebuchten Kreditforderungen

recovery of a debt   Forderungseinzug

recovery in the equity market   Erholung am Aktienmarkt

recycling of petrodollars   Rückführung der Überschußgelder, Wiedereinschleusung der Liquiditätsüberschüsse der OPEC-Staaten

red clause credit   Akkreditivbevorschussung

redeem (a) tilgen, ablösen (Anleihe, Hypothek); (b) zurückkaufen, zurücknehmen (Fondsanteile)

redeemable preference shares   rückzahlbare Vorzugsaktien

redemption (a) Tilgung, Ablösung, Rückzahlung; (b) Rücknahme

redemptions (a) Tilgungsleistungen, Tilgungszahlungen; (b) bei Investmentfonds:Mittelrückflüsse, Rücknahme von Anteilen

redemption
- arrears   Tilgungsrückstände, rückständige Tilgungsleistungen
- break   Aussetzung der Tilgungszahlungen
- by annual drawings   Tilgung durch jährliche Auslosungen
- commission   bei Anleihen: Einlösungsprovision
- commitments   Tilgungsverpflichtungen
- deferral   Tilgungsaufschub
- discount   Tilgungsdisagio, Rückkaufsdisagio
- fund   Tilgungsfonds
- funds   Tilgungsmittel
- holiday   tilgungsfreie Jahre, Tilgungsfreijahre
- notice   Tilgungsankündigung
- payment   Tilgungszahlung, Tilgungsleistung
- period   Tilgungsdauer
- premium   Tilgungsaufgeld, Tilgungsagio
- price (a) Tilgungskurs, Rücknahmepreis; (b) Rückzahlungswert
- requirements   Tilgungserfordernisse, Tilgungsbelastung
- service   Tilgungsdienst
- terms   Tilgungsmodalitäten

red herring   vorläufiger Emissionsprospekt

rediscount   Rediskont

eligible for - with (at) the Bank of England   rediskontfähig bei der Bank von England

rediscount v.   rediskontieren

to have bills rediscounted   Wechsel rediskontieren lassen

rediscount
- limit   Rediskontplafond
- line   Rediskontlinie, Rediskontrahmen

385

rediscount
- quota Rediskontkontingent
- rate Rediskontsatz
- undertaking Rediskontzusage

reduction Senkung, Verringerung; Rückführung
- of lending rates Senkung der Kreditzinsen
- of the loan to the limit agreed upon Rückführung des Kredites in den vereinbarten Rahmen

re-exchange Rückwechsel

reference bank Referenzbank (nach deren Geldmarktsätzen sich der Zinssatz für variabel verzinsliche Papiere richtet)

refinance v. refinanzieren
to - at matching maturities laufzeitkongruent (fristenkongruent) refinanzieren
to - in the capital market über den Kapitalmarkt refinanzieren

refinance bill Refinanzierungswechsel

refinance credit Refinanzierungskredit

refinancing Refinanzierung
- commitment Refinanzierungszusage, Refinanzierungsverpflichtung
- cost Refinanzierungskosten
- funds Refinanzierungsmittel
- line Refinanzierungsrahmen
- of lendings Refinanzierung des Aktivgeschäftes (der Ausleihungen)
- undertaking Refinanzierungszusage

refloat v. sanieren, umstrukturieren

reflow (reflux) of funds transferred abroad Rückfluß der ins Ausland abgeflossenen Gelder

refund v. (a) rückerstatten; (b) refinanzieren, umschulden (Anleihe)

refunding
- issue Refinanzierungsanleihe, Umschuldungsanleihe
- mortgage bond Refinanzierungspfandbrief

register v. eintragen, registrieren

registered debenture Namensschuldverschreibung

registered land certificate beglaubigter Grundbuchauszug

registered representatives qualifizierte Anlageberater bzw. Außendienstmitarbeiter von Brokern oder Wertpapierhändlern

registered shares (stock) Namensaktien

registration statement Anmeldung einer Emission bei der ⟶ Securities Exchange Commission

regular market organisierter Markt

regular way delivery Auslieferung von Wertpapieren vier Tage nach Abschluß des zugrunde liegenden Geschäftes

regulated investment companies Kapitalanlagegesellschaften, die in ihrer Anlage- und Dividendenpolitik gesetzlichen Richtlinien unterliegen (Br)

reimbursement (a) Rückvergütung, Rückerstattung; (b) Remboursbank entitled to claim reimbursement remboursberechtigte Bank
to obtain reimbursement from the foreign bank sich auf die ausländische Bank erholen

reimbursement
  to provide reimbursement on
  first call Rembours auf erstes
  Anfordern leisten

reimbursement
- authority Rembourszusage,
  Remboursermächtigung
- claims Remboursansprüche
- covering letter Rembours-
  schreiben
- credit Sichtakkreditiv
- instructions Remboursschrei-
  ben, Trassierungskredit
- recourse Remboursrückgriff

reimbursing bank Remboursbank,
  Remboursstelle

reinvestment Wiederanlage, Re-
  investition
- discount Wiederanlagerabatt

reinvoicing company Offshore-
  -Finanzierungsgesellschaft

REIT → real estate investment
  trust
related banking services Nebenleistungen einer Bank

release v.
  to - the documents die Dokumente freigeben
  to - the guarantor from his
  liability den Garantiegeber
  aus seiner Haftung entlassen
  to - liquidity Liquidität frei-
  setzen
  to - a mortgage eine Hypothek
  löschen

remargin v. nachschießen

reminder Mahnbrief

remission of debts Schuldenerlaß

remit v. (a) überweisen, über-
  senden; (b) anschaffen (Dek-
  kung); (c) erlassen (Schuld)

remittance Überweisung, Rimesse;
  Anschaffung
- by cable telegrafische Überweisung (Anschaffung)
- of cover Anschaffung der
  Deckung

remittee Empfänger, Begünstigter

remitter Überweisender, Auftraggeber

remitting bank überweisende (übersendende) Bank, Einreicherbank

renegotiable-rate mortgage Hypothek, bei der der Zinssatz alle
  drei oder fünf Jahre neu fest-
  gesetzt wird

renegotiate v. im Kreditgeschäft:
  den Zinssatz für ein Darlehen
  (eine Hypothek) den veränderten
  Geldmarktbedingungen anpassen;
  die Kreditkonditionen neu festsetzen (aushandeln)

renegotiated loan Anpassungs-
  darlehen

renegotiated loan business An-
  passungsgeschäft

renew v. erneuern, verlängern

renewal (a) Erneuerung, Verlängerung; (b) bei einem Wechsel:
  Prolongation
- bill Prolongationswechsel,
  Prolongationsabschnitt
- clause Verlängerungsklausel
- coupon Erneuerungsschein,
  Leiste, Leistenschein
- of a bill Prolongation eines
  Wechsels
- of a loan accommodation Darlehensverlängerung, Erneuerung
  (Verlängerung) eines Kreditverhältnisses, Kreditprolonga-
  tion
- rate Prolongationssatz
- undertaking Prolongationszusage

renounce v. to - an allotment auf eine Zuteilung verzichten

renounceable rights issue Bezugsrechtsemission, bei der für die Inhaber alter Aktien keine Zeichnungspflicht besteht

reopenings Ausgabe zusätzlicher Stücke zu bereits im Umlauf befindlichen Papieren

repatriation of capital Rückführung von Kapital

repay v. zurückzahlen

to - ahead of schedule (prior to maturity) vorzeitig zurückzahlen

to - at a premium mit einem Aufgeld zurückzahlen

repayable in full (a) vollständig rückzahlbar; (b) gesamtfällig (eine Anleihe)

repayment Rückzahlung, Tilgung, Ablösung, Abdeckung

upon repayment of the loan nach Rückzahlung des Kredites, nach Beendigung des Kreditverhältnisses

repayments on lendings Kreditrückflüsse, Rückflüsse aus dem Aktivgeschäft, Mittelrückfluß aus dem Kreditportefeuille

repayments required Tilgungserfordernisse, erforderliche Tilgungsleistungen

repayment
- charge Tilgungsbelastung
- free years Rückzahlungssperrfrist
- holiday tilgungsfreie Jahre
- of a loan Rückzahlung (Abdeckung) eines Kredites
- of principal Kapitalrückzahlung
- rate Tilgungsrate

- schedule Tilgungsplan
- terms Rückzahlungsbedingungen, Tilgungsbedingungen, Rückzahlungsmodalitäten

replacement Ersatz
- certificates Ersatzstücke, Ersatzzertifikate
- cheque Ersatzscheck
- cost Wiederbeschaffungswert

report v. (a) berichten; (b) ausweisen (in der Bilanz)

reporting
- date Stichtag; Bilanztermin
- requirements (a) Berichtspflichten, Meldevorschriften; (b) Bilanzierungsvorschriften

repos → repurchase agreement

repurchase Rückkauf, Rücknahme

repurchase v. zurückkaufen, zurücknehmen

to - in the market am Markt zurückkaufen

to - securities offered Wertpapiere aus dem Markt nehmen

repurchase
- agreement Pensionsgeschäft
- agreement on bills Wechselpensionsgeschäft
- at net asset value Rücknahme zum Inventarwert (Fondsanteile)
- commitment Rücknahmeverpflichtung
- discount Rückkaufsdisagio
- feature Rücknahmemöglichkeit, Rückkaufsoption
- option Rückkaufsoption
- price Rücknahmekurs, Rückkaufskurs
- privilege Rücknahmerecht

resale market Sekundärmarkt

reschedule v. umschulden

rescheduling Umschuldung
- accord (agreement) Umschuldungsabkommen
- exposure Umschuldungsengagements
- loan Umschuldungskredit
- package Umschuldungspaket
- terms Umschuldungskonditionen

rescission of contract Vertragsauflösung

rescue
- consortium Auffangkonsortium, Sanierungskonsortium
- operation Stützungsaktion
- scheme Sanierungsprogramm

reserve Rücklage
- balances (a) Rücklagen; (b) Mindestreserveguthaben von US-Banken bei einer Federal Reserve Bank
- carrying liabilities mindestreservepflichtige Verbindlichkeiten
- cost Mindestreservekosten
- facility Reservemittel, Reservemedium (IWF)
- management Reservehaltung
- requirements Mindestreserveanforderungen, Reservesoll
- statement Mindestreservemeldung
- unit Reserveeinheit (IWF)

resident Gebietsansässiger

residential
- banking ⟶ home banking
- finance Wohnungsbaudarlehen, Wohnungsbaufinanzierung
- lendings Wohnungsbaukreditgeschäft

- mortgage lending privates Hypothekenkreditgeschäft

residual
- amount Restbetrag, Spitze
- debt Restschuld
- exposure Restrisiko, Restengagement
- time to maturity Restlaufzeit
- value Restbuchwert

resolutive condition auflösende Bestimmung

resource stock Energiewerte, Rohstoffwerte

respite Stundung, Aufschub
- for interest payments Zinsstundung
- for principal (debt) repayments Tilgungsaufschub

respondent bank Korrespondenzbank

restitution claims Herausgabeansprüche

restrictions on borrowings abroad Beschränkung der Kreditaufnahme im Ausland

restrictive
- endorsement Rektaindossament
- loan provisions Auflagen für den Kreditnehmer
- monetary policy restriktive Geldpolitik

restructure v. umstrukturieren (Kredite); sanieren

retail
- account Privatkundenkonto
- area Privatkundenbereich
- asset portfolio Gesamtsumme der Ausleihungen an Privatkunden, Privatkundenkreditvolumen

389

retail
- banking Privatkundengeschäft, Mengengeschäft
- banking department (division) Privatkundenabteilung
- banking market Privatkundenmarkt
- banks auf das Privatkundengeschäft spezialisierte Banken; Sparkassen und Volksbanken
- branch network Zweigstellennetz einer Bank
- buying Käufe privater Anleger
- buying interest privates Kaufinteresse
- credit business Privatkundenkreditgeschäft
- customer Privatkunde
- deposit rates Zinssätze für Privatkundeneinlagen
- deposits Privatkundeneinlagen
- fund Publikumsfonds
- investment interest Anlageinteresse privater Anleger
- lending business (operations) Privatkundenkreditgeschäft
- lending demand Nachfrage nach Privatkundenkrediten
- liability portfolio Gesamtsumme der Privatkundeneinlagen
- loan Privatkundenkredit
- operations Privatkundengeschäft
- outlet terminal Kassenterminal
- products Dienstleistungen für Privatkunden
- side on the retail side im Privatkundenbereich
- Society kleine Genossenschaftsbank (Br)

retain v. einbehalten

retained earnings (a) einbehaltene Gewinne; (b) freie Rücklagen

retaining lien Zurückbehaltungsrecht

retention of profits Einbehaltung der Gewinne

retire v. (a) tilgen, ablösen, zurückzahlen (Anleihe, Kredit); (b) einlösen (Wechsel); (c) einziehen (Banknoten)

retirement Tilgung, Ablösung, Rückzahlung, Einlösung

retirement ahead of schedule vorzeitige Tilgung

retirement out of retained earnings Ablösung aus einbehaltenen Gewinnen

retirements Abgänge von Gegenständen des Anlagevermögens

retractable
- bonds Anleihen, bei denen alle drei bis vier Jahre eine Zinsanpassung erfolgt
- maturity vorverlegbarer Fälligkeitstermin

return (a) Verzinsung, Rendite; (b) Rückgabe; (c) Ausweis, Aufstellung

return on equity Kapitalverzinsung

returns nicht eingelöste Schecks und Wechsel, Scheck- und Wechselrückgaben

return v. zurückgeben, zurücksenden

to - unpaid unbezahlt zurückgeben, nicht einlösen

to - for lack of funds mangels Deckung zurückgeben

return-of-money bond Rückzahlungsgarantie

revaluation (a) Aufwertung;
(b) Neubewertung

- rate   Aufwertungssatz

revenue   (a) Einnahmen, Einkünfte; (b) Neubewertung

revenue bond   Schuldverschreibung, Obligation (in der Regel eine kapitalertragssteuerfreie Kommunalobligation)

reverse   v. stornieren, umbuchen

reverse

- annuity mortgage   Hypothek, durch die eine private Rentenversicherung finanziert wird

- arbitrage   Aufnahme eines Kredites, um einen höherverzinslichen Kredit abzulösen

- entry   Stornierung; Stornobuchung

- interest rate pattern   inverse Zinsstruktur

- split   Aktienzusammenlegung; Umtausch mehrerer Aktien in eine neue Aktie

- yield gap   inverses Renditegefälle

review   v. to - a loan exposure   ein Kreditengagement überprüfen

revocable credit   (a) Kredit, der jederzeit durch die ausreichende Stelle gekündigt werden kann; (b) widerrufbares Akkreditiv

revoke   v. widerrufen

to - the guarantee undertaking   die Garantiezusage zurücknehmen

to - a power of attorney   eine Vollmacht widerrufen

revolve   v. to - a credit line   eine Kreditlinie erneuern (verlängern)

revolving

- acceptance credit facility   revolvierender Akzeptkredit

- credit   revolvierender Kredit (Kredit, der sich bei Erfüllung bestimmter Voraussetzungen automatisch verlängert)

- documentary credit   revolvierendes Akkreditiv

- multicurrency credit   revolvierender Kredit, der in verschiedenen Währungen in Anspruch genommen werden kann

- term credit   revolvierender mittelfristiger Kredit

right of

- conversion   Wandlungsrecht, Umtauschrecht

- first refusal   Vorkaufsrecht

- recourse   Rückgriffsrecht; Regreßanspruch

- setoff clause   Klausel, die bei Zahlungsverzug des Schuldners dem Kreditgeber das Recht gibt, ausstehende Beträge mit vorhandenen Guthaben zu verrechnen

rights   Bezugsrechte

- agent   Bezugsstelle, Zeichnungsstelle

- financing   Finanzierung durch Ausgabe von Bezugsrechten

- holder   Bezugsrechtsinhaber

- issue   Bezugsrechtsemission

   on the basis of a one for ten rights issue   auf der Grundlage eines Bezugsrechtes im Verhältnis 10:1

- issue announcement   Bezugsrechtsankündigung

- letter   Bezugsrechtsangebot

- money   Bezugsrechtserlös

- offering   Bezugsrechtsangebot

- on   einschließlich Bezugsrechte

- quotation   Bezugsrechtsnotierung

- trading   Bezugsrechtshandel
- value   Bezugsrechtswert

right to
- call in a loan   Kündigungsrecht bei einer Anleiheemission
- payment under a credit   Akkreditivauszahlungsanspruch
- separate settlement   Aussonderungsrecht

risk   Risiko
- appraisal   Risikobewertung
- averse (risk-averting) investor   risikoscheuer Anleger
- capital   Risikokapital
- class   Risikogruppe
- hedging   Risikodeckung, Risikoabsicherung
- loving investor   risikofreudiger Anleger
- management   Risikomanagement, Risikosteuerung
- measuring (measurement)   Risikobewertung
- of default   Verzugsrisiko, Ausfallrisiko
- rating   Risikobewertung
- spreading   Risikostreuung

roll   v. to - over a loan
(a) einen fälligen Kredit verlängern (erneuern); (b) eine fällige Anleihe mit dem Erlös aus einer neuen Emission zurückzahlen

roll-over credit   Rollover-Kredit (Kredit, bei dem in bestimmten Zeitabständen eine Verlängerung bzw. Zinsanpassung erfolgt; in der Regel ist der Zinssatz an einen Interbankensatz, z.B. LIBOR, gekoppelt)

rounding-off buying   Arrondierungskäufe an der Börse

round lot   Hunderter-Einheit, Schlußeinheit von 100 Aktien

round tripping   Durchhandeln, d.h. Aufnahme von Geldern und anschließende Weitergabe zu einem höheren Zinssatz

RPs ⟶ repurchase agreements

RTC ⟶ revolving term credit

run   v.
to - the books   die Konsortialführung innehaben
to - cover   Deckungskäufe vornehmen

running
- account   Kontokorrentkonto
- account credit   Dispositionskredit
- days   laufende Kalendertage
- interest   Stückzinsen
- yield   Umlaufsrendite

S

safe custody (Depot-) Verwahrung

safe deposit (box) Schließfach, Safe, Tresorfach

safekeeping (Depot-) Verwahrung
- agreement Verwahrungsvertrag
- charges Verwahrungsgebühren, Depotgebühren

safety of principal Sicherheit des investierten Kapitals

sagging equity prices nachgebende (rückläufige) Aktienkurse

salary payment by bank giro credit bargeldlose Gehaltszahlung

sale Verkauf, Veräußerung; Verwertung

sale and repurchase agreement Pensionsgeschäft
- in bills Wechselpensionsgeschäft
- in securities Wertpapierpensionsgeschäft

sale
- by tender Verkauf auf dem Submissionsweg (einer Emission)
- in the open market Verkauf am freien Markt, freihändiger Verkauf
- of a collateral Verkauf (Verwertung) einer Sicherheit
- of mutual fund shares Mittelzuflüsse bei einem Investmentfonds, Verkauf von Fondsanteilen
- of subscription rights Verwertung von Bezugsrechten

sales load Ausgabeaufschlag

SAM ⟶ shared appreciation mortgage

same-day settlement Abrechnung (Regulierung) eines Effektenauftrages am gleichen Tag; taggleiche Verbuchung

Samurai bonds Yen-Auslandsanleihen; Yen-Anleihen ausländischer Emittenten auf dem japanischen Kapitalmarkt

sanction v. genehmigen, bewilligen (einen Kredit)

sanctioning Bewilligung
- limit Kreditbewilligungsgrenze
- power Kreditkompetenz

satisfaction (a) Befriedigung; (b) Löschung

selling securities in - of a debt Befriedigung aus Wertpapieren
- of a claim against the borrower Befriedigung eines Anspruches gegenüber dem Kreditnehmer
- of mortgage Hypothekenlöschung

satisfy v. to - a loan die Kreditansprüche befriedigen

savings
- account Sparkonto
- and loan association (S&L) Sparkasse (US)
- and loan industry US-Sparkassensektor
- bank Sparkasse
- bank lending Ausleihungen der Sparkassen

savings
- bond   Sparbrief
- book   (a) Sparbuch; (b) Spareinlagenvolumen
- certificate   Sparbrief
- deposits   Spareinlagen
- funds   Spargelder, Sparmittel
- rate   Sparquote
- scheme   Sparplan, Sparvertrag

SBA → Small Business Administration

scale v. to - down   repartieren

scale-down (scaling down) of purchase orders   Repartierung der Kaufaufträge, Geldrepartierung

scattered buying orders   vereinzelte Kaufaufträge

scheduled redemption   planmäßige Tilgung

schedule of borrowers   Verzeichnis der Kreditnehmer, Adressenliste

schedule of charges   Gebührenordnung

scheme-linked saving   Programmsparen

scoring system   Punktebewertungssystem (bei Kreditanträgen)

scout   Konsortialführer

scrip   vorläufiges Zertifikat, Interimsschein, Jungschein
- issue   Berichtigungsaktien, Gratisaktien

SDRs → Singapore Depositary Receipts

search of the Land Register (of the official title records) Grundbucheinsicht, Einsichtnahme in das Grundbuch

seasonal borrowing needs   saisonaler Kreditbedarf

seasonal loan   Saisonkredit

seasoned securities   gängige Emissionen (Wertpapiere, die sich bereits eine gewisse Zeit im Umlauf befinden; 120 - 360 Tage nach ihrer Emission)

seat on the exchange   Börsenmitgliedschaft

SEC → Securities and Exchange Commission

secondary
- banking   Finanzierungs- und Teilzahlungskreditinstitute
- capital   Vorzugsaktien mit begrenzter Laufzeit plus nachrangige Schuldtitel
- counters   Nebenwerte
- credit   Gegenakkreditiv, subsidiäres Akkreditiv
- distribution → secondary offering
- liquidity   Sekundärliquidität
- market   Sekundärmarkt, Zweitmarkt, Markt für bereits im Umlauf befindliche Titel
- market dealings   Handel im Sekundärmarkt
- market issue   Alt-Emission
- market securities   Sekundärmarkttitel, Zweitmarkttitel
- movements   sekundäre Kursbewegungen
- offering (offer)   Zeichnungsangebot für bereits im Umlauf befindliche Papiere; Verkauf eines Wertpapierpaketes im Sekundärmarkt
- reserves   Sekundärreserven einer US-Bank (setzen sich in erster Linie aus kurzfristigen Staatstiteln und leicht realisierbaren Papieren zusammen)
- stocks   Nebenwerte

second

- beneficiary Zweitbegünstigter
- line issues Nebenwerte
- mortgage nachrangige (zweite) Hypothek
- mortgage loan zweitstelliges Hypothekendarlehen
- of exchange Wechselzweitausfertigung, Sekundawechsel

sector index Branchenindex

secure v. sichern, besichern, absichern, unterlegen

to - the project with own capital resources das Projekt mit Eigenmitteln unterlegen

secured borrowing gedeckter Kredit

secured by blocked time deposits unterlegt durch gesperrtes Festgeld

secured by real security dinglich gesichert

secured by registration at the Land Registry grundbuchlich gesichert

secured debt besicherte Schuldtitel, abgesicherte Verbindlichkeiten

secured loan (lending) besicherter (gedeckter) Kredit

secured money Gelder, die die →eligible banks den discount houses zur Verfügung stellen

securities (a) Wertpapiere, Effekten, Stücke; (b) Sicherheiten

- assigned as collateral sicherungsübereignete Wertpapiere
- called for redemption zur Tilgung aufgerufene Wertpapiere
- delivered ausgelieferte Wertpapiere (Stücke), Effektenausgang
- deposited as collateral for a loan als Sicherheit für einen Kredit hinterlegte Wertpapiere, Sicherungsgut in Form von Wertpapieren
- drawn for redemption ausgeloste Wertpapiere
- due for redemption endfällige Stücke, fällige Wertpapiere
- eligible as collateral beleihbare Wertpapiere
- held as collateral als Sicherheit verwahrte Wertpapiere, Kautionseffekten
- held in custody (held in safekeeping) depotverwahrte Wertpapiere, Depotstücke
- listed on the stock exchange börsennotierte Wertpapiere
- pledged as collateral Deckungspapiere
- pledged under repurchase agreements in Pension gegebene Wertpapiere
- purchased under agreements to resell Wertpapiere, die im Rahmen von Pensionsgeschäften übernommen wurden
- redeemable by drawings auslosbare (verlosbare) Wertpapiere
- redeemed prior to maturity (redeemed ahead of schedule) vorzeitig getilgte Wertpapiere
- repurchased Rücklaufstücke, zurückgekaufte Wertpapiere
- sold at a discount mit einem Abschlag verkaufte Wertpapiere, Abzinsungspapiere
- traded for cash Kassapapiere
- traded in the USM im Freiverkehr gehandelte Wertpapiere

securities

- account Wertpapierkonto; Depot, Depotkonto
- account statement Depotauszug
- administration Wertpapierverwaltung, Depotverwaltung

securities
- and Exchange Commission US-Börsenaufsichtsbehörde
- at market values Wertpapiere zum Marktwert (Kurswert)
- clearing Effekten-Clearing, Effektengiroverkehr, Wertpapierverrechnung
- clearing corporation Effekten-Clearingstelle, Wertpapiersammelbank
- collateral Sicherheit in Form von Wertpapieren
- contract note Effektenkauf- bzw. -verkaufsabrechnung
- custody Verwahrung von Wertpapieren, Depotverwahrung
- dealer Wertpapierhändler
- dealings Wertpapierhandel
- delivery Auslieferung von Wertpapieren
- depository Depotbank, Hinterlegungsstelle
- escrow account Treuhanddepot, Anderdepot
- exchange Wertpapierbörse
- gains Gewinne aus Wertpapiergeschäften
- holdings Wertpapierbestand, Effektenbestand; Wertpapierbesitz
- income Wertpapiererträge
- investment Wertpapieranlage
- Investor Protection Corporation Schutzversicherung für Wertpapiersparer
- issue Wertpapieremission
- market Wertpapiermarkt
- market credit Effektenkredit
- offering Wertpapieremission, Zeichnungsangebot für ein Wertpapier
- order Effektenauftrag
- ownership Wertpapierbesitz, Eigentumsrechte an Wertpapieren
- portfolio Wertpapierportefeuille, Wertpapierdepot; Wertpapierbestand; Wertpapierbesitz
- prices Wertpapierkurse
- purchase Wertpapierkauf, Effektenkauf
- purchase price Effektenkaufpreis
- quotation Wertpapiernotierung, Wertpapierkurs
- regulation Wertpapiergesetzgebung
- sale Wertpapierverkauf
- trading Wertpapierhandel
- trading for own account Wertpapiereigenhandel
- trading income Wertpapierhandelsgewinne, Ergebnis im Wertpapiergeschäft
- trading operations Wertpapiergeschäft
- trading portfolio Wertpapierhandelsbestand
- transfer Wertpapierübertragung
- write-offs Abschreibungen (Wertberichtigungen) auf Wertpapiere

security (a) Sicherheit; (b) Wertpapier

as security for a credit line zur Unterlegung einer Kreditlinie, als Sicherheit für eine Kreditlinie

assigned as security sicherungsübereignet, als Sicherheit abgetreten

security deposited in support of a loan Sicherheitsleistung; für einen Kredit hinterlegte Sicherheit, Sicherungsgut

security ranking pari passu gleichrangige Sicherheit

security
- agreement (arrangement) Sicherstellungsvertrag, Sicherheiten-

vertrag, Kreditsicherungsvertrag
- code number   Wertpapierkennnummer
- denomination   Wertpapierstückelung
- deposit   hinterlegte Sicherheit, Sicherheitsleistung
- device   Besicherungsform, Sicherheitsform
- evaluation   Bewertung einer Sicherheit, Sicherheitenprüfung, Sicherheitenbewertung
- holdings   Wertpapierbestand, Effektenbestand
- interest   Sicherungsgut, Sicherungsgegenstand, Sicherungsrecht
- issue   Wertpapieremission
- liquidation   Verwertung einer Sicherheit, Verkauf des Sicherungsgutes
- offering   Wertpapieremission
- placing   Wertpapierplazierung
- proceeds   (a) Sicherheitenerlös; (b) Wertpapiererlös, Gegenwert der Wertpapiere
- sale   (a) Effektenverkauf, Wertpapierverkauf; (b) Verwertung einer Sicherheit, Verkauf des Sicherungsgutes
- value   (a) Sicherheitenwert, Wert des Sicherungsgutes; (b) Wert eines Wertpapiers

seesaw market   Schaukelbörse

segregation of securities   Streifbandverwahrung

seizure for security   Sicherungspfändung, Sicherungsbeschlagnahme

self-liquidating advance   Überbrückungskredit (wird aus bestimmten Verkaufserlösen zurückgezahlt)

self-sustaining upturn in the equity market   sich selbst tragender Aufschwung am Aktienmarkt

sell   v. (a) verkaufen; (b) verwerten (Sicherheit); (c) im Geldhandel: überlassen, geben

to - anti-marketwise   gegen den Markttrend verkaufen

to - at a discount   mit einem Abschlag verkaufen, als abgezinstes Papier verkaufen

to - at the market   einen Effektenverkaufsauftrag bestens ausführen

to - in the market   an den Markt abgeben

to - in the open market   am freien Markt verkaufen

to - off   abstoßen (Wertpapiere)

to - on a best efforts basis   auf Kommissionsbasis verkaufen (eine Anleiheemission)

to - on a no-load basis   ohne Ausgabeaufschlag verkaufen (Investmentfondsanteile)

to - out a declining stock   eine im Kurs rückläufige Aktie verkaufen (abstoßen)

to - out holdings   Bestände auflösen (abstoßen)

to - overnight funds   Tagesgeld überlassen

to - rights on   einschließlich Bezugsrechte verkaufen

to - short   Leerverkäufe abschließen

sell advice (recommendation)   Verkaufsempfehlung

seller   Verkäufer
- of a call (put) option ⟶ writer of a call (put) option
- of funds   Geber (auf dem Geldmarkt)

seller-repurchaser   Pensionsgeber

397

seller's market   Verkäufer-
markt

sellers only   Brief (Kurszusatz)

seller's rate   Sortenverkaufskurs; Briefkurs

selling   Verkauf, Verkäufe; Abgaben (Börse)
- agency bank   Verkaufskommis-
  sionsbank
- agent   Verkaufskommissionär
- bank   im Interbankengeschäft:
  Geberbank, geldgebende Bank
- commission   Bankenbonifika-
  tion, Schaltervergütung,
  Schalternutzen
- commitments   Verkaufsengage-
  ments, Verkaufspositionen
- concession → selling commission
- currencies forward   Devisen-
  terminverkäufe
- forward   Terminverkäufe
- group   Verkaufskonsortium,
  Plazierungskonsortium
- in light (quiet) trading   Abgaben bei geringen Umsätzen
- in the Fed funds market   Überlassung von Tagesgeld (US)
- markup   Ausgabeaufschlag (bei
  Fondsanteilen)
- on a best efforts basis   kommissionsweise Übernahme einer
  Emission
- overnight funds   Überlassung
  von Tagesgeld
- position   im Geldhandel:
  Gläubigerposition
- pressure   Abgabedruck, Verkaufsdruck
- price   Verkaufskurs; Ausgabepreis (bei Fondsanteilen)
- rate   Briefkurs, Verkaufskurs;
  Sortenverkaufskurs

- short   Leerverkäufe
- syndicate   Verkaufskonsortium,
  Plazierungskonsortium

sell-off   Glattstellung (von Be-
ständen)

sell order   (Effekten-) Verkaufsauftrag

senior
- creditor   bevorrechtigter Gläubiger
- debenture   erstrangige Schuldverschreibung
- debt   erstrangige Schuldtitel
- mortgage   im Rang vorgehende
  Hypothek; erststellige Hypothek
- securities   mit besonderen Vor-
  rechten ausgestattete Wertpapiere

sentiment in the market   Börsenstimmung, Marktklima

separate
- settlement   Aussonderung (bei
  einem Konkursverfahren)
- valuation   Einzelbewertung

separation of capacity → principle of single capacity

SEPON → Stock Exchange Pool
Nominees

serial bond   Serienanleihe

service   Dienstleistung, Service
range of services offered   Dienstleistungspalette

service   v. (a) bedienen, Zins-
und Tilgungszahlungen leisten,
den Schuldendienst übernehmen;
(b) betreuen, bedienen; (c)
Wertpapiere verwalten (Kupon-,
Tilgungstermine, etc. wahrnehmen)

service card   Bankomat-Karte
(→ servicetill)

service diversification   Diversifizierung des Dienstleistungsangebotes

servicetill   Bankomat (automatisierte Ausgabe von Scheckheften, Kontoauszügen, Geld, etc.)

servicing   (a) Bedienung; (b) Verwaltung (von Wertpapieren)

- a bond   Anleihebedienung, Wahrnehmung des Anleihedienstes

- a debt   Bedienung einer Schuld (eines Kredites), Schuldendienstzahlung, Schuldendienstleistung

- a mortgage loan   Bedienung eines Hypothekendarlehens, Entrichtung von Zins- und Tilgungszahlungen für ein Hypothekendarlehen

servicing ratio   Bedienungsquote

session   Börsensitzung

set v.

to - off against   verrechnen mit, aufrechnen gegen

to - up a line of credit   eine Kreditlinie eröffnen (einrichten)

to - up loan loss provisions   Risikovorsorge treffen, Rücklagen für Verluste im Kreditgeschäft bilden

settle v.   abrechnen, gleichen; abschließen, ausgleichen; abwickeln

settlement   (a) Abrechnung, Begleichung, Regulierung; (b) Abschluß, Ausgleich; (c) Abwicklung; (d) Vergleich (mit Gläubigern); (e) Erfüllung (von Börsengeschäften)

- bank   Abrechnungsbank, abwickelnde Bank

- currency   Abrechnungsvaluta

- day   Erfüllungstag, Liquidationstermin (bei Effektengeschäften); Abschlußtag, Abrechnungstag

- fractions   Abrechnungsspitzen

- note   Abschlußrechnung, Kauf- bzw. Verkaufsabrechnung

- of a deal   Erfüllung (Abrechnung) eines Börsengeschäftes

- of the debit balance   Ausgleich des Sollsaldos

- of fractions   Spitzenausgleich, Spitzenregulierung, Glattstellung von Spitzenbeträgen

- of interest and principal payments falling due   Begleichung der fällig werdenden Zins- und Tilgungszahlungen

- period   Abrechnungszeitraum

- price   Abrechnungskurs, Abschlußkurs; Liquidationskurs

- rate   Abrechnungskurs

- risk   Erfüllungsrisiko

settling day   →settlement day

seven-day

- deposits   Einlagen mit siebentägiger Kündigungsfrist

- money   Wochengeld

- rule   Bestimmung des Take-over Code: Aktienkäufe größeren Umfangs mit dem Ziel einer Firmenübernahme müssen sieben Tage im voraus angekündigt werden

shake-out   Glattstellung von Wertpapierpositionen

share   (a) Aktie; (b) Anteil, Beteiligung; (c) Fondsanteil

shares applied for   gezeichnete Aktien

shares deposited with the bank as collateral   bei der Bank als Sicherheit hinterlegte Aktien; Deckungspapiere, Kautionseffekten shares listed on the stock exchange börsennotierte Aktien

shares quoted in the USM im Freiverkehr notierte Aktien

shares repurchased (shares bought in) zurückgekaufte Aktien

shares sold in the open market am freien Markt verkaufte Aktien

shares tendered (shares on offer) angebotene Aktien

shares traded over the counter im Freiverkehr gehandelte Aktien

share
- account Bausparkassen-Anteilskonto (Br)
- account rate Zinssatz für Bausparkassenanteile
- allotment Aktienzuteilung, zugeteilte Aktien
- applicant (Aktien-) Zeichner
- application (Aktien-) Zeichnung
- application money Zeichnungsbetrag
- bid (Aktien-) Übernahmeangebot
- block Aktienpaket
- buyback Rückkauf von Aktien (durch das emittierende Unternehmen)
- capital Aktienkapital
- capital and reserves Eigenkapital (Aktienkapital plus Rücklagen)
- certificate (a) Aktienzertifikat; (b) Anteilschein

shared appreciation mortgage niedrigverzinsliche Hypothek, bei der der Hypothekengläubiger im Falle eines Verkaufs der als Sicherheit dienenden Liegenschaft am erzielten Gewinn partizipiert

share
- equity offering Aktienemission, Zeichnungsangebot für eine Aktie
- exchange (a) Aktientausch; (b) Umtausch von Aktien in andere Papiere (z.B. Fondsanteile)
- holder approval Zustimmung der Aktionäre
- holder of record eingetragener Aktionär
- holders' equity (funds) Eigenkapital
- holding (a) Aktienbesitz, Anteil am Aktienkapital; (b) Aktienbestand
- holding banks Aktionärsbanken
- issue Aktienemission
- offer (a) (Aktien-) Übernahmeangebot; (b) → share equity offering
- offering price (Aktien-) Emissionskurs
- option Aktienbezugsrecht
- option scheme Aktienbezugsrechtsplan
- ownership scheme Belegschaftsaktienplan
- placing Aktienplazierung
- portfolio Aktienportefeuille;
- premium Aktienagio, Aktienaufgeld
- price Aktienkurs
- price high (low) Höchststand (Tiefstand) eines Aktienkurses
- price making Kursbildung (Kursfindung) am Aktienmarkt
- rating Aktienbewertung
- split Aktiensplit
- stake Aktienanteil
- trading Aktienhandel
- warrant Aktienbezugsrechtsschein

sharp
- markdown deutliche Kursabschläge, Kursrutsch, Minusankündigung
- markup deutliche Kursheraufsetzung, wesentlich höhere Notierung, Plusankündigung
- price fluctuations (swings) starke Kursschwankungen, Kursausschläge
- setback (slide, slump, plunge) in equity prices Kurseinbruch (starker Kursrutsch) am Aktienmarkt
- upsurge (rise) in prices starker Kursanstieg, Kursexplosion

shed (a) abstoßen, verkaufen (Wertpapiere); (b) nachgeben (im Kurs)

shelf registration Rahmenregistrierung bei der → Securities and Exchange Commission (ermöglicht einem Unternehmen die kurzfristige Emission von Papieren)

shell Firmenmantel

shelve v. to - an issue eine Emission zurückstellen

shift v. (a) umgruppieren, umdisponieren, verlagern (Anlagen, Gelder); (b) überwälzen (Kosten, Steuern)

shift Umgruppierung, Verlagerung; Überwälzung
- in risk spreading Risikotransformation

ship mortgage Schiffshypothek

ship mortgage loan Schiffshypothekarkredit

shop Bezeichnung für ein Emissionshaus, das nach einer Wertpapierplazierung auch die Kurspflege für die jeweiligen Papiere übernimmt

shop selling Wertpapierverkäufe des Berufshandels

short (a) Kurzläufer;(b) Leerverkauf; (c) Baissespekulant

shortage Mangel, Knappheit; Defizit
- of buying orders Ordermangel (Börse)
- of cover fehlende Deckung
- of liquidity in the banking system mangelnde Bankenliquidität
- of offerings Materialmangel, Stückemangel (Börse)
- of security Unterbesicherung

short
- bill kurzfristig fällig werdender Wechsel (Wechsel mit einer Restlaufzeit von weniger als zehn Tagen)
- call deposits kurzfristig kündbare Gelder
- covering Deckungskäufe zum Ausgleich eines Leerverkaufs
- dated securities Kurzläufer
- deposits Einlagen mit kurzfristiger Kündigungsfrist
- end of the market (a) kurzer Bereich; (b) Markt für Kurzläufer

  borrower at the short end of the market Geld-, Interbankenmarkt: Nehmer im kurzfristigen Bereich

  interest rates at the short end of the market Zinsen am kurzen Ende
- exchange → short bill
- hedge Verkaufshedge
- interest Baisseengagement
- interest ratio Verhältnis zwischen den bei einer Aktie bestehenden Baisseengagements und den durchschnittlichen Tagesumsätzen in diesem Wert

short
- lendings   kurzfristige Ausleihungen, Kredite mit kurzer Laufzeit, kurzfristiges Geschäft
- life   kurze Laufzeit
- loan   kurzfristiger Kredit
- loan book   Volumen der kurzfristigen Ausleihungen
- maturity   kurze Laufzeit
- position   Baisseengagement
- sale   Leerverkauf, Blankoverkauf
- sale against the box   Form des Leerverkaufs, bei dem wohl die Papiere vorhanden sind, aber erst zu einem späteren Zeitpunkt ausgeliefert werden (z.B. aus Stimmrechtserwägungen heraus)
- seller   Leerverkäufer, Blankoverkäufer
- term borrowing requirements   kurzfristiger Kreditbedarf
- term borrowings   kurzfristige Kredite
- term credit line   kurzfristige Kreditlinie; im Geldhandel: Leihgeldlinie
- term currency borrowing   kurzfristiger Fremdwährungskredit; Leihdevisen
- term lendings   kurzfristige Ausleihungen, kurzfristiges Geschäft
- term rates   Zinssätze im kurzfristigen Bereich

shrinking interest margins   schrumpfende Zinsspannen

SIBOR → Singapore Interbank Offered Rate

side deal   bei Umschuldungen: inoffizielle (meist unerlaubte) Nebenabsprache, d.h. Bevorzugung eines Gläubigerlandes

sidelines   investors remained on the sidelines   die Anleger verhielten sich abwartend

sight
- bill   Sichtwechsel
- credit   Sichtakkreditiv
- deposits   Sichteinlagen
- liabilities   Sichtverbindlichkeiten
- negotiation credit   Sichtnegoziationskredit
- rate   Sichtkurs

sign   v. to - on an account   für ein Konto zeichnungsberechtigt (verfügungsberechtigt) sein

signature   Unterschrift
- book   Unterschriftenverzeichnis
- card   Unterschriftskarte
- verification   Unterschriftenprüfung

signing
- authority   Unterschriftsberechtigung
- officer   Unterschriftsträger, Zeichnungsberechtigter

simple
- credit   Akkreditiv, bei dem sich die auszahlende Bank direkt auf die eröffnende Bank erholen kann
- debenture   (a) unbesicherte Schuldverschreibung; (b) Schuldverschreibung ohne Wandlungsrechte
- note   einfacher Schuldschein, d.h. der Kreditnehmer verpflichtet sich zur Rückzahlung eines Darlehens zu einem bestimmten Zeitpunkt in einem bestimmten Betrag (US)

Singapore Depositary Receipts   Inhaberzertifikate, die bei

Emissionen ausländischer Kapitalgesellschaften in Singapur durch die örtlichen Emissionsbanken ausgegeben werden

Singapore Interbank Offered Rate Interbanken-Angebotssatz in Singapur

sinking fund Tilgungsfonds, Amortisationsfonds, Ablösungsfonds

- commitments Tilgungsfondsverpflichtungen

single

- capacity ⟶ principle of single capacity
- conversion rate nicht gestaffelter Wandlungskurs
- family mortgage revenue bonds kapitalertragssteuerfreie Kommunalobligationen zur Förderung des Eigenheimbaus
- signing authority Einzelzeichnungsberechtigung

SIPC ⟶ Securities Investor Protection Corporation

six-months'

- dollar Halbjahresdollar
- LIBOR Sechsmonats-LIBOR
- money Halbjahresgeld

size of the market bei Börsengeschäften: Schlußeinheit

skip-day settlement Abrechnung eines Wertpapiergeschäftes am zweiten Geschäftstag, der auf den Ausführungstag (trade date) folgt

sliding rate of interest gleitender (gestaffelter) Zinssatz

slippage of quotations Nachgeben der Notierungen, Kursrückgang

slump in equity prices Kurssturz, Baisse am Aktienmarkt

small

- account banks auf das Privatkundengeschäft spezialisierte Banken
- Business Administration US-Behörde (Finanzierungsinstitut) für die mittelständische Wirtschaft
- business lending scheme Kreditprogramm für die mittelständische Wirtschaft, Mittelstandskreditprogramm
- business loan Mittelstandskredit
- buying interest geringes Anlegerinteresse
- denominations kleine Stückelungen
- subscriber Kleinzeichner

soaring equity prices haussierende Aktienkurse

Society for Worldwide Interbank Financial Telecommunication (SWIFT) Internationales Datenfernübertragungsnetz für Auslandszahlungen

soft

- currency weiche (schwache) Währung
- currency countries Weichwährungsländer
- loan zinsgünstiger Kredit
- stock market rückläufig tendierender Aktienmarkt
- terms günstige Konditionen

sold note Effekten-Verkaufsabrechnung

solicit v. to - new business Kunden akquirieren

Solicitor Trust Account Notar-Anderkonto (Br)

solvency Zahlungsfähigkeit
- ratio Eigenmittelquote

soundness of a company gesunde finanzielle Lage eines Unternehmens

soundness of a guarantee Werthaltigkeit einer Garantie

source and application of funds statement Kapitalflußrechnung, finanzwirtschaftliche Bewegungsbilanz

sourcing customers Kundenakquisition

sovereign
- borrower staatlicher Kreditnehmer (Schuldner), Kreditnehmerstaat
- lending Ausleihungen an staatliche Kreditnehmer, Länderengagements
- loan Länderkredit
- risk staatliches Risiko, Länderrisiko

sparse trading geringfügige Börsenumsätze

spate of new issues Emissionswelle

special
- allowance (a) Sondervergütung; (b) Sonderwertberichtigung
- bracket Mitführer bei einer Anleiheemission
- call right Sonderkündigungsrecht
- charge for bad loans Sonderwertberichtigung auf Kredite
- credit Akkreditiv, über das nur bei einer bestimmten Bank verfügt werden darf
- crossing Scheckvermerk: Scheck kann nur bei einer bestimmten Bank eingelöst werden
- drawing right Sonderziehungsrecht
- features einer Emission: Sonderausstattung, Sonderkonditionen

specialist Kursmakler: betreut etwa 20 - 25 Aktiengesellschaften und ist für einen fairen und ordnungsgemäßen Handel in diesen Papieren zuständig (US)

special
- offering Zeichnungsangebot für bereits im Umlauf befindliche Papiere
- power of attorney Sondervollmacht; Einzelvollmacht
- presentation direkte Vorlage eines Schecks bei der bezogenen Bank
- purpose loan kurzfristiger zweckgebundener Kredit
- rate Vorzugskurs
- redemption außerplanmäßige Tilgung
- team ⟶ intensive care unit
- terms Sonderkonditionen
- write-offs Sonderabschreibungen, außerplanmäßige Abschreibungen

specialties Spezialwerte

specific provision for bad and doubtful debts Einzelwertberichtigung

specific reserve Sonderrücklage, zweckgebundene Rücklage

specimen signature Unterschriftsprobe

speculation in futures Terminspekulation

speculative buying spekulative Käufe, Meinungskäufe

speculative
- buying interest spekulatives Kaufinteresse
- counters Spekulationswerte
- markup spekulative Pluskorrektur

split
- investment company → split trust
- order Wertpapierkaufauftrag mit unterschiedlichen Kurs- bzw. Zeitlimits
- quotation Kursnotierung in Bruchteilen
- rate of exchange gespaltener Wechselkurs
- trust Investmentfonds, der unterschiedliche Anteile ausgibt (→ capital shares, → income shares)

sponsor (a) Konsortialführer; (b) Vertriebsfirma eines Investmentfonds; (c) bei Projektfinanzierungen: Projektauftraggeber; das an einem Projekt wirtschaftlich interessierte Unternehmen

sponsor v. to - a capital issue eine Emission übernehmen

sponsoring group Übernahmekonsortium

spot
- basis Begriff im internationalen Geldhandel: Erfüllungstermin ist der übernächste Arbeitstag - vom Schlußtag an gerechnet, zweitägige Valuta kompensiert
- commitments Kassapositionen
- deal Kassageschäft
- exchange Kassadevisen
- exchange market Devisenkassamarkt
- exchange rate Devisenkassakurs
- positions Kassapositionen
- rate Kassakurs
- trading Kassageschäfte

spread (a) Spanne (z.B. Kursspanne, Zinsspanne), Bandbreite; (b) Aufschlag auf den Kreditzinssatz (z.B. Aufschlag von 1 % auf LIBOR); (c) Gewinnspanne eines Eigenhändlers oder Kursmaklers; (d) Bankierbonifikation, Konsortialprovision

spreads between bids and offers Spannen zwischen Geld- und Briefkursen bei Aktien

spreads between buying and selling rates Spannen zwischen Devisenankaufs- und -verkaufskursen

spreads on domestic assets Zinsspannen bei Inlandsausleihungen (im Inlandsgeschäft)

spreads on new lendings Margen im Neugeschäft

spreads on traditional forms of lending Spannen im traditionellen Kreditgeschäft

spread v. streuen (Anlagen, Risiko)

spread lending Ausleihungen, deren Zinssätze an einen Aufschlag gekoppelt sind

spread price Spannungskurs

square v. to - positions Positionen glattstellen (auflösen)

squeeze on interest margins Druck auf die Zinsspannen

squeeze v. to - out of the capital market vom Kapitalmarkt verdrängen

stabilisation by the lead manager Kurspflege durch den Konsortialführer

stabilise v. stabilisieren to - the price by buying and

stabilise (continued)
and selling in the open
market   Kurspflege betreiben

stag   Konzertzeichner

stagging   Konzertzeichnung

stake   (a) Beteiligung, Anteil;
(b) Kapitaleinlage

stale
- bull   Haussier, der sich verspekuliert hat
- cheque   verfallener Scheck
- documents   veraltete Dokumente

stalemate in the equity market   Flaute am Aktienmarkt

stampede into shorts   Run auf Kurzläufer

stand v. to - at a premium   mit einem Aufgeld notiert werden

standardised lendings   normiertes (standardisiertes) Kreditgeschäft, Programmkredite

standard rates   Normsätze

standards of disclosure   Offenlegungsrichtlinien

standby
- arrangement   Bereitschafts-Kreditabkommen (IWF-Kreditzusagen); Garantiezusage
- credit   Bereitschaftskredit
- group   bei einer Emission: Garantiekonsortium, Garantiegruppe
- letter of credit   (a) Kreditbesicherungsgarantie; (b) Garantieakkreditiv
- syndicate   Garantiekonsortium
- underwriting   Verpflichtung zur Übernahme des nicht plazierten Teils einer Emission

standing   Bonität, Kreditwürdigkeit
- of the underwriter   Emissionskredit

standing order   Dauerauftrag

start-up dividend   Anlaufdividende

state v. ausweisen
to - at the lower of cost or market   zum Niederstwertprinzip ausweisen
stated profit (loss)   ausgewiesener Gewinn (Verlust)

state bank   einzelstaatlich zugelassene Bank

state charter   einzelstaatliche Zulassung

statement of account   Kontoauszug

status enquiry   Auskunftsanfrage

status information (report)   Kreditauskunft

statute-barred   to become statute-barred   verjähren

steels   Stahlaktien

sterile reserves   unverzinsliche Mindestreserven

sterling assets   ₤-Sterling Aktiva; ₤-Sterling Ausleihungen

sterling floater   variabel verzinslicher ₤-Schuldschein (Anleihe)

sticky price   unbeweglicher Kurs

stock   (a) Aktie; (b) allgemein: Wertpapier
stocks   Aktien, Aktienkurse
stocks advanced in active trading   Aktien zogen bei lebhaften Umsätzen an

stocks continued to benefit from speculative support Aktien profitierten weiterhin von spekulativer Nachfrage

stocks continued to lose ground on lack of interest Aktien gaben bei fehlendem Käuferinteresse weiter nach

stocks crumbled further Aktien bröckelten weiter ab

stocks drifted easier on lack of follow-through support Aktien tendierten bei fehlenden Anschlußaufträgen leichter

stocks drifted lower in thin trading Aktien waren bei geringen Umsätzen abgeschwächt

stocks eased across the board Aktien gingen auf breiter Front zurück

stocks edged forward a few points Aktien konnten sich um einige Punkte befestigen

stocks encountered lively interest Aktien stießen auf lebhaftes Interesse

stocks firmed in brisk trading Aktien wurden bei lebhaften Umsätzen höher notiert

stocks hardened at the close of the session Aktien zogen gegen Schluß der Börsensitzung an

stocks held up well in light trading Aktien konnten sich bei geringen Umsätzen gut behaupten

stocks improved sharply Aktien wurden mit Plus angekündigt

stocks moved higher across the board Aktien konnten sich auf breiter Front befestigen

stocks opened a shade lower Aktien eröffneten geringfügig leichter

stocks plotted an irregular course Aktien tendierten uneinheitlich

stocks plummeted to a new low Aktien sanken auf einen neuen Tiefstand

stocks rallied in after-hours trading Aktien erholten sich nachbörslich

stocks recorded heavy losses Aktien verzeichneten starke Verluste

stocks recouped early losses Aktien konnten Anfangsverluste wettmachen

stocks retreated on professional profit-taking Aktien tendierten nach Gewinnmitnahmen des Berufshandels schwächer

stocks shed a few points Aktien büßten einige Punkte ein

stocks trended downward on professional liquidation Aktien waren nach Glattstellungen des Berufshandels rückläufig

stocks turned sharply higher Aktien stiegen nach doppelter Plusankündigung

stocks were a fraction easier Aktien notierten geringfügig leichter

stocks were marked down Aktien notierten schwächer, Aktien wurden mit Minus angekündigt

stocks were mixed in thin trading Aktien tendierten uneinheitlich bei geringen Umsätzen

stocks wilted further Aktien gaben weiter nach (tendierten weiterhin rückläufig)

stock

- allotment Aktienzuteilung

- application (Aktien-)Zeichnung

- appreciation Wertzuwachs einer Aktie, Kursanstieg

- appreciation potential Kurschancen, Kurssteigerungspotential

- assessment Nachschußzahlungen auf Aktien

- brokerage Courtage

- capital Aktienkapital

stock
- category   Aktiengattung, Aktienkategorie
- certificate   Aktienzertifikat
- clearing agency   Abrechnungsstelle für Wertpapiergeschäfte
- collateral   Sicherheit (Sicherungsgut, Sicherheitsleistung) in Form von Wertpapieren
- consolidation   Zusammenlegung von Aktien
- corporation   Aktiengesellschaft
- corporation law   Aktienrecht
- denomination   Aktienstückelung
- discount   Aktiendisagio, Abschlag auf den Kurs einer Aktie
- dividend   Stockdividende
- exchange   Börse
- exchange clearing agency(house)   Abrechnungsstelle für Wertpapiergeschäfte
- exchange closing price   Börsenschlußkurs
- exchange committee on quotations   Börsenzulassungsausschuß
- exchange council   Börsenvorstand
- exchange daily official list   amtliches Kursblatt
- exchange dealings   Börsenhandel
- exchange floor   Börsenparkett
- exchange hours   Börsensitzung
- exchange introduction (launching)   Börseneinführung
- exchange list   Kursblatt
- exchange operator   Börsianer, Marktteilnehmer
- exchange pool nominees   zentrale Nominee-Gesellschaft der Börse (Br)
- exchange price (quotation)   Börsenkurs, Börsennotierung

- exchange rules and regulations   Börsenordnung
- exchange settlement day   Liquidationstermin
- exchange trading   Börsenhandel
- exchange turnover   Börsenumsätze
- exposure   Engagement (Anlage) in Aktien; Aktienbestand
- floatation   Aktienemission, Börseneinführung einer Aktie
- fractions   Aktienspitzen
- fund   Aktienfonds
- futures   Aktientermingeschäfte
- holder of record   eingetragener Aktionär
- holder proxy   Stimmrechtsvollmacht eines Aktionärs
- holders' equity   Eigenkapital, Aktienkapital plus Rücklagen
- holders' rights   Aktionärsrechte
- holding   (a) Aktienbesitz; (b) Aktienbestand
- index futures trading   Termingeschäfte in Aktienindizes
- in treasury   Aktien im Eigenbesitz der emittierenden Gesellschaft; Verwaltungsaktien
- issuance / issue   Aktienemission
- issuing premium   Aktienemissionsagio
- letter of application   Zeichnungsantrag
- list   Kursblatt
- loan   Effektenkredit
- lock-up arrangement   Aktienübernahmeoption, Vorkaufsrecht auf Aktien
- market average   Aktienindex
- market collateral   Sicherheit in Form von börsengängigen Wertpapieren
- market crash   Börsenkrach

- market credit Effektenkredit
- market downturn Kursrückgang am Aktienmarkt
- market investors Börsenpublikum
- market notices Börsenpflichtblatt; Börsennachrichten
- market prices Börsenkurse
- market rally ⟶ stock market recovery
- market rating Börsenbewertung
- market recovery Erholung am Aktienmarkt
- market trend Kursentwicklung am Aktienmarkt
- market upturn Kursaufschwung am Aktienmarkt
- market valuation / stock market capitalisation Börsenkapitalisierung
- market value Börsenkurswert, Börsenwert
- note Nachweis über zugeteilte Aktien
- offering Aktienemission, Zeichnungsangebot für eine Aktie
- of-record day Stichtag für die Ermittlung der dividendenberechtigten Aktionäre
- option Aktienoption; Aktienbezugsrecht; Bezugsrecht auf neue Aktien
- option trade Aktienoptionshandel
- placing Aktienplazierung
- portfolio Aktienbestand, Aktienportefeuille
- premium Aktienaufgeld, Aktienemissionsagio
- price Aktienkurs
- price average (a) Aktienindex; (b) Kursdurchschnitt
- price making Kursbildung (Kursfindung) am Aktienmarkt
- price range Kursspanne
- purchase Aktienkauf
- purchase plan Belegschaftsaktienprogramm (US)
- purchase warrant Aktienbezugsrechtsschein
- quotation Aktiennotierung
- rating Aktienbewertung
- repurchase Aktienrückkauf (durch das emittierende Unternehmen)
- retirement Aktieneinzug; ⟶ stock repurchase
- right Aktienbezugsrecht, Bezugsrecht auf neue Aktien
- sale Aktienverkauf
- split Aktiensplit
- subscription Aktienzeichnung
- subscription agreement (Aktien-) Zeichnungsvertrag; gelegentlich auch Übernahmevertrag
- swap Aktientausch
- take-over Aktienübernahme, Übernahme des Aktienkapitals
- trade Aktiengeschäft, Abschluß in Aktien
- trading Aktienhandel
- transfer Aktienübertragung
- transfer tax Börsenumsatzsteuer
- valuation Aktienbewertung, Bewertung von Wertpapieren
- warrant Aktienbezugsrechtsschein
- yield Aktienrendite

stop (a) Schecksperre; (b) limitierter Wertpapierauftrag; (c) Notlimit

stop v. to - payment on a cheque einen Scheck sperren

stop list Verzeichnis der gesperrten Schecks

stop-loss order   Auftrag zum Verkauf von Wertpapieren bei Erreichen einer bestimmten Kursgrenze

stop order   (a) → stop-loss order; (b) → stop payment order

stop payment order   Schecksperre; Auszahlungssperre

stop price   Kurslimit, Stopp-Kurs

stores   Kaufhauswerte

straddle   Stellage

straight
- bill of lading   Rektakonnossement
- bond   nicht wandelbare Anleihe
- debt / straight debt securities   nicht wandelbare Schuldtitel
- exchange terms   einfache Wandlungsbedingungen (ohne zusätzliche Vergünstigungen → kicker, sweetener)
- fixed-interest debt   festverzinsliche Schuldtitel ohne Wandlungsrechte
- line depreciation   lineare Abschreibung
- line interest computation   lineare Zinsberechnungsmethode
- line redemption   Rückzahlung in gleichen Tilgungsraten
- preferred stock   nicht wandelbare Vorzugsaktien
- prime floating (accommodation)   Kreditgewährung zur → Prime Rate ohne Aufschlag

straights → straight debt

strains on liquidity   Liquiditätsanspannung

street
- loan   kurzfristiges Darlehen
- market   Nachbörse
- papers   zweitklassige Schuldscheine
- price   nachbörslicher Kurs

strengthening
- the equity base   Stärkung der Kapitaldecke
- of prices   Kursbefestigung

stretch   v. strecken, verlängern (Laufzeit)

to - accounts payable   das Zahlungsziel bei Warenverbindlichkeiten voll ausschöpfen

to - out the repayment of a loan   ein Darlehen strecken

strike   v.
to - a deal   ein Börsengeschäft abschließen
to - the balance   saldieren

striking price   (a) Abschlußkurs, Abrechnungskurs (bei einem Wertpapiergeschäft); (b) Basispreis (im Optionsgeschäft); (c) Emissionskurs

stringent
- liquidity position   angespannte Liquiditätslage
- monetary policy   Politik des knappen Geldes

stripped bonds   leere Stücke; Wertpapiere nach Abtrennung der Wandlungsrechte bzw. Bezugsrechtsscheine

strongbox   Tresorfach, Schließfach, Safe

strong in after-hours trading   nachbörslich fest

strongly rising stock market
haussierender Aktienmarkt

strong market   feste Börse

strongroom   Tresor

strong upward trend   Haussetendenz, starker Aufwärtstrend

structural adjustment loan
Strukturanpassungskredit des IWF

structure of interest rates
Zinsstruktur

subaccount   Unterkonto, Nebenkonto

subbranch   Zweigstelle, Depositenkasse

subject
- to call   täglich kündbar
- to confirmation   bestätigungspflichtig, freibleibend
- to disclosure   berichtspflichtig, publizitätspflichtig
- to prior sale   freibleibend (bei einem Zeichnungsangebot)
- to a withdrawal notice   kündigungspflichtig (bei Spareinlagen)

sublimit   bei einer Kreditlinie: Abzweiglimit

submajors   Emissionsbanken, die in der Regel nicht als Konsortialführer tätig sind

subordinate v.   nachordnen, nachstellen

subordinated bond   im Rang nachgestellte Anleihe (in der Regel wandelbar)

subordinated collateral   im Rang nachgeordnete Sicherheit

subordinated debenture → subordinated bond

subordinated debt   im Rang nachgehende Forderung

subordinated debt securities
nachgestellte (nachgeordnete) Schuldtitel

subordinated loan   nachgeordnetes Darlehen

subordinated mortgage   nachrangige Hypothek

subordinated mortgage loan   nachgeordnetes Hypothekendarlehen

subordinated note   nachgeordneter Schuldschein, nachrangige Kassenobligation

subordination   (a) Nachstellung, Nachordnung, Nachrangigkeit; (b) Rangrücktritt
- agreement   Nachrangvereinbarung; Rangrücktrittserklärung

subpaying agent   Nebenzahlstelle

subscribe v.   zeichnen
invitation to subscribe   Zeichnungsangebot, Zeichnungsaufforderung
subscribed capital   gezeichnetes Kapital
fully subscribed issue   vollständig gezeichnete Emission

subscriber   Zeichner

subscribing bank   Zeichnerbank

subscription   Zeichnung, Bezug
- agent   Zeichnungsstelle, Bezugsstelle
- blank   Zeichnungsformular
- book   Zeichnungsliste
- charges   Zeichnungsgebühren
- money   Zeichnungsbetrag
- offer   Zeichnungsangebot, Bezugsrechtsangebot
- option   Bezugsrechtsoption, Zeichnungsoption
- period   Zeichnungsfrist, Bezugsfrist
- price   Zeichnungskurs, Bezugsrechtskurs

subscription
- ratio   one for six subscription ratio   Bezugsverhältnis 6 : 1
- rights   Bezugsrechte
- rights value   Bezugsrechtswert
- terms   Zeichnungsbedingungen
- to SDRs   Zeichnung von Sonderziehungsrechten
- warrant   Bezugsrechtsschein, Bezugsrechtsausweis, Bezugsrechtszertifikat

subsequent
- debit   Nachbelastung
- endorsement   Nachindossament
- endorser   Nachmann
- mortgage   nachfolgende (nachrangige) Hypothek

subsidiary   Tochtergesellschaft
- account   Nebenkonto

subsidise   v. subventionieren
subsidised loan   zinsverbilligter Kredit, Kredit aus öffentlichen Förderprogrammen
subsidising interest payments   Zinssubventionierung

substandard loan   (a) unzureichend besichertes Kreditengagement; (b) Kreditengagement, dessen Rückzahlung nicht gesichert erscheint

sub-syndicate   Unterkonsortium

sub-underwriter   Unterkonsorte

sub-underwriting share   Unterbeteiligung

successor borrower   Nachfolge-Kreditnehmer

suit upon a bill   Wechselklage

superior mortgage   im Rang vorgehende Hypothek

supervise   v. kontrollieren, überwachen

supervised loan   von einer Bankenaufsichtsbehörde beanstandetes und anschließend überwachtes Kreditengagement

supervision of banks   Bankenaufsicht

supervision of lendings   Kreditkontrolle, Kontrolle der Ausleihungen

supplemental reserve requirements   zusätzliche Mindestreserveanforderungen

supplementary financing   Zusatzfinanzierung

supply   Angebot; Zufuhr; Verfügbarkeit
- and demand in the capital market   Angebot und Nachfrage am Kapitalmarkt
- of fresh liquidity   Bereitstellung neuer (zusätzlicher) Mittel, Liquiditätszufuhr

supply   v. to - fresh funds   neue Mittel zuführen

support   (a) Unterstützung; (b) Stützung (Kurs, Währung); (c) Sicherung, Unterlegung (Kredit)
in - of a loan   als Unterlegung (Sicherheit) für einen Kredit
in - of the D-mark   zur Stützung der DM
the new issue found little -   die neue Emission stieß auf geringes Interesse

support   (a) unterstützen; (b) stützen; (c) unterlegen
supported by documents   unterlegt durch Dokumente
supported loan scheme   subventioniertes Kreditprogramm
the facility is supported by a bank guarantee   das Darlehen ist durch eine Bankbürgschaft unterlegt

support v.
loan supported by real security
durch eine dingliche Sicherheit unterlegter Kredit

support
- agreement (a) Kapitalintakthalteerklärung (Verpflichtung der Muttergesellschaft, das Kapital der Tochtergesellschaft nicht zu verringern; (b) Stützungsverpflichtung
- buying Stützungskäufe, Interventionskäufe
- commitment Stützungsverpflichtung
- fund Stützungsfond
- group Stützungskonsortium, Auffangkonsortium

supporting
- purchases Kursstützungskäufe
- voucher Beleg, Buchungs-(Rechnungs)beleg

support
- line Deckungslinie, Auffanglinie (gewähren Banken bei der Emission kurzfristiger Schuldtitel durch Industrieunternehmen)
- measures Stützungsmaßnahmen
- operation Stützungsaktion
- point Interventionspunkt, Interventionsschwelle
- scheme Stützungsprogramm, Besicherungsprogramm
- syndicate (a) Stützungskonsortium; (b) Kursregulierungs-Konsortium

surety (a) Sicherheit, Bürgschaft; (b) Bürge, Garantiegeber, Sicherheitengeber
- bond Bürgschaftserklärung
- deed Bürgschaftsurkunde, Sicherungsvereinbarung

surety's liability Haftung des Sicherheitengebers (des Bürgen)

surge Anstieg
- in equities Aktienhausse
- in interest rates Zinsauftrieb

surplus (a) Überschuß, Überhang; (b) Gewinn; (c) Rücklagen
- at the close of trading im Geldhandel: Tagesüberschuß
- cover Überdeckung
- dividend Dividendenzuschlag
- dollar holdings Dollarüberhang
- fund Rücklagenfonds
- funds überschüssige Kassenmittel, Überschußgelder
- liquidity Überliquidität, Liquiditätsüberhang
- money supply Geldüberhang
- of applications Überzeichnung (einer Emission)
- of deposits Passivüberhang, Einlagenüberschuß
- of lendings Aktivüberhang
- of offerings (of sell orders) Angebotsüberhang (Börse)
- on revaluation Gewinn aus Neubewertung
- proceeds Mehrerlös
- recycling Rückleitung (Rückführung) der Überschußgelder

surrender Auslieferung, Vorlage, Übergabe; Rücknahme
- charge Rücknahmegebühr
- facility (privilege) Rückgaberecht
- value Rücknahmewert

surrender v. (a) ausliefern (Wertpapiere); (b) vorlegen, übergeben (Dokumente); (c) abführen, rückführen (Gewinne)

surrogate forms of capital
Eigenkapitalsurrogate

suspend v. (a) einstellen (Zahlungen); (b) aussetzen (Notierung)

suspense
- account Interimskonto, transitorisches Konto, Cpd-Konto
- entry transitorische Buchung

suspension Einstellung, Aussetzung
- of debt service payments Einstellung des Schuldendienstes (der Zins- und Tilgungszahlungen)
- of payments Zahlungseinstellung
- of a quotation Aussetzung einer Notierung
- of redemption payments Tilgungsaussetzung
- price Kurs vor Aussetzung der Notierung

sustained rally anhaltende Kurserholung

swallow v. to - up an issue eine Emission vollständig übernehmen

swap (a) Swap, Swapgeschäft, Devisen-Reportgeschäft; (b) Umtauschaktion

swap v. tauschen, umtauschen

swap
- offer Umtauschangebot
- rate Swapsatz, Swapkurs
- terms Swapkonditionen
- transaction ⟶ swap

sweetener zusätzliche Vergünstigung bei einer Emission (z.B. Umtauschrechte, späterer Zinsaufschlag)

SWIFT ⟶ Society for Worldwide Interbank Financial Telecommunication

swings in interest rates Zinsschwankungen

switch Switch; Switch-Geschäft; Effekten-Kaufauftrag, dessen Ausführung an die gleichzeitige Abwicklung eines Verkaufsauftrages gekoppelt ist (oder umgekehrt)

switch v. to - out of the bond market into stocks von Renten in Aktien umsteigen

switch
- clause Währungsänderungsklausel (z.B. bei einem Roll-over-Kredit)
- ing securities Portefeuilleumschichtung, Umtausch (Umgruppierung) von Wertpapierbeständen
- premium Switch-Prämie
- reversal Annullierung (Stornierung) eines Switch-Geschäftes

syndicate Konsortium
a syndicate led by... ein Konsortium unter der Führung von...

syndicate v. syndizieren, ein Konsortium bilden

syndicated bid Gemeinschaftsgebot

syndicated guarantee credit Avalgemeinschaftskredit

syndicated loan Konsortialkredit, syndizierter Kredit, syndizierte Anleihe

syndicated loan business Konsortialkreditgeschäft

syndicate
- agreement Konsortialvertrag
- banks Konsortialbanken
- business Konsortialgeschäft
- leader Konsortialführer

syndicate
- manager   Konsortialführer
- member   Konsortialmitglied
- share   Konsortialanteil

syndication   Syndizierung, Plazierung (Kreditgewährung) durch ein Konsortium, Bildung eines Konsortiums
- agreement   Konsortialvertrag
- techniques   Syndizierungstechnik

T

take v.

to - on deposits Einlagen hereinnehmen

to - out a lien ein Pfandrecht bestellen

to - out a loan einen Kredit (ein Darlehen) aufnehmen

to - out a mortgage eine Hypothek bestellen

to - up a bill einen Wechsel einlösen

to - up documents which are in accordance with the terms and conditions of the credit akkreditivkonforme Dokumente aufnehmen

to - up an issue eine Emission übernehmen

to - up an option (stock right) eine Option (ein Bezugsrecht) ausüben

to - up new positions neue Engagements eingehen

to - up securities (a) im Emissionsgeschäft: Wertpapiere (Material) übernehmen; (b) im Rahmen der Kurspflege: Wertpapiere (Material) aus dem Markt nehmen

to - up stock rights Bezugsrechte ausüben

to - accommodation up to a pre-arranged limit einen Kredit im Rahmen eines Dispositionslimits aufnehmen

to - a charge over a policy eine Police belasten

to - delivery of stock Wertpapiere hereinnehmen

to - firm fest übernehmen (Emission)

to - an interest eine Beteiligung erwerben

to - profits Gewinne mitnehmen (Börse)

to - the rate in Prolongation nehmen, hereinnehmen (Börse)

to - securities into safekeeping Wertpapiere zur (Depot-) Verwahrung hereinnehmen

to - a shareholding eine Aktienbeteiligung erwerben

take-down Übernahme einer Konsortialquote

take or pay agreement bei Projektfinanzierungen: langfristiger Vertrag, in dem sich der Abnehmer zur Zahlung feststehender Beträge verpflichtet (gleichgültig, ob er Lieferungen erhält oder nicht)

take-out Kursgewinn (bei einem Aktienpakettausch)

take-over Übernahme

- bid Übernahmeangebot

- code Richtlinien der Londoner City für Unternehmenszusammenschlüsse

- deal Übernahmetransaktion

- price Übernahmekurs

- terms Übernahmekonditionen

taker Optionsverkäufer, Optionsgeber

TALISMAN ⟶ Transfer Accounting Lodgement for Investors, Stock Management for Jobbers

talon Talon, Erneuerungsschein

TAN ⟶ transaction number

tap Daueremission

to issue on -   im Wege der Daueremission begeben (auflegen), laufend emittieren

to turn the - off den Verkauf von→ tap issues einstellen

to turn the tap - on → tap issues abgeben

short (long) taps ⟶ tap issues mit einer Laufzeit bis zu fünf (zwanzig) Jahren

tap v.

to - the capital market   am Kapitalmarkt aufnehmen

to - the reserves die Rücklagen in Anspruch nehmen

tap bills laufend emittierte Schatzwechsel

tape quotation Ticker-Notierung

tap issues im Wege der Daueremission begebene Staatstitel (Schatzwechsel und festverzinsliche Wertpapiere)

tap stocks → tap issues

target company Gesellschaft, die Gegenstand eines Übernahmeangebotes ist

target range im Hinblick auf die Geldmenge: Zielkorridor

tariff of charges Gebührentabelle

taxable investment income steuerpflichtige Kapitalerträge

tax
- anticipation certificate (warrant) verzinslicher Staatstitel, der mit der Steuerschuld des Inhabers eines solchen Titels verrechnet werden kann
- benefits Steuervergünstigungen
- break Steuerfreijahre
- charge Steueraufwand, Steuerbelastung
- credit Steuergutschrift

tax-exempt steuerfrei
- fund Investmentfonds, dessen Ausschüttungen steuerfrei sind
- market kapitalertragssteuerfreie Wertpapiere
- notes kapitalertragssteuerfreie Kassenobligationen (in der Regel Papiere mit einer Laufzeit von 14 Monaten oder weniger)

tax-free exchange fund Investmentfonds, dessen Anteile gegen Einbringung von Wertpapieren gezeichnet werden können (der zuvor bei den Wertpapieren erzielte Wertzuwachs muß beim Tausch gegen die Fondsanteile nicht versteuert werden)

tax
- loss carryback steuerlicher Verlustrücktrag
- loss carryforward steuerlicher Verlustvortrag
- payment date (Abgaben auslösender) Steuertermin
- payment guarantee Steueraval
- privilege Steuervergünstigung
- selling (a) durch einen Steuertermin bedingte Abgaben; (b) Verkauf von im Kurs gefallenen Wertpapieren, um den Wertverlust steuerlich geltend zu machen

tax-sheltered
- account steuerfreies Anlagekonto
- accumulation of capital steuerfreie Vermögensbildung

tax-spared loans (quellen-)
steuerfreie Anleihen

tax switching steuerlich bedingte Portefeuilleumschichtung

tax treatment of equity securities Besteuerung von Dividendenpapieren

technical
- correction technische Kurskorrektur
- rally markttechnische Erholung
- rebound technische Reaktion auf vorangegangene Kurssteigerungen (oder Kursrückgänge)

technology stock Technologiewerte

teletext Bildschirmtext

teletext output of price information by computer elektronische Börsenkursanzeige

teller Schalterbeamter
- terminal Kassenterminal, Schalterterminal
- transaction Schaltergeschäft

temporary
- bridging finance (credit) Zwischenkredit, Überbrückungskredit
- cleanup of a loan vorübergehende Abdeckung eines Kredites
- home Parkplatz
  funds which are looking for a temporary home Gelder, die einen Parkplatz suchen
- repayment → temporary cleanup

tender (a) Ausschreibung; (b) Zeichnungsangebot, Tender; (c) Schatzwechseltender
  offering for sale by tender Angebot im Tenderverfahren

tender v.
  to - bills for discount Wechsel zum Diskont einreichen
  to - documents Dokumente andienen
  to - for an issue ein Zeichnungsangebot für eine Emission unterbreiten

tender
- bills Schatzwechsel, die wöchentlich zum Verkauf angeboten werden
- bond → tender guarantee
- guarantee Bietungsgarantie
- issue im Tenderverfahren angebotene Emission
- offer (a) Zeichnungsangebot (für Wertpapiere); (b) Übernahmeangebot
- offer financing Finanzierung eines Übernahmeangebotes
- sale Verkauf von Wertpapieren im Tenderverfahren (Submissionsverfahren)

tenor Laufzeit (eines Wechsels)

tentative agreement vorläufige Übernahmevereinbarung

term Laufzeit, Frist
  terms Konditionen, Bedingungen
  terms of issue Emissionsbedingungen
  terms of a loan (a) Kreditkonditionen; (b) Anleihemodalitäten
  terms of redemption Tilgungsmodalitäten
  issued for terms running from 2 to 10 years emittiert mit Laufzeiten von 2-10 Jahren

term
- account Termingeldkonto, Festgeldkonto
- business loan mittelfristiger Betriebskredit
- deposit investment Termingeldanlage

term
- deposits Termingeld, Termineinlagen, Festgeld, Festgeldeinlagen
- Feds terminiertes Tagesgeld (US)
- funds taken on deposit hereingenommene befristete Mittel

terminate v. aufkündigen, auflösen

term
- lendings mittelfristige Ausleihungen
- liabilities befristete Verbindlichkeiten
- loan mittelfristiger Kredit (in der Regel Laufzeiten zwischen 5-12 Jahren)

term money Termingeld
- account Termingeldkonto
- borrowings Termingeldaufnahmen
- contracts Termingeldabschlüsse
- deals (dealings) ⟶ term money contracts
- holdings Termingeldbestand
- lendings Termingeldhergaben
- placed im Geldhandel: Termingeldanlage
- rate Termingeldsatz
- yield Rendite bei Termingeldanlagen

term
- settlement Abrechnung von Wertpapiergeschäften in bestimmten Zeitabständen
- share Bausparkassenanteil mit festgelegter Laufzeit (Br)
- structure Laufzeitenstruktur, Fristenstruktur
- to maturity Restlaufzeit

territorial bonds von Gebietskörperschaften emittierte Anleihen

textiles Textilwerte

theoretical value of a right rechnerischer Wert eines Bezugsrechtes

thin
- branch Zweigstelle, Depositenkasse (US)
- margin unzureichende (knappe) Deckung
- market enger Markt
- trading geringe Umsatztätigkeit

third
- intermediate day letzter Börsentag vor dem Erfüllungstermin für Wertpapiergeschäfte
- market (ungeregelter) Freiverkehr; außerbörslicher Handel; Telefonverkehr
- mortgage an dritter Stelle stehende Hypothek
- of exchange Wechseldrittausfertigung
- party custodian Drittverwahrer
- party funds Fremdmittel
- window intermediäre Darlehensmöglichkeit

Three Cs of credit die drei Cs der Kreditwürdigkeitsprüfung: character - persönliche Kreditwürdigkeit; capacity - materielle Kreditwürdigkeit; collateral - angebotene Sicherheit

three months'
- bill Dreimonatswechsel
- funds (money, maturities) Dreimonatsgelder

thrift
- account Sparkonto
- business Spargeschäft

thrift
- deposits   Spareinlagen (in der Regel der Sparkassen US)
- institution   Sparkasse (⟶ thrifts, US)
- institution lending   Kreditgeschäft (Aktivgeschäft, Ausleihungen) der Sparkassen
- institution loan   Sparkassendarlehen
- passbook deposits   niedrigverzinsliche Spareinlagen
- promoting   Sparförderung

thrifts   Sparkassen (einschließlich Bausparkassen sowie Spar- und Kreditgenossenschaften - US); Sparkassensektor, Sparkassenwesen

thrifts' cost of funds   Refinanzierungskosten der Sparkassen

thrifts' deposit-taking business   Einlagengeschäft der Sparkassen

through bill of lading   Durchfrachtkonnossement

TIC   ⟶ true interest cost

ticket   (a) Aufgabe; (b) Scheckrückrechnung; (c) Kostenrechnung bei einem Wechselprotest

ticket day   Aufgabetag

tie v.   (a) binden, festlegen; (b) koppeln

to - up for a longer term   längerfristig anlegen

tied loan   zweckgebundener Kredit

tied to the prime rate   an die ⟶ Prime Rate gekoppelter Kredit

tied up for a longer period   längerfristig gebunden

tied up funds   festgelegte Mittel

tied up principal   blockiertes (gesperrtes) Kapital

tie-in transaction   Kopplungsgeschäft

tighten v. to - up the credit screw   die Kreditpolitik verschärfen

tightly held shares   Aktien, die von einem kleinen Personenkreis gehalten werden

tight market   enger Markt

tightness in the money market   Geldmarktanspannung

tight rein on money and credit   restriktive Geld- und Kreditpolitik

time

time allowed for payment   Zahlungsziel

times interest earned   Zinsdeckung

times over   xmal überzeichnet

time
- account   Festgeldkonto
- bargain   Termingeschäft
- bill   Nachsichtwechsel, Zielwechsel
- deposit account   Festgeldkonto, Termingeldkonto
- deposits   Festgeldeinlagen, Festgelder, Termingeld
- liabilities   Terminverbindlichkeiten
- loan   Kredit mit festgelegter Laufzeit
- note   Kassenobligation (Schuldschein) mit festgelegter Laufzeit
- purchase   Terminkauf
- table of new issues   Emissionsfahrplan, Emissionskalender

title   (a) Eigentumsrecht, Anrecht, Rechtstitel; (b) Kontobezeichnung

title

- deed   Eigentumsurkunde; Grundbuchauszug
- examination   Prüfung der Eigentumsrechte
- of account   Kontobezeichnung
- search → title examination

tombstone / tombstone advertisement   Emissionsanzeige

top v.

to - the subscription list   die Zeichnungsliste anführen

to - up a loan   einen Kredit aufstocken

top-heavy

- company   überkapitalisiertes Unternehmen
- market   künstliche Aktienhausse
- stock   überbewertete Aktie

TOPIC → Teletext output of price information by computer

topping up a loan   Aufstockung eines Krediles; Kreditnachschlag (IWF)

topping-up clause   Aufstockungsklausel (kann sich auf die Erhöhung der Kreditsumme oder einer bereits hinterlegten Sicherheit beziehen)

top-quality

- bond names   erstklassige Anleiheadressen
- borrowers   erste Adressen, erstklassige Kreditnehmer
- stocks   führende Aktienwerte, erstklassige Papiere

total

- assets   Bilanzsumme; Gesamtsumme der Aktiva
- borrowings   Gesamtverschuldung
- credit availability   Kreditrahmen
- exposure   Gesamtengagement, Gesamtobligo
- finance charge   Gesamtkreditkosten
- interest charge   Gesamtzinsbelastung
- lendings   Gesamtausleihungen, Kreditvolumen
- return   Gesamtertrag
- touch   der von → Jobbern genannte höchste Geldkurs und der niedrigste Briefkurs

town

- bill   Platzwechsel
- clearing   Platzgiroverkehr; interner Abrechnungsverkehr der Banken (durch Boten); Gegensatz: → CHAPS
- letter of credit   Platzakkreditiv
- practices   Platzusancen

trade   Handel, Abschluß

trades in equities   Abschlüsse in Aktien

trades in gilts   Abschlüsse (Umsätze) in Staatstiteln

trade v.   handeln; umsetzen

to - after hours   nachbörslich handeln

to - at a discount   mit einem Abschlag handeln

to - at unchanged prices   unverändert umsetzen

to - before hours   vorbörslich handeln

to - briskly   lebhaft handeln

to - for own account   auf eigene Rechnung handeln

to - in and out of the market   an der Börse spekulieren

to - in the premarket hours   vorbörslich handeln

trade v. (continued)

to - in the USM im Freiverkehr handeln

to - lower niedriger notieren, mit Minus ankündigen

to - off the floor (off the board) außerbörslich handeln

to - on margin Wertpapiere gegen Kredit kaufen

to - on the third market im Telefonverkehr (im ungeregelten Freiverkehr) handeln

to - over the counter im Freiverkehr handeln

to - sharply higher wesentlich höher notieren

to - the shorter market swings vorübergehende Kursschwankungen nutzen

traded call options gehandelte Kaufoptionen

traded options market Optionsbörse

traded put options gehandelte Verkaufsoptionen

contracts are traded in four currencies Abschlüsse erfolgen in vier Währungen

the issue traded at a discount of 1 point die Emission wurde mit einem Abschlag von 1 % gehandelt

the issue traded well in the market die Emission verkaufte sich gut

tradeable handelbar

trade

- bill Handelswechsel

- date Schlußtag, Ausführungstag (Effektengeschäfte)

- in fund Investmentfonds, dessen Anteile gegen Einbringung von Wertpapieren gezeichnet werden können

- investments Beteiligungen; Anlagewertpapiere

trader Händler

trading Handel, Handeln; Abschlüsse, Börsenumsätze, Börsengeschäfte

- ex rights Handel ex Bezugsrechte

- for account Wertpapiergeschäfte, die am folgenden → account day abgerechnet werden

- for cash Kassageschäfte, Kassaumsätze

- for account of third parties Abschlüsse für Rechnung Dritter

- for own account Eigenhandel, Selbsteintritt eines Kursmaklers

- in equities Aktienhandel, Abschlüsse in Aktienwerten

- in foreign issues Handel in Auslandswerten

- in futures Terminhandel, Terminabschlüsse

- in gilts Handel in Staatstiteln

- in options Optionshandel

- in rights Bezugsrechtshandel

- in secondary market securities Sekundärgeschäfte, Handel in Alt-Emissionen

- in shorts (longs) Handel in Kurzläufern (Langläufern)

- in the stock market Börsenhandel (→ trading the market)

- in unlisted securities Freiverkehrsmarkt, Handel in Freiverkehrswerten

- on terms of issue Handel per Erscheinen

- the market Börsenspekulation

- centred on speculative counters das Geschäft konzentrierte sich auf spekulative Werte

- remained at a low ebb Umsätze blieben gering, das Geschäft hielt sich in engen Grenzen

- went up das Geschäft hat sich belebt

trading

- account securities eigene Effekten
- account securities portfolio Effektenhandelsbestand
- costs Abschlußkosten
- day Börsentag
- difference Aufschlag bzw. Abschlag bei Kauf- bzw. Verkaufsaufträgen in→ odd lots
- downturn Geschäftsrückgang, Umsatzrückgang
- floor Parkett, Börsensaal
- hours Börsensitzung, Börsenstunden, Börsenversammlung
- loss Betriebsverlust
- lot Börsenschluß, Schlußeinheit
- portfolio Handelsbestand
- post Börsenstand
- profit Betriebsgewinn, Geschäftsgewinn
- record (a) Umsatzergebnisse; (b) Geschäftsergebnisse der zurückliegenden Jahre
- results Geschäftsergebnis
- session Börsensitzung, Börsenversammlung
- syndicate Vertriebskonsortium
- unit Börsenschlußeinheit
- upturn Geschäftsbelebung, Umsatzbelebung an der Börse
- volume Geschäftsumfang, Börsen-Umsatzvolumen

traditional banking services
Kernleistungen einer Bank

tranche of a loan (capital) issue Tranche einer Emission

transact v. abwickeln, durchführen

bargains transacted getätigte Abschlüsse

transaction Geschäft, Transaktion; Abschluß

transaction for cash Kassageschäft, Promptgeschäft

transaction for future delivery Termingeschäft

transaction for mid-month settlement Mediogeschäft

transaction on joint account Metageschäft

transactions for end-of-month settlement Ultimohandel, Ultimogeschäfte

transactions for new account Abschlüsse auf neue Rechnung (für die neue → account period)

transactions for own account Eigengeschäfte

transactions routed through the account Kontoumsätze, Kontobewegungen

transaction

- account Kontokorrentkonto (US)
- account services Kontokorrentfazilitäten
- charge Buchungsgebühr, Bearbeitungsgebühr
- exposure das mit einem Geschäft verbundene Risiko
- fee → transaction charge
- loan zweckgebundener kurzfristiger Kredit
- number Transaktionsnummer (beim Bildschirmtext)
- pricing Berechnung von Gebühren je Geschäftsvorfall
- value Auftragswert, Börsenwert
- volume → trading volume

transfer (a) Übertragung, Übertrag, Überweisung; (b) Umschreibung, Überschreibung

transfer v. (a) übertragen, überweisen; (b) umschreiben, überschreiben

to - into the name of XYZ auf den Namen von XYZ übertragen

to - to another account auf ein anderes Konto übertragen (umbuchen)

transferability Übertragbarkeit

transferable
- credit übertragbares Akkreditiv
- shares (stocks) übertragbare Aktien

Transfer Accounting Lodgement for Investors, Stock Management for Jobbers Clearing- und Verwaltungssystem für Wertpapiere (Br)

transfer
- agent (Aktien-) Transferagent, (Aktien-) Übertragungsstelle
- certificate Übertragungsbestätigung (bei der Übertragung von Aktien)
- charges Übertragungsgebühren; Überweisungsgebühren
- days Übertragungsfrist (bei Wertpapiertransfers)
- deed Übertragungsurkunde
- duty (a) Umschreibungsgebühr bei Aktienübertragungen; (b) Börsenumsatzsteuer

transferee Übertragungsempfänger

transfer
- fee Übertragungsgebühr
- form (Aktien-) Übertragungsformular
- office → transfer agent

transferor Übertragender
- company übertragende Gesellschaft

transfer
- receipt → transfer certificate
- risk Transferrisiko
- slip Überweisungsformular
- tax Börsenumsatzsteuer
- to reserves Einstellung in die Rücklagen, Dotierung (Bedienung) der Rücklagen

transhipment bill of lading Umladekonnossement

transit
- items Inkassopapiere, Distanzschecks
- number Bankleitzahl auf Schecks (US)

translate v. umrechnen

translation Umrechnung
- at historical rates Umrechnung zu den ursprünglichen Wechselkursen
- exposure Umrechnungsrisiko (bei der Umrechnung ausländischer Vermögenswerte in die Inlandswährung)
- gain Umrechnungsgewinn
- loss Umrechnungsverlust

transmission (a) Überweisung (von Geldern);(b) Übertragung (von Aktien)
- charges Überweisungsgebühren; Übertragungsgebühren
- order Überweisungsauftrag

transportation stocks (shares) Aktien von Verkehrsunternehmen, Verkehrswerte

treasuries Schatzpapiere, Schatzwechsel

treasury in the treasury of the company im Eigenbesitz der Gesellschaft (Wertpapiere)

treasury bill Schatzwechsel
- holdings Schatzwechselbestand
- issue Schatzwechselemission
- rate Schatzwechselrate (-zinssatz)
- yield Schatzwechselrendite

treasury
- bond (a) US-Schatzobligation (mit Laufzeiten von 10 - 40 Jahren); (b) von einer Gesellschaft zurückgekaufte eigene Schuldverschreibung
- certificate of indebtedness US-Schatzschuldbrief
- management Finanzmanagement, Gelddisposition
- note Schatzschein (Laufzeit zwischen 1 - 10 Jahren)
- stock (a) staatliche Schuldtitel; (b) mündelsichere Wertpapiere; (c) von einer Unternehmung zurückgekaufte eigene Aktien

triangular exchange Devisenarbitrage in drei Währungen

trigger v. to - a bull run in equities eine Aktienhausse auslösen

trigger rate auslösender Indexpunkt (⟶ drop-lock issue)

triple-A-rated borrower erstklassiger Kreditnehmer bzw. Anleiheschuldner

true
- cost of a facility (cost of borrowing) effektive (tatsächliche) Darlehenskosten
- interest cost effektive Zinskosten
- owner rechtmäßiger Eigentümer
- yield effektive Rendite

trust
- account (a) Treuhandkonto; (b) Nachlaßkonto
- agency Treuhandstelle
- agreement Treuhandvertrag
- and fiduciary investment income Erträge aus Treuhand- und Vermögensverwaltungsgeschäften
- assets Treuhandvermögen
- company (a) Treuhandgesellschaft; (b) Vermögensverwaltungs-Gesellschaft; (c) Verwaltungsgesellschaft eines Investmentfonds
- deed (a) Treuhandurkunde; (b) Vermögensverwaltungsvertrag

trustee (a) Treuhänder; (b) Vermögensverwalter; (c) Depotbank
- account Treuhandkonto, Anderkonto
- for a bond issue Anleihetreuhänder
- investments Treuhandanlagen, mündelsichere Anlagen
- securities mündelsichere Wertpapiere

trusteeship (a) Treuhänderschaft, Treuhandverhältnis, Treuhandverwaltung; (b) Vermögensverwaltung; (c) Nachlaßverwaltung

trust
- fund Treuhandfonds
- funds Treuhandgelder
- indenture Treuhandvertrag
- instrument Treuhandurkunde
- investments Treuhandanlagen
- management Vermögensverwaltung

trustor Treugeber

trust
- property Treuhandvermögen
- receipt loan / trust receipt inventory loan Warenbestandsbeleihung

- stock   mündelsichere Wertpapiere

turn   Provision (z.B. eines Jobbers)

 turn of the market   (a) Unterschied zwischen Geld- und Briefkurs; (b) Marktumschwung

turn   v.   to - into cash   verflüssigen

turnover   Umsatz; Börsenumsätze; Kontoumsätze

- commission   Umsatzprovision
- in equities (in bonds)   Umsätze in Aktien (in Rentenwerten)

turnpike bonds   kapitalertragssteuerfreie Kommunalobligationen zur Finanzierung des Baus von Autobahnen (US)

two-dollar broker   Ringmakler

two-tier market   zweigeteilter (gespaltener) Markt

two-way

- market   (a) Kauf- und Verkaufsgeschäft; (b) Wertpapier, für das ein Geld- und Briefkurs ermittelt wurde
- price   gespaltener Kurs, doppelte Kursnotierung
- voting   getrennte Stimmabgabe nach Stammaktien und Vorzugsaktien bei Hauptversammlungen

U

ultimate borrower Endkreditnehmer

unallocated storage Sammelverwahrung

unassented
- bonds Teilschuldverschreibungen, deren Inhaber die Zustimmung zu einer Änderung der Anleihemodalitäten verweigert haben
- stock Aktien, deren Inhaber die Zustimmung zu bestimmten Unternehmensentscheidungen verweigert haben

unassignable shares nicht übertragbare Aktien

unauthorised
- clerk Angestellter eines Brokers, der keine Abschlußvollmacht besitzt
- drawings nicht genehmigte Inanspruchnahmen
- overdraft nicht bewilligte Überziehung

unbalanced positions at the close of trading offene Positionen bei Börsenschluß

unbankable nicht bankfähig; nicht diskontfähig

unblocked funds freigegebene Gelder

unbroken dividend record regelmäßige Dividendenzahlungen, Dividendenkontinuität

uncallable securities unkündbare Wertpapiere

uncalled
- capital nicht eingezahltes Kapital
- portion of a loan nicht in Anspruch genommener Teil eines Kredites

unclaimed dividend coupons nicht eingelöste Dividendenscheine

unclean
- payments Zahlungen, die nicht im computergestützten Abrechnungsverkehr der Banken (CHAPS) sondern nur gegen Vorlage der effektiven Papiere abgerechnet werden können (Br)
- through bill of lading unechtes Durchkonnossement

uncleared items offene Posten (Positionen), nicht verrechnete Inkassopapiere

uncollateralised unbesichert, ungesichert

uncommitted
- credit facilities nicht zweckgebundene Kreditfazilitäten
- funds verfügbare (nicht zweckgebundene) Mittel
- reserves freie Rücklagen

unconditional
- acceptance uneingeschränktes Akzept
- and irrevocable guarantee unbedingte und unwiderrufliche Garantie

unconfirmed documentary credit unbestätigtes Akkreditiv

unconvertible bond   nicht wandelbare Anleihe

uncovered

- advance   Blankodarlehen, ungedeckter Kredit
- bill   ungedeckter Wechsel
- foreign currency borrowing
Aufnahme eines Fremdwährungs-
kredites ohne Abschluß eines
Kurssicherungsgeschäftes

undated securities   Wertpapiere
ohne festen Fälligkeitstermin

underfunding   Unterkapitalisierung, Unterfinanzierung

underlying

- lien   vorrangiges Pfandrecht
- mortgage   im Rang vorgehende
Hypothek
- securities   (a) Papiere, die
einem Wertpapiergeschäft zugrunde liegen; (b) Vorzugsaktien; (c) Wertpapiervermö-
gen eines Investmentfonds
- securities transaction   das
zugrunde liegende Wertpapiergeschäft

underpriced share   zu niedrig
bewertete Aktie

underpricing   Verkauf von Wertpapieren unter dem Emissionskurs

underrated share ⟶ underpriced
share

undersubscribed issue   nicht
vollständig gezeichnete Emission

undervalued currency   unterbe-
wertete Währung

underwrite   v. (a) übernehmen
(Anleihe); (b) versichern (Risiko)
amount underwritten   übernom-
mener Betrag, Konsortialquote

underwriter   (a) Konsorte; (b)
Emissionsbank; Emissionsinstitut;
(c) Versicherer

underwriting   Übernahme einer
Emission

underwritings   im Kreditgeschäft:
Unterschriften

underwriting

- agreement   Konsortialvertrag,
Übernahmevertrag; Emissionsvertrag
- banks   Konsortialbanken, Bankenkonsortium
- business   Konsortialgeschäft
- commission   Konsortialspanne,
Konsortialnutzen, Übernahme-
provision
- commitment   (a) Übernahmever-
pflichtung, Übernahmezusage,
Übernahmegarantie; (b) Konsortialquote
- commitments   Verpflichtungen
aus Konsortialgeschäften
- fee ⟶ underwriting commission
- group   Übernahmekonsortium
- guarantee   Übernahmegarantie
- house   Emissionsinstitut,
Emissionsunternehmer
- liability   Konsortialhaftung
- margin   Konsortialspanne
- price   Übernahmekurs
- prospectus   Emissionsprospekt
- risk   Übernahmerisiko, Risiko
des Emissionsunternehmers
- share   Konsortialquote
- syndicate ⟶ underwriting group

undertake   v.   zusagen, sich
verpflichten

undertaking   (a) Zusage, Verpflichtung, Verpflichtungserklärung, Versprechen; (b) Unternehmen
- to accept   Akzeptzusage

undertaking
- to buy   Ankaufsverpflichtung, Ankaufszusage
- to extend   Prolongationszusage
- to guarantee   Garantieversprechen
- to honour   Einlösungsgarantie
- to negotiate   Negoziierungsverpflichtung
- to pay on the part of the issuing bank   Zahlungsverpflichtung der Akkreditivbank
- to place   Plazierungsverpflichtung
- to take up documents   Dokumentenankaufszusage
- to take up an issue   Emissions-Übernahmeverpflichtung
- to take up the unsubscribed stock   Verpflichtung zur Übernahme der nicht gezeichneten Aktien

undisbursed
- dividends   nicht ausgezahlte (nicht ausgeschüttete) Dividendenbeträge
- loan   bewilligter, aber noch nicht ausgezahlter Kredit

undisclosed
- assignment   stille Zession
- borrowing   nicht publizierte Kreditaufnahme
- margin on a loan   nicht genannter Aufschlag auf einen Kredit
- principal   nicht genannter Auftraggeber
- profits   nicht ausgewiesene Gewinne

undiscountable   nicht diskontierbar

undoubted credit-worthiness   unzweifelhafte Bonität

undrawn loan (loan facility)   nicht in Anspruch genommener Kredit

unencumbered property   unbelasteter Grundbesitz

unfranked investment income   nicht besteuerte Zins- und Dividendenerträge

unhedged
- currency (exchange rate) risk   ungesichertes Währungs- (Wechselkurs-) risiko
- exposure   ungesichertes Engagement (Kredit,Devisen)

Uniform customs and practice for documentary credits   Einheitliche Richtlinien und Gebräuche für Dokumentenakkreditive

uniform interest rates   einheitliche Zinssätze

Uniform rules for collections   Einheitliche Richtlinien für Inkassi

uniform terms   (a) Einheitskonditionen; (b) einheitliche (standardisierte) Bedingungen

unimpaired stockholders   Aktionäre, die bei einer Unternehmenssanierung keine Verluste erleiden

uninstructed trust funds   Treuhandgelder, für die keine Anlagevorschriften seitens des Treugebers bestehen

unit   (a) Einheit; (b) Börsenschluß, Schlußeinheit; (c) Anteil, Fondsanteil; (d) Stück

units outstanding   im Umlauf befindliche (ausgegebene) Anteile, Anteilsumlauf

units redeemed (repurchased)   zurückgenommene (zurückgekaufte) Anteile, Mittelrückflüsse eines Investmentfonds

units sold   verkaufte Anteile, Mittelzufluß eines Investmentfonds

unit
- applicant Anteilszeichner
- assurance fondsgebundene Lebensversicherung
- banking system Einzelbankensystem (Banken ohne Zweigniederlassungen)
- certificate Anteilschein
- holder Anteilsinhaber, Anteilseigner
- holding Anteilsbestand, Bestand an Fondsanteilen
- ledger Anteilsregister, Verzeichnis der Anteilsinhaber
- of account Rechnungseinheit
- offering Emission von Fondsanteilen
- offering price Ausgabekurs (Ausgabepreis) von Fondsanteilen
- price Anteilskurs, Anteilspreis
- quotation Stücknotierung
- redemption Anteilsrücknahme, Rücknahme (Rückkauf) eines Fondsanteils
- redemption price Rücknahmekurs, Rücknahmepreis
- register ⟶ unit ledger
- trust offener Investmentfonds
- value (a) Stückwert;(b) Wert eines Fondsanteils

unlisted
- dealer Freiverkehrshändler
- market Freiverkehr
- securities Freiverkehrswerte, amtlich nicht notierte Werte
- securities market Freiverkehr
- securities market fund Investmentfonds, der die ihm zufließenden Mittel in Freiverkehrswerten anlegt

- trading Freiverkehr, Handel in Freiverkehrswerten

unload v.
to - holdings Bestände abstoßen
to - on the market auf den Markt werfen

unmanaged municipal bond fund Investmentfonds, dessen Anlagevermögen in Kommunalobligationen investiert wird und der nur während der Laufzeit dieser Papiere besteht

unmarketable securities nicht börsengängige Wertpapiere

unofficial market (ungeregelter) Freiverkehr; Handel unter Banken

unpaid cheque unbezahlt gebliebener (nicht eingelöster) Scheck, Scheckretoure

unplaceable nicht plazierbar

unplaced portion of a loan issue nicht plazierter Teil einer Anleiheemission

unqualified
- acceptance uneingeschränktes Akzept
- audit certificate uneingeschränkter Bestätigungsvermerk
- endorsement Vollindossament

unquoted
- company nicht börsennotiertes Unternehmen
- investments (a) nicht börsengängige Anlagepapiere; (b) Beteiligungen an nicht börsennotierten Unternehmen
- shares (stocks) nicht notierte Aktien

unrealisable assets nicht realisierbare (nicht verwertbare) Vermögenswerte

<u>unrealised gain</u>　nicht realisierter Gewinn

<u>unrecoverable debt</u>　nicht beitreibbare Forderung

<u>unredeemed bond</u>　noch nicht getilgte Anleihe

<u>unremoved title exceptions</u>　bestehende Eigentumsvorbehalte

<u>unseasoned</u>
- market operator　unerfahrener Marktteilnehmer
- security issue　(a) Neuemission; (b) wenig gängige Emission

<u>unsecured</u>
- debt　(a) unbesicherte Forderung; (b) unbesicherter Schuldtitel
- creditor　nicht abgesicherter Gläubiger
- loan　Blankokredit, unbesicherter Kredit
- loan stock　unbesicherte Schuldtitel
- note　unbesicherter Schuldschein
- overdraft　Blanko-Überziehungskredit, Dispositionskredit

<u>unsettled items</u>　offene Positionen

<u>unsold securities</u>　nicht plazierte Wertpapiere (Titel)

<u>unsubscribed shares</u>　nicht gezeichnete Aktien

<u>unsustainable</u>　the price level proved unsustainable　das Kursniveau konnte nicht gehalten werden

<u>until done for</u>　Limit gültig bis zur Abwicklung des Auftrages zum vorgegebenen Kurs

<u>untransferable shares</u>　nicht übertragbare Aktien

<u>unused line of bank credit</u>　nicht in Anspruch genommene Kreditlinie einer Bank

<u>unwilling market</u>　ein wenig aufnahmebereiter Markt

<u>upper</u>
- intervention rate　oberer Interventionspunkt
- lending limit　Obergrenze für Ausleihungen

<u>ups and downs</u> in interest rates　Zinsschwankungen, Zinsfluktuation

<u>upside</u>
- interest rate flexibility　Zinsspielraum nach oben
- price objective　Kursziel
- price potential　Kursspielraum nach oben

<u>upstream</u>　v. an die Muttergesellschaft abführen

<u>upstream</u>
- guarantee　Garantie einer Tochtergesellschaft zu Gunsten der Muttergesellschaft
- loan　Darlehen einer Tochtergesellschaft an die Muttergesellschaft

<u>upsurge</u>
- in interest rates　Zinsauftrieb
- in stocks　Aktienhausse, starker Kursanstieg

<u>upturn</u>　Aufschwung, Belebung
- in the bond market　Kursbefestigung am Rentenmarkt; Umsatzbelebung am Rentenmarkt

<u>upward exchange rate pressure</u>　Aufwertungsdruck

431

upward price correction Kurs-korrektur nach oben

usance Laufzeit (eines Wechsels)

USM ⟶ unlisted securities market

USM quote Notierung im Freiverkehr

usual terms and conditions
Normalkonditionen

utilities / utility stocks
Versorgungswerte

V

validity of the loan agreement Gültigkeit (Gültigkeitsdauer) des Kreditvertrages

valuable guarantee werthaltige Garantie

valuableness of a guarantee Werthaltigkeit einer Garantie

valuables Valoren, Wertgegenstände

valuation Bewertung, Wertbestimmung, Wertermittlung

- adjustment Bewertungsänderung

- date Bewertungsstichtag

- method Bewertungsverfahren

- of stock at cost or less Bewertung von Aktien zum Einstandspreis oder darunter

- of stock at market prices Bewertung von Aktien zu den aktuellen Kursen

- provisions Bewertungsvorschriften

value (a) Wert; (b) Valuta, Wertstellung

under good value mit alter Wertstellung

in terms of value wertmäßig

value v. bewerten

value

- adjustment Valutaberichtigung, Berichtigung (Korrektur)der Wertstellung, Wertberichtigung

- date Valuta, Wertstellung

- estimation Schätzung des Wertes

- for collection Inkassowert

- given clause Valuta-Klausel

- received Wert erhalten (in Rechnung)

- upon redemption Rückzahlungswert, Tilgungswert

variable annuity policy→variable life insurance

variable-coupon CDs variabel verzinsliche Einlagenzertifikate

variable-interest loan variabel verzinslicher Kredit

variable life insurance Lebensversicherung, bei der die Prämienzahlungen der Versicherungsnehmer in Aktien angelegt werden (ein Mindestwert wird garantiert; der effektive Auszahlungswert hängt hingegen von der Kursentwicklung der erworbenen Aktien ab - US)

variable-price

- market Schwankungsmarkt

- quotation variable Notierung, fortlaufende Notierung, Schwankungskurs

- securities Schwankungswerte

variable rate variabler Kurs, variabler Zinssatz

variable-rate

- bank loan variabel verzinslicher Bankkredit

- market variabler Markt, Schwankungsmarkt

- mortgage variabel verzinsliche Hypothek

variable-yield securities Wertpapiere mit variabler Rendite

variation Schwankung

variations in market price Kursschwankungen

variation margin variable Sicherheitsleistung

variation range Schwankungsbreite

vary v. schwanken

widely varying yields stark schwankende Renditen

vault Tresor

- cash im Tresor lagernde Gelder

VC-CDs ⟶ variable-coupon CDs

venture capital Beteiligungskapital, risikotragendes Kapital, Risikokapital, Wagniskapital

- company Kapitalbeteiligungsgesellschaft

- fund Kapitalbeteiligungsfonds

venture financing Beteiligungsfinanzierung, Wagnisfinanzierung

venture lending Kredite (Ausleihungen) an Kapitalbeteiligungsgesellschaften

verification ratios Bilanzkennzahlen

vest v. übertragen

the powers vested in the donee die dem Bevollmächtigten übertragenen Vollmachten

vesting deed (instrument) Übertragungsurkunde

viewdata Bildschirmtext

virgin shares neu emittierte Aktien

void adj. ungültig, null und nichtig

void v. annullieren, für ungültig erklären

volatility of interest rates Unstetigkeit in der Zinsentwicklung

volume (a) Volumen; (b) Börsenumsätze, Börsenumsatzvolumen

in terms of volume volumenmäßig

volume

- gains Zuwachs des Geschäftsvolumens (einer Bank)
- leader meistgehandelte Aktie, Umsatzspitzenreiter
- of business Geschäftsvolumen, Umsatzvolumen
- of dealings Umfang der Börsenabschlüsse
- of deposits Gesamteinlagen, Einlagevolumen
- of new issue activity Neuemissionsvolumen
- of trading→ volume of dealings
- shrinkage Umsatzrückgang; Rückgang des Gesamtbestandes

volumes control Volumensteuerung

voluntary adjustment (settlement) außergerichtlicher Vergleich (US)

vote (a) Stimme; (b) Abstimmung

vote-gearing Verhältnis von stimmberechtigten zu stimmrechtslosen Aktien

voting Abstimmung, Stimmabgabe

- by proxy Stimmrechtsausübung durch einen Bevollmächtigten
- capital stimmberechtigtes Kapital
- control Stimmrechtskontrolle
- instructions Stimmrechtsanweisungen

voting
- list   Stimmenliste
- power   Stimmrecht
- proxy   Stimmrechtsvollmacht, Stimmrechtsermächtigung
- right   Stimmrecht
- right transfer   Übertragung von Stimmrechten
- shareholder   stimmberechtigter Aktionär
- shares (stock)   stimmberechtigte Aktien; Stimm-Material
- trustee   Stimmrechtstreuhänder

voucher   Beleg

VRM ⟶ variable-rate mortgage

W

waiver   Verzicht, Verzichtserklärung

- clause   Verzichtsklausel
- of interest   Zinsverzicht, Zinserlaß
- of protest   Protesterlaß
- of recourse   Regreßverzicht

walks items   Inkassopapiere, die nicht über eine zentrale Abrechnungsstelle abgewickelt werden können

want-and-offer sheets   Kurslisten der Freiverkehrshändler (mit Geld- und Briefkursen)

warehouse   v. (a) ein größeres Aktienpaket zusammenkaufen (in der Regel unbemerkt); (b) einlagern, lagern

warrant   (a) Optionsschein, Bezugsrechtsschein; (b) Orderlagerschein

warrant exercisable at $ ... zum Kurs von $ .. ausübbare Option

warrants outstanding   im Umlauf befindliche (ausgegebene) Optionsscheine

warrant

- agent   Optionsstelle (für den Umtausch von Optionsscheinen in Aktien)
- bearing securities   Titel mit Optionsscheinen (z.B. Optionsanleihen)
- exercise period   Optionsfrist (für den Umtausch von Optionsscheinen)
- exercise price   Optionspreis
- holder   Inhaber eines Optionsscheines
- issue   (a) Emission von Optionsscheinen (Bezugsrechtsscheinen); (b) Optionsanleihe
- market price   Börsenkurs eines Optionsscheines
- premium   Unterschied zwischen dem Börsenkurs und dem rechnerischen Wert eines Optionsscheines

warrantor   Garantiegeber, Bürge

warranty   Garantie

way   Auftreten eines Brokers als Käufer oder Verkäufer

weaken   v. nachgeben, schwächer tendieren

weekly

- return   Wochenausweis
- tender of treasury bills   wöchentlicher Schatzwechsel-Tender

week order   auf eine Woche befristeter Wertpapierauftrag

well-maintained prices   gut behauptete Kurse

when issued   Vermerk bei einem Wertpapiergeschäft: Auslieferung der Stücke nach Erscheinen

when-issued contracts   Terminabschlüsse in noch zu emittierenden Papieren

wholesale

- banking   (a) Firmenkundengeschäft; (b) gelegentlich auch: Großkundengeschäft
- banks   große Geschäftsbanken; auf das Firmenkundengeschäft ausgerichtete Banken
- corporate lending   Ausleihungen (Kredite) an Firmenkunden

- factoring   Factoring im Zusammenhang mit großen Warenpartien
- financing   Großhandelsfinanzierung
- foreign exchange dealings   internationale Devisenhandelsgeschäfte
- investors   Großanleger
- money market   Interbankenmarkt
- paper   Finanzierungsinstrumente bei Großhandelsfinanzierungen
- sterling market   Interbanken-£-Sterling Markt

wide investment spread   breite Anlagenstreuung

widely disseminated stock portfolio   breitgestreutes Aktienportefeuille

widened parity bands   erweiterte Bandbreiten

widening of the interest rate spread   Erweiterung der Zinsspanne

wide price (quotation)   (a) stark variabler Kurs; (b) Kurs, bei dem eine große Spanne zwischen Geld- und Briefkurs besteht

widespread
- selling   Abgaben auf breiter Front
- shareholdings   breitgestreuter Aktienbesitz, Aktienstreubesitz

willingness to assume risks   Risikobereitschaft

willing to take stock   investors willing to take stock   aufnahmebereite Anleger

win v. to - new accounts   Kunden akquirieren

wind v. to - up   auflösen, liquidieren

windfall profit   unerwarteter (spekulativer) Gewinn

windmill   Kellerwechsel

window-dressing   Bilanzkosmetik

withdraw v. (a) abheben, entnehmen, abziehen, abdisponieren (Gelder); (b) zurücknehmen, zurückziehen (z.B. eine Garantiezusage); (c) einziehen (einen Wechsel)

withdrawal   Abhebung, Abzug; Rücknahme; Einzug
- at a three months' notice   Abhebung unter Beachtung einer dreimonatigen Kündigungsfrist
- behaviour   Abzugsverhalten
- notice   Kündigungsfrist (bei Einlagen)

withhold v.   einbehalten

withholding tax   Quellensteuer

without recourse   ohne Regreß

with rights   einschließlich Bezugsrechte

working
- capital requirements   Betriebskapitalbedarf
- capital restrictions   Auflagen, die der Kreditnehmer im Hinblick auf die Kapitalstruktur seines Unternehmens beachten muß
- funds   Betriebsmittel
- loan   Betriebsmittelkredit

workout   Kurszusatz: freibleibend

work-out department   auf Unternehmenssanierungen spezialisierte Abteilung einer Bank

write v.
to - a cheque   einen Scheck ausstellen

write
- to - back auflösen (Rückstellungen)
- to - down by $ ... um $ ... abschreiben (wertberichtigen)
- to - down on a straight-line basis linear abschreiben
- to - down the capital das Kapital vermindern
- to - off (a) abschreiben; (b) ausbuchen (als Verlust)
- to - off a loan einen Kredit (ein Engagement) abschreiben
- to - off as a loss als Verlust abschreiben
- to - off uncollectibles uneinbringliche Forderungen abschreiben (ausbuchen)

write-down Abschreibung, Wertberichtigung
- on securities Abschreibungen auf den Wertpapierbestand
- of the share capital Verminderung des Aktienkapitals, Kapitalschnitt

write-off (a) Abschreibung, Wertberichtigung; (b) Ausbuchung (uneinbringlicher Forderungen)
- of a loan Ausbuchung eines Krediets, Abschreibung eines Engagements als Verlust, Forderungsverzicht der Bank
- on fixed-income securities Abschreibungen auf den Rentenbestand
- on trade investments Abschreibungen auf Beteiligungen

write-off powers Ausbuchungskompetenz

write-off requirements Abschreibungsbedarf, Wertberichtigungsbedarf; erforderliche Abschreibungen (Ausbuchungen)

writer Aussteller; Verkäufer
- of a call option Verkäufer (Stillhalter) einer Kaufoption, Stillhalter in Aktien
- of a cheque Scheckaussteller
- of an option Stillhalter, Optionsverkäufer
- of a put option Verkäufer (Stillhalter) einer Verkaufsoption, Stillhalter in Geld

writing back provisions Auflösung von Rückstellungen

writing down → write-down

writing off → write-off

writing up security holdings Höherbewertung der Wertpapierbestände

wrong entry (post) Fehlbuchung

X

x.a. ex all ausschließlich aller Rechte

x.c. ex scrip issue ausschließlich (ex) Gratisaktien

x.cp. ex capitalisation issue ex Gratisaktien (Berichtigungsaktien)

x.in. ex interest ex (ohne) Zinsen

x.r. ex rights ex (ohne) Bezugsrechte

Y

Yankee(s) umgangssprachlich für US-Titel

Yankeebonds Anleihen ausländischer Emittenten am US-Kapitalmarkt

year-end
- position squaring Glattstellungen zum Jahresende, Jahresultimoglattstellungen
- settlement Jahresendabrechnung, Jahresultimoregulierung

yearling Kommunalschuldverschreibung mit zwölfmonatiger Laufzeit

years of grace tilgungsfreie Jahre, Tilgungsfreijahre

years to maturity Restlaufzeit

yield Rendite

  yields in the capital market Renditen am Kapitalmarkt

  yields on longs (shorts) Langläufer (Kurzläufer-) Renditen

yield v. abwerfen, erbringen, rentieren

yield
- adjustment Renditeangleichung
- calculation Renditeberechnung
- curve anticipation switch Portefeuilleumschichtung in Erwartung substantieller Renditeänderungen
- differential Renditegefälle
- expectations Renditeerwartungen

- floor untere Renditegrenze
- fluctuations Renditeschwankungen
- gap Renditegefälle
- increase at the short (long) end of the market Renditeanstieg im kurzen (langen) Bereich
- level Renditeniveau
- spread Renditespanne, Renditefächer
- to average life Rendite auf die durchschnittliche Laufzeit gerechnet
- to call date Rendite auf den Kündigungstermin gerechnet
- to maturity (to redemption) Rendite auf die Endfälligkeit
- upon issue Emissionsrendite

Z

<u>zero bonds</u> Zero-Bonds, abgezinste Schuldtitel, Abzinsungspapiere